A HISTORY OF
MODERN CRITICISM
1750–1950

4. *The Later Nineteenth Century*

Gregg   A.   Galley

A HISTORY OF MODERN CRITICISM 1750-1950

By

RENÉ WELLEK

The Later Nineteenth Century

CAMBRIDGE UNIVERSITY PRESS

CAMBRIDGE

LONDON   NEW YORK   NEW ROCHELLE

MELBOURNE   SYDNEY

Published by the Press Syndicate of the University of Cambridge
The Pitt Building, Trumpington Street, Cambridge CB2 1RP
32 East 57th Street, New York, NY 10022, USA
296 Beaconsfield Parade, Middle Park, Melbourne 3206, Australia

First published by Yale University Press 1965
First paperback edition published by Cambridge University Press 1983

Printed in Great Britain at the
University Press, Cambridge

Library of Congress catalogue card number: 82–12918

British Library Cataloguing in Publication Data
Wellek, René
A history of modern criticism.
Vol. 4: The later nineteenth century
1. Criticism—History
I. Title
801′.95′0903   PN86
ISBN 0 521 27075 8

CONTENTS

1: FRENCH CRITICISM: REALIST, NATURALIST, IMPRESSIONIST

FROM FRANCE come the two main slogans of later 19th-century literature: realism and naturalism. From there they spread to all the other countries, and in various disguises and modifications they are still with us. As "socialist realism" they challenge the whole tradition of aesthetics descended from antiquity and reformulated by the philosophers and critics of the Romantic Age.[1]

Realism was a philosophical term of long standing which meant a belief in the reality of ideas and was contrasted with nominalism, which considered ideas only names or abstractions. In the 18th century the meaning of realism was almost completely reversed. Schelling, in 1795, defines realism as "positing the existence of the non-ego," in contrast to idealism.[2] Schiller and Friedrich Schlegel were apparently the first to apply the term to literature. In 1797, in a then unpublished notebook, Schlegel says of the novel that "this realism is based on its nature" and he criticized Tieck for lacking in "matter, realism and philosophy."[3] In 1798 Schiller, in a letter to Goethe, asserts that "realism cannot make a poet."[4] In a printed aphorism in 1800 Schlegel says paradoxically that "there is no true realism except in poetry."[5] Similar statements can be found elsewhere in Schlegel and Schelling: they all refer to external reality and not to a specific period or style or school.

In France the term emerges in 1826. A writer in *Mercure Français* asserts that "this literary doctrine, which gains ground every day and will lead to faithful imitation not of the masterworks of art but of the originals offered by nature, could very well be called realism. According to some indications it will be the literature of the 19th century, the literature of the true."[6] Gustave Planche used the term after 1833 as an equivalent for exactitude of description. He refers to George Crabbe's "realism" and tells us that realism worries about "what escutcheon is placed over the door of a castle, what device is inscribed on a standard, and what colors are borne by a lovesick knight." [7] In 1834 Hippolyte Fortoul complains of a novel that it is written "with an exaggeration of realism that is borrowed from the manner of M. Hugo." [8] Thus realism at that time means an element—accuracy of detail—observed in writers whom we would today label romantic.

In the later forties the term was transferred to the minute description of contemporary manners: in 1846 Hippolyte Castille connects Balzac with a "realist school," [9] and in the same year a book on the history of Flemish and Dutch painting by Arsène Houssaye prominently uses the term.[10] But its establishment as a slogan is due to the commotion raised by the pictures of Gustave Courbet. They appear to us conventional and mediocre but in their time they not only aroused the antagonism of defenders of academic art but with their simple themes from peasant and bourgeois life were considered shockingly revolutionary. The novelist Champfleury (pseudonym of Jules Husson, dit Fleury, 1821–89) became Courbet's most vocal defender in articles published after 1850 and collected in 1857 as Le Réalisme. He defends Courbet against the charge of making his subjects uglier than reality: "the bourgeois are that way." The time of the pantheists is passed.[11] Champfleury as a novelist was an advocate of the village novel and appeals even to Auerbach's and Gotthelf's precedents.[12] In his theory he not only defends accuracy of description and interest in the lower classes but was among the first in France who wanted to "chase the author from his book as far as possible." [13] "The ideal for an impersonal novelist is to be Proteus, supple, changing, multiform, at the same time victim and executioner, judged and accused, who knows how to assume, in turn, the part of the priest, the magistrate, the saber of the soldier, the plough of the laborer, the naiveté of the people, the stupidity of the small bourgeois." [14] But Champfleury was not happy with the slogan "realism," and in the preface to the book with this title he practically disowned the term. He disliked all terms ending in "ism," because, he said, they were not part of the French language. In spite of the efforts of Stendhal the designation "classicism" could not be adopted. In "romanticism" we have a passing school if there ever was one. And realism as a term will "last hardly more than thirty years." He "does not love schools, flags and systems." [15] Courbet put a notice at the entrance of his 1855 exhibition: "Realism: Exhibit and Sale of 40 pictures and 4 drawings" but in the accompanying catalogue he protested that the "title of 'Realist' has been imposed upon me, in the same way that the artists of 1830 were labeled Romantics. Titles have never at any time given a true notion of the things themselves. If it were not so, works would be superfluous."[16] The year of Champfleury's *Réalisme* was that of the trial of *Madame Bovary*. The slogan was fixed by the debate but actually, even for criticism, the practice and theory of the great writers whom we in retrospect consider the masters of realism proved more important.

HONORÉ DE BALZAC (1799–1850)

Honoré de Balzac rightly holds the place of originator of the modern social novel. In the preface to *Comédie humaine* (1842) he stated his ambition to write "the history, so often forgotten by historians, the history of manners." Balzac thought of himself as a historian of contemporary society who would apply the method of Scott's novels to the France of his own day. Scott had "imprinted a gigantic *allure* on a kind of composition which before had been unjustly considered second-rate." Balzac, at least in the preface, conceived of his task as a search for a social typology; appealing to the achievements of zoology, he sees society as an analogue of the animal kingdom, an agglomeration of species: men are like varieties in zoology. Besides, his work has "its geography as it has its genealogy and its families, its persons and its facts."[1] But this sociological— or, as Balzac used the term, "physiological"—ambition is crossed by his conservative and Christian convictions: his novels are to support the social and religious order in depicting the anarchy of the time.

Balzac was hardly a thinker or critic, and even during his lifetime it was often observed that he did not live up to his scientific ideal: he was, rather, a creator of a world of imagination, a poet in the old sense of the word. Certainly in many contexts he upheld the most extravagantly romantic views of the role of the writer as an inspired prophet and showed, in spite of his encyclopedic ambitions, a consistent contempt for the intellect. In an early article, "Des Artistes" (1830), Balzac exalts the social role of the artist: "he commands entire centuries: he changes the face of things"; but genius is a disease like the pearl in the oyster. He is slave to a higher will, he has no character as he is "accustomed to make his soul a mirror in which the whole universe is reflected." The artist is condemned to suffer like Christ on the cross.[2] These are the themes of many of Balzac's stories of artists. Artists have their own peculiar faculty, which Balzac calls oddly "spécialité": a kind of intellectual vision or intuition. Thus Balzac often implies an aesthetics that is highly spiritualist or even Neoplatonic. The famous story "Le Chef-d'œuvre inconnu" (1831, expanded and revised 1837), assimilates a good deal of studio talk and artists' jargon, apparently with the help of Delacroix and Gautier; but in its pointed ending, the empty canvas displayed as the masterwork, Balzac appeals to inner vision with a vengeance.[3] In practice Balzac tried to organize writers and artists and wanted to assure himself and them fame and wealth on a large scale, often by fantastic schemes. But he also knew that the artist is lonely, that his insight is personal, and that art changes throughout history. He was acutely conscious of "the mutations of taste, the capriciousness of fashion, and the transformations of the human mind" [4] and shows even a sense for the variety of art which is far from romantic, classical, or realist dogmatism. Granted that Hugo's preface to *Cromwell* was in his mind, it still seems remarkable that he could praise the Chinese for having seen

the infertility of the Beautiful. The Beautiful can have only one line. Greek art is confined to a repetition of ideas. The Chinese theory has seen, a thousand years before the Saracens and the Middle Ages, the immense resources that the Ugly represents, a word that has stupidly been thrown into the face of the Romantics and which I use in opposition to the word Beautiful. The Beautiful is only one statue, one temple, one book, one play: the *Iliad* has been three times imitated, the same Greek statues have been copied over and over again, the same temple has been rebuilt *ad nauseam,* the same tragedy has walked the boards with the same mythologies, so as to make you sick with boredom. On the contrary, the poem of Ariosto, the romance of the trouvère, the play of the Spaniard or Englishman, the Cathedral and the town hall of the Middle Ages are the Infinite in art. For the thinker, are not the Gothic and the style of Louis XV cousins germane of Chinese art? [5]

This romantic universalism also inspires Balzac's idea of criticism. He detests the petty fault-finding critic who writes out of prejudice, and he recognizes a higher kind of criticism, "a whole science that demands a complete understanding of the works, a lucid view of the tendencies of the age, the adoption of a system, a faith in certain principles."[6]

One cannot say, however, that Balzac's own criticism lived up to this ideal. His critical opinions are wide-ranging and various, and even his formal literary criticism is more extensive than is generally known. But it is difficult to see why he should be labeled a "great critic" because of an early shrewd analysis of the improbabilities and absurdities of the plot of *Hernani* (1830) or for the long and in general favorable account of Stendhal's *Chartreuse de Parme* (1840). Lukács has exalted this "extraordinarily profound" review as "one of the great events in the history of world literature,"[7] but, soberly considered, Balzac does little more than retell the story and complain about the composition and the style while praising the central intrigue as Machiavelli's "*Prince* brought up to date."[8] Stendhal, understandably pleased to get the attention of a famous author but upset by Balzac's sharp words about his style, wrote him the well-known letter saying that "in order to catch the tone he used to read every morning two or three pages of the *Code Civil*."[9] But Balzac's review, however generous in its praise, can hardly be considered perceptive, as he dismissed the whole story of Celia or praised Stendhal for an exact observation of the "rules" of writing a novel. Still, the introductory classification of the literature of the time is of considerable interest: Balzac contrasts the "literature of images" (Hugo, Lamartine, Chateaubriand) with the "literature of ideas" of which Stendhal is a master and with whom he classes Mérimée and, oddly enough, Musset, Béranger and Nodier, while he considers himself as somewhere in between under the banner of "eclecticism" (an unfortunate term), with Walter Scott, Madame de Staël, Cooper, and George Sand as his fellow fighters.[10] It amounts to a contrast between the picturesque romantics and the common-sense reasoners deriving from the Enlightenment, with Balzac exalting himself as a synthesizer and reconciler. In his criticism certainly it won't do to make Balzac a realist or even a forerunner of realism. Observation, the depiction of contemporary manners, the interest in social typology, though hardly new as such, are only one strand in Balzac's thinking: he lacks the central technical prescription of the new realism, namely the absence of the author, detachment, *impassibilité*.

GUSTAVE FLAUBERT (1821–1881)

This factor, in theory and practice, was provided by Gustave Flaubert. *Madame Bovary* puzzled and shocked its contemporaries because of Flaubert's attitude; Armand Pontmartin, a conservative critic, complained that "the author has so well succeeded in making his work impersonal that one does not know after reading it to what side he leans." [1] Balzac, Dickens, Thackeray, etc. never left one in any moral doubt. Even Duranty, who was the editor of a short-lived magazine *Le Réalisme* (1856) and who shared Champfleury's views, did not welcome *Madame Bovary*. The book seemed to him cold and lifeless, more like a mathematical demonstration than a novel.[2] Sainte-Beuve, who knew about Flaubert's father being a surgeon, gave the cue: Flaubert "holds his pen like a scalpel. Anatomists and physiologists, I find you everywhere!" [3] At that time Flaubert's theoretical views could not have been widely known. Only the publication, first of his *Lettres à George Sand* (1884), introduced with a long preface by Maupassant, and then the *Correspondance* (4 vols. 1887), which contained the letters to Louise Colet written during the years of work on *Madame Bovary* (1851–56), presented his theories in any detail. Though necessarily unsystematic and often contradictory in different moods and in the contexts of different addressees, these letters have made a profound impression not only as a commentary on Flaubert's creative process or a running criticism of his contemporaries but as a statement of an aesthetic which, on a few points, strikingly formulates some of the perennial issues of novel writing and of all art.

The correspondence is the *locus classicus* for the "martyrdom" of the writer, for his struggle with language and recalcitrant matter. Flaubert over and over complains of the slowness of his progress, the grinding slavery of his work: five days in which he has written a single page, five or six pages in a week, twenty-five pages in six weeks, thirteen pages in seven weeks, a whole night spent in hunting for an adjective. "My God, what a struggle! Such drudgery! Such discouragement!" [4] He works in a kind of perpetual fury, with "the frenzied and perverse love for his work of an ascetic for the hair shirt which scratches his belly." [5] A cynic might suspect that Flaubert was given to exaggeration, writing as he did to a sentimental, prolific, and demanding woman writer. After all, he had constantly to advise her not to rely on inspiration, to write as little as possible and to write exactly and precisely. One must take "les affres de l'art" with a grain of salt. "His wild gesticulations, his plaintive, childish side" [6] belong to his temperament. His taste for seclusion, his secretiveness, his shyness, his distrust of the effusion of feeling correspond to his dislike for Lamartine, Musset, and Béranger. It is the self-criticism of the strong romantic streak in him.

Flaubert genuinely strove for objectivity in his art: both for impersonality and for *impassibilité*, detachment, indifference. These terms do not mean the same thing. Objectivity, known to the Germans, was felt as a pedantic neologism in French. Maupassant could call it a "vile word" in 1887.[7] "Impersonality" was primarily a technical device. The author must be absent from his novel, must not comment on his characters, must not moralize or philosophize about them. In a comparison anticipated in Hugo's preface to *Cromwell* Flaubert asks the writer to be like "God in the universe, everywhere present but nowhere visible. Art being a second nature, the creator of this nature should proceed by analogous procedures. One should sense in all atoms, in all aspects, a hidden and infinite indifference." [8] Flaubert said the same in different terms later: "the artist should no more appear in his works than does God in nature. Man is nothing, his work is everything." Flaubert thus thinks that "a novelist has no right to express his opinion about anything at all. Has God ever told his opinion?" [9] he asks. This divine objectivity, the Spinozistic deity of the artist-creator easily passes over into indifference, detachment, ironic distance, the impenetrability, *impassibilité*. Thus Flaubert's central concept wavers between two main tendencies of his time: scientism, objectivity, and aestheticism, art for art's sake. Impersonality opposes the novel with a purpose; *impassibilité* opposes the autobiographical novel of sentiment.

Much has been made of Flaubert's contempt for didactic art, of his distaste for the treatment of contemporary political and social issues, for his somewhat easy assumption that anything that is real art is *eo ipso* moral. But some of this art-for-art's-sake detachment is surely deceptive. The famous passage "Today I even believe that a thinker (and what is an artist if not a triple thinker?) should have neither religion nor fatherland nor even social conviction" [10] seems to come straight from Gautier's preface to *Mademoiselle Maupin*. But Flaubert had his political views, some even of extreme violence, such as the condemnation of the Commune; he held very definite social attitudes, such as a hatred for the *bourgeoisie*, which did not make him less contemptuous of the proletarian masses, and he had his religious, or rather nonreligious, views. They certainly were not confined to his private life but permeate the novels: who indeed can mistake the politics of *L'Education sentimentale* or *Bouvard et Pécuchet?* One must agree with him that "the reader is an imbecile or the book is false from the point of view of exactitude if the reader does not draw from it the morality which he should find there." [11] Thus the fury of "engaged" writers against Flaubert seems mistaken, even if they are right in condemning his social attitudes. It seems a strange naiveté of Sartre to say that "he holds Flaubert and Goncourt responsible for the repression which followed the Commune as they did not write a line to prevent it." [12] Flaubert's contempt and hatred for the mob deserves rather the opposite reproach made by Henry James: "He hovered forever at the public door, in the outer court . . . He should at least have listened at the chamber of his soul." [13]

Flaubert was primarily concerned with the problem of creating illusion: the illusion of a fictional world which need not arouse immediate emotion. This seems to him "something quite different and of an inferior order. I have wept at melodramas which are not worth four cents while Goethe has never moistened my eye, except with admiration." [14] "The illusion arises out of the impersonality of the work." Flaubert assures us of *Madame Bovary*, that "it is a totally invented story." [15] He tells us many times that he has "written tender pages, without love, and burning pages without any fire in his blood." [16] He sounds like Keats on the nature of the chameleon poet: "You may describe wine, love, women, or glory, on condition that you do not become a drunkard, a lover, a husband or a soldier. In the midst of life, you get a bad view of it: it either gives you too much pleasure or too much pain. The artist, in my opinion, is a monster, an unnatural creature." [17] It is Diderot's old paradox of the actor.

At times, Flaubert goes to great lengths to profess repulsion and profound distaste for the world of *Madame Bovary*, for its heroine, and for the very theme. The often quoted saying "Madame Bovary c'est moi" is obviously apocryphal and cannot be traced further back than 1909.[18] Rather he said that "the vulgarity of my subject matter often gives me nausea"; "The milieu is fetid," "I feel like vomiting physically" and, in letters, he did not conceal his opinion that Madame Bovary is "a woman of false poetry and false sentiments."[19] Usually he defends his choice of theme as a "prodigious tour de force," as an exercise, a "work of criticism or rather anatomy," "an act of crude will power," "a deliberate, made-up thing."[20] He defends it also on the general theoretical ground that all subjects are equal. "Yvetot is worth as much as Constantinople," as "an artist must raise up everything."[21] When naturalism was victorious, Flaubert turned the maxim around and used it against Huysmans' early novel *Les Sœurs Vatard*. "The Ganges is no more poetic than the Bièvre. But the Bièvre is no more so than the Ganges. Beware lest we return once more to exclusive subjects and the precious vocabulary of classical tragedy. It will then be thought that a style is enhanced by the use of vulgar expressions when formerly it was embellished with choice phraseology."[22] Henry Miller and Company have made the prophecy come true.

But the saying "Madame Bovary c'est moi" was not invented for nothing. The detachment and impartiality is often matched by a sense of identification, if not with the heroine, then, at least, with a mood or scene or physical sensation. Flaubert can say that "nothing pertaining to myself interests me" and that "Homer, Rabelais, Michelangelo, Shakespeare, and Goethe seem to me pitiless."[23] But he has his romantic moods. Writing the scene of Madame Bovary's first "fall" with Rodolphe in the woods he says almost ecstatically: "today, for instance, man and woman, lover and beloved, I rode in a forest on an autumn afternoon under the yellow leaves, and I was also the horses, the leaves, the wind, the words my people spoke, even the red sun that made them half-shut their love-drowned eyes."[24] The famous letter to Taine, which is an answer to a scientific questionnaire, describes the same identification in physiological terms. "When I was describing the poisoning of Emma Bovary, I had a taste of arsenic in my mouth, was poisoned so effectively myself, that I had two attacks of indigestion one after another—two very real attacks, for I vomited my entire dinner." [25] It is useless to try to reconcile these statements. There are simply these two sides to Flaubert's nature and theory: detachment and involvement, realism and romanticism.

Flaubert comes nearest to a reconciliation when he grasps the unity of content and form, subject and object. From his earliest days he saw that "there are no beautiful ideas without beautiful forms and vice versa. The Idea exists only in virtue of its form." [26] "The distinctions between idea and style" he declares are "a sophism." [27] "Form is cloak. No. Form is the flesh of the idea, just as the idea is its soul, its life," or form and content are "two entities which never exist without each other." [28] But often Flaubert loses this insight. In one well-known passage he goes to the extremes of formalism. "What seems to me beautiful, what I should like to do, is a book about nothing, a book without external support which would sustain itself by the internal power of its style as the earth is sustained in the air, a book that would have hardly any subject or at least a subject that would be almost invisible, if possible. The most beautiful works are those that have least matter in them." But this is an isolated pronouncement: it envisages a distant ideal, which justifies the axiom that there are "neither good nor bad subjects." [29] Flaubert's own books are actually full of matter, even researched documentation, ballast, dead weight.

Thus Flaubert's reaction to realism is extremely ambiguous. In aesthetics he often sounds like a Platonist in search of ideal beauty. The sight of the Parthenon was for Flaubert one of the deepest experiences of his life. "Art is no illusion whatever they say." [30] Years afterward he remembered with violent pleasure one of the walls of the Acropolis, a wall that is completely bare. "Well, I wonder," he tells George Sand, "whether a book, quite apart from what it says, cannot produce the same effect. In a work whose parts fit precisely, which is composed of rare elements, whose surface is polished, and which is a harmonious whole, is there not an intrinsic virtue, a kind of divine force, something as eternal as a principle?" And he adds expressly: "I speak as a Platonist." [31] Flaubert's distaste for the real and for realism become obsessive in spite of all the fierceness with which he tried to observe and to reproduce, to analyze and to anatomize what he knew. "I am supposed to be enamored of the real," he protests, "while I actually detest it. I undertook this novel [*Madame Bovary*] out of hatred for realism." [32] Even twenty years later he wrote George Sand: "I detest what is usually called realism, though I have been made one of its high priests." [33] Naturalism seemed to him an equally empty term: "Why has one abandoned the good Champfleury with his 'realism,' which is an ineptness of the same caliber, or rather the very same ineptness?" [34] In many contexts Flaubert tried to dissociate himself from his disciples. "Reality in my view must not be anything but a springboard. My friends are convinced that it constitutes the whole of art. I am indignant at such materialism and almost every Monday I have a fit of irritation reading the articles of our good Zola. After the Realists, we get the Naturalists and the Impressionists. What progress! These jesters who want to persuade themselves and us that they have discovered the Mediterranean!" [35]

Though Flaubert was often struck by the power of Zola and called *Nana* "a colossus with dirty feet, but it *is* a colossus," [36] he felt that Zola's theories were wrong or narrow and that he cramped his own work by the theories he imposed on it.

Actually Flaubert, at least in ambition, was himself a theorist and critic. It is easy to collect the usual irritated pronouncements against critics and criticism, but he had a deeper insight into its needs and even into its history than was usual at that time. He even thought once of writing a "History of Poetic Sentiment in France." "One should write criticism as one writes natural history, without any moral idea. It is not a question of declaiming about this or that form, but of explaining in what it consists, how it connects with other forms and what it lives by." [37] He even sketched the two main stages of French criticism: grammatical with La Harpe, historical with Sainte-Beuve and Taine. He then asks, "but when will the critic be an artist? Nothing but an artist, but a real artist? Where do you know of a critic who cares about the work itself, in an intense way? One analyzes finely the environment in which it is produced and the cause that brought it about. But the unconscious poetics? Where does it come from? Its composition, its style? The point of view of the author? Never." [38] He criticizes Taine perceptively. His *History of English Literature* has a wrong starting point. "There are other things in Art than the environment in which it moves and than the physiological antecedents of the worker. With such a system one can explain a series, a group, but never an individuality, the special fact which makes a man *this man*. This method leads necessarily to a slighting of talent. The masterwork has no other mean-

ing than as a historical document." [39] Flaubert thus proposes to replace rhetorical and historical criticism with something we might
call today stylistic criticism. "Aesthetic criticism has remained behind historical and scientific criticism because it has had no foundation. The knowledge that they all lack is an anatomy of style," [40] or
as he rephrases it: "They might know the anatomy of a sentence,
but they understand nothing of the physiology of style." [41] Very
early, Flaubert arrived at the striking formula that "every work of
art has its special poetics by which it is made and subsists." [42]

In practice, Flaubert was extremely conscious of the concrete
problems of French prose. He wanted to give it "the consistency of
verse. A good prose sentence must be like a good line of verse,
unchangeable, as rhythmic, as euphonious as verse." [43] The choice
of words, the right word, is the first step; but Flaubert cares also
about the purity of tone, the rhythm of a paragraph, the clash of
assonances. Proust and others have admired the way Flaubert
exploited the resources of the French system of tenses.[44] The
elaborate counterpoint achieved in the scene of the agricultural
show in *Madame Bovary* comes nearest Flaubert's highest ideal—
that is, synthesis, the "harmony of disparate things." It reminds him
of "Jaffa, where I smelled the odor of lemon trees and corpses simultaneously; the deep-dug cemetery let you see half-rotten skeletons,
while the green bushes swayed with golden fruit above our heads.
Don't you feel how this poetry is perfect and here is the great
synthesis?" [45] Flaubert anticipates Eliot's "unified sensibility":
falling in love, reading Spinoza, with the noise of the typewriter or
the smell of cooking.[46] But this synthesis seems only a juxtaposition.
Ultimately there is an unresolved conflict between, on the one hand,
Flaubert's scientific or would-be scientific observation, his Olympian detachment, and, on the other, the passionate search for
Beauty, for calculated purity of effect and structure. It is the contrast
between the gray-on-gray *Education sentimentale* and the gory and
golden *Salammbô*. The synthesis of realism and aestheticism fails in
Flaubert, both in theory and in practice.

GUY DE MAUPASSANT (1850–1893)

This synthesis was achieved, in a derivative way, on a lower level,
and at the expense of tension, by Flaubert's devoted disciple, Guy

de Maupassant. In two prefaces, one to Flaubert's Correspondence with George Sand (1884) and another to his own novel, *Pierre et Jean* (1887), Maupassant expounded his master's theories with a different emphasis. *Madame Bovary*, Maupassant declares, constitutes a "revolution in literature." Flaubert was the first real artist of the novel who composed with style, the first who achieved "impersonality." [1] Still, Maupassant is far from dogmatic. Flaubert was to him no realist in the school sense and he admits the possibility of an idealist novel. Novelists want truth but "not the trite photography of life." They must aim at the "more complete, more gripping, more probing vision than reality itself," they must give relief to events, must produce "a profound sensation of truth," "a complete illusion of the true." Realists who have talent should be called "illusionists." Maupassant is a relativist, or rather subjectivist, in his theory of knowledge, if one can use such a pretentious term for his feeling that "our different eyes, our ears, our organs of smell and taste create as many truths as there are men on earth." "The great artists are those who impose their particular illusion on humanity." Maupassant distinguishes between the "objective novel" and the novel of pure analysis. The objective novel is his own ideal: a novel that avoids all complex explication, all discourse about motives, and lets persons and events pass by our eyes. What matters is patience and concentration on the object. "In order to describe a burning fire or a tree on a plain, we must look at the fire or a tree until they cease to resemble, for us at least, any other tree or other fire." "Particularize" is Flaubert's and Maupassant's main advice to the novelist. He must make us see in what way "a carriage horse does not resemble fifty other horses that follow and precede it." There is only one right word to express a thing, one adjective to qualify it. In gross contradiction to philosophical or temperamental solipsism, Maupassant asks for one right relation to the reality outside of us and peremptorily asks the critic to limit himself. He "must be nothing but an analyst without purposes, without preferences, without passions, and like an expert on pictures, must appreciate only the artistic value of the art object submitted to him." [2]

Maupassant gave currency to Flaubert's doctrine of the single "right" word and the novelist's *impassibilité,* but the stress on objectivity goes poorly with the "illusionism" and the assumed solipsism.

Still, enmity toward open didacticism or social purpose draws the line against the new "naturalism" that had in the meantime been formulated by Zola.

EMILE ZOLA (1840–1902)

Emile Zola is judged, as a theorist, almost always by the introductory essay to *Le Roman expérimental* (1880). Sympathetic recent students of his novels, Angus Wilson and F. W. J. Hemmings, have called it "peculiarly silly," and "embarrassingly naive" and they want us to believe that "nothing Zola ever wrote has damaged his reputation more than the six volumes of literary criticism that he published in a block in 1880 and 1881." [1] But surely this cannot be true. At most, the initial pages and the leading theme of the essay on the experimental novel may be dismissed in such terms. Obviously there is no "experimental" novel in the sense in which there is an experiment in a scientific laboratory. Zola—by quoting Claude Bernard's *Introduction à l'étude de la médicine expérimentale* (1865), sometimes merely replacing the term "physician" by "novelist"—suggests not only an analogy but an identity between novel writing and a physiological experiment, a novelist and a scientist. "Since medicine, which is an art, is becoming a science, why shouldn't literature itself become a science, thanks to the experimental method?" [2] Clearly the comparison limps. A novel can be only a mental construct, an imaginary experiment. The figures of the novelist, even though he has carefully defined their heredity and milieu and, in imagination, construed their behavior according to a scientific knowledge of human motives, cannot be pressed to yield an unequivocal answer, as the laboratory experiment may. The imagination remains free. But we do an injustice to Zola in taking him literally. Quoting or paraphrasing Bernard was a rhetorical device—possibly an unfortunate device—to cloak his theories with the prestige of contemporary science. It tells us simply that the novel Zola advocates should be "a general enquiry into nature and man," [3] which assumes the doctrines of scientific determinism. Man is governed by laws of heredity, by the pressure of the environment, by the whole causal structure of the universe; the novelist must not violate these laws and must study the structure.

Even in this article Zola admits that "the method is only a tool." "What remains is skill, genius, the *a priori* idea." [4]

The "experimental novel" was only a new slogan added to the general theory of naturalism that Zola had developed since the sixties. He had named it then, and the term carried his views everywhere long before the 1880 essay. Zola, however, was right when he disclaimed inventing the term. "It is found in Montaigne, with the meaning we give it today. It has been used in Russia for thirty years, and by twenty critics in France, particularly by M. Taine." [5] No such passage can be found in Montaigne, but naturalism was an old philosophical term for materialism or any secularism. In a literary sense it can be found in Schiller, in the preface to *Die Braut von Messina* (1803), as something Schiller finds worth combating, because in "poetry everything is only a symbol of the real." [6] Zola may have heard from Turgenev that the term was used in Russia. Belinsky usually spoke of the "natural" school in Russian literature, but in the 1847 "Survey of Russian Literature" he also uses "naturalism" as an opposite of "rhetorism." [7] In French, as in English, naturalist means, of course, student of nature, and the analogy between the writer and the naturalist, specifically the botanist and zoologist, was thus ready to hand. Taine in the essay on Balzac (1858) draws the comparison when he says that "the naturalist lacks any ideal; even more does the naturalist Balzac lack one." His tradespeople and provincial types are "the proper object of a naturalist." His worst people are the most successful. "They are in effect the heroes of the naturalist and the crude artist who is not repelled by anything." [8] Hugo in the preface to *La Légende des siècles* (1859) drew another parallel. "A poet or a philosopher is not forbidden to attempt with social facts what a naturalist attempts with zoological facts: the reconstruction of a monster according to the imprint of a nail or the cavity of a tooth." [9] Cuvier's speculations on extinct antediluvian fauna struck the imagination of the time forcibly. It is the parallel that both the early and the late Zola has in mind. "Today," Zola wrote in 1866, "in literary and artistic criticism we must imitate the naturalists; we have the duty of finding the men behind their works, to reconstruct the societies in their real life, with the aid of a book or a picture." [10] The critic and the novelist do not differ basically and both are, or want to be, scientists. In

the preface to a new edition of his novel *Thérèse Raquin* (1868),
Zola most conspicuously expressed his scientific aim. The book is
"an analytical labor on two living bodies like that of a surgeon on
corpses." It is substantially what Zola meant later by the "experimental novel." The scientific parallel serves two main purposes: it
defends the treatment of any subject matter, however low or
repulsive, and it wards off charges of immorality. A doctor cannot
be criticized for studying a revolting venereal disease and cannot be
accused of immorality for investigating its causes and cures. The
preface ends with Zola proudly claiming "the honor of belonging
to the group of naturalist writers." [11] The term was established and
has survived: at first without much distinction from realism and
later, in the twentieth century, mainly with a limitation to Zola's
deterministic, scientific theory, in distinction from the much larger
and looser concept of realism applicable to any art concerned with
the representation of reality.

Zola was right when he claimed in 1882 never to have changed.
"The method has remained the same, the aim, and the faith." [12] The
differences between the early Zola of 1866–68 and the Zola of
1879–81 are at most those of emphasis. In the early writings he
preserved a strong concern for the personality of the writer. The
well-known definition "A work of art is a corner of creation seen
through a temperament" [13] occurs in the early collection of critical
articles, inappropriately named *Mes Haines* (1866), even though
the theological "creation" was later replaced by "reality." Zola,
even at a later stage, did not, however, deny the role of the individual. He was too proud of being a writer, a benefactor of mankind
and a "worker"; he was, too, avid for fame, in spite of the impersonal
implications of his theories, which required the "dethronement" of
the imagination, the profession of impartiality toward the characters and issues of his novels, and in general a belief in the typical
and universal. Zola spread the slogans "the human document," "the
slice of life," and "the protocol." [14] They fostered the writing of novels
without arrangement, selection and, even more, idealization. The
distinctions between art and life, reportage and fiction are abolished.
But much of this is polemics against romanticism and fervid propaganda art. In practice, Zola in spite of his study of government reports
and his observations in mines, saloons, brokerage offices, vegetable
markets, barracks, brothels, railway shops, and so on, knows very well

that a novelist is no mere reporter, that he "gains immortality by setting forth living creatures, by creating a world according to one's image."[15]

Zola is a better and finer practical critic than is usually recognized. He can be exasperating in his Philistinism toward the more distant past: "I do not care for beauty or perfection. I don't give a hoot for the great centuries. I care only for life, struggle, excitement. I feel at ease among our generation."[16] He leaves Shakespeare to his glory, bored as he was by a performance of *Macbeth*. He dismisses Goethe as a museum piece.[17] But he is good at criticizing and characterizing his contemporaries and immediate ancestors. Stendhal and Balzac are his masters. Zola called Stendhal in 1867 "our greatest novelist" and praised him for his observant detachment: Stendhal studied "men like strange insects, driven by fatal forces. His humanity does not sympathize with that of his heroes; he is content to do his work of dissection simply displaying the results of his labor."[18] The Stendhal fashioned after Zola's own ideal or the image of Flaubert is, in a later long essay, replaced by a more accurate and critical picture. Stendhal mystifies and puzzles also by his pose of an amateur but is basically simple. He is not an observer but rather a logician still untouched by modern science. Zola now feels strongly that Stendhal's novels are excogitated, willed, deduced. Julien Sorel, for instance, seems to him "complicated like a machine whose function one finally does not clearly know." The end of *Le Rouge et le Noir* is pure invention. Julien causes "the same surprises as d'Artagnan." *La Chartreuse de Parme* is a fairy tale. Stendhal finally goes against Zola's grain. "He is the Father of us all, like Balzac. He has brought us analysis, he is unique and exquisite, but he lacks the good nature of the powerful novelists. Life is simpler."[19]

The admiration for Balzac is warmer and more intimate, though Zola wrote little about him. Balzac is hailed as "the father of naturalism," the writer who has described the whole of France and saw everything and said everything.[20] But Zola disapproved of his political opinions and construes a sharp contrast between his conscious intentions and his unconscious sympathies. In an article dating from 1870 Zola put it extravagantly: "Balzac is ours: Balzac, the royalist and Catholic, worked for the Republic, for the free societies and religions of the future."[21] In the Balzac article of the series *Les Romanciers naturalistes* (1881) which is largely an account of the Correspondence with Mme Hanska, he speaks of Balzac's "lack of consciousness" which comes primarily from his "lack of critical sense." He has written "the most revolutionary work, a work where, under the ruins of a rotten society, democracy grows and affirms its place." In spite of his political opinions "Balzac, willy nilly, sided for the people against the king, for science against faith." [22] Finally, in a programmatic article, "Le Naturalisme" (1882), Zola again says that Balzac "could openly profess Catholic and monarchical opinions, while his work is nevertheless scientific and democratic, in the broad sense of the word." [23] With a deep insight into what today would be called the intentional fallacy, and possibly with some consciousness of the dualism between his own work and his theories, Zola marvels "how the genius of the man can run counter to the convictions of that man." [24]

Friedrich Engels must have known these passages (or some of them) when he wrote his famous letter to Miss Harkness [25] about the conflict between Balzac's political sympathies and the implied drift of his work, so closely does he reproduce Zola's main argument. It seems a quirk of history that Zola's idea has become a standard doctrine of Marxist criticism while Zola's naturalism is condemned by authoritative Marxist critics like Lukács.

For Zola, Balzac and Stendhal are the two pioneers of the naturalist novel. Sainte-Beuve and Taine are the masters of modern criticism. Sainte-Beuve is the founder of scientific criticism: the use of biography makes him a determinist. But Zola, of course, cannot agree with his low estimate of Balzac and jeers at his preference for second-rate men, "for his secret horror of loud things, whether books or men." [26] Zola dislikes "the pretty falsity, the perfect politeness, full of hidden malicious meaning, the persistent smile which disguises the severity of his judgments." [27] Sainte-Beuve, to Zola's taste, is too feminine, too flaccid.

Rather, Taine was "the chief of our criticism." [28] In 1866 Zola proclaimed himself a "humble disciple," [29] and the influence of Taine on Zola's deterministic theories need no elaboration. But later Zola was disappointed with Taine's cautious attitude toward his admirer and with his political development. The early essay in *Mes Haines* (1866) makes much of Taine the artist, of his "love of power and splendor," of his "passionate aspirations toward force and the free life." Taine, he admits modestly, is too learned for him, and even the reservation that his system has "something rigid and tense, something generalized and inorganic" [30] in it is voiced with diffidence. But later Taine's "spirit of system" became a genuine grievance. Taine, we hear, "wears a professor's gown," has become "a timid academician, a waverer in philosophy, an equilibrist of criticism." [31]

Zola, early and late, knew who is important and who will matter in history. He trusts evolution, progress, and sees himself and his doctrines as part of an inexorably flowing stream. The novel rides the crest of the wave. It mirrors the new world and uses the methods of science. The theater, Zola argues, lags behind: in a long career as a theatrical critic he chastises the timidities and conventionalities as well as the sentimental and romantic extravagances of the Paris stage, always hoping and prophesying that the drama will, at last, catch up with the novel. The theater is "the last citadel of convention." Sardou produces only "a curious, amusing toy"; the younger Dumas is a preacher. The theater, Zola warns, "will be naturalist or it will be nothing." [32]

Poetry must have disappointed Zola. It stubbornly refused to become naturalist. Zola, in his youth, had written reams of romantic verse. Hugo was the obvious model. But Zola soon criticized him for "putting a veil between the objects and our eyes" [33] and later savagely attacked the last collections of his poetry for their obscure, contradictory, occult philosophy. *L'Âne* seemed to him "incredible gibberish." Hugo is "colossal and empty," a man from the distant past completely lost in the age of science.[34] But the fierce attacks are prudently silent on Hugo's novels. Zola could hardly have denied that he himself had learned from *Notre Dame de Paris* and *Les Misérables*. On the whole, poetry seemed to Zola an inconsequential, puzzling game. Not surprisingly, Mallarmé's verse seemed to him a string of mere words.[35] But, condescendingly, he permitted poets "to make music while we work." [36]

"Work" means the realist novel and the new painting. Early, Zola came to the defense of Courbet as a painter, and argued against his exploitation by the radical anarchist Proudhon. Courbet is a "painter of flesh," like Veronese and Titian, while Proudhon admires only the content.[37] Zola helped to defend Manet, at first for his defiance of academic convention but increasingly with a real sympathy for his art. Zola does not merely appreciate his "nature as it is" painting but knew how to characterize his "surprisingly elegant awkwardness," the color juxtapositions of "Le Déjeuner sur l'herbe" or the contrast effects in "Olympia," where the girl's nude body is "indecent, just as it should be." [38] But later Zola was disappointed with Manet and the Impressionists in general: they had fled into the country and had not fulfilled his hopes of being painters of modern urban civilization. His old school friend Paul Cézanne seemed to him only an "aborted genius." [39]

Art criticism, though voluminous, was only an episode in Zola's great campaign for the new art of the century. The novel was the actual battleground or the great workshop. Flaubert was the great fellow champion whom Zola admired also as a person and friend. As early as 1866 he hailed him as a "chemist-poet," "mechanic-painter," [40] and after his death he described him, moved and movingly. With Flaubert the "naturalist" formula passed into the hands of "a perfect artist," a stylist, a rhetorician. Zola's reservations come out in the obituary essay. Flaubert is too nihilistic, too gloomy; he lacks a sense for the "evolution of literature," which he falsely conceived as independent of society. He lacks Zola's great confidence in the future. [41]

Comprehensibly Zola is most generous toward his followers. He praises Daudet on all occasions, though for autobiographical reasons he would complain about Daudet's liking for the Provence which included even the *mistral*. [42] He has nothing but praise for Maupassant, who contributed "Boule-de-Suif" to *Soirées de Medan* (1880), a volume designed as a display of the wares of the school. [43] And he praises J.-K. Huysmans, at least for the early naturalistic novels, though he soon recognized that Huysmans "refines too much, torments and works his sentences too much like jewels." [44] Zola constantly refused to be considered the head of a school, as he had a horror of authority and stagnation and a genuine sense of history, which he knew would surpass him and batter him with something new and hostile.

Such blows fell hard on Zola later in life. He must have enjoyed the outcries of the Philistines against the morals of his novels, as he liked to stir up the waters and shock the bourgeoisie. He must have dismissed as British prudery the prosecution to which his translator and publisher Henry Vizetelly was subjected in England. [45] But he must have been distressed by the "Manifesto of the Five against *La Terre*" (1887), written apparently by J.-H. Rosny, which bluntly accused him of compensating for sexual impotence by the brutal and lewd fantasies of his peasant novel.[46] Then came the apostasy of J.-K. Huysmans, who in *Là Bas* (1891) denounced Zola for his "materialism," for "eulogy of brute force and apotheosis of the strongbox," for "the new Americanism of morals." [47]

Less personal though no less indicative of a change were the anti-naturalist critics attracting attention at that time. Melchior de Vogüé's *Le Roman russe* (1886) proved a great antinaturalist force. Zola knew and admired Turgenev, as did Flaubert and Henry James: they all welcomed what they read of Tolstoy. But de Vogüé's preface presented the Russian novel as an antidote against the immorality and scientific indifference of the French naturalist novel. De Vogüé (1848–1910) was a conservative French nobleman who had served with the Embassy in St. Petersburg. He admired Turgenev and Tolstoy for their spirit of compassion and Christian forgiveness, which he opposed to the cynicism and pessimism of the French. He concentrated his fire on Flaubert's *Bouvard et Pécuchet,* on its realism "without faith, without emotion, without charity." The Russians and the English (George Eliot in particular), though "personally detached from Christian doctrine, keep its strong imprint, as bells of the church that always ring out things divine, even when turned to profane uses." [48] They are ever present witnesses of the Infinite. De Vogüé's sympathy stops short of Dostoevsky whom he treats with a puzzled air as "the Jeremiah of the jail," "the Shakespeare of the lunatic asylum." He speaks perceptively of *Crime and Punishment* but all the later novels seem to him monstrous and unreadable.[49]

De Vogüé admires Tolstoy as one of the greatest masters: but he sees in him a "propagandist of nihilism" or, contradictorily, combining "the mind of an English chemist with the soul of a Hindu Buddhist." [50] De Vogüé established the unfortunate pattern which made the Russian novelists some sort of exotic, inspired madmen, but his book made the decisive breakthrough. Limited as it is in critical insight, it was a turning point in East-West literary relations.

While de Vogüé was anticipating the Catholic religious revival of the turn of the century, other critics began the dissolution of the objective world assumed by Zola, also in criticism. Jules Lemaître

and Anatole France memorably expressed the complete relativism
to which a solipsistic psychology can lead.

JULES LEMAÎTRE (1853-1914)

It is difficult to distinguish between the basic theories of Lemaître
and France. Both come from Renan's skepticism and dilettantism
and continue the skeptical side of Sainte-Beuve. France expressed
himself possibly more memorably and sharply, but Lemaître preceded him and was no doubt the better literary critic, in that he
engaged more texts more closely, while France's literary criticism
was only a comparatively minor activity accompanying his rich
fictional production. Lemaître's eight volumes of *Contemporains*
(7 vols. 1887–99; Vol. 8, 1914), though interspersed with trivia, range
widely and contain substantial studies. The four volumes of Anatole
France's *La Vie littéraire* (1888–94) are lighter fare. Oddly enough,
the two writers—so nearly related by temperament, methods and
taste—moved to the opposite ends of the intellectual spectrum:
Lemaître became an ardent anti-Dreyfusard and finally a member
of the *Action française*. France pronounced the funeral oration at
the grave of Emile Zola and became a Communist.

In the beginning, however, the two engaged the same enemies,
dogmatism and naturalism, and came to the same conclusions.
Lemaître apparently transferred the painters' term "impressionism" to literary criticism and argued from a similar subjectivist
theory of knowledge. "Works pass by the mirror of our mind; but
as the procession is long, the mirror changes, in the meantime, and
when by chance the same work returns, it no longer projects the
same image." [1] In his youth Lemaître adored Corneille and almost
disliked Racine: later he adores Racine and Corneille left him cold.
Man is changeable, inconsistent, and the critic can do no more than
"define the impression which, at a given moment, this work of art
has made on us where a writer himself has put down the impression
which he in turn has received from the world at a particular hour." [2]
Thus today's impression cannot commit the impression of tomorrow. Criticism is "the representation of a world as personal, as
relative, as vain, and hence as interesting as that which other literary
genres constitute." [3] It can be nothing but "the art of enjoying books
and of enriching and refining one's impressions of them." [4]
Criticism which believes in system or a body of doctrines such as

Brunetière's is mistaken. There are no genres and no hierarchy of genres. There is no evolutionary history. The divorce between admiration and liking accepted by Brunetière is not only deplorable but false. "One calls good what one loves." [5] The critic is not a judge but only a reader. He needs "sympathetic imagination" to enjoy all kinds of works of art even in the distant past. Lemaître is strongly aware of the modern historical sense, of the survival of the past within us. "The modern mind seems made up of several minds; it contains, one could say, the minds of centuries gone by." [6] Lemaître himself began as an academic literary historian with studies of French 18th-century comedy and of Corneille's interpretation of Aristotle.[7] His late, rather slight books on Fénelon (1908) and Racine (1910) were a return to this early love. But, in arguing against Brunetière he objected strongly to the whole notion of tradition and the worship of the past. He resolutely, even blatantly, declared his "modernity." "Is it my fault that I'd rather reread a chapter by M. Renan than a sermon by Bossuet, *Nabab* than *La Princesse de Clèves,* or a comedy by Meilhac and Halévy than even a comedy by Molière himself?" [8] In an article on Gaston Paris, Lemaître launched a full-scale attack against antiquarianism: "the most futile of human occupations," fit for people who "amuse their intelligence with easy difficulties." At bottom the scholar "despises the poets, novelists, critics, and journalists." Actually "philology prevents him from understanding literature." "Three quarters of the texts of the Middle Ages ooze an insufferable boredom." Antiquarianism is sentimental ancestor worship designed to prove one's good heart.[9] The tone of disappointment and defiance is unmistakable: Lemaître enjoys the Paris of his time, enjoys the daily chore of literary journalism, and enjoys almost all kinds of modern art: the Parnassians, Sully Prudhomme, François Coppée, Baudelaire, in spite of his "puerile search for extravagant opinions," [10] the Goncourts, and even Zola. Lemaître dismisses Zola's theories and ridicules his crudities and improbabilities, but finally comes to the conclusion that he composed an impressive "pessimistic epic of human animality." [11] Lemaître thoroughly enjoyed the contemporary theater and published ten volumes of his *Impressions du théâtre* (1888–98). He welcomes Huysmans and Anatole France as well as Maupassant. His sympathies stop short only at the frontiers of France. A later article "De l'Influence récente des littératures du Nord" attacks the admiration for Ibsen and the Russians. He makes valid points when he protests that saintly prostitutes are not a Russian invention; that women like Nora, who follow the voice of their heart, were well known to George Sand; that motifs and ideas come back in a new disguise to France from which they originally emanated. He tones down his exercise in "literary chauvinism" at the end and recognizes (I believe for the first time) that criticism is judgment, which, however, is "an impression controlled and enlightened by preceding impressions." [12] He begins to turn toward classicism and conservatism. The highly laudatory essays on Lamartine and Veuillot testify that there was always an undercurrent of emotional Catholicism in him. The attitudes of the early 20th-century French classicism are foreshadowed.

ANATOLE FRANCE (1844–1924)

Anatole France put the argument for complete subjectivism with the greatest epigrammatic force and grace. In the preface to the first volume of La Vie littéraire (1888) he formulated the position most memorably:

> The good critic tells the adventures of his soul among masterpieces. There is no more an objective criticism than there is an objective art, and all those who flatter themselves that they have put anything other than themselves into their work are the dupes of the most deceptive illusion. The truth is that one never gets outside oneself. This is one of our greatest afflictions. What would we not give to see, for a minute, the sky and the earth with the faceted eye of a fly or to understand nature with the crude, simple brain of an orangutan? But this is denied us. We cannot, like Tiresias, be a man and remember having been a woman. We are enclosed in our person as if in a perpetual prison. . . . The critic should say if he is candid: Gentlemen, I am going to speak about myself in connection with Shakespeare, Racine, Pascal, or Goethe.[1]

Obviously aesthetics and theory are delusions. "Aesthetics is not based on anything solid. It is a castle in the air." [2] "We know today little more about the laws of art than the troglodytes of the Vézère who traced the mammoth and the reindeer with the point of the silex on bone and ivory." [3] Criticism never can become a science, as it must learn that "every book has as many different copies as there are readers and that a poem, like a landscape, changes with the eyes that see it, in the minds that conceive it." [4] The only thing a critic can do is to record the pleasure a work gives him. "Pleasure is the only yardstick of merit," but it also is "the cause of the eternal diversity of our judgments." [5] There is no such thing as tradition or universal agreement. France admits that "almost universal opinion favors certain works. But this is due to prejudice, and not at all to choice or spontaneous preference." [6] France, in his polemic with Brunetière, denies his contention that there is a minimal agreement of what is art and what is non-art: when it comes to drawing up the two lists, no understanding is possible.[7] France ridicules the superstition of great names. "Ossian as long as he was regarded an ancient seemed equal to Homer. He is despised because one knows he is MacPherson." [8] There is simply no opinion in literature which cannot be easily contradicted. Only rarely does France recognize that extreme skepticism defeats itself. "If one doubts, one must fall silent." [9] Candidly he denies being a critic. "I shall never know how to manage the threshing machines into which some nimble men feed the literary harvest in order to separate the grain from the chaff." But there are fairy tales. He is writing "tales about literature." [10] After all, criticism is the daughter of imagination, and in a way, a work of art.[11]

It is all put wittily and sharply and may convince those who accept the theory of knowledge implied in these statements: the distrust of reason and the doubt about reality. Actually France, of course, as any other critic, claims that his impressions are of interest to others. His own taste has some aspiration to authority, though in theory he praises an all-embracing historical tolerance that allows us to love both Shakespeare and Racine.[12] In a destructive review of Zola's *La Terre* he can say: "he lacks taste, and I have come to believe that a lack of taste is the mysterious sin mentioned in Scripture, the greatest sin, the only sin for which there is no forgiveness." [13] France's own taste would be easy to define. He disapproves of naturalism: it outrages nature, modesty, and beauty.[14] In the review of *La Terre* he goes so far as to deplore Zola's ever having been born, though he always recognized a "vigorous, crude talent" in him. Actually he praised *La Bête humaine* and *La Débâcle*, with reservations, long before he forgave Zola everything for his defense of

Dreyfus.[15] France certainly admired the classical virtues of lucidity, brevity, and simplicity: *Daphnis and Chloë, La Princesse de Clèves, Candide,* and *Manon Lescaut* are light enough "to fly through the ages." [16] France praises Baudelaire, though he agrees that he was "a very bad Christian" and even a "despicable man." "But he was a poet and hence divine." [17] But all this is hardly new or unusual. What was important, besides the radical anti-theory, both in Lemaître and France, was rather the form: the perfection they attained in critical *causerie*.

The deftness and charm of these hundreds of articles, often on ephemeral topics, is impossible to overstate. Sainte-Beuve succeeded in the form before but within more fixed patterns, with more historical and intellectual baggage. Lemaître and France indulge in all the devices developed since Hazlitt of autobiographical reminiscence, personal allusion, metaphorical fancy, impressionist evocation, parody, and satire, to achieve their aim of engaging and persuading the reader. Lemaître's review of Zola's *Le Rêve,* for instance, retells the plot of the novel in the apparently unstudied style of a medieval legend or fairy tale and then suddenly quotes the "physiological" passages in order to conclude with the genuinely critical perception that there is "an enormous discrepancy between the content and the form" which is unpleasant and disgusting.[18] Lemaître has made his point and has demonstrated it amusingly in a short space. France achieves the same thing in a brief essay on Flaubert's *Correspondance.* He starts with the memory of a visit to Flaubert, a description of his person and the violent opinions he pronounced, and then turns to the *Correspondance* to find his memory confirmed. Flaubert was "coarse and kind, enthusiastic and laborious, a mediocre theorist, an excellent worker and great, good man." He writes to Louise Colet as if she were a good dog; he had only one passion, literature.[19] It is only a tiny sketch made up of a seemingly artless mosaic of reminiscences, quotations, and opinions, but it serves its purpose very well: we know the man and the book and what the critic thinks of them. This is surely one task of criticism. Lemaître and France denied the age-old struggle for a theory of literature, for any intellectual understanding of the art but they have, in practice, reasserted one of the main functions of criticism: the definition and formation of taste.

2: HIPPOLYTE TAINE

TODAY THE NAME TAINE (1828–93) almost compulsively evokes three words: race, milieu, and moment. He is known as the founder of a sociological science of literature. But one has the impression that at least outside of France he is not read any more. Writers on English literature hardly ever refer to his *History of English Literature*. Even in France his reputation is under a cloud. Except for specialists his peculiar, highly complex position in a history of criticism seems to be unknown or misunderstood.

The formula "race-milieu-moment" has been severely criticized. "Race" owing mainly to its abuse by the Nazis, seems a discredited concept today, at least, in literary studies. We doubt that there is a necessary link between physical traits and specific mental habits. We cannot believe in a French, English, or German "race," and even less in the stability and complete distinctness of respective psychic characteristics and hence literary traditions. "Moment" seems either an obscure or a superfluous concept. In the introduction to the *History of English Literature,* the *locus classicus* of Taine's theory, "moment" is defined as "the acquired speed" or "the acquired impulsion" [1] of the historical process. "Moment" is identified with speed, on the analogy of mechanics, and thus, combined with mass, would make up the resultant force. It can, however, be argued that the term is "entirely unnecessary and even inappropriate," [2] that using it is like saying that water is made up of three components—H_2, O, and water. "Moment" is the sum of race and milieu, or sometimes simply the milieu of a particular time.

The term "milieu" is the only one that has preserved its usefulness and has survived intact. It is a catch-all for the external conditions of literature: it includes not only the physical environment (soil, climate) but also political and social conditions. It is a conglomerate of everything that can even remotely be brought into contact with literature. Taine, it is argued, never properly analyzed it, never made up his mind which one of its components is the "starter" of the historical process, or what their exact relationships, their comparative weights, are.

It is not surprising that those who believe in a social determination of literature have gone to Marxism for a more rigorous method and more concrete analysis, with apparently far more certain results. Taine is recognized only as a pioneer, as a precursor of a genuine sociology of literature. When literary historians such as Georg Brandes, Edmund Gosse, and Vernon Parrington make definite acknowledgments to Taine, they seem to pay tribute mainly to his stimulation: but in reality Brandes and Parrington are largely inspired by political fervors of their own, and Edmund Gosse came to see that he had really learned nothing from Taine's method.[3] Taine does not satisfy those whose ideal is a social science of literature.

Others doubted the whole enterprise: the claim that literature is primarily a product of society, that a work of literature is a social document that can be reduced to its social causes. In Taine's own time, Sainte-Beuve and many others voiced such objections. Faguet formulated them in a well-known essay.[4] The personality of the artist, it is argued, cannot be explained. With Taine's method we might be able to account for the mind of a burgher from Rouen in the 1630's, and even for Thomas Corneille, but not for the genius of Pierre Corneille. Mediocre writings may serve as social documents but the greatest works of art are poor historical evidence. Moreover, Taine's whole method minimizes the fact and value of art, for, with him, art becomes only a piece of life. Its essence—form and the specific angle of imagination—is ignored. Thus sociologists, aestheticians, and formalists have united in rejecting Taine and (with the passing of time) in ignoring him. One must grant the justice of these criticisms against vague racial theorizing, against the loose reduction of literature to influences from climate and social conditions. Taine's claim that "if these forces could be measured and deciphered, one could deduce from them, as if from a formula, the characteristics of the future civilization" and his contention that "when we have considered race, milieu, and moment, we have exhausted not only all real causes but, even more, all the possible causes of movements"[5] have not been convincing. On every point he fails to show the complete concrete determination of literature by race-milieu-moment.

But while this criticism of Taine is well-founded, a closer examination shows that it gives a highly simplified account even of the race-milieu-moment triad and entirely ignores the many other motifs of his critical thought.

"Race" in Taine is not open to the usual objections: it is not a fixed integer, a mysterious biological factor; Taine does not preach the purity or superiority of a race. It is, rather, a shifting term, which sometimes refers to the main human races but more often to the difference between the Germanic and Latin nations and most frequently to the national characteristics of the main European nations: English, French, and German. Taine's race is simply the old *Volksgeist,* the genius of a nation.[6] Every nation, Taine agrees in reproducing the view of the German classical scholar Otfried Müller, is "a moral person."[7] Taine saw that this "race" has come about by a long process, often hidden in the darkness of prehistory.[8] "A race exists having acquired its character from the climate, from the soil, the food and the great events that it underwent at its origin."[9] Race, he recognizes, does not explain an individual. He chides Michelet for his attempt to explain the characters of Maximilian and Charles V "by combining the qualities of the five or six races that furnished their ancestors."[10] "Race" with Taine is simply the French mind or the English character.

Taine felt acutely the differences among the main European nations. From his reading and environment he had inherited the contrast between the Latin and the Germanic nations, between the North and the South as a central problem in modern literary history. Madame de Staël, Stendhal, Philarète Chasles, Emile Montégut had been or were preoccupied with this question, and all around Taine historians like Augustin Thierry, Michelet, Renan, and Froude were disentangling the racial strands in French, English, and ancient history. Taine, in bewildering profusion, ascribes to the English race the most diverse and often contradictory characteristics: stoic energy and basic honesty, heroic severity, a somber and passionate imagination, a sense of the real and the sublime, a love of solitude and the sea, an instinct of revolt, depth of desires, gravity and vehemence, concentrated passion, sensibility and lyrical exaltation, a phlegmatic temper, an exact knowledge of precise detail, and a strong sense of the practical.[11] Taine shifts to and fro from physical characteristics, such as the large feet of English men and women or the rosy cheeks of their children,[12] to generalizations about the intensity of their sensations and feelings, the power of their will, and even to highly specific cultural predispositions and convictions. He can speak of the "great English idea," "the persuasion that man is primarily a moral and free person"; he can assume that the English are somehow naturally Protestant, and that they have no talent or interest in metaphysics.[13]

Similarly, the portrait of the French is drawn in the most diverse ways: according to mood, soberly or satirically. They are a "light and sociable race,"[14] "the need of laughter is a national trait."[15] "A facile, abundant, curious mind is the genius of the race."[16] In a passage defining the French spirit that came to England with the Normans, Taine generalizes boldly: "When a Frenchman conceives an event or an object, he conceives quickly and *distinctly*. The movement of his intelligence is nimble and prompt like that of his limbs; at once and without effort he seizes an idea. But he seizes that alone. He is deprived or, if you prefer, he is exempt from those sudden half-visions that disturb a man, and instantaneously open up to him vast depths and far perspectives. Images are excited by internal commotion; he, not being so moved, imagines not. He is moved only superficially. He is without sympathy. That is why no race in Europe is less poetical."[17] Late in life Taine can say that a Frenchman is a "rhetorician and a gabbler,"[18] can deny his nation "the madness and genius of imagination,"[19] and can even proclaim his political incapacity and call "stupid vanity" his national disease.[20] Within the French spirit a distinction is sometimes drawn between the original Gallic spirit and the Latin mind that was imposed upon it. But curiously enough whole pages of the characterization of the Gallic spirit in the book on La Fontaine are transferred bodily to the *History* and there ascribed to the French spirit in general.[21] In the book on art in the Netherlands, Taine draws a distinction between race and nation, but in the two separate chapters devoted to these concepts he fails to keep to the distinction he drew between them: between "race with its fundamental and indelible qualities that persist through all circumstances and in all climates . . . (and) the nation with its original qualities . . .

transformed by its environment and history." [22] The chapter on race considers habits of eating and physical traits but also discusses the regard for the marriage tie, the difference between the classical and romantic traits of the European nations, and the question of Catholicism and Protestantism; the chapter on the people speaks of the influence of soil and climate, of labor conditions, politics, and so on. Taine's attempt to establish the national psychologies of the main European nations is purely impressionistic. He achieves only an agglomeration of traits drawn from all kinds of sources: from travel impressions, travelers' accounts, anecdotes; from a study of art and literature whose characteristics are freely assigned in haphazard selection to the nation that produced the author sometimes centuries before. Differences of epochs, social classes, regions, and gifts (genius or casual encounter in street?) are ignored: little details are accumulated, always with the assumption that they are somehow symptomatic. One cannot dismiss the problem of national character: one must admit the truth of many of Taine's observations, but one must be dissatisfied with the lack of system, order, and evidence in Taine's typology. The nations remain figures that assume colors or change them as the argument or the need of contrast or balance seems to require. Though central to his literary theory, the concept of race remains elusive, shifting, and ultimately opaque.

Moment is also a much more complex concept than the definition of speed of evolution in the introduction to the *History of English Literature* seems to imply. Taine never again speaks of acquired speed. Mostly ("moment" is not used often) the term means something very different: the age, the *Zeitgeist*. The passage in the introduction seems to suggest another related meaning: the position of a work of art in tradition; Taine refers to the contrast between Corneille and Voltaire, Aeschylus and Euripides, Lucretius and Claudian, da Vinci and Guido Reni [23] as "moments," distinguishing between a precursor or a successor. But then again he seems to think of "moment" as a period when a particular conception of man prevails: the knight or the monk are ideals in the Middle Ages, while the courtier and the fine talker become the models in the French 17th century. Oddly enough Taine then speaks of ages in which there is a concordance of forces: in the French 17th century the "sociable character and spirit of conversation innate in France encountered the habits of the *salon* and the moment of rhetorical analysis,"[24] as if the *salon* and rhetorical analysis existed somehow as given entities that converge with the national character. Moment remains as baffling and shifting a concept as race. It points to the unitary spirit of a time or to the pressure of a literary tradition. Its main function is to serve as a reminder that history is dynamic while milieu is static.

The term milieu occurs prominently in Balzac's preface to the *Human Comedy* (1842), where it is used in the sense of habitat of an animal. Balzac took the term from the zoologist Geoffroy Saint-Hilaire, who in turn drew it originally from physics. Comte also used the term prominently.[25] But the idea of explaining literature by its environment, especially by climate and social conditions, is age-old. It goes back to antiquity and the Renaissance and is in full flower in the 18th century, notably with Dubos, Marmontel, and Herder and in Madame de Staël's early work, *De la Littérature* (1800). Taine, in many respects, continues the work of Madame de Staël. His leading theme is also the contrast of the Latin and Germanic nations and the relation of national character to social conditions. But Taine writes in a different mental climate, with different assumptions and methods. The theory of milieu in Taine has scientific pretensions: it aims at a complete deterministic explanation of literature (and all mental life). Taine always emphasized that he is an absolute determinist,[26] and he often repeats the doctrine that "the work of art is determined by a totality of the general state of mind and surrounding manners."[27] Taine is convinced as to the identity of the method of the natural and moral sciences.[28] He defines even his "main idea" as the "assimilation of historical and psychological research to physiological and chemical researches."[29] He can even say, "I apply physiology to moral matters, nothing more. I have borrowed from philosophy and the positive sciences methods which seem to me potent and applied them to the psychological sciences."[30] All of Taine's writings are permeated by analogies between mental and physical events. He speaks of the history of art as a sort of applied botany, or he carefully parallels "mental climate" and "moral temperature" with examples of zones of vegetation.[31] One passage that excited much comment and prompted accusations of materialism says that "vice and virtue are products like vitriol and sugar."[32] Taine had to explain, even years afterward, that he did not say that vice and virtue were chemical products or even like chemical products, but that they were products explainable in terms of their causes, which may not all be physical.[33] Taine held fast to this view: everything is determined by causes. The aim of every science and its only valid method is the demonstration of a universal law of causation.

But how concretely does Taine show the causal dependence of literature on its milieu? Has he analyzed the strands within the milieu and the mutual dependencies of climate, soil, and social and political conditions? At times he assumes that the physical conditions of life are the starter of the causal process. In discussing Holland, he construes an amusingly simple series of causes and effects: "It might well be said that in this country water makes grass, grass makes cattle, cattle make cheese, butter, and meat; and all these, with beer, make the inhabitant. Indeed, out of this rich living, and out of this physical organization, saturated with moisture, spring the Flemish temperament, the phlegmatic nature, the regular habits, the tranquil mind and nerves, the capacity for taking life easily and prudently, the unbroken contentment, the love of well-being, and, consequently, the reign of cleanliness and the perfection of comfort."[34] Climate is often spoken of as causing specific mental states: Taine can say that rain "leaves no room for other than sinister and melancholy thoughts,"[35] and that "the amount of inconvenience which the [English] climate imposes upon man, and the endurance it requires of him are infinite. Hence arise melancholy and the idea of duty."[36] Taine plays constant variations on the theme of the depressing influence of the English climate, its changeability, the rain, the fog, the cold, the mud, the storms at sea, often contrasting it with the sunny, balmy South. The book on La Fontaine (in the revised edition of 1861) starts with a travel chapter that compares landscapes of the Picardy, Flanders, the Rhine, and the Ardennes with that of Champagne. Here everything is "on a small scale, in agreeable proportions, without excess and contrasts."[37] Thus man and in particular La Fontaine "takes on and keeps the imprint of the soil and the sky."[38] Taine never doubts the accuracy of his climatic information and generalizations [39] and never asks how far man could emancipate himself from its influence. He is content with the broad truth of the contrast between North and South: sadness and joy.

When Taine approaches literature itself more closely, he usually tries to relate it more concretely to social and political conditions. Thus Renaissance art is depicted against the background of the politics of the Borgias and Machiavelli. French 17th-century literature is always connected with the court of Louis XIV, and Restoration comedy with the manners or rather bad manners of the court of Charles II. Almost always, at least a sketch of the social and political conditions is given as a background of the literature or art.

But Taine attempts a causal explanation seriously only when he focuses on the audience of literature. He proclaims that "literature always adapts itself to the taste of those who can appreciate it and pay for it," [40] and makes a real effort to give concrete descriptions of several audiences: thus he contrasts the popular audience of Shakespeare with that of Restoration comedy [41] or the new audience of artists and professionals in France with frequenters of the *salons* of the 17th and 18th centuries.[42] Most strikingly Taine depicts the audience of Tennyson—the family circle, the world-wide travelers, the connoisseurs of antiquity, the sportsmen, the lovers of the country, the wealthy, cultivated free businessmen and their ladies— and confronts it with that of Musset—the intellectuals, the Bohemian artists, the earnest specialists, the hectic women of leisure.[43] Implicitly, at least, he shows how these two poets satisfy their respective audiences by incorporating preferences of their readers in their writings. Still, Taine does not expressly claim that a specific audience evokes a specific literature: often he seems to consider the public rather an obstacle to the artist. Dryden, for instance, had "the worst of publics, debauched and frivolous, devoid of individual taste." [44] A harmony between the artist and the audience is assumed to be ideal. "The character who weeps on the stage only rehearses our own tears; our interest is but that of sympathy; and the drama is like an external conscience." [45] Tragedy was impossible with an audience of drunkards, prostitutes, and old children (like Charles II), and Dryden thus had to fail as a tragedian. But even if one admits the light that these observations shed on the influence of the audience on literature, one must conclude that Taine does not provide a systematic scientific sociology of literature and fails even to formulate the problems it raises. He is content with indicating a variety of external circumstances under which literature is pro-

duced without ever clearly analyzing the exact relevance of each
component element or the degree of dependence.

If Taine's achievement could be described merely as an attempt
to establish a sociology of literature, we should have to assign him
only the role of a dilettantish and impressionistic precursor.
Though he made much of race-milieu-moment, we must, however,
interpret him on different grounds, on a different intellectual basis,
since his real greatness and importance as a critic of literature lies
elsewhere. Taine is not easy to place in a history of ideas. Clearly
he was not a materialist in the sense of Hobbes or Helvétius.[46] He
can say rightly: "I am so little a materialist that in my eyes the
physical world is nothing but appearance." [47] He is also, contrary to
the usual opinion, no positivist, obviously not a positivist in any
school sense. One cannot find any mention of Comte in all of
Taine's voluminous and fully preserved early papers.[48] Taine
studied Comte only in 1860, when Taine's views were settled on
practically all decisive questions. Later he severely criticized Comte
not only as "probably one of the worst of all bad writers," but as
"entirely a stranger to metaphysical speculations, to literary culture,
historical criticism, and psychological feelings." [49] Taine was more
favorably impressed by Mill, but his examination of the *Logic*
culminates in an elaborate criticism of Mill's central concept of
cause.[50] Taine finds it entirely unacceptable because it is purely
empirical, an observed sequence of events, a total heterogeneity of
cause and effect. When reviewing Spencer, Taine dismisses his
agnosticism, his whole idea of the Unknowable.[51] Still, admitting
Taine's rejection of many central doctrines of the most eminent
positivists, one could argue that he was positivist in a wide and loose
sense. The worship of the natural sciences and their methods points
in this direction: seen in the wide perspective of 19th-century intellectual history, Taine seems to belong to the reaction against early
idealism. He seems to go back to Condillac and Cabanis even
though he does not share the exact views of Comte, Mill, and
Spencer. He is certainly imbued with the psychological and biological ideas of his time.

But on many points Taine does differ profoundly from positivism: one could even argue that he is almost isolated in his time and
place. He believes deeply in an "intelligible universe." He is con-

vinced that we know reality as it is, in itself, and that we are capable of "absolute and limitless knowledge," that "metaphysics is possible," [52] that "existence itself is explicable." [53] He believes in a single system of the world, in an identity of thought and being, essence and existence, and ultimately in some kind of pantheism. The eloquent conclusion of the *French Philosophers,* which glorifies the world as a unique, indivisible being whose "eternal axiom" or "creative formula" [54] the philosopher seeks to discover, leaves no doubt about his pantheistic leanings. The same fervent belief in the intelligible world, tempered sometimes with a recognition of our distance from the ultimate goal of complete knowledge, fills the last pages of both *De l'Intelligence* and *Thomas Graindorge.*

In short, Taine was basically a Hegelian. We have abundant evidence of his close study of the *Aesthetic,*[55] the *Logic,* the *Philosophies of History, Religion,* and *Right.*[56] We have many pronouncements of high admiration and professions of personal adherence. Hegel is "a Spinoza multiplied by Aristotle"; [57] he is the philosopher "who came nearest the truth." [58] More importantly, in many central passages Taine definitely proclaims as his aim the translation of Hegel (or the "Germans") into modern scientific terms.[59] The Hegelian influence (apart from the problem of knowledge) is most important in two respects: in Taine's idea of history and in his central aesthetic conceptions.

Taine himself tells that Hegel taught us "to conceive historical periods as moments, to look for internal causes, spontaneous development, the incessant becoming of things." [60] Taine's view of history is Hegelian in its emphasis on dynamic change, though far less consistently than Hegel's, seen in terms of dialectical oppositions, which Taine calls "volte face"; [61] and in triads of thesis, antithesis, and synthesis. It is Hegelian also in its view that mind or mental change is the motive power of history. Contrary to the usual assumption that he is a materialist, Taine believes that "all great change has its root in the soul," [62] that the "psychological state is the cause of the social state." [63] But "cause" in Taine is used in a way quite different from the ordinary naturalistic explanation by antecedent forces. Taine uses cause (as Hegel does) as a synonym for law or concept, essence, substance, or even "fact." Taine's causal explanations are baffling because he does not trace causal sequences but, rather, reduces a phenomenon to its logical precedence, its law, its essence.

Thus when he tries to explain the rise of Protestant church music, he gives as its causes a changed view of the cult, a new idea of conduct, and finally a new idea of God.[64] "The causes of events are the innate laws of things." [65] Like Hegel, Taine thinks of history mainly in collectivist terms—the development of large forces, nations, races, philosophies, literatures, arts—though, contrary to Hegel, he does not glorify the state. Like Hegel, he tries to combine such collectivism with individualism; the collective forces are expressed and represented by great individuals. As in Hegel, the identification of force and success with greatness is implicit. As in Hegel, the evolution of humanity is conceived as tightly organized: history is thought of as a sequence of periods which are organic unities and which manifest a complete parallelism of all human activities. There is such a convergence, for instance, in the age of Louis XIV. "Between a hedge at Versailles, a philosophical and theological reasoning of Malebranche, a prosodic rule prescribed by Boileau, a law of Colbert on mortgages, a compliment in the waiting room of the king at Marly, a statement of Bossuet about the kingship of God, the distance seems infinite and unsurmountable," [66] but actually all these diverse events are expressions of one and the same spirit. There is a close parallelism between Lydgate's poetry and the costumes and flamboyant architecture of his age.[67] Like Hegel (and Vico) Taine believes that history moves in cycles: that civilizations rise, flower, and decline like organisms,[68] and that France in the 19th century corresponds to the age of Alexandria, the age of decadence.[69] Only in one point of the conception of history does Taine differ profoundly from Hegel: he does not share his optimism, his view that the universal progress toward liberty (or rather consciousness) was accomplished in Hegel's own time. Taine has too pessimistic a view of the nature of man: he believes in scientific progress, but he has despaired of moral or artistic advancement. As he has lost religion (though he became more and more aware of its historical role and its desirable effects on social stability) he shares the gloomy pessimism and even personal despair of many men of his and all ages. Marcus Aurelius is his favorite remedial reading; his sympathy for Byron, Musset, and Heine has its explanation in this survival of the romantic *Weltschmerz*.[70] Scientism and pessimism often go hand in hand but in Taine they are overlaid by a Hegelian sense of history and historical development.

If one understands Taine's Hegelian view of history and art, the argument most frequently voiced against Taine that art, and especially great art, is no "social document" becomes irrelevant, and his view of the important critical problem of the "representativeness" of a work of literature is clarified. Taine (and Hegel) equate historical and artistic greatness. The very nature and definition of art is precisely the concrete universal, the union of the particular and the general. From the very first pages of his thesis on La Fontaine (1853) Taine constantly paraphrased and translated Hegel's definition of art as "das sinnliche Scheinen der Idee." Poetry is "the art of transforming general ideas into small sensuous facts"; [71] art is "a general idea become as particular as possible." [72] Art is thus a form of knowledge, though sensuous knowledge, and the artist (like the philosopher) grasps the essence and nature of things. Art conveys truth, and necessarily historical truth, truth about man at a certain time and place. Works of art "furnish documents *because* they are monuments." [73] Taine believes that ages crystallize in great works.[74] A harmony between genius and age is postulated: in Racine we come upon an "exact correspondence between the public and the private manner of feeling. His mind is like the abridgment of the mind of others." [75] The very different fables of La Fontaine are also "the whole century abridged." [76] Taine can conclude that "the deeper [a poet] penetrates into his art, the more he has penetrated into the genius of his age and race." [77] Though mediocre or average works of art may seem to us better social documents, Taine finds them inexpressive and hence unrepresentative. "Representativeness" and "expressiveness" of an age, a nation, and thus historicity and nationality are, by definition, both a result and a cause of artistic value.

The entire novelty of his criticism (and that of his precursors) lies in these concepts, for in Taine's mind the birth of the historical spirit in Germany and the new subtle psychology of Stendhal and Sainte-Beuve unite to form the criticism he was practicing himself.[78] In a study of Carlyle he defines his method of considering the poet, the writer, as a "revealer of the infinite, as a representative of his century, his nation, his age." He continues: "You recognize here all the German formulae. They signify that the artist detects and expresses better than any other the salient and durable features of the world that surrounds him, so that we may draw from his work a theory of man and of nature together with a picture of his race and of his time. This discovery has renewed criticism." [79]

But historicism easily leads to complete relativism. Taine often emphasizes the historical spirit as a spirit of universal toleration. He criticizes classicism for thinking that man is everywhere the same [80] and the English (with Walter Scott) for their inability to achieve the historical spirit because they consider their civilization the only rational one.[81] Taine defines the "historical spirit" as "sympathy for all forms of art and all schools . . . as manifestations of the human spirit" [82] and fortifies historical relativism by the analogy of scientific objectivity. "Science neither pardons nor proscribes: it verifies and explains." "It is analogous to botany, which studies the orange, the laurel, the pine, and the birch, with equal interest." [83] But Taine does not, of course, consider all works of art to be of equal value and he had to recognize that at all times and at every step he was making judgments.[84] He does not lose sight of the central problem of his criticism, that of representativeness.

This criterion of representativeness was, from the very first, Taine's way of overcoming relativism. In the book on La Fontaine he had tried to rank authors according to the following standard: do they represent merely a passing fashion (such as Voiture), a historical genre (such as Racine), or the spirit of the whole race (such as La Fontaine)? [85] Later, when he came to repeat the scheme, he modified it. Lowest in the scale still stood literature as representing a mere fashion of three or four years' duration, then the same as representing a generation, then a historical period, then a race. This time humanity appeared as the highest value.[86] Taine does not quite face the implications of the new scale with a purely all-human literature as the highest point. The new scale seems to reject the concrete universal and would end up in good classicism: it certainly would belie the emphasis on nationality repeated in the same book. "The greater the artist, the more deeply does he manifest the temper of the race." [87]

But whether complete universality or nationality or expressiveness of a particular age is the standard, the work of art is always considered a sign or a symbol of humanity, nation, or age. Art and literature are in Taine not a social document, though he often says so. Rather they are the essence, the summary of history.

This assumption explains a puzzling feature of Taine's practice:

his astonishingly uncritical use of evidence. As a symbol or sign of a
mental state, the work of art is never isolated and fixed as an object
(the method of positive science) and needs, in Taine's mind, no
comparison with other nonartistic documentary evidence. The
truth behind an anecdote (however unverifiable) is symbolic truth.
We can draw indiscriminately on all sources: fiction, history, documents, anecdotes, etc. The brutal sensuality of the Elizabethans is
"proved" by referring to the brothel scenes in *Pericles,* to the
wooing of Catherine by Henry V, and to Marston's *Dutch Cour-
tezan,*[88] just as the dying speech of Mithridates in Racine's tragedy
"proves" the dignity and composure of the 17th-century French-
men.[89]

Still, Taine often seeks corroboration for his impressions and
theories from a harmony between historical and literary evidence.
He was, for instance, highly pleased to discover Madame d'Aulnoy's
Voyage en Espagne (1691). "Neither the books nor the pictures
lied: the persons of Lope, Calderón, Murillo, and Zurbaran walked
the streets." [90] Taine might have been disconcerted to hear that the
Voyage had been drawn mainly from literary sources and that
Madame d'Aulnoy may never have been to Spain.[91] Still he could
not have abandoned his central insight; Calderón and Lope, he
would have to say, tell us more about the essential Spain of the
Golden Age than all the documents in archives. "I would give fifty
volumes of charters and a hundred volumes of state papers for the
memoirs of Cellini, the epistles of St. Paul, the table talk of Luther,
or the comedies of Aristophanes." [92]

The assumption that lies behind Taine's conviction is that the
artist is necessarily the man of the deepest insight into truth, not
only truth in a general or transferred sense, but also the truth of an
age or a nation. Thus to Taine, Byron is great and representative
because he saw into the essence of things, even though he was a rebel
against society, alone against all, repudiated and persecuted. But
with other figures, Taine rather assumes a harmony with an age of
a more obvious kind: "By representing the mode of being of a
whole nation and a whole age, a writer rallies round him the
sympathies of an entire age and an entire nation." [93] "Success" with
his contemporaries is the correlate of representativeness, expressiveness. The writer succeeds because he expresses his time, because he
holds up the mirror or erects the ideal implicitly recognized by his

society. The author or rather his characters become models which are imitated as he in turn has drawn his ideal from the instinctive desires of his society.

Almost all of Taine's interest in literature focuses on fictional characters because characters are to him the concrete-universal itself, the type, the ideal. The type, a "fragment of universal man," or a representative of the instincts of the race or the principal traits of a period, is the most important result of art.[94] The ideal or the "purified idea" of the poet becomes the "reigning personage, the model," [95] a creature of the imagination, which is historically and socially significant because there is a "fixed correspondence between what man admires and what he is." [96]

Taine develops a theory from many germs that came to dominate practical criticism, especially in Russia. The term "type," in the sense of a great universal figure of mythical proportions, is used by August Wilhelm Schlegel and Schelling when they discuss Hamlet, Falstaff, Don Quixote, or Faust. In this sense it was imported into France by Charles Nodier in an essay entitled "Des Types en littérature" [97] and used pervasively in Victor Hugo's rhapsody on Shakespeare (1864). The term occurs with the meaning of social type (in the place of the old *caractère*) in a discussion of the rising novel of manners in Balzac's preface to the *Comédie humaine* (1842) and in the preface to George Sand's *Le Compagnon du Tour de France* (1851). The two main strands combine in Taine: there are traces of both the Hegelian ideal and the social type in his conception. His standard of judgment shifts away from the more recent concept back toward the ideal type when he formulated his theory for the lectures at the *Ecole des Beaux-arts* (1867). Taine never thinks of his types merely as realistic pictures, as sources of information about social stratification, although he goes through the characters of La Fontaine's fables, of Shakespeare, Balzac, Dickens, and others with this question in mind. He has little use for realism in the usual sense. Comic characters or simple realistic figures are rated lowest because they represent the most transient social types.[98]

What Taine admires most in art is the depiction of the "hero," and even the superman, the powerful, elemental, passionate man whom he finds everywhere in Shakespeare and Balzac. Taine—himself the most upright and sensitive of men—worships force in history as did Burkhardt and Nietzsche. Force seems to Taine admirable in itself, whatever its ethical consequences. "Wherever there is life, even bestial and maniacal, there is beauty." [99] Force, splendid power, is good in art. "I would rather meet a sheep than a lion in the open country; but behind bars, I would rather see a lion than a sheep. Art is such a bar." [100] Art, one could parody Taine, provides us with a collection of beautiful monsters in a zoo: the railings and cages "by taking away fear . . . preserve the interest." "We can contemplate the superb passions." "It takes us out of ourselves." "Our soul grows with the spectacle." [101] But in life and history Taine increasingly saw the viciousness of such monsters, and he drew acid portraits of Robespierre and Napoleon as maniacs of vanity and egoism. Even his early admiration for the splendid super-men of Shakespeare and Balzac or for Stendhal's ruthless climbers was modified by moralistic and utilitarian standards, in the lectures on the ideal. Here Taine ranks types according to their social value (the scale agrees with the scale of heroes based on the progress from the local to the universal and ends likewise with the most gener-alized, most ideal art as the highest) . Powerful men are preferred to realistic types, but the true heroes, the benefactors of mankind, are rated highest.[102]

This new scale of the "beneficence" of characters leads to conse-quences in literary judgments that seem quite inconsistent with the permanent tendencies of Taine's taste. Forced by the logic of his scheme, he has to rank "complete persons, true heroes" above the great passionate criminals or monomaniacs. He has to list ideal women like Miranda, Imogen, and Goethe's Iphigenie, martyrs like Polyeucte, and finally heroes of the ancient epics: Siegfried, Roland, the Cid. "Further up, and in a higher sphere, are the saviors and gods of Greece or of Judea and Christianity represented in the Psalms, the Gospels, the Apocalypse, and that continuous chain of poetic confessions of which the last and purest links are the *Fioretti* [of St. Francis] and the *Imitatio Christi.*" [103]

Taine links this triad of types (realistic, characteristic, ideal) with a triadic scheme of history. In highly cultivated and refined ages, in mature epochs, when society is at its fullest development, when man stands midway, as in Greece in the 5th century B.C., in Spain and England at the end of the 16th century, in France in the 17th century, and in Taine's own time, appear the lowest and truest types in comic and realistic literature, the most robust and enduring types in dramatic and philosophical literature. But creations truly ideal are abundant only in primitive and simple ages. We must always go back to remote ages, to the origin of peoples amidst the dreams of human infancy in order to find heroes and gods.[104] With a lapse in consistency, Taine, who never particularly valued primitive heroic art, refuses to rank pure heroes, beneficial models, as aesthetically highest. He still finds in Shakespeare and Balzac the most profound works of literature: "They manifest better than others the important characters, the elementary forces, the deepest layers of human nature." [105] The moral scheme is merely superimposed by Taine and not really reconciled with the aesthetic.

Taine, at first, seems to have held very strict views on the distinction between art and ethics. He ridiculed Cousin for the term "moral beauty" and the view that the artist is "a master of virtue." [106] He often asserts that "the artist aims only at creating beauty," [107] that aesthetics and ethics are entirely distinct.[108] He constantly reproaches critics and novelists for moralizing. Thus Macaulay's criticism seems to him very limited, since Macaulay (whom he otherwise admired extravagantly) appears always as a "judge of the righteous and the sinners"; [109] and Thackeray is severely taken to task for sermonizing and preaching.[110] Taine greatly prefers Madame Marneffe in *Cousine Bette* to Becky Sharp. Part of his objection to moralizing is aesthetic: he sides with objective art: with the "sympathetic" Shakespeare against the "concentrated," subjective art of a Milton.[111] In the drama and the novel at least, Taine is a pronounced partisan of objectivity in the sense of the author's absence from the book. The novelist should be a psychologist who "enjoys through contemplation the greatness of a harmful feeling or the organized mechanism of a pernicious character." [112] He praises Stendhal's *Le Rouge et le Noir* for the supposed complete disappearance of the author behind the work.[113] His admiration for Flaubert's *Madame Bovary* and for the stories of Mérimée is based on the same motive. Mérimée "effaces himself. He does not play the cicerone of his treasures." [114] Taine felt that the author's commentary weakens illusions. "Art is attenuated, poetry disappears." [115] He was also personally averse to the display of emotion. "I believe the great principle of Gautier and Stendhal to be true; do not display your feelings on paper . . . It is indecent to reveal one's heart: it is better to be accused of having none." [116] But Taine's objection to moralistic art is not only personal and aesthetic: it comes also from a conviction that "the essential in man is hidden far below moral labels" [117] and that "whether Peter or Paul was a villain concerned only their contemporaries," [118] who had to live with them.

Apparently Taine's outlook changed, and in the lectures on the ideal (1867) he tries to arrive at a reconciliation of aesthetic and moral standards. His solution, with its scale of beneficence of the hero, seems peculiarly unsatisfactory. The moral significance of a work of art, not to speak of its aesthetic value, cannot be judged by the beneficence of the leading character apart from the work itself. Monime is a better person than Phèdre, but that does not mean that *Mithridate* is either aesthetically or morally superior to the other play.

Actually Taine's standard of representativeness, of the truth value of the work of art, of its social usefulness is much modified in practice by his belief in individuality and the expression of individuality. In the aesthetic and historical scheme (derived from Hegel) in which Taine moves there is no contradiction between imitation and expression, truth and feeling. Art is both representative of reality and expressive of personality. The author expresses himself, his particular view of the world, and thereby depicts the world around him and penetrates into the essence of things. "Essence," Taine tells us, is a technical term that he would like to replace by the "capital character, some striking and principal quality, an important point of view, an essential [sic] manner of being of the object." [119] The aim of art is thus to represent the "characteristic," which is both the individual and at the same time that which is significant of reality. Contrary to the usual opinion, Taine does not want to explain away or dissolve individuality. In a letter to Sainte-Beuve, who had made this criticism, [120] Taine asserts, "I have never intended to deduce the individual, to demonstrate that a Shakespeare, a Swift had to appear at such and such a moment in a certain place." [121] On the contrary, Taine's main purpose as a critic is precisely to grasp the individuality, not only of a person but also of an age or a nation: "My fundamental idea was that one must reproduce the emotion, the particular passion of the man one describes . . . in short to paint him in the manner of artists and at the same time to construe him in the manner of reasoners." [122] This is what Taine means by psychological criticism (in contrast to the moralistic English criticism). In a passage in which he characterizes man as "a spiritual machine" he says, "I calculate the play of its motors, I feel with it the impact of obstacles; I see beforehand the curve that its motion will trace out; I experience for it neither aversion nor disgust. I have left these feelings at the threshold of history, and I taste the very deep and pure pleasure of seeing a soul act according to a definite law, in a fixed environment with the whole variety of human passions." [123] Taine is looking for the soul and mind of the writer, and he wants to understand and analyze it as a kind of system dominated by a "master faculty."

The term "master faculty" has been usually understood as a principle of order, as an intermediary link between the collective forces of race-milieu-moment and the psychic events. It can be thought of also as another naturalistic deterministic principle, as a device of classification by which men are put into the proper pigeonholes according to individual types: passionate, imaginative, intellectual, etc. No doubt Taine thought of the human mind often in terms of mechanistic analogies: "A man's particular genius is like a clock," he would say. "It has its mechanism, and among its parts a mainspring. Seek out this spring, show how it communicates movement to the others, pursue this movement from part to part down to the hands in which it ends." [124] Even more frequently he thinks in terms of analogies derived from zoology: thus the dominant trait of the lion is that of a great flesh-eater, and this quality determines the shape and size of his teeth and jaw, his muscles and eye, his stomach and intestines, as well as his "moral" traits. Taine learned from biologists to speak of a law of organic balance or of a connection of interdependence of characters.[125] He suggests that men could be classed in families and species, as in zoology.[126] Here is one of the reasons for the attraction of La Fontaine's fables and the many comparisons between men and animals: men are lions, wolves, foxes, monkeys; and man in general is even called "a ferocious and lewd gorilla." [127]

But "master faculty" is not merely a mechanical or biological principle. It is most often just the principle of individuality: "the dominant and persistent psychic state." [128] Each talent has a master faculty like an eye that is "sensitive to only one color." [129] It is both within the author and what the author discovers and brings out in the world around him. The artist chooses a principal trait: he himself sees things only through his master faculty. The term "master faculty" seems not a happy one to indicate this dominator of a mind. It has obvious ancestors in stoic theory; "ruling passion," versified by Pope, can under various names (e.g., *forme maîtresse*) be found in Montaigne,[130] Bacon, and Pascal.[131]

But the theory clearly exaggerates the oneness and exclusiveness of the master faculty. Taine (who seems a logician to many observers) actually has a profoundly irrationalistic view of human nature. "Strictly speaking, man is mad by nature, as the body is sick; reason and health come to us as momentary success, a lucky accident." [132] External perception, memory are hallucinations: man's real life is "that of a lunatic, who now and then simulates reason, but who is in reality 'such stuff as dreams are made on.' " [133] Taine agrees with what he conceives to have been Shakespeare's psychology. "Man is a nervous machine, governed by a temperament, disposed to hallucinations, transported by unbridled passions, essentially unreasoning, a mixture of animal and poet. His mind is but vigor, his virtue but sensibility, and imagination is his prompter and guide; he is led at random through the most determinate and complex circumstances to pain, crime, madness, and death." [134] This sounds overdrawn and lurid, but Taine conceived of the great poets and writers as monomaniacs obsessed by their one ruling passion, imagination, which rules also the characters they imagine. Shakespeare's imagination is described as "freed from the shackles of reason and morality"; [135] Balzac is depicted as a passionate monomaniac obsessed by work, greed, and lust who envisages (like a visionary) a similar world of monomaniacs: Philippe Brideau, the old Grandet, Hulot. (In *Gambara* and *Masimilla Doni,* a small novel in two parts, Taine counts seven monomaniacs.) [136] Even Dickens, though Taine recognizes his sentimental and moralistic traits, appears as a creator of a world of oddities, humors, criminals, and fools. Sometimes the concept of "master passion" is used by Taine with great skill: Julien Sorel is analyzed in terms of his master passion, pride, and all the apparent contradictions of his behavior are resolved. But often the "master faculty" serves only as a mechanical formula that reduces the complex to the simple. Thus, in the whole book on Livy, Taine insists monotonously on one trait, "an orator turned historian"; or he repeats, for satirical purposes, that Cousin is a "man of eloquence" and nothing else, in order to draw a caricature almost as exaggerated as Daumier's big-nosed lawyers.

The term "master faculty" links the mind of the artist and the character of his world. The work of art is thus also a personal expression. Taine is rarely interested in biography as such, and when corrected by Jean-Jacques Jusserand on details of the *History of English Literature,* he congratulated himself on having stressed the works themselves.[137] Taine (in 1856) was quite content to do without biographical information on Dickens: "Forty volumes, more than suffice to know a man . . . his talent is in his works." [138] Only occasionally did Taine use biographical knowledge: but even here it is used rather as a source of information on the manner of life and on the physique of the man than as systematic narrative. The portrait of Pope is a mosaic carefully pieced together from anecdotes largely culled from Johnson's *Life,* depicting Pope as a malicious, vain, and insincere dwarf.[139] But Taine knows that all this information should not tell against the poetry. He can only say: "I truly wish I could admire Pope's works of imagination, but I cannot." [140] But with Milton and Shakespeare the biographical interpretation becomes much more important. Taine adopts the old view, known to Blake, Coleridge, Shelley, Chateaubriand, and Keble, that Milton "lent Satan his republican soul"; [141] and he can say, absurdly, though also with some precedence (e.g., in essays by Jones Very, in 1838) that "Hamlet *is* Shakespeare" [142] or that Jaques is a "transparent mask behind which we can see the face of the poet." [143] Taine drew from Philarète Chasles [144] what he considered a new biographical interpretation of the *Sonnets* [145] and, on the whole, gives a heightened, extremely lurid picture of a passionate Shakespeare conjectured from the tragedies and the assumed romance of the *Sonnets.* Croce has angrily protested against this characterization where "at the end one does not know whether poets or murderers, artistic contrasts and harmonies or quarrels and dagger blows file past us." [146] But while Taine's identification of Shakespeare with his heroes and criminals seems extravagant and the characters themselves are seen too much as savages and madmen, Taine by no means ignores Shakespeare's aloofness and creativity:

> Metaphor is not his whim, but the form of his thought. In the height of passion he imagines still. When Hamlet, in despair,

remembers his father's noble form, he sees the mythological pictures with which the taste of the age filled the very streets. He compares it to

A station like the herald Mercury
New-lighted on a heaven-kissing hill. [Act iii, sc. 4]

This charming vision, in the midst of fierce invective, proves that there lurks a painter under the poet. Involuntarily and out of season, he has torn off the tragic mask that covered his face; and the reader discovers, behind the contracted features of this terrible mask, a graceful and inspired smile of which he had not dreamed.[147]

The contrast between poet and painter (by painter is meant the artist contemplating his work) may not be drawn very happily, but Taine, we see, is not oblivious to the artist's power of metamorphosis and surrender to the world around him.

Often in Taine art seems to be just personal emotion. Discussing Michelangelo, he speaks of the artist as compulsively mimicking an inner sensation [148] and argues that Michelangelo changed the ordinary proportions of the human body under such internal pressure. Distortion is expressive of emotion. With Taine emotion and emotional sincerity are often standards of good art. "A spring of living ideas and frank passions is needed to make a true poet." [149] "Force in a work of the mind comes only from the sincerity of a personal and original sentiment." [150] Taine excuses Wordsworth (who bores him) by saying "after all, the man is convinced"; [151] and Surrey is chided for thinking "less frequently of loving well than of writing well." [152] Taine does not consider the objection that the lover Surrey would be forgotten and that we remember him only because he thought of writing well. There is even an odd passage describing La Fontaine's manner of composition: he sees "bits of landscapes, gestures, comic or touching figures as if in a dream. During that time, his hand has written unfinished lines concluded with similar syllables; and it happens that the lines are the same as the dream; his sentences have merely noted down emotions." [153] La Fontaine, as traditional and sophisticated a poet and craftsman as one could find anywhere in literary history, is turned into a dreamer and almost into an automatic writer. "La Cigale et la fourmi" becomes something like "Kubla Khan." As Taine was to say, poetry is "the involuntary cry of vivid sensation, the solitary disclosure of an overfull soul." [154]

With such a conception of poetry it is not surprising that Taine very rarely recognizes the importance of form and unity in a work of art. He does so, professedly, in the section of the *Philosophy of Art* that adds a criterion of "convergence of effects" to those of the importance and beneficence of characters. On occasion he praises an author for his sense of form. Thus Spenser and Chaucer are said to have been the first English authors who had "a sensation of totality; they understand proportions, relations, contrasts; they *compose*." [155] But plot or action is always minimized. It is "just a series of events and an order of situations arranged to bring out the characters." [156] When Taine arrives at the discussion of modern lyrical poetry, he embraces a purely emotionalistic point of view. In speaking of Burns he says that "at this moment, the form seems to dissolve into nothing and to disappear; I dare say that this is the great trait of modern poetry." [157] Form, plot, structure mean little to Taine, but he has strong interest in one element of the aesthetic surface: in diction. In a nontechnical but often acutely observant way he can describe style, saying "one judges a mind by its style." [158] Throughout the book on the French philosophers he uses stylistic observations for his satirical purposes, showing, for example, amusingly and devastatingly how the lucubrations of Maine de Biran could be translated into comprehensible ianguage. He accumulates observations on the metaphors and the broken sentence structure of Saint-Simon,[159] the exact choice of words in La Bruyère [160] and the pedantic, obscure, and bombastic jargon in the reflective passages of Balzac.[161] He describes the bare style of Stendhal sympathetically and seems to accept, at this point, the novelist's disparagement of the metaphorical style as un-French and unreasonable,[162] even though his own style was neither bare nor unmetaphorical.

In his critical analyses Taine always returns to his central contrast between genuine poetry—poetry of emotion and passion, individual, "characteristic" writing, the poetry of the North, of England, of Shakespeare and Byron—and the rhetoric of the French tradition, whose classical spirit is rationalistic and hence unpoetic. From the very first of his writings, in *La Fontaine* (1853) , as well as in his last extended pronouncement on literature, the section on the classical spirit in *L'Ancien Régime* (1875), Taine fought this classical spirit and described it with complete consistency. An early letter contrasts French 17th-century tragedy, an art of oratory and analysis in which we do not come to know people, with the art of Shakespeare, which creates illusion, individuals, in short "the characteristic." [163] The oratorical style that extends from Malherbe and Guez de Balzac to Delille and Fontanes, the "reasoning reason" that does not want to embrace the fullness and complexity of things [164] is, for Taine, not only the great blight of poetry but also the intellectual force that brought about the French Revolution, Napoleon, and ultimately the fall of France in 1870. The classical spirit combined with the new scientific spirit furnished the lethal explosive: the concept of the rights of man and the whole absurd idea of a new and rational society, a rootless inhuman Utopia, a centralized despotism whether Republican or Imperial. Taine grossly overrates the rationalism and Cartesianism of French classicism and the whole effectiveness of literary influences on the Revolution. But he seems to me clearly right when he says that the Revolution grows out of the 18th century, continues (also in its fashions, jargon, and taste) the tradition of classical France, and must not be interpreted as the result of the nascent 18th-century romanticism. But whatever the justness of his opinions on these large questions, he does judge the literature of the 17th century by this abstract model and praises only those authors who have succeeded in escaping it: La Fontaine, whom Taine sees as a lone survivor of the Gallic spirit, Pascal, a sublime suffering recluse, and Saint-Simon, a passionate rebel of violent sensibilities. Racine is taken as the representative of the classical spirit, of the rhetorical reason that fails to create living characters and presents only generalized abstractions mouthing commonplaces. But Racine is saved in Taine's eyes by the delicacy and vivacity of his feelings, by his restless, timid, and almost feminine sensibility.[165] Boileau, however, is definitely unreadable or, at best, readable only as a historical document.[166] Madame de la Fayette's style and sentiments seem to him "so remote from ours that we have trouble understanding them. They are like too refined perfumes: we do not smell them anymore; so much delicacy seems to us coldness or insipidity." [167] Taine has to strain his historical imagination to sympathize: but one feels his lack of ease in this world of scruples and unsuspected, mixed feelings.[168]

Taine as a critic has paid hardly any attention to the French

18th century if one excepts the purely ideological accounts of Voltaire, Diderot, and Rousseau in *L'Ancien Régime*. His interest in French literature reawakens with the Romantic Age. Musset is to Taine the greatest of all French poets: [169] a revealing judgment not only because it is voiced with genuine fervor but because it points to Taine's own ideal of poetry. But his main preoccupation was with the rising French novel: with Stendhal and Balzac. Taine was one of the early admirers of Stendhal, of his psychology and his cult of force. He forgave Balzac all his faults of taste and good sense in a rush of admiration for his power and imagination. Mérimée also, another worshiper of splendid animal force, excited his (somewhat more moderate) admiration, as did *Madame Bovary* by his friend Flaubert. Taine's letters to Zola show his sympathy even for the author of *Thérèse Raquin,* though he warned him against the danger of writing "nightmares" and advised him to "take pity on poor mankind." [170]

But though Taine's knowledge of French literature was obviously extensive and intimate, Taine always tried to emancipate himself from what he felt to be the incubus of its classical spirit and to recommend Nordic, or rather English, poetry to his nation for emulation.[171] In glowing terms which strike one often as overdone in their astonished admiration, he praises the man of the North, the Teuton and Englishman, as the "passionate, concentrated, interior man," [172] the born poet. To Taine all distinctions disappear: he sees a continuity from Caedmon to Byron. Byron appears as a "skald transported into the modern world." [173] He hears the "paganism of the North, the intimate confession of Marlowe, Byron, and the ancient sea kings" even in the dying speech of Mortimer, who, in good Senecan terms, denounces the wheel of Fortune. [174] The English berserker, sea king, and skald is strangely enough also a man of gloomy Protestant piety, who has "an anxious idea of the dark beyond." [175] At every point Madame de Staël's concept of Nordic grandiose, melancholy, passionate poetry survives in spite of Taine's concrete knowledge of many authors who cannot possibly fit the picture. But then, English neoclassicism is consistently disparaged: Dryden (in an inferior disjointed chapter of the *History*) appears as a transitional figure who emerges as the English were quitting "the age of solitary imagination and invention, which suits their race, for the age of reasoning and conversation, which does not suit their race." [176] Dryden is a failure in everything except a few odes. Pope is treated harshly as an artificial, mechanical versifier, who lacks even delicacy and taste [177] and is redeemed only by his craftsmanship and his sense of nature. Dr. Johnson is a comic, grumbling bear who wrote moral essays of which Taine could say that "they suit the taste of the Englishman because they are insipid and dull to us." [178] Swift alone is treated with real sympathy as the "great and unhappy genius, the greatest of the classical age," in the extravagance of his pride and the solidity of a positive mind.[179] But Taine sees only the masculine, naked crudeness, the bitter misanthropy, the vehemence in his dryness and nothing of the charm and intellect in *Gulliver* or the rhetorical art of the *Tale of a Tub*.[180]

All the *History of English Literature* seems to work up to the conclusion that there are, on the one side, "the plain men of science, the popularizers, orators, men of letters—in general the classical ages and the Latin races," and, on the other, "the poets, prophets and usually the inventors—in general, the romantic ages and the Germanic races." [181] Put in such terms, the contrast of light and shade seems drawn so crudely that Taine's *History* would appear almost as an anticlassical pamphlet, a panegyric of the most unrestrained, passionate, emotional romanticism.

But such an appearance is deceptive. Taine obviously is uncomfortable with the extremes to which he has committed himself. His own taste is much more restrained and even more classical than many of his enthusiasms seem to indicate. There is a mental reservation even in his characterizations of the most highly admired authors. The very exaggeration of the picture of Shakespeare: the emphasis on the horror and madness, the disregard of logic and classical reason suggest some aloofness. It is an admiration for the lion behind the bars who must remain forever incarcerated behind them. Also the praise of Swift (whose picture seems similarly overdrawn) is tempered by horror and even disgust; of Byron by a sense of tragic waste; of Dickens by a knowledge of his vulgarity and sentimentality; and of Carlyle by distaste for his fanaticism and violence. The portrait of Balzac which ranks him with Shakespeare and defends even his style makes many reservations, not only as to his opinions, which to Taine seem those of a charlatan, but also as to his taste and even his manners. There is a streak of Victorian prudery or just ordinary modesty in Taine: not only does he sometimes suppress or drop a passage from his translations of an English text, possibly out of regard for the conventions of his audience (all chapter of the *History* were first published in periodicals), but he is genuinely shocked and horrified by the gross brutalities of Restoration comedies and the sentimental indecencies of Balzac's heroines.[182] When Taine says that Balzac "has bad manners; is gross and a charlatan,"[183] we might still think that he is simply characterizing the lion: the naturalist must say something of his sharp teeth and predatory habits. But when Taine says that "he lacks true nobility; delicate things escape him; his anatomist's hands soil bashful creatures, he makes ugliness even uglier,"[184] we feel that Taine's sense of propriety is offended, that he cannot deeply sympathize with the new, crude naturalism. Even Shakespeare or the supermen of the Renaissance are seen from a distance: Taine's ideal of man is not that depicted by his most admired writers, is not a creature of force or power and madness. Actually his model man is a sensible, stoic scholar and an upright, objective scientist. He exalts what fundamentally he must consider "savage" art, because he is convinced that man is basically irrational, that his intellect illuminates only a very small upper layer of the life of his mind.

It is paradoxical that Taine, in history and art, minimizes the intellect so much. He is weak and obviously negligent in what today would be called the history of ideas. He was capable of philosophical analysis and knows (not only in *De l'Intelligence*) how to argue closely on technical points. The chapters on Cousin and Jouffroy are masterpieces of destructive analytical power; the account of Mill's *Logic* is professionally competent. But when Taine turns to literary history, he shows little interest in the subtler problems of the history of thought. He is content with rough sketches of medieval, Renaissance, and rationalist mentality. What he says of the Middle Ages, which he considers a "terrible night"[185] where people lived a brutal life "on a dunghill"[186], is almost grotesquely inadequate. He fastens on passages from Thomas Aquinas, posing conundrums on the virginity of the Mother of Christ,[187] and dismisses the whole enterprise of medieval scholasticism as a cardhouse of quibbles. But while we may explain Taine's low opinion of the medieval intellect by his early anticlericalism, we are surprised by his extremely simplistic view of the Renaissance: he is content to accept a diluted version of Michelet and Burckhardt, which operates only with the contrast between paganism and the Reformation. It is equally surprising to see how little he says of Locke, Berkeley, or Hume [188] and how little he seems to understand or care to understand the exact intellectual position even of his most discussed literary figures. Swift appears as a man of no definite opinions at all except a general misanthropy and irony toward religion and science. Dr. Johnson is described only as a person, and his writings are dismissed, though Taine used Johnson's *Life of Pope* extensively.[189] He has read much of Dryden, quotes him and translates him (even his prose) but has nothing to say about his position in criticism or religion with the exception of some references to his Catholicism. On one occasion a comment by Dryden on *Phèdre* [190] serves the purpose of showing the crudity of the English understanding of French 17th-century civilization. The brilliant chapter on Milton also fails to give any insight into his thought. It is construed on the usual triad: Milton represents a synthesis of Renaissance and Reformation. Much effort and wit is expended to show that the figures in *Paradise Lost* are very much like contemporary Englishmen. Taine laughs at Adam and Eve. "I listen, and I hear an English household, two reasoners of the period—Colonel Hutchinson and his wife. Good Lord! Put clothes on them at once!" [191] "Adam had entered paradise *via* England; there he seems to have learned *respectability,* and there he studied moral speechifying." [192] The archangel "eats like a Lincolnshire farmer," [193] is badly bored when put to watch at the doors of Hell and is overjoyed to be back in Heaven.[194] Jehovah is a grave king who maintains suitable state, something like Charles I,[195] a schoolmaster who, foreseeing the solecism of his pupil tells him beforehand the grammatical rule. Milton's heaven is like a Whitehall filled with bedizened footmen. The angels are the chapel singers.[196] We hear nothing of the theology of Milton, nor even of the argument of *Paradise Lost*. Similarly, the essay on Tennyson that treats him as "an idle singer of an idle day" gives no hint of the content of *In Memoriam* and ignores his patriotic poetry completely.

We hear as little of literary history in a narrow sense as of intellectual history. There is hardly anything in Taine on sources, influences, continuities of genres or devices, prosodic forms, or stock characters. He occasionally alludes to such things: to Aristophanes in connection with Ben Jonson, to Horace with Addison, to

Spenser with Milton. Because of his preoccupation with nationality, he shows hardly any sense of the totality of the European literary tradition or of comparative literature as the interchange of themes, ideas, and forms between the European nations. The English tradition must appear indigenous at any price, and the influences Taine cannot help recognize must either be minimized or represented as interferences which disturbed and weakened the native tradition. Thus the point of an elaborate account of Molière [197] in introducing the Restoration dramatists is to demonstrate the distance between the ideal of the French *honnête homme* and the brutality of the English imitation. Wycherley's plays are a "defamation of mankind," pictures of animal ferocity and brutal debauchery which, contrasted with the models in Molière, show the difference between the two societies and the two countries. Wycherley must be "genuinely English, that is, energetic and somber," [198] vigorous and crude. More surprising is another of the rare comparisons in the *History:* the parallel Taine draws between *Faust* and Byron's *Manfred.* It shows insight into the difference between Goethe's myth of nature and Byron's titanism, but it culminates in an odd comparison between the two main characters. Faust, we are told, has no character. "In what mediocrity and platitude the Faust of Goethe sinks compared to Manfred! He is no hero. His worst action is to seduce a seamstress (*grisette*) and to go dancing at night in bad company—two exploits all students have accomplished. Compared with him, what a man is Manfred!" [199] The method is that of Chateaubriand and Saint-Marc Girardin: a character is compared quite outside the context of a play as if he were a person in real life and is judged by ethical standards that in the case of Taine are those of the ethics of individualism.

Taine, though imbued with the scientific ideals of his time, did not understand (or rather rejected) the basic scientific method: the treatment of the work of literature as a "thing," a projected object that thus can be handled as a totality, can be compared with other works, can be seen as a link in a series, and can be isolated from the mind of its creator or reader. Rather, Taine treats literature as a symptom of an age or nation, or an individual mind, and dissolves the work of literature into an assemblage of characters.

Taine as a critic is at his best when he can describe this fictional world of characters as a symbolic social picture of the time. Thus the book on La Fontaine treats the hero as a kind of erratic boulder isolated from his contemporaries by temperament. The early verse is ignored and only the Fables are analyzed as a social picture of the age: with the king, the nobility, the monk, the bourgeois, the magistrate, the physician, the professor, the merchant, the peasant, all disguised as animals. But Taine understands that the Lion, while king of the beasts, is not Louis XIV, that an idealization, purification, or heightening has taken place in the artistic process: "La Fontaine is a moralist and not a pamphleteer: he has represented kings and not the King. But he had eyes and ears and must one believe that he never used them? One copies one's contemporaries in spite of oneself." [200] The poet is a sociologist, but an unconscious one.

The brilliant essay on Balzac is the high point of Taine's criticism: it links the man, "a businessman in debt," [201] his greed for money, his sensuality, his ambition, his capacity for sheer work, with his society, the imaginary world of his characters, his style, and his philosophy. The unity in contrariety, the interconnections and linkages are established convincingly: the sensation of the totality of the writer, his work, and the civilization he represents is powerfully conveyed. Other essays or chapters in the *History* fall short of this success, but on occasion approach it: the Dickens piece, even the unsympathetic essay on Tennyson or the overdrawn and oddly distorted account of Shakespeare.

But Taine always fails with authors who do not lend themselves to this method. Thus the surprisingly enthusiastic account of Spenser is merely descriptive, metaphorical; it is largely filled with quotations, strangely helpless as characterization. The attention given to English lyrical poetry, though rather full in the number of names and quotations, seems often out of focus. Taine dismisses 17th-century poetry (Donne and others) as bad taste. He has little use for neoclassical poetry, which seems to him imitative of the French. He has a perspective on the romantics that even at the time of writing was quite obsolete. All the emphasis falls on Burns and Cowper as the precursors and Byron as the representative genius. Taine does not know Keats, though he mentions him twice; [202] he praises Shelley but vaguely; [203] he almost ignores Coleridge as a poet and critic; [204] and he considers Wordsworth as an inferior Cowper.[205] The praise of Byron, who is compared to Aeschylus, is so extravagant that it can hardly be taken seriously today.[206] One is confirmed in a low opinion of Taine's sense of poetry (or at least English poetry) when one encounters his high praise of *Aurora Leigh*,[207] which he had read, he tells us, twenty times. He has a pronounced romantic sensibility, obvious in his admiration for the gloomy Byron, his praise of Musset, or his treatment of Thackeray. Taine is shocked by the latter's cynicism and admires *Henry Esmond* most because this book is freest of it. He admires not only the book but also the dreary character of Henry Esmond himself.[208] All the, often incongruous, preferences for the romantically sentimental must be explained by Taine's much deeper and very genuine pessimism: his bitter sense of man's subjection to death and fate, unreason and depravity.

Taine thus presents, contrary to the usual view which reduces him to a kind of pseudo-scientist, an extraordinarily complex and even contradictory mind at the crossroads of the century: he combines Hegelianism with naturalistic physiology, a historical sense with an ideal classicism, a sense of individuality with universal determinism, a worship of splendid force with a strong moral and intellectual conscience. As a critic he has suggested questions in the sociology of literature, but has much more successfully characterized an individuality and analyzed the world of a writer, his types and ideals. A sense of individual detail, of the "small significant fact" often oddly clashes with the general structure of bold generalization: a worship of passionate, colorful imaginative art is often mitigated by traditional good sense and taste.

From a modern point of view Taine seems much more relevant than Sainte-Beuve: he raises more issues; he formulates more theories; but he lacks Sainte-Beuve's easy grace and sense of proportion. He is a violent writer, fond of extreme formulas and loud colors. His style (influenced by Michelet and Macaulay), metallic and monotonous, reflects the disturbance of his mind, the tension and clash of ideologies and sympathies. But just because of this complexity, Taine assumes the stature of "representativeness" for which he himself was always searching in literature and art.

THE REPUTATION of Ferdinand Brunetière is today in eclipse. He is neither widely read nor quoted nor highly regarded. He suffers in part from an inevitable reaction to the great practical power he wielded during his own lifetime. From 1893 on, he was editor-in-chief of the *Revue des Deux Mondes,* to which he had been a major contributor since 1875. He was the main professor at the *Ecole Normale* from 1886 to 1900. He became a member of the Academy in 1893. From such key positions he spoke with the voice and tone of authority. He turned to the great French tradition, to the model of the 17th century, to the classical and moral ideals of the past. In the last years of his life, mainly for social and political reasons, he became a convert to Roman Catholicism, which seemed to him the only antidote against modern anarchy.

Thus Brunetière can be described, and dismissed, as one more exponent of French traditionalism, as a successor of Désiré Nisard, who must have influenced him profoundly in his youth. His glorification of the French 17th century and his attacks on French realism and naturalism as well as on romanticism were neither new nor striking. Realism and naturalism ran counter to his moralism and idealism; romanticism, with its exaltation of the ego, its indulgence in the personal, its moral and literary subjectivism, violated the principle of authority and tradition. Moreover, Brunetière is also ignored because he surprisingly adopted—in a possible contradiction of traditionalism—the scientific ideas of his time. Early in his life he became a fervent adherent of Darwinism and tried to apply its principles to the study of literature. He evolved the theory of the evolution of genres. But this theory, for which he is perhaps best remembered today, is almost always dismissed as being based on a bad analogy; it no longer excites much interest. Thus Brunetière is doubly buried.

But some injustice is done here, not only to Brunetière's important historical position but to the permanent value of his ideas. I
shall not try to defend him as a traditionalist, a moralist, and
classicist, although he does present lucidly and persuasively many
arguments for this point of view. For example, his theory of commonplaces [1] is a striking defense of classical generalities; his stoic
morality, in its emphasis on the victory of will over the instincts and
appetites, is practically the same as that of the American new
humanists; and he defends the French tradition well against the
modern hypertrophy of individualism and the crudities of naturalism. His first book, *Le Roman naturaliste* (1883), has been
wrongly described as simply an attack on naturalism and its principles. It is true that Brunetière consistently disapproves of Zola for
moral and artistic reasons and that he has no use for Zola's theory
of the experimental novel, that he constantly—in a wide historical
perspective—minimizes the novelty of naturalistic claims and procedures. He also attacks both the journalistic *reportage* in the
novel and the impressionistic technique of the Goncourt brothers,
which seem to him illicit and ultimately unsuccessful attempts to
blur the differences between the arts.

Le Roman naturaliste presents a sympathetic and highly laudatory analysis of *Madame Bovary,* several novels of Daudet, and the
stories of Maupassant, and contains an admirable and admiring
account of George Eliot. His attitude toward Flaubert is somewhat
ambivalent: he has no use for Flaubert's later manner, which he
considers a decline into mere virtuosity, but he does analyze and
praise *Madame Bovary.* Though his theoretical disquisitions and
histories create a contrary impression, Brunetière has an extraordinary capacity for observation in stylistic matters. He describes,
for example, Flaubert's way of translating sentiment by an exactly
corresponding sensation.[2] He shows that the comparison is no
longer an ornament of the discourse and even less a personal intervention of the narrator in his story; it becomes rather a kind of
instrument of analysis and psychological experimentation, "the
expression of an intimate correspondence between the sentiments
and the sensations of the characters who are being described. And
why should we not say, in almost metaphysical terms, that it does
not serve merely to indicate a secret link between a human being
and his environment, but that it unites him, or, better still, reunites

him with this very environment?" [3] Brunetière then comments upon
Flaubert's unusual use of the French imperfect tense "to blend and
to merge even more intimately the story of a human being with
the description of the environment into which circumstances have
placed him," [4] a use which allows us to enter *in medias res,* into the
mind of the person himself. Though Brunetière does not yet use the
term, he describes *le style indirect libre* and admires the distribution of the prizes at the agricultural fair for the way in which it is
presented from twenty different viewpoints.[5] Brunetière also well
understands Flaubert's attitude toward his characters: his irony,
the way in which "the devices of romanticism themselves serve as
instruments for this ridicule of romanticism." [6] Brunetière is surely
not wrong when he sees both Flaubert's strength and his limitation
in his preoccupation with a psychology in which "sentiment is still
involved with sensation in which will is confused with desire." [7]
This, he thought, explains the success of *Madame Bovary:* Flaubert
never again achieved this convergence of devices and subject, form
and matter.[8] Brunetière is extraordinarily harsh on *Trois Contes—*
Le Cœur simple is spoiled by the grotesque detail of the parrot as
the Holy Ghost; the two other tales seem to him mere exercises in
orientalism or erudite reconstructions.[9] Yet the high appreciation of
Maupassant's stories and novels shows that Brunetière was no ordinary, squeamish moralist. He actually shares the pessimism about
human nature evident in Flaubert, Taine, and Maupassant. Late in
his life (1906) Brunetière wrote a whole book on Balzac, which
breathes deep sympathy not only for his opinions but for his art
and the aims of his art. Brunetière, in spite of his polemics against
Zola, thought of himself as a realist—the right kind of realist who,
like all good classicists, wanted to discover the really real.

But he is not correctly labeled if we call him a classical realist.
Brunetière even sympathized with symbolism, which he welcomed
as an ally against the victorious naturalism.[10] He understood the
theory and expounded it lucidly. Symbol precedes comparison and
allegory: what they "distinguish and divide and separate . . . the
symbol unites, joins together, and makes into one and the same
thing." [11] But Brunetière argues that symbolism is age-old, the procedure of all art, in all ages, from the Diana of Euripides to the
Beatrice of Dante and the Eloa of Vigny.[12] There is no boundary
line between late 19th-century "symbolism" and romantic symbol-

ism such as we find it in Vigny, Lamartine, and Hugo or in the *Antigone* of Ballanche; and the theory goes back even to Görres and Creuzer.[13] In practice, Brunetière praised mainly a few poems by Henri de Régnier [14] and Verlaine. He was puzzled by Mallarmé and had his doubts about the talent of most poets in the group.[15] With all his sympathy for symbolism—which extends even to an exposition of its affinities with Wagner, the Pre-Raphaelites, Carlyle, and Ruskin—Brunetière tries hard to separate Baudelaire from the symbolists and to make of him a mere decadent, a "roi des mystificateurs." [16] Not that Brunetière denies the originality and talent of Baudelaire: he sees the point of the theory of correspondences and the novelty of his interest in smells, but, on the whole, he is much too shocked by the sadism, the satanism, and the interest in homosexuality to view Baudelaire without prejudice as a poet. His distaste for Baudelaire as a person extends to the poet's theory of decadence and artificiality: Brunetière sees in symbolism a means of reaching nature, true nature, inner nature; Baudelaire appears to him to have cut off art from all reality and to have willfully exalted personal and technically contrived art. Brunetière cannot see beyond the dandyism: Baudelaire remains for him a charlatan, and nothing seems to him more untrue than Barbey d'Aurevilly's attempt to make the poet appear as a Christian.[17] Brunetière's sympathy with symbolism is thus far from complete. Still, it shows enough comprehension to refute the opinion that he is simply a neoclassicist, a rationalist who has no feeling for poetry. Brunetière, one must grant, has no power of evocation, little wit or grace or simple imaginative sympathy.

His strength lies not in what today would be called practical criticism but in the theory of criticism and in literary history. Here he made a real and important contribution. No other critic, at least in France, has stated so clearly what seems to be central, critical truths. He believed that criticism must focus on the works of literature themselves and must distinguish the study of literature from biography, psychology, sociology, and other disciplines. Moreover, he courageously defended the final aim of criticism as that of judging and even ranking, and he distinguished this act of judgment sharply from any purely personal preference, impression, or enjoyment. Finally, he expounded and illustrated a theory of literary history that at least raises (whatever its extravagances and extremes) the central problem of an internal history of literature that would not simply be a dictionary of facts chronologically arranged or a disguised social history. Even the concept of the evolution of genres (though pressed too closely along biological analogues) is a fruitful one and is wrongly ignored at the present time.

Brunetière saw clearly that criticism cannot become anything like a branch of knowledge with a systematic framework unless it defines its object: and that object is clearly the work of literature itself and not the soul of the author or the social background. Otherwise it would become (as it has in practice) psychology or sociology or social history. "In fact, works of literature and art can indeed be signs, but they are first of all works of literature or art which must be considered as such. . . . While a poem may bear witness to the soul of the poet, a poem is a poem, and if criticism forgets this when it claims to refrain from judgment, it is no longer criticism but history and psychology." [18] The object of criticism is to judge, to classify, and to explicate the work of literature. Explication is the first step: very few people know how to read a text. Only then can one go outside and compare the work of art with the mind of the author or the environment. But style is not the man and a work is not a sign, a testimony, and faithful image of what an author was in reality.[19] Brunetière is fond of quoting the example of Bernardin de Saint-Pierre, whose life makes a totally different impression from that which we gain from *Paul et Virginie*.[20] Classification and comparison are the next step. Brunetière recommends even the comparison of the drama of Shakespeare with the tragedy of Racine, or the lyric of Musset with that of Heine, where there are no genetic relations, as an indispensable procedure of all literary criticism. He constantly defends the necessity of comparative literature, of seeing French literature as a part of European and general literature.[21] After classification and comparison comes critical judgment. Brunetière has to defend the necessity of critical judgment against two points of view: the strictly scientific view, using the analogy of the science that does not prefer the butterfly to the toad or the spider, or the rose to the moss or weed; and the impressionistic criticism that denies any values except purely personal statements of preference or descriptions of experiences and of enjoyment. Brunetière, who is often charged with wrongly identifying works of art with organisms, actually knew very well that this identification was only a metaphor and that works of art are not living beings.[22] They are works made more or less well by men for men. Hennequin's attempt to make criticism "scientific," in the sense of abstaining from praise or blame, is doomed to inevitable failure. Brunetière can easily show that Taine, to whom Hennequin appeals, has always pronounced judgments and that Hennequin himself judges constantly when he says, for instance, that Flaubert "composes sentences and paragraphs perfectly, chapters in a mediocre way, and books poorly." [23]

Brunetière argued more insistently against the impressionists. Anatole France in the preface to *La Vie littéraire* had stated the case in extreme terms. "Man can never get outside himself." Unfortunately, we cannot see the world with the eyes of a fly or comprehend nature with the brain of an orangutan.[24] Brunetière answers that we are neither flies nor orangutans, but men, and "we are men largely by the power which we have of going outside ourselves in order to seek ourselves, to find ourselves again, to recognize ourselves in others. The dupery is to believe and teach that we cannot get outside ourselves, when, on the contrary, life is employed in doing precisely that. Otherwise there would be no society, no language, no literature, no art." [25] Actually the impressionists themselves judge all the time and their mocking of doctrinaire critics should not obscure the fact that there are differences of rank between Racine and Campistron, that one cannot put Victor Hugo below Madame Desbordes-Valmore, or Balzac below Charles de Bernard. "Neither M. France nor M. Lemaître nor M. Desjardins has ever tried it and never will try it." [26] Brunetière is well aware that "personal" criticism leads to an ignoring of "the books about which one talks and the subjects they treat." [27] With such criticism literary history perishes, and with it, tradition. Brunetière, however, too easily exaggerates the stability of human nature denied by his adversaries. He sees in criticism (as T. S. Eliot later did, using almost the same words) a "common effort,"[28] and he minimizes the actual disagreements.

> Opinions are not free. . . . one is not free to have an opinion and, as they say, one's own taste; there is always a criterion, an objective foundation of critical judgment. One can err in the application of the criterion, and this is one of the sources of

the diversity of opinions among men. One might not know the criterion itself, in which case we are faced with the obligation of searching for it. But that it exists is beyond doubt. [29]

Brunetière can be this confident because he draws a distinction between personal opinion and recognition of value, and, correspondingly, between beauty and perfection in the work of art. Beauty to him is something subjective, perfection something objectively ascertainable. Mere enjoyment is not a criterion of value. "One laughs more . . . at the *Voyage de M. Perrichon* than at the *Misanthrope.*" [30] "We can step outside ourselves; we can raise ourselves above our tastes; we must do so." [31] "The beginning of criticism," he can say, "is first to judge our personal impressions in order to approve of them afterward, but more frequently to contradict them." [32] We must ask about certain works if "it may be that we have no right to enjoy them, and, on the other hand, if certain works displease us, it may be that *we* are wrong." [33] The divorce between sympathy and judgment, sensibility and reason is here dangerously overstated: it must have been the conflict of Brunetière's own mind that led him to this position. It is not refuted, however, by saying that appreciation must grow out of sympathy, that love and praise are one and the same thing. Though the close link between heart and head is undeniable, it often snaps in life (when we love what we disapprove of) and in art (when we are bored with what we know is great and enjoy what we know is cheap or ephemeral) .

It is another question as to whether Brunetière has described the norms of judgment very fruitfully. He recognizes that "criticism which is not the application of an aesthetics is not criticism," [34] but he himself hardly thought much about the general principles of aesthetics except to emphasize constantly the differences between the arts. "They do not aim at the same end, whatever one may say; they do not use the same means; and they do not address themselves to the same senses, they do not achieve the same effects." [35] Brunetière stands at the opposite extreme to Croce not only in believing in the sharp distinctions between the arts but also in believing in the distinction of the literary genres and in approving of their purity. "For each has its laws, determined by its very nature." [36] Brunetière is not only ready to describe these distinctions but to judge works by adherence to them. He also accepts the neoclassicist table of the hierarchy of genres with tragedy at the top and the lyric as an inferior kind.[37] Late in his life he concluded that he did not know whether there was a hierarchy of genres.[38] Though stated more systematically and clearly than any of the critics of the 17th or 18th centuries had done, the condemnation of the confusion of the arts and genres, its constant devaluation of hybrid or mixed forms, is just good neoclassicism. But it is given a different meaning, because Brunetière, unlike the neoclassicists, has a strong historical sense, a feeling for the history and evolution of literature. He knows that criticism and aesthetics and literary history are closely bound up with one another.[39]

Brunetière's theory of literary history is his greatest achievement. He sees, first, that the usual accumulation of information about the past does not sufficiently define literary history. He is content to leave this antiquarianism to "histoire littéraire" as opposed to "histoire de la littérature," a distinction he has taken from Nisard. Most literary histories are not histories but dictionaries where the names are classed in chronological rather than in alphabetical order.[40] Other literary histories, under the pretext that literature is an expression of society, confuse the history of literature with the history of manners.[41] One must resolutely envisage the ideal of an internal history of literature. "A history of literature has in itself and from the first the sufficient principle of its development."[42] The central preoccupation of the literary historian is thus "a filiation of works. At all time, in literature as in art, it is the past which presses with the heaviest weight upon the present."[43] What is to be established is the inner causality. In literature—after the influence of the individual—"the greatest operating force is that of works on works."[44] It is a double influence: positive and negative; we imitate or we reject. "The Pléiade of the 16th century wanted to do 'something other' than the school of Clément Marot. Racine, in his *Andromaque* wanted to do 'something other' than Corneille in his *Pertharite;* and Diderot in his *Père de famille* wanted to do 'something other' than Molière in his *Tartuffe.* The romantics in our time wanted to do 'something other' than the classicists."[45] Literature, we would say, moves by action and reaction, convention and revolt. This movement is, of course, not automatic but the result of human forces: an original work changes the direction of the development; a conventional work continues or repeats it. Individuality is thus given an enormous historical role in this scheme of a good neoclassicist; thus individuality "introduces into literary history . . . something that did not exist before it, that would not exist without it, and that will continue to exist after it." [46] But change comes also with the change of social and historical conditions. Development is thus "the new disposition of identical elements; a 'change of front,' if I may say so; a modification of the relations which keep the parts of the same whole together: this means all that the word 'evolution' means; it does not mean anything else." [47] The method of literary history will be the method of determining and selecting the points of change, the *moment* which, with a special twist given to Taine's term, now assumes precedence over *race* or *milieu*. "Do you want to find the true cause . . . of the tragedy of Voltaire? You must first look for it in the individuality of Voltaire, and mainly in the necessity that weighed upon him, as he followed in the traces of Racine and Quinault to do something other than they." [48] The work that changes the direction gets all the attention. Brunetière has the courage of his conviction when he ignores Madame de Sévigné and the Duc de Saint-Simon in his *Manuel* because they could not influence the immediately subsequent evolution: their works were published in 1734 and 1824 respectively, long after they were written.[49] Thus literary periodization will not follow a chronological scheme by centuries or reigns of monarchs but must be based on these literary turning points.[50] Finally a general map of the whole evolution of literature will emerge. Works will be understood, placed, situated, and ultimately judged in the stream of history.

It seems impossible to disagree with this aim and with the general method. Brunetière, however, lived at the time in which Darwinism made its deepest impression, and he adopted from it not the idea of historical evolution alone but specifically the idea of the evolution of species. Though literary genres exist as institutions exist and one can write their history, they are not biological species, and the analogy between the history of genre and the evolution of a species is a tenuous one. We must distinguish between two kinds of evolution: that of the growth of an egg to a bird and that exemplified by the change from the brain of a fish to that of a man. In the first concept (ontogeny) a specific animal is born, grows, changes, matures, declines, and dies; in the second sense (phylogeny) no series of brains develops one from another, but only some conceptual abstraction, "the brain," definable in terms of its function, can be compared and shown to change. The brains of animals can be arranged in a series leading up to an ideal drawn from the human brain. Brunetière assumes the truth of both analogies. "A genre is born, grows, attains its perfection, declines, and finally dies." [51] To give his own example, French tragedy was formed in the time of Jodelle and Garnier, reached its maturity with Corneille and Racine, declined with Quinault and Voltaire, and died with La Harpe and Lemercier. But in what sense can one speak of the evolution of a genre in terms of such a close analogy with human life? The *tertium comparationis* for the birth of tragedy is merely the fact that there were no tragedies in French before Jodelle. And tragedy died only in the sense that according to Brunetière no *important* tragedies were written after Lemercier. He therefore has to judge the later attempts of François Ponsard to revive classical tragedy as abortive.[52] He has to define tragedy in such a way that Hugo's plays, however tragic in mood and conclusion, must be excluded as a new and different genre.

In fact, genres do not die like individuals: in a review of the situation of poetry in 1852, Sainte-Beuve recognized that even the oldest genres were still being cultivated: classical tragedies, fables in the style of La Fontaine, epics, chansons, burlesque poems. "The genres do not die out: they can be in eclipse, they can be dominated by others more in fashion; but they last, they perpetuate themselves and they are there in reserve ready for new talent when it comes, with frameworks and points of departure all prepared." [53] There is always the possibility that great tragedy will be written in French in the future. Racine's *Phèdre*, in Brunetière's scheme, stands at the beginning of the decline of tragedy, but it will strike us as young and fresh compared to the learned and frigid Renaissance tragedies, which according to Brunetière represent the "youth" of French tragedy. The analogy between the evolution of a genre and the life cycle of an individual breaks down at every point: it is only a series of metaphors, dangerous in its implication because it suggests the fatality of decline and death and because it enforces the view that all change is only slow continuous change like biological change—that there are no breaks or jumps, no sudden reversals into the past, only growth and decline. *Natura non facit saltum* is a principle not applicable to art (nor to history). As an argument for inevitable decadence or inevitable progress it is still doing very practical damage to human thinking (Marx, Spengler, Toynbee) and behavior.

The second concept of evolution cannot be dismissed so easily. Brunetière did not always clearly distinguish this concept from the first, but he used it much more frequently, consistently, and successfully. It recognizes that no actual transformation of an entity called a genre takes place, but that we can arrange works of art (as we can arrange brains of animals) in a series leading to a specific goal. This goal must be postulated to be a value or norm and that allows us to split up an apparently meaningless series into its essential and unessential elements, to apply a "regulative concept," an underlying pattern, which is real, that is, effective, because it actually molds the writing of concrete works. From his dogmatic neoclassical point of view Brunetière constantly runs into the danger of postulating only one aim, one culminating point of a series, and thus of lowering all works preceding the model to mere unindividualized stepping stones, all mere repetitions of the pattern as symptoms of decay and dissolution. He has not avoided the difficulty of accounting for the role of individuality in the morphological approach. His concept of value is too static: it is brought in as if from outside and does not quite recognize that the historical process will produce ever new forms of value, hitherto unknown and unpredictable. Brunetière is an absolutist who sees the historical process only as a working-out of eternal values: as steps toward the Temple. But the idea of evolution itself, though often applied mechanically and rigidly, is unimpeachable. It is not true that Brunetière merely postulated it theoretically: he carried it out at least in outline for all of the three genres that he recognized, for tragedy, the lyric, and the novel, and he gave examples for the evolution of an individual. The two volumes of lectures on Hugo and the earlier sketch, "L'Evolution d'un poète: Victor Hugo," [54] show the poet passing through different stages from the oratorical to the lyric, then to the dramatic, and finally the epic, in a schematic way which is assumed to be also that of general history. (The poet is something like an abbreviation of history.) The evolution from the subjective to the objective, from romanticism to "naturalism" [55] (oddly used here) is also the ethical progress of the man.

The evolution of the novel is sketched several times. At first he merely enumerates the successive types, *chansons de geste, roman courtois, roman épique* (by which he means those baroque monsters by La Calprenède, Madame de Scudéry, and others) , and finally the novel of manners,[56] without more than a suggestion that each successive stage is prepared by the preceding one. For example, the heroic novel of the 17th century becomes slowly more realistic by masquerading as a historical novel or by incorporating contemporary scandals in the *roman à clef*. The second sketch, in the same preface,[57] describes the rise of the novel in terms of its assimilation of matter from other genres: Brunetière adopts the suggestion from Darwinism of a struggle for existence, of a rivalry between the genres. Though hardly more than another metaphor, this raises a neglected and very real problem: surely genres do change their position in a hierarchy in different ages, and the intensity and extent of their cultivation varies with the times. Lesage and Marivaux enriched themselves with "the successive losses of comedy, comedy of character, comedy of manners, comedy of intrigue." [58] With Prévost and Rousseau the novel absorbs the matter of tragedy, with Madame de Staël and George Sand it achieves the right to treat moral and ideological questions. The scheme is tenuous and hardly precise, and Brunetière abandoned it when in his last book on Balzac (1906) he described concretely the rise of the novel. The picaresque novel, the epistolary novel (both focused on the one teller) , the "confession," which led to the analytical psychological novel of the type of *Adolphe,* the exotic and historical novel of Chateaubriand and Scott, and finally the subliterary novel of intrigue (what we call the Gothic romance), all contributed to the social novel of Balzac. Balzac is pictured so distinctly as the culminating point of the novel that the earlier forms serve only as steppingstones toward his height. To say that there are "genres or species whose very fortune and existence are linked to circumstances, to a precise moment of their evolution, and which die of their victory" [59] repeats the false analogy to the struggle of the species. The historical novel has been revived in many countries and will without doubt continue to the end of time.

The evolution of lyric poetry in France during the 19th century is the theme of a two-volume series of lectures at the Sorbonne (1893–94) . The exaltation of personal sensibility and the revival of eloquence in Rousseau, the exoticism, the local color, the enlargement of the feeling for nature, and the reintegration of the religious sentiment in Bernardin de Saint-Pierre and Chateaubriand—all build up to the achievement of Lamartine and the early Hugo. The origins of the modern lyric served Brunetière as an example for another favorite analogy with biological evolution: genres supposedly become transformed into other genres. French pulpit oratory of the 17th and early 18th centuries was transformed into the lyrical poetry of the romantic movement. According to Brunetière tragedy and oratory had, in those years, crowded out the lyric: oratory then diminished and disappeared. He even asserts that for half a century (from 1704 to 1749) it would be impossible to find a single "eloquent" page of French prose.[60] Rousseau, in a different genre, revives the form and matter of pulpit eloquence, which then is somehow instilled into verse, into the poetry of Lamartine and Hugo. But the analogy will not stand close inspection: at most, one could say that pulpit oratory expresses feelings similar to the modern lyric (for example, the transience of things human) or that it fulfilled similar social functions (the definition of the sense of the metaphysical).

Tragedy is a subject much more closely related to the demands of its audience than are written forms, and it thus lends itself best to the approach through genre history. Brunetière sketched it several times, outlining the Greek and then the French developments. The limited source material from antiquity and the highly selected series of plays from the French 17th century allow the construction of a number of stages. Whatever may be said in detail to correct Brunetière's outline (elaborated in a series of lectures centered around representative plays, *Les Epoques du théâtre français*, 1892) the method is surely justified. We can trace such an evolution; we can find a similar one in Elizabethan drama, from mysteries and interludes through hybrid forms like Bale's *King John* to Marlowe and Shakespeare, just as we can describe the rise of perspective painting in the late Middle Ages. We are confronted with the problem of an internal history of the art of literature. Brunetière has raised the problem clearly and tried to answer it courageously, but unfortunately the prestige of Darwinism seduced him into far too close an imitation and transfer of concepts from biology; literary genres are not species, and do not transform themselves into higher species. The innovations caused by genius are not comparable to the mechanistic variation of characteristics, to the Darwinian "sport," or even the "mutation" of De Vries. Literary values cannot be reduced to mere novelty or to maturity and purity. Though Brunetière's biological analogy is not convincing, he has seen a problem that is still with us and that surely must again become a central preoccupation of any future history of literature conceived as an art, changing in the course of history.

GUSTAVE LANSON (1857-1934)

For the 20th century Gustave Lanson became the symbol of French academic literary history. He is considered even today the head of "positivist" French literary scholarship: the sponsor and mentor of all the *thèses* about the lives and works, the sources, influences, and reputations of the great and less than great French authors treated with an exclusive regard for conscientiously established facts. Lanson's thesis on *Nivelle de La Chaussée et la comédie larmoyante* (1887), his *Bibliographical Manual of Modern French Literature,* his elaborate critical editions of works by Voltaire and Lamartine support this claim.[1] In a formal pronouncement on "L'Esprit scientifique et la méthode de l'histoire littéraire" (1909), he recommends "the healthy discipline of the exact methods" for literary history, "their disinterested curiosity, severe honesty, laborious patience, and submission to fact" and wants us to "reduce to an indispensable and legitimate minimum the share of personal feeling in our knowledge"[2] of literature. Lanson had become a great authority, a pedagogical leader who traveled to the United States in 1911—one of the first French professors to do so—and reported, with sympathy and a certain condescension, on American university life.[3]

Lanson's prestige was established mainly, however, by his *Histoire de la littérature française* (1894), which became the standard manual of French literary history. It has all the virtues of a manual: accurate information, lucidity, equity, proportion. Actually it is far more than a textbook, and there is some irony in the conventional image of Lanson as the instigator of strict research methods; for the *History* combines sweeping historical generalizations with psychological portraiture, characterization, and critical judgment. The prefaces to the *History* and to a collection of papers, *Hommes et livres* (1895), proclaim that literary history "has as its object the description of individualities." [4] The aim of literary study is not in any strict sense scientific: it strives, rather, for intellectual pleasure and the shaping of man's interior culture. Lanson rejects Taine's triad as insufficient, doubts the rigidities of Brunetière's theories, deplores Renan saying that "the study of literary history is destined in large measure to replace the direct reading of the works of the human mind," [5] and insists on distinguishing "the literary monument from the historical or philological document." [6] The literary phenomenon and not the biography of the author or the social background is his central concern. Individuality must be found in the work. In practice, Lanson does exactly that: he characterizes ideas, sentiments, moods, and attitudes; describes, expounds, interprets, but also judges, often with epigrammatical sharpness and personal concern. It speaks for his candor that in subsequent editions he added notes and postscripts in which he often revoked or modified his earlier opinions without abandoning his generally classical and mildly romantic preferences. The tone of equity and calm is seldom broken, the judicious weighing of all sides is rarely abandoned. Adjectives such as "baroque" for Chateaubriand's arguments in defense of Christianity, of "puerile" for Hugo's family poetry, or of "mediocre" for Gautier's intelligence come as small surprises.[7] Quite explicitly all literature is judged by a combination of realist, rationalist, and classicist criteria. The chapters on the Middle Ages impose a strict selection. Even the *Chanson de Roland* is considered "dry and rude" in its form and "stiff and poor" in language,[8] and the bulk of the *chansons de geste* as well as the chivalrous romances are assigned to oblivion.[9] Lanson admires Jean de Meung as a precursor of Rabelais and Voltaire but does not hesitate to call the *Roman de la Rose* "a jumble, a chaos." [10] Villon appeals by his "absolute sincerity," which makes the rogue Villon palatable to "us honest people, peaceable burghers." [11]

The directness of the criticism in the discussions of the texts and persons is somewhat counteracted and diluted, in its effect, by Lanson's framework around his portraits: the sketches of social and intellectual history, the generalizations about the French spirit or the character of the French regions. The French are intellectual, sensual, realist; they are not lyrical and not metaphysical. "These great loves such as Tristan and Yseult were not made for us French-men." [12] The *fabliaux* (and not the courtly love of the troubadours) represent "a form of the spirit of the race," and the *salon* society, two hundred pages and three hundred years later, represents also "a necessary form of the French spirit." [13] Boileau's naturalism, in which "a positivist rationalism combines with a search for aesthetic form and which proposes three terms, pleasure, beauty, and truth as identical or inseparable" is, Lanson concludes, "the literary doctrine which answers best the permanent qualities and needs of the French spirit." [14] Even Racine is assimilated through an emphasis on his domestic, bourgeois qualities and his psychological realism.[15] These are found not only in Molière, La Fontaine, and Bossuet but also in the 18th century, which, unlike Brunetière or Nisard in their histories, Lanson never denigrates at the expense of the 17th century. Rather, he was one of the first students of the French *philosophes* who defended them against Taine's charge of a priori abstract Utopianism and traced the real origins of their ideas.[16] He gives a sympathetic exposition of Rousseau's doctrines. Lanson is too judicious not to see the greatness of Voltaire and Diderot, though he carefully exposes their limitations: the inchoate verve of Diderot or the dryness of Voltaire's intellect.

The 19th century receives a rather hurried treatment. Lanson's taste is either elegiac, pessimistic or mildly realist. He praises Lamartine and Vigny on the one hand and Flaubert on the other. Renan and Michelet are his most admired heroes. He shares Sainte-Beuve's reservations against Balzac and Stendhal and shies away from Hugo and Zola. He treats Baudelaire harshly as the representa-tive of "low romanticism, pretentiously brutal, macabre, immoral, artificial in order to confound the bourgeois." [17] Mallarmé is, in passing, dismissed as of "slight value" [18] and Rimbaud is not even mentioned in the first edition. This was in 1894, when the symbolist line may have been obscure, but in the later editions hardly any amends are made: Mallarmé is treated coolly as an "incomplete artist who has not succeeded in expressing himself," and Rimbaud is barely mentioned in a footnote.[19] This antisymbolist prejudice must have done more harm than anything else to damage Lanson's reputation as a critic.

The book was deservedly such a success that Lanson had to bring it up to date several times. What in the first edition was a brief, noncommittal survey of "the present hour" became in the seventh edition (1902) an ambitious section on the literature of the last decades, which was expanded and revised as late as 1922. Verlaine and Verhaeren are praised among the new poets; and among the novelists, oddly enough, Paul Adam carries away the honors: we are told that he has more creative power than Zola or Balzac.[20] There is much mere enumeration of names and titles with polite and meaningless praise. Pierre Louÿs is called, for instance, "a fine artist, so Greek in his so French prose."[21] The 1922 edition culminates in a peroration on "eternal France" and the "victory of the Latin spirit over the Germanic spirit" in 1918.[22] Additions made to the body of the text now show populist preoccupations; thus a hymn on Michelet's book *Le Peuple,* "the true catechism of a Frenchman," has an incongruous fervor, though even in the first edition Michelet was considered among "the two or three greatest writers of the century."[23] These surveys of recent literature show that possibly the identification of Lanson with the academic mind is not quite unjustified: he becomes disoriented, even willful when faced with the new literature of his time. He illustrates the danger of writing contemporary literary history, though it is difficult to know where the line separating the past from the present can be drawn and why the task should have been beyond his power. But this collapse of standards need not obscure the fact that the original *History of French Literature* succeeds in a wise combination of history and criticism, scholarship and interpretation. It will remain the best French literary history of the 19th century.

Lanson has been singled out here as representative of the enormous expansion of French literary historiography and research in the second half of the 19th century—work that cannot be divorced from criticism, though much of it was purely antiquarian: textual, editorial, bibliographical, biographical, source study, etc. It soon covered all periods of French literary history and almost all foreign literatures. The greatest scholars were those who were practiced and schooled in the preparatory labors of literary scholarship, but who then took wider views, attempted bold syntheses, and felt the need of communicating the results of their lifework to an academic public that sometimes broadened into the literary public in general.

A few names will suffice. Old French studies were organized in France by Gaston Paris (1839–1903), who had spent two years

(1856–58) at Bonn with Friedrich Diez, the founder of Romance philology, and then produced the fundamental *L'Historie poétique de Charlemagne* (1865), a lively erudite account of the Emperor's odd fortunes as a figure in literature. Paris was one of the founders of the *Société des anciens textes français* (1875) ; he edited innumerable Old French texts himself; he indefatigably wrote papers on questions of sources, dates, and migration of themes, and he supervised the production of other scholars in his field for decades in countless reviews and reports. His *La Littérature française au moyen âge* (*XIe-XVe siècle*, 1888) and the lectures, *La Poésie du moyen âge* (2 vols. 1885, 1895), carried his name beyond the confines of the group of Old French specialists and helped to make the French conscious of their great medieval heritage. Paris combines intellectual history with literary history. He is always soberly descriptive, though not averse to bold theories of epic or lyric origins that today are considered obsolete. (The Germanic origins of the *chansons de geste,* the spring song as the source of the European lyric, etc.). His only goddess is truth: "We are less concerned with appreciating the Middle Ages and having them appreciated than with knowing and understanding them." [24] But this appreciation is what Paris helped to achieve, because his love of truth and his contempt for romantic falsification were the right way of teaching interest and admiration for the literature of the Middle Ages.[25] Paris accomplished the aim of all good historians of literature, who, by removing obstacles in our way, by making us see things as they are, make us more readily feel the beauty and splendor of the past.

In French literary history since the Middle Ages the men who combine literary history and criticism were obviously far more numerous. Brunetière and Lanson are the best examples. In their time Emile Faguet (1847–1916) was their most serious rival but today his fame seems to have faded badly. Partly this is due simply to his prolific production—his books must number somewhere between fifty and sixty—but more seriously it is due to the impression of didacticism and impersonality which his work conveys. The slightly ironic classroom tone, the prolixity of much exposition, quotation, and description do not help matters. Faguet seems to conceal the reasons for his judgments and the criteria for his distinctions almost deliberately. He is extremely distrustful of theory; in characterizing himself he says: "he rejects, probably because he lacks it, the art of pulling together totalities, of disengaging the general spirit of an age, of following the sinuous lines of filiations and influences, in a word, the art of general ideas in literature, and the 'spirit of literary laws.'" [26] At most he would accept that of action and reaction, recognize that one generation likes to do the opposite of what the preceding did.[27] His objections to Comte, Taine, and Brunetière are well taken but are not replaced by anything specific other than a general concern for individuality. Faguet is something like a minor Sainte-Beuve: he shares his view that criticism is "work and art, but not science, or not yet, and no doubt never." [28]

Faguet, however, lacks the art of Sainte-Beuve and much of his psychological insight and power of characterization. The enthusiastic monograph on *Flaubert* (1899) , for instance, labors an elementary contrast between the realistic and the romantic books and adds a chapter: "What remained of the realist in the romantic and of the romantic in the realist." [29] In characterizing the figures in *Madame Bovary,* Faguet speculates fancifully on what Rodolphe and Léon might have told later in life about their relations with Emma.[30] An article from as late as 1910 made a disgraceful, unperceptive attack on Baudelaire which had the merit of exciting Gide's spirited defense.[31] But, strangely, he is at his best when he expounds and analyzes ideas. The three volumes of *Politiques et moralistes du XIXe siècle* (1891, 1898, 1900)—particularly the last with its studies of Sainte-Beuve, Taine, and Renan—are the work that has best preserved its value. Paradoxically, the logical analyst of ideas turns in his literary studies most sharply against the ideologists of the past. Of the four collections of portraits, each devoted to a century (*Dix-septième siècle,* 1887, *Dix-neuvième siècle,* 1887, *Dix-huitième siècle,* 1890, and *Seizième siècle,* 1893) , the one on the 18th century has most character. The whole century is disparaged as "singularly pale compared to the preceding and following ages." It is "neither Christian nor French." It is "all new, all primitive and as if all raw." It lacks tradition: it is childish or adolescent.[32] The chapter on Voltaire plays up his contradictions as a thinker and his egoism as man. He lacks "profundity, imagination, sensibility" as a critic and writer.[33] Diderot is a "half-artist, half-thinker." [34] Only Rousseau and Montesquieu are considered very great writers in that age. Rousseau's *Contrat social* is interpreted strikingly as in conflict with the basic tendencies of his thought.[35] A later book, *La Politique comparée de Montesquieu, Rousseau et Voltaire* (1902), develops the contrast of the three thinkers: Rousseau, the advocate of popular tyranny; Montesquieu, the liberal nearest to Faguet's preference; and Voltaire, the constitutional monarchist. Five later, mildly critical books on Rousseau [36] got lost in the shuffle of the violent anti-Rousseau agitation of Lasserre, Charles Maurras, and the Baron Seillière in 1912. Faguet, though he condemned generalization in theory, can even be criticized for his concentration on ideas and arguments and for the lack of historical background in his books. The posthumously published lectures on *Histoire de la poésie française* (11 vols. 1923–36), show a complete lack of continuity. They are leisurely, discursive examinations of texts; yet valuable in that Faguet discusses obscure 17th-century or 18th-century poets, quotes and praises them with some indulgence to the taste of their time.[37]

Faguet is completely absorbed in French literature; other literatures, as with Brunetière or even Sainte-Beuve, appear only at the margin. Taine had written the most important history of English literature in the 19th century, and his example excited competition and opposition in France. Taine was hardly a specialist. The *Histoire littéraire du peuple anglais* (2 vols. 1894, 1904) of Jean-Jacques Jusserand (1855–1932) points up the change of barely thirty years. Jusserand writes a solid descriptive account of cultural history before the outbreak of the Civil war, based on much original research. He had already written *La Vie nomade et les routes d'Angleterre au XIVe siècle* (1884) and a book on Langland (1893). He had closely studied the English medieval drama and the novel at the time of Shakespeare (1887) and later wrote a firsthand book on *Shakespeare en France* (1898).[38] The book on *English Wayfaring Life* shows his main interest: in the setting and background of literature, in the picture of the society it presents. There is no sociological explanation, nor is there any real aesthetic interest.

The aesthetic point of view was strongly reasserted by Auguste Angellier (1847–1911) in a polemical introduction to his book on *Robert Burns* (2 vols. 1893). He argues against Taine. We don't know anything concrete about the race of Burns; we do know the landscape setting and the society. "But in reality how does this even in the least contribute to an explication of his genius?" A work of art is unique, and because of this "there is no scientific criticism nor will there ever be any, at least in regard to the flower of genius, the proper flavor of a work." [39] Emile Legouis (1861–1937) is also suspicious of grandiose theories and cares mostly for the art of poetry and the mind of a poet. His book *La Jeunesse de Wordsworth* (1896) was the first close study of *The Prelude,* and his books on Chaucer and Spenser glowingly expounded their art for a French public. Legouis late in life wrote the first part (up to 1660) of *Histoire de la littérature anglaise* (1924) in collaboration with Louis Cazamian and produced a not unworthy pendant to Lanson's French history. Legouis, unlike Taine and Jusserand, concentrates on the actual literature, and he knows how to expound, describe and characterize quietly, soberly, but also warmly and even enthusiastically. His sympathy goes out to a visual, bright, well-composed art, particularly to Chaucer, who seems to him, as to Montégut, French in spirit as in name. "He descends directly from our trouvères and belongs to them except for his language." [40] Legouis loves Spenser, in whom he sees largely a painter of pageants, a musician of verse who "poses as a professor of morals." [41] Legouis' sympathy stops before the Jacobean drama, its loose composition, its gross buffooneries, its indulgence in melodramatic effects, its profusion of physical horrors and macabre subjects. Even Shakespeare has his faults: intemperance, an excess of lyricism.[42] Anglo-Saxon literature, Legouis argues, does not belong to English literature at all. It is divided by a gulf from Middle English literature. Its gloom contrasts with the new brightness introduced by the French. A whole chapter on the general traits of Old French literature is inserted which Legouis lifted bodily from his *Défense de la poésie française* (1912), a spirited plea against the English underestimation of French poetry, against Matthew Arnold, Landor, and others.[43] Legouis as a professor at the Sorbonne organized the academic study of English literature in France and created a school that bore rich fruit in the 20th century.

English literature was the nearest to French, but French students went farther afield and established "comparative literature" as an academic discipline. The term *littérature comparée* comes apparently from Villemain, but the thing itself is much older. One could argue that even ancient or Renaissance comparisons between Homer and Vergil are "comparative." Surely Herder and the Schlegels conceived of literature as a totality in its interconnections.

In 1870 De Sanctis called his chair at Naples (originally meant for the German poet Georg Herwegh) "letteratura comparata." Hutcheson Posnett wrote a book in 1886 called *Comparative Literature*. In 1886 Max Koch established the first periodical devoted to comparative literature in Berlin.[44] But Joseph Texte (1865–1900) inaugurated the first French chair of comparative literature at Lyon in 1896. He had written on *J.-J. Rousseau et les origines du cosmopolitisme littéraire* (1896), a thorough study of English-French literary relations prior to and including Rousseau, and he was to collect his *Etudes de littérature européenne* (1898), which range widely from Italian influences on the French Renaissance to Sir Thomas Browne, Keats, and the German influence on French romanticism. In a programmatic statement, "L'Histoire comparée des littératures," he sees the discipline as a study of the totality of all literatures in their interrelationships and acknowledges that it arose in Germany from "the revolt against the despotism of the French yoke."[45] His ideal is generous and has been carried out in many countries since then. Texte established a French school which, with Fernand Baldensperger, Paul Van Tieghem, and Jean-Marie Carré, developed a specific character. It narrowed the original grand conception to a study of influences conceived in a factual manner as study of translations, intermediaries, reviews, echoes, etc. Its concept of literature is external and the spirit nationalistic: a computing of cultural riches, a credit and debit calculus in matters of the mind.[46] But as originally conceived, comparative literature is surely a major postulate of a new age. Literature has to be seen as one stream, as a whole. Goethe's ideal of world literature must also be the ideal of literary scholarship and criticism.

IT WOULD BE an exaggeration to say that the scientific ambition of Taine, Brunetière, and Lanson dominated the time. Critical activity in France (or rather in Paris) was so diversified that one could illustrate the whole gamut of 19th-century attitudes, aesthetic and ideological, with a study of the minor critics of the time who have today been forgotten or are beginning to be forgotten. It will be hard to revive them, though one should recognize the high level maintained by the well-known critics of the time: the great skill of characterization, the deftness and clarity of exposition, the breadth of horizon, and, most prominently, the boldness of their judgments. At the risk of some injustice to many writers important in their time and place—such as Paul Saint-Victor (1827–81), whom Saintsbury called "a very famous writer"[1] but who seems to me florid and empty, or Francisque Sarcey (1828–99), who decided the success of plays on the Parisian stage for decades—I shall single out a few figures of marked individuality and considerable scope.

JULES BARBEY D'AUREVILLY (1808-1889)

We can locate Barbey d'Aurevilly at one end of the spiritual spectrum. He was a violent and flamboyant writer who for decades upheld conservative principles derived, in substance, from the Catholic restoration, particularly from Joseph de Maistre. His criticism belongs to his later years and was, in part, collected only after his death, in 17 volumes under the general title, *Les Œuvres et les hommes* (1860–1909). As Barbey d'Aurevilly was admired by Léon Bloy and Léon Daudet, he represents a channel of transmission from the France of the Bourbons to the tendencies of the 20th century which culminated in the *Action française*. Barbey d'Aurevilly is primarily a polemicist, a harshly satirical judge of his time, who indulges freely in passionate outbursts, verbal fireworks, and witty gambols, often couched in animal metaphors, in order to destroy his ideological and personal enemies. But along with the theatrical display of his prejudices and hatreds there is often genuine insight into the weaknesses and limitations of much 19th-century thinking and feeling. We sense the support of a fervently held positive creed and of a taste that allows him enthusiasms and recognitions which are sometimes perceptive and even prophetic.

Barbey d'Aurevilly is simply extravagant when he deals with enemies of his religion and politics, particularly if they are foreigners. The little book on *Goethe et Diderot* (1880) is an extreme case. Diderot appears not only as an atheist, materialist, sensualist, and disreputable pornographer, but as a complete cynic, a foreigner, a "German" in spirit, who gave his ideas to Goethe, who, in turn, is nothing but an inferior Diderot—boring, dry, cold, and pedantic at that. Diderot is "the serpent of naturalism," Goethe his "snail." [1] Goethe's whole fame is a fraud perpetuated on the French, who suffer from his "occupation" as they did from the Prussian army in 1871. One can imagine what d'Aurevilly has to say about Hugo, whom he also hated for political reasons, or about Zola. Hugo is an "ass accompanied by trumpets," "a Prussian poet" (because he wrote *L'Année terrible*). Zola "carved in human excrement." [2]

But even where d'Aurevilly's involvement seems slight, his judgment is extraordinarily harsh. Thus Turgenev's *Sportsman's Sketches* are dismissed as inconsequential; Gogol surprisingly seems to him a mere imitator of Jean Paul and Voltaire, and Leopardi is a mere rhetorician and not a poet of despair. "The sadness of the eagle in his eyrie is not that of the penguin and Leopardi is only a penguin." [3]

But fortunately Barbey d'Aurevilly did not only master the art of invective. The volume on the French critics, *Les Critiques ou les juges jugés* (1885), characterizes, analyzes, and judges Villemain, Sainte-Beuve, Philarète Chasles, Taine, and others, harshly but often accurately. Even the malicious essay on Sainte-Beuve, which insists on Sainte-Beuve's lack of principles, slippery skepticism, love of gossip, and worship of small facts, contains more than a grain of truth. [4]

Barbey d'Aurevilly's taste is rooted in his romantic youth. Chénier and Lamartine are his favorite poets, and he admires

Musset and Vigny. He was a friend and discoverer of Maurice de Guérin.[5] Considering his general hatred of realism, his admiration for Balzac can be explained by his welcome for a political ally, but the praise of Stendhal is more unusual and surprising, though Stendhal's love of passion and power is a sufficient point of contact.[6] The review that Barbey d'Aurevilly wrote of *Madame Bovary* at the time of publication was not unfavorable (certainly less so than Sainte-Beuve's), but later Barbey d'Aurevilly treated Flaubert consistently as a man who has lost all of his original talent. His writings show only surface glitter, technical dexterity, inner coldness, and emptiness.[7] D'Aurevilly admired Baudelaire as "an atheist and modern Dante" with whom he shares the doctrine of the fall of man and his contempt for modern civilization.[8] A specific positive taste emerges from d'Aurevilly's writings, loves as well as hatreds, and both are argued with a fierce independence and candor that give life to the rigid ideological framework compounded of monarchy, the Catholic religion, and the French tradition.

EDMOND SCHERER (1815–1889)

Edmond Scherer provides an obvious contrast. He was a Protestant theologian in his early years, but lost his faith and became a literary critic after 1861, when he was 46. A selection of the articles he wrote for *Le Temps* was published in 10 volumes as *Etudes critiques sur la littérature contemporaine* (1863–95), and there are other volumes on 18th-century topics as well as religious questions. One could make Scherer sound like a dour Calvinistic moralist, who did not shed his parsonic habits. He certainly is disillusioned, suspicious of popular democracy and of faith in progress, convinced, as was Barbey d'Aurevilly, of French decadence. But unlike d'Aurevilly, Scherer saw the incarnation of French decadence in Baudelaire. "He has given me the feeling for it, he has revealed its nature." Decadence is like senility, when man becomes ugly, driveling, and impotent. The distinction in art between beauty and ugliness is abolished. "The horrible once exhausted, you arrive at the disgusting. You paint unclean objects. You pursue them furiously; you wallow in them. But this rottenness itself grows rotten. This decomposition engenders a fouler decomposition, until finally there remains an indescribable something that has no name in any language—and that is Baudelaire." [1] Baudelaire is neither an artist nor a poet. He lacks mind as well as soul, spirit as well as taste. He has no genius. There is nothing sincere, simple and human in him. At bottom he is a pure Philistine, a dupe of himself, a judgment that Scherer repeated even in 1882. Baudelaire perpetuated "a hoax": his only claim is to have contributed to "an aesthetics of the debauch," to a "poem of the house of ill fame." [2] Zola offends Scherer not only as "the Balzac of the pot-house" who cannot write and who propounds a ridiculous theory of the experimental novel, but also because of his "horrible certitude," his fanatical zeal, which for Scherer portends the disappearance of literature, at least as it was understood throughout history. [3]

Still, Scherer does not merely recoil from the new, the violent, and the horrible as a gentleman and scholar. He also examines the past and finds it full of hollow idols. He bravely touches upon national palladia. Bossuet is the "most sterile genius of our literature." [4] Chateaubriand is even emptier. "His vanity has a scorching harshness which makes it evil and terrible." [5] The ideas and the character of a fervent Catholic rub Scherer the wrong way. But Scherer propounds also a "literary heresy" about Molière, criticizing him for slovenly versification and for lapses in style, as well as for the improbabilities of the *Misanthrope,* "a maniac who should be shut in an asylum." [6]

Foreign classics do not fare better. One can sympathize with Scherer's impatience with the German cult of Goethe. There is justice in some of Scherer's reflections on Goethe's taste, his political opinions, or his deference to King Ludwig of Bavaria. One may grant the dull stretches in *Wilhelm Meister* and can see that Scherer must disapprove of Goethe's cult of experience, of an existence that has no other aim than personal fulfillment. Old objections against the unity of *Faust* and the success of the second part are restated trenchantly. But Scherer becomes insensitive and merely captious when he surveys the plays and poems concluding that Goethe has "no ingenuousness, no fire, no invention: he lacks the dramatic vein and is no creator." He has left us no distinct character. [7] The date, 1872, of Scherer's essay accounts for the acerbity of the tone.

Scherer is not much kinder to English idols, though English literature was his favorite interest: his mother was partly English, he had spent a year in England as a youngster, and he knew the language well. Still, the essay on Milton (1868), in spite of Scherer's admiration for the man, amounts to a sharply worded condemnation of *Paradise Lost* as "an unreal, grotesque and boring poem." Scherer sees a complete contradiction between the epic poem and the theodicy, between the Renaissance and the Puritan element in Milton. He condemns the explanation of the problem of evil as verging on the grotesque and, though he knows that one cannot separate the form from the content, ends by praising only certain episodes and similes and Milton's mighty line.[8] In passing, Scherer demolishes Byron as "one of the French superstitions" [9] and attacks Carlyle for his jargon as a "prophet and buffoon" [10] and Ruskin for his "affectations of profundity" and "studied poses of charlatanism." [11] Little seems to remain.

Scherer nevertheless admires much in English literature: Shakespeare, whom he defends against biographical interpretations; Laurence Sterne, whose irony tempered by melancholy seems to him the essence of humor; [12] Wordsworth; and George Eliot. The essay on Wordsworth (1881), which contains a tribute to Arnold's "limpid clearness and unaffected grace," [13] shows a real insight into a poet then very remote from French interests. Scherer sees that he is not merely a didactic or descriptive nature poet, however fine, but that in the dialogue of the mind with the spirit of things Wordsworth achieves not only health but "higher knowledge, a *gnosis* which mere reasoning could not reach." [14] George Eliot's wisdom and serenity appeal to Scherer strongest. She, to his mind, wrote "the most perfect novels ever written" and is "the most considerable literary personality since the death of Goethe." He praises *Adam Bede* most highly and isolates the story of Gwendolen Harleth from *Daniel Deronda* (anticipating F. R. Leavis) as the best work of her later years.[15]

Yet, after all, Scherer was most at home in the French tradition, though he often criticized it harshly. "We lack," he can say, "the poetic force and the originality of the English, the science and speculative power of the Germans." [16] Somewhat contradictorily, he cares for two types of French writing: the elegiac poets and 18th-century prose. He praises Racine in the highest terms and complains that he "never met an Englishman or German who felt Racine." [17] He admires Lamartine, who seems to him greater than Wordsworth; Musset and Maurice de Guérin are poets after his own heart (oddly agreeing with Barbey d'Aurevilly) ; and he is attracted to Amiel for his lyrical despair and his experience of depersonalization.[18] But he can also glorify the 18th century for its ideals of tolerance, equality, and human solidarity, and write sympathetically about Diderot.[19] There is much solid information, even erudition and good critical sense, in Scherer's articles on many French figures.

Clearly he has learned from Sainte-Beuve, whom he considers "decidedly the greatest of our modern critics" and whom he praises unstintingly for "justness, lack of malice, suppleness" and exactitude. He rightly rejects the view that Sainte-Beuve was always a skeptic and recognizes that, for a time, he genuinely cared for spirituality and piety.[20] Scherer's position seems quite unequivocal from his discussions of Taine. He disapproves of what he considers his deductive method, his wild generalizations about the English or his chamber-of-horrors picture of the French Revolution. He can say, not unjustly in this case, that Taine's *Philosophie de l'art grec* contains "not a word of art nor a word of philosophy."[21] But the closeness to Sainte-Beuve is deceptive. Actually, at least in theory, Scherer upheld evolutionism and demanded of literary history a "sentiment of development" which meant not necessarily progress but rather transformation. He criticizes Nisard for his static picture of French literature and Saintsbury's *History of French Literature* (which he shoots full of holes) for its lack of a truly historical method and a sense of evolution.[22]

Scherer demands impersonality from the critic, since understanding means "leaving oneself in order to transport oneself as far as possible into the heart of things as they really are."[23] "We must react against the mere sensations of our taste, try to dominate them, endeavor to see things in their very essence, i.e., in their necessity," their laws.[24] The scientific ideal of the time is thus also Scherer's ideal. It leads to tolerance, even relativism. "I can enjoy both Shakespeare and Racine without any need of comparing them."[25] The universe is in eternal flux, and absolutism is as impossible in aesthetics as in philosophy. Ranking of poets is a puerile game.[26] But here Scherer is aware that everything would seem to become individual and arbitrary, and he answers that the masterpieces which are admired by all generations refute complete skepticism. From an "analysis of the character of the writer and the study of his age arises spontaneously an understanding of the work. Instead

of a personal and arbitrary estimate, made by whomsoever, we see
the work, in some way, pronouncing judgment on itself, and taking
the rank that belongs to it among the productions of the human
mind." [27] Scherer does not see that he has begged the question, that
he has shifted the burden to the sum of other people's judgments,
which make up the universal consensus explicable only on the
assumption of a common human nature judging by common
standards. There is a glaring contradiction between Scherer's
historistic and evolutionary theories and his practical criticism,
which is either determined by a personal taste or by social and moral
concerns that often have a Kantian or simple Protestant rigidity.

EMILE MONTÉGUT (1826–1895)

There is nothing rigid about Emile Montégut. He is an extremely
versatile, sympathetic, widely read essayist who has considerable
merits as a propagator of English and American literature in France.
Montégut has been called "the only great essayist of the nineteenth
century" [1] (presumably in France), but he is in danger of being
forgotten, not only because his books have not been reprinted and
are all only collections of articles that he wrote for the *Revue des
Deux Mondes,* with their accepted prolixity and leisurely approaches, but also because he lacks the strong individuality, either
as a theorist or a judge, which alone conveys a name to posterity.
He has sympathy with his subjects, rhetorical skill in exposition,
and great variety of information, but he lacks a center and a deeper
coherence. At first sight he might strike us as an adventurous dealer
in paradox, not lacking in boldness. He likes pushing arguments
and theories to their extremes. In his long review of Taine's *History
of English Literature,* for instance, he makes some reservations
against Taine's "brilliant hardness" and excessive determinism but
then swallows his racial theories hook, line, and sinker and recklessly speculates about the Saxon, Norman, Italian, and Celtic spirit
in English literature. "The taciturn and free" Anglo-Saxon was the
only strain that produced the great English poets, except "Chaucer,
who was nothing but a Frenchman who expresses himself in the
English language." Lord Byron "joins himself directly over the
centuries to the Old Saxon poets and the primitive Scandinavians." [2]
Similarly, Montégut goes Lamb's argument against the presentation

of Shakespeare's plays on the stage one better, denying that "the drama was the necessary form of his genius." Shakespeare's plays are "not unfaithful to the laws of art and poetry, but unfaithful to the laws that are particularly constitutive of the theater and the dramatic kind." [3] The essay on Alexander Pope romanticizes him excessively. Pope was "a real heretic hidden under the most scrupulous forms of classical orthodoxy." Montégut admires *The Rape of the Lock,* "Eloisa to Abelard," and "Elegy to the Memory of an Unfortunate Lady," but dismisses the ethical and satirical poetry. Pope supposedly had no other passions than literary ones; and one can read him without knowing anything of the history of his time.[4] In all these instances paradoxes are pushed to extremes that cannot withstand closer inspection, but we feel that the conclusions are not proposed very seriously and that they are not supported by any general scheme.

Montégut was a tolerant Catholic of liberal and even mystical tendencies who took a favorable view of Protestantism for its moral concern with concrete life and reality. He began his career with laudatory articles on Emerson and Carlyle. He brings out Emerson's Platonism and individualism, deploring his implied destruction of history, but he minimizes or misunderstands Emerson's equalitarian and democratic convictions.[5] Montégut was apparently soon disappointed, however, with the new idealistic reaction in England and America and welcomed realism if it stayed within the confines of Christianity. Dutch painting and the English novel are his prime examples, and George Eliot is his heroine, though he also wrote sympathetically of Charlotte Brontë, Trollope, and even Charles Kingsley.[6] English realism serves as contrast to French realism and naturalism, which, for Montégut, as for Scherer or Barbey d'Aurevilly, are the symptoms of French decadence, of the new godless society speeding toward destruction. In 1861 he could write that France has "neither a great novelist nor a great dramatic writer nor a genuine poet",[7] at a time when Hugo, Flaubert, and Baudelaire were at the height of their powers. Montégut is thus definitely a man of the past, of the later romantic movement, who admires Lamartine, Hugo, Musset, Gautier, and the Guérins with some reservations. He looks at the 18th century as the unpoetical and rationalistic age that destroyed old Catholic and classical France. Montégut preserves, however, a definite aesthetic sensibility within his

religious view of the world. He can say that God and religion are
the true aims of art, but he clearly distinguishes between aesthetic
and social criticism [8] and is by no means a mere moralist. He
defends, for instance, Gautier's *Mademoiselle de Maupin* for its
innocent, adolescent animality [9] and reflects genially on Boccaccio's
tale of Alaciel, the betrothed of the King of Garbo.[10] He can be
witty and sensible, criticizing Michelet's *De l'Amour,* for its economic implications and naivetés, though he loved the man and
admired him extravagantly as "the greatest imagination of this
time." [11] He can review Hugo's *Chansons des rues et des bois,* suggesting that it is less a revelation of senile sensuality than a
deliberate self-aggrandizement of a poet filling a gap in the genres
of his all-inclusive work.[12] Montégut has some passing words of praise
for *Madame Bovary,* which he considers a milestone in social history.
Parallel with *Don Quixote,* it has put an end to the "sensuous sentimentality" made fashionable by the romantic school,[13] just as
Cervantes put an end to the chivalric craze in Spain.

Madame Bovary joins the series of literary types that are the
theme of Montégut's most coherent book, *Types littéraires* (1882).
He discusses Don Quixote, Hamlet, Werther, and Wilhelm Meister
as the key figures in literary history, and would include Alceste in
the sequence. Don Quixote appears as the personification of Spain,
at once heroic and picaresque. He is more than a literary symbol, he
is a historical person who "really lived" in the 17th century.[14]
Similarly, Hamlet is treated as a Renaissance figure with the shadow
of the Middle Ages hovering over him and is defended as a living
human being with all his contradictions: he is "simultaneously
meditative and energetic, masculine and irresolute, melancholic
and brutal." [15] Werther is the most appealing figure to Montégut,
because he is a bourgeois character who in effect put an end to
chivalric and aristocratic literature; he is a man of Montégut's own
flesh and blood, with whom he can identify himself even better than
with Hamlet and Alceste, the prince and nobleman who anticipate
him as types embodying the modern divorce between the inner and
outer world. Werther has nothing to do with the flamboyant heroes
of Chateaubriand and Byron who are supposed to be descended
from him. They are desperadoes on quite another scale than the
meek Werther suffering from the smaller ills of life.[16] For Montégut
draws a line against apparently unmotivated pessimism and athe-

ism. He admired Hawthorne and described the novels, particularly *The Blithedale Romance*, with genuine understanding. But he recoiled at his complete gloom about human nature and would not have shared Henry James' view of Hawthorne's sense of detachment and aesthetic play.[17] He was genuinely puzzled and upset by Vigny's universal pessimism. He searches desperately for biographical reasons for his gloom and seems completely unable to understand Vigny's sense of man's solitude and personal tragedy.[18] The limitations of the bourgeois, Catholic, mildly romantic outlook are apparent to our time. They are not compensated for by Montégut's large tolerance, his wide horizon, and his historical merits as an intermediary among the great literatures of the West.

PAUL BOURGET (1852–1935)

Barbey d'Aurevilly, Scherer, and Montégut belong to an older generation; the younger men bear the imprint of Taine, share the scientific ambition of the time, the diagnostic view of literary study. Paul Bourget's *Essais de psychologie contemporaine* (2 vols. 1883, 1885) stand out for their insight and skill of presentation. Unfortunately Bourget later became a fashionable novelist of Parisian high life and an advocate of Catholic and monarchical traditionalism. An aura of strong erotic perfume hangs about his novels; they are justly forgotten today. But the two volumes of early essays, though they show some affectation, and point to the later novels in their sensibility, are a virtuoso piece of cultural diagnosis drawn from literary evidence. Bourget traces the sources of modern pessimism, the whole phenomenon of "decadence," by studying the writers who influenced him and his generation most deeply: Baudelaire, Renan, Flaubert, Taine, and Stendhal in the first volume, and the younger Dumas, Leconte de Lisle, the Goncourt brothers, Turgenev, and Amiel in the weaker second volume. Bourget is concerned with the "psychology", or rather the sensibility, of these authors and analyzes their effect on himself and, explicitly, on his own time. Though each essay is independent, they all pursue the one theme of decadence, carefully assembling the diverse traits of modern despair, the new *mal du siècle*, which differs, in Bourget's mind, mainly in heightened self-consciousness from its romantic ancestor. Its main ingredients are seen very clearly: dilettantism, which means relativism and indifference; cosmopolitanism, which uproots man from his certainties; science, which destroys religion and personality; analysis, which cripples creation; and finally pessimism or nihilism, which leads to suicide of the individual and of civilization.

Stendhal is the distant precursor, who was not appreciated in his own time because he had a shocking power of analysis. Stendhal's hero, by his very nature, "acts and sees himself acting, feels and sees himself feel." [1] Besides, Stendhal was a cosmopolitan when France was still self-centered in her Napoleonic glories. Analysis poisons the loves of Baudelaire. His disillusionment with sex and religion leads him to nihilism and to decadence as a creed which Bourget explains as literal, physical decay. The organic metaphor is exploited somewhat perversely: the artistic and social health and unity of older times contrasts with the unhealthiness, dispersion, and fragmentation of modern writing. The style of decadence is found where "the unity of the book decomposes to make room for the independence of the page, where the page decomposes to make room for the independence of the sentence, and the sentence to make room for the independence of the word." [2] Flaubert still clings to literary romanticism, but it is a disillusioned romanticism, which leads to suicide and despair. "Emma and Frédéric have read novels and poets; Salammbô is nourished with the sacred legends recited by Schahabarim." They all suffer from having known the image of reality before knowing reality itself. "The abuse of the brain is their great disease." [3] Flaubert, like his heroes, is a bookish man whose self-consciousness paralyzes his will. His characters are all passive, like "walking associations of ideas." [4] Each image is isolated, each word separate like a stone in a mosaic. Flaubert's *impassibilité* fits in with the determinism of Taine and the dilettantism of Renan. Renan's dilettantism is interpreted as relativism and skepticism, as the "extreme of civilization" which has "slowly abolished the faculty of creation in order to substitute the faculty of comprehension." [5] Renan understands religion but does not believe in it, Leconte de Lisle has sympathy for all religions and all, even animal, life, but ends with Buddhism, a total nihilism in which all history appears as a meaningless progress toward death. The Goncourt brothers display the collectors' mania, which is another form of dilettantism, and have the power of analysis that destroys the will and the spontaneity of feeling as well as the coherence of traditional composition and style. Amiel presents the image of the will-less modern man undermined in his certitude by the conflict of the French and German spirit within him and by the pessimistic philosophies of Schopenhauer and Hartmann. He is "too full of the inner life." [6] "Analysis," said Amiel himself, "kills spontaneity. The grain ground to flour can never more germinate or rise." [7]

Two authors, in Bourget's gallery, let some light into the dark room of decadence. Turgenev—who is as disillusioned, weak-willed, and uprooted as his French friends—differs by being healthily Russian. His cosmopolitanism is always concerned with Russia, with Europe in Russia; his pessimism has a touch of tenderness; and his women keep the feminine mystery totally dissipated by the modern French novel. The younger Dumas is the writer who has most critically described the new inability to love, our illness "by an excess of critical thought, from too much literature, from too much science." [8] But Bourget discerns in Dumas glimmers of hope: a rigorous moralism and an almost Manichaean mysticism. The caricature of the irresponsible intellectual, the positivistic philosopher Sixte in Bourget's novel *Le Disciple* (1889), is outlined in these essays, and even his later conversion is faintly adumbrated.

The colors are often put on crudely; the division of each essay into three parts, each with a single theme, often seems mechanical; the evidence is sometimes arranged or distorted; and certainly the gloom is too monotonously thick. Stendhal was no pessimist in Bourget's sense. But the books diagnosed a real *malaise* impressively. Nietzsche quoted and used Bourget's concept of decadence. [9] Also, Bourget's method is an innovation, at least in this degree of purity. It comes from Taine's concept of the work as a sign and goes back to any idea of the moral influence of books. Bourget clearly focuses on the writers preceding his generation (Amiel is out of place here) who shaped the mood of his youth: a very specific Parisian intellectual youth which, however small in numbers, set the tone of the age. Bourget was a good critic if criticism is the confession of a man and, simultaneously, the mouthpiece of a time.

EMILE HENNEQUIN (1859-1888)

Another attempt at a systematization of criticism was made by Emile Hennequin in his small book *La Critique scientifique* (1888).

Hennequin is little known today. His three short books were not reprinted. They repel by their tortuous style full of archaisms and neologisms, scientific terms and far-fetched adjectives. Hennequin died at the age of 28 in a bathing accident, and the great impression of his personality lasted only long enough to ensure the publication of his theoretical book and the collection of two volumes of his scattered essays, *Ecrivains francisés* (1889) and *Quelques Ecrivains français* (1890). Hennequin found one great admirer abroad in the eminent Czech critic, F. X. Šalda (1867–1937), who translated him and kept his memory green in my student years at the University of Prague in the 1920's.[1]

La Critique scientifique attempts to put criticism on a scientific basis by treating the work of art as a "sign" of the mind of the author or the society from which he came or the audience which he addresses. Hennequin devices the term "esthopsychologie" to indicate his central concern for the aesthetic emotion, which he describes in Kantian terms as an end in itself. "Art is the creation in our heart of a powerful life without action and without pain."[2] Only later, in retrospect, will the aesthetic emotion provide motives for human conduct. Hennequin criticises Taine's triad. The belief in a stability of a national character or race is mistaken. The influence of *milieu* and *moment* is uncertain, obscure and variable. Hennequin argues that with the growth of individualism and the increasing conflict between the artist and society the influence of the *milieu* decreases so much as to become almost nonexistent in the flowering of a free society. He uses the standard argument that *milieu* cannot explain such geniuses as Rembrandt or Leonardo da Vinci and that Taine himself does not even try to account for them. Nor is he convinced that Chateaubriand owes anything to Britanny or Flaubert to Normandy. "Does Flaubert or Corneille represent the physical and picturesque features of Rouen?"[3]

Hennequin then makes his most fruitful suggestion: study not the background of an artist but his admirers. The work of art is, in part, "the expression of the faculties, of the ideal, of the internal organism of those who are moved by it."[4] A work appeals to its audience because it is its mental analogue. If an audience considers it truthful and lifelike, it need not actually reproduce reality faithfully: for example, *La Dame aux camélias* was accepted as a marvel of realism by the theater public of its time. Laborers hardly believe in the truth of *L'Assommoir* but easily recognize the ideal mason or blacksmith of the popular novelist. A novel thus will be appreciated "when it realizes the subjective truth of which it renders the ideas and does not contradict the imagination." [5] Hennequin then makes rather obvious comments on the different kinds of public or age groups to which different poets appeal: Musset and Heine to youth, Horace to old age. He suggests that literary history should rather study the succession of fictional types: they precede and anticipate the evolution of the national mind, they express a nation because they are admired. The glory of an artist and the victory of a national hero are analogous phenomena because the individual in both cases realizes a type and excites imitation, approbation, and admiration. The artist and the hero are at the same time the causes and the types of the movement they provoked. Rather incongruously, Hennequin concludes that art hinders the moral progress of man, as it helps him to remain addicted "to the practice of his atavistic inclinations." Art softens manners, weakens nationality and patriotism. "The most civilized nations are the easiest to conquer." [6] The defeat of 1870–71 still rankled.

The proposal of a sociology of taste or audience reaction is, however, not carried out in the two collected volumes of Hennequin's practical criticism. The better of the two, *Ecrivains francisés*, has a striking theme: the foreign writers who, in recent times, were translated, read, and admired in France. Dickens, Heine, Turgenev, Poe, Dostoevsky, and Tolstoy, in that order, are the subjects of the book. But with the exception of a few pages toward the end, no attempt is made to study the impact of these writers on France. We hear something of the influence of Heine and the German *lied* on Catulle Mendès, François Coppée, and Villiers de l'Isle-Adam, and a feeble suggestion is made that Dostoevsky appeals to the "higher categories of the readers of Dickens, in the well-to-do and enlightened bourgeoisie, particularly in the Protestant bourgeoisie." [7] But this is all. Actually, the foreign writers are classified as psychological types in a very schematic manner. Poe is the absolute intellect, Heine represents a balance of intelligence and sensibility, Dickens the extreme of sensibility, with Dostoevsky going beyond him into mysticism. [8] All these generalizations of the conclusion strike me as afterthoughts. They do not describe the essays justly, which at their best achieve brilliant characterizations of the mind and style of the authors under consideration with an art which must be called Taine's. Hennequin, in spite of his misgivings about Taine's theories, is his disciple. The extreme formulas, the loud colors, a certain rigidity and schematism remind us of chapters in the *History of English Literature* or the essay on Balzac.

Hennequin's essay on Poe pursues the idea of Poe's absolute intellectuality so dear to his French admirers from Baudelaire to Valéry. Hennequin believes in the old legends: Poe solved the mystery of Marie Roget, deciphered all the cryptograms, led a life of adventure in Europe, and died of hunger. "Steely mechanism," "metallic," "machine-like," rigid, icy, etc. are the key terms of the characterization.[9] The Heine essay is far better: it makes Heine very French, "one of ours," and succeeds in describing his irony, his emotional instability and his coquetry even in dying.[10] Hennequin's concept of poetry is "symbolist" in the sense in which the word was understood for a time, for example, by Verlaine. Poetry should aim at vagueness, suggestion, music, and thus Heine (and Baudelaire, whom Hennequin *preferred to Heine) presents a problem. He thinks that they ceased to write poetry when they became psychological analysts. They are poetically, though not literally, below the impersonal ideal poetry of a Shelley or Hugo.[11]

But the essays on Dickens and the three Russian novelists represent Hennequin at his best. Dickens is characterized very much as Taine or George Henry Lewes depicted him, as a caricaturist and visionary. His limitations are strongly insisted on: sensuality and the intellect are excluded from his world. The affinities to vaudeville and melodrama are brought out and the types of Dickensian characters are classified. Hennequin prefers the later Dickens: *Great Expectations* and *Our Mutual Friend*.[12] Turgenev is labeled "the elegiac poet of realism." His fragmentary, reticent procedure, moving slowly by an accumulation of tiny traits and the moral malady of his heroes,[13] is sketched well enough, but one has the impression, as in the better essays on Dostoevsky and Tolstoy, that Hennequin had little understanding or sympathy for the Russian situation. Still, the two essays on Dostoevsky and Tolstoy are most symptomatic of the reaction of the first Western readers to the Russian novel just because Hennequin speaks so frankly and critically and conveys the surprise and shock of novelty which has worn off for us with the years the Russians have become familiar figures. Hennequin did not know *The Possessed* and *The Brothers Karamazov* and hardly understood Dostoevsky's complex doctrines.

But he brings out strongly the nightmarish phantasmagoric quality of Dostoevsky's world "where the streets, the houses, and the people, so permanent or firmly walking at first, suddenly begin to tremble and soar, like shadows or black outlines of dreams. And this miracle never happens but that a breath of another world vaporizes all this matter into an indistinct mirage." [14] The mixture of the real and the phantastic, the monotony of the situations and the moods in the different books are made an implicit reproach, as is the "disproportion between sensibility and reasoning." [15] Hennequin, a good French rationalist at heart, considers mysticism—the exaltation of "madness, idiocy, imbecility, the candor of idiots and the goodness of criminals" [16]—simply nonsense.

This rationalistic incomprehension damages also the fine essay on Tolstoy, which was one of the first to treat *War and Peace* adequately. Hennequin makes "life" the keyword of his characterization: life in transition, in flux, in slow evolution. Even the main characters are fluid, subject to the variations of their surroundings. Hennequin points to Tolstoy's sense of the physical person and to his success in describing men losing their individuality in hospitals, on the battlefield, or in the prison compound.[17] Many of Hennequin's observations were later elaborated by Merezhkovsky. But Hennequin makes at the end a curious final reservation:

> The reader of Tolstoy feels himself in the course of the work vaguely but surely repelled by the spectacle it represents. The writer seems incessantly to gird himself for the great effort to encompass his immense subject and incessantly he fails, turns aside and detaches himself as if he did not care for the work he has undertaken; scenes are sketched unfinished, hardly pointed up by a few strokes; the great crises of the characters are indicated in confused and vague words; the descriptions of the principal actions which started with a feverish ardor, weaken in jumbled sentences; an immense lassitude betrays itself in the exposition of ideas, discolors the psychologies, blunts the dialogues, blurs the physiognomies.[18]

Hennequin strongly senses "the vague and menacing presence of a transcendent nihilism." He is simply shocked by Tolstoy's "absurd" philosophy of history and by Tolstoy's then recent religious conversion, which is "at the point of touching the shrill irrationalism of the worst fools." [19] Hennequin's sympathy completely fails before the phenomenon of religion, but he seems to put his finger on the limitations of Tolstoy's art.

The collection of essays *Quelques Ecrivains français* (1890) is an act of piety on the part of Hennequin's friends. The three main essays on Flaubert, Zola, and Hugo are the most schematic and formulaic pieces among Hennequin's writings. Each author is characterized by a set of leading traits. Flaubert is a writer enamored of words, which with him always precede ideas. He builds his books like mosaic. They resemble "enormous cubes of glittery granite." [20] Zola works by enumeration of details, intoxicated by a love of life and force which, in its very excess, leads to disillusionment and pessimism. Hennequin has no use for Zola's theories on art expounded in *L'Œuvre* and condemns naturalism, but he admires Zola's "gigantic abstractions" and his "supreme gift of life." [21] Hugo, similarly, is characterized by his technique of incessant repetitions, antitheses, divisions within his characters—but in a much more hostile mood. Hennequin ridicules his exploitations of the hoariest commonplaces and enjoys reciting his silly theories: "He explains the rictus of corpses by the joy of the dead in re-entering the great whole and the positions of the eyes of toads by their desire to see the blue sky." [22]

Hennequin belongs to the many critics in the 19th century and today who want to make criticism scientific, impersonal, free from value judgments. But these passages and many others show that Hennequin was a critic with a considerable power of analysis, skill of characterization, and clear definition of taste and judgment. His recommendation of a study of the audience of a work of art, his sense of the analogue between the fictional hero and his public, remained only a suggestive proposal. But he offers in his scheme of criticism a way out from the purely causal thinking of most of his contemporaries into a "synthetic" literary scholarship that would include an aesthetic, a psychology, and a sociology in a discipline he would call anthropology.[23] From our point of view it is conceived too narrowly as a descriptive science, oblivious of what centrally matters: meaning, value, beauty, which have to be discerned and discriminated critically. It seems a pity that Hennequin did not live to develop his ideas.

5 : FRANCESCO DE SANCTIS

In ITALY Francesco De Sanctis (1817–83) is considered *the* critic, a
national classic whose voluminous works are being republished in
three rival editions—one even on bad paper, cheaply produced for
"the people." [1] Benedetto Croce, by far the most influential Italian
critic of the 20th century, has done most to establish his fame: he
has edited, expounded, and fervently defended De Sanctis throughout his long writing life. He considers him as a "critic and historian
of literature without rival," and rejects comparisons with Lessing,
Macaulay, Sainte-Beuve, and Taine as inadequate.[2] A veritable cult
of De Sanctis has come into being: Giuseppe Borgese has proclaimed
the *History of Italian Literature* "the masterpiece of Italian culture
in the 19th century." [3] Giovanni Gentile advocated a return to De
Sanctis as a polemical weapon against Croce. Marxists and students
of stylistics today try to reinterpret his teachings to suit their own
purposes.[4]

Outside of Italy De Sanctis is practically unknown: he is not even
mentioned in recent histories of aesthetics; and Saintsbury, in his
History of Criticism, treats him quite mistakenly as a mere follower
of Sainte-Beuve.[5] A German student of early Italian literature,
Adolf Gaspary (1849–92), studied with De Sanctis in Naples and
admired him greatly, but his own work on early Italian literature
(*Geschichte der italienischen Literatur,* 1882–88) shows hardly any
influence, as it is largely philological and historical; while the
English critic, John Addington Symonds, in the literary parts of his
Renaissance in Italy (1875–83), drew on De Sanctis not only for views
and information but often for whole paragraphs of paraphrase.[6]

Brunetière referred to the *History* with high praise.[7] But the
American translation of the *History* (1931) caused no ripple,
though F. O. Matthiessen read it and acknowledged his debt for the
distinction between allegory and symbol which pervades his fine
book *American Renaissance* (1941). There is a descriptive Colum-

97

bia University dissertation on De Sanctis, and more recently the essays on Dante were translated.[8] But one cannot speak of any sustained interest in De Sanctis outside of Italy.

The reasons for this neglect are not far to seek: De Sanctis wrote almost exclusively on Italian literature, and Italian literature, with the exception of Dante, has, strangely enough, almost ceased to excite critical interest in the rest of the world. De Sanctis, moreover, is so definitely an Italian patriot of the *risorgimento*, so passionately concerned with the political, intellectual and moral rebirth of his country, and so strongly identified with Naples and the South that he might appear provincial, pedagogical, and didactic to an outsider. His style, often highly involved and repetitious, is sometimes rhetorical in a manner grating to Anglo-Saxon ears.[9] But more profoundly, the neglect of De Sanctis must be due to the real difficulties of his position, the ambiguities of his terminology, the very complexity of his thought. Still, his achievement of a synthesis of criticism and literary history is so unique and great that an effort must be made to disentangle the web of his thinking.

Croce and his followers emphasize De Sanctis' aesthetic doctrines, which anticipate Croce's position on several points: the autonomy of art and the concept of form. De Sanctis himself disclaimed any ambition to formulate an aesthetic and prided himself on his bent for the concrete and his distrust of any system.[10] But he does pronounce, though only in passing, on the nature of art. Art "has its own aim and value in itself and must be judged by the special criteria deduced from its nature." [11] The phrase "autonomy of art" asserts the distinction between art on the one hand and emotion, morality, science, conceptual knowledge, philosophy, and factual truth on the other. Art is not a direct expression of sentiment. "Sentiment is not aesthetic in itself. Sorrow, love, etc. . . . as long as it has no power to transform itself and idealize itself, may be eloquent in its expression but may not be artistic. Not only is emotion not the substance of art, but in order that it be capable of arousing the aesthetic faculty it must be kept in just measure. Emotion must not trouble the soul, deprive it of self-control, serenity, disturb its inner harmony." [12] Art is not subservient to morality, as "morality is not the consequence but the presupposition, the antecedent of art." [13] Art is not an idea or concept, nor science or philosophy in disguise. "Reasoning, doctrinal form are the negation of

art." [14] "Thought as thought is outside of art." [15] Nor is art an imitation or passive reflection of reality: it would have no function of its
own and would always necessarily remain inferior to reality.[16] Art
aims at truth, but only at artistic truth, ñot at the real, and we can
speak of reality in art "only on condition that it is the artistic real
and not the natural or historical real." [17] Historical truth is extrinsic
to art and anachronisms are thus immaterial. "Historical interest
has nothing to do with poetry, which can represent even extraordinary and unnatural things, provided it presents them with such a
coloring that we have no time to defend ourselves from enthusiasm
and to ask: is it true?" [18] Rather, art is a "shadow, an image, a
semblance of the real," "reality raised to illusion." [19]

   Art is Form, Form with a capital F. It must not be confused with
"forms"—language, diction, tropes and figures—or style.[20] Form
is simply the work of art itself, a concrete, individual substance, a
living organic unity. De Sanctis, in variations on the same theme,
asserts the unity, the wholeness of a work of art; either by saying that
the whole is contained in its parts, fused and interpenetrated, or
merely by proclaiming that it is alive, that it is life itself.[21] At times
De Sanctis would draw an analogy between the work of art and the
works of nature.[22] In other contexts he would ask for the complete
identity of form and content in a perfect work of art.[23] Sometimes
the emphasis is shifted to the origin of the Form in the mind of the
poet. "This inner process constitutes what in scientific language is
called 'form,' which must not be confused with the similar word
used by rhetoricians to mean its grossest appearances." [24]

   The "unconsciousness and spontaneity" of the artist is the main
condition of his greatness.[25] The poet creates by imagination a
poetic "world." This poetic world is above all individual, concrete: art "individualizes"; [26] "poetry must come down to earth
and take on flesh." [27] Even Dante should "paganize." [28] Concreteness and individuality are with De Sanctis not merely qualities
of the work as a whole but they apply, for instance, to fictional characters. A poetic character must always be "such a magistrate, such a
priest, such a soldier; in this 'such a' is the whole secret of artistic
creation." [29] Hence, De Sanctis completely rejects the view that
"type" is the highest creation of art. In poetry, for him, there are no
types but only individuals. "To say that Achilles is the type of force
and courage, and that Thersites is the type of cowardice, is inexact,

as these qualities may have infinite expressions in individuals. Achilles is Achilles and Thersites is Thersites." [30] At most, he would allow type to be an early form of art, "its cradle," [31] or perhaps the result of a process of dissolution achieved by time in which individuals such as Don Quixote, Sancho Panza, Tartuffe, Hamlet are reduced to mere types in popular imagination.[32] But true art is always individual and creates individuals. Thus allegory, symbolism, and personification are all inartistic. Allegory is condemned because there is no "interpenetration of the two terms. The thought has not descended into the image: the figured has not descended into the figure." [33] "Allegory dies and poetry is born" [34] is an early formula on which De Sanctis insists throughout his *History*.

As art is spontaneous creation, De Sanctis rejects any judgment made on the basis of plans, theories, or intentions of the author. "One thing is to say, another to do." [35] One must "distinguish the intentional world and the effective world—what the poet willed and what he has made." [36] Thus "the safest and most conclusive method is to look at the book itself and not at the intentions of the author." [37]

This aesthetic of an organic, concrete, individual work of art, in which form and content are ideally indistinguishable, created by genius in an act of imagination, is matched by an analogous theory of criticism. De Sanctis distinguishes three stages in the critical act: first an act of submission, a surrender to first impressions, then recreation, and finally judgment. Criticism must not, so he says, "falsify or destroy the ingenuousness of my sentiments." In the theater we should forget Aristotle and Hegel, cry and laugh, be simply men. "Just as poetics cannot take the place of genius, so criticism cannot take the place of taste, and taste is the genius of the critic. Just as one says that poets are born, so also are critics born: in the critic there is also a kind of genius which must be a gift of nature." [38] The critic should identify himself with the artist and the work of art, even recreate it, "give it a second life, and say with the pride of Fichte:—I create God." [39] In more sober terms, De Sanctis wants the critic "to remake what the poet has done, to remake it in his own manner and by other means." [40] Usually this remaking is conceived of as translating from the unconscious to the conscious. "Criticism is the consciousness or eye of poetry, the same spontaneous work of genius reproduced as a work reflected by taste.

It must not dissolve the poetic universe, it must show the same unity become reason, self-consciousness . . . It is the poetic conception itself seen from another point of view . . . creation re-thought or reflected." [41] But this recreation must not be arbitrary. "Criticism does not create; it recreates; it must reproduce." It should become a "science" or a "superior science," though De Sanctis speaks of it also as a form of art, with the science understood.[42] Once De Sanctis even thought of the critic as a performer on the analogy of the actor. "The critic picks up the few syllables and divines the whole word." Critic and actor "do not simply reproduce the poetic world, but integrate it, fill its gaps." [43]

Beyond this recreation, whether translation into consciousness or an acting out of the poet's words, there is the final critical judgment. "After the critic has acquired a clear awareness of the poetic world, he can determine it, assign to it its position and attribute to it its values. And that is what is properly called *judging or criticizing*." [44] The critic must define the "intrinsic value of a work," and "not what it has in common with the times, a school, or with its predecessors but what it has that is peculiar and untransferable." [45] In art De Sanctis does not admit mediocrity because "there is no more-or-less alive. It is alive or dead; there is the poet and the non-poet, the eunuch brain." [46]

One can see why Croce could claim De Sanctis as his precursor. Croce also stresses the autonomy of art, the individual, concrete, unique work itself, which is not a concept or idea or copy of reality; and he conceives of criticism as identification with the work and as discernment of what is living and what is dead, what is poetry and what is nonpoetry. These doctrines in De Sanctis are sufficiently pervasive to refute any attempt to make him a "materialist", or even a forerunner of Marxist aesthetics. But they are not part of a system like Croce's: there is no continuity between art and ordinary intuition in De Sanctis; there is no sharp distinction between literature and poetry, no identification of intuition with expression and of poetry with lyricism, no reduction of criticism to the definition of sentiment, and no rejection of the very possibility of literary history. On the contrary, De Sanctis, the defender of the autonomy of art, could be described rather as a moralist who sees literature, charged with a high social mission, symbolize a great historical process. The critic who is to mete out sentences of life and death is actually a historian who sees each work of art justified in its place, fatefully needed, inescapably great or small. The propounder of this "formalism" actually devised a whole scheme of conflicts between content and form and a whole series of terms describing the various stages and aspects of a work of art.

De Sanctis is no monist or idealist in Croce's sense. His epistemology is clearly dualistic, generally Kantian: a subject orders an objective world.[47] The artist does not create *ex nihilo*. In spite of occasional phrases about creative genius, De Sanctis' poet is not like the Christian God but rather more like the Platonic *demiurgos* imposing order on chaos. There is for De Sanctis a material existing before art, though he insists that the material becomes transformed in art and that any material can become art. "Everything is the matter of art." [48] "There is nothing in nature which cannot become art." [49] Even an immoral, absurd, frivolous content can become form and thus become immortal.[50] The ugly is not only a possible subject of art but actually preferable to the beautiful, as "the beautiful is only itself; the ugly is itself and its contrary." [51] In his revulsion against abstract neoclassicism and its vacuous ideal, De Sanctis goes so far as to say that Thaïs (the strumpet briefly presented in *Inferno,* xviii) is "more alive and poetic than Beatrice, insofar as she is a mere allegory" and that Iago is "one of the most beautiful creatures of the poetic world." [52] Mephisto is superior to Faust, hell to paradise. A virtuous woman is not a good subject for poetry,[53] since perfection or the ideal is, for De Sanctis, an abstraction and hence unpoetic.

The poet imposes form on matter, but there is often a conflict between matter or content, and form. De Sanctis postulates a perfect identity of form and content but only as a kind of limiting concept, an ideal. The identification has the consequence of equating content and form and making the terms interchangeable. "As the content, so the form." [54] "In poetry there is really neither form nor content, but as in nature, the one is the other." Paradoxically De Sanctis concludes that "the great poet annihilates the form so that it is itself the content." [55] "Content is thus not neglected. It appears twice in the new criticism [= De Sanctis]: first, as natural or abstract, as it was; the second time, as form which it has become." [56] Usually De Sanctis operates not with an identification of the two terms but with a conflict between them. Matter can sometimes be so resistant that the poet fails to subdue it. In Dante's *Comedy* there remains "an abstract and pedantic base which resists all efforts of the imagination." [57] In Alfieri "the political and moral content is not a mere stimulus or occasion for artistic formation, but is its substance, and invades and spoils the work of art." [58] In the 18th century "content appears not as art, already formed and transfigured, but as if divided from art, anterior and superior to art." [59] Sometimes the content is conceived of as existing independently, demanding its form. "When the content exists, it knocks and knocks again, and in the long run it makes its way, and creates its own form." [60] But just as often form can somehow become independent, indifferent to any content, "a pure play of forms." [61] At other times content and form are thought of as warring within the work of art itself. In Leopardi, we are told, there is a "disharmony of content and form," [62] or "an inner division in his poetic form," which gives a dramatic character to his lyrics—"laughter and tears, life and death." [63]

De Sanctis recognizes that a work of art has an "argument," which is by no means a *tabula rasa* on which the poet can write; "it is rather a marble, already shaped and carved, which contains its own concepts and laws of development. The chief quality of genius is to understand its argument." [64] Argument is "a conditioned and determined matter containing in itself virtually its own poetics, i.e., its organic laws, its concept, its parts, its form, its style." [65] De Sanctis even criticizes a poem because the author "has not seriously considered his argument." [66]

Content, argument, or what we would call theme generates the "situation." "Matter, in a concrete and determined position, acquires a character, becomes a 'situation.'" [67] Situation leads to "the unity of design, the structure and agreement of the parts." "It determines the appearance, the style [of a work of art]." [68] Sometimes situation refers to personality, the soul of the poet.[69] In other contexts "situation" seems merely a synonym for genuine organic form. "Poems that do not come from the soul, from inside, but are a mechanical and artificial product do not have 'situations' and therefore have no form in the elevated sense of the word." [70] Only rarely does the term mean something more specific. We are even told that a specific situation is "inaesthetic, or incapable of representation." [71] Foscolo's "Sepolcri" has a "genuine lyrical situation," shows "a soul in a determined condition, which sets in motion its inner world"; in contrast, his "Grazie" gives a history and metaphysics of its inner world and simply loses "situation," concreteness, and ceases to be poetry.[72] The term is simply an alternative for form, unity, individuality, or concreteness. It comes from Hegel's *Aesthetics*, where, in the section on the Ideal, it is discussed as one of the qualities of action.[73] Its implication of fixedness and stasis makes it hardly useful for more complex works of art, and De Sanctis himself uses it extensively only in the *Essay on Petrarch*, where he surveys the "situations" of various sonnets and *canzoni* or (to use a more familiar vocabulary) classifies the poems by themes. It is hard to see why the term should have recently been singled out as a great discovery central to De Sanctis' practice and capable of further application.[74]

De Sanctis speaks much more frequently of the work of art as a special "world" and discusses fictional characters in terms of the opposition between the ideal and the real, the characteristic and the general, the image and the phantasm. De Sanctis always condemns the abstract ideal, the "perfect, dead ideal," but defends the ideal entering the real, fused and interpenetrated with it.[75] In Manzoni he admires this fusion of the ideal and the real and finds even in Zola "the living sentiment of the human ideal and the strong constructive and representative imagination" that makes him an artist.[76] A fictional character should be "characteristic"—his individuality should stand out; but precisely the more individual the character, the more completely is the ideal incorporated in him. Every individual has his ideal, even the bandits in *I Promessi sposi*.[77] Contrary to his usual stress on the concretely individual and unique, De Sanctis would often recognize that great poets such as Dante and Leopardi, "by raising their feelings to general significance succeeded in fusing into a single personality what in their soul is most peculiar and intimate with what in the concept is most extrinsic and abstract." [78]

More frequently De Sanctis asserts that "image is the proper field of the poet." [79] Even higher than "image" is the "phantasm," which De Sanctis sometimes distinguishes from image on the grounds that there are two kinds of imagination, the lower *immaginazione*, which is mechanical and analytical, and the higher *fantasia*, which is organic and synthetic. [80] Once he defines "phantasm" as "this spiritualized image, that half reality." [81] Boccaccio's *Filocolo* is criticized for giving us the image but not the "phantasm," "those underlying meanings and shades which give us the feeling and music of things." [82] Guerrazzi is condemned for "lacking the immediate and direct intuition of the phantasm." [83] Thus the true poet is dominated by his phantasm, lives in this world of *fantasia,* and must forget himself in it. Instead of saying to his creature: "Arise and walk: . . . leaving it all its liberty as a person" Guerrazzi, the author of a bad historical novel on Beatrice Cenci, says, "You are my work: you belong to me." [84] "Phantasm" thus seems identical with the successful fictional character who must live his own life, must be seen objectively.

De Sanctis prefers objective to subjective art, the impersonal imagination of a Homer or Ariosto to the "manner" of subjective poets such as Petrarch or Tasso. Irony in the sense of destruction of illusion is condemned by De Sanctis as it was by Hegel. "In this smile, in this presence and awareness of the real, among the creations of genius, is the negative side of art, the germ of its dissolution and death." [85] Humor also seems to De Sanctis a negative art form. It "has, as its meaning, the destruction of the limit, together with an awareness of that destruction. It is the sentiment that nothing is true or serious, that every opinion is as good as any other." [86] Even the comic is not ranked with highest art. In an elaborate classification of the forms of the comic in Dante's *Inferno,* De Sanctis tries to establish some kind of scale of the comic, with buffoonery as the lowest and caricature as the highest form. But even higher than all forms of the comic is "sarcasm," a term used by Vischer for "annihilating scorn," "the door through which we turn our backs on the comic and enter again into great poetry." [87] Sarcasm must consume and purify itself, must become impersonal anger. Seriousness, passion, tragedy are to De Sanctis the highest forms of art.

De Sanctis cares little for traditional genre distinctions, as he always stresses the individual and the particular against the general and universal. But he does not reject the three main categories, lyric, epic, and drama, or such traditional kinds as idyll, elegy, and satire, and constantly operates with these terms either as basic psychological attitudes or as historical forms. Epic is for De Sanctis the earliest art form. It "draws its life from the intimate center of a nation." [88] It implies a traditional history, a social atmosphere in which the poet lives. Dante's Ugolino is considered epic, "primitive and integral epic, into which lyric and drama have not yet penetrated," [89] and the Napoleon of Manzoni's ode on his death ("Il Cinque Maggio") is also epic.[90] Farinata is "still the epic stuff of man, not the dramatic. Eloquence and the inner life of the soul are lacking." [91] Thus drama means to De Sanctis the highest form of art, as it is action, liberty, free personality. "Without human liberty, poetry, not to mention drama, is destroyed." [92] Necessity, lack of freedom is to De Sanctis always "prose." Thus Satan frozen into the icy sea at the bottom of Hell is "an absolutely prosaic character." [93] The lyric is for De Sanctis the last stage of art. "Art dies in a lyrical accent, in a musical sigh. The lyric, music, are the last forms of art." [94] All literary history is seen in the large categories of epic, drama, and lyric, but with a changed order, compared to Hegel's, where drama comes last. But the minor genre forms are rarely discussed in De Sanctis. Only the sonnet is singled out as "the poem of a quarter of an hour," similar to spatial art, which has the advantage of being "better able to represent the simultaneous than the successive." [95]

But such a reflection on outer form is very rare indeed. One finds occasional remarks on sound effects, or on the role of a stress on the sixth and seventh syllable in a sonnet by Petrarch, or on the Italian decasyllable in Berchet, or on the disappearance of rhyme and stanza in Foscolo's "Sepolcri." [96] A well-known passage on the classical period in Boccaccio assumes a contradiction of form and content: Boccaccio's world "would be intolerable, would be deeply disgusting, but art clothes its nakedness in these ample Latin forms as in a veil blown by lascivious winds." [97] Much more frequently De Sanctis recognizes the unity of content and form, of subject matter and style, in order to ignore the second term of the dichotomy. Style is "not constructed *a priori*. It is the consequence of a given way of conceiving, feeling, and imagining." [98] It is not "an arbitrary, isolated phenomenon." It is in "intimate connection with the whole design of the composition." [99] But De Sanctis strongly opposes the dictum that "style is the man." It is rather the "argument," the thing, the subject matter, "the expression that takes its substance and its character from the thing it wants to express." [100] To De Sanctis, outer form and style are ideally indistinguishable. "The form is a mirror that makes you pass immediately to the

image, so that you do not notice there is a glass between you." [101]
"This transparence of form consists in its annihilation, when it becomes a simple transmission and does not attract the eye to itself.
It is like a mirror in which you do not stop at the glass. . . . It is
limpidity. Limpid water is water that allows you, as if it were not
there, to see the bottom. Limpid form allows the object to emerge
from it without attracting the reader's attention." [102] Objectivity
thus is imperceptibility of form, undistorted "imitation." "The
motto of a serious art is: let's speak little ourselves and let the things
speak much. *Sunt lacrimae rerum*." [103] It is high praise when De
Sanctis says of Leopardi that he "forgets the word," that the "word
is for him nothing but an instrument . . . a diaphanous medium
in which the thought is reflected in all its limpidity and clearness." [104] De Sanctis sees through the glass. The self-styled "formalist" actually studies feelings and characters, arguments and situations. Form with De Sanctis is really inner form or *eidos*, a term
that oscillates, in the neoplatonic tradition, between the meaning of
the Platonic "idea" and the Aristotelian forming principle.

Similarly, the aesthetician who defends the autonomy of art
rejects art for art's sake as "an excessive formula." [105] It is true only
in the sense that art is the aim of art. "The bird sings in order to
sing, well and good. But the singing bird expresses his whole self,
his instincts, his needs, his nature. A man singing also expresses his
whole self. It is not sufficient to be an artist; he must be a man." [106]
Throughout De Sanctis' works the whole man is contrasted with the
partial man, the "poet" with the "artist." His ideal is a sort of humanism in which art plays only a role subordinate to the totality of
man's strivings for rational, ethical, religious, and philosophical
ideals. De Sanctis' greatest work, *The History of Italian Literature*
(2 vols. 1870–71) is a history of the Italian conscience, "conscience"
in the double sense of intellectual and moral awareness, "consciousness" and "moral sense," being the center of total man, just as "imagination" is the central faculty of the artist. The historical scheme
underlying the book is implicit also in many of the individual *Saggi
critici*. Several of the essays must be considered as elaborations of
points in the *History,* even though they may have been published
before the actual writing of the great synthetic work. Also, the
lecture courses given at Naples when De Sanctis held the chair of
comparative literature (1871–76), which trace Italian literary

history in the early 19th century, must be treated as a continuation of the *History* and its scheme. This scheme had early crystallized in De Sanctis' mind. Only the lecture courses given in his private school at Naples (1839–48) before his long prison term and his banishment can be dismissed as immature and largely derivative. From the time of his exile in Turin and Zurich (1854–60), all his work is dominated by this general scheme, which cannot be interpreted as a concession to the times or as a mere pedagogical device to link the individual chapters of the *History* on the great Italian writers. On the other hand, one cannot call the scheme "sociological," as hardly any attempt is made in the *History* to show a causal relationship between social change and literature. There are occasional remarks which assume that literature is a social document: De Sanctis recommends for example, that we study Renaissance comedies to "penetrate the mysteries of that Italian corruption," [107] or tells us that in Boccaccio "this society, unchanged, is introduced into the *Decameron,* as it were, caught red-handed in the act of life." [108] He can also proclaim his general adherence to the saying that "literature is an expression of society." "Art is something more than individual caprice; art, like religion and philosophy, like political and administrative institutions, is an intrinsic part of society, a natural result of culture and of national life." [109] But here, and throughout the book, no naturalistic determinism is assumed: rather, the hero of the book is a unitary national mind or conscience whose bearer and ideal is the total man, both religious and moral, who, if he is an artist, has high imagination to express this conscience or consciousness. Italian literature is not used as a document to study the changes of Italian society, nor is the social change studied in order to throw light on the literature, but rather the assumption is made that Italian literature constitutes the very essence or summary of Italian history itself. De Sanctis does not write *Kulturgeschichte:* he barely alludes to political or social events or situations; he practically ignores the other arts and expressly refuses to write a history of Italian philosophy.[110] In his *History,* literature itself, without any need for comparison with political, social, or art history, enacts a great spiritual drama: the fall and redemption of Italy.

The developmental scheme is not one of simple progress or decline. It is not exhaustively described by De Sanctis when he defines the "ruling principle" of his *History* as "the successive rehabilitation of matter, a gradual coming closer to nature and the real." [111] The change from the ideal to the real, from transcendence to immanence, is one of the themes of the *History,* but it is not the only nor is it the dominant one. It is far more complex and can best be described by briefly going through the stages of the scheme.

De Sanctis begins—in rather lame, introductory chapters that suffer most from gaps in information and lack of sympathy—by describing the main themes and genres of early Italian medieval literature: chivalry, the love lyric, scholastic learning, visions, mystery plays, political chronicles, all of which Dante is said to have synthesized and exalted in the *Divine Comedy.* Dante is the first great Italian poet, a total human being, a man, an imagination: "the beautiful unity of Dante who saw life in the harmony of intellect and action achieved through love." [112] Dante has all the human and poetic virtues: faith, the "preliminary and necessary condition of poetry," [113] sincerity, truth, a vivid sense of reality, the ardent passion of the patriot, and high imagination. But he is, in De Sanctis' view, too much implicated in his age: too medieval. He has an obsolete transcendental view of the world that puts the aim of life into the hereafter; he has a false intellectualistic concept of poetry that makes him invent a world of allegories and symbols. He has a static concept of human personality and knowledge that does not allow him to create free moving human beings or to think independently of his authorities.

The *Comedy* is seen as the result of a conflict between the poet in Dante who created such human beings as Francesca da Rimini, Farinata and Ugolino, and the philosopher, or rather scholar, who expounded without question an inherited doctrine in shadowy lifeless allegories. "But Dante was a poet, and he rebels against allegory." [114] "This artistic world, born from a contradiction between the intention of the poet and his work, is not thoroughly harmonious, is not pure poetry." [115] De Sanctis recognizes that the other world and the earthly world are, in Dante, indivisible and correlative, that his human beings with their passions, vices, and virtues remain human, though eternized, in the other world. But this eternizing, this rigidifying into statues, is to De Sanctis also one of Dante's limitations. "These mighty figures standing on their pedestals, rigid and epic like statues, are waiting for the artist who will take them by the hand and throw them into the turmoil of life, and make them dramatic beings. And that artist was not an Italian: he was Shakespeare." [116] In this imaginary projection to Shakespeare, the *Inferno* must be greatly preferred to the *Purgatorio* and *Paradiso,* and even within the *Inferno* a regress of life is evident. There is a constant diminishing of life and hence of poetry from the great individualities of the upper Hell to the groups of sinners in Malebolge and finally to its extinction in the ice of the lowest circles. "The Devil vanishes at the door of Purgatory and the flesh dies— and with the flesh, a good deal of the poetry disappears also." [117] De Sanctis describes *Purgatory* almost entirely in terms of images, paintings and sculpture, dreams and visions, as a world of quiet affection, of melancholy, resignation, as a lyrical effusion of pain, hope, and love. In the *Paradiso* "we reach the final dissolution of form. It was corporeal and material in the *Inferno,* picturesque and fantastic in the *Purgatorio;* here it is lyrical and musical: the imminent appearance of spirit, absolute light without content, not spirit itself but its covering and boundary." [118] In the final vision of God, Dante has words but not the form. His intellect is still alive, but his imagination, which had lighted him like a torch, has gone. " 'High fantasy' loses its power, and with the death of imagination poetry dies too." [119] Dante is the great ancestor, the wellspring of Italian poetry. But he was also representative of his time, of the Middle Ages, which De Sanctis sees as a way of life and thought from which man has finally freed himself for his own good.

After Dante there comes decline and fall, the fragmentation of the human being, the decline of high imagination, the shriveling of the great ethical substance, but also a rise, a liberation from the shackles of the Middle Ages, a new humanity and a new, more humane art. Both in the brief chapter of the *History* devoted to Petrarch and in the earlier book, *Saggio critico sul Petrarca* (1869), which is based on lectures delivered at Zurich in 1858–59, De Sanctis sees Petrarch as the artist (in contrast to the poet Dante) who has lost the totality of the greater man: lost his content and acquired the cult of form for form's sake. Petrarch's world is much narrower than Dante's: it is an inner world of a solitary and contemplative nature. But this inner world is, in De Sanctis' scheme, somehow more real, more human than Dante's. In apparent contradiction to earlier pronouncements about Dante, De Sanctis declares that with Petrarch "man is found," [120] that in him "the real appears for the first time in art," [121] and that we detect "the dawn of reality" in the very contradictions of Petrarch's mind.[122] Petrarch, to De Sanctis' regret, did not, however, free himself completely from the world of the Middle Ages. He seems like a man pulled here and there by contrary currents. His intellect still belongs to the Middle Ages, and his feeling, original and new as it is, is a resigned and weak melancholy. De Sanctis ignores or dismisses the humanist and politician and concentrates only on the *Canzoniere* (with a short, disparaging treatment of the *Trionfi*) . The Italian poems are discussed in terms of this psychological conflict between spirit and flesh: with the spiritualism considered "not an aspiration, but an obstacle which Petrarch cannot overcome." [123] The medieval spiritualism survives in personifications, reflections, and allegories, in the part of the poetry that lacks reality and concreteness. This, to De Sanctis, is the dead part of Petrarch, while Petrarch brooding tenderly and sensuously over the dead Laura is alive and new. Though De Sanctis constantly appeals to the criterion of "sincerity," he well understands that this does not concern the empirical biography of the author. He completely dismisses all questions as to the identity and historicity of Laura. "I confess that I cannot answer such or similar questions for the simple reason that I don't know and that Petrarch has not taken me into his confidence." [124] Petrarch's individual human sentiment and his concern for form are his great historical contributions, but they were achieved at a price. "Dante who ought to have been the beginning of a whole literature, was the end of one. Petrarch's world, so perfect on its surface, was divided and feeble within, and was merely artistic contemplation where once it had been faith and feeling."[125]

Petrarch is a figure of transition: with Boccaccio we are in another world. A revolution has been accomplished. The Middle Ages are not only rejected, they are laughed at.[126] The world of transcendence has disappeared. Here is a secular world, real, natural, a parody of the *Comedy*, "an anti-Comedy," a human Comedy.[127] It is a cynical, malicious world of the flesh, gross in its feelings but polished and embellished by fancy.[128] God's providence has disappeared from it and nothing but pure chance remains, and result of chance: "adventures," "extraordinary cases," which might be tragic but are so in a very different, external, and superficial sense. No ideal remains but a certain liberality and gentility of the soul, and an observance of social customs called "honor." [129] What remains of the immense shipwreck of conscience is a sense of literary integrity, of artistic feeling and the irony of the artist: the comic ideal implied. "The motive of the comedy, however, comes not from the moral world but from the intellectual world." It is "culture blossoming for the first time, and conscious of itself, turning the ignorance and malice of the lower classes into a joke." [130] Art is the only thing in life that Boccaccio feels seriously about: he is "a writer but not a man." [131] He is thus the wellspring of decadence, of the enfeeblement of Italian conscience. The whole of the Renaissance is seen as a development from Boccaccio.

Renaissance, for De Sanctis, means formalism, artistry, divorce between form and content. Content becomes indifferent; "what matters is not what one has to say but how to say it." [132] The whole humanist movement remains on the surface: "It does not come from the people and it does not descend to the people." [133] In the greatest poet of the 15th century, Poliziano, there is only the sense of form and a voluptuous dream of the Golden Age. Ariosto escapes into a world of mere fancy, which is saved from complete emptiness only by his "adult, materialist, realist spirit, incredulous, ironical [which] amuses itself at the expense of its fancy." [134] But De Sanctis has an enormous (in view of his scheme, somewhat incongruous) admiration for the art of Ariosto and defends him sharply against objections made by Cesare Cantù on grounds of probability, historical accuracy, and morality.[135] De Sanctis sings the praises of Ariosto's objectivity and clarity with which he depicts his golden dream, his enchanted castle, but he denies him any "sentiment of fatherland, family, humanity, and even love and honor." [136] He can sympathetically describe even the cynical *Maccaronea* of Folengo and give an account of the venal and depraved Aretino which does not fail to single out his acute modern sensibility, yet they must both symbolize the further descent of the Italian conscience. It logically led to a loss of independence and to a long stagnation, during the Counter Reformation, in the backwaters of Europe. The one great poet of that age, Torquato Tasso, is, like Petrarch, a sick man who felt the pain of two worlds and was unable to reconcile them. He is lyrical, subjective, elegiac, sentimental, incapable of reaching the heroic. "His seriousness, like his religion, is superficial and literary."

"He seeks the epic and finds the lyric; he seeks the true or the real and creates the fantastic; he seeks history and meets up with his own soul." [137] After Tasso there came only Marino, *marinismo,* "the corpse" of Tasso and Petrarch.[138]

But in the gloom of the Renaissance there is one ray of light; one great man who, alone and singlehanded, rejected both the Middle Ages and the Renaissance: Machiavelli. He knew that the mission of man is on this earth, that his prime duty is patriotism, the glory, greatness, and freedom of his fatherland. Machiavelli is a man completely emancipated from the supernatural world who, different from the artists around him, has found a new content. He has discovered the program of the modern world: intellect, the science of man, the nation, the state, progress, and the future.[139] With Machiavelli the redemption of Italy begins. But he was alone in his time: Guicciardini is merely an intellectual, an ineffective egotist whose ideal man, described also in a special essay,[140] is the man without ideals, the utilitarian, the indifferent modern individualist.

While Italian literature descends into the trough of Marinism and its continuation in the equally empty pastoral "Arcadia," individual philosophers and scientists—Bruno, Campanella, Galileo and later Vico—prepare the new content of the future literature, the "new science." Bruno discovers the "organic method," the very essence of science.[141] Vico discovers history as a science, and criticism which is neither dogmatism nor skepticism.[142] But these Italians were persecuted or were, like Vico, bookish professors in a library. The intellectual movement passed to France and England, where it became a great historical force. Italian literature of the 17th century is "empty of passion and action and empty of conscience," [143] without even a consciousness of its decadence. The last poet of the old literature is Metastasio, whom De Sanctis—as he often does with pure artists—appreciates highly for his clarity and harmony but whom he considers the end of a line: just before the dissolution of poetry into music.[144] For music is to De Sanctis mere form, without ideas or images, the last stage of Italian decadence. "The old literature had found its tomb in music." [145] Music is the only contribution of Southern Italy even as late as the early 19th century. "Here was our genius!" exclaims De Sanctis, alluding to Bellini and Donizetti.[146] The tone of regret and even contempt is obvious.

But the regeneration, at least in the North, was on the way by the middle of the 18th century. The revolt against empty form begins with Goldoni, the Galileo of the new literature.[147] He restored reality and the word (which is neither music nor the empty word of "Arcadia"). Unfortunately, he still lacked "an inner world of conscience," "sincerity and force of convictions." [148] Only with Parini "is man reborn" (in contrast to the mere artist). "Content is to him the substance of art, and the artist is to him the man in his integrity, as patriot, believer, philosopher, lover and friend." "Poetry has regained its ancient meaning and is again the voice of the inner world." "The form itself becomes the idea, a harmony of idea and expression." [149] A special essay on Parini elaborates this conception, with some reservations as to Parini's ironic, bookish, imitative, neoclassical forms, in order to conclude that "the man was worth more than the artist." [150] Similarly, Alfieri had the new moral and political content, the fire of the soul; yet somehow he failed to achieve the proper form, remained in a world of abstractions: his hatred of tyranny is too individualistic, his patriotism too abstract. "He lacks the science of life." [151] But De Sanctis, in his early writings, had defended Alfieri against the disparagements of foreign critics (Veuillot, Janin, Gervinus),[152] showing that his ideals were those of his time, that his classicism was not mere rhetoric but the classicism that also inspired the French Revolution, and that his tragedies are not comparable to Racine's but have another aim and another form. Still, in Alfieri the new content has not yet achieved its organic form. Even Foscolo has achieved it only once—in the "Sepolcri," which announces the resurrection of the inner world, the return of religion to a "people oscillating between hypocrisy and negation." [153] Foscolo's other works, discussed at length in a special essay, do not achieve totality. *Jacopo Ortis* lacks analysis, the fullness and variety of real life. "You hear a single chord, the orchestra is lacking. Above all, grace, delicacy, suavity, a certain inner measure and peace are lacking, wherein lies the secret of life." The "Grazie" is not poetry but a lecture with poetic embellishments.[154]

Only with Manzoni has the new literature come into its own. Here the content is restored in full, the ideal and the real reconciled. Manzoni—as the series of essays and lectures show—is for De Sanctis the crucial figure of the new Italy. His religion is interpreted as a democratization and humanization of Christianity, as "liberty, equality, fraternity evangelized." [155] In *I Promessi sposi,* "this ideal world is enveloped in a historical world, which gives all the illusion of a full and concrete existence, becomes its true living center, the unity of the whole work." [156] De Sanctis, however, condemns Manzoni's poetics and his final rejection of the historical novel. Manzoni is an artist in spite of his system. The ideal is realized in his work, and it is "the purest and at the same time the most modern of all ideals, not of the reaction but of the Restoration of Europe." [157] *I Promessi sposi* is one of those masterworks which in the history of art inaugurate a new era, the era of the real, a monument next to the *Divina Commedia* and *Orlando Furioso.*[158]

Alongside Manzoni stands only the great solitary Leopardi. He was De Sanctis' favorite poet in his youth; throughout his life he commented on him and to him he devoted his last unfinished book, a close genetic and even biographical study of Leopardi. De Sanctis sees Leopardi as heralding a new age, the end of theology and metaphysics, the aridly true, the really real. But Leopardi's skepticism leaves his moral world inviolate. This tenacious life of his inner world, in spite of the death of every philosophical and metaphysical world, is the original quality of Leopardi, and gives his skepticism the stamp of religion.[159] In an eloquent passage at the end of an early, highly critical and even satirical exposition of Schopenhauer's philosophy,[160] De Sanctis had suggested this positive side of Leopardi. "He does not believe in liberty, and he makes you love it. Love, virtue, glory he calls illusions, and he kindles in your breast an inexhaustible passion for them . . . He is a skeptic and he makes you a believer—and while he calls all life empty and deceptive, you somehow feel more firmly attached to all that in life is noble and great." [161] The contrast between the cold and negative intellect and the warm heart yearning for the ideal is the central theme of the late book. "This dualism is the dynamic force of Leopardi's poetry, the lever that sets it in motion and makes of it an original organism." [162] De Sanctis thus minimizes the philosophical poems and the prose and emphasizes the idylls, finding even an "almost childish good nature in their profundity." [163]

The remainder of Italian literature of the 19th century is divided by De Sanctis into two groups: the liberal and the democratic school: the liberal Catholic school embraces the followers of Manzoni, while the democratic school is headed by Mazzini. The division often seems arbitrary but serves the purpose of emphasizing the political alignment of the authors, especially since De Sanctis in these late lectures includes many publicists, historians, and philosophers (Rosmini, Gioberti) in largely ideological discussions. Here and in several early essays De Sanctis musters contemporary literature and severely handles the imitators of the masters: F. D. Guerrazzi for a sensational novel on Beatrice Cenci, Padre Bresciani for a Jesuitical historical romance, *L'Ebreo di Verona,* and Giovanni Prati for his pretentious pseudo-Faustian epics.[164] De Sanctis saw the exhaustion of the romantic tradition and, late in life, sought for a remedy in the rise of naturalism. He wrote favorably on Zola, praising his objectivity, his social concern, defending his morality and welcoming his exposure of the corruption of Second Empire France.[165] But disturbed by the rapid spread of naturalism and positivistic science, he tried, in the last years of his life, to restore the balance. He lectured on the need of the ideal and deplored the new "animalism," the cult of force, the usurpations of science.[166] Consistently throughout his mature work De Sanctis upholds a humanism that is ethical and realistic in the sense of a rejection of the abstractness of neoclassicism and the cloudiness of fantastic romanticism. He felt that such "realism"—filled with an ethical pathos salvaged from Christianity—is an excellent antidote "for a fantastic race, fond of phrase-making and display, educated in Arcadia and rhetoric." [167]

Thus a historical vision that has a practical end inspires all of De Sanctis' work. The great *History* concludes with an exhortation to Italians: "The new century can already be seen taking shape within the old. When it comes we must not be found last in the line, nor yet in the second place." [168] The *History* traces both a fall and a slow reconstruction, and points to the future. There is no linear progress, at least in literature, for De Sanctis. Rather, an original totality breaks up and is again reunited. Content and form, fused in Dante at his best, dissolves, to be fused again in Manzoni and Leopardi. But the false transcendence of the Middle Ages gives way to reality. An empty formalist art for art's sake literature—from Boccaccio to Metastasio—is finally replaced by one inspired by life and the nation; a literature of the learned or the upper classes becomes one comprehensible to the people, speaking with its voice. There is in De Sanctis' scheme a strong secular immanentism, a trust in progress, in development, in the march of mind which is almost as fateful as Providence. There seems no possibility of revolt against the *Zeitgeist*. In the 15th century no drama could arise, not because Italians have no dramatic genius but because "that light-hearted and sensual world could not give you anything except the idyllic and the comic." [169] In the 16th century Italy no longer had the power to produce the heroic or the tragic. "Nothing shows more the frivolous basis of Italian life than these vain attempts of Tasso to achieve seriousness. Whether he wanted to or not, he remains a follower of Ariosto." [170] Similarly, Marino could not help being the "corrupter of his age." Rather, the age corrupted him, or more exactly, "there were no corrupters and no corrupted. The age was that way and could not be any other. It was the necessary consequence of no less necessary premises. Marino was the genius of his age, the age itself in the great force and clarity of its expression." [171] Even the Jesuits who represent the "intellect in its ultimate depravity" were both the cause and the effect of the corruption, and therefore still "were a progress, a natural result of history." [172] Romanticism, which De Sanctis usually condemns as reaction, is still "a serious movement of the spirit; according to the eternal laws of history." [173]

Complementary to De Sanctis' trust in the *Weltgeist* and *Zeitgeist* is his trust in the people, in the *Volksgeist*. The people are called "the inappealable judge of poetry." [174] De Sanctis never fails to buttress his views with the popularity of a work or figure, and at one point he even considers popularity proof of absolute aesthetic value. Speaking of Metastasio, he says that "no other poet was so popular, no other poet has so deeply penetrated into the spirit of the people. There is then in his dramas an absolute value, superior to the passing moment, a value that even the dissolvent criticism of the 19th century has not destroyed." [175] But this trust in the people should not be confused with a belief in popular poetry or in folklore: De Sanctis recognizes that so-called popular literature is in a state of petrifaction, is literature descended to the people rather than rising out of it.[176] His ideal of a popular literature, "drawn from the heart of the nation," [177] implies rather the belief that the great poet is the voice of the people and the age. "Ariosto and Dante are the two standard-bearers of two opposed civilizations . . . the syntheses in which their times were completed and closed." [178]

Especially in the early essays a strong historical relativism prevails. We must judge according to the spirit of the time and not by extraneous criteria: we must not make a retroactive judgment, nor transport into the past the needs and ideas of the present.[179]

But this is precisely what De Sanctis does. His "historicism" is constantly modified by this consciousness of the need of his time and the future. History for him is contemporary history. If we criticize his scheme (even accepting its basic assumptions), the distortion of the Renaissance will strike us most sharply. His views seem impoverished by failure to recognize Italian achievements in the plastic arts (despite some allusions to Michelangelo, Raphael, and Da Vinci) and by his strange conception of music as empty sound.[180] The Renaissance is seen as a purely literary phenomenon, and even its literary achievement is seen as mere form, rhetoric, or fancy, while whole strands of these times (for example, the Platonic academy) are slighted or ignored. Machiavelli and Bruno are taken out of their context in order to be made precursors of the New Science. In spite of its Vichian associations and De Sanctis' great admiration for Vico, the New Science means to him, in practice, merely the Enlightenment conceived in the simplified terms of a progress from Bacon to Darwin. The Counter Reformation is condemned as a time of mere naturalism with a hypocritical varnish.[181] De Sanctis, like his time, has no taste for the baroque. Up to the 18th century De Sanctis had hardly alluded in his *History* to foreign influences, and he had treated even the revival of the classics only in the most general terms. But now he suddenly shifted attention to international intellectual history, sketching the development from Descartes to Rousseau and the rise of European romanticism. The perspective seems false, however, when Manzoni is given the role of the initiator of realism. *I Promessi sposi,* however fine a book, does not deserve the key position assigned to it by De Sanctis. But there is little point in taking issue with the details of De Sanctis' scheme and judgments. His triumph is the success with which he has integrated concrete criticism into this historical scheme. The historical scheme, with its dialectics of content and form, ideality and reality, transcendence and immanence, poetry and artistry, enters directly into the concrete criticism. In almost every case—Dante, Petrarch, Ariosto, Machiavelli, Tasso, Parini, Alfieri, Foscolo, Manzoni, Leopardi, and many others—De Sanctis has posed the problems that have since been debated and elaborated by Italian criticism.[182]

Strangely enough, in a review of Luigi Settembrini's *History of Italian Literature* (1869), written when De Sanctis was working on his own book, he seems to envisage some kind of distant synthesis of knowledge: to be the immense labor of an entire generation. "It will be possible when there is a monograph or study about every epoch and every important writer which will say the last word and solve all questions." [183] But such a positivistic ideal of accumulation of knowledge postponed to a distant future was actually quite alien to his mind. He must have felt that he was able to provide a proper synthesis singlehandedly; certainly nobody can deny his wide erudition in Italian literary history and his close knowledge of the great texts. His errors are quite minor,[184] and the gaps in his knowledge and the distortions of perspective are rather due to the state of knowledge in his time and to De Sanctis' scheme of values than to any personal ignorance. He knew that literary history is not merely a summary of knowledge. What is needed, he pleads, is a philosophy of art. "We do not yet know what is literature and what is form." [185] We lack also "a history of criticism, one of the important works still to be done." [186] We need a "history also of the criteria by which writers and artists have been guided. Every writer has his aesthetics in his head, a certain special way of conceiving art, and his predilections in method and performance." [187] Such a history is evolutionary. "History, like nature, does not proceed by jumps; progressive steps generate at last the great poet who gives a definite form to the whole series. Thus Dante is the great poet of religious visions; Petrarch the great poet of the troubadours; Ariosto put the last touches on the chivalric series." [188]

The early lectures, *La Poesia cavalleresca* (1858–59), trace "a genuine progression" to the summit of Ariosto,[189] just as the *History* traces an evolutionary scheme of alienation and reconstitution; he believes, as he says, in "the poetical Real which I call Form, the living Reason taken in the act of life, Reason-History." [190] Nothing is further from his mind than a Crocean denial of the possibility of literary history, for he thinks all the time in totalities and continuities, sometimes in ways that offend our sense of reality. Thus Dante is said to have had his successors outside of Italy because no figures in Italian literature created after Ugolino show such family feeling. [191] Hence Dante's earthly paradise is "the stuff from which later the Spanish drama was to arise." [192] And *Gerusalemme Liberata* contains "the presentiment of a new poetry which one day will be called *I Promessi sposi*." [193] Taken as literary history, such relationships are merely fanciful: but they must be seen as analogies in the totality of a historical scheme where everything hangs together and even melts into one great unity.

This unity is obviously Hegelian—Reason-History, spirit as development. Surely the concept of history in De Sanctis remained Hegelian (in a liberal interpretation, like that of the Hegelian Left) all his life, even if the scheme of Italian literature seems to be drawn rather from Edgar Quinet's *Les Révolutions d'Italie* (1848) .[194] In Quinet we find the same interpretation of Italian history in terms of a conflict between conscience and art, and even the positions of Dante and Petrarch, Machiavelli and Tasso in the general scheme are identical. But Quinet hardly wrote *literary* criticism: his book is, rather, a dirge for Italian decadence, a meditation on Italian history. It is vaguely Hegelian in its view that all art is the manifestation of religion and history is the road to freedom.

On aesthetic and critical questions De Sanctis, however, reacted sharply against orthodox Hegelianism. The early lecture course (1845–46) on the history of criticism contains an exposition of Hegel's aesthetics, which De Sanctis read in Bénard's French summary (1840). While in prison (1850–53) De Sanctis studied German, made lengthy extracts from Hegel's *Logik,* and translated the Hegelian *Allgemeine Geschichte der Poesie* by Karl Rosenkranz.[195] But in Zurich—where he had contacts with F. T. Vischer, whose *Aesthetik* he must have read, at least in part—he came to reject Hegelian aesthetics. He wrote a rather elaborate criticism (which remained unpublished) charging Hegel with the intellectualistic misunderstanding of art. De Sanctis recognizes that Hegel himself had fine taste and that he kept within certain just limits, which were exceeded by his disciples. But the system pressed Hegel to seek the idea in the form, even though he knew the organic unity of idea and form. "His major glory was to have loftily proclaimed the contemporaneity of the two terms in the spirit of the poet, and to have located the excellence of art in the personal unity, in which the idea is encased and almost forgotten. Nobody speaks more than he of the individual and of incarnation . . . but because of his system this free and poetic individual is, in fact, an individual manifestation, or, to speak with the language now in fashion, the transparent veil of the idea; the principal, the important thing is always the thing manifested." [196] Hegel admits that ideas in art are no longer idea, but form, not the general, but the particular; yet in practice the particular of Hegel becomes "a veil of the general, his form an appearance of the idea." "The content, the inner significance, the idea, the conception is the calamity of the Hegelian critic." As an example De Sanctis quotes the interpretation of Goethe's *Iphigenie* as a kind of allegory of the triumph of civilization over barbarism.[197] De Sanctis clearly feels that he has grasped the original insights of Hegel from which Hegel and especially the Hegelians deviated at their peril. De Sanctis' dissatisfaction with the drearily schematic *History* of Rosenkranz and the "unaesthetic" *Aesthetik* of F. T. Vischer [198] is justified, even though it may exaggerate the gulf between De Sanctis and Hegel, who, at his best, recognized the concreteness of art as well as De Sanctis himself.

De Sanctis, especially in later years, saw that the Hegelian system had crumbled under the impact of modern science. He felt more strongly his own affinity with a tradition that could be called loosely Vichian. De Sanctis himself, however, thought of Vico's literary criticism as intellectualistic: "he looked in art for ideas and types." [199] De Sanctis did not know Herder but knew Kant and Schiller, who had first defined the autonomy of art, the unity of form and content. He usually disparaged the Schlegels, though they had most clearly reasserted these very doctrines. De Sanctis recognized the enormous influence of A. W. Schlegel in changing literary criteria, in exalting Shakespeare and Calderón and disparaging French tragedy. He calls A. W. Schlegel "the founder of a new criticism": he knows that the Schlegels have the merit of making the aim of art art itself, and that they (together with Madame de Staël) saw literature as an expression of society.[200] But De Sanctis, while sharing their rejection of the unities, severely trounced August Wilhelm's comparison between the two Phaedras as a relapse into the old-fashioned rhetorical criticism which misunderstands the essence of art.[201] Except in his earliest speculations [202] he thought the whole debate about classicism and romanticism obsolete polemics. His sympathy for the Schlegels was necessarily imperfect, as he saw them far too exclusively as spokesmen of the European reaction and even classed the skeptical August Wilhelm with the "fanatical panegyrists" of Christianity.[203]

Oddly enough, De Sanctis considered Hegel as propounder of an unhistorical view of art, as wanting art to be considered outside of space and time.[204] Thus he often contrasts German philosophical *a priori* criticism with French historical and psychological criticism. The German school concentrates on the concept and has the air of a dissertation; the French school tarries complacently over the historical form and sticks to narrative.[205] In practice, De Sanctis, however, makes finer distinctions among the French critics: he always dismisses old-fashioned rhetorical criticism such as La Harpe's,[206] and elaborately attacks what he calls "the criticism of parallels" of Saint-Marc Girardin.[207] De Sanctis ridicules his method of confronting, for instance, Corneille's Horatius with Hugo's Triboulet as examples of fatherly love. Girardin compares the incomparable: he measures individualities against an abstract moral ideal. But while De Sanctis goes so far as to say that he "hates the criticism of parallels," [208] he confines his hatred to this specific rhetorical method derived from Chateaubriand. De Sanctis' own criticism is itself constantly "comparative": but he compares totalities, works, poets like Dante and Boccaccio, Ariosto and Tasso, in order to characterize and to individualize, and not, like Girardin, in order to moralize about fictional characters or prove the superiority of the classics over the romantics. Of the historical French critics De Sanctis valued Villemain most highly. His *History of Eighteenth Century Literature* is praised for the skill with which principles and judgments are suggested in what seems merely straightforward narration. Still, Villemain is pronounced to be without creative power and without vigor: "a man of letters in the old sense of the word, to whom rhetoric, the art of speaking well, matters most." [209] De Sanctis casually alludes to Taine's "exaggerated" theory of milieu.[210] We hear nothing, in detail, of the French "psychological" critics. Sainte-Beuve is mentioned only three times for his "defective and mediocre" essay on Leopardi.[211] Alfred Mézières' book on Petrarch is considered a warning example of psychological criticism. "The author is isolated from his work and studied in the facts of his life, in his defects and virtues, in his qualities. A more or less exact judgment of the man, but not of the work, can come of it." [212]

Still, De Sanctis himself practiced psychological criticism of a different sort. He rejected biographical explanation but was deeply concerned in many of his best-known essays with the psychology of the characters created by his poets. Thus the essay on Racine's *Phèdre* rejects all abstract requirements about probability, historical color, and morality, concluding that "a tragedy may have all these traits and still be utterly mediocre." [213] What matters is that Racine has created a living character, a woman alive in all her contradictions and vacillations. The criticism is purely an analysis of the psychology of Phèdre: the play as a play is neglected and the mythical setting is dismissed as mere trapping. The realistic taste of the 19th century, which would make Racine something like a forerunner of Sardou or Ibsen, determines the whole conception.

The highly admired essays on the *Inferno* are also psychological character studies and are often frankly evocative. They all start by removing obstacles to proper comprehension, by dismissing historical and allegorical interpretations. They all center on a psychological analysis of the characters and an explanation of the poet's attitude toward them. Thus De Sanctis defines the character of Francesca da Rimini—her passion and shame, her feminine tenderness, and Dante's pity and knowledge of her sin. [214] The Farinata essay retraces the action, explaining how Dante prepares for the impression made by Farinata rising from his burning coffin, and the role the interruption by Calvacante's father plays in heightening the imperturbable grandeur of the man who "holds hell in great despite."[215] The Ugolino essay also comments, step by step, even line by line, on the narrative. It draws attention to linkages and anticipations in order to explain character. The man who furiously bites his own hands in the tower is the same man who will gnaw the skull of his betrayer in hell.[216] De Sanctis builds up an impression of the gigantic and vague and, contrary to his usual stress on clarity and definiteness, he admits and develops the ambiguities of the verse

Poscia, più che il dolor, pot'il digiuno.[217]

The criticism becomes evocative, even impressionistic, but it keeps its basis in a close reading of the text directed toward a psychological explanation. De Sanctis answers such questions as, What are the feelings of Ugolino toward his sons? toward Ruggiero? toward Dante? The offense of Ruggiero is not Ugolino's death but the death of his sons. Dante's outburst of hatred against Pisa corresponds to the inhuman, colossal proportions of Ruggiero's guilt.[218] De Sanctis goes badly astray, however, when he makes Pier della Vigne speak in metaphors, conceits, and antitheses "because he is not moved by what he says." [219] It would be hard to imagine a grosser anachronism and more blatant confusion between life and art. Here the specific feelings and the motivations of the characters are the main concern of De Sanctis' criticism.

But this is obviously only one aspect of De Sanctis' practical criticism. His greatness lies in his successful combination of a historical vision and scheme with an intensely searching criticism of a poet's world. Within this scheme he suggested the essentials of an aesthetic that developed and pointed up motifs of romantic criticism (organicity, concrete form, the autonomy of art) so successfully that he was able to exert a powerful influence on Croce and his followers. But De Sanctis' position is not so much that of a forerunner: rather, he is a synthesizer who fuses Hegelian history with romantic dialectic aesthetics and translates them both into a new context in which the metaphysics are dropped and the new positive and realist spirit has been assimilated. His historical position (though he of course differs widely in his theories and practice) is similar to that of Belinsky in Russia and Taine in France. All three, De Sanctis, Belinsky, and Taine, absorbed Hegelian historicism and romantic aesthetics and transformed them for the needs of their time and place, preserving their essential truths and thus handing them on to the 20th century. But De Sanctis' achievement far transcends his historical role: in spite of lapses into didacticism and emotionalism, he wrote what seems to me the finest history of any literature ever written. It successfully combines a broad historical scheme with close criticism, theory with practice, aesthetic generalization with particular analysis. While a historian, De Sanctis is also a critic, a judge of art.

AT THE TIME of its publication De Sanctis' great *History of Italian Literature* was, strangely enough, not reviewed, and suddenly De Sanctis was dismissed or ignored as a critic and aesthetician who does not live up to the requirements of modern positive literary scholarship. In the very year of his death (1883), *Il Giornale storico della letteratura italiana* started publication with a programmatic declaration that asserts, rather sweepingly, that Italian literary history had made no progress since Tiraboschi, that the "more or less ingenious syntheses, instead of relying on a direct study of facts, relied on some aesthetic, political, and philosophical preconceptions, with the help of which they tried to interpret and order facts badly ascertained and badly observed, and even to reconstruct history systematically." The new history will draw on a "direct study of the monuments" and "shy away from any systematic construction." [1] A whole group of erudite scholars made their appearance about that time. They transformed the mental climate completely. Criticism retired into daily reviewing or polite essay-writing, while literary history— antiquarian research, editing, sources and influences, biography, and historical explanation in terms of origins and backgrounds— assumed the center in literary studies. One can speak even of a "historical school" grouped around a few great scholars who were not critics and even were often enemies of criticism, though critical preconceptions and theories survived in their work without their apparently questioning or realizing them clearly.

The emphasis inherited from German romanticism on the popular element and on origins is strongest in the intensive research devoted to the beginnings of Italian literature and to the tradition of Italian folk song. Alessandro D'Ancona (1835–1914), who had started his folk song researches in the fifties, defended two main theses in his *La Poesia popolare italiana* (1878) : the spread of Italian popular poetry from a single center, Sicily, and the evolution of its metrical schemes from an original four-line verse to ever more complex forms.[2] Biological analogies, Spencerian formulas permeate the vocabulary, but the emphasis is less on the theories than on the communication and description of much new material as it is also in his other great work, *Le Origini del teatro in Italia* (1877), as well as in his many pioneering studies of the precursors of Dante.[3]

Domenico Comparetti (1835–1927) has more historical imagination and literary feeling. His *Virgilio nel Medio Evo* (1872) traces the myth or image of Vergil in the Middle Ages with great learning, and in a chapter on Dante finely explains Dante's choice of Vergil as his guide through the other world. The sharpness with which Comparetti distinguishes between the learned tradition on which Dante drew and the popular legends of Vergil that supposedly derive from oral Neapolitan tradition has been criticized as a romantic superstition,[4] but whatever may be objected to the details of Comparetti's book, it succeeds in evoking the mentality of the Middle Ages. It is a reputation study, which is not merely an accumulation of opinions but a sympathetic explanation of the reasons for the genesis of an image and a fame.

Though as learned as the others, Pio Rajna (1847–1930) seems to represent a stage of lower critical awareness. His *Le Fonti dell'Orlando furioso* (1876) assumes that Ariosto's epic can be broken up into its antecedents and that something damaging is being proved because this episode comes from Boiardo, another from an old romance, and others from Ovid, Vergil, or Statius. Rajna asserts that "there are no creators in the absolute sense of the word. The products of imagination do not elude the universal laws of nature. Also what is new, considered closely, is nothing but the metamorphosis of the old. Every form presupposes a chain of preceding forms; the additions may be more or less rapid, but they are always gradual." Ariosto's invention is often deficient, and hence Rajna would not answer the question whether Ariosto's borrowing does not diminish his merit with a decisive "no." "If he had himself invented the plenty which he has from others, more than one laurel leaf would be added to the crown of his glory."[5] The evolutionary dogma underlies also the more speculative but equally erudite *Le Origini dell'epopea francese* (1884), which argues in favor of the derivation, ultimate and unprovable, of the *chansons de geste* from assumed Germanic epics of the time of the Merovingians. In both books the reduction of works of art to individual thematic motifs, themes, etc., which the poet merely combines like a mosaic layer, has progressed so far that the very existencé of individual form is lost to sight.

Formal, verbal, and metrical problems, almost totally absent in Rajna, attract the attention of Francesco D'Ovidio (1849–1925), but they have become also external, isolated, and are treated atomistically. *Le Correzioni ai Promessi sposi* (1878) was the authoritative minute examination of the two versions of the great novel and thus of the whole vexing "questione della lingua." *Versificazione italiana e arte poetica medievale* (1910) laid the foundation for a history of Italian metrics: a field sadly neglected even today. Many erudite writings on Dante comment closely on passages—sometimes, as on the Ugolino canto, in open polemic with De Sanctis' views. But when D'Ovidio attempts criticism, he does not go beyond moralizing and verbal caviling. The severe attack on Tasso as lacking in intellect and character and writing incorrect Italian seems totally misdirected.[6]

The one man of the group who wrote a general history of Italian literature was Adolfo Bartoli (1833–94). His *Storia della letteratura italiana* (7 vols. 1878–84) reached only Petrarch, but was a first-hand re-examination of all texts and documents often in a skeptical spirit suspicious of legends and traditions. The first volume, based on the research embodied in his parallel *I Primi due secoli della letteratura italiana* (1880), is a skillful survey of medieval genres that attempts to build up to a picture of medieval mentality, and the last volume on Petrarch was the first general study of the man and all his scattered writings. The underlying critical assumptions are, however, strangely simple. Bartoli is secular, anti-clerical, anti-ascetic, and favors anything that he can consider "pagan," "realist," or "modern." He looks for such traits in the *fabliaux*, in Goliardic poetry, in burlesque satires, and always hails any praise of physical love or nature as anti-medieval. Even the lack of an Italian epic is interpreted as a proof of Italian positivism, its repugnance to any "legendary labor, to any poetic elaboration of the saga." "Realism is the characteristic of Italian art; there is no salvation outside its bosom."[7] There is much learning acquired with enormous diligence, much organizational power, much acumen in all these authors, but also a strange incapacity for aesthetic analysis or even sensitive reaction, a lack of insight into critical problems, which they share, of course, with the whole trend of positivistic scholarship of the time, whether in Germany or France or the United States.

Still, De Sanctis had his pupils and followers. D'Ovidio was one of them; he reacted against his method at first but later gave a sympathetic account of "De Sanctis as a lecturer and teacher" (1903), emphasizing, probably with some justice, that De Sanctis did not encourage work in criticism by his pupils and was unable to communicate his method. D'Ovidio takes the comfortable view that De Sanctis' method is simply incommunicable and personal and that the need of the time is collective research, to which even mediocre students can contribute something valuable.[8] The admiration for the teacher remains distant or rather purely personal.

This is not the case of Francesco Torraca (1853–1938), one of De Sanctis' pupils in Naples. He defended De Sanctis' work eloquently, emphasizing the sides in De Sanctis that should have appealed to the new time: his recommendation of research, even collective research, his concern, particularly in the late lectures on Manzoni and Leopardi for the study of the historical setting and psychological development.[9] Torraca held fast to some of De Sanctis' central doctrines. He sees, for instance, that "the supreme end of criticism is to examine the work of art in itself, what it has peculiar to itself and by which it is alone alive." He sharply rejects the view that the artist has necessarily to contribute to the betterment of society. He would then become a critic, a philosopher, and not an artist. "His only task is to give body and life to his images, which he cannot, if he is really an artist, construct a priori on the pattern of preconceptions." [10] Torraca was one of the first critics who admired Verga precisely for his power of representation, while he dismissed his theories.[11] The mass of Torraca's writings is, however, purely erudite. Much is "comparative literature," studies of sources and influences, or research on the medieval theater, Sicilian lyrics, and Dante, to whom Torraca devoted a detailed commentary full of historical erudition and sensible observation.[12] But in all his many learned books there is a sound core of critical judgment and common sense. A paper, "Donne reali e donne ideali," argues excellently, for instance, against the false necessity of choosing, set up by Rodolfo Renier, between ideal and real women in medieval poetry. Women, Torraca shows convincingly, were idealized in very similar

ways in all ages without therefore ceasing to be real.[13] Torraca also
sensibly doubts the literal application of the concept of evolution
to literature, recognizing the fact of sudden transformations and
reforms, and he is clearly aware of the precariousness and purely
preparatory function of all source studies.[14] Unfortunately, he is
often diffuse, unfocused, and colorless compared with the edge and
power of his teacher. Still he is the best of De Sanctis' disciples,
unless we prefer Vittorio Imbriani, who sins on the other extreme
in being bizarre, willful, extravagant.

Imbriani (1840–86) had known De Sanctis in Zurich and had
become at the age of twenty-three, Docent of German literature at
the University of Naples. He gave an inaugural lecture eloquently
pleading for the need of studying foreign literatures and containing
the argument that all the great Italian writers are the culmination
points of long developments preceding them abroad. Petrarch summarizes troubadour poetry, Boccaccio the fabliaux, Ariosto the
chivalric romances. Manzoni would not exist without Walter
Scott.[15] In a little book, *Le Leggi dell'organismo poetico e la storia
della letteratura italiana* (1869) , Imbriani develops this idea within
an evolutionary scheme. Everything great in literature is the organic
product of a long national gestation. Every work of art is necessary
and logical in its place. A triadic scheme of "intuition," "imagination," and "characterization" is devised. These three progressive
stages correspond to the epic, the lyric, and the drama and, at the
same time, to the three stages of Italian literature represented by
Dante, Ariosto-Tasso, and Alfieri. Each stage has its dominant
meter: the *terzina,* the *ottava,* and the *verso sciolto.* All this sounds
like Hegelian schematism and is reduced to absurdity by the extremism with which Imbriani upholds a collectivist view. Every masterwork proceeds from the people and cannot help being an integral
part of the national organism. All other works are, as it were, drafts
for the masterworks. Within this evolutionary scheme Imbriani
holds fast, however, to the distinctness of art. The poet is an unconscious creator of characters and scenes, not a disguised philosopher
or moralist, and every work of art should be a unity, an organic
growth.[16]

This demand for "organic unity" underlies also Imbriani's
assault on Goethe's *Faust* as "Un Capolavoro sbagliato" (1865).
The criticism, though extravagant in its violence and damaged by

humorous digressions and gambols, can hardly be dismissed. *Faust,* Imbriani argues, lacks an organic concept. It is made up of three disparate strands: an epic of God and man, a little romance (that of Faust and Gretchen) , and a legend, the pact with the devil. Imbriani shows the inconsistencies in the characterization of Faust. There is nothing in common between the Faust of the first soliloquy and the Faust who enters Gretchen's bedroom. Often Faust is "really the most contented person one can imagine, really a comic figure." In general Imbriani judges by neoclassical criteria, of harmony, decorum, unity of tone, dominant sentiment. Goethe—Imbriani feels—oscillates too much between the comic and the sublime, the tragic and the humorous. Besides, Imbriani (like De Sanctis and Vischer) considers anything allegorical or symbolic as unpoetic and thus dismisses the second part of *Faust* as "senile," since art must never be general, must always achieve an image, a determined idea, a particular "fantasma." The application of the criterion of organicity and concreteness is so rigid that *Faust* can be saved only as a series of lyrical passages, an album of poetic beauties.[17]

Imbriani used his considerable polemical powers also against contemporary poetic reputations, for example against Aleardi and Zanella, both with Goethe classed as *Fame usurpate* (1872) . He also effectively applied his criterion of unity to the "close reading" of poems. In an excellent short paper, which contrasts a poem on the same theme by Ippolite Pindemonte, a mere mosaic of reminiscences, with a poem by Alessandro Poerio, an organic work of art, Imbriani demonstrates the difference between poet and versifier.[18] Later, out of his spirit of contradiction, Imbriani engaged in researches on Dante which attempt to take an unfavorable view of his character but amount to little more than unverifiable speculations.[19] Imbriani died early, not yet forty-six. He remains an oddity, a crusty polemicist, in character and style reminiscent of Baretti and Tommaseo, a real critic but one who, like Goethe's masterwork, did not quite come off.

In the last thirty or forty years of the century one figure dominated the Italian literary scene: Giosuè Carducci (1835–1907). His authority as a poet and public figure increased the impact of his erudite and polemical criticism. Carducci's activity extends over fifty years—from the seventeen-year-old young man who announced his battle against romanticism to the last article "Dello Svolgimento dell'ode in Italia" (1902). In his early years in Florence, Carducci edited Italian classics, and from 1860, as Professor of Italian at the University of Bologna, he held a key position, which was both academically honorable and nationally influential. With the decline of Carducci's reputation as a poet, mainly since Enrico Thovez's brilliant onslaught in *Il Pastore, il gregge e la zampogna* (1909), his critical work has necessarily lost some of its luster as a reflection on the man and his poetry which before had appeared as the major glory of modern Italian literature. But apart from Carducci's achievement as poet, the criticism has preserved its independent value. Still, today we need to make sharp discriminations among the many introductions, speeches, lectures, essays, and treatises that fill some twenty-three of the thirty volumes of the Edizione Nazionale. We can dismiss many polemics which, in the old leisurely way, comment, often sentence by sentence, on the writings of some ephemeral adversary. It is also best to draw a veil over much of the official rhetoric. For instance, a speech in honor of Leopardi (1898) is only a repertory of empty phrases, such as "avanti, avanti per la patria e per civiltà," singularly inappropriate to the man who is being commemorated.[1] For our purposes we need not pay detailed attention to Carducci's many merits as an editor and even as a research scholar who investigated such problems as Bolognese popular poetry of the 13th century, the early reputation of Dante, and the textual tradition of Petrarch's poems.[2] Carducci, with part of his mind and a good deal of his labor, belonged to the historical movement and, in his theoretical pronouncements, often proclaimed "historical criticism" to be "his genre." In a lyrical passage he recommended to Italian youth the "disinterested pleasure in the discovery of a fact or a new monument of our history" and evoked the air and solitude of libraries as "healthy and full of visions as the air and the sacred gloom of ancient forests."[3] Carducci could even proclaim his ideal to "raise literary history with the severest historical method to the rank of natural history," and one could collect several passages in which Carducci disclaims the role of the critic as judge. "Judgment? That is too pretentious a word for me. I combat, I admire, I comment; I do not judge,"[4] is a characteristic passage that seems to confirm his inclusion in 19th-century skeptical, relativistic, antiphilosophical, positivistic historical movements.

But though there is no need to doubt Carducci's desire for accuracy and objectivity or his suspicion of aesthetics and peremptory verdicts, in practice he goes constantly beyond the assumptions of the historical school in the direction of both a speculative literary history and a judicial analytical criticism. His historical conception of Italian literature is simply romantic. Art and literature are "the moral emanation of civilization, the spiritual irradiation of the people."[5] In his eloquent discourses, "Dello Svolgimento della letteratura nazionale" (1868–71), Carducci traces a scheme of the evolution of older Italian literature in terms that are clearly derived from his romantic predecessors, such as Gioberti in Italy, and the French historians, such as Ginguené, Fauriel, Quinet, J.-P. Charpentier, Ozanam, and others.[6] Literature is conceived as representing historical forces which are also social and racial forces. Dante, Petrarch, and Boccaccio are supposed to represent respectively the three Italian "people" in Tuscany: the old people of citizens; the new people, the burghers and the peasant; and finally the small people, or the mob.[7] This social stratification, which is also a temporal sequence, is crossed by racial categories. Carducci sees "Etruscan religious imagination, the Roman social intellect, the Germanic individual sentiment, the Provençal and French light spirit, the practical and progressive instinct of the Lombard communes," all of which are present in the Florence of the 13th century.[8] Even years later he would speak of Dante as combining the Etruscan sacerdotal race with the Roman civil race and the German warrior race.[9] The Roman, the Teutonic, and the Italian popular forces appear in literature as the ecclesiastic, the chivalrous, and the national elements, which correspond to the usual distinctions among the main medieval genres (legends, romances, the lyric).[10] These shifting terms and sweeping generalizations can hardly withstand modern criticism. The overcharged picture of the year 1000, when all Christianity supposedly awaited the end of the world, and the vignette of the lean wandering Italian humanists searching for manuscripts in monasteries jeered at by German barons, are only fanciful embroidery.[11] What lends critical interest to these discourses, however, is Carducci's defense of humanism, the pagan and classical Italy that he feels to be the true Italian tradition.

Here obviously was the point of disagreement with De Sanctis. Carducci referred to De Sanctis rather condescendingly as a "gran

valent-uomo" who had his "preoccupations and prejudices, prejudices, of course, of a philosophical, aesthetic, and critical nature,
which are the worse because they are embraced and followed
fervently," but who was somewhat deficient in learning.[12] But surely
Carducci rather disagreed specifically with De Sanctis' whole scheme
of the course of Italian literature. Since an early introduction to an
edition of Poliziano (1863), Carducci consistently defended humanism, the cult of form and the word, the imitation of the classics,
minimizing any conflict with the popular tradition. He denies
emphatically that "the erudite movement of the fifteenth century
was outside of the national tradition." [13] It appears to him a genuine
"restauratio," a return to ancient Rome, a return to the popular
and national sources of Italian strength. The whole early Italian
literature from Guinizelli to Ariosto is called "indigenous and
national," and the 16th century is proclaimed "one, classical,
Italian," while the 14th century was still "individual and Tuscan"
and the 15th "partial and federal." [14] These slightly contradictory
statements seem a tour de force of Carducci and of many of his
contemporaries to assimilate Dante, Petrarch, and Boccaccio to
humanism and the Renaissance, to play down their medieval
elements and, at the same time, to emphasize their nationality,
Latinity, as well as the popularity of the whole tradition. In the case
of Poliziano and Lorenzo de Medici, Carducci succeeds in bringing
out the popular, festive, pageant-like character of their poetry, but
with Dante and Petrarch, Carducci obviously has difficulties, which
he hides behind very general assertions setting off Dante against the
Dark Ages which preceded him. Actually, in a close study of Dante's
miscellaneous poems (1865), he attempts to trace Dante's evolution as an abbreviated version of older Italian literature. The
chivalric principle predominates in the early courtly love lyrics, the
mystic and religious elements in the middle period, and the learned
theology in the late scholastic lyrics.[15] By a strange sleight of hand
the last period appears also the most classical and hence national,
though Carducci's good taste made him prefer the religious and
mystical poems as the best from an aesthetic point of view. There is,
in Carducci, often a conflict between aesthetic predilections and an
ideology that, at any price, has to find nationality, classicity, and
Latinity in every great Italian poet.

Carducci as a critic is at his best when the ideology can cooperate with his taste, when he can defend and trace the formal, rhetorical tradition of Italian poetry and can indulge in his genuine craftsman's interest in poetic diction, rhetorical devices, and metrical schemes. Recently his concern for these matters has made him something like a venerated ancestor of the new Italian students of stylistics who appeal to him against the sharply antirhetorical and antiformalist teaching of Croce. They can find many scattered pronouncements on the central importance of form in poetry, of technical skill, of the choice of the right meter.[16] Carducci, no doubt, frequently disparaged raw emotion and inspiration and, in general, upheld classicism against romanticism.[17] But all this as theory seems hardly new or even unusual and is never exemplified by a systematic study of style. The nearest we ever get to such an ideal is Carducci's monograph on Parini's poem *Il Giorno*. The bulk of *Storia del Giorno* (1892) is taken up with biography, social background, literary history in the sense of sources, and an account of the reception of the poem. The study then attempts something more narrowly critical in comments on Parini's irony and something formalistic in remarks on the poetic language (its Vergilian elements) and the metrics. We get a sketch of the history of the Italian *verso sciolto* and comments on alliteration, run-on lines, half-verses, etc.[18] But all this is not modern stylistics but unsystematic commentary—impressionistic appreciation of individual passages or historical explication.

Still, in his rather loose way, Carducci does re-examine and revaluate the Italian poetic tradition. He sees Parini as a culmination point of the Arcadia and not merely as its negation as De Sanctis and others had seen him, for they emphasized only his new ethical content and earnestness. Early Carducci compiled valuable anthologies, with introductions, of the erotic poets of the 18th century and of the classicist lyrical poets of that century, and late in life he traced the history of the Italian ode.[19] These collections and essays are not merely erudite literary history but acts of taste as they singled out poets (for example, Savioli) and poems neglected since the romantic reaction. Also, the essay on the early poetry of Foscolo which characterizes the intimacy and modernity of Foscolo's classicism and the high appreciation of Monti as well as the admiration for Metastasio fits into this taste.[20] Even the attempt to rescue Leopardi's early patriotic odes [21] from the aspersions of De Sanctis and A. C. Cesareo, though inspired by patriotic motives and personal animosities, agrees with his whole campaign (if one can use so strong a word) in favor of the humanistic, neoclassical tradition of Italian poetry. Carducci is, of course, very well aware of the association of this tradition with Italian moral and political decadence. He himself is far too conscious of his own role as a teacher of the nation to embrace an art for art's sake point of view, but he does often protest against narrow didacticism [22] and, as to older literature, takes simply a historistic view, annoyed at attempts to judge or to deplore things that seem to him simply facts of history. "Also in criticism, I am something of a fatalist." Under certain conditions of government, he argues, only certain things could be done. "I love, for instance, the Latinists of the 15th century; I like the academicians of the 16th century; I have fun with the 17th century poets; I find consolation among the Arcadians; and I am amused at the Frenchified poets." "The beautiful is, to my mind, relative and moral by itself."[23]

This relativistic universal tolerance is, however, far from complete. Carducci's secularism is too strong; he cannot tolerate *The Imitation of Christ* or Calderón, whose *Life is a Dream* he criticized severely.[24] He keeps his distance from Manzoni, as he thought of him mainly as the fountainhead of romantic conservative Catholicism. He admired Manzoni's poetry (though he had reservations about the ode on Napoleon), but he criticized the dramas and, goaded by inflated claims for Manzoni's greatness, tried even to reduce the importance of *I Promessi sposi*.[25] Some of Carducci's arguments are directed against the whole genre, against the modern novel. The lack of an Italian novel seems to Carducci a proof of the poetic nature of the Italians. His distaste for the "prosaic" novel extends also to Stendhal, against whom he could not have had anticlerical objections. Stendhal, Carducci asserts, writes a "false and affected style" and is "impotent" to create living characters.[26] We hardly need add that later Carducci disapproved of Zola's experimental novel as "neither fiction nor science," just as the historical novel was "neither an epic nor history."[27]

Carducci's glorification of the Italian-Latin tradition is also inspired by his ardent nationalism, which, at first, took the forms of almost comic xenophobia but later was transformed into a juster appreciation of the position of Italian literature.[28] Still, he always rejected the ideal of a European literature. This seemed to him merely the indication of a historical fact of the dominance, from time to time, of one literature: of France in the 12th and 13th centuries, of Italy in the 16th, of France again in the 17th and 18th centuries.[29] More and more his own interests extended beyond the frontiers of Italy: he knew and admired Victor Hugo very early, but later he learned to read German and some English. His translations and imitations of Heine (even of jokes in his prose) , the influence of German classistic metrics on his experiments in *Odi barbare* bear testimony to his interest in three poets: Goethe, Heine, and Platen.[30] Later Carducci wrote a warmly commendatory introduction to an Italian prose translation of Shelley's *Prometheus Unbound,* and in a letter he even recognized that the English and the Germans are today "truer poets" than the Italians.[31]

Carducci, in spite of all the incoherencies of his thought, is an extraordinarily representative and, in many ways, appealing figure. He combines romantic historiography with its center in the "spirit of the people" with a humanistic, "pagan" classicism, a sweeping grandiose vista of the Latin tradition with a minute attention to close reading, interpretation, textual variants, metrical schemes, and shades of verbal meanings. The commentary to Petrarch's *Rime* (1876), which reprints and comments on preceding commentaries like an English Variorum edition, contrasts sharply with the fanciful generalizations about races, people, classes, and spirits of the lectures "Dello Svolgimento della letteratura nazionale." Somewhere in between is Carducci's best critical work: the ample comment on Parini, the essay on Dante's *Rime,* the defense of Tasso's *Aminta,* and the study of the early Foscolo.[32] They are historical characterizations animated by a definite taste. They lack the psychological finesse and individualizing power of Sainte-Beuve (whom Carducci greatly admired) ; [33] they lack the evocative magic and theoretical firmness of De Sanctis; but they, especially if taken in their totality, made an important contribution to a reinterpretation of the history of Italian poetry and are, at their best, fine examples of sympathetic historical criticism.

Around Carducci arose a whole group of essayists (one hesitates to call them critics) who did much to make foreign literatures known in Italy. Two were Carducci's personal friends: Giuseppe Chiarini (1833–1908) and Enrico Nencioni (1837–96) . Chiarini is a sober, informative student who wrote extensively on Byron, Shelley, Carlyle, Heine, largely with a biographical emphasis,[1] and studied Shakespeare sensibly though hardly with any original perception. Most of the essays in *Studi Shakespeariani* (1896) are biographical or source studies, while the long paper on *Romeo and Juliet* is little more than an extended retelling, with extracts and comments on other commentators. Chiarini declares that "art criticism is something essentially subjective which reduces itself in the last analysis to that where one says, 'I like it,' and the other says, 'I do not like it.'" Criticism is presumptuous, as nothing assures us that our way of seeing is superior to that of the great men of the past.[2] Nencioni is uncritical in a different way: he is a sentimentalist and moralist, who, for instance, thinks that Shelley's drowning was Divine punishment for the drowning of Harriet. With strange innocence he assures us that there is nothing indecent in Goethe or Burns, and that Byron's relationship to Teresa Guiccioli was platonic. But Nencioni has merit in introducing the Brownings as early as 1867, and in writing for the first time in Italy of Swinburne, Whitman, Hawthorne, and others.[3]

Chiarini and Nencioni are only cultivated middlemen, while Bonaventura Zumbini (1836–1916) and Arturo Graf (1848–1913) are scholar-critics who aim at a compromise between the historical school and appreciative criticism. Zumbini's main work concerns Petrarch and Leopardi,[4] but he also wrote on Bunyan and Milton, Goethe and Lessing. The essay on *Paradise Lost*, though highly respectful, criticizes the unity and organization, complains of the clash of motifs—such as the metamorphosis of Satan into a hissing serpent, which Zumbini traces to Ovid's Cadmus story—and points out disparities in the characterization of Satan, which are explained, somewhat too easily, as a conflict in Milton between "spontaneity and reflection," clearly discernible in the distinctions between "the hero put in action and the hero described."[5] Zumbini, in a harsh review of Settembrini's *Lezioni*, suggests that a correction of De Sanctis' criticism should aim at defining "the aesthetic value of a work but at the same time should recognize the importance of content," as Zumbini admits "natural poetry, what I would call the natural poetry of the idea."[6] Croce, in his first book on literary criticism (1894),[7] took Zumbini to task as the horrid example of the confusion that set in after De Sanctis, but somewhat unjustly he

singled out a man of great erudition and acute analytical powers
who leaned to compromise solutions in aesthetics.

Graf is more representative of the confusions and vacillations of
the later 19th century. He adopted simultaneously or successively
the most discordant philosophies, from extreme idealism to positivism.[8] He ranges from purely erudite researches in cultural history,
such as *Anglomania e l'influsso inglese in Italia nel secolo XVIII*
(1911), to rather commonplace pronouncements on the theory of
literary history.[9] His main work, *Foscolo, Manzoni, Leopardi*
(1898), is largely biographical and "psychological," with the psy-
chiatrical and physiological emphasis of the time. Thus Graf studies
the diverse "sensory attitudes" of Leopardi: his sight, hearing, taste,
etc.[10] The early essay on *Hamlet* (1878) is little more than an
elaboration of the old thesis that the prevalence of intellect paralyzes Hamlet's capacity for action. The emphasis on Hamlet's
attempts to reduce everything to "system" seems, however, overdone.[11] Graf, an erudite, cultivated, sensitive man, lacks a position
that could be defined as his own; ultimately he seems only a reflex
of the French psychological critics, an inferior Bourget.

Almost none of this intensive critical activity of the last decades
of the 19th century was related to the contemporary Italian literary
situation. At most, D'Ovidio studied the meters of *Odi barbare,* and
Chiarini wrote a biography of Carducci.[12] But new concepts emerge
with the Italian "verismo," a variant, at least in theory, of French
naturalism. Luigi Capuana (1839–1915), a second-rate novelist, is
usually considered its theoretical spokesman, while its best writer,
Giovanni Verga (1840–1922), made only a few programmatic pronouncements. In a general history of criticism neither seems important, but Capuana has a certain interest precisely because he refused
to be classified and kept a firm grasp on the nature of art. He complained that he is being considered a strenuous "champion of
naturalism" merely because twenty years ago he had dedicated a
novel to Zola.[13] He wrote a whole book, *Gli 'ismi' contemporanei
(Verismo, simbolismo, idealismo, cosmopolitismo)* (1898), in
which he rejects all such slogans as abstractions. Actually Capuana
has a well-defined position, which he described in early theatrical
reviews and many articles on contemporary novels and poets collected in several miscellaneous books.[14] Capuana consistently
defends the main tenets of naturalism: a scientific approach to the

object of observation, impersonality, contemporaneity, and prox-
imity of subject matter. He praises Zola, his generous purpose, and
finds in *L'Assommoir* "a sensation which does not remain a simple
state of sensation but raises itself, purifies itself and becomes sentiment, poetry." Capuana was one of the first critics to admire Verga
for similar reasons: his perfect impersonality, his familiarity with
his subjects, "the immense sadness" which emerge from his writings.[15] Capuana differs, however, from Zola and other naturalists in
France by a strong hold on the concrete nature of art, which is, in
part, due to the visible influence of De Sanctis. Capuana constantly
emphasizes the necessity of "form," in De Sanctis' sense, which is
"sentiment" and "life," terms he uses almost interchangeably.[16]
Differing also from realist theory, Capuana rejects anything in art
that is not concrete and hence anything "typical" or "tendentious."
Echoing De Sanctis almost literally, he says that "type is an abstract
thing; it is a usurer, but not Shylock; it is a suspicious man, but not
Othello; it is a hesitant, chimeras-hunting man but not Hamlet." [17]
This rejection of the typical extends to anything abstract; it extends
to any overt philosophical or social purpose, to any symbolism; and,
in its concreteness, it finds also arguments against cosmopolitanism,
the type of "Parisian" literature represented by D'Annunzio,[18]
arguments in favor of the depiction of Italian reality and ultimately
of regionalism, the art of Verga rooted in Sicily, focused on the
elementary passions of relatively simple men. Capuana is a day-by-
day literary journalist who writes often on topics for which he is ill
prepared. He does much that must be described as trivial reporting,
but his basic position is so clearly distinct from the pseudo-scientific
pretensions of the naturalists and still so deeply sympathetic for
their concern with reality, with the concrete life around them, that
something like a distinct (though limited) theory of Italian naturalism emerges.

It is also defined in Verga's few prefaces and letters of a theoretical
nature. "The hand of the artist must remain completely invisible";
the work of art should seem "to have made itself, to have matured
and issued spontaneously, like a natural fact, without any point of
contact with its author."[19] But Verga knows well that this perfect
impersonality is a "willed artifice which is sought for (pardon the
word-play) in order to avoid any artifice, in order to give a complete
illusion of reality."[20] This realism that is so objective and detached

from the author's mind thus cannot lead to a polemical work. Its humanitarian mission is only implicit— "a plea for the humble and disinherited without the need to preach hate or to deny the fatherland in the name of humanity."[21] The modesty of the claim, the firmness with which the concern with illusion is upheld, give to these pronouncements their special tone of sobriety and intensity, which is also the virtue of Verga's art, so distinctly breaking as it does with the rhetorical tradition of Italian literature.

Still, one can understand why Benedetto Croce, confronted with the situation of Italian literary criticism in the early 1890's, felt that criticism is merely a collective name for the most diverse operations of the mind and that many of those, such as the biographical approach or the scientific method, are completely irrelevant to a meaningful conception of criticism. He had discovered De Sanctis, but in his first publication, *La Critica letteraria* (1894), he still came to surprisingly relativistic conclusions as to the possibility of aesthetic judgment. His diagnosis of the ills of a purely positivistic historical scholarship is acute and pertinent even today, but it took Croce some eight years before he produced the remedy with his *Estetica,* and only in 1903 did he start his review, *Critica,* with articles revaluating modern Italian literature. Croce clearly belongs to the new century, and the writers described in this chapter must serve rather as a foil for Croce's activity than as a source. He returns to De Sanctis and the Germans for inspiration.

7: ENGLISH CRITICISM:
HISTORIANS AND THEORISTS

IT WOULD NOT BE UNFAIR to say that around 1850 English criticism
had reached a nadir in its history: the great romantics, Coleridge,
Hazlitt and Lamb, had died in the thirties; Carlyle, the strongest
figure after them, had relinquished criticism for history and social
pamphleteering; Macaulay and Mill were no longer concerned with
criticism. The camp followers of the great romantics, De Quincey
and Leigh Hunt, both lived till 1859, but were only pale ghosts of
their youth. Poetic theory was practically nonexistent or simply a
remote derivative of popularized romanticism: genius, imagination,
sincerity of feeling, the moral and finally social function of the poet
were the constant themes of perfunctory discussion ultimately
derived from Wordsworth.[1]

Still, a revival of English criticism was just around the corner. It
came about in various and often devious ways. One could sort out
the different motives by pointing to a new historicism, a new
classicism, a new realism, and finally a new aestheticism which
opposed the all-pervading Victorian atmosphere of didacticism and
moralism. But these motives are not clearly set off from one another:
they combine, they enter into compromises, they attempt genuine
syntheses.

Historicism radiated mainly from Germany and was felt first in
classical philology and most conspicuously in theology.[2] Its power
was strengthened, though its direction and spirit was changed with
the victory of Darwinian evolutionism in the sixties. But in literary
history its immediate achievements were disappointing. Carlyle's
suggestions were not followed up systematically: no coherent and
firsthand history of English literature was written until the 1890's.
Antiquarianism flourished and found new support in the analogy
of the natural scientist's disinterested objectivity, ambition for
completeness of evidence, and meticulous accuracy. But the human-

ists of the Renaissance or the Jesuit and Benedictine scholars of the 17th century had cultivated these scholarly virtues without much attention to the model of physical science. When a scholar such as F. J. Furnivall (1825–1910), who founded the Early English Text Society, the Chaucer Society, the New Shakspere Society, and the Browning Society, proclaimed himself a "scientific botanist,"[3] he was merely trying to buttress the validity of his metrical tests for the determination of the chronology of Shakespeare's plays. In his violent controversy with Swinburne, he rudely ridiculed the poet's reliance on his "long, hairy, thick and dull ear,"[4] because Swinburne had dared to doubt some of his findings. The influence of academic German scholarship worked in the same direction. Facts, parallels, influences became the preoccupation of scholars and tyros. Attempts at synthesis and criticism were being discouraged or postponed to a distant future. In England, A. W. Ward (1837–1924), who himself had written a factual *History of Dramatic Literature* (1875), became the main exponent of this point of view, which he called significantly *Realpolitik*.[5] The successes and limitations of this attitude can be seen in the growing flood of dictionaries, monographs, contributions, notes and queries. They always imply a static conception of literature and hence are inimical to the writing of literary history. The use of contemporary psychological conceptions was also of little importance for criticism or literary history proper. William Minto (1845–93), in his solid books on *English Prose* (1872) and *Characteristics of English Poets* (1874), could analyze only random details of literary form, because he had adopted the purely atomistic psychology of Mill and Bain.[6]

Sociological and biological concepts began to penetrate literary history almost simultaneously. Positivists in the Comtian sense studied not so much literary history as intellectual history, as reflecting social evolution. John Morley (1838–1923), who wrote intellectual biographies of *Voltaire* (1872), *Rousseau* (1873), and *Diderot and the Encyclopaedists* (1878), thought of art as "only the transformation into ideal and imaginative shapes of a predominant system and philosophy of life." The aim of criticism, which he calls "synthetic criticism," is to "trace the relations of the poet's ideas . . . through the central currents of thought, to the visible tendencies of an existing age."[7] In a lecture "On the Study of Literature" (1887) Morley recommends that the student of literature undertake "an ordered and connected survey of ideas, of tastes, of sentiments, of imagination, of humour, of invention . . . and the manifold variations that time and circumstances are incessantly making in human society." [8] Among his essays on literary figures, collected in *Critical Miscellanies* (3 vols. 1886), and *Studies in Literature* (1890), a sympathetic portrait of Byron succeeds best, while essays on Carlyle, Macaulay, Wordsworth, and Emerson are dominated either by the polemical intent of a liberal or the apologetics of a rationalist for romantic illusions.

Much more fruitful for literary history was the attempt to transfer the concept of biological evolution to the history of literature. On a small scale, in literary biography, we find Spencerian ideas of integration in Edward Dowden's *Shakspere: His Mind and Art* (1875). Shakespeare's development is conceived of as a moral self-integration, an illustration of a general human pattern. Using the terminology of Spencer's *Biology,* Dowden attempts to show how "the structural arrangement of Shakespeare's whole nature became more complex and involved" until his work became "the expression of a complete personality." The technical vocabulary often hides a moralistic conception: Shakespeare arriving at "a temper liberal, gracious, charitable, a tender yet strenuous calm." [9] The Spencerian thesis of a progress from communal to individual life permeates H. M. Posnett's *Comparative Literature* (1886), the first book in English expressly devoted to that subject. It is a concept of comparative literature that still survives in the Slavic countries: an attempt to survey oral poetry on an international scale within a scheme of evolution. In Russia about the same time, Alexander Veselovsky tried something similar, with much greater concrete learning than the New Zealand judge could command.[10] But the main exponent of an evolutionary literary history in Victorian England was John Addington Symonds, whom we shall discuss in detail later.

In Symonds we see naturalism rampant; literary history became a branch of biology. However, there was considerable opposition to such naturalism in the Victorian Age. It came first from the whole aesthetic movement, from writers such as Swinburne, Saintsbury, and Gosse. Edmund Gosse (1845–1928), who was a versatile but trivial critic, characteristically paid lip service to the evolutionary ideals of the time. In his *Short History of Modern English Literature* (1897), he professes to show the "movement of English literature"

and "above else" to "give a feeling of the evolution of English literature," [11] but in practice supplies us only with information and
some critical impressions on authors and their work. In a moment of
candor Gosse later rightly disclaimed any interest in Taine and
stressed his indebtedness to Sainte-Beuve.[12] Swinburne and Saintsbury deserve extended treatment.

In literary history the old romantic concept of literary development as a history of the national mind was most fruitful. It was suggested by Carlyle and is echoed all over the Victorian age, for
instance in the writings of David Masson (1822–1907), who later
produced the monumental *Life of Milton,* and in the popular books
of Henry Morley (1822–94). Masson can use phrenological jargon
about the "national brain of Britain which had suffered a sudden
contraction in the frontal organs of ideality, wonder and comparison." He can, as early as 1859, speak about "self-contained evolution" as "a natural law by which genres detach themselves" or
rather are "thrown off" from a nondescript original form. He can
fatuously ask his students to study "that vital and essential something—a clear transparency . . . which we call the mind or spirit
of the time." [13] Morley thinks of English literature as the "national
biography," "the story of the English mind," "the continuous
expression of one national character." In Morley these conceptions
were, in practice, overshadowed by considerations of a purely
pedagogical nature. Literature becomes a system of national virtues,
"an embodiment of the religious life of England," [14] a collection of
uplifting passages and inspiring lives.

At the end of the century, W. J. Courthope (1842–1917) wrote
his *History of English Poetry* (6 vols. 1895–1910), which skillfully
combines the leading historiographical concepts of the time.
"National imagination" is at the center, but its history mirrors the
development of society and politics, which are conceived as growing
like a biological organism. Politics and literature are thought of as
springing from one common source: the evolution of national
character. The evolution itself is seen as a long dialectical process,
as a conflict between individualism and collectivism which goes
right through English history. Their perfect synthesis and harmony
is Courthope's own political and poetical ideal. In the Middle Ages
there was an unhealthy preponderance of collectivism. During the
Renaissance a harmony was established: while in modern times,

mainly through romanticism, individualism tends to prevail both in poetry and in politics. The English constitution, with its harmony of freedom and authority, is to Courthope a model of the ideal harmony between the individuality of the poet and the national tradition. Courthope impressively evokes long vistas into intellectual history. The flexibility of his general conception and the boldness with which it is carried out put Courthope's monumental work probably into the first place of English literary histories. But his critical power is frequently cramped by rigid moralism and academic classicism. His main defects come out in the analyses of individual writers: his sense of poetic form is weak, and the final impression prevails that the history of English poetry is an abstract play of massive intellectual movements and tendencies, in which the art of poetry seems almost completely lost.[15] Compared to the achievements of a Taine or Hettner or Brandes, not to speak of De Sanctis on the Continent, English literary history failed to achieve the proper balance of criticism and history which keep these books alive even today in spite of their shortcomings.

But historiography was, at least in England, on the fringes of literary criticism. In the Victorian setting, which had a streak of deep distrust toward speculation and theory, theory of literature remained also on the outskirts, on the other extreme of the intellectual map.

Almost alone among Victorian critics, Eneas Sweetland Dallas (1828–79) attempted a systematic theory of poetry with scientific aspirations. This theory consists largely of an elaborate classification of genres in a triadic scheme, in the manner of the German aestheticians. Oddly enough, the scheme overlays a highly irrationalistic psychology that locates the origin of art in the unconscious or the "hidden soul." The incongruous mixture of psychology of the unconscious with insistently symmetrical schematization makes Dallas' books piquant dishes not to be missed by connoisseurs of the history of criticism.

Dallas wrote two books: *Poetics* (1852) and *The Gay Science* (2 vols. 1866); the second book was a development of the first but was left unfinished, with two more volumes to come. The second volume of *The Gay Science* shows the author's fatigue: toward the end it includes loosely related discussions about the literary situation quoted from the author's own abundant reviews for the

London *Times*. At Edinburgh, Dallas had been a student of Sir William Hamilton, whom he never ceased to admire as "the greatest thinker of the nineteenth century." [16] Dallas' books are steeped in the general tradition of British empirical psychology and in his teacher's skeptical common-sense antirationalism. He frequently jibes at the Germans who "see further into a millstone than most men" and complains that "the German [Hegel or Schelling] constructs art as he constructs the camel out of the depths of his moral consciousness." [17] Through Hamilton, however, who claimed to have been the first after the Germans to develop the concept of the unconscious,[18] Dallas draws from the romantic irrationalist strain in German aesthetics. He knew A. W. Schlegel and Jean Paul's *Vorschule der Aesthetik* [19] firsthand, and he knew, of course, the general Platonic tradition with its emphasis on unconscious inspiration: Sidney and Shelley in particular. The early Ruskin is often in Dallas' mind: Arnold is too intellectual for his taste.[20] His fair knowledge of the history of criticism enlivens the whole exposition.

The unassimilated strands in Dallas' work may be easily disentangled. British psychological empiricism claims to erect poetics into a "science of pleasure." The Gay Science of his second book is interpreted to mean "the joy science." The end of art is "its own good pleasure." Imagination is "the house of pleasure"; "dreamland" is "essentially a land of bliss." The pleasure of art is the pleasure of imagination.[21] The poet brings—and Wordsworth is the great exemplar—"a gospel of its kind,—glad tidings of great joy, glad tidings of smaller joys, but always pleasure." [22] Like Jeffrey and his models Dallas defends poetry as a school of sympathy. "The student of poesy . . . is taught to sol-fa through the gamut of human emotions. The poet preaches a gospel, kindles love, and trusts in the force of those sympathies which lead one man to imitate another." [23] Like his predecessors Dallas struggles awkwardly with "pure pleasure," "mixed pleasure," "hidden pleasure," and puzzles over the "painful pleasure" of tears and tragedy.[24]

But Dallas criticizes the traditional empirical account of the imagination because it identifies imagination too closely with memory, passion, or reason (in the sense of invention). For Dallas imagination is simply the general term for all the unconscious activities of the mind, for the involuntary memory, for subconscious emotion, and unconscious reasoning. This "hidden soul" is the

source of the artist's strength, since Dallas is convinced that consciousness is detrimental to action and creation. "What we try to do,
we cannot do; when we cease trying, we do it." [25] Not only is the
subconscious the source of art: it is also the explanation of its appeal
and the measure of its worth. "Art is poetical in proportion as it has
this power of appealing to what I may call the absent mind, as
distinct from the present mind, on which falls the great glare of
consciousness, and to which alone science appeals." [26] Hence,
Dallas must consider "self-consciousness hurtful to poetry" and
exclude "didactic, artistic, satiric writing" from genuine poetry.[27]
"Artistic" here obviously means artificial, contrived, calculated art
of any sort. Lyrical poetry logically enough is "the most perfect
poetry" [28] and poetry above all must be "sincere." Dallas complains
of the contemporary tendency in Tennyson and others, toward
dramatic lyricism. "There are drinking songs by teetotalers who
trespass in ginger-beer; home-songs by the veriest idlers; hunting-
songs by those whose noblest game have been rats and mice, and
such small deer; war-songs by gentle ladies; sea-songs by landsmen
who get sick in crossing a river . . . and sacred-songs by men who
are never in church." [29]

Dallas' insight into the unconscious free play of the imagination,
and the spontaneous sincerity of the poet drawing on his hidden
soul, comes to very little. A statement such as "all good poetry has a
latency of meaning beyond the simple statement of facts" [30] sounds
like an anticipation of psychoanalysis but actually leads only to an
acceptance of vagueness and suggestiveness in poetry. Dallas can say
that "the finest poetry has scarcely any definite meaning whatever"
and quotes from Wordsworth's *Intimations* ode, which, supposedly,
contains "many lines comprising a kind of essence of poetry, but to
which it is scarcely possible to attribute any distinct signification.
The often-quoted passage about the 'fallings from us, vanishings,
blank misgivings of a creature moving about in worlds not realized,' etc., are exquisitely beautiful, but are altogether without
any special meaning." [31] Dallas is finally content with a gesture
toward "magic," toward "an occult power which lurks in the [poet's]
words." [32]

Dallas has no tools to penetrate or even to describe the unconscious, and when he comes to discuss the theory of genres he indulges
in speculative classifications that are quite unrelated to his funda-

mental insight. He divides the genres, traditionally enough, into Play, Tale, and Song, but then he argues—apparently with Jean Paul's scheme in mind [33]—that the play has to do with the present, the tale with the past, and the song with the future. Drama uses the second person plural, the epic the third person singular, the lyric the first person singular. Dallas insists at length that it must be the second person *plural* in the drama and not singular, as the Quakers' "thee" merely proves their egotism.[34] It never occurs to him to think of Latin, French, and German. Drama is linked with "plurality," epic with "totality," and lyric with "unity"—that is, Kant's categories of quantity must be dragged in to make another triad. As if this were not enough, Dallas must tell us that drama is "romantic" (in the wide sense of "modern") , the epic "classical," and the lyric "divine," and that drama is "beauty," epic "truth," and the lyric "the good." [35]

This scheme of the *Poetics* is not repeated in *The Gay Science,* but there another triadic scheme is developed. Three forms of the tendency of the mind to similitude are distinguished. They are: (1) I am that or like that; (2) That is I or like me; and (3) That is that or like that. The first of these forms contains the ruling principle of dramatic art: sympathy. The second contains the ruling principle of epic or historical art: imagination.[36] The wider meaning of "imagination" as the automatic action of any and every faculty is suddenly forgotten in favor of something more conventionally representational or image-making. But the scheme is worked out fully to account for types of imagery as well. The assimilating tendency of sympathy is displayed in the drama by the poet's identification with his characters in dramatic or metaphorical "personations." The assimilating tendency of egotism shows in the lyric as "the sort of imagery which is known as anthropomorphism and personification." Ruskin's "pathetic fallacy" is no fallacy at all.[37] And finally there is an objective class of similitudes which seems to be epic according to the scheme but is exemplified by what we would call synaesthesia, the community of the senses, an "amalgam of metaphors." [38] Beyond this discovery of similitudes there is also a final stage of poetic activity: the perception of unity. Dallas, with his usual ingenuity, distinguishes three sorts of poetic wholes—the whole of intension, the whole of protension, and the whole of extension, and these are again correlated to the genres. "The intensive whole is the favourite of the lyrical mood; the protensive whole dominates in the epic; and the extensive whole is the very life and essence of dramatic art." [39] This leap of the mind "from the particular to the universal, from the accidental to the necessary, from the temporal to the eternal, from the individual to the general," accounts for the creation of types in art, for "symbolism." [40] It is hard to see how this speculative triadic scheme of genres and kinds of imagery is related to the original emphasis on the unconscious, since the lyric has obviously ceased to be the highest genre. The drama is even described as the peculiarly Christian art, because Greek tragedy is interpreted, oddly enough, as basically epic. It all ends with a sentimental "theology of art." [41] Great poetry is religious in temper, even "Protestant" in tone.[42] Milton is Dallas' hero. In Thackeray and Victorian fiction Dallas deplores the "withering of the hero": the predominance of anecdotal biography and false individualism.[43]

The modern discoverers of Dallas have been delighted to unearth an early psychoanalyst and even "an earlier and less harassed D. H. Lawrence"; [44] but that interpretation ignores the fact that Dallas has no unifying vision, that the "hidden soul" remains hidden, and that he constructs an ingenious triadic system of genres and images that is hardly tenable in detail and is derivative from the Germans in its method. Dallas erected a Victorian style Crazy Castle, a thing of rags and patches that cannot come to life again and remains a curiosity of the time.

There was still another theorist who attempted to put criticism on a scientific basis: George Henry Lewes (1817–78), who is known also for his popular biography of Goethe (1855) and his association with George Eliot. Lewes' *Principles of Success in Literature* (1865) was a series of articles, which only much later were reprinted independently. The essays made, I believe, little impact, though they are characteristic of the time and the man. Lewes wants to find the "method of literature" founded upon psychological laws: involving principles which are true for all peoples and all times. He has a rather surprising faith in "success as a test of merit," [45] though he does, of course, discriminate between various kinds of success. The principles of success are simply the principles of literature of which he distinguishes three: that of vision, the intellectual form; that of sincerity, the moral form; and that of beauty, the aesthetic form. He does not seem to notice that he has renamed Truth, Goodness, and Beauty. Everything turns around the principle of experience, authenticity, direct vision on the side of truth; sincerity, uprightness on the side of goodness; and economy, simplicity, sequence, climax, and variety of style on the side of beauty. The whole scheme has a representative "common sense" quality, but it is too simple.

Lewes did not have, however, an unphilosophical or provincial mind. He was an extremely versatile, popular philosopher who wrote a *Biographical History of Philosophy* (1845–46) and many books on psychology and physiology. He wrote much criticism for the *Westminster Review* and theatrical reviews for *The Leader*. His point of view can be called "classical" or rather rationalist, positivistic, and certainly antiromantic. His early articles on Hegel's aesthetics [46]—not an unfavorable descriptive account, on A. W. Schlegel's *Dramatic Lectures*,[47] and on the works of Lessing [48] not only show his German interests, which culminated in the *Life of Goethe,* but also define his position very clearly. A. W. Schlegel seems to him only a popular writer who merits the applause he has received, "but as an oracle—as a rational, serious, philosophic critic" must be considered "one of the most dangerous guides the student can consult." Lewes has no use for Schlegel's affectation of philosophical depth. "Bad analytical criticism seems better than mediocre philosophy." [49] Lessing is the right counterweight. Lewes likes his "direct and practical tendencies," he finds his mind "of a quality eminently British." "Of all Germans, he is the least German," is Lewes' highest praise, meaning presumably by "German" anything obscure, pseudo-profound, and pedantically learned. Lewes found Friedrich Schlegel's enthusiastic essay on Lessing "most offensive," because it was "an indirect eulogy of the 'New School' as it was called which launched into those extravagances which it christened Romanticism." [50] When Lewes came to write on "The Errors and Abuses of English Criticism," he attacked the still uneradicated practice of anonymous reviewing but has an occasion to define the office of criticism as "the translation of the poet's emotions into their fundamental or correspondent ideas." [51] Criticism is rationalization, translation into concepts.

It seems thus logical that Lewes became the first English exponent of the theory of realism in the novel, though we must remember that he was a fervent admirer of French classical tragedy and the acting of Rachel only a few years before.[52] There was nothing in England comparable to the French debates when Lewes, in 1858, expounded realism for the first time. "Art is Representation of Reality." "Realism is the basis of all art." Lewes judges contemporary German novelists very severely: he trounces Gustav Freytag and Otto Ludwig as unrealistic and mawkish and praises Paul Heyse and Gottfried Keller with some reservations.[53] In other contexts he attacked the unreality of Hugo's *Travailleurs de la mer,* the "melodrama and improbability" of *Jane Eyre,*[54] and the fantastical exaggerations and wooden puppetry of Dickens. Dickens, whom he knew personally, is described as "seer of visions" with an imagination of such compulsive vividness as to approach hallucination.[55] Still, Lewes cannot be described as a defender of literal naturalism. He disliked what he called "detailism"[56] and speaks always of a selection of typical elements. The appeal is to "the necessary coherence of reality," to "the true relations of things,"[57] which does not exclude properly directed fantasy or the creation of humorous types which excite and direct the imagination of the reader as Dickens succeeds in doing.

Clearly George Eliot (Mary Ann Evans, 1819–80) held very similar views, which were not necessarily all derived from Lewes. She wrote a good deal of criticism that has little to do with literary theory or even the novel. It can be surprisingly harsh or slashing: she comments, for instance, on "the insolent slovenliness" of Lord Brougham's biographies and "the bad opera" quality of Tennyson's *Maud,* or satirically depicts Edward Young, the author of *The Night Thoughts*—hardly a provoking target even a hundred years ago— as "excogitating epigrams or ecstatic soliloquies by the light of a candle fixed in a skull," devising "monstrous absurdities" of insincere hyperboles.[58] But her quiet advocacy of realism mattered in its time: particularly the passage in *Adam Bede* (1859) in which she expresses contentment "to tell my simple story, without trying to make things better than they were; dreading nothing indeed but falsity." Truth is her hero, as it was for Tolstoy in the Sebastopol stories a few years before. "The faithful representing of commonplace things" is her definition of the novel.[59] But her aesthetic is also one of sympathy and love. "Art is the nearest thing to life; it is a mode of amplifying experience and extending our contact with our fellowmen beyond the bounds of our personal lot," could have been said by Wordsworth or Tolstoy. "A picture of human life such as a great artist can give, surprises even the trivial and the selfish into that attention to what is apart from themselves, which may be called the raw material of moral sentiment." [60] This realism which wants to make an emotional and humanitarian impact is defended on two fronts: against the sentimentalists who falsify reality, "Silly Novels by Lady Novelists" to whom she devoted an amusing essay,[61] and against the mere moralists. In a curious exchange of letters with the positivistic philosopher Frederic Harrison, George Eliot defends "aesthetic teaching as the highest of all teaching." "If it ceases to be purely aesthetic—if it lapses anywhere from the picture to the diagram—it becomes the most offensive of all teaching." [62] She defends, for instance, the morality of Goethe's *Wilhelm Meister* as a "large tolerance" and attacks "the parsonic habit" [63] of Charles Kingsley while privately admitting that she had "sinned against her own laws" in her own novels often enough.[64] Her ideal is aesthetic effect, convincingness, illusion. She complains about an episode in a novel that it is "merely described and not presented." [65] But she has no doctrinaire conception about the correct method of story-telling. She asks: "Why should a story not be told in the most irregular fashion that an author's idiosyncracy may prompt?" [66] and she cites *Tristram Shandy* without qualms. Her realism is hardly concerned with theoretical refinements or even requirements. She was no Henry James.

The more surprising is a recently published fragment that shows George Eliot speculating on "Form in Art" (1868) with a psychological and biological vocabulary—possibly derived from Lewes. Form in poetry is interpreted as a complex organism, "by which no part can suffer increase or diminution without a participation of all other parts in the effect produced and a consequent modification of the organism as a whole." The principle, ultimately descended from Plato, is proclaimed a standard of criticism. "By this light, forms of art can be called higher or lower only on the same principle as that on which we apply these words to organisms; viz. in proportion to the complexity of the parts bound up into one indissoluble whole." [67] Here a criterion of complexity used, for instance, by the New Criticism is announced, though George Eliot makes much more of the biological parallelism. It seems a pity that she did not pursue this train of thought, which would have modified or at least supplemented her theory of realism in the novel.

Novelistic theory was in general realistic. Dramatic theory hardly existed. The essay usually cited with high praise, George Meredith's *Essay on Comedy and the Use of the Comic Spirit* (1877) is a whimsical ramble through the history of comedy praising Molière and Congreve but yielding very little for general theory. We are merely told that Comedy flourishes best in civilized society with no "marked social inequality of the sexes." Some attempt is made to tie the Comic Muse to the intellect and to distinguish it from satire and irony, but I fail to see the illumination in a definition which asserts that "irony" is "the humour of satire" or in a distinction in which the juxtaposition of knight and squire in *Don Quixote* is called a "Comic conception," while the opposition of their natures is "most humorous." [68] I find myself in agreement with Croce that these psychological classifications lead nowhere in literary criticism.

Nor did the poets of the time get far in attempts to describe the nature of poetry. Robert Browning wrote one critical essay on Shelley (1852), originally an introduction to a collection of *Letters of Percy Bysshe Shelley* which turned out to be forgeries. It takes up the distinction between the objective and the subjective poet in highly Platonizing terms. The subjective poet "is impelled to embody the thing he perceives, not so much with reference to the many below, as to the One above him, the supreme Intelligence which apprehends all things in their absolute truth." "Not what man sees, but what God sees—the Ideas of Plato, seeds of creation, lying burningly on the Divine Hand—it is toward these that [the poet] struggles." "He digs where he stands—preferring to seek [the primal elements of humanity] in his own soul as the nearest reflex of the absolute Mind." In vocabulary highly colored by Platonizing idealism Shelley's inward turn is defended as "a presentment of the correspondency of the universe to Deity." [69] Browning's own practice is at stake. Shelley is used as an occasion to make Browning's own ambition clear: when he is most individual he is most universal. The subjective becomes objective. But this is simply the dialectics of the universal and the particular. The poet is God's witness, is speaking for God.

A humbler poet, Gerard Manley Hopkins (1844–89), when he

reflected on poetry, also had an overwhelming religious concern. The poet's function is to glorify God by reproducing the "inscapes" of objects and people. The striking term seems sometimes to mean any pattern in nature, any reflection of the creator in creation, sometimes something in art, "a species or individually distinctive beauty of style," or sometimes simply "a design or pattern," both in nature and art.[70] Hopkins sounds extremely like Ruskin in his concern for truth of observation and minute notations of natural phenomena, or like Arnold when he demands high seriousness. But most of his reflections on poetry are of a technical character: he distinguishes levels of style: "the language of inspiration," "Parnassian language," and "the language of verse," renaming the traditional three levels,[71] and he is, most centrally, concerned with prosodic theory. I cannot here enter into a history of metrics, but it seems that the basic concepts of Hopkins' theory of "sprung rhythm" are far from clear or exact, and it remains valuable chiefly as a defense of his own practice and of the tradition of Anglo-Saxon and alliterative verse in English. He sees many important points, such as the parallelism of sound and meaning and the counterpoint of metrical scheme and language stress, but "sprung rhythm" itself is merely an odd name for the use of counterpoint to the extreme of destroying the conventionally fixed metrical scheme.[72] Hopkins' theory reacts against Coventry Patmore's *Essay on English Metrical Law* (1857) which identifies metrical and word accent and stresses the dipodic nature of English meter.[73] But we cannot solve such questions of poetic practice and technique. We should rather turn to the professional critics. The central figure of the age is obviously Matthew Arnold.

8: ARNOLD, BAGEHOT, AND STEPHEN

MATTHEW ARNOLD (1822–1888)

THE POSITION OF Matthew Arnold (1822–88) as the most important
English critic of the second half of the 19th century seems secure.
His eminence is due not only to his literary criticism but also to
his standing as a poet and general critic of English society and
civilization. Today both in England and in the United States—
especially in academic circles—his influence is still felt. It is rather
the influence of his *Kulturphilosophie* than of his literary criticism,
but among critics of the 20th century Irving Babbitt, T. S. Eliot,
F. R. Leavis, and Lionel Trilling show marked affinities with his
outlook. Arnold provides us with an apology for culture, a restatement of the Greek ideal of *paideia* modified by Christianity; he
makes a defense of the study of the humanities against the growing
encroachments of scientific and vocational training; he gives a
satirical picture of the Anglo-Saxon middle classes: their Philistinism and their religion with its anti-aesthetic bias; he provides a
defense of poetry and literature, a defense of the critical spirit and
the exercise of criticism; and finally—though this part of his activity
is most dated—he advocates an undogmatic religion.

If we examine these views more closely, we may conclude that
what Arnold propounds is neither novel nor distinctly Arnoldian.
One can say that he merely restates the ideal of German *Bildung* as
it was formulated by Goethe and Wilhelm von Humboldt: he
shares their emphasis on antiquity as the model, their praise of
disinterestedness, their European horizon, and their central conception of the ideal man as the total man, in whom a unity of
faculties, intellect, and sense constitute what Arnold termed
"imaginative reason." We may feel that the defense of the humanities against the sciences must be put on a different basis than in the
19th century and that Arnold's picture of the English middle classes
is obsolete and overdrawn; we can classify his religion as an unhappy
hybrid of stoicism and evangelicalism, of Goethe and Schleier-

macher. We may feel (as I do) that both his and our own latter-day
preoccupation with the defense of letters is superfluous and tiresome. Arnold repeats over and over again that literature educates,
that it forms man, makes him see things, makes him know himself,
gives him serenity. We may feel that Arnold loses all perspective
when he tries to extend the claims of literature and voices the hope
that it will replace religion. "The future of poetry is immense,"
begins the famous passage which culminates in the statement that
"most of what now passes with us for religion and philosophy will
be replaced by poetry."[1] Taken literally, this aim may seem absurd
or undesirable if it merely means that people will cease to believe
in religion and philosophies and will be provided by poetry with a
sufficient interpretation of life. Implicitly, Arnold recommends his
own *Weltanschauung,* which refuses to accept any dogma and any
systematic philosophy. He wants us to rest content with a "poetic"
view of life, one that is neither traditionally religious nor systematically philosophical but rather moralistic and emotional. "Morality touched by emotion" was Arnold's definition of both religion
and poetry.

But for our purposes—confined as always to literary criticism—
much of this, however important for the great debate on religion
and culture, is irrelevant. We must rather try to define Arnold's
contribution to thinking about literature and poetry.

Arnold is, first of all, a very important apologist for criticism.
Criticism, of course, means for him not simply literary criticism but
rather the critical spirit in general, the application of intelligence
to any and all subjects. Arnold is an eloquent advocate of "disinterestedness," curiosity, flexibility, urbanity, a free circulation of ideas.
Specifically he attacks British provincialism and recommends an
opening of doors to European, mainly French and German, winds
of doctrine. It was and is a valuable plea, which must be seen in its
historical setting. Arnold's ideal of "disinterestedness" must not be
understood as Olympian aloofness or escape to the ivory tower. It
is easy to show that Arnold himself was deeply absorbed in the
problems of his age and was not above engaging in polemics and
even losing his temper.[2] But "disinterestedness" surely means for
him something quite specific: a denial of immediate political and
sectarian ends, a wide horizon, an absence of prejudice, serenity
beyond the passions of the moment. The famous formula for the

aim of criticism, "the endeavour . . . to see the object as in itself it really is," [3] may raise more questions than it solves, but it is a good antidote to "over-vehemence in liking and disliking," [4] to eccentricity, to "individual fancy"; [5] it defines "the right tone and temper of mind" [6] for good criticism. "Disinterestedness" is also intellectual "curiosity," an "instinct prompting [us] to try to know the best that is known and thought in the world, irrespectively of practice, politics, and everything of the kind." [7] The term "best" may be another begging of the question, but again it means something concrete and good: an escape from the bondage of one's time and place, a sense of the whole tradition of the West, of the presence of the great classics, and a feeling for Europe as "one great confederation." [8] Arnold's own "curiosity" may have fallen far short of the ideal of Goethe's world literature (to which he alludes), but one should recognize that Arnold knew his Homer and Sophocles in the original, welcomed Leopardi, Heine, and Tolstoy, and was steeped in the French criticism of his time. (He knew not only Sainte-Beuve and Taine, but also Planche, Nisard, Villemain, Scherer, Vinet, Saint-Marc Girardin, and many others.) His erudition is often slighted; his acquaintance with older English literature outside of the greatest names seems surprisingly meager. He had the gentleman-scholar's dread of pedantic learning and disparages his own erudition with some mock humility. But while one should admit that he was no Sainte-Beuve, Dilthey, or Croce (he was, after all, a poet and a busy inspector of schools), he read Greek and Latin, German and French (and some Italian), and knew enough for a critic who does not even pretend to be a professional literary historian or classical philologist. Arnold's advocacy of the critical spirit, of an atmosphere conducive to the free exchange of ideas, his praise of objectivity, disinterestedness, and curiosity (properly understood) are valuable and sound even today.

Arnold also said important things about the theory of criticism. His point of view is not entirely consistent and may have shifted toward the end of his life. He often seems to have believed in a purely descriptive, interpretative criticism. "The judgment which almost insensibly forms itself . . . is the valuable one." The critic should "communicate fresh knowledge, and let his own judgment pass along with it"; he should be "a sort of companion and clue." [9] Arnold even said: "I wish to decide nothing as of my own authority;

the great art of criticism is to get oneself out of the way and let humanity decide." [10] The main function of criticism is "to make an intellectual situation of which the creative power can profitably avail itself." [11] The process of criticism is thus conceived as informative, liberating, preparatory to creation. Arnold defined the perfect critic when he praised Sainte-Beuve: "a critic of measure, not exuberant; of the centre, not provincial; of keen industry and curiosity, with 'Truth' (the word engraved in English on his seal) for his motto; moreover with gay and amiable temper, his manner as good as his matter." [12] But this cheerful temper and cosmopolitan tolerance is only one side of Sainte-Beuve's mind and it is only one side of Arnold's. Especially in his later years Arnold strongly asserted the judicial function of criticism. His early defense of the French Academy is made in the name of a "high, correct standard in intellectual matters," of "severe discipline," [13] and he early believed that "in the literary opinion of Europe, if not in the literary opinion of one nation, in fifty years, if not in five, there is a final judgment." [14] In "The Study of Poetry" Arnold defends the "real estimate" against the historical and personal estimate, both of which seem to him fallacious. By personal estimate he means an estimate in terms of "our personal affinities, likings, and circumstances," [15] a judgment in the light of our personal history, which seems to him inadequate because it is purely subjective. The rejection of the historical estimate needs much fuller substantiation. It is the overestimate that comes from seeing a work as a stage in the development of literature, especially in the early development of a national poetry. Arnold criticizes the "attempt to acquaint oneself with the time and life and historical relationships" of a genuine classic as "mere literary dilettantism unless it has . . . clear sense and deeper enjoyment for its end." [16] Elsewhere, discussing Edmond Scherer's praise of the method of historical criticism, Arnold calls it a "perilous doctrine, that from such a study the right understanding of [Milton's] work will 'spontaneously issue.' In a mind qualified in a certain manner it will—not in all minds." Arnold gives Macaulay (one of his pet aversions) as an example of a critic with a knowledge of biography and history who is still deficient as a critic. "Let us not confound the method," he concludes, "with the result intended by the method—right judgments." [17] In part Arnold simply wants to reject the growing and to him extravagant claims of the antiquarian enthusiasts of his time. He thinks the *Chanson de Roland,* medieval romances in general, and Marot overrated, and he protests against the German worship of the *Nibelungenlied.*[18] In part, however, Arnold genuinely desires to escape his own historicism and that of his time with its danger of falling into a complete relativism of values. "Real estimate" may again conceal a *petitio principii,* may merely posit and not solve the problem of reality, but Arnold sees, at least, the need of such an estimate, and he states it impressively.

It would be a mistake to think that Arnold himself was not a historical critic. He had been imbued with the historical point of view since his youth, which was spent in the shadow of his father, Dr. Thomas Arnold, one of the first expounders of the science of classical antiquities and the historical sense in the German tradition. Arnold's inaugural lecture at Oxford, "On the Modern Element in Literature" (1857, published 1869), presents a scheme of history that must be characterized as deterministic and schematic in an almost Hegelian way. Arnold surveys a sequence of ages and nations which he judges in terms of their political and intellectual greatness, vigor, and life, along with a sequence of literatures that are rated according to the adequacy with which they express their particular age and nation. The term "adequacy" seems to mean both "representativeness," sympathy with the age, and "greatness" in a moral and artistic sense. Such an "adequate" literature is then pronounced to be "modern," regardless of chronology. This terminological innovation has little to recommend it, as both usage and etymology (*modo,* just now) are opposed. But it allows a scheme of almost Vichian *corsi e recorsi.* First there was the Homeric Age, with Homer "a greater power than even Sophocles or Aeschylus; but his age is less interesting than himself." [19] He was a great poet living in an age that was not adequate to him. Then came the Greece of Pericles, the age of a perfect, adequate, "modern" literature, "modern" because of its pacific attitude, toleration, intellectual maturity, and critical spirit, an age that came to an end with the defeat of Athens in the Peloponnesian War. Afterward "the intellectual and spiritual life of Greece was left without an adequate material basis of political and practical life; and both began inevitably to decay." [20] In Rome there was a great age but no adequate literature. Lucretius "withdraws himself," was "overstrained, gloom-weighted, morbid; and he who is morbid, is no adequate interpreter of his age." [21] Virgil, similarly, is "conscious, at heart, of his inadequacy for the thorough spiritual mastery of that world"; he has "a sweet, a touching sadness," a nostalgia for the past.[22] Horace is a man without faith, without enthusiasm, a skeptical man of the world.[23] Arnold did not continue the scheme systematically beyond antiquity in this lecture, but it is obvious from his other writings how it would continue. Dante, like Homer, would be a poet living in an age inadequate to him. As to the Elizabethan Age, Arnold seems to have been of two minds. In the inaugural lecture he quotes Sir Walter Ralegh's *History of the World* in order to demonstrate its intellectual inferiority to the history of Thucydides and, by implication, the inferiority of Ralegh's time to that of Pericles. In a letter he speaks of Shakespeare as an "infinitely *more than adequate* expression of a *second class* epoch." [24] But in the essay on Heine (1863) the Elizabethan Age is considered as an example of the time when "English society at large was accessible to ideas, was permeated by them, was vivified by them. Hence the unique greatness in English literature of Shakspeare and his contemporaries. They were powerfully upheld by the intellectual life of their nation." [25] There was, then, a great literature adequate to the age. In Arnold's scheme English 18th-century literature appears as "a provincial and second-rate literature," in contrast to the French literature of that age, "one of the most powerful and pervasive intellectual agencies that have ever existed," [26] and one that "fulfilled a great mission victoriously." [27] Arnold recognizes the historical importance of English 18th-century literature as a reaction to the poetic exuberance of the Elizabethan Age and as the creator of a sober modern prose style. And, in a letter, he admitted that Pope's poetry was "adequate to Pope's age—that is, it reflected completely the best culture and intelligence of that age." But it "was a poor time after all." [28] But the whole century is obviously considered an "inadequate" age which stifled such talents as those of Gray or Bishop Butler. The English romantic period is similarly considered as lacking in "intellectual atmosphere." English poetry of the first quarter of the century—in a famous phrase—"did not know enough." [29] Arnold introduces here a conception slightly different from his earlier idea of adequacy. There is the main current of literature and ideas represented, for instance, by Goethe and Heine, but the English poets "do not belong to that which is the main current of the literature of modern epochs, they do not apply modern ideas to life; they constitute, therefore, *minor currents.*" [30] The Germans are similarly handicapped by their lack of a great national life, though apparently a "sort of equivalent" for it is provided "in the complete culture and unfettered thinking of a large body of Germans." [31] The cumbersome German (and Italian) style is ascribed to the "want of the pressure of a great national life, with its practical discipline, its ever-active traditions." [32] In a rare mood of irreverence for Goethe, Arnold describes his *Maerchen* as a "piece of solemn inanity, on which a man of Goethe's powers could never have wasted his time, but for his lot having been cast in a nation which has never lived." [33]

Contrary to the usual opinion, Matthew Arnold is thus primarily a historical critic who works with a historical scheme in his mind. Society is often conceived as an independent, fixed, given force that even genius cannot change. In an early letter, for instance, he explains the elaboration of 17th-century style by the limited number of ideas accessible at that time. He assumes a set number of ideas at a particular age which have to be elaborated by imagination and are elaborated more curiously and fancifully when there are fewer of them.[34] "The creative power," he asserts, "works with elements, with materials," "the best ideas current at the time." [35] Addison is not up to La Bruyère and Vauvenargues because of "the atmosphere in which he lives and works; an atmosphere which tells unfavourably, or rather *tends* to tell unfavourably (for that is the truer way of putting it) either upon style or else upon ideas." [36] The *Zeitgeist* is one of Arnold's favorite terms. Only on occasion will he recognize that a lonely spirit can escape it. He tells Clough: "I took up Obermann, and refuged myself with him in his forest against your *Zeit Geist* [sic]." [37]

Yet Arnold does not think merely in terms of genius versus age, individual versus society, poet versus current or staple of ideas. He just as often thinks in collectivist terms of race and the march of history. He is preoccupied almost as much as Taine with racial theories. All his writings play variations on the contrasts appearing among the Latin, Celtic, and Germanic races, or in that between the Hebraic and the Greek spirit. But the distinction between national spirit (*Volksgeist*) and race is not clear to him. He sketches the history of France in terms of the conflict between Gaul, Latin, and Teuton.[38] His lectures *On the Study of Celtic Literature* turn upon the concept of race. He rejects a purely social explanation. "Modes of life, institutions, government, climate, and so forth . . . . will further or hinder the development of an aptitude, but they will not by themselves create the aptitude or explain it." [39] He confidently assigns to the Celts (with whom he sometimes includes the French) specific literary characters: a turn for style, a turn for melancholy, and a turn for natural magic,[40] while he denies them other literary abilities, such as a sense of over-all form. He never raises the obvious question whether these qualities could not be found elsewhere in the world where there were no Celts—in the Orient, for instance—and he never seems to doubt the cogency of his argument that the occurrence of these qualities in English literature is a proof of Celtic nature in the English.[41] It is never clear what Celtic nature is supposed to be: Celtic blood in the English? Celtic influence? or simply a "note," a quality, which Arnold calls Celtic. Arnold distinguishes between a Greek and a Celtic way of handling nature in English poetry without recognizing the implicit contradiction to his basic thesis. If there is Greek cultural influence without racial admixture why must there be Celtic blood rather than merely Celtic influence? Shakespeare and Keats are the main sources of Arnold's examples for natural magic, but Arnold does not definitely assign Celtic blood to them as individuals. The whole theory is much vaguer. It is a breakup of certain broad characteristics of poetry into elements labeled Anglo-Saxon, Norman, and Celtic. It would be easy to show the circularity of Arnold's argument, the difficulties with which he is confronted in case of the supposedly Celtic French, the whole airiness of his historical and literary structure. Obviously he did not know a single Celtic language, and even his secondhand information is very meager and handled very freely. One should recognize that Arnold was drawing on many contemporary sources: Renan, Michelet, Thierry, Edouard Martin, Taine. One should also realize that he was reacting against the Teutonism of Freeman and Carlyle. He was pleading, too, for good sense and tolerance in the Irish question. He had a very specific aim in mind: the creation of a Chair of Celtic at Oxford. His book was called *On the Study of Celtic Literature* and was not and did not claim to be a survey of the Celtic literatures. In spite of its

meager information and in spite (or because) of its fanciful generalizations about racial characteristics, it had an immense (though
slightly absurd) influence on the Irish Renaissance soon after
Arnold's death.[42]

One side of the equation is race: the other is the "stream of
history," the "natural current in human affairs," [43] "the natural and
necessary stream of things," [44] the "fatal law of development," [45]
the "*moment.*" [46] The last is a term Arnold borrowed from Taine
(though Taine is for him too systematic, too deterministic). One of
the critic's highest functions is to grasp this development. The critic
has "to ascertain the master-current in the literature of an epoch,
and to distinguish this from all minor currents." [47] The critic not
only discerns the wave of the future, he can share in making and
directing it. "A time of true creative activity . . . must inevitably
be preceded amongst us by a time of criticism." [48] "Out of this stir
and growth [of new ideas], come the creative epochs of literature." [49]
This is Arnold's belief and hope for the future. He believes that he
is preparing a new flowering of English literature, and that England
needs nothing more than criticism, the critical spirit, an influx of
new ideas from abroad and from the past. "Centrality" is Arnold's
term for the opposite to "provinciality," [50] and provinciality means
a dearth of ideas, a stifling atmosphere that does not allow an adequate literature. Gray was his oddly selected example for the suffo-
cation of talent by his age. His own time seemed to him an unpoetic
age, an "arid" time.[51]

Arnold had a low opinion of most of his contemporaries and
would have been surprised by the mid-20th century glorification of
the Victorian Age. Carlyle seemed to him a "moral desperado," [52]
"too willful, too turbid, too vehement" to be a great writer.[53] Ruskin
was "eccentric" and "dogmatic" (like himself) "but *wrong.*" [54]
Tennyson, though called on occasion a "most distinguished and
charming poet," [55] is rated below Musset and Heine,[56] and *Maud*
is a "lamentable production," "thoroughly provincial, not European." [57] Arnold rated Browning higher, though more as an intellect
than a poet. Swinburne was a "pseudo-Shelley," [58] and the novelists
hardly interested him. He read *David Copperfield* for the first time
in 1880 [59] and thought burying Dickens in Westminster Abbey "a
monstrosity." [60] Thackeray seemed to him a "first-rate journeyman
though not a great artist." [61] To judge from "Haworth Church-

yard," Arnold did admire *Jane Eyre* and *Wuthering Heights,* but a private letter on *Villette* is most damning.[62]

Arnold's personal melancholia and even defeatism is only thinly overlaid by the vague cosmic optimism of his more public prose writings. His hopes for poetry are "immense," but poetry is conceived on the one hand so widely that it is simply religion (in Arnold's diluted sense) and on the other hand so narrowly that it is reduced to didactic poetry, to poetry as "criticism of life."

This famous phrase, if taken literally, seems indefensible; it would be a gross intellectualistic and didactic misinterpretation of the nature of art. But Arnold pointed out that it was not meant to be a definition of poetry in contrast to prose [63] and later revised the formula to read: poetry is criticism of life "under the conditions fixed for such a criticism by the laws of poetic truth and poetic beauty." [64] The supplement shifts the whole issue to these laws, which Arnold, however, never defines or describes, at least not explicitly. The alternative phrase "poetry is at bottom a criticism of life" [65] can be defended as saying merely that all literature gives an interpretation and evaluation of life. It thus was useful as a protest against the view that literature is only an amusement or game. It was an assertion that literature provides knowledge.

Arnold knows that a world-view implicit in poetry must not be confused with a systematic philosophy. He rejects, for instance, Leslie Stephen's attempt to abstract a system of Wordsworth's ethics. Wordsworth's philosophy seems to him an "illusion," "so far, at least, as it may put on the form and habit of 'a scientific system of thought,' and the more that it puts them on." [66] Elsewhere he protests that "no one will be much helped by Wordsworth's philosophy of Nature, as a scheme in itself and disjoined from his poems." [67] He knew that Wordsworth speaks "with a truth far beyond any philosophic truth of which he has the conscious and assured possession." [68] In spite of the phrase "criticism of life" Arnold did not actually confuse poetry and philosophy, creation and criticism.

But it is hard to defend Arnold against a more general charge of didacticism. Poetry may not be philosophy but it must, to be truly great, have "high seriousness." The phrase—by which he translates Aristotle's *spoudaiotes* [69]—has a strong implication of solemnity and sublimity and is thus excessively narrow as a definition of great poetry. Arnold certainly laid himself wide open to criticism when he denied "high seriousness" to Chaucer but allowed it to Gray and Shelley.[70] Chaucer gives a "large, free, sound representation of things," he has "truth of substance," [71] but not the "high seriousness" that Arnold finds, though fitfully, in Villon. One suspects that Arnold knew only parts of Chaucer, or that, in this particular context, "high seriousness" meant Villon's sense of the transitoriness of life, his acute feeling for the presence of death. Actually, Arnold values many poets and among them his greatest favorites, Wordsworth and Goethe, for their consoling, "healing power," for the "joy" and even optimism they radiate. Leopardi, whom Arnold admired highly, loses out against Wordsworth and Goethe because of his pessimism,[72] and Coleridge is criticized for his lack of joy, which seemed to Arnold "something unnatural and shocking." [73] The emphasis on "joy" (as opposed to pleasure) surely derives from Wordsworth (though Arnold also quotes Schiller) ,[74] as the idea of "healing power" (*vis medica*) comes from Keble's *Lectures*. The recurrent stress on "joy," which is clarified by his speaking of poetry as addressed to the "great primary human affections," to "the elementary part of our nature," [75] seems to refute an interpretation of "high seriousness" as churchyard solemnity.

Very often Arnold conceives of poetry very widely: as all human utterance at its best. It "is simply the most beautiful, impressive, and widely effective mode of saying things," [76] "the most delightful and perfect form of utterance that human words can reach," [77] the "most perfect speech of man." [78] He usually distinguishes two functions of poetry: poetry as the interpretation of the natural world, and poetry as the interpretation of the moral world.[79] Poetry interprets either the physiognomy and movement of the outward world or the ideas and laws of the inward world of man's moral and spiritual nature. "In other words, poetry is interpretative both by having *natural magic* in it, and by having *moral profundity*. In both ways it illuminates man; it gives him a satisfying sense of reality; it reconciles him with himself and the universe." [80] Arnold greatly preferred the second way: but he appreciated Keats and Maurice de Guérin, who seemed to him poets of natural magic, and he saw, most of the time, the dangers of mere didacticism. Clough, trying to solve the riddle of the universe, irritated him, though he was dissatisfied with Tennyson's sensuous poetry of surface, overwhelmed and baffled by Shakespeare. The famous sonnet "Others abide our question. Thou art free!" is illuminated by an early letter which says that "Shakespeare is as obscure as life" and that his "attempt to re-construct the Universe is not a satisfactory attempt." [81] There are then these three kinds of poetry: the questioning and restless, like Clough's; the sensual and superficial, like Tennyson's; and the obscurely grand, like Shakespeare's. But there are other kinds too. There are Wordsworth and Goethe, the consolers, the dispensers of joy, and there are such poets as the uniformly grand Homer, Milton, and Dante and even the gloomy, but free and daring, Byron.

Arnold often speaks of poetry as "the noble and profound application of ideas to life," [82] and sometimes he speaks even of the application of "moral ideas." But he explains carefully that he uses "moral" in a wide sense to include the whole question, "how to live?" [83] But even the unfortunate term "application," with its suggestion that ideas are applied like plasters, should not obscure the fact that Arnold is explicitly clear in the belief that poetry is not simply didactic. He knows that poetry must be concrete. He quotes Milton to the effect that poetry should be "simple, sensuous, passionate" (though he changes the last term to "impassioned") , and he criticizes Emerson's poems for being "seldom either simple, or sensuous, or impassioned." Emerson's poetry "lacks concreteness, it lacks energy." [84] Often Arnold speaks of the collaboration of man's faculties in producing poetry: of emotion and reason, or imagination and reason, "imaginative reason." [85] Such is the achievement of the Greeks, and Arnold hopes that by it "the modern spirit, if it would live right, has chiefly to live." The term "imaginative reason" becomes clearer when we hear that the poetry of later paganism "lived by the senses and the understanding," while that of medieval Christianity lived by "the heart and imagination." [86] Neither combination is completely satisfying. Rather a union of intellect and emotion, of imagination and reason, is stipulated, though it is hardly envisaged with clarity.

One kind of poetry is definitely disparaged: the poetry of reason, the poetry of the English 18th century, poetry "conceived and composed in [the poets'] wits," as opposed to genuine poetry "conceived and composed in the soul." [87] Arnold's calling Dryden and Pope "classics of our prose" [88] has aroused much criticism in our age, which once more admires neoclassical poetry. Arnold is vulnerable when he quotes isolated prosy passages from Pope and Dryden and when he disparages an accurate image in Goldsmith's *Deserted Village*.[89] He is hardly right (though he has the precedent of Wordsworth) in denying the 18th century an "eye on the object"; one finds it difficult to understand the excessive praise of Gray, especially of the two odes (which Arnold prefers to the *Elegy*). But one should understand the specific meaning of Arnold's criticism: the term "soul" in his formula means not the Christian soul but something like the German *Gemüt*, the heart. Dryden and Pope do not offer the kind of spiritual consolation Arnold was seeking, and surely he is not wrong in saying that the share of intellect in composing poetry is with them very strong. Pope wrote some of his poems first in prose: he *is* "clever," "argumentative," "ingenious," and even "artificial." (All these are adjectives used by Arnold, the last in the special sense which it has in the Bowles-Byron controversy or in Hazlitt.)

The contradictions in Arnold's concept of poetry and its limitations—the alternatives of mere didacticism or soulful religious seriousness—are connected with Arnold's lack of clarity on such central problems of poetics as the relation between content and form, between totality and local detail. Arnold (like his time in general) has a feeble grasp of the difference between art and reality. Imagination, illusion, the special world of art, mean little to him. In some sense he acknowledges the unity of form and content, but mostly he conceives of the subject of poetry as something given and fixed, something capable of being judged as poetic or unpoetic outside a work of art. Form just as often is conceived of as a hard vessel into which the poet pours his content. Even reality is often seen as something given and fixed, either good or bad for the artist, and art often means only artifice, technique, virtuosity. The poet, Arnold assumes, should deal with a beautiful world, but, unfortunately, he is not always able to do so. The world of Robert Burns, for instance, was a "harsh, a sordid, a repulsive world."[90] Or said more strongly in a letter: "Burns is a beast, with splendid gleams, and the medium in which he lived, Scotch peasants, Scotch Presbyterianism, and Scotch drink, is repulsive."[91] Arnold disliked the new French realism intensely. He criticized *Madame Bovary* even more severely than Sainte-Beuve did, though several points are taken from Sainte-Beuve's essay.[92] Arnold likes *Anna Karenina* because he likes the people and world Tolstoy depicts, even though he has no high opinion of Tolstoy's art. "We are not to take *Anna Karénine* as a work of art; we are to take it as a piece of life." [93]

Arnold began his critical career by arguing that "all depends upon the subject," [94] the choice of a fitting action. He chose the subject of *Merope* because it is an ancient story from Hyginus, "this rich mine of subjects for tragedy," and because it contains "a recognition of the most affecting kind." [95] Belief in a poetic subject or situation existing prior to a work of art is the complement of the belief that there is a style independent of subject matter and that there are metrical forms that have value and meaning outside of a poem. Arnold's criticism is deeply entangled in these old fallacies. His persistent disparagement of the French alexandrine and the English rhymed couplet is the clearest instance of such blindness. Arnold tells us many times that the alexandrine and the English couplet constitute a "form radically inadequate and inferior," or that "true tragic poetry is impossible with this inadequate form." [96] Arnold believes in a fated, inherent character in such meter. "Pope's brilliant gift for versification is exercised within the limits of a form inadequate for true philosophic poetry, and by its very presence excluding it." [97] Arnold even argues that it was the sway of the French alexandrine that hindered Molière from being a tragic poet, "in spite of his having gifts for this highest form of dramatic poetry which are immeasurably superior to those of any other French poet." Molière had "far too sound an instinct to attempt [tragedy] with inadequate means" and therefore "confined himself to comedy." Forced by this hypothesis (though it is, to say the least, unverifiable) Arnold suggests that Molière was even in his comedies "hampered and lamed" by the alexandrine, "so that this true and great poet is actually most satisfactory in his prose." Yet if it is true that Molière's temper was tragic, one must seek for it in the rhymed plays, *Le Misanthrope* and *Le Tartuffe,* which come nearest to tragedy, and not in *L'Avare, Georges Dandin,* and *Les Fourberies de Scapin,* which Arnold singles out for praise.[98] The condemnation of the alexandrine extends to all French poetry, a judgment for which Arnold has, of course, much English and French precedent, even in Sainte-Beuve. "Set [a Frenchman] to write poetry, he is limited, artificial, and impotent" [99] is Arnold's generalization, several years after the publication of *Les Fleurs du mal,* which heralded the great movement of modern French poetry.

The whole discussion *On Translating Homer* into English shows Arnold's constant assumption of inherent fixed characteristics in special metrical forms. He considers the ballad meter essentially inferior to the hexameter and argues that Homer *must* be translated in hexameters. Arnold himself provided several rather wooden specimens of a hexameter translation which are surely inferior as poetry to Pope's "inadequate" couplets and even to Tennyson's later blank verse. Arnold does not recognize that the English hexameter is quite different from Homer's and thus just as "inadequate" as blank verse or Chapman's long line, and that insistence on a particular metrical pattern begs the question of *English* poetry. The whole theory of the grand style is vitiated by this belief in form apart from meaning. Arnold is convinced of the uniform nobility and elevation of Homer whatever the subject matter or theme, and uses this preconception as the main argument against the translation of F. W. Newman. Newman, in his rebuttal, to my mind rightly, argued that Homer "rises and sinks with his subject and is often homely and prosaic." [100] But Arnold in his reply implicitly denies that the grand style in his sense is the high style of antiquity, the opposite of *sermo pedestris;* he can still argue that Homer "sheds over the simplest matter he touches the charm of his grand manner; he makes everything noble." [101]

Similarly Milton is often treated as "a great artist in the great style whatever may be said as to the subject of the poem." [102] Arnold's last critical pronouncement, the address on Milton (February 1888), is a hymn to the artist in the grand style who provides an increasing mass of readers ignorant of Greek and Latin the vicarious experience of ancient grandeur. *Paradise Regained* is cited as an example of "the incomparable charm of Milton's power of poetic style which . . . makes a great poem of a work in which Milton's imagination does not soar high." [103]

But mostly the theory of the grand style (derived from Sir Joshua Reynolds) takes up the Longinian motif of the sublime style as the expression of a great soul. It allows him to speak of Richelieu as a "man in the grand style" [104] or of Spinoza as "a character in the grand style." [105] The literary meaning is submerged in a common metaphor. More often style in a poet means something moral and ethical as well. What is valuable in Sophocles is "the grand moral effects produced by the style. For the style is the expression of the nobility of the poet's character." [106] In Keats he finds "that stamp of high work which is akin to character, which is character passing into intellectual production," [107] and sees "the *ethical* influences of style in language,—its close relations . . . with character." [108]

Grand style requires a grand subject. The grand style is stated to "arise in poetry when a noble nature, poetically gifted, treats with simplicity or with severity a serious subject." [109] Thus two distinct types of the grand style are allowed: a simple grand style represented by Homer, and a severe grand style represented by Milton. Arnold prefers the simple Homeric style as more "magical." The severe style has something "intellectual" [110] about it, and is thus presumably less poetic. Dante is allowed to have both the simple and the severe style in alternation.[111] But the term "grand style," Arnold admits, is ultimately "indefinable." [112]

Ideally, at least, Arnold often requires a balance between content and form. In Wordsworth there is "a balance of profound truth of subject with profound truth of execution." [113] "A congruity between conception and expression, which when both are poetical, is the poet's highest result." [114] At times, though rarely, Arnold has insight into the reciprocity of metrical form and matter. In discussing Wordsworth's "Lucy Gray" and "Ruth," Arnold draws attention to the more complex stanza of the latter poem. "Who does not perceive," he comments, "how the greater fulness and weight of his matter has here compelled the true and feeling poet to adopt a form of more *volume* than the simple ballad-form?" [115]

Arnold is well aware of the central importance of totality and unity in art. The idea of "totality" appears early in his critical vocabulary: the 1853 Preface makes much of the "grandiose effect of the whole," the "total-impression" (Arnold spells the term with a hyphen) and of *architectonice,* something suggested to him by Goethe's reflections on dilettantism. The ancients are contrasted with the moderns on this point. "They regarded the whole, we regard the parts." [116] These terms recur in later essays and are varied by the addition of such phrases as the "spirit which goes through her [George Sand's] work as a whole," [117] or "a supreme total effect," [118] or "the *symmetria prisca* of the Greeks," [119] or "composition," or "grouping" used in a painter's sense. These terms are used to express standards of judgment. *Paradise Lost* has "architectonics," [120] as have *Lear* and *Agamemnon,* but Keats was not ripe for the "architectonics of poetry." [121] *Faust* is disjointed and "can never produce the single, powerful total-impression"; [122] Emerson's poems fail, as he never produces a "plain, forcible, inevitable whole"; [123] Byron was an improviser. His poetic work could not have "first grown and matured in his own mind, and then come forth as an organic whole." [124] The *Giaour* is "a string of passages, not a work moving by a deep internal law of development to a necessary end." "Our total impression from it cannot but receive from this, its inherent defect, a certain dimness and indistinctness." [125] *Anna Karenina* suffers from having too many characters "if we look in it for a work of art in which the action shall be vigorously one, and to that one action everything shall converge." [126]

Arnold's more celebrated proposal to use "touchstones," "infallible touchstones," "short passages, even single lines" [127] as a norm for judging poetry is an obvious contradiction of the insight into unity, an atomistic principle that may be used to justify the most willful and erratic prejudices. Arnold himself, however, warns against a mechanical application of the touchstones. "These few lines, if we have tact and can use them, are enough even of themselves to keep clear and sound our judgments about poetry, to save us from fallacious estimates of it, to conduct us to a real estimate." [128] But he admits that it is not easy to apply such lines to other poetry. "Of course we are not to require this other poetry to resemble them; it may be very dissimilar." [129] The touchstones enumerated in "The Study of Poetry" are eleven passages, three each from Homer, Dante, and Milton, two from Shakespeare, all in a tone of sadness, melancholy, or resignation. A whole book has been written to show that the mood and theme of each can be found almost everywhere in Arnold's own poetry and notebooks and in his prose writings, and that they are thus based rather on a "personal" than on a "real" estimate.[130] They are, no doubt, all fine passages but, as specimens of great poetry, extremely limited in range. They are not always representative of their authors and often hardly comprehensible outside of their context. But touchstones can be defended as a "tip for mobilizing our sensibility, for focusing our relevant experiences in a sensitive point, for reminding us

vividly of what the best is like." [131] Yet they are of very limited usefulness in practical criticism and they have been frequently abused
by Arnold's admirers, almost comically by learned but insensitive
scholars such as Albert S. Cook [132] and Lane Cooper, [133] and even by
T. S. Eliot, who is not above quoting one of Arnold's touchstones,
Dante's "E'n la sua voluntad è nostra pace," [134] as a kind of critical
blunderbuss. Arnold is not responsible for the mistakes of his followers, but he plays bad tricks with touchstones himself. Thus he
takes two prosaic lines from Pope and the first two lines from
Dryden's *The Hind and the Panther* and "overthrows" them by
quoting against them a line from *Hamlet*, another from *Paradise
Lost,* and a third from the *Prioress' Tale,*[135] and just before this he
has thrown the Dante verse at Chaucer. "The accent of such verse
is altogether beyond Chaucer's reach." [136] In the essay on Gray a
single line from Shakespeare is used to demonstrate the falseness of
a single line from Goldsmith, and three lines from Pindar show up
Dryden's ode on the death of Mrs. Killigrew.[137] The method becomes patently absurd when two lines each from French, English
and German poetry are supposed to prove the inferiority of French
poetry in general.[138] Arnold quotes a song from Beaumont and
Fletcher's *The Bloody Brother* and a bit from Heine's *Lazarus* ("Der
Sterbende") against two poorish lines from the *Journal* of Eugénie
de Guérin,[139] a writer who has no status whatever even among the
minor French poets of the Romantic Age. Almost as bad is the
attempt to prove the deficiency of German poetry in style, "its style
of prose as much as poetry," by taking two sententious lines from
Goethe's *Tasso,*

> Es bildet ein Talent sich in der Stille,
> sich ein Character in dem Strom der Welt,[140]

and quoting against them the passage on blindness, rolling out
"Blind Thamyris and blind Maeonides" from *Paradise Lost.*[141] One
could easily invent counter-examples—two lines, for instance, from
the chorus of angels in *Faust* against some prosy speeches of God the
Father in *Paradise Lost.* One could produce some fine passages in
Hugo and Musset and quote them against a tortured quibbling
piece from *The Rape of Lucrece,* as Emile Légouis has done in his
defense of French poetry.[142] But the game is not worth the candle.
Single passages prove nothing. Even "E'n la sua voluntad è nostra
pace" is no longer poetry taken out of context and is not even verse.

It is comparable to "And the peace of God which passeth all understanding" or "And our hope of you is stedfast" [143] as an impressive
and memorable formula, but it is no infallible touchstone of poetry.
Voluminous authors like Dante cannot be represented by one or
two lines, nor can centuries or whole national traditions.

Arnold's stereotyped phrases and formulas are unfortunately the
best remembered side of his criticism. He knew it himself and
treated his pet phrases with proper irony. In "A Liverpool Address"
(1882) he draws his accepted image as a "nearly worn-out man of
letters," "with a frippery of phrases about sweetness and light,
seeing things as they really are, knowing the best that has been
thought and said in the world, which never had very much solid
meaning, and have now quite lost the gloss and charm of novelty." [144]
The range and variety of Arnold's criticism belie such a superficial
indictment. It seems necessary to survey his essays in an attempt
to rank them and to point out some of their virtues and shortcomings.

The two early prefaces (to the *Poems*, 1853, and to *Merope*, 1858)
are manifestoes of neoclassicism, reassertions of the superiority of
the ancients over the moderns, defenses of right subject matter, of
action, *mythos*, in the Aristotelian sense. The *Merope* preface is the
only passage in Arnold I know of where he discusses a genre theory:
he believes the aim of tragedy is to conduct us to "a sentiment of
sublime acquiescence in the course of fate, and in the dispensations
of human life." [145] Temperamentally Arnold had to accept the stoic
version of Aristotle, even though he had just read Jakob Bernays,[146]
who might have taught him a more accurate interpretation.

In 1857 Arnold began his lectures as Professor of Poetry at Oxford
with "On the Modern Element in Literature." It was a memorable
occasion for two reasons: English instead of Latin was used for the
first time, and his lecture with its sweeping survey of history
announced the arrival of historicism in official English literary
history. That lecture and the two printed lecture series, *On Translating Homer* (1861) and *On The Study of Celtic Literature* (1867),
have already been discussed sufficiently. The *Essays in Criticism*
(1865) came in between and are made up of essays published in the
two preceding years. The two first essays in the volume, "The Function of Criticism at the Present Time" and "The Literary Influence
of Academies," are Arnold's most formal and most eloquent pleas
for criticism and the critical spirit. The whole volume clearly shows

the influence of Sainte-Beuve; not only are the essays on the two Guérins and on Joubert suggested by Sainte-Beuve's essays on these writers: they are also (as is the essay on Marcus Aurelius) portraits in Sainte-Beuve's sense: deft blends of biography, liberal quotation, and psychological observation. Arnold has been blamed for wasting his energy on three minor French writers, but he wanted to paint unknown figures as part of his program of arousing "curiosity," and he was drawn to them by sympathetic interest in the religious and contemplative temper of his sitters. This was enough. We may object only to the English parallels drawn by Arnold. Maurice de Guérin, we are told, had "more distinction and power" than Keats,[147] and Coleridge comes off second best to Joubert in "delicacy and penetration" as well as "joy." [148] The whole conception of Joubert as "a French Coleridge" (the original title of the essay) must be explained by Arnold's deliberate ignoring of Coleridge's poetic achievement and by his quite insufficient knowledge of the whole scope of Coleridge's philosophical and critical work. The essay on Academies, which presents the moderate thesis that the institution of an academy might have done something to combat the eccentricities of English literature, was suggested by Sainte-Beuve's review of a new edition of the history of the French Academy by Pellison and d'Olivet.[149]

The essay on Heine, which has been much admired, seems to me the least satisfactory of the literary essays in the volume. Arnold, from a perspective which is French in its sources, considers Heine the follower and heir of Goethe, on whom "incomparably the largest portion of Goethe's mantle fell." [150] The emphasis on Heine as the "brilliant soldier in the Liberation War of humanity" [151] is quite speciously linked up with Goethe's very differently meant saying about himself that he had been the Liberator of the Germans.[152] The admiration for Heine's "culture" ("he had all the culture of Germany; in his head fermented all the ideas of modern Europe") [153] seems excessive if one knows Heine's gross simplifications of German philosophy, while the condescending attitude to his morals strikes one as unpleasantly smug. Arnold consistently disparaged German romanticism, of which he could have had only an indistinct notion. Coupling Novalis and Rückert [154] seems sufficient proof of his ignorance, as is the opinion that Heine had "a far profounder sense of the mystic and romantic charm of the Middle Age than

Goerres, or Brentano, or Arnim." [155] In a letter to Sainte-Beuve, Arnold ridicules the idea (advanced by Madame Blaze de Bury in an article in the *Revue des Deux Mondes*) that his own poetry and that of his contemporaries was derived from Shelley's. "It is as if one ascribed to Jean Paul and Novalis rather than to Goethe and Schiller the whole literary movement in Germany in the last fifty years." [156] But in 1854 this would have been much nearer the truth: E. T. A. Hoffmann, Stifter, Keller (whose *Grüner Heinrich* came out in 1854), and even Heine himself show much more clearly the influence of Jean Paul and the romantics than that of Goethe and Schiller. Arnold takes Carlyle to task for overrating the German romantics in comparison with Heine; but when Carlyle's articles and translations were done (1827–30) Heine was only beginning to emerge from obscurity. Arnold does not, to my mind, see the real greatness of Heine's poetry and quotes quite mediocre specimens from *Reisebilder* and *Romancero*. Arnold fails precisely in his professed aim "to mark [Heine's] place in modern European letters, and the special tendency and significance of what he did." [157] For Arnold has, strangely enough, a purely ideological, liberal perspective on German literature and interprets even Goethe as "that grand dissolvent," the propounder of a "profound, imperturbable naturalism," a man "radically detached from this [old European] order." [158] But Goethe was neither a dissolvent nor a naturalist nor an enemy of the old order.

Arnold had a very wide acquaintance with Goethe's writings; he quotes him many times and enters many of Goethe's sayings in his *Notebooks;* he knew not only the famous works, such as *Werther, Wilhelm Meister,* and *Faust,* not only Eckermann and Riemer, but also many nooks and corners of Goethe's writings, including the *Geschichte der Farbenlehre, Anmerkungen zu Rameaus Neffe,* and many of his scattered articles on literature. But he cares for Goethe obviously rather as a sage than as a poet and interprets his wisdom far too uniformly in support of his own liberal religion and "active" stoicism.[159] No doubt other motifs in Goethe appealed to Arnold and influenced him. He admired Goethe's critical spirit so highly that he called him "the greatest critic of all times," [160] the "supreme critic." [161] He admired Goethe's cosmopolitanism, his devotion to antiquity and, above all, his ideal of culture, of self-realization and humanity. But Arnold wavered on Goethe's status as a poet: he quotes and approves of Wordsworth's saying that Goethe's poetry is not "inevitable enough" [162] and summarizes, without much disagreement, the extremely cool essay by Scherer. He endorses Scherer's low opinion of the second part of *Faust*,[163] which may seem to us preposterous but was, at that time, shared even by German critics such as F. T. Vischer.

Almost half of the *Essays in Criticism* concern literature only marginally and foreshadow Arnold's growing absorption in religious problems. Ten years elapsed after the publication of the book on *Celtic Literature* (1867) before Arnold returned to literary criticism. He did so cautiously at first, reproducing, with little comment, two reviews by Edmond Scherer on Milton and Goethe (1877). The only other literary piece in *Mixed Essays* (1879) is an obituary of George Sand, a glowing tribute to her generosity and humanitarianism rather than a criticism of her works. The only literary essay that appears in *Irish Essays and Others* (1882) is the very interesting piece on "The French Play in London" (1879), Arnold's fullest pronouncement on French tragedy and Molière on occasion of a visit of the *Comédie Française* to London. Between 1882 and 1884 Arnold wrote unsigned letters ("Letters of an Old Playgoer") to the *Pall Mall Gazette* which show his remarkable presentiment of a rebirth of the English stage and contain his curiously adverse comments on *Hamlet*. It is a "tantalizing and ineffective play," it is not a "drama followed with perfect comprehension and profound emotion . . . but a problem soliciting interpretation and solution." [164]

During these years a definite change in Arnold's techniques and attitudes took place. He emancipated himself completely from the influence of Sainte-Beuve.[165] He found a new tone of judicial criticism. Even the essays that preserve the earlier method, the late pieces on "Amiel" (1887) and on "Shelley" (1888), show the change. The essay on Amiel is surprisingly unsympathetic. Arnold, apparently reacting against the praise lavished on Amiel by Scherer and Arnold's own niece, Mrs. Humphry Ward, treats his philosophy as "perfectly futile," [166] "unprofitable," [167] ridicules his desire for totality and infinitude, deplores his pessimism, and finds value only in his literary opinions. The essay on Shelley is a review of Dowden's two-volume *Life*: it is professedly concerned not with Shelley's work but with his biography and character. Arnold deplores Dowden's attempt to whitewash Shelley in his relation to Harriet; he has to take refuge in French words like *bête* and *sale* to express his horror at Shelley's set and world; [168] he calls Shelley's actions "not entirely sane"; still he concludes by repeating his earlier phrase about "the beautiful and ineffectual angel, beating in the void his luminous wings in vain." [169] It is hard to see how Arnold could, on his own terms, have defended such a complete dualism in viewing Shelley's life and poetry, his ethics and art. But Arnold died before he could write the essay on Shelley's work he had intended.

The essay on Tolstoy (1887) is Arnold's only piece of criticism on a novelist. It seems disappointing today as it is largely *reportage,* an account of the plot and characters of *Anna Karenina* and of Tolstoy's first tracts after conversion, which Arnold had read in French translation. Arnold's sense of the continuity between *Anna Karenina* and the post-conversion Tolstoy is sound. The whole essay must be judged historically as an example of Arnold's "curiosity" for what was then a new literature.[170] It must be seen also as instigated by Arnold's distaste for the French realistic novel. The contrast between the French "bitterness, cruelty, and lubricity" illustrated by *Madame Bovary* and the wholesomely clean moralism of Tolstoy is always in Arnold's mind.

But Arnold's newly found certainty and authority are most boldly and memorably expressed in the series of essays devoted to the English romantic poets: the introductions to his anthologies of Wordsworth (1879) and Byron (1881) and to the selections from Gray and Keats in Humphry Ward's *English Poets* (1880). The actual ranking of the romantic poets was long settled in Arnold's mind; it is publicly announced in the Heine essay,[171] but it is argued fully in the later essays. It is too well known to require more than the briefest summary: Wordsworth and, after him, Byron are the two greatest poets of the age; Keats—though falling short of actual accomplishment—is a great promise. Shelley and Coleridge are definitely inferior.

Arnold's preference for Wordsworth is admirably defended. The anthology shows in detail that he loved the pastoral, serene Wordsworth above the speculative and mystical. The protest against the attempt to extract a philosophy of nature and ethics from Wordsworth is perfectly defensible if one remembers Arnold's desire to dismiss Wordsworth's *formal* philosophy. But one should not forget that Arnold actually values Wordsworth for the cognitive element in him, for "seeing into the life of things." [172] Arnold, however, does not quite recognize the intellectual subtlety and profundity of Wordsworth's poetry and overstates his "provincialism" and lack of book learning. He told John Morley that Wordsworth was a "boor," [173] and he reproached Wordsworth for not having read Goethe.[174] But Wordsworth, who knew no German or very little, did read *Wilhelm Meister* and "The Bride of Corinth," in translation and was disgusted by Goethe's "inhuman sensuality." [175]

The preference for Byron as the second greatest poet is harder to defend. Arnold understands the arguments against Byron's artistry and mind, citing examples of the "slovenliness and tunelessness of much of Byron's production." He considers Byron's "most crying faults as a man—his vulgarity, his affectation,—as akin to the faults of commonness, of want of art, in his workmanship as a poet." [176] Outside of the essay in question Arnold refers even more sternly to Byron's "deep grain of coarseness and commonness, his affectation, his brutal selfishness." [177] He constantly disparages his intellect, quoting Goethe's saying that Byron is a child when he reflects.[178] Byron seems to Arnold "an ordinary nineteenth-century English gentleman, with little culture and with no ideas." But in spite of all these reservations Arnold exalts Byron as "the greatest natural force, the greatest elementary power" in English poetry since Shakespeare.[179] His admiration has mainly political motives: Byron is an enemy of cant and Philistinism, a great fighter in the war for the liberation of mankind. Byron, Arnold feels strongly, is fundamentally sincere in spite of all his theatrical preludings. While he admits Byron's ill success in creating characters and actions and in making artistic wholes, he admires him also as a poet for his "wonderful power of vividly conceiving a single incident, a single situation." [180] Arnold's anthology shows clearly what he liked in Byron: descriptive and narrative passages, rhetorical reflections. But any defense of Byron as a poet must be based largely on *Don Juan* and *The Vision of Judgment*. Arnold gives only small fragments of the satires and thus cannot present a persuasive argument for Byron's importance as a poet. Arnold's Byron is still the Byron of *Childe Harold* and even of the *Giaour* and *Lara*. The precedent of Goethe and Taine, the preoccupation with liberalism which in

Arnold's mind made the oddly assorted succession Goethe-Byron-Heine the main current of European literature, and the polemical intent against the exaltation of artistry among his contemporaries help to explain Arnold's desire to preserve Byron's reputation as the greatest figure of the early 19th century. But these considerations hardly justify Arnold's comparative disparagement of Keats, Shelley, and Coleridge, who all nowadays seem much greater poets than Byron.

Keats stands highest among these poets in Arnold's eyes. Arnold, with the Victorian gentleman's smugness toward despair and passion, deplores the letters to Fanny Brawne, "their abandonment of all reticence and dignity," in which he sees "something underbred and ignoble, as of a youth ill brought up." [181] At the same time Arnold recognizes "elements of high character" in Keats,[182] even of "flint and iron," [183] and "lucidity," which "is in itself akin to character." [184] He acknowledges that Keats' passion for the Beautiful was "an intellectual and spiritual passion." [185] He emphasizes, however, Keats' "natural magic," in which "he ranks with Shakespeare." [186] He underscores, excessively to my mind, the idea that Keats was not ripe for "moral interpretation." He admires rightly the great odes for their "rounded perfection," but does not think *Hyperion* a success.[187] Keats, though greatly admired, is seen too much as a mere promise.

Shelley is criticized as a man and hardly as a writer. But there are scattered passages that concern his work. To say that the pieces by Shelley in Palgrave's *Golden Treasury* are "a gallery of his failures" [188] shows a complete lack of appreciation even for the best in Shelley, and to prefer the translations, the "delightful Essays and Letters," to the poetry seems puzzling. One may perhaps suppose Arnold was thinking mainly of the *Defence of Poetry*.[189] Arnold is quite unjust when he contrasts Shelley's choice of topics—Queen Mab, the Witch of Atlas, The Sensitive Plant—with Byron's George the Third, Lord Castlereagh, the Duke of Wellington, and Southey. Shelley wrote on the same people even better, and Byron has his own fancy Orient and Tahiti, as unreal as anything in Shelley.[190] One must admit, however, that Arnold genuinely felt Shelley to be inferior in his handling of words (i.e., diction), while he admitted the musical (prosodic) qualities of his poetry,[191] and that Arnold, while accepting Byron's liberalism, was repelled by

Shelley's "nonsense about tyrants and priests." [192] The neglect of Coleridge as a poet is puzzling; as far as I know, the poetry of Coleridge is never mentioned by Arnold.

But however much we may disagree with Arnold's ranking of the poets and ages, he accomplished the main task of a practical critic: the sifting of the tradition, the arrangement or rearrangement of the past, the discrimination among currents, major and minor. The table of the English poets was fixed by Arnold for a long time to come. But Arnold's defense of the critical spirit, his theory of criticism with its emphasis on the real estimate, and even his discussion of the concept of poetry (limited as it is by his didacticism) were a great contribution to English criticism. Arnold, almost single-handedly, pulled English criticism out of the doldrums into which it had fallen after the great Romantic Age.

With Arnold we can group two critics, Walter Bagehot and Leslie Stephen, who, in general, share his concerns. As they are fundamentally didactic in outlook and conservative in taste, they may be contrasted with the aesthetic movement that we shall treat below.

WALTER BAGEHOT (1826–1877)

Bagehot has been called by a good judge "one of the freshest and alertest of the neglected Victorian writers," [1] and some twenty years ago a well-argued thesis [2] proposed him as a significant critic who anticipated American neohumanism. But Bagehot seems not very important today, though he is sane, representative, and symptomatic enough to deserve some attention. For him the center of literature is occupied by the great normal geniuses, the "painters of essential human nature" [3] such as Shakespeare and Scott. Shakespeare is a universal man who conveys a "general impression of entire calmness and equability." [4] Scott has a steady insight, "a peculiar healthiness," "a conservative imagination" whose principal object is "the structure—the undulation and diversified composition of human society." He has an accurate knowledge of political economy—high praise from an editor of *The Economist;* Scott knows that the world is neither a world of exact justice nor an "uncared-for world" deserted by God. [5] Bagehot sees Scott's failings and limitations: his sentimental view of woman, his lack of a searching, abstract intellect, his indifference to the deeper reaches of the soul. But even these

deficiencies are paradoxically virtues. In politics and theology
Bagehot praised "stupidity," the prejudice of Burke or the ignorance of Bishop Butler, who were his intellectual masters. Bagehot
sees, for instance, the national appeal of the poetry of Cowper in
"these exact delineations of what the English people really prefer,"
"torpid, in-door, tea-tabular felicity." [6]

Compared to these "normal" authors most others seem to
Bagehot eccentric, "unsymmetrical." Dickens "has been led by a sort
of pre-Raphaelite *cultus* of reality" into error: he gives us caricatures instead of people. "You could no more fancy Sam Weller, or
Mark Tapley, or the Artful Dodger really existing, than you can
fancy a talking duck or a writing bear." His poor people "have taken
to their poverty very thoroughly." "A tone of objection to the
necessary constitution of human society" [7] displeases the Tory
critic. He prefers Thackeray for his "stern and humble realism,"
but also objects that Thackeray "thought too much of social
inequalities" and distinctions but in his writings "was too severe on
those who, in cruder and baser ways, showed that they also were
thinking much." [8] Bagehot classes Laurence Sterne with Thackeray
for his pity and humanity, but is repelled by Sterne's oddity: his
"antediluvian fun," his indecency, his utter lack of form and order.
Since Bagehot pronounces that "an imperative law of the writing
art is that a book should go straight on" and that "eccentricity is no
fit subject for literary art," he must conclude that *Tristram Shandy*
is an example of "barbarous, provincial art": "redolent of an
inferior society." [9]

Bagehot's toleration for deviations from his ideal, well-centered
man varies in different essays. Hartley Coleridge is treated with
sympathy as a charming dreamer who never "grasped the idea of
fact and reality." [10] Clough is admired for his struggles with an
undefinable religion, and his poetry defended as "intellectual
poetry" of limited appeal but genuine merit.[11] On the other hand,
Béranger is disparaged as a common, genial, skeptical, democratic
man who appears to Bagehot particularly French in his limitations.
He lacks "*back* thought." He has no access to the "strong, noble
imagination," "the solid stuff" [12] in which the English excel.

Surprisingly, and possibly inconsistently, there comes a point at
which Bagehot transcends this somewhat commonplace ideal of
normal art. Off and on he adopts the romantic concepts of the

imagination and nature: mainly, it would appear, from Hazlitt, whom he greatly admired and whose style and method must have influenced him.[13] Imagination is "a living thing, a kind of growing plant" beyond the limits of consciousness, working unseen, in a state of "stealing calm." Imagination "detects the secrets of the universe, explains Nature, reveals what is above Nature." [14] It is "a glancing faculty" which loves contrasts and opposites. Shakespeare's imagination, says Bagehot, dimly echoing Coleridge's formula, "seems to be floating between the contrasts of things." [15] Bagehot sees no evidence for any difference between imagination and fancy, but assigns to fancy a subordinate role of amplification and ornamentation.[16] Wordsworth and Shelley represent this realm of imagination, which is for Bagehot the realm of the highest and purest poetry. He chides Jeffrey for dismissing Wordsworth's mysticism. "The misfortune is that mysticism is true," that there is "a religion of Nature, or more exactly, the religion of the imagination." [17] Wordsworth's "works are the Scriptures of the intellectual life," because of "this haunting, supernatural, mystical view of Nature." [18] Though Bagehot disapproved of Shelley's politics and religion, he classes him with Wordsworth for his "classical," pure imagination: simple, abstract, aspiring to the unconditioned. He treats him sympathetically even as a person: his impulsive temperament "passes through evil, but preserves its purity." Keats contrasts with Shelley as a fanciful, ornamental, romantic poet. Keats used to pepper his tongue, "to enjoy in all the grandeur the cool flavour of delicious claret," while Shelley was a "water-drinker." [19] Surprisingly, and most unjustly, S. T. Coleridge is found lacking in the proper romantic nature worship: he was, after a brief Wordsworthian phase, "utterly destitute of any perception of beauty in landscape or nature." [20] Equally unjustly Bagehot condemns Pope as the "poet of fashionable life" which has "no reference whatever to the beauties of the material universe." "The poetry (if such it is) of Pope would be just as true if all the trees were yellow and all the grass flesh-colour." [21]

In Bagehot's most ambitious literary essay, "Wordsworth, Tennyson, and Browning: or Pure, Ornate and Grotesque Art in English Poetry" (1864), this typology is elaborated at length. The pure, imaginative, classical Wordsworth contrasts with the ornate, fanciful, romantic Tennyson and with the grotesque, realistic, medieval

Browning. Keats would be grouped with Tennyson, Shelley with Wordsworth. Milton is brought into the scheme as combining a simple classical subject matter with ornate, profuse imagery.[22] The details of the characterization seem often doubtful: the medievalism of Browning is overplayed for the sake of the thesis—it apparently means only something like the minute realism of the pre-Raphaelites—and obviously the term "classical" applies to Wordsworth and Shelley in too peculiar a meaning to find acceptance. The historical continuity from Wordsworth to Tennyson, from Shelley to Browning is ignored. But the game of contrasts among the three poets gives occasion for Bagehot's most interesting proposal: "We want a word *literatesque,* fit to be put into a book," on the analogy of *picturesque,* "fit to be put into a picture." "Literatesque" would mean "that perfect combination in *subject-matter* of literature, which suits the *art* of literature." It is the "typical form, the rememberable idea." "The business of the poet is with types; and those types are mirrored in reality." "The poet must find in that reality, the *literatesque* man, the *literatesque* scene, which nature intends for him, and which will live in his page." [23] Bagehot is well aware of the ancestry of his notion: he appeals to the debate between Schiller and Goethe on the *Urpflanze.* The symbolic plant is the type and "Goethe was right in searching for this in reality and nature; Schiller was right in saying that it was an 'idea.' " In modern poetry this "type" is the poet himself. Of course the poet does "not describe himself *as* himself: autobiography is not his object; he takes himself as a specimen of human nature . . . He takes such of his moods as are most characteristic, as most typify certain moods of certain men, or certain moods of all men." Poets describe what is "generic, not what is special and individual." [24]

In a different context Bagehot arrived at this personal but typical poetry by way of a history of genres. "Poetry begins in Impersonality. Homer is a voice." Dramatic art, Greek drama in particular, is a transition to the lyric, which expresses some one mood, some single sentiment, some isolated longing in human nature. It deals not with man as a whole, but with man piecemeal. Lyrical poets must not be judged literally from their lyrics, since these are "discourses" (what I suppose would be called in German *Rollenlyrik*). But the modern poet is neither epic, nor dramatic, nor lyric in the old sense. He is "self-delineative": he depicts his mind "viewed as a whole." Modern "egotistical" poetry, that of Wordsworth or Shelley or Byron, is actually "allied to the epic," [25] since it is concerned with the delineation of one character, one hero, as Homer with Achilles or Vergil with Aeneas.

Bagehot returns to the portrait or character of the poet in all his essays but to the representative, universalized character—for "art can only deal with the universal," with the idea, the typical and representative.[26] In practice this often means the average national type: Béranger or Cowper, neither of whom expresses the highest possibilities of his respective nation; or it means the universal man represented by Shakespeare. In an essay "Shakespeare—the Man" (1853) Bagehot defends the view that personality must be discernible through writings even where we have no biographical evidence. "A person who knows nothing of an author he has read, will not know much of the author whom he has seen." He quotes the description of the fleeing hare from *Venus and Adonis* (lines 679–708) and comments: "It is absurd, by the way, to say that we know *nothing* about the man who wrote that; we know that he has been after a hare. It is idle to allege that mere imagination would tell him that a hare is apt to run among a flock of sheep, or that its so doing disconcerts the scent of hounds." Shakespeare is contrasted with Scott, who had a much more limited "organization," and with Goethe, who seems to Bagehot "always a man apart from life." Goethe went to every scene "with a reserve and as a stranger. He went there *to experience*." Shakespeare was not merely "with men, but of men," a universal man, but also a man of the people. Though Bagehot sees something of Shakespeare's latent melancholy, his "insight into the musing life of man," his general portrait is disconcertingly Victorian: a "substantial man," "a judge of dogs," "an outdoor sporting man," a patriot distrusting the mob, etc.[27] Bagehot is too wary of the abnormal: he disparages even Falstaff as an artistic misconception and complains of Hamlet as a divided nature who seems to him an inferior subject for art.[28] Bagehot's central thesis about personality in writing may be right, but in practice he is unable to see in Shakespeare more than what he is looking for: the social and moral ideals of his time.

Bagehot's taste is limited, preoccupied with the normal, distrustful of everything eccentric, even Philistine in the Arnoldian sense. But in theory Bagehot hit upon an important theme: the "type," which almost simultaneously engaged the attention of Taine in France and Dobrolyubov in Russia. He gave it an original twist with the concept of "egotistical," "self-delineative," but representative poetry.

LESLIE STEPHEN (1832–1904)

No one can doubt the general distinction of Leslie Stephen in various fields: he was the first editor of the *Dictionary of National Biography* who alone contributed 378 articles; he wrote five volumes (Johnson, Pope, Swift, George Eliot, Hobbes) for the English Men of Letters series; he was a moral philosopher who expounded agnosticism and an evolutionary *Science of Ethics* (1882); and finally and most eminently he was an intellectual historian whose *History of English Thought in the Eighteenth Century* (1876) and the *English Utilitarians* (1900) put him possibly first among the neglected band of Victorian intellectual historians: Buckle, Lecky, John Morley, Flint, Merz, Adamson, to name only a few.

Strictly from the point of view of literary criticism Stephen's position and importance are debatable. Desmond MacCarthy in a lecture on Leslie Stephen (1937) called him "the least aesthetic of noteworthy critics" and complained that he is "deficient in the power of transmitting emotions he had derived himself from literature; he seldom, if ever, attempted to record a thrill." [1] Q. D. Leavis, on the other hand, thought such deficiency an asset, as criticism is "not a mystic rapture but a process of intelligence." [2] Stephen for her is a great critic precisely because he is a sturdy moralist, the true "Cambridge critic," presumably a spiritual ancestor of her husband. Noel G. Annan, in his excellent book on Stephen (1952), tried to strike a balance. He admits Stephen's limitations but still claims him as "Arnold's disciple" who "did for English fiction what Arnold had tried to do for poetry." [3]

The comparison with Arnold will not, however, withstand inspection. Stephen does not share his faith in classical humanism, either ancient or Goethean. He does not advocate culture, criticism, or an opening of doors to Continental winds of doctrine, and he does not believe in the future of poetry. As the review of Taine shows, he doubts the value of racial types, Celtic, Teutonic, and Latin, so prominent in Arnold's criticism. He never uses touchstones. In a lecture on Arnold (1893) Stephen himself says that Arnold's intellectual type was different from his own. "Had Arnold been called upon to pronounce judgment upon me, he must, however reluctantly, have put me down as a Philistine." [4] Philistinism surely means here Stephen's own basic utilitarianism, which he tried elaborately to reconcile with Darwinian evolutionism. It means, in literary criticism, a frank intellectualism and moralism.

The essay on "Wordsworth's Ethics" begins characteristically: "Under every poetry, it has been said, there lies a philosophy. Rather, it may almost be said, every poetry is a philosophy." [5] Anticipating the very phrasing of A. O. Lovejoy's statement that "ideas in literature are philosophical ideas in dilution," Stephen studies literature because "it holds a number of intellectual dogmas in solution." [6] He tries to extract from Wordsworth's poetry an ethics which, he confidently believes, will "fall spontaneously into a scientific system of thought." [7]

Stephen, however, is well aware of the difference between a philosophical treatise and a piece of imaginative literature. The whole aesthetic doctrine seems to him "a misstatement of the very undeniable and very ancient truth, that it is the poet's business, to present types, for example, and not to give bare psychological theory." [8] The poet must incarnate his thought in concrete imagery. "The morality, for example, of Goethe and Shakespeare appears in the presentation of such characters as Iago and Mephistopheles." [9] The role of criticism, or at least one of its roles, will be a translation into intellectual terms of what the poet has told us by characters and events. The title of one of Stephen's essays, "Pope as a Moralist," could analogously be given to almost all his other articles.

Of course Stephen is not content with this role of translator: he judges and ranks his authors according to their implied moral philosophies. The standard is that of a secular, social morality which teaches us to recognize the "surpassing value of manliness, honesty, and pure domestic affection" [10] but still has a sense of evil and a feeling for man's impotence and of the mystery around him. Shakespeare, Wordsworth, George Eliot, Scott meet these specifications, and of all writers Dr. Johnson appeals to Stephen most by his morality and his sense of personal doom. On a lower level are the good common-sense moralists like Pope and Fielding, who have their limitations. "We scarcely come into contact with man as he appears in presence of the infinite." [11] And then there are the writers whom Stephen calls morbid, great, and bitter men like Swift, warped, protesting women like Charlotte Brontë, extravagant cynics like Balzac, cloudy idealists such as Shelley, and insincere buffoons such as Sterne.

This is, no doubt, moralistic criticism, but it is literary criticism because it is concerned with the "world" of the poet, with his characters and events as they affect the characters, and with the literary value of the books, for Stephen is convinced of the basic identity of moral and aesthetic value. "The highest poetry must be that which expresses not only the richest but the healthiest nature," and "vicious feeling indicates some morbid tendency, and is so far destructive of the poetical faculty." "The vigour," he asserts, "with which a man grasps and assimilates a deep moral doctrine is a test of the degree in which he possesses one essential condition of the higher poetical excellence." [12] Within the limits of this conception Stephen analyzes the psychology of characters and the implicit morality of the chief English novelists from Defoe to Stevenson and applies the same procedure to dramatists like Shakespeare or Massinger, to poets like Pope, Gray, or Shelley and to essayists like De Quincey or Hazlitt. The criticism of books quite naturally passes into biography, into a judgment of the man rather than the work, for Stephen does not believe in the distinction. He can say that "the whole art of criticism consists in learning to know the human being who is partially revealed to us in his spoken or his written words." [13] He can identify the study of the life of Charlotte Brontë with the study of her novels,[14] and he can become involved in the most awkward conundrums about Pope's "sincerity," since he admires him as a moralist and still has to accept the evidence, accumulated by Elwin, of his "lying on the most stupendous scale." [15]

Though Stephen has a professional grasp of British empirical philosophy, he shies away from an analysis of the metaphysics, ontology, or even theory of knowledge of the writers he discusses. He brushes off Wordsworth's "mysticism," sneers at Coleridge's philosophy, and treats Shelley's Godwinian sensationalism and Platonic idealism as mere romantic moonshine. Nor do we get, of course, any analysis of technique, language, or composition, whether in poetry or in fiction. He does on occasion recognize that "the technical merits of form can hardly be separated from the merits of substance," [16] but usually he "leaves such points to critics of finer perception and a greater command of superlatives." [17] The essay on Sterne has nothing whatever to say about *Tristram Shandy* as a novel—its parody of the novel form, its handling of time, etc. The essays on Shelley and Coleridge shirk any discussion of the poetry. When Stephen recommends the address to Chaos from *The Dunciad*,[18] he quotes other people's opinions but carefully refrains from endorsing their praise. Occasional comments on Defoe's devices to enhance credibility [19] or Richardson's difficulties with the epistolary form [20] or Massinger's prosaic blank verse [21] are so rare that MacCarthy's conclusion about Stephen's criticism as the "least aesthetic" seems amply justified.

The moralistic point of view overrides also the historical and social point of view in Stephen. At first sight he seems imbued with the historical method of his time. Certainly *English Thought in the Eighteenth Century* contains passages that define the character of imaginative literature as a "function of many forces" [22]—the current philosophy, the inherited peculiarities of the race, its history, its climate, its social and political relations. The late lectures *English Literature and Society in the Eighteenth Century* (1904) treat literature "as a particular function of the whole social organism," [23] and Stephen's biographer, F. W. Maitland, reports that "I have heard him maintain that philosophical thought and imaginative literature . . . are but a sort of by-product of social evolution, or, as he once put it, 'the noise that the wheels make as they go round.' " [24] But however closely Stephen studies the relations between literature and history or between literature and the audience to which it was addressed, he is never willing to embrace the consequences of a sociological method—its complete determinism, its moral indifference, its relativistic suspension of judgment, its elimination of the individual. He complains that the "exaltation of the historical method threatens to become a part of our contemporary cant" [25] and ridicules the historical method if it means "accepting beliefs as fact without troubling about their reasons." [26] Even while he strongly recommends the study of English history and intellectual currents to the student of English literature, he recognizes that there is "a vast difference between what is called knowing a thing's history and really knowing the thing itself." [27] He holds firmly to a fixed standard of morality which alone lifts him above the flux of history and allows him to judge literature, even though he himself, paradoxically enough, in his *Science of Ethics* tried to explain even ethics as a result of the process of evolution.

But apart from morality and truth Stephen has no standards or theory for literature. He expressly denies that there can be a science of aesthetics or any general rules or principles of criticism, even though he recommends that the critic proceed in a scientific spirit, with due regard to facts, dispassionately, with "a certain modesty in expression and diffidence in forming opinions." [28] At most, he grants "that there is surely no harm in a man's announcing his individual taste, if he expressly admits that he is not prescribing to the tastes of others." [29] He can even say that "all criticism is a nuisance and a parasitic growth upon literature." [30] "The one great service a critic can render is to keep vice, vulgarity, or stupidity at bay." [31] It seems significant that we hear nothing of ugliness or bad art.

Ultimately Stephen simply distrusts art. Like his utilitarian and evangelical friends he concedes that "there is a good deal to be said for the thesis that all fiction is really a kind of lying, and that art in general is a luxurious indulgence, to which we have no right whilst crime and disease are rampant in the outer world." [32] He defends the author's comments in the novels of Fielding and Thackeray with an argument which makes him hardly a safe guide to fiction. "A child dislikes to have the illusion broken, and is angry if you try to persuade him that Giant Despair was not a real personage like his favourite Blunderbore. But the attempt to produce such illusions is really unworthy of a work intended for full-grown readers." [33]

This basic skepticism and even nihilism about the value of literature and the rights of criticism are the reasons for the present neglect of Stephen as a critic. His certainties are purely moral, not metaphysical or aesthetic, and even his acute moralistic criticism will be felt today narrowly circumscribed by his view of human nature and history. His moral vision, earnest, public-spirited, upright as it is, seems cramped by the complacencies and facile assumptions of his positivistic and utilitarian creed. We can fully recognize his great historical merits, especially in his defense of the kindred values of 18th-century literature. We can admire the sober analytical skill of many of his essays (especially in *Hours in a Library*, a collection greatly superior to the *Studies of a Biographer*) . But we must admit the grave limitations of a sensibility that treats literature either as a moral statement in disguise or as a social and psychological document. It is hard to believe that Stephen's criticism can be made to speak to our time.

OUR IMAGE of American criticism in the thirties and forties (Volume 3 of this *History*) was organized around the contrast of Poe and Emerson. After the fifties the picture changes. Transcendentalism is on the wane; Poe has died. Criticism is dominated by the Boston, or rather Cambridge, "Brahmins," among whom James Russell Lowell is the most learned, prolific, and representative critic. In New York there flourished a now forgotten school of violently nationalistic critics.[1] Walt Whitman grew out of this environment, accomplishing a strange fusion of "Yankee Transcendentalism and New York rowdyism."[2] Only very late, in the eighties, did a critical movement propounding realism as a definite doctrine arise. Its hesitant spokesman was William Dean Howells. But even earlier Henry James had slowly begun to formulate his critical creed, which, though not doctrinaire realism, drew strength from realism to elaborate an organistic, illusionist aesthetics of the novel which still speaks to our time.

WALT WHITMAN (1819–1892)

Walt Whitman called for a poetry of the future, for a clean break with the past, for democratic poetry written for the masses about the masses, for poetry inspired by modern science and technological progress, for poetry freed from the shackles of rhyme and traditional meter, from any restrictions in subject matter and reticence about sex. At first Whitman was ridiculed and ostracized; but he won devoted disciples and, slowly, critical recognition, particularly in Europe. For a time he loomed almost as the founder of modern poetry, the inventor of free verse. His influence on Lindsay, Sandburg, and Hart Crane in America, on Dylan Thomas, Laforgue and Verhaeren, Arno Holz, and Mayakovsky in Europe (to cite only representative names) was highly important. Now the Whitmanians have mostly receded into limbo, ousted by a new race of poets for whom Baudelaire and Mallarmé might rather be claimed as the ancestors.

The impression created by Whitman's pronouncements of a revolution in poetry and of a total rejection of the past is in many ways deceptive. His prophetic voice is also a voice from the past. His appeal to individual intuition, to the "inner light," owes something to his Quaker background. Much is due to the inheritance of the Enlightenment, to Jeffersonian and Jacksonian democracy, of which the young Whitman was an ardent propagandist. His "populism" has surprising French affinities in the flushed rhetoric of Jules Michelet's *Le Peuple,* and the vague socialism of Pierre Leroux mediated by George Sand. It has even been argued that Whitman's assumed personality or mask (unfairly described as a "pose") is derived from the ideal artist described in *Consuelo* and *La Comtesse de Rudolstadt.*[1] But Whitman's main inspiration was clearly Emerson's version of Transcendentalism. Whitman said himself that his main purpose was "the religious purpose." The "new theology," "the supreme and final science, the science of God," will accept natural science, and will grow out of science, superseding any conflict between philosophies, to reach "the eternal soul of man (of all else too) , the spiritual, the religious,"[2]

> I believe materialism is true and spiritualism is true,
>   I reject no part . . .
> I adopt each theory, myth, God, and demi-god.[3]

A monstrous syncretism transposes transcendentalism in a different key: the distinctions between nature and man, soul and body disappear. Yet the original debt to Emerson seems undeniable.

As early as 1847 Whitman wrote that Emerson joins "on equal terms the few great sages and original seers. He represents the freeman, America, the individual"[4]—just as Whitman wanted to represent them. Whitman heard Emerson lecture in 1842 and in 1855 sent him a copy of the first edition of *Leaves of Grass,* which elicited the famous enthusiastic letter. Emerson sought him out in New York several times; and Whitman accompanied the second edition of *Leaves of Grass* (1856) with a long open letter addressing Emerson as "dear Friend and Master."[5] In 1860 Whitman visited him in Boston, and Emerson's attempt to dissuade Whitman from including "The Children of Adam" in the third edition did not dim the personal relationship of the men. Whitman was a guest in Concord in 1881 and the next year wrote a moving obituary.[6] Even in 1881 he declared Emerson to be "unmistakably at the head" of all American poets; and he had early recognized that Emerson had helped him to "find himself." [7] Whitman nonetheless saw the temperamental and social differences that divided him from Emerson. There are always reservations in his praise: Emerson is "too perfect, too concentrated," "best as a critic or diagnoser." He holds "a singularly dandified theory of manners," shows "too great prudence, too rigid a caution." "Cold and bloodless intellectuality dominates him." [8] But when Whitman tries to minimize Emerson's influence, saying that "I began like most youngsters to have a touch (though it came late, and was only on the surface) of Emerson-on-the-brain" and that he "address'd him in print as 'Master,' and for a month or so thought him as such," he was definitely covering up his traces, and he was falsifying history when he denied having read Emerson before starting *Leaves of Grass*.[9]

Placing a distance between himself and Emerson ran parallel with Whitman's new desire to identify himself with German idealism. He stated that he "had read Kant, Schelling, Fichte and Hegel" before the publication of the first edition of *Leaves of Grass*, calling himself "the greatest *poetical* representative of German philosophy" and his book "the song of idealism." [10] He claimed that the "history of [*Leaves of Grass*] not only resembles and tallies, in certain respects, the development of the great system of Idealistic Philosophy in Germany by the 'illustrious four'—except that the development of *Leaves of Grass* has been carried on within the region of a single mind—but it is to be demonstrated, that the same theory of essential identity of the spiritual and material worlds . . . are expressed and stated in *Leaves of Grass*, from the poet's point of view." [11] Whitman's enthusiasm for Hegel, in particular, went to astonishing lengths. Hegel is "Humanity's chiefest teacher and the choicest loved physician of my mind and soul." [12] Whitman proposed that all the principal works of Hegel and Carlyle be "this day" collected and "bound up under the conspicuous title: *Speculations for the Use of North America, and Democracy there*," [13] since, oddly enough, Whitman thought Hegel "fit for America—large enough and free enough." He "most fully and definitely illustrates

Democracy." "The formulas of Hegel are an essential and crown-ing justification of New World Democracy." [14] German philosophy "is the most important emanation of the mind of modern ages and of all ages, leaving even the wonderful inventions, discoveries of science, political progress, great engineering works, utilitarian comforts etc. of the last hundred years in a comparatively inferior rank of importance—outstripping them all." [15] A poem written "after reading Hegel" has the comforting thought:

> I saw the little that is Good steadily hastening
>   towards immortality,
> And the vast all that is call'd Evil I saw hastening
>   to merge itself and become lost and dead.[16]

An examination of Whitman's knowledge of the German philos-ophers reveals, however, that he knew hardly more than a few secondhand accounts in a history of German literature, an anthol-ogy, and encyclopedias.[17] He did not even go to the translations that were then available. His enthusiasm is due in part, no doubt, to his desire for support by the prestige of philosophy; and at that time the St. Louis Hegelian movement had helped to transplant Hegel's fame to America when it was on the wane in Germany. On the other hand, it was also a genuine sense of kinship. Hegel advocates evolu-tion, progress, freedom, a reconciliation of science and religion: he was an optimist and determinist. What more was needed for Whitman, who could not see and would not have cared for the differences?

This attempt by Walt Whitman, compounded by worshipful disciples and interpreters, to make himself a philosopher or even an exponent of German philosophy could not succeed. Whitman has no coherent metaphysics, aesthetics, or theory of criticism. But there is a concept of poetry and a program for poetry and an ideal of the poet that give him a position in the history of criticism. Like many others, he preaches contemporaneity, nationalism, and realism; but with him these slogans are in the service not of a critical, social realism (as it was formulated in France or Russia) but of a poetry of the future, a worship of nature, of the world, America, the masses, science, and technology.

In ever new variations, in the prefaces and postscripts to the various editions of *Leaves of Grass,* in *Democratic Vistas* (1871), and in any number of articles and pronouncements, Whitman rhapsodically proclaims the hope for this new poetry which "needs tally and express Nature, and the spirit of Nature," which must incarnate America, "its geography and natural life and rivers and lakes," [18] its teeming humanity, its masses, men and women, soul and body, and especially sex, which had hitherto been excluded from poetry. These poems "must vocalize the vastness and splendor and reality with which Scientism has invested Man and the Universe." The scientists "are the lawgivers of poets and their construction underlies the structure of every perfect poem," for "in the beauty of poems are the tuft and final applause of science." [19]

This new American, democratic, scientific, optimistic poetry will make a clean break with the past. When Whitman says that "in these *Leaves*, everything is literally photographed," he adds immediately "nothing is poetized, no divergence, not a step, not an inch, nothing for beauty's sake—no legend, or myth, or romance, nor euphemism, nor rhyme." [20] The photographic realism means mainly a rejection of the themes and spirit of older poetry. "No, I do not choose to write a poem on a lady's sparrow, like Catullus—or on a parrot, like Ovid—nor love-songs like Anacreon—nor even . . . like Homer—or the siege of Jerusalem—nor . . . as Shakespeare. What have these themes to do in America?" [21] The new poetry of the West is insistently opposed to the feudal poetry of the East, i.e., Europe. The "petty environage and limited area" of European poets contrasts with the "cosmic and dynamic features of magnitude and limitlessness" [22] open to the American. Whitman wants a poem "altogether our own, without a trace, or taste of Europe's soil, reminiscence, technical letter or spirit." [23]

English literature, in particular, seemed to Whitman inferior to others: "material, sensual, cold, anti-democratic" or "moody, melancholy," with no first-class genius except Shakespeare.[24] Whitman's own favorite English authors—Shakespeare, Scott, Tennyson, Carlyle—"exhale that principle of caste which we Americans have come on earth to destroy." [25] Shakespeare is "offensive to democracy," he represents "incarnated, uncompromising feudalism, in literature." "The democratic requirements are not only not fulfilled in the Shakespearian productions, but are insulted on every page." [26] Tennyson supplies "the last honey of decay (I dare not call it rottenness) of that feudalism." He is "the poetic cream-skimmer of our age's melody, *ennui* and polish." He contains "never one democratic page." [27] Carlyle, though admired as a prophet and as "a perfectly honest intellect," is "feudal at the core." [28] A very early paper, "The Anti-Democratic Bearing of Scott's Novels," [29] has no trouble in establishing the thesis of the title.

The wholesale condemnation of feudalism in literature includes dogmatic theology, aestheticism, and "culture." Goethe seems to Whitman not only a courtier but also a cold aesthete who "operates upon the world" and whose view that "the artist or poet is to live in art or poetry alone apart from affairs, politics, facts, vulgar life, persons and things—seeking his 'high ideal' " is enough to incapacitate him forever from "suiting America and the forthcoming years." [30] Whitman has only contempt for Arnold. "He brings to the world what the world already has a surfeit of: is rich, hefted, lousy, reeking, with delicacy, refinement, elegance, prettiness, propriety, criticism, analysis." [31] Whitman is no admirer of Dr. Johnson, "a sycophant of power and rank," "a vile low nature." [32] Milton's *Paradise Lost* is "nonsense" and "offensive to modern science and intelligence." [33] The only exceptions are Burns, in spite of his sentimental Jacobitism, and Dickens, a "truly democratic writer," in spite of his satire on the United States.[34]

But Whitman's break with European literature is by no means so clear-cut as these or similar quotations might suggest. He knew and loved precisely the authors he attacked most—Shakespeare, Scott, Tennyson, and Carlyle; and he admired Italian opera— hardly a democratic art in his sense. In Whitman we feel a nostalgia for the European past, most often for something dead and buried, as in "Song of the Exposition.":

> Pass'd, pass'd, for us, for ever pass'd,
> that once so mighty world, now void, inanimate,
>   phantom world . . .
> Pass'd to its charnel vault
> Blazon'd with Shakspere's purple page,
> And dirged by Tennyson's sweet sad rhyme.

After the Civil War, moreover, when Whitman's high hopes were dashed and he saw too much of the corruption of the Gilded Age, he recognized the need of literary continuity. Americans "need just the precipitation and tincture of this entirely different fancy world of lulling, contrasting, even feudalistic, anti-republican poetry and romance." He knows that "what has been fifty centuries growing, working in, and accepted as crowns and apices for our kind, is not going to be pulled down and discarded in a hurry." [35] His nationalism becomes more tolerant; his concept of poetry becomes that of diverse national poetries, each representing its national spirit. Whitman appeals to Herder and Friedrich Schlegel.[36] Poetry is "Voices of the Nations in Song." Folk poetry in this broad sense includes even the Indian epics, the Bible, Homer, Ossian (of whom Whitman must be the last important admirer), the *Cid*, the Arthurian romances, the *Nibelungenlied*, and the English and Scottish ballads.[37] Even this ideal is finally expanded to include all poetry as one poetry, one great tradition:

> The whole earth's poets and poetry—*en masse*—the Oriental, the Greek, and what there is of Roman—the oldest myths—the interminable ballad-romances of the Middle Ages—the hymns and psalms of worship—the epics, plays, swarms of lyrics of the British Islands, or the Teutonic old or new—or modern French—or what there is in America, Bryant's, for instance, or Whittier's or Longfellow's—the verse of all tongues and ages, all forms, all subjects, from primitive times to our own day inclusive—really combine in one aggregate and electric globe or universe. All poetry becomes essentially, like the planetary globe itself, compact and orbic and whole.[38]

As he himself recognized, Whitman was obviously not a historian or critic. He was mainly a manifesto writer: a defender of his own art and inspiration and a propagandist for a similar poetry of the future. The poet's role is conceived in the most grandiose fashion. He is to define his nation, give it "moral identity," [39] help to unify it truly after the ordeal of the Civil War. Poetry "alone is to define the Union (namely, to give it artistic character, spirituality, dignity). What American humanity is most in danger of is an overwhelming prosperity, 'business,' worldliness, materialism: what is most lacking, East, West, North, South, is a fervid and glowing Nationality and patriotism." A "class of loftiest poets" will fill this lack in the future. The danger is, however, that they may be voices crying in the wilderness: "To have great poets, there must be great audiences, too." [40] "The best literature is always the result of something greater than itself—not the hero but the portrait of the hero. Before there can be recorded history or poem there must be transaction. Beyond the old masterpieces, the Iliad, the interminable Hindu epics, the Greek tragedies, even the Bible itself, range the immense facts that preceded them, their *sine qua non*—the veritable poems and masterpieces of which, grand as they are, the word-statements are but shreds and cartoons." [41] This view of literature as a dimmer mirror of reality, as a passive recorder of the past (which may have been fortified by Whitman's interest in Taine) [42] is inconsistent with his usual mood of ascribing to the poet a creative function. The poets are not only "divine mediums" through whom "come spirits and materials to all the people, men and women," [43] but "a few first-class poets, philosophs, and authors, have substantially settled and given status to the entire religion, education, law, sociology, etc. of the hitherto civilized world." They must also "stamp, and more than ever stamp, the interior and real democratic construction of this American continent, today, and days to come." [44] The means to achieve this Whitman envisages to be largely the creation of "an American stock personality," [45] or of "national, original archetypes." [46] He appeals to the experience of the past: "In all ages, all lands, have been creators, fashioning, making types of men and women, as Adam and Eve are made in the divine fable." Whitman lists, as instances, Achilles, Ulysses, Prometheus, Hercules, Aeneas, Plutarch's heroes, the Merlin of Celtic bards, the Cid, Arthur and his knights, Siegfried and Hagen, Roland and Oliver, and so on to Milton's Satan, Cervantes' Don Quixote, Shakespeare's Hamlet, Richard II, Lear, Marc Antony, and the modern Faust. He does not forget female characters: Cleopatra, Penelope, the portraits of Brunhilde and Chriemhilde; Oriana, Una, the modern Consuelo, Walter Scott's Jeannie and Effie Deans.[47] As in France and in Russia at the time, all hopes for literature are centered on the social power of the fictional hero held up as a model for human behavior. With his "personalism," his desire to create one representative American man who is himself, his nation, and humanity, Whitman gives this view a special formulation.

In an unguarded moment Whitman said that he "sometimes thinks the *Leaves* is only a language experiment." [48] But he surely was mistaken; his experimenting is an extension to language of his desire for all-inclusiveness, for an equalitarianism, for freedom from restraints and taboos. "An American Primer," lecture notes which seem to date from 1856, is a celebration of the English language as spoken in America. "Words follow character, nativity, independence, individuality": words have beauty and texture. Whitman would like to have slang words among fighting men, gamblers, thieves, and prostitutes collected: he would like to get rid of names like St. Lawrence or St. Louis in order to substitute the original Indian names. He likes new words which "would give that taste of identity and locality which is so dear in literature." [49] A much later small piece on "Slang in America" defends slang as the "lawless, germinal element, below all words and sentences, and behind all poetry," and as "an attempt of common humanity to escape from bald literalism, and express it illimitably, which in highest walks produces poets and poems." [50] But what Whitman wants is not metaphor but local color and freedom. Throughout his writings he rejects all metaphors, all ornamentation, and all similes and wants a style of perfectly, transparent clearness, "a plate-glassy style." [51] Language must be free as poetry must be free. "A great poet is followed by laws—they conform to him." [52] Freedom is spontaneity, instinct. "To speak in literature with the perfect rectitude and insouciance of the movements of animals and the unimpeachableness of the sentiment of trees in the woods and grass by the roadside is the flawless triumph of art." [53]

Freedom is also metrical freedom. "The rhyme and uniformity of perfect poems show the free growth of metrical laws and bud from them as unerringly and loosely as lilacs or roses on a bush." [54] "Rhyme" must mean "verse" here, since Whitman rejects rhyme violently as obsolete and feels it must be restricted to comic effects. He thinks that the "time has arrived to break down the barriers of form between prose and poetry." [55] His own free verse, which is often that of dipodic *versets* modeled on the English Bible or Ossian, drops sometimes into prose. Its rhythms overflow into the professed prose writings, which are often a string of rhapsodic, incoherent, long-breathed exclamations and enumerations, far from the coveted ideal of clarity. Whitman himself seems to have wavered on this point; he sometimes defended a measure of obscurity, "vista, music, half-tints." [56] But his main rhetorical device in both his poetry and his prose is metonymy: examples, specimens of the elements comprising democratic inclusiveness,[57] an enormous spreadout of names—of insects, birds, animals, diseases, places, countries, parts of the body, and so on. It all serves to assert a suffused pantheism in which the Platonic ladder has been pulled down. Body and soul, spirit and flesh, heterosexual "amativeness" and homosexual "adhesiveness," nature worship and the glorification of machine technology are elaborately confounded. Poetry melts into religion and philosophy, into life, and into nature.

JAMES RUSSELL LOWELL (1819–1891)

Whitman read the *Iliad* "in the full presence of Nature, under the sun, with the far-spreading landscape and vistas, or the sea rolling in." He exhorts us to read poetry and his own poems "in the open air every season of every year of our life." [1] Lowell called his collections of essays *Among My Books* (1870, second series 1876) and *My Study Windows* (1871). The contrast between the two men could not be more sharply marked, but it could be deceptively overdrawn, for Whitman was actually a wide reader and Lowell was not merely a "bookman"[1] (as he called himself). He was a man of the world and its strife: an ardent abolitionist in his youth, United States minister to Spain and to the Court of St. James. The professorship at Harvard (1856–72) was only a long episode in his busy life and he chafed under its yoke every day of his tenure.

Still, Lowell was the first American critic who was also an academic scholar: neither George Ticknor, the learned historian of Spanish literature, nor Henry Wadsworth Longfellow—his predecessors in the Harvard professorship—can be called critics. Lowell knew well not only French, Italian, Spanish, and German: he had studied Old French, Middle High German, and Middle English and could draw on philological research with assurance. But his learning was worn lightly and always served a humane purpose.[2] It was matched by a power of picturesque presentation and a gift of witty formulation, and was backed by a critical creed nourished by the best doctrines of the great romantic tradition. Yet, in spite of all the erudition, brilliance, wit, and good taste, his critical work has faded inexorably. Few today will call him, as Saintsbury did, the "premier critic of America." [3] He has been elaborately attacked as an "impressionist," a mere "appreciator" but "no critic," and the attempts by neohumanists to rescue him have not succeeded.[4]

It is quite true, however, that Lowell was not an impressionistic critic. He was not absorbed in his own sensibility; he was not even interested in defining a personal point of view. Though he had imitated the methods of Lamb, Hazlitt, and Leigh Hunt in his earliest critical writings—the papers on "The Old English Dramatists" (1842) and the discursive *Conversations on Some of the Old Poets* (1844)—he became very conscious of the limitations of Lamb's preference for the "intense focus of passionate phrase" at the expense of "unity of design and balanced gravitation of parts." Lowell concedes that recording "our impressions may be valuable or not, according to the greater or less ductility of the senses," [5] but he makes no claim to a special "ductility" of his own senses. He always asks the critic "to recall that total impression . . . which is the only safe ground of judgment." [6] His reputation as an impressionist is due to his love of elaborate picturesque similes, which incrust almost every page of his prose. For instance, he compares the mind of Milton to "the trade-wind" which "gathers to itself thoughts and images like stately fleets from every quarter" and then develops the comparison with fleets relentlessly: "some deep with silks and spicery, some brooding over the silent thunders of their battailous ornaments," etc. On the very same page, Lowell switches to the trite "organ" simile, "mighty in compass, capable equally of the trumpet's ardors or the slim delicacy of the flute." [7] Fortunately, humorous and witty similes come off much better. Thoreau, for instance, "looks at the country sometimes (as painters advise) through the triumphal arch of his own legs, and, though the upsidedownness of the prospect has its own charm of unassuetude, the arch itself is not the most graceful." [8] The aim of all these images is always characterization by graphic analogy, even though we feel today that Lowell enjoys his own ingenuity too much and often loses sight of his object.

Lowell even thought it wise "to eliminate the personal equation from our judgments" [9] and asserted constantly the need for objective standards. In an early review (1847) he rejects "liberal criticism" as a misnomer. "There can be no such thing, any more than there can be a liberal inch or a liberal ell." [10] The Dante essay (1872) says substantially the same: a poet "must be judged primarily by his poetical qualities" and "he must be judged by them absolutely, with reference, that is, to the highest standard, and not relatively to the fashions and opportunities of the age in which he lived." [11] On occasion Lowell makes concessions to "two ways of measuring a poet, either by an absolute aesthetic standard, or relatively to his position in the literary history of his country and the conditions of his generation." [12] But while he often admits that "the spirit of the age must enter as a modifying principle" [13] and uses historical arguments, Lowell always aims "to appeal a case of taste to a court of final judicature whose decisions are guided by immutable principles." He finds these principles in the Greeks, who "furnish us with our standard of comparison" [14] and in Dante, Shakespeare, Cervantes, and Goethe. The latter are the modern classics because they are universal. Though his own poetry was probably most successful when it was most local, as in *The Biglow Papers,* Lowell had little sympathy, in spite of his patriotism, with the attempts to create an American national literature. "We were busy growing a literature. We watered so freely, and sheltered so carefully, as to make a soil too damp and shaded for anything but mushrooms; wondered a little why no oaks came up, and ended by voting the mushroom an oak, an American variety." [15] Lowell felt that "human nature is everywhere the same" and that nationality would take care of itself.

Lowell's main criterion of greatness is the imagination, which he uses in many shades and distinctions as a term of praise for all writers he admires: from the shaping, constructive imagination of the greatest to the mere willful fancy of the small poet.[16] Lowell knows that the unity of imagination is not superimposed but organic, grown, not made, that form and substance "are manifestations of the same inward life, the one fused into the other," that "form is not a garment but a body." [17] He knows that there is an "intimate and genetic relation between words and thoughts," [18] that imagination results in style, "a perfection as a whole." [19] One can agree with his neohumanist defender that Lowell has "the sanest and most comprehensive conception of literature in America prior to the 20th century." [20] All these principles—creative imagination, unity of form and substance, a central absolute standard modified by historical considerations, universality of meaning—are not any the worse for being derivative. Lowell clearly learned from Coleridge, Lamb, Hazlitt, Goethe, and August Wilhelm Schlegel, and learned his lessons well.

The deficiencies of Lowell's criticism are not in his admirable theories but in his failure to carry them out in practice. Though Lowell believes in the unifying imagination, he is unable to describe it except in most general terms when confronted with his texts. Though he asserts the necessity of conveying a total impression, in practice he is constantly reduced to commenting on isolated passages, to anthologizing, to guiding us to individual beauties. His search for absolute standards remains content with abstract declarations, and the historical point of view serves only as an apology for shortcomings. His essays never achieve the coherence and unified point of view of the best in Arnold, Pater, Sainte-Beuve, or even his friend Leslie Stephen.

The essay on Chaucer (1870), for instance, takes very long to settle down to its ostensible topic. We get Lowell's views on the troubadours, the trouvères, the Anglo-Saxon character, the Norman contribution; we get comparisons between Chaucer on the one hand, and Dante, the English medieval romances, Gower, and Langland on the other; we get reflections on Chaucer's role in the stabilization of the English language and an elaborate discussion of his metrics before we ever meet the texts. Chaucer's descriptions are then contrasted with Shakespeare's, Blake is quoted about the universality of his types, and we end with a declaration of love for the man: "If character may be divined from works, he was a good man, genial, sincere, hearty, temperate of mind, more wise, perhaps, for this world than the next, but thoroughly humane, and friendly with God and men." [21] *Troilus and Criseyde* is not even mentioned, and the character of Chaucer's poetry is obscured by such old clichés as "gracious worldliness." [22]

The same kind of analysis could be made for most of the essays. They vary in range and information from the solid Dante essay (1872), based on "twenty years of assiduous study," [23] to the essay on Lessing (1866), which is little more than a summary of a German biography.[24] These essays had importance and value in their time. The sympathetic admiration for Dante was especially unusual in Protestant New England. But as criticism the essays show too many traces of lecture-room considerations and reticences and too little analytic skill and power of characterization to survive. They suffer also from Lowell's inability to keep to an orderly scheme of exposition and to make up his mind on ultimate values. This is particularly true of the essays on Dryden (1868) and Pope (1871), for Lowell could neither rid himself of romantic preconceptions about neoclassicism nor deny his sympathetic interest in these poets. The Dryden essay, which keeps a thread of biography and chronological description of the works, goes completely to pieces toward the end: we get quotations from the prefaces, reflections on Dryden's prose style and supposed gallicisms, a paragraph on his conversion to Roman Catholicism, an account of his physical appearance, and finally a summing-up of his stature that ends on a note of embarrassed irresolution. Similarly, the essay on Pope expounds first the old view, dating back to Joseph Warton, that Pope was most eminent in a lower kind of poetry, the artificial and conventional. Lowell seems to agree that there are either "born Popists or Wordsworthians," a view that has found adherents even in our time.[25] But then he retracts, asserting that there is only one kind of poetry and that, according to Warton, Pope was really no poet at all. Lowell, however, demurs at this conclusion and tries to rescue Pope on a single issue: he is a great poet of fancy in *The Rape of the Lock*, but all his other works are thrown to the romantic wolves. In detail, Lowell criticizes only *An Essay on Man* for its logical inconsistencies (as Lessing had done a century earlier) and throws up his hands in horror at the filth of *The Dunciad* and the irreverence toward women displayed in the satire "Of the Characters of Women." [26] Lowell grants Pope lack of malice [27] and constantly apologizes for him on historical grounds: the age was prosaic, artificial, and gross, and Pope eagerly fulfilled its needs. The final judgment, however, is indecisive and ambiguous, and the correlation to the time and even to the literary tradition remains tenuous.

Yet there is genuine criticism in Lowell's writings. It has one theme: distaste for sentimentalism, egotism, pessimism, and romantic nature worship. It is ethical and cultural rather than aesthetic in inspiration, but it gives a point to his essays on his predecessors and contemporaries. The sentimentalist "is the spiritual hypochondriac, with whom fancies become fact." "He loves to think he suffers, and keeps a pet sorrow, a blue-devil familiar." He "substitutes his own impression of the thing itself; he forces his own consciousness upon it." He "disjoins deed from will, practice from theory," [28] living a life of illusion. Petrarch is the fountainhead of this "degenerate modern tendency," [29] Rousseau, Chateaubriand, Wordsworth, and Shelley its modern representatives. In America Thoreau is one of the tribe. Carlyle is also "essentially a sentimentalist": and Heine's cynicism is "sentimentalism soured." [30] Yet Lowell is again unable to keep this point of view in focus. Even the almost wholly unsympathetic essay on Thoreau (1865), which satirizes him as an unhealthy eccentric who "registers the state of his personal thermometer thirteen times a day," ends with an enormous flourish of sudden praise ranking him with Donne, Sir Thomas Browne, and Novalis.[31] One might suspect that Lowell considers these three also to be eccentrics, but he did admire Donne highly.[32] The essay on "Rousseau and the Sentimentalists" amusingly ridicules the exhibitionist pose. "Rousseau cries, 'I will bare my heart to you!' and, throwing open his waistcoat, makes us the confidants of his dirty linen." [33] Nonetheless, on the central issue Lowell wavers again helplessly. In the early part of the paper we are assured that "genius is not a question of character," that biography does not matter; but at the end we get a laborious defense of Rousseau's sincerity as a man of "fitfully intense convictions." [34]

Though the fine essay on Wordsworth (1875) comes to much closer grips with a familiar poet, it is even more irresolute. Lowell attacks Wordsworth's "system of a Nature-cure, first professed by Dr. Jean Jacques and continued by Cowper." He finds something ludicrous "in the spectacle of a grown man running to hide his head in the apron of the Mighty Mother." [35] He expounds the view since made familiar by J. K. Stephen's humorous verses that there are "two voices" in Wordsworth: a Jeremiah and his scribe Baruch, the voice of thunder and the bleating of sheep.[36] Lowell belabors Wordsworth's limitations: his lack of humor and of dramatic power, his insularity, provincialism, even parochialism. "He was the historian of Wordsworthshire." [37] But in spite of all these criticisms (voiced, in milder terms, even in the Presidential address before the Wordsworth Society, 1884) [38] Lowell recognizes that Wordsworth "seems to have caught and fixed forever in immutable grace the most evanescent and intangible of our intuitions, the very ripplemarks on the remotest shores of being," and concludes that Wordsworth is "now enrolled as fifth [presumably after Shakespeare, Chaucer, Milton, and Spenser] in the succession of the great English

Poets." [39] The figure of an inspired village yokel contradicts Lowell's usual exalted conception of the poet as an imaginative teacher and total man.

Lowell prefers man to nature, universality to particularity, a classically designed whole to a loose series of gleaming passages, but he held these intellectual preferences as a man of literary culture and a responsible citizen who saw the evil social consequences of romanticism, not as a poet deeply imbued with the romantic worship of nature nor as a critic brought up on Coleridge's concept of imagination. His hostility to the feeling of continuity between man and nature in Wordsworth and Thoreau clashes with his recognition of creative imagination and his whole residual transcendentalism. Even the antiromantic essays leave us dissatisfied: they expose the conflicts in Lowell's mind, his indecisions, vacillations, and incoherences, his feeble grasp of ideas, his fatal lack of critical personality, however appealing and useful Lowell was as a lover and expositor of good literature.

WILLIAM DEAN HOWELLS (1837–1920)

The theory of realism was imported from Europe very late, though the practice of close observation and realistic techniques in local-color fiction, Western humor, and even the sentimental novel was widespread long before. Americans could also draw on the solid English tradition of the novel of manners. Poe, Hawthorne, and Melville, who today seem the greatest writers of the age, were romantic and symbolistic artists who either escaped their society or transmuted its problems in a manner very different from what proponents of literature as a "mirror of society" require. Hawthorne, in his preface to *The House of the Seven Gables* (1851), defended his type of "romance," with its allegorical features, against the novel, which "is presumed to aim at a very minute fidelity, not merely to the possible, but to the probable and ordinary course of man's experience." [1] Melville, who admired Hawthorne greatly and wrote a review, "Hawthorne and his Mosses" (1850), praising the "great power of blackness in him," [2] also protested against the preconceptions of realism. His ideal readers "want nature, too; but nature unfettered, exhilarated, in effect transformed. . . . It is with fiction as with religion: it should present another world, and yet one to which we feel the tie." [3] But the advent of the French theory of realism was hardly slowed by the lessons of these masters. The long resistance against French realism was rather due to moral and religious objections: to the "lubricity" of French fiction and its pessimistic, irreligious implications.[4]

William Dean Howells succeeded in formulating a theory of realism for the America of his time precisely because he emphasized the difference of his views from those of the French and drew support instead from the masters of realism in Russia, Italy, and Spain. His little book of rather random reflections, *Criticism and Fiction* (1891), is usually considered the manifesto of American realism, but it was actually only a skirmish in a long campaign for his doctrines.[5] In *My Literary Passions* (1895) Howells told the story of his course of reading beginning with the bookcase in his home in Ohio which contained Cervantes and Goldsmith to the day in 1886 when Tolstoy struck him like a revelation. In the course of these years he read the standard authors, passed through various enthusiasms, and, during the years of his consulship in Venice (1860–65), discovered Italian literature. Howells' first book of criticism, *Modern Italian Poets* (1887), is rather impersonal, descriptive, and colorless. He had the good taste to quote De Sanctis [6] at crucial points, but he did not care for Foscolo and Leopardi and even the admiration for Alfieri and Manzoni remains distant and forced: the book reads like a self-imposed task inspired by political sympathy for the new Italy. Among the Italians, Howells really loved only Goldoni, "the inventor of realistic Italian comedy." [7]

Howells' theory of the novel crystallized in the early years of his editorship of the *Atlantic Monthly* (1866–81), when he became acquainted with the French, the German peasant novelist Berthold Auerbach, and Turgenev. At that time Howells' main theoretical concern was the principle of noninterference by the author, of complete objectivity of presentation. In 1869 he praised one of Auerbach's stories for "telling itself." "One does not think of the author till the end." [8] He describes his own ideal when he tells us that Turgenev is "the most self-forgetful of the story-telling tribe, and he is no more enamored of the creations than of himself; he pets none of them; he upbraids none; you like them or hate them for what they are; it does not seem to be his affair." Turgenev "leaves all comment to the reader"; he cares for character and minimizes plot; he uses "the play method"—that is, he dramatizes and does not comment and explain.[9] Henry James realizes this ideal in America: "artistic impartiality" is his "characteristic quality" and, as with Turgenev, "it is the character, not the fate of his people which occupies him." [10] In an essay on James (1882) Howells expressly contrasts the new fiction and the old:

> The art of fiction has, in fact, become a finer art in our day than it was with Dickens and Thackeray. We would not suffer the confidential attitude of the latter now, nor the mannerism of the former, any more than we could endure the prolixity of Richardson or the coarseness of Fielding. These great men are of the past—they and their methods and interests; even Trollope and Reade are not of the present. The new school derives from Hawthorne and George Eliot rather than any others . . .
>
> It is largely influenced by French fiction in form; but it is the realism of Daudet rather than the realism of Zola that prevails with it and it has a soul of its own which is above the business of recording the rather brutish pursuit of a woman by a man, which seems to be the chief end of the French novelist. This school, which is largely of the future as well as the present, finds its chief exemplar in Mr. James; it is he who is shaping and directing American fiction, at least.[11]

Criticism and Fiction (1891) hardly says anything new. Literature and art are "the expression of life," and "are to be judged by fidelity" to it. What is needed in criticism is not reference to other artists or the tradition of art, but an appeal to life: comparison with the things that the readers have known. Negatively this means a condemnation of romanticism, or rather of romantic devices; positively, an emphasis on probability of motive, a rejection of catastrophes and accidents. Fiction should minimize plot and center on character. It should reflect life as it is, in the United States, and hence it should not be so tragic and gloomy as Dostoevsky's novels. In a well-known passage—often quoted outside its context of the contrast with Dostoevsky's criminals and revolutionaries—Howells asserts his optimistic, democratic faith in human nature and America. "Our novelists, therefore, concern themselves with the more smiling aspects of life, which are the more American, and seek the universal in the individual rather than the social interests. It is worthwhile, even at the risk of being called commonplace, to be true to our well-to-do actualities." These actualities include a cleaner and saner view of the relation between the sexes than prevails in the French novel. Howells admits that "there is vicious love beneath the surface of our society" but insists that it is not characteristic. In the novel sex should be minimized. Passion is not only sexual passion: "the passion of grief, the passion of avarice, the passion of pity, the passion of ambition, the passion of hate, the passion of envy, the passion of devotion, the passion of friendship; and all these have a greater part in the drama of life than the passion of love, and infinitely greater than the passion of guilty love." Finally, this basically optimistic, democratic, decent art of the American novel must serve the good of humanity, must make men "kinder and better." [12] Tolstoy has become Howells' "final consciousness." "The supreme art in literature had its highest effect in making me set art forever below humanity." Compared to the early reviews of Turgenev and Henry James, Howells has lost interest in technical prescriptions for the novel. Tolstoy seems to him the only writer who has "no manner" at all, whose fictions "seem the very truth always," whose "frank and simple kindliness is what style is in the merely literary author." [13] Howells criticizes Tolstoy only when he deviates from this straightforward recording: when he becomes parabolical, as in his late peasant tales, or "descends to exegesis," as in *The Kreutzer Sonata* and applies to all marriages "the lesson of one evil marriage." In general, Howells feels that Tolstoy's art is so simple, so unassuming, so "real" that it ceases to be "literature in the artistic sense at all" and becomes life itself.[14]

Howells' scattered later writings clarify and elaborate his point of view but hardly modify it. A lecture, "Novel-Writing and Novel-Reading" (1899, not published until 1958) expounds the creed again. "Truth is the prime test of a novel," and truth means life and is the guarantee of beauty. Howells defends its going into the "dark places of the soul, the filthy and squalid places of society, high and low." "Let all the hidden things be brought into the sun, and let every day be the day of judgment. If the sermon cannot any longer serve this end, let the novel do it." But he recognizes that direct instruction will not achieve this end. "If it is a work of art, it promptly takes itself out of the order of polemics or of ethics and primarily consents to be nothing if not aesthetical. Its story is the thing that tells, first of all." What matters is "the effect of life," which Howells seems to think of as triumph of deception. Theoretically he knows that art is not life but the art of the novelist is something like a *trompe d'œil,* an optical illusion. "The effect is like that in those cycloramas where up to a certain point there is real ground and real grass, and then carried indivisibly on to the canvas the best that the painter can do to imitate real ground and real grass. . . . If we are very skilful and very patient we can hide the joint." With a different figure Howells says the same when he says that "the business of the novelist" is "arranging a perspective for you with everything in its proper relation and proportion to everything else." But he adds immediately, it is also the novelist's function "to help you to be kinder to your fellows, juster to yourself, truer to all." The type distinctions sketched in Howells' lecture make this ideal of illusionism with a didactic purpose much more concrete. There are "truthful" and "untruthful" novelists. Jane Austen, George Eliot, Anthony Trollope, Thomas Hardy; Flaubert, Maupassant, the Goncourts, Daudet and Zola, Turgenev and Tolstoy are all "truthful." Thackeray, Dickens, Bulwer, Reade, Dumas, and "measurably" Dostoevsky are "untruthful." There are three types of novels in descending order of greatness: the novel, the romance, and the "romanticistic" novel, a different classification, which allows for Hawthorne as a writer of romance. *Pride and Prejudice, Middlemarch, Anna Karenina, Fathers and Sons* belong to the first class; the novels of Dickens and Hugo, to the third and lowest. Another threefold classification Howells introduces in the lecture has the same value criterion: the autobiographical form is the most narrow, the most difficult as to keeping of illusion: it includes *Gil Blas, Barry Lyndon* (Thackeray's best book in Howells' estimate), *Henry Esmond, The Blithedale Romance,* and *David Copperfield.* There is, secondly, the biographical novel with one central figure, of which Howells gives only one example: Henry James' *Roderick Hudson;* and there is, thirdly, the "historical" novel, by which Howells means the novel told as if the material were real history, by a universal intelligence, the omniscient author. It is by far the highest form, though it is "almost shapeless, as it is with the greatest difficulty, with serious limitations of its effects, that you can give it symmetry. Left to itself, it is sprawling, splay-footed, gangling, proportionless and inchoate; but if it is true to the life which it can give no authority for seeming to know, it is full of beauty and symmetry." [15] An unreal solution is propounded: its trust in the ultimate artistic success of deception, formlessness, literal truth, seems constantly withdrawn by a realization that art is not life, that the artist has to choose and arrange, has his technique and point of view.

Howells even attempted a sketch of something like a history of fiction. At first glance, the central theme of *Heroines of Fiction* (1901) is most unpromising. Howells argues that the English novel has established "the right of innocence in a true picture of manners, and honors the claim of inexperience to be amused and edified without being abashed." Goldsmith was the pioneer, and three women—Jane Austen, Fanny Burney, and Maria Edgeworth— "forever dedicated [the novel] to decency; as women they were faithful to their charge of the chaste mind." "They imagined the heroine who was above all a Nice Girl." With its glossy illustrations and sentimental reflections on such heroines as the blind girl Nydia in Bulwer's *The Last Days of Pompeii, The Heroines of Fiction* seems a mere bookmaking job destined for the drawing-room tables of the prim American women readers of the time. It begins by excluding Defoe. "Because of his matter, and not because of his manner or motive, his heroines must remain under lock and key, and cannot be so much as named in mixed companies. DeFoe's [sic] novels cannot be freely read and criticized." [16] But once Howells has arrived in the 19th century, on safe ground morally, he makes his discriminations freely and acutely. He downgrades Scott, Dickens, and Thackeray and praises Jane Austen, Trollope, and George Eliot. He has no use for Cooper but admires Hawthorne, whom he can defend by drawing a distinction between good romance and bad romanticism. "Romance, as in Hawthorne, seeks the effect of reality in visionary conditions; romanticism, as in Dickens, tries for a visionary effect in actual conditions." [17] Howells even likes the "bullied heroines" of the Brontës and is lavish in his praise of Hardy's *Jude the Obscure,* though he is afraid to quote it: "No greater and truer book has been written in our time or any." [18]

There are many inconsistencies in Howells' later criticism: fits of mawkish prudishness are followed by generous praise for Zola as "one of the greatest and most heroic of French citizens." His books, "though often indecent, are never immoral, but always most terribly, most pitilessly moral." [19] Grossly exaggerated praise for trivial women short-story writers alternates with severe censure of the greatest masters. Howells' critical standards are relaxed, uncertain, and wavering, because basically, in spite of his enormous output, he did not care for criticism as analysis and judgment. It comes out most clearly in his ambiguous judgment on Henry James' books; his constant preference for James' least original writings.[20] Still, Howells was a propagandist of the new novel and a generous patron of such newcomers as Hamlin Garland and Stephen Crane.[21]

In relation to the Italian and Spanish novel he similarly conceived his role as that of an enthusiastic middleman. He introduced Verga's *I Malavoglia*[22] but found the Spanish novel more congenial. He established personal contacts with Armando Valacio Valdés, quoted some trite reflections in *Criticism and Fiction* as if he had found the crown witness for realism,[23] introduced *Doña Perfecta* by Pérez Galdós, and praised Juan Valera's *Pepita Jiménez*. As late as 1919 he was carried away by Blasco Ibañez' *La Catedral*. Ibañez seems to him "easily the first of living European novelists." The book is "one of the fullest and richest in modern fiction, worthy to rank with the greatest Russian work and beyond anything yet done in English." [24] Howells is prone to overrate his Spaniards, partly because they were new to him and his audience and partly because they served (like the Russians) as a stick to beat the French with: "the ugly French fetich which has possessed itself of the good name of Realism to befoul it." [25] Howells, with all his blind spots, found an inclusive and generous, though lax, creed of "reticent realism." His younger friend Henry James went much further into the theory of the art.

10 : HENRY JAMES

THERE IS an extreme divergence of opinion, even among presumably sympathetic critics, about the stature of Henry James as a critic. T. S. Eliot considers Henry James "emphatically not a successful *literary critic*. His criticism of books and writers is feeble. . . . Henry was not a literary critic." Eliot recognizes that James, in his novels, is a fine critic of persons but denies him access to ideas. In Eliot's paradoxical language, "he had a mind so fine that no idea could violate it." [1] On the other hand Percy Lubbock in *The Craft of Fiction* pronounces James "the novelist who carried his research into the theory of the art further than any other—the only real *scholar* in the art," [2] while Morris Roberts in a little book on *Henry James's Criticism* declares that "no critic has ever gone more deeply into the philosophy of art." [3] R. P. Blackmur, finally, praises James' *Prefaces* to the New York edition of his novels as "the most sustained and I think the most eloquent and original piece of literary criticism in existence." "Criticism has never been more ambitious, nor more useful." [4]

Eliot's opinion and that of the diverse Marxist or patriotic American detractors of Henry James seem to me quite wide of the mark. James to my mind is by far the best American critic of the nineteenth century who—*pace* T. S. Eliot—is brimful of ideas and critical concepts and has a well-defined theory and a point of view which allow him to characterize sensitively and evaluate persuasively a wide range of writers: largely, of course, the French, English, and American novelists of his own time. But on the other hand, the exaltation of the *Prefaces* to the greatest piece of criticism ever written seems to me extravagant. The *Prefaces*, as a totality, judged as criticism, are disappointing: they are, no doubt, of great interest to the student of James' life and career as a writer, and they have the almost unique distinction of being an author's extended commentary on his own work. But the *Prefaces* are primarily reminiscences and commentaries and not criticism. They tell us where and when a book was written, what the "germ" of the story was—a remembered figure, an anecdote told at dinner, a mood recaptured—or they explain, expand, and develop the theme of the novel or indulge in general reflections on manners and life. Actual criticism is rare in the *Prefaces*: it is confined to the early novels, when James objects to the hurried wind-up of *Roderick Hudson* or disparages *The American* as romantic and untrue to life. Moreover the *Prefaces* contain reflections on the relation of art and life and do—though only intermittently—analyze and defend James' novelistic technique: particularly the need of a central intelligence, of a steady focus of narration.

But these passages—particularly the preface to *The Ambassadors*—form part and parcel of James' general, critical work. To isolate them would overemphasize a single technical device, the "point of view," with which James has become identified with a vengeance and would obscure the totality of his critical achievement which contains discussions of most issues of literary theory in relation to many writers. We must examine primarily the five volumes of criticism published by James himself: *French Poets and Novelists* (1878), *Hawthorne* (1879), *Partial Portraits* (1888), *Essays in London and Elsewhere* (1893), and *Notes on Novelists* (1914), and we must supplement these with the many scattered reviews beginning as early as 1864, introductions and pronouncements in letters, not quite completely collected in *Views and Reviews* (1908), *Notes and Reviews* (1921) and, recently, *The Future of the Novel* (1956), *American Essays* (1956), and *Literary Reviews and Essays* (1957). It will be best, within our limits, to take James' critical work as a whole, from his first reviews in 1864 to the articles on "The New Novel" in 1914, fifty years later, and to consider it as a unity in which the criticism of his own novels takes only a minor place. No doubt there are some shifts of doctrine and marked changes of style during these fifty years: in particular, the earliest stage of James' reviewing in the *Nation* and the *North American Review* in 1864–66 differs in being more pronouncedly moralistic and intellectualistic. The last writings are often overrun by "cobwebs," elaborate and sometimes strangely empty circumlocutions, or indulge in intricate similes almost for their own sake. On the whole, though, James' critical views are remarkably coherent and consistent and show, at most, changes of emphasis due to a difference of audience or the changed atmosphere of the time.

Henry James, for a time, hoped to become the American Sainte-Beuve. In a letter he proposes "to do for our dear old English letters and writers *something* of what Ste. Beuve [*sic*] and the best French critics have done for theirs." He does not want to "imitate him, or reproduce him in English": rather he wants to do something analogous to his work, which, it seems to him, belongs to the past; James, on the other hand, very self-consciously feels himself a man of the future, an American who has the advantage of looking at Europe from the outside. "We can deal freely with forms of civilization not our own, can pick and choose and assimilate and in short (aesthetically) claim our property wherever we find it." He hopes for "a vast intellectual fusion and synthesis of the various National tendencies of the world." [5] Surely James by his work, both fictional and critical, remained faithful to the dim program of this youthful, boasting letter. All his life he was acutely conscious of the low status and condition of English and American criticism, and the need of a revival of criticism, especially of the novel. He constantly recognized the superiority of France on this point and derived, no doubt, his general method and style from the French critics, at least in his early stages. But we must not underrate the tremendous impression of Arnold's *Essays in Criticism* (1865), which James recalled reading first in the proof sheets of the American reprint,[6] or the life-long admiration for Lowell, whose essays seemed to him "miracles of evocation, of resurrection, of transmission, of insight, of history, of poetry." [7] Nor must we forget the influence of the American and English reviewing media of his time and men like Leslie Stephen (whom James knew well) and Edmund Gosse (whom he admired extravagantly).

James' opinion of Sainte-Beuve shifted and was far from uncritical. In an early review (1865), James distinguishes "small criticism" and "great criticism." "Great criticism seems to us to touch more or less nearly on pure philosophy. Pure criticism must be of the small kind. Goethe is a great critic; M. Sainte-Beuve is a small one. Goethe frequently starts from an idea; M. Sainte-Beuve starts from a fact: Goethe from a general rule, M. Sainte-Beuve from a particular instance." Though James says that Sainte-Beuve "may be called the first of living critics," he deplores that he is "not a philosopher in so far as that he works with no supreme object," has no "deliberate theory of life, of nature, of the universe." [8] In a review of an English translation of *Portraits de femmes* James complains that Sainte-Beuve is "very little of a moralist and, in a really liberal sense of the word, not overmuch of a thinker." He is a psychologist, an empiric of great literary merits. "He is a little of a poet, a little of a moralist, a little of a historian, a little of a philosopher, a little of a romancer." He is a "wonderful man in flagrant default of imagination, of depth, of sagacity, of constructive skill," but there remains "his passion for literature—in which we include both his insatiable curiosity and his eternal gift of expression—his style." [9] But after Sainte-Beuve's death James' tone changes: a review of *Premiers Lundis* calls him "the acutest critic the world has seen" and complains only of an "impression of almost formidable sagacity," of his being, even in his early reviews, "too shrewd, too old, too *posé*." [10] A review of *English Portraits* then seems to appreciate more highly the "subtle interfusion of science and experience." "Most erudition beside Sainte-Beuve's seems sterile and egoistic; none was ever turned to such infinite account, so put to use, so applied, so controlled by life." James admires his relish for temperance, his perfect taste, his sense of measure in which he feels even a touch of Philistinism. He disagrees only with his low estimate of Balzac, whom Sainte-Beuve "detested, without ever suspecting, apparently, the colossal proportions of the great novelist's genius." [11] In James' longest essay on Sainte-Beuve, the same motifs are developed further: Sainte-Beuve had "the passion for scholarship and the passion for life. He was essentially a creature of books, a *literatus;* and yet to his intensely bookish and acquisitive mind nothing human, nothing social, was alien . . . He valued life and literature equally for the light they threw upon each other." Again we hear of his just and comprehensive perceptions with the reservation that Sainte-Beuve was unjust to Balzac and George Sand and overgenerous to Baudelaire and Feydeau. But now James voices more strongly his reservations as to Sainte-Beuve's character, his malice, his feline innuendos, his insinuations. Still, he admires his fierce independence, his concept of the critic, not as "the narrow lawgiver or the rigid censor," but as "the student, the inquirer, the observer, the interpreter, the active, indefatigable commentator, whose constant aim was to arrive at justness of characterization. Sainte-Beuve's own faculty of characterization was of the rarest and most remarkable; he held it himself in the highest esteem; he valued immensely his *impression*." [12]

This is why James finally preferred Sainte-Beuve to Scherer and Taine. Early James thought Scherer "a solid embodiment of Mr. Arnold's ideal critic." He preferred him to Sainte-Beuve "because his morality is positive without being obtrusive." [13] But later he thought Scherer disappointing. "He lacks imagination, and he is subject to odd lapses and perversities of taste." James disapproves of his calling Thackeray "a cold, *ennuyeux* writer," and chides him for "a strange dulness of vision" when Scherer "declares he can see nothing but dreariness in *Wilhelm Meister* or indeed in all [Goethe's] literary works except the lyrics and *Faust*." [14] Taine from the very beginning seems to James not pre-eminently a critic but rather "alternately a philosopher and a historian." [15] Taine's theory seems to him "decidedly a failure" even though he admits that "a group of works is more or less the product of a 'situation.'" James complains of Taine's "inordinate haste to conclude," of his "monstrous cumulative violence of expression," and judges him "thoroughly a stranger to what we may call the intellectual climate of our literature." [16] He deplores his "want of *initiation*," his "failure to apprehend the native code of aesthetics," crassly exhibited by his extravagant praise of *Aurora Leigh* and Lord Byron.[17] James, however, always admired Taine's essay on Balzac, "so much the finest thing ever written on our author," [18] but concludes that Sainte-Beuve, "the least doctrinal of critics," had "by his very horror of dogmas, moulds and formulas," contributed more effectively than Taine to the science of literary interpretation. Sainte-Beuve's "truly devout patience with which he kept his final conclusion in abeyance," "his frank provisional empiricism" seems to him "more truly scientific than M. Taine's premature philosophy." [19]

What James said about Sainte-Beuve—of his anxiety to preserve his impression intact, his "provisional empiricism," his aim at a "justness of characterization"—describes also James' own ideal of criticism. "The critic," he wrote in 1868, is "simply a reader like all the others—a reader who prints his impressions." [20] "Nothing will ever take the place of the good old fashion of 'liking' a work of art or not liking it: the most improved criticism will not abolish that primitive, that ultimate test." [21] Criticism is "the only gate of appreciation, just as appreciation is, in regard to a work of art, the

only gate of enjoyment." It is an appeal "from the general judgment, and not to it; is to the particular judgment altogether." [22]
The true method of criticism is always that of sympathy, of identification with the work of art. "To criticise is to appreciate, to
appropriate, to take intellectual possession, to establish in fine a
relation with the criticised thing and make it one's own." [23] Criticism is "the principle of understanding things. Its business is to urge
the claims of all things to be understood." [24] There is no use quar-
reling with an author's subject, which is "given him by influences,
by a process," which is finally mysterious. We are concerned
critically only with the treatment.[25] The aim of the critic is to "catch
a talent in the fact, follow its line, and put a finger on its essence."
Thus James deplores the decline of the fashion of the literary
portrait whose aim is "to fix a face and figure, to seize a literary
character." [26] Literary portraits were Sainte-Beuve's special *forte*
and *Partial Portraits* is the title of one of James' own collections and
could be the title of each of them. But submission to the author,
sympathy, even the art of portraiture do not exclude judgment.
James recognizes that "we never really get near a book save on the
question of its being good or bad, of its really treating, that is, or
not treating, its subject." [27] But he seems, theoretically at least, to
know only one criterion of judgment: there is "*à priori,* no rule for
a literary production but that it shall have genuine life." [28]

This theory of criticism, so tentative, so empirical, so conscious
of all the difficulties of what James calls "the most postponed and
complicated of the arts, the last qualified for and arrived at, the one
requiring behind it most maturity, most power to understand and
compare," [29] does not, however, do justice to James' practice. Actually he has an extraordinarily clear grasp of the nature of art, its
relations to reality and the other activities of man; he has very
definite, though often implicit, requirements for successful art, and
he has the power to apply his standards to the authors he examines.
His theoretical position seems clear-cut and coherent. He is neither
a "realist," the label pinned on him in most histories of literature,
nor a "formalist," a devotee of art for art's sake, for which he is
often dismissed.

James definitely disapproved of "art for art's sake": its creed
seemed to him to exhibit "a most injurious disbelief in the illimit-
able alchemy of art," [30] to presuppose a false divorce of art from

reality and morality. James, no doubt, admires Gautier and quotes the poem "L'Art" as "a case of an aesthetic, an almost technical, conviction, glowing with a kind of moral fervor," [31] but he dismisses the preface to *Mlle de Maupin* as ridiculous [32] and chides Gautier for the hardening of his moral feelings. His pictures of Spanish bull fights show "what length *l'art pour l'art* can carry the kindest-tempered of men." [33] The rags of the beggars on the Spanish steps in Rome, which Gautier could "see and enjoy for ever," remain for James "but filth, and filth is poverty, and poverty a haunting shadow, and picturesque squalor a mockery." As Gautier is a "master of a perfect style which has never reflected a spiritual spark," [34] so Baudelaire is merely another inordinate cultivator of the sense of the picturesque which he found even in darkness and dirt. Baudelaire (whom James obviously misinterprets as a mere sensationalist) offers a proof for "the crudity of sentiment of the advocates of 'art for art.' " [35] The representatives of the aesthetic movement in England did not appeal to James either: he reviewed Swinburne's drama *Chastelard* most unfavorably [36] and severely trounced *Essays and Studies* as "simply dabbling in the relatively very shallow pool of the picturesque." "The author does not understand morality—a charge to which he would be probably quite indifferent; but . . . he does not at all understand immorality." [37] Pater seems to him "curiously negative and faintly-grey . . . . He is the mask without the face," [38] and Wilde "was never in the smallest of degree interesting" to him but had become so in the trial only because of "this hideous human history." [39] D'Annunzio finally gave an occasion for a summing-up on the aesthetic movement: a spectacle "strange and finally wearisome," that of "beauty at any price," [40] which James sees confirmed by the example of D'Annunzio. James' criticism of D'Annunzio is, no doubt, directed not only against his "exclusive aestheticism" which is "bound sooner or later to spring a leak" [41] but against D'Annunzio's sexuality, his cruelty, insolence, and ultimate vulgarity. The objections are not disentangled, though at the end James asks whether the aesthetic adventure *"need* give us no more comforting news of success" than what he considers the failure of D'Annunzio.[42]

The criticism of the aesthetic movement is directed at the moral obtuseness and its falsity to a full reality. But James cannot be described simply as a realist or a moralist. Certainly, there are many passages in his writings which, in general, indicate approval of realism and profess his admiration for what are usually considered its masters: Balzac, Flaubert, Maupassant, Daudet, George Eliot, and Turgenev. Over and over James repeats that "the only reason for the existence of a novel is that it does attempt to represent life," [43] that it has the "large, free character of an immense and exquisite correspondence with life." [44] "Art," he says in a well-known passage, "plucks its material . . . in the garden of life—which material elsewhere grown is stale and uneatable." [45] James criticizes George Sand for lacking "exactitude—the method of truth" [46] and, as early as 1864, recommends "the famous 'realistic system' " for study and advises the author of a picturesque novel, Miss Harriet Prescott, to "cultivate a delicate perception of the actual." [47] In his last survey (1914) he praises "The New Novel" for "hugging the shore of the real," its "appetite for a closer notation, a sharper specification of the signs of life." He constantly welcomes "exactness—truth of detail," "saturation," "specification," in Balzac and Flaubert. He admires Wells and Bennett for being each "immersed in his own body of reference," for "being saturated" which "is to be documented," for the "smell of packed actuality" emanating from their books.[48]

But this insistence upon the reference of art to reality does not, in James, mean an obfuscation of the difference between life and art: art is not a mirror, art cannot be "an amorphous slice" [49] of life as Zola would want us to have it. Nor can "real people" be transferred into a novel. "The original gives hints, but the writer does what he likes with them." [50] James objects specifically to D'Annunzio's *Il Fuoco* "for the impression of a direct transfer, a 'lift,' bodily, of something seen and known." [51] Art, even the art of the novel, is not copying, not imitation but a selection from life, a transformation, a creation, "life being all inclusion and confusion, and art being all discrimination and selection." [52] Art is a "chemical process, the crucible or retort from which things emerge for a new function," [53] or, in another metaphor, art must be "the tempered and directed hammer that makes the metal hard" [54] or, with the grandest claim, the artist is the modern alchemist who "renews something like the old dream of the secret of life." [55]

Art actually can only achieve the illusion of life and can achieve it only by the "authority" of the writer, inducing conviction, belief, acceptance in the reader. James is constantly preoccupied with this problem of plausibility, "the strong internal evidence of truthfulness" he found, for example, in George Eliot[56] while he thought it absent in Hugo's *Les Travailleurs de la mer*[57] and *Marie Tudor*.[58]

James found it difficult, however, to define the limits of plausibility, of probability in Aristotle's sense. On the one hand, he certainly admired much unrealistic art and cultivated the ghost story as for him the "most possible form of the fairy-tale."[59] In his discussion of *The Turn of the Screw* he expressly rejects the reduction of his ghosts to psychic phenomena amenable to study by the Society for Psychic Research, as his ghosts were precisely "goblins, elves, imps, demons."[60] James also often recognizes the distinction between the novel and the romance: he ranks the romance lower, thinks it an excuse "to relieve the writer of all analysis of character, to enable him to forge his interest out of the exhibition of circumstance rather than out of the examination of motive,"[61] but in later years he treated "romance" and "romanticism" with increasing tenderness. He admired Stevenson quite inordinately both as a heroic person and as an accomplished writer with style and imagination; he appreciated Rostand and his "happy romantic principle," though wondering and anxious at his "deflection" from reality.[62] He dismisses, among the definitions of romance, that of "a matter indispensably of boats, or of caravans, or of tigers, or of 'historical characters', or of ghosts, or of forgers, or of detectives, or of beautiful wicked women, or of pistols and knives" and is not satisfied with reducing it to the "idea of the facing of danger." He prefers to think of it as "experience disengaged, disembroiled, disencumbered, exempt from the conditions that we usually know to attach to it." Whimsically he pictures us readers as sitting in the balloon of experience tied to earth by a rope while "the art of the romancer is, 'for the fun of it,' insidiously to cut the cable, to cut it without our detecting him."[63] But James cannot quite believe that the trick of cutting the cable without detection can be brought off successfully. *The Scarlet Letter* suffers from "a want of reality and an abuse of the fanciful element,"[64] and in *The Marble Faun* Hawthorne has "forfeited a precious advantage in ceasing to tread his native soil. Half the virtue of *The Scarlet Letter* and *The House of the Seven Gables* is in their local quality; they are impregnated with the New England air."[65] Still, James has trouble with "fixing the measure of reality." He finds it hard to accept Don Quixote or Micawber. Their "reality is a very delicate shade; it is a reality so coloured by the author's vision that, vivid as it may be, one would hesitate to propose it as a model." [66] He refers to Dickens' characters as performing "a feverish dance to the great fiddling of Dickens." Dickens made them dance but "he couldn't make them stand or sit *at once* quietly and expressively." [67] *Our Mutual Friend* seemed to him, in 1865, crowded with grotesque creatures and gratuitous distortions which have no humanity in them.[68]

On occasion James can say that the novelist must regard himself "as an historian and his narrative as a history," [69] but mostly he sees the fallacy of this appeal to what really happened. He certainly considers the historical novel an impossible feat "of completely putting off one consciousness before beginning to take on another." [70] It is "a mere *escamotage*": even such a master as Flaubert failed dismally with his historical novels. A New England regionalist writer, Sarah Orne Jewett, who tried her hand at a historical romance, is solemnly exhorted: "go back to the dear country of the Pointed Firs, *come back* to the palpable present *intimate* that throbs responsive." [71] The historical novel must fail precisely in the illusion of life, the cultivation of which seems to him "the beginning and the end of the art of the novelist." [72]

But why should the novelist try to create this illusion of life? What is the ultimate function of art? It is certainly not in James' mind simply that of a social mirror or propaganda. He deplores the prose fiction that now (1914) "occupies itself as never before with the 'condition of the people,' a fact quite irrelevant to the nature it has taken on," with the result that "its nature amounts exactly to the complacent declaration of a common literary level." [73] But James is acutely aware of the social roots of art. "The flower of art blooms only where the soil is deep . . . it takes a great deal of history to produce a little literature." [74] That is the insistent theme of the book on Hawthorne: his having lived in a crude and simple society. "No State, in the European sense of the word, and indeed barely a specific national name. No sovereign, no court, no personal loyalty, no aristocracy, no church, no clergy, no army, no diplomatic service, no country gentlemen, no palaces, no castles, nor manors." [75] The nostalgia for Europe with its snobbish overtones has its deeply felt seriousness: a concern for the isolation of the artist, particularly in the United States, and a fear of leveling, of the smoothing off of edges, of the decay of character which James still finds in Balzac and Dickens but begins to miss in an egalitarian democracy.[76] James can then go to extremes of illusionism and escapism. The function of the novel will be "to provide another world," "an experience that, as effective as the dentist's ether, muffles the ache of the actual." [77] But art can hardly be only a pain-killer. James himself adds immediately: "what we get of course, in proportion as the picture lives, is simply another actual—the actual of other people," though he professes not to know why that should be a relief. Usually James understood that we return to reality fortified, that the artist, in allowing us "to live the life of others," [78] not only extends our experience but gives us a view of the world and a knowledge of ourselves. "The great question as to a poet or a novelist is, How does he feel about life? what, in the last analysis, is his philosophy," since his work is an "expression of a total view of the world" [79] and "imaginative writers of the first order always give us an impression that they have a kind of philosophy." [80] In a letter to G. B. Shaw James summarized his "suspicion" of "the 'encouraging' *representational* work," the one-track mind of Shaw, while maintaining the high civilizing function of art: its contribution to man's self-awareness and hence also to his moral decisions. Works of art "are capable of saying more things to man about himself than any other 'works' whatever are capable of doing." We artists "enable him to pick and choose and compare and know, enable him to arrive at any sort of synthesis that isn't, through all its superficialities and vacancies, a base and illusive humbug." [81]

Synthesis, a total view of the world and of man, presupposes an inclusiveness of art, forbids a partial view of reality: implies an artist speaking as a whole man. This is where morality, conscience, comes into James' scheme and literary standards. Art must not be purely descriptive, mere local color, a mere reproduction of the surface of the world. Gautier and Loti are great masters of the picturesque but they ignore the soul of man. But man, James demands, must not be represented partially, as a mere animal. He must appear as a total human being, moral and intellectual. On the question of "decency," the treatment of sex in fiction, James seems to contradict himself—but only apparently so. He deplored the unspoken censorship that excluded large tracts of life from the novel; he regretted

the spinsterish restrictions of the time, and often pleaded for freedom on such matters, as he pleaded for freedom in the arts in general. But confronted with the themes of Baudelaire or even Maupassant, James beats a hasty retreat into what must be described as
his basic puritanism or rather into a simple aversion for the animal
and the perverse—but often also for the universally, healthily
human. A late essay on Matilde Serao puts the matter very clearly:
James deplores the "conspiracy of silence" [82] in English and American fiction but treats Matilde Serao as a warning example of what
complete license will lead to: a literature which will be predom-
inantly erotic with "no place speedily . . . left for anything else." [83]
James concludes somewhat whimsically that "unmistakably we turn
round again to the opposite pole, and there before we know it have
positively laid a clinging hand on dear old Jane Austen." [84] These
are dead issues today, long ago resolved in favor of freedoms
undreamt of even by the flamboyant Matilde Serao. James always
held two views he felt perfectly compatible: discontent with the
timidity of the Anglo-Saxon conventions and embarrassment and
even horror at the eroticism of the French novel. It became particularly acute in the case of Maupassant, whom James calls "a lion
in the path," as it seems to him "discouraging to find what low views
are compatible with mastery," that one can be "at once so licentious
and so impeccable." [85] Baudelaire is another case of a "rare combination of technical zeal and patience and of vicious sentiment." [86]
Even the admired Balzac, we are told, "had no natural sense of
morality, and this we cannot help thinking a serious fault in a
novelist," [87] and Flaubert is elaborately criticized for the limits of
his moral vision, culminating in the extravagant charge of "inexperience and indifference in regard to the phenomena of character and
the higher kinds of sensibility." [88] In ever new variations James
develops a contrast between, on the one hand, the English and
American novel and the Anglo-Saxon character, and, on the other,
the French novels, in which the French appear as masters of craft
and form, as painters of the surface of the world, of sensations and
instincts and desires, of the relations between men and women, but
as utterly deficient in depicting "the operation of character, the
possibilities of conduct, the part played in the world by the *idea*." [89]
"When they lay their hand upon the spirit of man, they cease to

seem expert." [90] The contrast between the English novel and the French is drawn so sharply that the English appear as the blundering, formless, prudish psychologists and moralists and the French as the shallow, immoral masters of the surface and of sensations. Sometimes James is somewhat put out by the presence of Paul Bourget, "who notes with extraordinary closeness the action of life on the soul" [91] and admits that "if there were not a poet like Sully-Prudhomme or a moralist like M. Renan, the thesis that the French imagination has none but a sensual conscience would be made simpler than it ever is to prove anything." [92] But, on the whole, James speaks always of "we of the English faith," [93] "we of the English tongue" with "our Anglo-Saxon theory," [94] identifying himself with the English moralists and psychologists but chiding them for their neglect of art, for "being a little weak in the conjuring line." [95] The implication of the contrast is obvious. James himself aims at righting the balance; he himself is creating the psychological, moral novel which is also a work of art and form.

But the synthesis has been accomplished or approached before: in James' three masters, Turgenev, George Eliot, and Hawthorne. *A Sportsman's Sketches* "offers a capital example of moral meaning giving a sense to form and form giving relief to moral meaning." [96] "A certain middle field where morals and aesthetics move in concert" [97] is also occupied by George Eliot, though the novel was too often for her "not primarily a picture of life, capable of deriving a high value from its form, but a moralised fable." [98] Also Hawthorne, who deeply influenced James' own novels,[99] succeeded in transmuting "his heavy moral burden into the very substance of the imagination," [100] though James felt that he failed when he used allegory— never "a first-rate literary form" in spite of Bunyan and Spenser. Allegory is a deviation into didacticism: "It is apt to spoil two good things—a story and a moral, a meaning and a form." [101]

This union of morals and aesthetics seems to James peculiarly personal. "The deepest quality of a work of art will always be the quality of the mind of the producer . . . No good novel will ever proceed from a superficial mind; that seems to me an axiom which, for the artist in fiction, will cover all needful moral ground." [102] Thus James cannot accept Flaubert's insistence on complete "impersonality" and rejects Zola's reliance on scientific procedure.

"Vision and opportunity reside in a personal sense and a personal history, and no short cut to them in the interest of plausible fiction has ever been discovered." [103]

Still, James means by "personality" something individual which may be hidden, concealed, and implied, and he actually disapproved of the preoccupation with biography. He deplores the "complete intellectual muddle" which has made the pitiful story of the Brontë sisters cover and supplant "their matter, their spirit, their style, their talent, their taste." "Literature," he protests, "is an objective, a projected result; it is life that is the unconscious, the agitated, the struggling, floundering cause. But the fashion has been, in looking at the Brontës, so to confound the cause with the result that we cease to know, in the presence of such ecstasies, what we have hold of or what we are talking about. They represent, the ecstasies, the high-water mark of sentimental judgment." [104]

James, on this point, pleads for a sharp distinction between the main literary kinds. " 'Kinds' are the very life of literature, and truth and strength come from the complete recognition of them." "The confusion of kinds is the inelegance of letters and the stultification of values." [105] James was never particularly interested in poetry: he seems to lack the descriptive vocabulary in speaking of Musset, Morris, or Lowell. But he has his special genre theory for lyric poetry, a recognition of its peculiarly personal character. "The Poet is most the Poet when he is preponderantly lyrical, when he speaks, laughing or crying, most directly from his individual heart . . . It is not the *image* of life that he thus expresses, so much as life itself, in its sources—so much as his own intimate, essential states and feelings." [106] Thus he relishes the "intensity and closely personal savour" of Musset [107] and the "great gift of passion" in Byron and criticizes Lowell for being "too literary." His poetry is often "more the result of an interest in the general form than of the stirred emotion." [108] The intense egotism of Whitman, however, offended James, and he lectured him that art "requires, above all things, a suppression of one's self, a subordination of one's self to an idea." "You must forget yourself in your ideas" in order to be a poet. "Your personal qualities . . . are impertinent. You must be *possessed*, and you must strive to possess your possession." [109] The theoretical inconsistency is, no doubt, due to James' objection to a particular personality—the distastefully pagan, barbaric Whitman. He could,

however, relax his insistence on the purity of kinds, admitting that
for a particular effect lines may be crossed [110] or that an author such
as Kipling proves "that there are just as many kinds, as many ways,
as many forms and degrees of the 'right,' as there are personal points
in view." [111]

Still, in the novel James, while granting an ultimate personal
quality, insists on extreme objectivity, on illusion even to the degree
of delusion. The novel must not appear to be a novel; the author
must not interfere. He commends Turgenev for being "superior to
the strange and second-rate policy of explaining or presenting [his
characters] by reprobation or apology." [112] He comes down hard on
Trollope for taking "a suicidal satisfaction in reminding the reader
that the story he was telling was only, after all, a make-believe." [113]
Trollope, he complains, "admits that the events he narrates have not
really happened, and that he can give his narrative any turn the
reader may like best. Such a betrayal of a sacred office seems to me,
I confess, a terrible crime." [114] Miss Harriet Prescott in her novel
Azarian fingers her puppet to death. "'Good heavens! Madam!'
we are forever on the point of exclaiming, 'let the poor things
speak for themselves!' " [115] James, one must conclude, would have
no use for Sterne deliberately breaking the artistic illusion or for
Thackeray fingering his puppets.

The insistence on objectivity makes James condemn also the first-
person narrative or the fictional autobiography. *Gil Blas* and *David
Copperfield* are examples of the "terrible *fluidity* of self-revela-
tion." [116] But he is not satisfied with the usual narration by an
omniscient author. One way to eliminate him would be to approxi-
mate fiction to drama, to let dialogue grow, to compose by scenes
rather than by summary panoramic narration and description.
James' *The Awkward Age* is an experiment in this technique. In
general, however, James does not approve of an attempt to emulate
the drama. His own unlucky dramatic experiments sharpened his
consciousness that a play and a novel are eternally distinct and have
their own rigid laws. His admiration for the drama is largely due to
the demands for unity, economy, and concentration made by the
stage. In 1875 he considered the "dramatic form of all literary
forms the very noblest" and indulged in an elaborate comparison
between the drama and "a box of fixed dimensions and inelastic
material, into which a mass of precious things are to be packed

away." "To work successfully beneath a few grave, rigid laws, is always a strong man's highest ideal of success." [117] James' own plays are attempts to conform to the conventions of the well-made play imported from Paris: his articles on the younger Dumas and Rostand owe their tone to a genuine envy for their mastery of stage-craft and to James' overwhelming consciousness of its difficulties. He admired the *Comédie française* and some of its actors, such as Coquelin, almost unreservedly and took a dim view of the London stage and what he felt to be the amateurishness even of its most prominent actors, Henry Irving and Ellen Terry. He welcomed Ibsen for all sorts of reasons but especially because Ibsen "with his curious and beautiful passion for the unity of time (carried in him to a point which almost always implies also that of place), condemns himself to admirable rigors." [118]

Thus it seems hardly surprising that drama and dramatic unity in the novel are frequent terms of praise. Among George Eliot's novels, *The Mill on the Floss* has "most dramatic continuity," in distinction from descriptive, discursive narration.[119] The terms "scenic" and "scene" occur most frequently in contradiction to "picture." James speaks with approval of some of his stories as demeaning themselves "as little constituted dramas, little exhibitions founded on the logic of the 'scene,' the unit of the scene, the general scenic consistency." [120] In discussing *The Awkward Age* he praises the beauty of the conception "in this approximation of the respective divisions of my form to the successive Acts of a Play" [121] and its abiding "without a moment's deflexion by the principle of the stage-play." [122]

But James himself considered *The Awkward Age* an experiment and, in general, thought of scene as simply some concentrated action, not necessarily in dialogue form. Usually he disapproved of too much reliance on dialogue.

> Admirable for illustration, functional for illustration, dialogue has its function perverted, and therewith its life destroyed, when forced, all clumsily, into the constructive office. It is in the drama, of course, that it is constructive; but the drama lives by a law so different, verily, that everything that is right for it seems wrong for the prose picture, and everything that is right for the prose picture addressed directly, in turn, to the betrayal of the "play."

Dialogue, for instance, in the novels of the elder Dumas seems to James "the fluid element" "with so little wrought texture that we float and splash in it; feeling it thus resemble much more some capacious tepid tank than the figured tapestry, all overscored with objects in fine perspective, which symbolizes to me (if one may have a symbol) the last word of the achieved fable." [123] James complains of the "preposterous pretension of [dialogue], this most fatuous of the luxuries of looseness to acquit itself with authority of the structural and compositional office." He argues that spoken words in a novel should "live in a medium, and in a medium only," meaning apparently by medium a surrounding descriptive setting and analytical preparation, while a play "lives exclusively on the spoken word— not on the report of the thing said but, directly and audibly, on that very thing . . . it thrives by its law on the exercise under which the novel hopelessly collapses." [124] Thus a novel like Galdós' *Realidad,* which is completely in dialogue, or a story like Hemingway's "The Killers" would have met with James' disapproval as he insists on an alternation of narrative, description, and dialogue. Dialogue is only a means toward a general effect which James often calls the "picture," and "picture," at almost any turn, is "jealous of drama," as "drama is suspicious of picture." [125]

"Picture" is used rather shiftingly by James: at times it is only the descriptive part of a novel, inferior to the "scene"; at others it is a metaphor for the total composition, the general "presence" of the novel, sometimes with a definite parallel to painting in James' mind. The analogy of perspective or "foreshortening" seems to strike him most. "The mystery of the foreshortened procession of facts and figures . . . is but another name for the picture governed by the principle of composition" in contrast to the usual method of "the juxtaposition of items emulating the column of numbers of a schoolboy's sum in addition. It is the art of the brush, I know, as opposed to the art of the slate-pencil; but to the art of the brush the novel must return, I hold, to recover whatever may be still recoverable of its sacrificed honor." [126] But this analogy to painting and picture is strictly an analogy. "Foreshortening" in the novel means merely the author's skill of subordinating some events and characters, the perspective created by a focus of narration. James disapproved of the Goncourts' attempt to "poach" on the art of painting [127] and was always severely critical of writers merely interested in pictorial descriptions and local color. "Picture" is not enough. "Every good story is of course both a picture and an idea, and the more they are interfused the better the problem is solved." [128] James requires of D'Annunzio that we should "feel a general idea present" [129] and disparages Balzac as an intellect even though James recognizes that his books purvey a great many ideas. "But we must add that his letters make us feel that these ideas are themselves in a certain sense 'things.' " They are "pigments," [130] and pigments are obviously not enough. Ideas must not merely serve a decorative scheme; a human and intellectual meaning must arise from them.

If illusion and idea in the novel must be achieved by objective means, but not dramatically, neither by dialogue nor by a first-person narrative, no alternative remains but James' panacea: the use of an observer or, as he sometimes calls him, a "reflector." As early as 1868 James found it "good to think of an observer standing aloof, the critic, the idle commentator of it all, taking notes, as we may say, in the interest of truth." [131] Both in theory and in his novelistic practice James emphasized more and more a single focus of consciousness, a single "point of view," a "central light." [132] The *Prefaces* define these "centers": Maisie as the "ironic center" of *What Maisie Knew*,[133] Lambert Strether as "the register," the "reflector" of *The Ambassadors*, within whose compass everything is kept,[134] the "successive centers" in *The Wings of the Dove*, "portions of the subject commanded by them as by happy points of view," [135] and two characters, the Prince and the Princess, in the two halves of *The Golden Bowl*.[136] The point of view in James is not, however, just a technical device serving the "economy of treatment," permitting "recording consistency." [137] It serves to heighten the consciousness of the character and hence to increase the reader's identification with him. Ultimately it is another device to achieve the general effect of illusion. "The figures in any picture, the agents in any drama, are interesting only in proportion as they feel their respective situations." [138] They must therefore be "intense *perceivers*" [139] to serve their purpose. There must be a "mind of some sort—in the sense of a reflecting and colouring medium." [140] This insistence on the mind and intellect of the "reflector" explains James' criticism of both *Madame Bovary* and *L'Education senti-*

mentale. Emma Bovary suffers from the "poverty of her consciousness" and Frédéric Moreau is a nonentity, an "unconsciousness." It
was a mistake to present Madame Arnoux only through Moreau's
eyes, "a moral mistake," since Flaubert did not even realize that he
made it.[141] Everything depends on the quality of the consciousness
and not on the mere device of the focus or an intermediary narrator.
James thus did not approve of the technique of Conrad's *Chance,*
since he apparently did not admire the mind of Marlow. He thought
the book "an exhibition of method" and Conrad "a votary of the
way to do a thing that shall make it undergo most doing." [142] This
seems to describe James' own technique in later years, though not
apparently in James' own mind. He thought that in Conrad (whom
he admired for other reasons) [143] "objectivity is definitely com-
promised" by the complex reference to several narrators. There is a
"baffled relation between the subject matter and its emergence
which we find constituted by the circumvalations of 'Chance.' " [144]

The moral scrupulosity of Lambert Strether or again the very
innocence of Maisie set against the monstrous behavior of the grown-
ups make them fit subjects as "reflectors," but they can serve as
reflectors only because James considers them types. "Type," in
James, is both the specific and the general, the concrete universal,
the "eminent instance" [145] which thus achieves the universalizing
function of art. Turgenev's characters are praised for being particular and general, as is Homais in *Madame Bovary,* while Dickens'
characters are "particular without being general; because they are
individuals without being types; because we do not feel their continuity with the rest of humanity." [146] George Eliot "proceeds from
the abstract to the concrete"; her characters are often "disembodied
types," [147] or really not proper types but concepts. James, strangely
enough, considers Emma Bovary not a type in his sense: she is too
"specific," she does not even attain the average, the "middling."
"Hers is a narrow middling"; she is not sufficiently "illustra-
tional." [148] James seems to underrate Flaubert's implication in
Emma; he does not see the universality of her disillusioned romanticism and thinks too purely of the localized setting and the conventional plot of adultery and suicide.

James, in theory, would not, however, admit the isolation of a
character or type from the novel as a totality. He rejects Trollope's
preference for "novels of character" in opposition to "novels of

plot." It is "an idle controversy," as "character, in any sense in which we can get at it, is action, and action is plot, and any plot which hangs together, even if it pretend to interest us only in the fashion of a Chinese puzzle, plays upon our emotion, our suspense, by means of personal references." [149] In his best-known essay, "The Art of Fiction" (1884), James emphatically rejects the distinction. "What is character but the determination of incident? What is incident but the illustration of character? What is either a picture or a novel that is *not* of character?" [150] But often enough James does exalt character against description. "An author's paramount charge is the cure of souls, to the subjection, and if need be to the exclusion, of the picturesque. Let him look to his characters: his *figures* will take care of themselves." [151] The defense of character means a defense of psychology in the novel. "What we want is Passion's self . . . What do we care about the beauty of man or woman in comparison with their humanity? . . . The only lasting fictions are those which have spoken to the reader's heart, and not to his eye." [152] James somewhat indignantly defends himself against a critic of "An International Episode" [153] for showing "Bostonian nymphs" rejecting English dukes "for psychological reasons." "A psychological reason is, to my imagination, an object adorably pictorial," [154] it is an "adventure" as "it is an incident for a woman to stand up with her hand resting on a table and look out at you in a certain way." But this adventure or incident is "at the same time an expression of character." [155] James would not admit any such thing as an "adventure pure and simple; there is only mine and yours, and his and hers," [156] an adventure felt and experienced, "felt life." [157] Action and character, incident and motivation, romance and psychology collaborate and cannot be conceived separately. "The soul of a novel is its action," [158] but action may be merely the look of a woman standing up. Action is *"line,* bony structure and palpable, as it were, tense cord." *"I* like a rope (the rope of the *direction and march of the subject,* the action) pulled, like a taut cable between a steamer and a tug, from beginning to end." [159] He complains of a novel by Hugh Walpole that *"line* (the only thing *I* value in a fiction etc.) is replaced by a vast formless featherbediness" [160] and he objects to Tolstoy for the same reason. Tolstoy is a "wonderful mass of life . . . an immense event, a kind of splendid accident . . . a monster harnessed to his great subject—all human life!—as an elephant might be harnessed." [161] Tolstoy's and Dostoevsky's novels are "fluid pudding, though not tasteless, because the amount of their own minds and souls in solution in the broth gives it savour and flavour, thanks to the strong, rank quality of their genius and their experience." But he deplores their "lack of composition, their defiance of economy and architecture." [162]

The comments on Tolstoy show that James held a narrow view of form and even kept an untenable divorce between form and substance, form and life-content when confronted with works of art in a different tradition. He obviously did not recognize the complex composition and stylistic mastery of Tolstoy, since it was another kind of "form" and "style" than Turgenev's or his own. There was, one must admit, also a curious sentimental streak in James, which made him resent the supposed cruelty of the two great Russians and the cynicism of Flaubert and Zola. James preferred Turgenev's maudlin story *Mumu* to Flaubert's *Un Cœur simple* [163] and admired even such an absurdly contrived fantasy as Turgenev's *Phantoms*.[164]

But theoretically, James was perfectly aware of the unity of content and form. He complains of "the perpetual clumsy assumption that subject and style are—aesthetically speaking, or in the living work—different and separable things." [165] He often argues that "the grave distinction between substance and form in a really wrought work of art signally breaks down," that it is impossible "to mark any such joint or seam," or to "disintegrate a synthesis" such as his novel *The Awkward Age*.[166] It is the highest praise for him to say of *Madame Bovary* that "the form is in *itself* as interesting, as active, as much of the essence of the subject as the idea, and yet so close is its fit and so inseparable its life that we catch it at no moment on any errand of its own." [167] The harmony of form and substance is James' constant requirement: as "form alone *takes*, and holds and preserves, substance," [168] while "any claimed independence of 'form' on its part is the most abject of fallacies." [169] This is why James considered translating impossible and disliked being translated. He wrote to a prospective translator most discouragingly: "I feel that in a literary work of the least complexity the very form and texture are the substance itself and that the flesh is indetachable from the bones! Translation is an effort—though a most flattering one!—to *tear* the hapless flesh." He rejoiced that his memoirs, *A Small Boy and*

Others, "is locked fast in the golden cage of the *intraduisible.*" [170]

"Form" in James means most often composition, architecture—
for example, the right distribution of conversation, narration, and
pictorial matter. He finds Howells deficient in it [171] and lauds his
own *Ambassadors* as "the most proportioned of his productions"
alongside *The Portrait of a Lady,* which is "a structure reared with
an 'architectural' competence." [172] But often also James contrasts
"form" in the sense of composition with "texture" and style. Texture is something else than style. Dumas, George Sand, Trollope
"weave a loose web," while Balzac "weaves a dense one." The "tis-
sue of his tales is always extraordinarily firm and hard" and even
shows "fantastic cohesiveness." [173] But texture is not style and style
is not form. "Madame Sand's novels have plenty of style, but they
have no form. Balzac's have not a shred of style, but they have a great
deal of form" (and, we have been told, texture) .[174] But surely
"style" is here conceived very narrowly, as Balzac has style (or
several styles) . It is hard to see how James could deny both style
and form to Emerson and find him "a striking exception to the
general rule that writings live in the last resort by their form." [175]
Though Emerson's *Essays* have their compositional principles, they
struck James as a mere mosaic of desultory sentences: but surely
Emerson has an unmistakable and memorable verbal style. James
admires style and even "manner" in Stevenson and D'Annunzio.[176]
But evidently he has a whole gamut of uses for the term; he can
praise George Sand's style: "That is what it is really to *have* style—
when you set about performing the act of life," [177] where the term
means simply the power of creation, of giving life to art, or he can,
on the other hand, protest against Flaubert's worship of style. "Style
itself moreover, with all respect to Flaubert, never *totally* beguiles;
since even when we are so queerly constituted as to be ninety-nine
parts literary we are still a hundredth part something else." [178]

But in spite of all these shifts of terminology James has an excellent hold on the concept of organic form. He tells us that he
delights "in a deep-breathing economy and an organic form," [179]
refers complacently to his own "organic form," [180] and writes criticism from the very beginning of his career with the concept and
metaphor in mind. "A genuine poem is a tree that breaks into
blossom and shakes in the wind," while George Eliot's *The Spanish
Gipsy* is rather "like a vast mural design in mosaic-work." [181] "A

novel," he goes on, elaborating the metaphor, "is a living thing, all one and continuous, like any other organism, and in proportion as it lives will it be found, I think, that in each of the parts there is something of each of the other parts." [182]

Unity is a requirement of organic art, but in a proper organistic theory it is unity in variety, an inner, living unity. James recognizes this when he praises Flaubert for being "the devotee of the phrase" which is "properly part of something else that is in turn part of something other, part of a reference, a tone, a passage, a page." [183] He praises *Silas Marner* because it has "that simple, rounded, consummate aspect, that absence of loose ends and gaping issues, which marks a classical work" [184] and is pleased with Arnold's *Essays* for having a definite topic with a beginning, middle, and end, for today, on the whole, "a book or an article is looked upon as a kind of Staubbach waterfall, discharging itself into infinite space." [185] But this legitimate demand on all art becomes a denial of different organizations when James tells of his "mortal horror" of two stories in one and compares a novel without a single center to a "wheel without a hub." [186] *Daniel Deronda* is described, in an appreciative dialogue, as a two-center novel,[187] and *War and Peace,* he complains, has no "center of the interest." [188] James' criticism of *The Ring and the Book* assumes this same rigid standard: James proposes to retell Browning's story from a single point of view, the consciousness of Caponsacchi.[189] James, one fears, violates here his own rule to grant the artist his theme, as Browning's main interest was precisely in the multiplicity of perspectives from which he told his story several times over.

Unity in James is not only of perspective but also of tone. Reflecting on Balzac's *Curé de village* he complains of the "fatal break of 'tone,' the one unpardonable sin for the novelist," [190] about the middle of the book, while he praises Gautier's travel books: "each of his chapters of travel has a perfect tone of its own and that unity of effect which is the secret of the rarest artists." [191] The analogy to a painting, its "keeping," its harmony, is again in James' mind. "Form," "unity," "tone" create "illusion," the illusion of a "world." Mrs. Gaskell's *Wives and Daughters* has "reared a new and arbitrary world over [the reader's] heedless head—a world insidiously inclusive of him (such is the *assoupissement* of his critical sense), complete in every particular." [192] But this illusory world of fiction (and art in general) must be, James feels, a joyous and good world. This is why he chides Turgenev for his gloom and Flaubert for his hatred of the *bourgeoisie* and his tortured martyrdom for style. "We hold to the good old belief that the presumption, in life, is in favour of the brighter side. . . . The artist . . . should have at least tried his best to be cheerful. . . . We value most the 'realists' who have an ideal of delicacy and the elegiasts who have an ideal of joy." [193] James could, in his early years, say, somewhat crudely, "To be completely great, a work of art must lift up the reader's heart," and "Life is dispiriting; art is inspiring." [194] Similarly, he remonstrates with Vernon Lee about her novel *Miss Brown* that "*life* is less criminal, less obnoxious, less objectionable, less crude, more *bon enfant*, more mixed and casual, and even in its most offensive manifestations, more *pardonable*" [195] than it appears in her novel. Flaubert's intense hatreds surprise and distress James. "How can art be so genuine and yet so unconsoled, so unhumorous, so unsociable? How can it be such a curse without being also a blessing? . . . Why, in short, when the struggle is success, should the success not be at last serenity?" [196] James cannot share Flaubert's "puerile dread of the grocer, the *bourgeois*. . . . That worthy citizen ought never to have kept a poet from dreaming." [197] *Bouvard et Pécuchet,* James felt, "is surely, in the extreme juvenility of its main idea, one of the oddest productions for which a man who had lived long in the world was ever responsible." [198] Flaubert's hatred of his public was so excessive that it amounted to a betrayal of art. "He hovered forever at the public door . . . He should at least have listened at the chamber of the soul." [199] The tone of self-consolation is obvious; James was deeply discouraged by the growing indifference to his own work; he retired more and more into the chamber of the soul and hoped only vaguely that the spread of the reading public, especially in the United States, would lead to the rise of "individual publics positively more sifted and evolved than anywhere else" which would then "contain shoals of fish rising to more delicate bait," [200] such as, presumably, his own novels offered. The prophecy, in a manner, has been fulfilled and James has today his devoted public and acute analysts who have risen to his bait.

James, in spite of his awareness of evil, preserved an ideal of optimism, of serenity, of trust in nature and human nature, a final almost Olympian perspective. This temper, so curiously similar to his brother's and father's, is also at the roots of his aesthetic, which is, in its basic positions, organistic, illusionist, i.e., asking the artist to create a world that is somehow like life and to create it on the analogy of nature in order to support man in a belief in the moral and social order of the universe. On these two points, aesthetics and the general temper of serenity, the parallel to Goethe seems striking. (James' own optimism was rudely shaken only by the outbreak of the First World War.) [201] There is no need to make much of a direct contact, since Arnold and (in parts) Sainte-Beuve achieved a similar combination, even though James seems to me nearer in temper and aesthetic doctrine to Goethe than either of these models. James, we must remember, had praised Goethe as the "great critic"; and he had early written a review of *Wilhelm Meister* in which he voiced his admiration, in spite of many reservations regarding Goethe's novelistic skill, for Goethe's power of creating human beings, for the "luminous atmosphere of justice which fills the book," for his plan: *non flere, non indignari, sed intelligere.*[202] James later chided the younger Dumas for his violently nationalistic and moralistic preface to a French translation of *Faust,* proclaiming his agreement with Goethe's "immense respect for reality," and admiration for his use of facts, "the mysterious music he drew from them." [203]

Intelligence, reality, "nature" which is also form and illusion in art, the joy of art and its civilizing power, are also James' preoccupations. James alone in his time and place in the English-speaking world holds fast to the insights of organistic aesthetics and thus constitutes a bridge from the early nineteenth century to modern criticism.

11: THE RUSSIAN RADICAL CRITICS

NIKOLAY CHERNYSHEVSKY (1828-1889)

AFTER THE DEATH of Belinsky (1848) a vacuum seems to have existed in Russian criticism for a few years. But in the middle fifties a devoted follower of Belinsky, Nikolay Chernyshevsky, began writing on aesthetic theory and criticism. His critical activity lasted only a few years, as his interests were more and more absorbed in economics and politics. In 1862 he was arrested and later deported to Siberia. His young disciple, Nikolay Dobrolyubov, began writing criticism in 1857 but died four years later of tuberculosis. Just about the time the careers of Chernyshevsky and Dobrolyubov had come to an end, Dmitri Pisarev began his short writing life, of which four years were spent in a fortress: he committed suicide by drowning, aged only 28.[1]

The continuity between these critics and their master, Belinsky, is obvious. Still, they differ sharply from him, however sincerely they may have thought that they were only developing the ideas and conceptions of Belinsky's last stage. The intellectual atmosphere had changed greatly in the short time since Belinsky's death: Belinsky had grown up in the shade of German idealism and had never abandoned its basic doctrines on art and history. Chernyshevsky, Drobrolyubov, and Pisarev had no understanding of the German romantic views. Their philosophy precluded this: it is frequently called Feuerbachian and considered identical with that of the latest stage of Belinsky. But I cannot see any evidence that these writers adopted the specific doctrines of Feuerbach, a highly sentimental, fervid theologian, imbued with Hegel's ways of thinking. They must rather be described as materialistic monists, most deeply influenced by such popularizers of the scientific outlook as Vogt, Moleschott, and especially Büchner, and by the English Utilitarians. They propounded a materialism substantially identical with that of Holbach and Cabanis: mental processes are physical processes, hence all action is completely determined by them. Religion is superstition. This deterministic materialism is paradoxically combined with great fervor for social reform: and even with a spirit of sacrifice, unexplainable by the hedonism, enlightened egoism, and utilitarianism of their theories.

But we must confine ourselves to their literary theory and criticism, and make sharp distinctions between them, on this point. Chernyshevsky, though a commanding figure in the Russian revolutionary movement, eminent also as an economist, must be ranked lowest among the group as a literary critic. He seems to have been a man with hardly any aesthetic sensibility: a crude, harsh thinker, preoccupied, even when speaking of literature, with immediate politics. Chernyshevsky does not even believe in the social role of art. It is apparently no mere smokescreen for the censor when he argues at length and with many examples that "not by books or periodicals or newspapers is the spirit of a nation awakened—but only by events."[2] Rather, literature induces a peaceful and reasonable disposition in the mind aroused by events. Those who wish for the preservation of existing customs should not be afraid of literature. It cannot incite new demands and promote new tendencies.[3] Though this might almost seem to be said with tongue in cheek, we must conclude from Chernyshevsky's other writings and his philosophical position that he actually thought of literature as a mere surrogate, *Ersatz* for life, a passive mirror of society.

Chernyshevsky's theoretical views are most fully stated in his dissertation *The Aesthetic Relations of Art to Reality* (1855). There he argues against Hegelian aesthetics, or rather against isolated Hegelian formulas in F. T. Vischer's volumes. His own position is then stated simply and clearly. Art is an inferior reproduction of reality. The only function of art is that of spreading knowledge about reality: to remind us of it or to inform those who have not experienced it. The purely aesthetic is dismissed as mere sensual pleasure, trivial at its best, reprehensible at its worst. Beauty is simply life, and not a quality distinguishable from it: thus almost all young women are beautiful.[4]

His views of the individual arts are similarly crude. Sculpture is quite useless: any number of persons walking the streets of Petersburg are more beautiful than the most beautiful statue. Painting is even more inferior to reality: greenish and reddish colors on a picture cannot compare with the real color of a human body or face.[5] Chernyshevsky recognizes music as the direct outpouring of feeling only in song: but then it is not art but nature itself, like the song of birds. All music that deviates from natural song, especially instrumental music, is a mere substitute for song and hence inferior.[6] Poetry, as it does not affect the senses directly but appeals to imagination, fares even worse compared to reality. The strength and clarity of its impression is far below that of the other arts, as words are always general and hence pale and feeble. The poet's invention must not be overrated: the more we know about the poet, the more we have to conclude that he is a historian, an author of memoirs.[7] Nor is plot-invention anything to boast of: any French or English crime gazette contains more interesting and more intricate real-life stories than any writer can devise.[8] All the superiority of literature over an exact report can be reduced to a greater fullness of details supplied by literature, to a "rhetorical amplification" of the facts. Why then is art valued at all? asks Chernyshevsky, and he can answer only that man values what he has made himself, out of vanity, or because art satisfies his propensity for daydreaming, his innate sentimentality, or simply because art reinforces his memory. A portrait reminds us of an absent friend; a picture, of the sea. Imagination is weak: we need reminders. Art may acquaint us with what we could not experience ourselves. But basically art does no more than any reasonable discussion of a subject. Art is, at most, a "handbook" for those beginning to study life: it prepares us for the reading of the original sources and, from time to time, serves as reference.[9] Here, surely, aesthetics has reached its nadir: or rather it has been asked to commit suicide.

Similar crude views are propounded on less general questions. What is tragic? asks Chernyshevsky and answers: simply any suffering or death; even a chance death.[10] What is sublime? Anything that is larger in comparison to what we expect in a given context.[11] Form and content are entirely separate. The content of art is all reality, however ugly by old standards; and who cares for form? [12]

These views are matched by opinions about specific works of art: Homer is incoherent, offends by his cynicism and lacks all moral feeling. Aeschylus and Sophocles are rude and dry. Beethoven is often incomprehensible and wild; Mozart's *Don Giovanni* is boring.[13]

In short this famous dissertation still admired in Soviet Russia and by Georg Lukács, which makes a show of scholarly rigor with its parade of definitions, is a crude act of defiance by a young provincial who wants to thumb his nose at what the world has hitherto considered great and beautiful, worth their time and supreme effort. But Chernyshevsky is deadly serious in exalting reality, worshiping fact and knowledge, rejecting everything sensual, artificial, and useless, and asserting the complete identity of art and life.

Some of the positions of the dissertation are elucidated, in their historical relationships and applications, by an early review of a Russian translation of Aristotle's *Poetics* (1854) and by the long series of articles called *Studies in the Age of Gogol* (1855). The review of Aristotle makes an appeal to Plato's rejection of art but finds something valuable in Aristotle's theory of imitation, though Aristotle is criticized for his dry formalism. Chernyshevsky violently rejects Plotinus' aesthetics as the source of contemporary (German) mystical aestheticism. Though Chernyshevsky's knowledge of the ancients is largely secondhand,[14] the paper shows insight into the eternal relevance of the positions taken by the main Greek philosophers and a sense of the unity of theory and history. "Without history," says Chernyshevsky, "there is no theory, without theory no history."[15] But as in the dissertation, Chernyshevsky constantly minimizes and distributes the values of art. He recognizes that art causes pleasure but argues that "sitting and chatting on the bench in front of the house among peasants or around the samovar among the townspeople has done more to develop good humor and good feeling toward other people than all the paintings, from the bast pictures of peasants to the 'Last Day of Pompeii.' "[16] A curious new argument is put forward for identifying novel and drama. "A dramatic work can just as well (or even better) be told in epic form." Yet he admits that the converse is not quite true, because a novel turned into a stage play would become even more tiresome. Boredom is multiplied a thousandfold by the presence of a thousand bored spectators.[17]

Studies in the Age of Gogol shows that Chernyshevsky had the makings of an intellectual historian. He gives accurate and firsthand descriptions of the critics of the time, Polevoy, Senkovsky, Shevyrev, Nadezhdin, in order to introduce a full exposition of Belinsky's ideas. Much of the book is quotation: but one must realize that

Belinsky's writings could not be collected at that time and that
quoting them from the periodicals in which they had been printed
was, in itself, a great service to his audience. One cannot expect a
dispassionate attitude from Chernyshevsky: he was a publicist
defending and promoting a cause. But his claims for Belinsky seem
to me reasonable and even moderate. He emphasizes the fact that
Belinsky was the first genuine historian of Russian literature who
had clear conceptions about the nature of literary history.[18] He
defends the good sense and restraint of the reputedly "furious"
Belinsky; he tries to demonstrate the logic and continuity of
Belinsky's development; and he rightly asserts that criticism in
Russia has a much wider function than in the West. In Germany
there are special publics, for instance, for the novel. In England
there are philosophers, jurists, economists read by the layman.
"With us," says Chernyshevsky, "literature constitutes the whole
intellectual life of the nation." In Russia, then, writers and poets
should feel their obligations a thousand times more strongly than
in the West.[19]

It is sometimes difficult to distinguish what is exposition and
what is commentary in Chernyshevsky's text: he wanted to shield
himself behind the authority of Belinsky or, to put it more kindly,
to fuse the master's authority with his own. But if we take into
account long reviews of editions of Pushkin and Gogol [20] and other
scattered pronouncements, a picture of Chernyshevsky's views on
the main Russian classics emerges.

Though Chernyshevsky wrote a laudatory *Life of Pushkin* for
popular consumption and honored his work and name, he looks at
him as a figure of the past, a pure artist who has only historical
significance. Pushkin is praised as the founder of Russian literature, "as the first among us who raised literature to national significance. He was a man of extraordinary intellect and excellent
education, though he was neither a thinker nor a scholar. Every page
of his overflows with good sense and the life of an educated mind,
though one must not seek deep meaning, clearly discerned or coherent ideas in his writings." Besides, Pushkin seems not original
enough: he reminds one too much of Byron, Shakespeare, and
Scott.[21]

The main praise goes to Gogol as the founder of the "critical
tendency" in Russian literature, the creator of a school, who made

Russian literature independent of foreign influences and made it an organ of national self-knowledge.[22] Chernyshevsky approaches Gogol's literary evolution in the spirit of a historian of ideas. Using the letters first collected at that time, he shows that one cannot speak of a betrayal of the liberal cause by Gogol, as his later views were prepared and anticipated from the first. Chernyshevsky analyzes the second volume of *Dead Souls,* stressing its continuity with the first. It seems to him as good as the first as long as Gogol moves in the old sphere. He shows some literary discernment in pointing out the passages and scenes where Gogol does this but strangely enough admires extravagantly the dreary concluding speech of the Governor General against corruption.[23] While Chernyshevsky is right in seeing the continuity of Gogol's evolution, he is, as a liberal democrat, inclined to dismiss Gogol's ideas. For instance, he pays no attention to Gogol's early essays, which show a respectable knowledge of conservative, largely German romantic theories of history and art. Chernyshevsky ascribes Gogol's reactionary views to his poor education, the "narrow horizon" of his youth, his expatriation and isolation, and his association with writers such as Shevyrev and Zhukovsky during his later years.[24] Still, within the limits of Chernyshevsky's incomprehension of the religious and conservative outlook on life, his view of Gogol even as a political writer shows considerable historical insight and psychological sympathy.

The exposition in *Studies in the Age of Gogol* of Belinsky's last writings allows Chernyshevsky to restate his views of the relation between literature and society. His attack on "pure art," art for art's sake, is, we see more clearly than in his dissertation, not a reasoned rejection of German theories of the autonomy of art or even a rejection of the flaming proclamations of French romantics, but an attack on the view that art is pleasure. Chernyshevsky cannot think of pure art as anything but drinking songs and erotic conversation;[25] art, I should say, not for art's sake but for the sake of wine or sex. It is easy for him to argue that this Epicureanism lacks a vital link with the rational needs of the modern age, an age devoted to humanity, to the struggle for the betterment of human life. In obvious contradiction to his usual skepticism as to the social effect of art, Chernyshevsky says now that "poetry is life, action, struggle, passion," and that literature cannot help serving the tendencies of an age.[26] He admires and recommends the social writers of his age: Béranger, George Sand, Heine, Dickens, Thackeray, without making much distinction between them.

Chernyshevsky's attitude toward his Russian contemporaries was defined in many reviews during the next years: one hesitates to call the bulk of these articles literary criticism. He shows, for instance, the detrimental influence of the Slavophiles on Ostrovsky,[27] and he attacks the flabby liberalism of Turgenev in the guise of a review of the story of *Asya*. This article, "The Russian at a *Rendezvous*" (1858), is too characteristic of his method and the methods of the whole group not to merit description. Turgenev's protagonist (not hero surely), a weak man who retreats before the love of an ardent girl, is declared the representative of Russian society, a symbol of the decaying aristocracy. The scene of Asya's rejection is considered a "symptom of the disease that corrupts all our actions."[28] This melancholy story of an abortive love is used as an allegory of Russian will-lessness, as a peg to hang on a warning to the aristocracy to heed the needs of the time. The general attitude is blatantly set forth in an often-quoted passage: "Goodbye erotic questions! A reader of our time, occupied with problems of administrative and judiciary institutions, of financial reforms, of the emancipation of the serfs, does not care for them."[29] The reader is Chernyshevsky, and the public for which he spoke either rejected art as sensual pleasure or wanted to use it as an instrument of propaganda. Turgenev's delicate art did not interest them at all.

But it would be a mistake to deny to Chernyshevsky all literary sensitivity and ability in analysis. His review of Tolstoy's *Childhood, Boyhood* and *Sebastopol Stories* (1856) shows that there were the germs of a good critic in him. Tolstoy is praised as a psychologist who describes the "psychic process, its forms, its laws, its dialectics accurately." Chernyshevsky quotes a passage describing the feelings of a soldier waiting for the fall of a shell and calls it "interior monologue."[30] He then compares Tolstoy's art with that of a painter who catches the sparkling reflection of light on quickly bouncing waves or the shimmer of a ray of light on rustling leaves. Something similar seems to him to have been achieved by Tolstoy in describing the mysterious movement of the life of the soul.[31] Chernyshevsky points out what has been elaborated since: Tolstoy's technique has affinity with impressionism. But it is typical of Chernyshevsky and his audience that after praising Tolstoy's moral purity, Chernyshevsky suddenly turns to an embarrassed defense of Tolstoy's theme of childhood. *Childhood,* he says at length, is about a child and not about issues such as war or social reform, but it is still worth reading.[32]

NIKOLAY DOBROLYUBOV (1836–1861)

It is to Chernyshevsky's credit that he himself saw that literary criticism was not his strong point or main interest and that he ceded the literary department of the *Contemporary* to his young disciple, Nikolay Dobrolyubov, in 1857. After that he wrote hardly any literary criticism. The book *Lessing, His Time, His Life, His Work* (1857), though obviously devised to exalt the role of the critic in national life, is a disappointing compilation from Danzel and Guhrauer.[1] It is preoccupied with history and biography and never gets to a proper discussion of Lessing's works or significance.

Dobrolyubov was, of course, just as little interested in art as his master, though he wrote much more exclusively about belles-lettres. But he applied more consistently, more systematically and consciously the point of view indicated by Chernyshevsky. He was the most important of these critics as a literary theorist, though he had as little literary taste and sensibility and was as diffuse and repetitious as Chernyshevsky. He is even more lumpish and stodgy, and lacks all literary grace and intellectual agility; he is strangely unctuous in his violently secular way.

Dobrolyubov never tires of repeating the view expounded by Chernyshevsky that literature is only a mirror of life which reflects but cannot change reality. This view expressed in an early discussion of Saltykov-Shchedrin's *Provincial Sketches* (1857) and just as emphatically in his last essay on Dostoevsky's *Insulted and Injured* (1861), runs through all of Dobrolyubov's writings. Sometimes he refutes absurdly inflated claims for the effect of literature on society: Virgil, he says, could not change Tiberius into Aeneas, Demosthenes could not save Athens from Philip of Macedon.[2] Literature did not raise the question of the emancipation of the serfs: rather it was raised by life, and then literature brought about a "calm contemplation, a reassessment of all the aspects of the problem."[3] At times, Dobrolyubov points to a vague future, to social action for the solution of a problem posited by literature. Thus Ostrovsky's plays, he shows at great length, describe types of domestic tyrants and down-trodden women: they make us see this "realm of darkness" among the Russian merchant class. But the way out of it must be found by life itself: "Literature only reproduces life, it never portrays what does not exist in reality."[4] Similarly Dostoevsky (Dobrolyubov, of course, knew only the early Dostoevsky, up to *Insulted and Injured*) shows us forgotten, oppressed people, whose human dignity has been humiliated and insulted, but offers no solution or way out. Dostoevsky needs supplementation and commentary, presumably of a kind Dobrolyubov was anxious to supply. The essay concludes with a call to follow the "uninterrupted, harmonious, powerful, irrepressible stream of life," the wave of the future in which all these critics believed.[5]

But in spite of these many declarations of the humbleness of literature's role as a mere passive mirror of life, Dobrolyubov, almost as often, assigns it a slightly more active role. The influence of literature, he says early, is only indirect; it spreads slowly; but still it helps to clarify existing tendencies in society.[6] Literature is " the only way of knowing what is defeated and what is victorious, or what is beginning to permeate and predominate in the moral life of society."[7] It may even be useful in "quickening and giving greater fullness to the conscious work of society."[8] "Literature is an auxiliary force, the importance of which lies in propaganda, and the merit of which is determined by what it propagates and how it propagates it." Once he goes further: the very greatest writers have grasped the truths of philosophers and depicted them in action. Representing a higher stage of human consciousness in a given age, they rise above the auxiliary role of literature and enter the ranks of historical leaders who have helped mankind to become clearly conscious of its vital strength and natural inclinations. Shakespeare is Dobrolyubov's one example of such greatness; he considers Dante, Goethe, and Byron to be of lower rank: none of them so fully symbolizes an entire phase of human development as Shakespeare did.[9] Occasionally, Dobrolyubov would even express a touching trust that the dissemination of ideas by literature might be easily "expressed in administrative activity";[10] that "at a certain point of evolution, literature becomes one of the powers moving society." Literature tells "society of honorable and useful activity. It chants always the same song: Get up! wake up! look at yourself!"[11] Thus Dobrolyubov runs the gamut from complete pessimism to messianic hopes: from the view that literature is a passive mirror to the view that it incites to direct action, transforms society.

An early essay, "On the Share of the People in the Development of Russian Literature" (1858), ostensibly a review of A. Milyukov's *Studies in the History of Russian Poetry,* suggests a historical scheme according to which Russian literature moves toward becoming truly national, all-national, representative not only of one class but of the whole people. The ideal is phrased in terms of romantic nationalism, but its implications are much more concretely social. "Literature," he says, "cannot anticipate life, but it must anticipate the formal, official manifestation of the interests active in life. As long as an idea is only in the minds of people, as long as it is seen as realizable only in the future, literature should evaluate it from various sides and from the point of view of different interests. But as soon as the idea has become an act, has been formulated and solved definitely, literature has nothing more to do. It can at most only praise what has been done." [12] This awkward passage well illustrates Dobrolyubov's pervasive dilemma: his theoretical conviction that literature is mere words which cannot affect reality, and the practical impossibility of the resignation implied, the need of demanding from literature a discussion of what he considered new and progressive ideas in the hope that they may prevail after all.

The same hesitation runs through the historical survey: on the one hand, the development of literature is said to reflect the changes of society passively and inertly; on the other, it seems to him shameful that literature has not expressed what he considers the real needs and character of the nation. Dobrolyubov wants an all-national literature, above parties and cliques, but recognizes that literature has "always expressed the interests and opinions of those whose job was the writing of books or of those who supported them ever so little." [13] In glancing at Old Russian literature he can see only a complete lack of poetry, deadness, abstractness.[14] In discussing a religious tract, he complains that one could hardly have chosen anything more remote from the life of the nation than the theme of ritual.[15] Lomonosov is chided for not "feeling for the class from which he has risen." [16] Pushkin, though praised for his historical role and his artistry, is considered as lacking in true national spirit. His aristocratic prejudices, his epicurean tendencies, his French education, his dilettantism (he was a man to whom "strenuous activity of the mind was unknown")—all this prevented him from being permeated by the spirit of Russian nationality.[17] He acquired only its form, not its substance. Gogol came nearer to Dobrolyubov's ideal but did not reach it. He achieved a truly national point of view but did so unconsciously.[18] Thus the proper fusion of literature and nationality is still an ideal in the future.

Dobrolyubov wavers between a romantic conception of nationality as something uniquely Russian and a hope for a literature written for the peasant masses, representing them and comprehensible to them. He has a very real sense of the thinness and smallness of contemporary Russian literary culture; he says that there are only 20,000 subscribers to all Russian magazines and only 15,000 school teachers in the whole country. It is, he admits wryly, an illusion to think that Russian literature is truly national. "Our interests, our sufferings are remote and funny, incomprehensible to the mass: our enthusiasm seems to it even comic."[19] Feeling his isolation as an intellectual, Dobrolyubov raises the question of popular art, which was to find such radical answer in Tolstoy and in Soviet policies.

But Dobrolyubov rarely turns to these problems. In his practical criticism he centers mainly on one problem: the trueness to life of the novels and plays he discusses. Often, he quite consciously applies the realistic standard of the "slice of life." He complains that Ostrovsky does not show us how a character in a play "grew and was brought up, what influenced him in his youth."[20] He disparages strictly coordinated and logical plots and consistent characters such as Tartuffe, Richard III, and Shylock, because presenting them on the Russian stage would mean ascribing to Russian life something it does not contain. "Suppose," he asks, "that naturalness precludes consistency?"[21] He never doubts that "naturalness" has precedence over unity and coherence. Dobrolyubov thus attacks the demands made on the drama by the French well-made play. Why should there not be subordinate figures if they help to explain the situation?[22] There is no need of poetic justice, as there is no justice in real life.[23] He defends Ostrovsky's *Storm* against critics who complain of a dispersion of interest in the conflict with the mother-in-law or of the parallel love affairs.[24] All this may happen in life and thus can be represented on the stage.

The criterion of lifelikeness is equally applied to Dostoevsky: *The Double* is unfortunately fantastic;[25] Natasha in *Insulted and Injured* sounds like the author;[26] her love for the depraved Alyosha is unnatural;[27] and the psychology of the narrator is obscure.[28] Dobrolyubov would like to praise Dostoevsky for his pictures of downtrodden humanity but cannot bring himself to consider *Insulted and Injured* as a work of art at all. It cannot be studied from an aesthetic point of view;[29] the result, he implies, would be entirely negative. He takes Dostoevsky's or rather the narrator's disparaging remarks about his novel writing very literally and is pleased by his lack of aesthetic pretensions. Besides, he argues, "as long as literature has the slightest possibility of even distantly serving social interests and of expressing even obscurely and feebly its sympathy with them, one cannot get excited even by the most brilliant of aesthetic exercises."[30] In the case of Ostrovsky, Dobrolyubov feels that aesthetic canons have happily been violated in favor of realism (and hence should be discarded). Confronted with Dostoevsky's art, he cannot approve its deviations from the canon of the realistic novel. He throws him easily to the aesthetic wolves.

For the most part, Dobrolyubov cheerfully admits his lack of interest in literary matters. He constantly repeats that subject matter alone decides: he condemns Fët for writing about babbling brooks and prefers Tyuchev for his interest in principles and social questions.[31] Pushkin, we are told, would not attract any attention in the present day if he appeared with the same contents.[32] Dobrolyubov says that he himself writes "pathological studies of Russian society,"[33] that he looks for the moral in a fable.[34] In a suppressed conclusion to the essay on Ostrovsky's "Realm of Darkness" Dobrolyubov boasts that he uses metaphorical expressions out of necessity: he is obliged to deal mainly with the products of an author's imagination and not directly with the phenomena of life.[35] Censorship, he implied, prevents him from writing on society and politics: literature is only a pretext.

Still, Dobrolyubov made a contribution to the theory of the social study of literature. He, apparently for the first time, thought clearly of "social types" as revealing an author's world-view, independently of or even contrary to his conscious intentions. The actual world-view of a writer must be sought in the living images he creates. He concentrates the facts of real life into them.[36] "In these images the poet may, imperceptibly even to himself, grasp and express an inner meaning long before his mind can define it. Sometimes the artist may even fail to grasp the meaning of what he himself is depicting. It is precisely the function of criticism to explain the meaning hidden in the artist's creations."[37] The contrast between the social import of Gogol's characters and the theories formulated later by the author is Dobrolyubov's stock example. The author's intention may remain forever unknown, and even if it be clearly expressed, it may not be in complete harmony with what his artistic nature has imbibed from the impressions of real life. The conscious intention of an author remains a secondary and personal question.[88]

This method of studying social types, with its dismissal of what today is called the "intentional fallacy," seems a valuable technique; it distinguishes between an overt and a latent meaning of a work of art somewhat as, in different contexts, Freud, Pareto, or Mannheim distinguish them. It is a call to penetrate hidden assumptions, to identify the crystallizing points of social change. Social types—in the sense of general types like the gentleman, the intellectual, the peasant—had already begun to attract consideration in French literary discussions. The German romantic critics, especially A. W. Schlegel and Schelling, had discussed the great mythical types of humanity: Faust, Hamlet, Don Quixote, Sancho Panza. Schlegel and other German critics had dismissed conscious intention as a criterion of value.[39] But these motifs had not, I believe, coalesced, as they did in Dobrolyubov.

Unfortunately, Dobrolyubov was unable to keep steadily to his central insight, either in theory or in critical practice. He thought of literary images, with his pat utilitarianism, as "facilitating the formulation of correct ideas about things and the dissemination of these ideas among men." [40] He conceived the truth of these images often very narrowly, blandly identifying truth with morality: voluptuous scenes and dissolute adventures or the glorification of war are simply "untrue." The artist, he implies, should be a moralist, but at the same time apparently also a scientist. Science and poetry should merge, but science to Dobrolyubov means "correct" social and moral ideas. What seems to be a Platonic fusion of the true, the good, and the beautiful, in practice becomes simple didacticism, and even a crude allegorizing to serve immediate polemical purposes.

We can show Dobrolyubov's method at work by discussing his most famous critical papers. "What is Oblomovism?" (1859) takes Oblomov and abstracts from him one quality, indolence, and declares this to be the key to the riddle of many manifestations of Russian life.[41] "Oblomovka is our motherland: a large portion of Oblomov is within every one of us." [42] Dobrolyubov sees the continuity between Oblomov and the type of "superfluous man" depicted in Onegin and Pechorin, yet he wants to dismiss these two fictional types as belonging to a dead past. "They have lost their significance, they have ceased to mislead us with their former mystery and enigmatic dissonance."[43] Instead of pursuing the theme and analyzing Oblomov, Dobrolyubov dismisses Goncharov's obvious sympathy for his hero and his psychological explanation of the growth of his weakness and declares him a "disgusting nonentity."[44] At the end he can only hold him up as a kind of warning example, a bogeyman, an allegory of Russian backwardness. He has lost sight of the book and the figure.

Next he uses his technique in analyzing Ostrovsky's early comedies in a very long piece, "The Realm of Darkness" (1859). Here Dobrolyubov does not have to deal with a complex character such as Oblomov: he is faced with a great variety of figures, which he can reduce to a few types and for which he then tries to define the social causes that created them.[45] He can easily show that Ostrovsky depicts a type of domestic tyrant and bully (samodur) and the abject, ignorant wives and girls surrounding him. He is anxious to show that Ostrovsky—though in his political ideas affected and, in his opinion, corrupted by Slavophile views—actually exposes and ridicules tyranny and oppression at every point. Ostrovsky must be claimed as an unconscious liberal and ally. But when Dobrolyubov starts to give causal explanations of these conditions, he loses sight of the plays completely: he argues about a false respect for law and order and talks about the economic dependence of the victims on the merchant tyrants. He darkly hints that he could say more if censorship allowed it, and one must recognize that his description of tyranny and despotism (though ostensibly limited to the plays under discussion) could easily be and certainly was read as a general indictment of Russian autocracy. The plays are used to document tyranny, oppression, ignorance, superstition, downtrodden resignation, vices which Dobrolyubov with the Rousseauistic faith of his time ascribes to bad social conditions, since "baseness and crime are not inherent in human nature." [46]

The later article on Ostrovsky's *Storm* (1860) shows the method at its insensitive worst. Dobrolyubov sets himself to see the heroine of the play, Katerina, as the "representative of a great national idea" and to glorify her suicide and her defiance of her tormentors as "the height to which our national life is rising in its development." [47] Her drowning herself in the Volga is interpreted as a "challenge to the power of tyranny," and her character is seen as a "reflection of a new movement of national life." [48] Dobrolyubov, conscious of the paradox of his interpretation, defies those who charge him with having made "art the instrument of an extraneous idea." He asks and expects affirmative answers: Does the interpretation follow from the play? Does living Russian nature find expression in Katerina? Are the demands of the nascent movement of Russian life truly reflected in the meaning of the play? Ostrovsky, he concludes triumphantly, "has challenged Russian life and Russian strength to take determined action." [49] But if my own reading of the play is anywhere near the text, Katerina must rather be considered as a pitiful figure, dominated by dark instinct, who rushes into an adulterous adventure, trembles before the wrath of God, shudders at a thunderstorm and pictures of hell-fire, and finds refuge, from her sense of sin and guilt, in the waters of the Volga. The atmosphere of the play is that of a fairy tale. The evil mother-in-law, the stupid husband, the lover at the gate, the watchmaker who tries to discover the secret of perpetual motion, the gossipy pilgrim-woman, the half mad lady shouting "All of you will burn in unquenchable fire" give the play a tone of weird unreality like that of a story of E. T. A. Hoffmann. To make Katerina, an adultress and a suicide, a superstitious ignorant woman pursued and crushed by a sense of guilt and doom into the symbol of revolution seems the very height of what could be called "loss of contact" with the text. Anything must serve the cause, and if it does not it must be made over to fit.

The slightly earlier article, "When will the day come?" (1860), dealing with Turgenev's novel *On the Eve,* is somewhat subtler. Dobrolyubov has not quite surrendered his critical sense and sees that the Bulgarian hero is rather shadowy.[50] No action of Insarov's is shown. The story cannot be considered a rebuke to the young

Russian generation; it is impossible to hold up Insarov as a model of civic courage. Turgenev did not want to write and could not write a heroic epic.[51] Dobrolyubov admires the scenes in Venice preceding the sudden death of the hero and comments favorably on the love story as a story. His analysis of Yelena is quite sympathetic, but suddenly and in flat contradiction to what he has said just a few pages before, he goes off into his usual allegorizing. Why is Insarov a Bulgarian and not a Russian? The answer is, of course, that Turgenev has to import him from Bulgaria because there are no rebels and no need of rebels in Russia. With heavy irony, Dobrolyubov tells his readers and the censors how everything in Russia is peaceful, orderly, governed by law; that Russians would not dream of cutting the limb of the tree on which they are sitting. But this ironical disclaimer of a Russian Insarov is then openly revoked in the expression of the "hope that there will be soon an opportunity for actions." "We need a man like Insarov, but a Russian Insarov." The ominous phrase "The day will come" concludes the piece. The insight of the critic (shown also in his sympathetic analysis of Yelena) is lost; the lay figure Insarov serves as a pretext for a call to revolution.[52]

One can discover some signs of growth in sensibility in Dobrolyubov's last article, called "Forgotten People" (1861), dealing with Dostoevsky's *Insulted and Injured*. Though Dobrolyubov disparages Dostoevsky as an artist, he shows some power of analysis and characterization, not only of the novel that is the ostensible subject of the review, but of the other writings of the early Dostoevsky. Even *The Double* is considered with some attention to the motivation of the split in Golyadkin's personality.[53] There is one passage that displays a sudden recognition of the role of imagination in art. An artist, says Dobrolyubov, is not a "photographic plate." "He supplements the isolated moment with his artistic feeling. He creates a whole, finds a vital link, fuses and transforms the diverse and contradictory aspects of living reality." The poet's work is "something that must be so, and cannot be otherwise."[54] The power of Dostoevsky's imagination, the personal tone, dark and diseased though it seemed to Dobrolyubov,[55] had its effect. Dobrolyubov began to glimpse the nature of art as creation and to use ideas from Belinsky which might have led him to a deeper understanding. But, unfortunately, he died in the year of this article (1861), aged not yet 26.

DMITRI PISAREV (1840-1868)

Dmitri Pisarev first rose to prominence as a rival of Dobrolyubov. He established his critical reputation by contradicting and refuting the views and interpretations of Dobrolyubov. But this rivalry should not obscure the fact that Pisarev was also a pupil of Chernyshevsky and of Belinsky in his later stage, and that on matters of literary theory and general philosophical outlook there is little difference between Pisarev and Dobrolyubov. Pisarev in the Soviet Union today is not so highly valued or so widely studied and reprinted as Chernyshevsky or Dobrolyubov, mainly because he is suspected of radical individualism and even anarchism. Even Masaryk compares him with Stirner and Nietzsche.[1] But there seems to me very little justice in all this. Pisarev was a radical Utilitarian who believed in a rational egoism finally working toward the common good. He differs from Chernyshevsky in having little hope in the peasant. After four years in the Peter-and-Paul Fortress, he apparently became also much more skeptical as to the imminence of revolution; all his hopes were put into the dissemination of rational and scientific ideas, into the slow creation of a materialistic intelligentsia. He was distrustful of utopias in the style of Fourier's phalansteries, and kept up an early fear of the omnipotent state.[2] But in his writings there is hardly any trace of romantic individualism or exaltation of genius. Pisarev shares the basic outlook of Chernyshevsky and Dobrolyubov. He is, like them, a rigid naturalistic monist. He devotes much of his writing to exposition and popularization of the writings of Vogt, Moleschott, Büchner, and, later, Huxley and Darwin. He has cut off all connections with the idealistic romantic past, and has done so more completely than they. He ridicules Heine's prophecy of the revolutionary importance of German philosophy as a bad jest and dismisses the German romantics as completely dead figures.[3] When he discusses Belinsky, whom he reveres as the father of realism, he wants to take off the shell of Hegelianism. He rejects the idea of organic development as a mere delusion: Belinsky's attempt to show the inevitable evolution from Derzhavin through Batyushkov and Zhukovsky to Pushkin seems to him arrant nonsense.[4] He is completely nonplussed by the idea of a parallel development of all the arts and activities of man expressing a common spirit of the time. He argues that you can never explain why, for instance, people wore full-bottomed wigs under Louis XIV and powdered their hair with starch under Louis XV. It was only individual caprice and not the expression or reflection of any world-view.[5] Like his fellow critics, Pisarev has ceased to understand the role of imagination, the wholeness of a work of art, the distinction between life and fiction. He ridicules the inspiration theory and the whole idea of unconscious creation.[6] A poet thinks up an idea and then fits it into a chosen form. That costs labor. He is like a tailor who cuts his cloth, adds to it, snips this bit off and another there, changes this or that.[7] One can become a poet as one can become a lawyer, a professor, a journalist, a shoemaker or a watchmaker. A poet or artist is an artisan like any other.[8]

Form and content are completely divorced in Pisarev's mind. Form is, at most, necessary in order not to obstruct content.[9] Language is communication to be valued only as we value the telegraph wire.[10] Thus Pisarev quite consciously brushes aside questions of artistic merit: to distinguish the manner of one writer from another would mean writing dreary stylistic investigations. What interests him is only what a writer did for our social awareness.[11]

On aesthetic matters, Pisarev pushes the ideas of Chernyshevsky to even greater polemical extremes. His notorious paper "The Destruction of Aesthetics" (1865) is an enthusiastic endorsement of Chernyshevsky's dissertation. Pisarev draws its logical conclusions. If beauty is life, he says, then "every healthy and normal person is beautiful," and aesthetics dissolves, to Pisarev's apparent satisfaction, into physiology and hygiene.[12] If art expresses everything that interests man, we must ask what interests man. Criticism will be an argument not about art but about natural science, history, politics, and moral philosophy.[13] Chernyshevsky is right in showing that an aesthetician can judge only the form of a work of art and thus can have no opinion of its substance. The true critic is a thinking man who judges the contents, i.e., the phenomena of life represented in a work of literature.[14]

Aesthetics to Pisarev thus means the view that form is more important than content;[15] it means aestheticism, art for art's sake. By a sleight of hand, aesthetics can mean to him any theory of art. But such a theory is impossible because all art appeals to a purely subjective feeling of pleasure[16] and thus is not and cannot be science. This "destruction of aesthetics," with Pisarev, easily widens into a destruction of art itself. First of all, he rejects what he considers the purely ornamental sensuous arts of music, painting, and sculpture, for which he sees no possible social use. In a famous *boutade* he finally concedes that drawing may be necessary for making plans for houses or illustrations to works such as Brehm's *Tierleben*.[17] Next, poetry as verse seems to him completely outmoded, and in his attack on Pushkin he purposely prints all verse as prose. Poetry is a dying art, and we should rejoice at it. "No man of our generation of real intelligence and talent can spend his life piercing sensitive hearts with killing iambs and anapaests." [18]

What remains is only the novel and the drama with a social purpose. Even these, though they are the main topics of Pisarev's literary essays, are considered temporary expedients, makeshift instruments of propaganda useful to shape the world view of readers,[19] but of no intrinsic value. The general decline in the status of belles-lettres is consistently hailed as a sign of social progress.[20]

Some of Pisarev's statements against art and aesthetics were undoubtedly rhetorical flourishes, polemical extravagances designed to shock the reader (*épater le bourgeois*). But I think Pisarev is quite serious in his rejection of art: he must be grouped with a long line of thinkers that begins with Plato, goes through the Elizabethan puritans, the "geometrical" partisans of the Moderns under Louis XIV, to the Benthamite Utilitarians and men like Proudhon, who all wanted to banish the poets from the Republic. Pisarev was concerned with the economy of society and of the Russian intelligentsia in particular. He was shocked by the existence of a conservatory of music in a nation that lacked sufficient bread to prevent famine or by a "scientific expedition to the shores of the Tigris to decipher cuneiform inscriptions at a time when the ordinary Russian could not make out printed letters in his own language." [21] Young men should be warned off the arts. They should revere Darwin, Liebig, Claude Bernard, rather than Bryulov (a painter), Glinka, and Mochalov (an actor).[22] Today science and the spread of science is the one thing needful, at least in Russia. Pisarev's slogan, "realism," is simply analysis, criticism, intellectual progress.[23] A realist is a "thinking worker." [24] Literature and especially the art of the novel is, at most, recognized as a means of communicating and disseminating such ideas. "Literature raises psychological problems, shows the clash of passions, characters, and situations, leads the reader to thinking about these conflicts and the means of abolishing them." [25] Literature, in short, helps in forming public opinion: novels change the morals and convictions of a society, though they do so very slowly, like drops wearing out a stone.[26] In his general condemnation of art, Pisarev makes an exception in favor of writers who are "knights of the spirit." [27] They need not be "imaginative writers." He is pleased to note that Belinsky and Dobrolyubov have become famous without writing poetry, novels, or dramas. He concedes even that Nekrasov may continue to write verse if he cannot express himself in any other manner; that Turgenev may continue to write novels if he cannot explain but only depict his Bazarov; that Chernyshevsky may put into fictional form what might have been a treatise on sociology.[28] But this is only a temporary concession to the deplorable weaknesses of human nature. Pisarev sees art consistently as a past form of human endeavor that has been vanquished or should be vanquished shortly by science.

Pisarev's attitude toward history and literary history in particular is thus completely negative. All historical novels are useless.[29] So is all literary history. He ridicules a man devoted to the study of Old Russian literature.[30] What of it even if he were as great as Grimm? Grimm might have accomplished something if his study of German folk speech had induced him to write on science in popular language. But what is the use of antiquarianism? "I say with all sincerity that I would rather be a Russian shoemaker or baker than a Russian Raphael or Grimm." [31] Pisarev was himself a student of history: he compiled a great number of articles on history, e.g., on Metternich, on the history of the press in France, on Erckmann-Chatrian's *Histoire d'un paysan*. But they all serve a purely practical purpose. The historical novel by Erckmann-Chatrian allows Pisarev to retell the story of the French Revolution for his starved readers.

Pisarev's extreme views on general questions—his blatant enmity toward art, his rejection of all the central insights achieved in the history of criticism—bode ill for the value of his practical criticism. But strangely enough, he has genuine critical insights and a considerable power of analysis. In spite of many doctrinaire aberrations and blind spots he seems to me a more sensitive practical critic and a far more lively writer than either Chernyshevsky or Dobrolyubov. He even has wit and polemical brilliance. One must, of course, make large allowances: the famous attack on Pushkin (in "Pushkin and Belinsky," 1865) is often downright silly. It is the kind of brutal execution, the jeering verbal quibbling that defeats its own purpose. The picture of Onegin as a shallow, cowardly dandy whose boredom is not genuine dissatisfaction with life but simply *Katzenjammer* [32] is an amusing tour de force, but is marred by a constant attempt to identify Pushkin and Onegin. It leads to the conclusion that "we modern Russians have nothing in common with the type which Onegin represents." [33] The insensitive mauling of Tatyana and Lensky is merely coarse. In the dissection of several poems Pisarev tears words and phrases out of context, ignores the fictional framework, and shows a literal-mindedness that seems to me only deplorable. The harmless poem "October 19, 1825" is pressed quite mercilessly as evidence for snobbery. Still, one understands why Pisarev disliked Pushkin's claims to supernatural inspiration, his contempt for the crowd, and his anti-Polish patriotism. The conclusion that Pushkin reveals his "inner vacuity, his spiritual poverty, and intellectual impotence," [34] that he was "unable to analyze and to understand social and philosophical problems," [35] does not differ very much from what had been said by Dobrolyubov and even by Chernyshevsky. But everything in Pisarev is said so bluntly and indiscriminately that the modicum of polemical truth becomes a falsehood.

The treatment of Pushkin is paralleled in the frequent references to Goethe, for whom Pisarev conceived a similar dislike and whom he also saw as the representative of a past aristocratic art. Pisarev simply adopts the views of Börne and never enters into a close discussion. His one essay on a foreign poet, that on Heine (1867) ,[36] is by no means imperceptive of aesthetic values or obtuse in psychological insight, as are the essays on Pushkin. Pisarev gives a good description of the violent transitions in Heine's prose: "Colors of extreme brightness are suddenly replaced by the face of a charming woman, then by the demoniac eyes of a hideous satyr; these turn into a bushy tree, and instead of a tree, there appears a porcelain tower and below it a Chinaman on a fantastic dragon; and then all this is obliterated and the author looks at us with a contemptuous and melancholy smile." [37] Thus Pisarev can, on occasion, write evocative criticism, a kind totally inaccessible to his fellow critics.

He can see Heine's inner division and see through his posturing about his innumerable mistresses.[38] But the focus of the essay is on Heine's political and aesthetic opinions. Pisarev sees them both as ambiguous, undecided, wavering. Heine wants to be a "courageous soldier in the war of humanity" but at the same time wants to be a pure artist and even an irresponsible clown. He is horrified by the mob: he tells us that he has to wash his hands everytime he has brushed against somebody in the crowd. Heine is a liberal tied to the decaying corpse of the *Gironde*.[39] His attitude toward art is similarly vacillating. We find in him all answers, today this and tomorrow the opposite. "When the poet sings like a nightingale without purpose, Heine feels the smell of fresh hay. If he puts himself under the banner of a definite idea, Heine shouts that the world is being flooded with Rumford's Utility Soup."[40] Heine praises "nightingales" such as Uhland, Tieck, and Arnim, but also propagandists such as Laube and Gutzkow. Pisarev defends Heine's sincerity and tries to give a historical explanation of his confused position. Writers of the 18th century like Voltaire or Diderot passionately believed in political revolution. Writers of our time believe in "economic regeneration," Pisarev's euphemism for socialism. But Heine lived in the in-between, dark zone filled with disillusionment, doubt, and vague aspirations. He has lost the old faith and has not acquired the new one.[41] He lacks faith as he lacks a public and roots in his own nation. Voltaire and Diderot were whole men; Heine is divided, tragically torn apart.[42] Today we have whole men again: Proudhon, Louis Blanc, Lassalle—and, we might add, Pisarev.

The definition of the new whole men in Russia is Pisarev's main concern in analyzing current Russian fiction. He begins his literary career by rejecting Dobrolyubov's analyses. Oblomov, he finds, cannot be considered a representative type: he is abnormal physically and temperamentally.[43] Stolz is not a man but a puppet, and so is Olga.[44] Goncharov is a man without ideas, an ironical skeptic who does not sympathize with any one of his figures, though he understands them all.[45] He is a pure artist, of no relevance to the "new men" of Pisarev's persuasion.

Turgenev, before *Fathers and Sons,* is judged more sympathetically than Goncharov, but still severely. Pisarev likes his women, especially Asya, but disagrees with Dobrolyubov about *On the Eve*. Insarov is entirely impossible, a mere synthetic figure of heroism who offers no hope that the day will come.[46]

When Dobrolyubov died, literary criticism in the *Contemporary* was taken over by Maxim Antonovich (1835–1918), who reviewed *Fathers and Sons*, denouncing Bazarov as a monster, a caricature, a libel on the young generation. Pisarev saw further and better. He hailed Bazarov as the representative of the new man and analyzed him sympathetically and penetratingly. In the article "Bazarov" (1862) Pisarev recognizes Bazarov's brutality, ill manners, and cynicism, but praises his forthrightness, his scientific outlook, and his sturdy independence. He is even independent of what he professes; he is capable, as shown by his behavior at Mme Odyntsov's and his duel with Pavel, of making a fool of himself.[47] His feelings of love on his deathbed are not a symptom of weakness; rather they show that he has become a man instead of being only the embodiment of the theory of nihilism. His rationality has been extreme, but it disappears in the time of approaching death.[48] He has struggled against this love because he felt he might become unfaithful to his image of life.[49] Bazarov's death is pure chance. The story is broken off, to be completed by the future, in reality.[50] Pisarev sees that the author's attitude toward his hero is what we would call today ambivalent. Turgenev does not fully sympathize with any one of his figures; he is not content with either fathers or children.[51] Turgenev cannot share Bazarov's ruthless negations, but he respects them. Though he himself inclines toward idealism, none of the idealists in the book is comparable even to Bazarov in strength of mind and character.[52] In creating Bazarov, Turgenev might have wanted to lower him, but his artistic integrity made him pay the tribute of just respect.[53]

In a later development of this characterization, in "The Realists" (1864), Pisarev, on the whole, repeats the early analysis but elaborates on the relation between Bazarov and Mme Odyntsov. He makes a wholehearted defense of Bazarov's high-mindedness and respect for the woman he loves, mostly because Bazarov has been attacked for immorality and cynicism. Pisarev shows that Turgenev depicts a strong and even sublime passion, but in the process he somehow deprives Bazarov of his original vigor and crudity; he makes him too much of a hero "without stain and reproach," even defending his courting of Fenichka.[54] Whatever one may object to details of Pisarev's interpretation, his recognition of Bazarov's significance was important: it has its personal touch of pathos. In Bazarov, Pisarev discovered himself and his generation. His criticism was a genuine act of self-knowledge, a justification of a method that treats a fictional figure as a symbol quite apart from the overt

... e that Pisarev's interpreta-
... toward his own creation:
... th greater sympathy and

... with Bazarov can be seen
... Turgenev about *Smoke*.
... not like the scenes ridicul-
... r leader Bubarev, a carica-
... em aside, recognizing that
... w at the reactionaries more
... hero of the novel, Litvinov,
... the weak student-friend of
... has happened to Bazarov?"
... t Bazarov actually died in

... ssion of Bazarov in all of
... the dead Dobrolyubov is
... early satires of Saltykov-
... re entertainer whose influ-
... l he gives him blunt advice
... eful, such as translating or
... nce.[57] Pisarev is on firmer
... terpretation of Ostrovsky's
... rather, "a Russian Ophelia
... acts, commits the last and
... Volga."[58] Pisarev becomes

most satirical when he shoots at targets hardly worth aiming for: at a novel, *A Woman's Fate*, by Stanitsky, the pseudonym of Mme Panaeva, at the bad novels of a lesser Tolstoy, Theophil, or at novels such as Leskov's *No Exit*, caricaturing the radicals. He waxes most enthusiastic, deliriously so, when he praises Chernyshevsky's *What Shall We Do?* He finds even artistic value in this dreary revolutionary tract.[59]

His reviews of Dostoevsky and Leo Tolstoy are the most interesting to us. Pisarev reviews the *Memoirs from a Dead House* and contrasts them maliciously with *Sketches* by Pomyalovsky describing life in a priests' seminary. Pisarev shows or pretends to show that the life of the chained convicts in the Siberian stockade is, to judge from Dostoevsky's account, much freer and much more hopeful and less degraded than that of the cowed and oppressed seminarists. The title of the article, "The Dead and the Dying" (1865), reverses ordinary expectations: the inhabitants of the House of the Dead have a chance of recovery; the seminarists have perished utterly.[60]

When Pisarev came to review *Crime and Punishment* as "The Struggle for Life" (1867), he knew Dostoevsky's convictions and must have looked upon him as a political enemy. A letter shows that he was completely carried away by the book,[61] but his review pays only very perfunctory compliments to Dostoevsky's psychological insight and announces that he will ignore the point of view of the author and discuss only the manifestations of social life depicted in the book.[62] The method is Dobrolyubov's, the same that Pisarev had used on Bazarov. Pisarev assumes that the author, if he is a good writer, reflects life accurately, and that his attitudes and mere theories are irrelevant: intentions, logical schemes do not count. He has succeeded well with Bazarov, but he fails with Raskolnikov. His polemical purpose made him ignore the obvious fact that Dostoevsky does not merely impose his ideology upon his figure (he does little of that), but actually presents a drama of ideas in the actions and persons of the novel itself. Pisarev, sensing that Dostoevsky wants to show up the "new men," adopts the strategy of proving that Raskolnikov's crime was entirely due to poverty. His convictions had no influence on the action;[63] the root of his illness was not in the brain but in the pocket.[64] His share of freedom was exceedingly small.[65] His views have nothing in common with those of the "new men." Pisarev takes Raskolnikov's article, discovered by the police, and demonstrates that Raskolnikov has illicitly expanded the term "criminal" to include every historical leader. In Pisarev's mind a great man who spills blood wantonly and commits crimes against humanity, ceases to be a great man. And the whole view that individuals can change the stream of history is mistaken.[66] Raskolnikov's theory is not the cause of the crime, any more than hallucination is the cause of an illness.[67] Raskolnikov, after the crime, goes to pieces and puts himself under the tutelage of a good-natured but uneducated girl. The implication is obvious. One need not take Raskolnikov's regeneration and final conversion seriously. All this is cleverly devised by Pisarev and is an effective argument against an interpretation of the novel as saying, "Look—these new ideas lead to crime." But it is not good literary criticism because it ignores the bulk of Dostoevsky's text. Dostoevsky ascribes the crime not to poverty but to a complex of motives which includes Raskolnikov's theories—not only romantic titanism, which Pisarev dislikes, but also Utilitarianism (or rather an extreme version in which anything is permissible if its leads to the ultimate good of society), a thing that Pisarev believes in. Dostoevsky did not and could not write a novel à la Zola, with the thesis "poverty leads to crime," because he believed in human self-determination, in moral freedom. Pisarev distorts the book because he ignores half of Raskolnikov's motivation and almost all that follows after the crime. There, after all, is the real emphasis of the book. Pisarev's method of discussing a situation as if it were one in real life, from the point of view of his own determinism, breaks down in face of a book that is a closely knit and complex drama of ideas.

He fails even worse with Tolstoy. "The Blunders of an Immature Mind" (1864) is a review of some of Tolstoy's early writings: *Childhood, Boyhood, Youth; A Landlord's Morning;* and *Lucerne.* The "immature mind" is Tolstoy's hero Nekhlyudov in the last two stories. Pisarev shows him to be a transitional type, less inactive and passive than Rudin, less active than Bazarov. He is trapped by his aristocratic education, incapable of sound and practical views of the world because he lacks scientific training. Nekhlyudov is given advice as if he were a real person: it was a foolish idea to stay on his estate; he should have liberated his peasants and moved away completely. His behavior in Lucerne, inviting a singer into the elegant hotel, was merely hysterical, impractical, and foolish.[68] Though Pisarev sympathizes with Tolstoy's humanitarianism and professes admiration for his power as a writer, he has no comprehension of his mental struggles nor any perception of the Rousseau-istic criticism of civilization that runs through all of Tolstoy's work. Still, the article has something to say: the placing of Irtenev-Nekhlyudov as a type in Russian social history is roughly correct.

The late review of *War and Peace* (1868), or rather of its first half then published, shows a definite decline of Pisarev's powers. "The Old Nobility" of Pisarev's title includes merely two characters of the novel: Boris Drubetskoy and Nikolay Rostov, who are used to show up the crudely scheming, ambitious, spoilt, and lazy old aristocracy. Again Pisarev professes to ignore the intentions of the author,[69] but again, as in the review of *Crime and Punishment,* it is the bulk of the actual text which is ignored. The whole atmosphere of nostalgia for the past is completely missed. In Pisarev's defense, one must say that the article was only the first of a projected series which would have taken up Pierre, Andrey, and Natasha.[70] But nothing came of it. During the last two years of his life Pisarev was obviously at a dead end. Most of his articles are mere compilations— for instance, from W. H. Dixon's *Spiritual Wives* and from Sismondi's *History of the Italian Republics.* An unfinished article, recently published, on "Diderot and his Time"[71] is only an abstract from the book by Karl Rosenkranz. Pisarev found it difficult to publish after the suppression of the *Russian Word,* the periodical that had printed most of his work. He tried to get into the *Contemporary.* But he was, as he says in the letter to Turgenev, now quite alone, and he perished soon afterward, in despair.

Looking back at our three critics, we should admire their devotion to their cause. We must recognize that they were not primarily interested in literature at all. They were revolutionaries, and literature was only a weapon in the battle. They did not see and did not want to see that man is confronted with questions that surpass those of his own age; that the insight art provides into the full meaning of existence does not necessarily grow out of his immediate social preoccupations.[72] As critics they constantly lose sight of the text, confuse (sometimes deliberately) life and fiction, treat figures in novels as if they were men or women on the street, or allegorize the fictional character, make it evaporate to represent some generalization: the decadent aristocrat, the desire for freedom, the new man, and so on. They constantly succumb to two not unrelated fallacies: naturalism and intellectualism. They lose hold on the concrete universal, the fusion of the particular and general in every work of art. Content and form are divorced: the unity of the work of art broken up, imagination reduced to a mere combinatory intellectual power. Art in short is denied as a value in itself. It is distributed between a despised sensual pleasure of form and a purely cognitive or hortatory content. Art, at bottom, is superfluous, and Pisarev spoke only the truth, like any *enfant terrible*.

But this tendency, destructive of the very nature of literary criticism and art in general, should not make us ignore the real contribution of Pisarev and his fellows to a social study of literature. Their analysis of social types was something new and important methodologically. One must, besides, recognize that Russia at that time was actually producing a social novel, that poetry was then derivative, and the drama rather a reflex of the novel. Our critics helped to define and describe the nature of the social novel, the obligation of the writer toward social truth; his insight, conscious or unconscious, into the structure and typical characters of society. It seems a pity that they did so in narrow local terms shackled by their gross utilitarianism. The noise of the battle deafened them.

THERE IS some injustice in our concentrating on the radical critics and neglecting the parallel series of conservative Russian critics. They are, for obvious reasons, forgotten in Soviet Russia and most of their writings have never been reprinted. They are thus doubly unknown in the West. At least Apollon Grigoriev was a critic of great gifts who in terms of theoretical awareness and literary perceptions, if not in historical influence, seems to excel the radical critics. In 1914 Leonid Grossman thought that "there is no doubt of his primacy in Russian criticism." He considered him as more profound than Sainte-Beuve, less quirky and "pathetic" than Carlyle, and less rigid and dogmatic than Taine. He saw him as a forerunner of Bergson who has still something to say to his time.[1] A recent student of Russian literature, Vsevolod Setschkareff, thinks that a close study of Grigoriev could even today put literary scholarship on a firmer basis.[2]

Grigoriev claims attention for his main position: what he himself called "organic" criticism. It is not original with him, but is eloquently and clearly elaborated and set off against rival theories. It seems largely derived from a study of Schelling, whom Grigoriev called "the Plato of the new world," "the greatest of the world's thinkers."[3] With rare insight he associates Carlyle, Emerson, and Hugo for his book on Shakespeare with Schelling.[4] Grigoriev understands that all these writers hold a view which was discussed here as "historicism" or "organology." The central concept is "Life" conceived as a unity of the biological and psychic. "Art is the ideal expression of Life."[5] It is omnipresent in all nations, as Grigoriev insists in quoting Schelling: "Wherever there was life there was poetry."[6] Art grows out of life, spontaneously, organically. It must be, then, concrete, personal, sincere, but also local and national. It is involved in the life of a nation, expresses its ideals and aspira-

tions, but does so unconsciously, naturally. Grigoriev believes with
Schelling and Carlyle that "unconsciousness gives creative works
their unfathomable depth." [7] Every work of art is part of a huge
organism and "almost never can any literary phenomenon be con-
templated in its isolated particularity." [8] Organic criticism will be
looking at "art as a synthetic, total, immediate, and perhaps even
intuitive understanding of life," [9] and will itself be intuitive, immediate. The aim of the critic will be to grasp the individuality or
tone of an author or of an age: its particular atmosphere or "drift." [10]
The critic will feel (and not only know) this relation, for Grigoriev
will not recognize a divorce between feeling and judging.[11]

The theory is clearly romantic, "historistic" in the sense of
Herder, the whole German historical school, or Carlyle in his early
stage. Life, growth, individuality, nationality, originality, spontaneity, sincerity are the key terms. The central point of view serves
also a polemical purpose. Grigoriev rejects formalism, art for art's
sake, as abstract, negative (in the Schellingian sense) and purely
technical.[12] It is a complete misunderstanding of his position to
consider him "aesthetic" or "formalistic." But the "organic" point
of view serves also to set him off against the Hegelians and the Russian radicals who believe in progress and reason. Grigoriev carries
on a constant warfare against what he calls "historical criticism,"
i.e., historical relativism and evolutionism. It denies aesthetic laws,
has "no criterion, no eternal ideal," and is at bottom "indifferent-
ism and fatalism." [13] Historical criticism is false if it means relativism which accepts and would have to accept any rubbish in its
historical place. It would obliterate what to Grigoriev is the eternal
difference between the art of Shakespeare and the pseudo-art of the
French drama.[14] Historical criticism is condemned to a constant
change of temporary idols: Pushkin the day before yesterday, Gogol
yesterday, Goncharov today, etc.[15] The worship of an abstract general humanity leads only to gross materialism: to "a slavish service
to the life" of the moment.[16] Historical criticism has actually lost
faith in history, as "faith in history is faith in eternal, unchanging truth." [17] In constant variations Grigoriev repeats this main
thesis: historical criticism is false, the historical sense is right. It is a
"feeling for the organic linking of the phenomena of life, a feeling
for the harmony and wholeness of life." [18] This sense of individuality, locality, nationality is, however, always transcended by

reference to a single, unchanging, eternal ideal. It cannot be relative, for truth cannot be relative.[19] "Evolution of the ideal" is a phrase which actually means its negation.[20] Grigoriev denies that there can be new art. "The dreams of a new art are the convulsions of the exhausted Germanic-Romance world in its most conscious representatives, George Sand, Liszt, etc. They do not see and cannot see that life is exhausted and that a new life begins" with Orthodoxy, in Russia. It will not be a new art, but a "Homeric, Dantesque, and Shakespearean art of the new world." Its beginnings are in Pushkin and Mickiewicz.[21]

Unfortunately there seems to be some lack of clarity to Grigoriev's conservativism: one understands his ideal of beauty in the past and sees how his intense and sympathetic study of folk poetry works into the scheme. He can sound like Herder or Grimm. He wants "nationality," he feels that with Schelling "their total self-responsible meaning has been returned to the nations and persons in order to destroy the idol of the abstract spirit of humanity and its evolution."[22] But at the same time the leading theme of his practical criticism is the succession of Russian types, an evolution which is as "progressive" as that sketched, with a different goal in mind, by his enemies, the radical critics. The poet proves his objectivity, i.e., his insight into reality, by his ability to create types; and "type, whatever he may be" (ugly, immoral?) "is in itself the beautiful," is art.[23] In Grigoriev's view there are two kinds of knowledge: discursive and intuitive, by logical deduction or by types. Vital works, vital types express what is alive in an age. Thus art is prophetic. "Everything new is brought into life only by art; it embodies in its productions what is invisibly present in the air of an age. Even more, art often feels what is approaching in the future, just as birds feel fine or inclement weather approaching."[24] Grigoriev alludes to Hegel's concept of *Göttertrauer,* the sadness of the Olympic gods sensing their doom, and quotes then the concluding passage of Schelling's *System des transzendentalen Idealismus,* accepting it as his own "philosophical-aesthetic confession of faith."[25] Grigoriev does not seem to recognize the difference between the early Schelling who looked for the "Odyssey of the spirit" in nature and art and the later expounder of the philosophy of a revelation in the dim past. His own theory is riddled with this contradiction between the Platonic and static absolute of emanationism and the evolutionism

which he embraces in practice and which underlies his whole
history of Russian 19th-century literature.

Belinsky is Grigoriev's master, but it is obviously the early Belinsky, before he acquired his trust in progress and the spirit of the
time. Grigoriev likes best the very early writings, the "Literary
Reveries" (1834) and would have wanted him to stop writing by
1844.[26] Pushkin is the great wellhead of Russian literature: the
creator of the two types Grigoriev sees struggling for mastery over
the Russian soul: the predatory Hermann of *The Queen of Spades*
and the meek Belkin of the *Tales*.[27] Grigoriev admired Gogol as the
representative figure of his age. He even defended *Selected Passages
from a Correspondence with Friends* at the very beginning of his
literary career.[28] Perversely to my mind, he exalts Gogol as a humor-
ist full of love for life with a hunger for the ideal, who is misunderstood as a gloomy caricaturist.[29] Gogol's later despair was caused
by his recognition of the lifelessness of his positive types, his failure
to embody his ideal.[30] Realism seems to Grigoriev false as theory,
but a necessary stage in the development of Russian literature. It is
a technical achievement like the discovery of perspective in painting. It must be exhausted to the bottom. No novel is today possible
without an exact knowledge of the *milieu*.[31] Thus Grigoriev can
praise Pisemsky and many other writers while preserving some
reservations against their literalism. Grigoriev attacks only Lermontov's Pechorin as negative, as an obsolete descendant of René and
Obermann. Pechorin is actually a comic type made poetic by
Lermontov's passionate nature.[32] Of all recent writers Grigoriev
valued Ostrovsky most highly: he expected from him the "new
word" in 1851, praised him consistently for his firm view of the
world (he uses the term *Weltanschauung*), his truly Russian feeling
and atmosphere, and defended him against Dobrolyubov's attempt
to claim him for the reformers as a satirist of the "Realm of Darkness."[33] Grigoriev hailed the hero of Turgenev's *Nest of Gentle-
folk*, Lavretsky, as a "new, living, positive" Russian type.[34] His
return to the soil agreed with his own formula, *pochva* (soil), with
the curious Christian naturalism which seemed to him and Dostoevsky the right reconciliation of Westernism and Slavophilism. Compared to Lavretsky, Oblomov is dismissed as abstract and contrived,
while Turgenev's ineffectual, meek hero is given the highest praise
Grigoriev can bestow on any fictional figure: "he was born, not

invented." [35] Also Tolstoy is praised by Grigoriev as a psychologist, particularly for *Family Happiness,* but Grigoriev seems to resent Tolstoy's excessive preference for the meek type in which he sensed a contradiction to Tolstoy's real temper: some insincerity or divorce from contemporary life.[36] Dostoevsky was received at first coolly by Grigoriev: he thought *Poor People* derivative from Gogol and *The Double* repulsive like a corpse. But he came to admire *The Insulted and the Injured* and in his last years collaborated closely with Dostoevsky's journalistic ventures.[37] But we must not forget that Grigoriev died before he could know the mature Dostoevsky and Tolstoy.

Grigoriev seems thus as a theorist an offshoot of German romanticism who, like the early Carlyle, developed one point of view with striking force and applied it to the history of Russian literature. But there is an unresolved conflict in Grigoriev's thought that must have diminished his impact, and his criticism of individual writers remains within the curious circle of preoccupation with social types. It is difficult to find Bergsonism anticipated unless Schelling did so, or to see him as an impressionist merely because he stresses intuition. His criticism suffers also from the besetting sins of the time, and not only in Russia: inordinate prolixity, repetitiveness, constant polemics, digressions, and concern with writers who are forgotten even in their homeland. But Grigoriev had one great disciple: Dostoevsky.

FYODOR DOSTOEVSKY (1821–1881)

From a present-day point of view Grigoriev is totally overshadowed by Fyodor Dostoevsky, who, next to Tolstoy, appears as the greatest figure of Russian literature in the later half of the century. He has been studied and debated endlessly not only as a novelist and person but as a thinker and prophet of religion, psychology, morals, politics, and even metaphysics. Strangely enough, his critical and aesthetic views have been neglected, though they throw considerable light on his practice and are far from incoherent and opinionated. In contrast to some of Dostoevsky's views on politics and religion, they may strike us as sweetly reasonable, as achieving a balance of good sense between the warring factions of the time.

One must recognize, however, that Dostoevsky's aesthetics (as distinguished from his literary criticism) is extravagantly idealistic: its sources may be in Plato, Schiller, and Belinsky, but Dostoevsky's tone is so rapturously worshipful of ideal beauty, his celebration of the beauty of the world, of the paradise in which we live or could live, is so strained that we feel the kinship between the aesthetic ecstasy and the mystical illumination sometimes associated with the epileptic fit. There is a mawkish streak in Dostoevsky's vision, whether Myshkin is made to say that "Beauty will save the world" [1] or Claude Lorrain's hazy picture of Acis and Galatea serves as an image of the Golden Age or Raphael's Sistine Madonna is extolled to the sky. In a sober context Dostoevsky argued that "art is as much a necessity of man as eating and drinking. The need for beauty and creation embodying it is inseparable from man and without it man would perhaps have refused to live in the world. Man craves it, finds and accepts beauty without condition." "In beauty there is harmony and the promise of tranquillity, it is the embodiment of man's and mankind's ideals." [2] But Dostoevsky is also fully aware of the danger of beauty: the famous reflection of Dmitri Karamazov about the majority of men finding beauty in Sodom [3] is only one of many pronouncements about the terror, the temptation, and the delusion of beauty. Beauty with Dostoevsky clearly has immediate ethical and religious implications: the Platonic identification of Beauty, Goodness, and Truth is taken literally.

At first sight this aesthetic seems to have little to do with literary theory or criticism. But it surely lies behind Dostoevsky's constant aspiration for the universal and eternal in art, his desire to create types rather than individuals, and his rejection of the current realism. "The novelist, the poet has other tasks than the depiction of everyday reality: there is the universal, the eternal and—it would seem—the forever unexplorable depths of human character and spirit." [4] Dostoevsky complains that "they say Reality should be represented as it is, whereas there is no such reality, never has been on earth because, to man, the essence of things is inaccessible, while he experiences nature as it reflects itself in his idea after having passed through his senses. This is why one should give more leeway to the idea and not fear the ideal." [5] That is why he always defended the right of the fantastic in literature and deplores the contemporary tendency of asking for a "copy of real facts" and rejecting "poetic truth." [6] He praised E. T. A. Hoffmann, greatly preferring him to the more material Edgar Allan Poe.[7] He ridiculed the note-taking of novelists, or the imitation of tricks of speech on the stage.[8] He strongly felt his difference from the realistic writers of his time: from Goncharov, Turgenev, and Tolstoy, and engaged in open or covert polemics against them. Dostoevsky was shocked by the "smallness and banality of Goncharov's vision of reality."[9] His complex attitude toward Turgenev is too highly colored with personal animosity to be conclusive as criticism,[10] but he never met Tolstoy and admired him greatly as an artist. The more significant is his almost envious disapproval of the whole "landowners'" literature, of the harmonious family life of *War and Peace* which belongs to an irrevocable past.[11] Dostoevsky attacked Tolstoy openly only for his views on the Southern Slavs, voiced by Levin at the end of *Anna Karenina*.[12] Dostoevsky constantly protested that art must not be confined to realistic contemporary subjects. "We are bound up with our historical past and with universal humanity."[13] He quoted a poem, "Diana," by Fët with the highest praise, defending its mythological subject. "Art is not always true to reality."[14] Somewhat timidly Dostoevsky tried to propound an alternative meaning for realism to describe his own art. While finishing *The Idiot* he wrote two letters claiming a higher kind of realism: "I have quite a different conception of reality and realism than our realists and critics. My idealism is more real than their realism. Don't you think if one told what we other Russians have lived through in these last ten years in our spiritual development, our realists would shout that these are fantasies! But it is pure, authentic realism. Here exactly is realism, only it is in depth, while with them it is on the surface." "I have my own idea of reality in art; and what most people will call almost fantastic and an exception sometimes constitutes for me the very essence of realism. The ordinariness of events and the conventional view of them is not realism in my opinion but, indeed, the very opposite of it."[15] Strakhov, the addressee of this letter, later reported that Dostoevsky said: "They call me a psychologist. It is not true. I am rather a realist in a higher sense, i.e., I depict all the depths of the human soul."[16]

Much of this has to be understood in the polemical situation of the time. Dostoevsky in the sixties attacked Chernyshevsky and Dobrolyubov for their utilitarian view of art. He parodied Chernyshevsky's *Dissertation* in a mock session of authors. The speaker asks the others "to instil in yourself the principle that a real apple is better than a painted apple, the more so as one can eat a real apple, but cannot eat a painted apple. Consequently art is nonsense and a luxury and only serves to amuse children." "Shoes are better than Pushkin." What matters is only the belly.[17] More seriously, in a long article in 1861, directed against Dobrolyubov, Dostoevsky argues that the dilemma of "art for art's sake" versus "social utility" is false and falsely formulated. He concedes to the Utilitarians that art may be out of place at a certain moment (the earthquake at Lisbon, the battlefield) and that it has a high social value. But this value can be achieved, he argues, only by complete freedom of inspiration and creation. "Everything that has been imposed from above, everything that has been obtained by force from time immemorial to our own day has never succeeded and, instead of being beneficial, has only been harmful." [18] The utilitarians with their demands for immediate usefulness defeat their own purpose. Dostoevsky shows that the story about a serf-girl, *Masha,* by Marko Vovchok, extolled by Dobrolyubov, is not only bad art but completely unconvincing and ineffective as propaganda for the emancipation. He concludes perceptively: "The truth is that you despise poetry and true art; all you are concerned about is your cause; you are practical men." [19] The utilitarians do not recognize that art is an "organic whole," having an "independent, inseparable, organic life of its own." [20] Using the terminology of Grigoriev, with whom he was then closely associated, Dostoevsky pleads for a deeper unforeseeable usefulness. "How can we possibly determine, measure, and weigh the benefit the *Iliad* has conferred on humanity as a whole?" Even "Laura at the piano can be of some use." [21] Dostoevsky was particularly upset by the radical critics' disparagement of Pushkin, as he revered him not only as the greatest Russian poet but as the ideal Russian: the universal man, whose utility cannot be measured. The famous Pushkin speech (1880) extols him as the man who has absorbed and overcome all of Europe, as the great reconciler and synthetizer. Dostoevsky himself says that he is "not speaking as a literary critic," and some of his arguments would seem unconvincing in their simplicity. Thus much of Pushkin's universality is proved too easily by the variety of Pushkin's subject matter and sources, drawn as they are from many lands. *"Don Juan (The Stone Guest)* could have been written by a Spaniard"; the genius of England is in *The Feast at the Time of the Plague*,[22] etc. More convincingly, Dostoevsky develops the idea of Pushkin as the creator of the Russian types, of Aleko and Onegin as the Russian wanderers, of Tatyana as the apotheosis of Russian womanhood, etc. Dostoevsky adopts the pervasive method of Russian criticism, which seems one of the most striking of the features that set it off from the preoccupations of the West: the constant attempt, first made by Belinsky, to derive from a few fictional figures a spiritual history of the Russian and the social types of the time: the superfluous man, the nihilist, and later the Underground Man, or the positive revolutionary hero. The distinctions between fiction and reality, art and life, are abolished or minimized, partly because attention could focus on a few figures who had become representative, while in the West similar attempts would bog down in a welter of fictional figures giving contradictory evidence. A list such as Tom Jones, Uncle Toby, Elizabeth Bennett, Edward Waverley, David Copperfield, Becky Sharp, etc. simply would not make the same sense and could not attract the emotional attachment of the great Russian fictional heroes. But the task is the same everywhere. Don Quixote, Hamlet, Faust show that there are fictional figures who have become almost historical personalities. Dostoevsky attempted himself to create such mythical figures and skillfully anchored them in the past of literature: Myshkin, the Idiot, refers to Don Quixote, Raskolnikov to Rastignac; the *Brothers Karamazov* are permeated with quotations from Schiller, and Faust and Mephistopheles reappear in a different key as Ivan and his shabby devil.

NIKOLAY STRAKHOV (1828–1896)

Grigoriev died in 1864; Dostoevsky after the failure of his two periodicals, *Vremya* (Time) and *Epokha* (1861–64), did not engage in literary criticism; in *The Diary of the Writer*, his later journalistic venture (1876–77, 1880–81), he says quite definitely that he had made up his mind that "literary criticism would have no place in it."[1] Still, in the seventies and eighties the conservative, substantially Slavophile point of view was represented well by Nikolay Strakhov, an extremely versatile philosopher, popular scientist, and ideologist who wrote voluminously against the nihilists and criticized the positivism and evolutionism that was being introduced from Europe. His long articles on Renan and Taine (whom he considered greatly inferior to Renan) are often incisive and spirited polemics. Ideologically Strakhov was very close to Grigoriev and Dostoevsky. He became Dostoevsky's first biographer, but strangely enough, during the composition of his reminiscences of Dostoevsky, turned sharply against him as a human being. As he told Tolstoy in a notorious letter, Dostoevsky was "neither a good nor a happy man." He was "malicious, envious, and dissolute," and in support Strakhov told the hardly verifiable story of Dostoevsky's supposed rape of a young girl. Dostoevsky, it seems to him, resembles the hero of *The Notes from Underground,* Svidrigailov in *Crime and Punishment,* and Stavrogin in *The Possessed.*[2] Earlier Strakhov had praised Dostoevsky consistently as an enemy of nihilism who looks at nihilism with understanding and pity. His main theme is "penitent nihilism": Raskolnikov, Shatov, Ivan Karamazov.[3]

Still, Strakhov would not require our attention if he were simply one of the numerous ideologists discussing West versus East at that time. He was also a literary critic and, I think, a good literary critic at a time when the other critics of any standing had been silenced either by death or exile. Strakhov commented perceptively on the great works of Russian literature of the sixties and seventies, admittedly within the limits and preoccupations of the scheme he had taken over from Grigoriev, whom he admired as "our best critic" and whose works he edited in 1876.[4]

Strakhov's general concept of Russian literature is very much like Grigoriev's. He sees it as a struggle between native and foreign elements in which Russia is to achieve its true nationality and spiritual independence by an absorption of Western influences. Strakhov, however, different from Grigoriev and Belinsky, defends 18th-century Russian pseudo-classicism as a necessary preparation of the great 19th-century literature and as an expression of newly found Russian self-confidence,[5] and he exalts Pushkin, anticipating closely the general argument of Dostoevsky's famous speech. Pushkin absorbed and surpassed his European models. Strakhov sensitively comments on Pushkin's virtuosity and detachment toward his models and emphasizes the playful, parodistic attitude which comes through, e.g., in his "Imitations from the Koran" or the versions from Dante. Strakhov also makes much of the late prose of Pushkin. He finds the beginnings of Gogol in "The Undertaker," of Dostoevsky in "The Postmaster," and of Tolstoy in *Captain's Daughter*.[6]

By far his best critical work is devoted to Turgenev and Tolstoy. Strakhov is of two minds about Turgenev: he admires him as an artist but does not, of course, like his ideology. He wants to rescue him from the clutches of the nihilists, and when Turgenev himself professed agreement with them, blandly declared that "a poet does not know himself what he wants to say." [7] Strakhov, rightly to my mind, interprets *Fathers and Sons* in universal terms. It is a novel not about nihilism but about the clash of generations and the conflict between theory and life. Bazarov is defeated by life and love. Bazarov's enmity toward art is a necessary feature of his character, as art always takes us out of our time into the eternal, away from the excitement of the day to the calm of contemplation.[8] Strakhov could not like *Virgin Soil*: it seemed to him a failure and a feeble apology to the younger generation. But Turgenev was not a nihilist; he embraced "a light Schopenhauerism." Strakhov's obituary of Turgenev seems ungenerously nationalistic: Turgenev does not express the true spirit of Russia.[9]

Tolstoy became Strakhov's ideal writer, though he disagreed with his later religious and political views. The review of *War and Peace* succeeds in bringing out the greatness of the book: its humanity and universality. Strakhov argues convincingly that it is not an historical novel but rather a family chronicle or an epic, and he explains its moral message as that of a true heroism: an acceptance of suffering, of submission which he sees embodied in the peasant Platon Karatayev. He must have been one of the first critics to assign him a symbolic eminence. Strakhov even defends Tolstoy's philosophizing: he rightly interprets his fatalism not as a modern determinism but as a kind of pantheism.[10] *Anna Karenina* impressed Strakhov as a picture of moral chaos. Both Anna and Levin are suicidal types. The book is seen as much more gloomy and depressing than it seems at least to one reader today. Strakhov disagrees with De Vogüé about Tolstoy: he is mistaken in invoking mysticism and Buddhism when old Christianity is sufficient to account for Tolstoy's views.[11]

This is only a small indication of Strakhov's critical work, which is always sane and lucid, free from the turgidity of Grigoriev, but also lacking something of his *finesse* and passion. Strakhov, in spite of his religious convictions, was an intellectualist, a rationalist like Tolstoy. Dostoevsky knew it when, in 1869, he welcomed Strakhov as "the only representative of our contemporary criticism to whom the future belongs" and remarked on his "immense, spontaneous sympathy for Leo Tolstoy." [12]

An actual understanding of Dostoevsky, at least as a thinker, began with Vladimir Solovyov (1853–1900), who delivered three speeches in Dostoevsky's memory in 1883 in which he hailed him as a prophet of God, a mystical seer,[13] and with V. V. Rozanov, who in 1890 examined "The Grand Inquisitor" for the first time almost as a religious text and interpreted its bearing on a philosophy of history.[14] The radical intelligentsia, however, had turned against Dostoevsky. The populist, Nikolay Mikhailovsky (1842–1904), found a formula: Dostoevsky is a "cruel talent" (the title of his article, 1882), a sadist who enjoys suffering, a defender of the order of things which creates torturers and tortured. Dostoevsky, he declared, is most successful in describing the sensations of a wolf devouring a sheep and of a sheep devoured by a wolf. His picture of Russia and the Russian revolutionaries is totally false: he missed the most interesting and most typical features of our time.[15] Thus Russia split on Dostoevsky again into two widely divergent camps: the radical and the conservative, the secular and the religious. Dostoevsky, the prophet of a new religion, became the rallying point of the Russian symbolists. Though some of their writings precede the year 1900, a consideration of symbolist criticism will be best left to the 20th century.

An erroneous conception of the Russian 19th century would be created, however, if we thought of it entirely in terms of the warring ideological factions. Apart from this turmoil, a very active academic scholarship was built up. Slavic philology, which had been founded as an encyclopedic science by Joseph Dobrovský (1753–1829) in Bohemia, developed in Russia rapidly with a study of old Russian literature and folklore, and the literary history of the modern period was put on secure foundations by many diligent investigators. Still, it is characteristic of the Russian situation that A. N. Pypin's (1833–1904) most successful *History of Russian Literature from the Beginnings to Gogol* (4 vols. 1898–99) is not only erudite, factual, "positivist," but also fervently liberal in tone and emphasis.

Pypin can be compared to Hettner and Brandes rather than to Taine, to whose example he appealed on occasion.

ALEXANDER POTEBNYA (1836-1891) AND ALEXANDER VESELOVSKY (1838-1906)

But there were two scholars who made important contributions to literary theory which were appreciated only in the 20th century. Alexander Potebnya was rather a linguist than a literary theorist, but he was one of the very first linguists who were seriously concerned with the problem of poetic language. He drew from Wilhelm von Humboldt the distinction between language as product or work, (*ergon*) and language as activity (*energeia*) and argued that poetry is a constant activity disturbing and overcoming the conventions of language as work. Poetry is identified with linguistic creation. While thought tries to reduce a word to a mere label signifying an object, poetry tries to bring out the multiple meanings of a word: it aims at exploiting the similarities in sound of a word with other words, or similarities in derivation or grammatical categories, etc. A word, and particularly a poetic word, is a multivalent sign, a true symbol.[1] In this basic theory Potebnya interestingly anticipates Croce and the so-called "idealist philology" of Karl Vossler, which identifies linguistic with poetic creativity. The conception became important in Russia for symbolist theory and later for the formalists. Potebnya himself lived all his life in provincial Kharkov and exercised his main influence only after his death. In his general outlook he harks back to German romantic linguistics, even though he studied in Berlin in 1862 with Steinthal as another compatriot of his did in the same year.

But Alexander Veselovsky went quite a different way. He became immersed in the new social sciences, in *Völkerpsychologie,* in ethnology, in comparative folklore. He spent several years in Italy and eventually produced a two-volume study of Boccaccio.[2] In Petersburg since 1870, as Professor of General Literature, Veselovsky put out a steady stream of studies on the migration of themes and plots ranging all over the Western and Eastern world: from dimmest antiquity to romantic literature. But we are not here concerned with erudition, even though Veselovsky must be classed among the greatest literary scholars of the century in breadth of knowledge and scope of competence. He is important for our topic because he resolutely tried to see literature as a totality of works: he always considered a work of literature as an object divorced from the psychic events of its origins or effects, as a kind of "thing" which can be set among other things in the world, compared with them, and explained by causes and consequences. His ultimate aim, particularly in later life, was the construction of what he called "historical poetics," a universal evolutionary history of poetry in which the history of poetic devices, themes, forms and *genres* would be traced through all literatures: oral and written.[3] The overambitious task remained necessarily incomplete, but the many partial contributions amount to a general scheme impressive not only by the wealth of documentation but by the ingenuity and suggestiveness of the problems raised.

Veselovsky assumed an original syncretism of genres: not a mixture but rather an undifferentiated original oral poetry which he construed just as the Indo-European philologists construed the supposed parent language from which all "Aryan" languages are descended. Veselovsky described the process of scission very concretely, drawing examples in one paragraph from a story originating in the Faroe Islands, from Homeric hymns, from Longus, etc. Poetic language is assumed to have been created only in these prehistoric times. It even now reflects the conceptions of primitive man: animism, myth, rituals, ceremonies, etc. Thus the "psychological parallelism" between man and nature in much popular lyrical poetry reflects an original, animistic view of the world.[4] The scheme assumes a hardly tenable divorce between content and form. Poetic languages and forms are given: content changes with social and intellectual changes. The role of the individual in literary creation is severely limited; he can only modify the inherited poetic language in order to give expression to the changed content of his time. Thus Veselovsky combines a sociological point of view with formalism, which allows him a close study of the techniques, particularly of oral, anonymous poetry. Metaphor and meter, as well as *motif* and plot, or topic (*sujet*), which he sharply distinguishes from the subject matter in reality, are analyzed on a wide canvas.[5] Veselovsky has assigned a task to scholarship which can hardly ever be solved. The Russian formalists, however, have taken up his challenge. But Veselovsky bears the stamp of his time too strongly to be still relevant with his concrete solutions. He has no proper grasp of the unity of form and content, the organicity of a work of art, and he ignores, too blandly, the problem of individual creation. Characteristically, when he studies modern writers like the romantic Russian poet Zhukovsky,[6] he chooses a man who is an eclectic and intermediary, who reflects his times and the currents almost passively. Veselovsky worships objective facts and science so excessively that he cannot deal with aesthetic value. The central problem of criticism remains outside his ken. He transmitted an all-embracing universalism, an anti-individualistic, almost collective approach, a concern for literary evolution and its social causes to later Russian literary scholarship, but he also saddled it with a technological methodology that tries to drain literature of its aesthetic and thus finally of its deepest human appeal. Veselovsky is the patron of comparative literature in Russian and one of the originators of Russian formalism. He is almost unknown in the West.

LEO TOLSTOY (1828–1910)

It is usual to treat Tolstoy's little book *What Is Art?* (1898) as an aberration of a great old man: to consider it as "one of the least intelligent books ever written,"[1] to dismiss it as a fanatical pamphlet against art. It certainly is written with a satirical violence, with a lack of tolerance and imaginative sympathy which can be excused only by Tolstoy's craving for truth, for absolute sincerity, and his genuine concern about the position of art and literature in society. But this attitude, while comprehensible in view of Tolstoy's frequently obtuse judgments and brutal condemnations, will not do. One must recognize that *What Is Art?* is not merely an outburst of the old man after his conversion but grows out of the totality of his life and art: is a logical consequence of his constant, basic preoccupations. And these preoccupations, however disinclined we may be to agree with his solutions, raise very important, still unsolved problems of the function of art in society.

Tolstoy starts out by describing the enormous role art plays in a modern economy: the time and labor spent on it by hundreds of thousands of workmen, carpenters, masons, paperhangers, tailors, hairdressers, jewelers, typesetters.

> Hundreds of thousands of people devote their lives from child-
> hood to learning to twirl their legs rapidly (dancers), or to
> touch keys and strings very rapidly (musicians), or sketch with
> paint and represent what they see (painters), or to turn every
> sentence inside out and find a rhyme to every word. And these
> people, often very kind and clever and capable of all sorts of
> useful labor, grow savage over their specialized and stupefying
> occupations, and become one-sided and complacent specialists,
> dull to all the serious phenomena of life and skilful only at
> rapidly twisting their legs, their tongues, or their fingers.[2]

And Tolstoy asks the question whether art is so important that such
sacrifices should be made for its sake. The point raised, at first, is
thus economic: Tolstoy, preoccupied with the Russia of his day,
sees art as luxury, as a drain on national resources of labor and men,
and then he sees modern art as a dehumanizing speciality, as a
technicality which breaks up the unity of man, makes him a partial
man, a virtuoso who suffers as any workman at a machine from the
evils of the division of labor.

Then Tolstoy asks, "What is art?" and surveys the definitions of
art and beauty which he found in a multitude of books. He picks—
largely from Schasler's *Kritische Geschichte der Aesthetik* (1872)—
definitions of beauty and art in order to conclude that they are all
foolish or irrelevant, for art is not concerned with objective beauty
at all. He has also no use for metaphysical definitions that seek the
nature of art in something supernatural. Rather he adopts a definition of art which he derives from Eugène Veron's *L'Esthétique*
(1878), at least in substance. To quote Tolstoy:

> To invoke in oneself a feeling one has once experienced and
> having evoked it in oneself then by means of movements, lines,
> colors, sounds, or forms expressed in words, so to transmit the
> feelings that others experience the same feeling—this is the
> activity of art. Art is a human activity consisting in this, that
> one man consciously by means of certain external signs, hands
> on to others feelings he has lived through, and that others are
> infected by these feelings and also experience them.[3]

Veron similarly considers it a mistake to make either physical or
moral beauty the foundation of aesthetics and, like Tolstoy, thinks

that "an artist has but to abandon himself to his emotion and it will become contagious." [4] Veron's position leads him to conclusions and critical judgments quite different from Tolstoy's, but he shares with him a distaste for the specialized, technical, modern art, for academicism, and agrees with the emphasis on the sincerity of the artist. In Veron empathy with the artist is central: "art is the result," he says, modifying his initial position, "less of communicated emotion, than of the participation of human personality in that emotion." [5] In Tolstoy the communication, the infection, is primary. He then immediately raises the question what kind of emotion is conveyed by art and answers it by saying that art must communicate good emotions. "Art is not, as the metaphysicians say, the manifestation of some mysterious Idea or Beauty or God; it is not, as the aesthetic physiologists say, a game, in which man lets off his excess of stored-up energy; it is not the expression of man's emotions by external signs; it is not the production of pleasing objects; and, above all, it is not pleasure; but it is a means of union among men joining them together in the same feelings, and indispensable for the life and progress towards well-being of individuals and of humanity." [6]

This theory has a respectable ancestry: art as communication of emotion is a conception known to Dennis, Dubos, Diderot, and many writers of the 18th century in the Longinian tradition. We can find the closest parallel in a writer whom Tolstoy could hardly have read—Wordsworth. The poet must "bind together by passion and knowledge the vast empire of human society," he "widens the sphere of human sensibility for the delight, honour, and benefit of human nature," he produces an "accord of sublimated humanity." [7] The common denominator between Wordsworth and Tolstoy is their Rousseauism, their enmity toward urban civilization, their concern for the effect of literature on the masses of humanity, their hope for literature as an instrument of unification in a spirit of love. Neither can escape the obvious difficulties raised by the criterion of sincerity and the attendant impossibility of drawing any kind of boundary between art and emotional persuasion. Nor did they face the fact that in limiting the emotions to be aroused by art to those they consider good and right, they shifted the criterion of evaluation to ethics, politics, and religion and ran into the constant danger of mere didacticism, judgment by good intention, and right subject matter.

Tolstoy tries, then, to show how the false view of art arose. He glances back at the Greeks, puzzled by the conception of the identity of goodness and beauty which to Tolstoy was completely refuted by reality and Christianity. He ridicules the worship of the Greeks: "a small, semisavage, slave-holding people who lived 2000 years ago, imitated the nude human body extremely well, and erected buildings pleasant to look at." [8] He has more sympathy with the Middle Ages: though his general distaste for Catholicism and organized religion also makes him look back at the Middle Ages as a superseded stage of humanity and the arts. Still, medieval art was true art, since it corresponded to the religious view of life held by the people among whom it arose.[9] Tolstoy, in spite of his basic primitivism and strong antihistoricism, is strangely affected by the belief of his time in progress and by the basic Hegelian view of the coherence of ages: the view of art as a collective expression of its society.

Renaissance art is to Tolstoy as to Ruskin the beginning of bad art in the sense of constituting an art divorced from the people, an art for mere pleasure's sake, an art limited to the upper classes. Tolstoy then concentrates his fire on modern art which serves now only the upper classes. He asks: "But if art is an important matter, a spiritual blessing essential for all men like religion (as the devotees of art are fond of saying), then it should be accessible to everyone. And if, as in our day, it is not accessible to all men, then either art is not the vital matter it is represented to be, or that art which we call art is not the real thing." [10] Instead of pursuing this argument, Tolstoy, however, chooses the easier way out of attacking the specific evils (or what he considered evils) of the art of his time. He gives a highly colored, grossly oversimplified account of contemporary decadence: in a tone of outrage and with an incomprehension of contemporary idiom which lays him wide open to the charge of Philistinism, prudery, or simply insensitivity. He tries first to show that modern art has shrunk in its subject matter, has given up such wide range of feelings and themes as those of religion and labor, and concentrates only on three simple feelings: "the feeling of pride, the feeling of sexual desire, and the feeling of weariness of life." [11] He refers in shocked terms to current French books such as Remy de

Gourmont's *Les Chevaux de Diomède,* or Pierre Louÿs' *Aphrodite* and argues that just as the content of modern art is all either sexual or pessimistic, its form has become more and more involved, affected, and obscure. Tolstoy quotes poems by Verlaine, Baudelaire, Mallarmé, and Maeterlinck to prove his point. Similarly, modern drama is ridiculed: Ibsen, Maeterlinck, Hauptmann, as well as modern music, Wagner and Strauss. The condemnation is sweeping and indiscriminate: even the attack on the very real cult of obscurity is weakened by Tolstoy's examples. It is difficult to see anything unintelligible, for instance, in Baudelaire's prose-poem "Le galant tireur," which Tolstoy quotes.[12] But obviously Tolstoy objects to the whole method of suggestion, the whole device of indirection, insisting always on literal interpretation, on blunt direct information about intent and meaning.

With his usual sincerity, Tolstoy grants, however, that what is incomprehensible to him might not be so to others and that what he considers comprehensible might not be so to the masses. He admits that he belongs to the people who grew up in the first half of the 19th century admiring Goethe, Schiller, Musset, Hugo, Dickens, Beethoven, Chopin, Raphael, da Vinci, Michelangelo, etc., who are unable to make head or tail of the art of the time and wish to ignore it. But modern art, he recognizes, is too important, spreading also to Russia, to be ignored, and it must not be dismissed merely because he does not understand it.

"The only advantage the art I acknowledge has over decadent art lies in the fact that the art I recognize is comprehensible to a somewhat larger number of people than present-day art." [13] One would think that Tolstoy is now on the way of understanding the process of artistic education, however much he might want to reverse its trend toward greater exclusiveness. But this is not so. In his desire to have this universal art, he simply denies that art which is not universally comprehensible is art at all. "To say that a work of art is good but incomprehensible to the majority of men is the same as saying of some kind of food that it is very good but most people can't eat it." "Great works of art are only great because they are accessible and comprehensible to everyone." Tolstoy recognizes that scientific knowledge requires preparation and a certain sequence, so that one cannot learn trigonometry before knowing geometry, but art, he asserts without any proof, "acts on people independently of their state of education, infects any man whatever his stage of development." [14]

Thus all art except art comprehensible to all is condemned, and Tolstoy can return to his assault on counterfeit art. Much of modern art is mere imitation, or is copied from reality, or is merely striking and interesting; criticism is obviously superfluous, since art is immediately comprehensible. What do critics explain? "The artist, if a real artist, has by his work transmitted to others the feelings he experienced. What is there, then, to explain?" [15] You either feel it or don't. Tolstoy even launches into a diatribe that charges critics with having established the inflated reputation of much pseudo-art. The Greek tragedians, Dante, Milton, Shakespeare owe their present-day standing to the deference for criticism. A special chapter is then devoted to Wagner and to a comic description of a performance of *Siegfried* in Moscow. After this long assault on pseudo-art, which not only includes the decadent art of the late 19th century but takes pot-shots at the later works of Beethoven, at Michelangelo's Last Judgment, at Shakespeare's *Hamlet,* etc., Tolstoy returns to a more positive analysis of what he considers art. The main criterion is infectiousness, the affective power of art. "A real work of art destroys in the consciousness of the recipient the separation between himself and the artist, and not that alone, but also between himself and all whose minds receive this work of art. In this freeing of our personality from its separation and isolation, in this uniting of it with others, lies the chief characteristic and the great attractive force of art." [16] Art, then, is empathy, but also a surrender of individuality in the sense in which Schopenhauer conceived of art as an escape from the principle of individuation. Tolstoy tries to define the conditions of infectiousness and sees it in the "individuality of the feeling transmitted," in the "clearness with which the feeling is transmitted" and in the "sincerity of the artist, i.e., the greater or lesser force with which the artist himself feels the emotion he transmits." The first condition is somewhat paradoxical and surprising in view of Tolstoy's general defense of absolute universality. Tolstoy states dogmatically that "the more individual the feeling transmitted, the more strongly does it act on the recipient," [17] a view that shows the large residue of romantic subjectivism in Tolstoy's poetics. Clearness of expression is less surprising, though it could be argued that much emotional effect is often achieved by obscurity, by indirection, and by suggestion. But Tolstoy will have nothing to do with this. "Sincerity" seems to be an alternative term for successful, convincing, emotionally effective art. This central term "infectiousness" involves and conceals for Tolstoy the whole problem of form, though at times he accepts more traditional criteria, like that of oneness. He accuses Goethe's *Faust* of lacking "the chief characteristic of a work of art—completeness, oneness, the inseparable unity of form and content expressing the feeling the artist has experienced," [18] a statement which seems to imply that individual, clear, sincere feeling must lead to a well-organized, complete work of art. Elsewhere in discussing Hauptmann's *Hanneles Himmelfahrt,* Tolstoy tries to establish some distinction between mere excitement of feeling, as in seeing the poor girl Hannele mistreated by her drunken father, and a genuine infection of man by man. He asserts that in the case of Hannele we have only "a mingled feeling of pity for another [human being] and of self-congratulation that it is not I who am suffering; it is like what we feel at the sight of an execution, or what the Romans felt in their circuses." [19] But while one may grant Tolstoy's criticism of Hauptmann's play as a sentimental tear-jerker, it is quite unclear how on his theory it is possible to distinguish between such pity for Hannele and genuine artistic emotion.

Tolstoy can get at anything like a standard of values only by classifying the feelings with which art is to infect us. He distinguishes bad and good feelings; and among good feelings, the only legitimate province of art, Tolstoy distinguishes two kinds: simple feelings of common life, such as merriment, pity, cheerfulness, tranquillity, and so forth, and religious "feelings flowing from a perception of our sonship to God and of the brotherhood of man." [20] The two are one and the same: the simple feelings are the feelings of community among men and thus eventually of human brotherhood. Yet Tolstoy distinguishes between universal and religious art. In a famous passage which has done much to expose his theory to ridicule, he gives modern examples of these two kinds of art: first of "the highest art flowing from the love of God and man I should give Schiller's *Robbers,* Victor Hugo's *Les Pauvres Gens* and *Les Misérables;* the novels and stories of Dickens—*The Tale of Two Cities, Christmas Carol, The Chimes,* and others—*Uncle Tom's Cabin;* Dostoevsky's works—especially his *Memoirs from the House of the Dead*—and *Adam Bede* by George Eliot."[21] As good universal art Tolstoy mentions *Don Quixote,* Molière's comedies, *David Copperfield,* and the *Pickwick Papers* by Dickens, Gogol's and Pushkin's tales, and some things of Maupassant's. To this rather amazing list one should add what elsewhere is quoted as examples of good ancient art—the *Iliad* and *Odyssey*; the epic of Genesis, especially the stories of Isaac, Jacob, and Joseph; the Hebrew prophets; the Psalms; the Gospel parables; the story of Buddha, and the hymns of the Vedas; and Tolstoy gives a blanket endorsement to folklegends, fairy tales, and folk songs. Tolstoy consigns his own artistic production to the category of bad art, excepting the story *God Sees the Truth but Waits,* which seeks a place in the first class (religious art), and a *Prisoner of the Caucasus,* which belongs to the second.[22]

Tolstoy at the end sketches his hopes for art in a new and better Christian society. There will be no specialized artists, no professionals; artistic activity will be accessible to all men, first, because it will not demand the technique now required, but also because all men will learn music and drawing together with reading and writing. The art of the future will be produced by all members of the community who feel need of such activity, but they will occupy themselves with art only when they feel such need. The artist of the future will live the common life of man, earning his subsistence with some kind of labor. He will receive no payment for his activity. The task of art is by no means small. "Through the influence of real art, aided by science, guided by religion, that peaceful cooperation of man which is now maintained by external means—by our lawcourts, police, charitable institutions, factory inspections, and so forth—should be obtained by man's free and joyous activity. Art should cause violence to be abolished." "The task of art is to make that feeling of brotherhood and love of one's neighbor, now attained only by the best members of society, the customary feeling and the instinct of all men." The last sentence of Tolstoy's treatise is: "The task of Christian art is to establish brotherly union among men."[23]

The treatise on art here described and analyzed can be supplemented from the mass of Tolstoy's other writings and the reports of visitors and interviewers. *What Is Art?* is not merely the peculiar anti-aesthetic revulsion of the late Tolstoy but substantially represents the views of even the young man. A diary entry of 1851 says: "The people have their own fine, inimitable literature. They don't want any higher literature and there is none." [24] An early story, *Lucerne* (1857), sets the beauty of primitive art against self-complacent civilization. When Tolstoy taught his peasant children (1862–63), he attacked the problem of artistic education in practice and reached highly primitivist conclusions. He was surprised to discover that two hardly literate peasant boys of 11 showed considerable gifts in composing stories. He printed a story in his Magazine, *Yasnaya Polyana,* and not only praised it as "equal to anything in Russian literature" but, reflecting on it, drew the most extreme conclusion: all contemporary art is addressed only to the upper classes. He dismisses, as he did later in *What Is Art?,* the argument that artistic training is necessary to appreciate it. "Who said this? Why? What proves it? It is only a shift, a loophole to escape from the hopeless position to which the false direction of our art, produced for one class alone, has led us. Why are the beauty of the sun, of the human face, the beauty of the sounds of a folk song, and of deeds of love and self-sacrifice accessible to everyone, and why do they demand no preparation?" [25] Tolstoy complains that there is a complete lack of suitable reading for peasant children. He doubts whether so long as no suitable literature is produced for the people, it is worth their while to learn to read.

What is said in *What Is Art?* thus can be supported from almost all periods of Tolstoy's life and can be illustrated from other occasional writings. Of these the best-known is "Shakespeare and the Drama" (1906), which was written as a preface to a pamphlet by Ernest Howard Crosby, a New York judge, called *Shakespeare and the Working Classes.* Crosby expounded there the old view that Shakespeare's outlook was aristocratic and hostile to the people. Tolstoy's essay agrees with Crosby's argument and buttresses it by a general attack on Shakespeare's morality: it amounts to an endorsement of the strong, to the espousal of the principle that the end justifies the means, etc. Shakespeare, moreover, was indifferent to religion. But Shakespeare, besides being immoral, was also a bad artist. Tolstoy elaborately ridicules, by retelling in a tone reminiscent of Rymer or Voltaire, the plot of *King Lear,* concluding that the old play, *King Leir,* is much more reasonable and touching. While Tolstoy has no trouble in proving the improbability of *King Lear,* or the baffling lack of explanation in Hamlet's behavior, he is surely mistaken in asserting that there is no individuality in the language of Shakespeare's characters, with the exception of Falstaff. A preposterous history of Shakespeare's reputation, which Tolstoy drew from German sources, tries to persuade us that Shakespeare was forgotten, and unearthed only by the Germans, who wanted a stick to beat the French with and wanted to justify objective art—that is, the amoral and immoral art of the German classics. Goethe is the main culprit. At the end Tolstoy deplores the divorce of drama from religion, the decline of drama to an empty and immoral amusement. He vaguely hopes for a new form of modern drama which will serve for the elucidation and confirmation in man of the highest degree of religious consciousness.[26]

The other surprising document is Tolstoy's introduction to a Russian selection of Maupassant's stories (1894). It precedes the publication of *What Is Art?* and gives a slightly different definition of the requirements for good art. The first condition of infection was "individuality," but this is here said to be "a correct, that is, a moral, relation of the author to his subject," a knowledge of the difference between good and evil. The other two requirements are identical with those in *What Is Art?*—clearness of expression and sincerity. Tolstoy then gives an extremely sympathetic discussion of Maupassant's novels, among which he discriminates quite soundly. He likes *Une Vie*, the best French novel since *Les Misérables*. Maupassant's moral relation to his figures is right: he really hates the coarse debauchee who destroys the happiness and peace of a charming family, and, similarly, *Bel-Ami* is praised because it shows righteous indignation at the prosperity and success of a sensual brute. But the later novels are evidences of a moral and artistic decline, bear the stamp of indifference, haste, and unreality and cater to the taste for the dirty and obscene. Yet Tolstoy discerns in Maupassant a man who thinks right: who saw through the society of his time and saw the evils of life and sex. "Maupassant had talent, that is to say, he saw things in their essentials and therefore involuntarily discerned the truth." There was a conflict in Maupassant between theory and practice. "He wished to extol sexual love, but the better he came to know it the more he cursed it." [27] Like Dobrolyubov, Tolstoy sees art as involuntary unconscious insight into truth which the artist might try to falsify by his theories but which he cannot do, if he is a true, upright and sincere artist.

Tolstoy applies the same principle to Chekhov's story "The

Darling" (1905) . There he uses the Bible passage telling of Balaam blessing the people of Israel, though he had come up on the mountain to curse them (Numbers 33–34) . The same happened to Chekhov: he wanted to ridicule the poor ignorant woman who always repeated parrotlike the views of her three husbands, but he involuntarily clothed that sweet creature in the radiance of love. "He wanted to knock down Darling, and directing the close attention of a poet upon her he has exalted her." [28] Tolstoy, though right in his interpretation of the story, does not see that Chekhov is not far from his point of view and that there was probably no such conflict in him: Chekhov could both laugh at her and admire and sympathize with her.

Tolstoy's criticism of Maupassant and Chekhov counteracts somewhat the impression of crudity and mere didacticism of the most obvious sort which one might derive from many of Tolstoy's pronouncements. One could, however, fortify one's condemnation of Tolstoy's views by collecting pronouncements, mostly from the later years, on his contemporaries, which are almost always contemptuous and smugly conservative in taste.

Nietzsche is condemned for his "immoral, coarse, inflated, incoherent chatter" and considered literally a madman.[29] Ibsen was also on Tolstoy's list of aversions. "I read all his dramas and his poem 'Brand': all are contrived, false and badly written in the sense that all his characters are not true and not consistent." [30] Kipling, Strindberg, Wilde are also dismissed; for example, *Salome* is called "perfect madness, a mere string of words." [31] Similarly Tolstoy disliked and condemned the Russian symbolists: Merezhkovsky, Shestov, Rozanov, etc. He found something good in Kuprin and in the early Andreyev and, among his younger contemporaries, he admired Chekhov and Gorky.[32] But the admiration of Chekhov did not extend to the dramas. He told Chekhov that they are "even worse than Shakespeare's." [33] In most cases Tolstoy only gives opinions without any substantiation. Only rarely is there a glimpse of his principles. For example he disliked Flaubert and condemned the *Legend of Saint Julian* as a "revolting piece of nastiness." [34] He gives his reasons elsewhere, in the introduction to S. T. Semenov's *Peasant Stories*. "The last episode, intended to be the most touching in the story, is one in which Julian lies down in the same bed with the leper and warms him with his own body. This leper is Christ, who carries Julian off to Heaven with him. All this is told with great mastery, but I always remain perfectly cold when I read that story. I feel that the author himself would not have done, and would not even have wished to do, what his hero does, and therefore I myself do not wish to do it and do not experience any agitation when reading of this amazing exploit." [35] The argument *ad hominem,* of literal identification with a figure, could hardly be pushed further. After all, Flaubert is not Saint Julian.

Tolstoy's views of art and literature formulate very radically an affective, emotionalist theory of art where all emphasis is put on three elements: the sincerity of the artist, the emotional effect of the writing, and the truth, the honesty of his reproduction of reality. The work of art as a structured object of linguistic signs is ignored, and so is the inventiveness, the imaginative power of the artist, the role of tradition, and convention. Tolstoy sees in his theory the only salvation against the alienation of the artist from society, the modern professionalism, and with it the insincerity, untruthfulness, fantasticalness, and obscurity of modern literature. Possibly more clearly than anybody else in his time, Tolstoy put the question of the divorce between the artist and the masses, the whole problem of popular universal literature. In our time Soviet Russia solved the problem of literature for the masses, in very different terms. It was done at the expense of both the religious values dear to Tolstoy and the aesthetic subtleties he condemned.

13: GERMAN CRITICISM

IN THE WEST, German literature of the second half of the 19th century is a complete *terra incognita* until the advent of Nietzsche. Even such fine poets and novelists as Gottfried Keller, C. F. Meyer, Wilhelm Raabe, and Theodor Fontane are known only to a few specialists. German criticism of the time is necessarily even more obscure. No single figure stands out as a spokesman of the country as do Sainte-Beuve and Taine in France, De Sanctis in Italy, and Brandes in Denmark. Still, not only was this the time of the great expansion of specialized literary scholarship, the period in which *Goethe-philologie* became almost a branch of learning, but literary studies also flourished in forms closely related to criticism proper: literary historiography, literary biography, and technical poetics. In the traditional form of critical activity, namely the critical essay, Germany at this time produced little of enduring value. Only Karl Hillebrand seems comparable to the essayists in the West, and he remained by choice very much at the margin of things German. There were, of course, the day-by-day militant critics such as Julian Schmidt and Paul Lindau in Berlin, and Ferdinand Kürnberger in Vienna. Theodor Fontane had a long record as a theater critic in Berlin before he welcomed the new movement of naturalism in the 1880's. The wave of naturalism, which seemed a radical break with the past, subsided very quickly, however; and before the turn of the century the circle around Stefan George had changed the literary situation again in a very different direction. The George circle felt the impact of the thought of a man who first emerged in the '70's: Friedrich Nietzsche, the most original, radical, and baffling critic of the time. We can conclude our considerations with him, since the literary criticism of the George circle belongs mainly to the 20th century.

The achievement of German literary history in this period is impressive, particularly the work of Hermann Hettner (1821–82).

His *Literaturgeschichte des achtzehnten Jahrhunderts* (6 vols. 1856–70) successfully combines narration, characterization, and criticism. The six volumes are not confined to German literature: the first two on English and French literature serve as an introduction. The four volumes on German literature are much superior, partly because Hettner improved in his stride and partly because he was much more at home in Germany. The French volume (1860) was an act of courage in its time, since "in England and Germany," as Hettner complains, "one no longer reads or knows 18th-century French literature, but vilifies it." Hettner recognizes an "indestructible core of truth, a high-minded enthusiasm and energy" [1] in the thought and activity of the *philosophes* and sees the Enlightenment as a positive phase of world history. He protests against the German habit of dismissing a thinker such as Voltaire because of his lack of system and levity of tone, and he gives sympathetic accounts of the thought of Voltaire, Montesquieu, Diderot, and Rousseau. In the German volumes he strongly stresses their influence, particularly that of Rousseau on Herder, Goethe, and Schiller. Hettner's main lesson is that "it is time to stop talking endlessly about the disintegrating, destructive, negative nature, the frivolity and impudence of the French *philosophes*." [2]

The earlier volume on the English 18th century (1856) is least distinguished: Hettner does not appreciate the "extremely flat and drily rational" poetry of Dryden and Pope: and he makes the usual objections against the morals and the incoherence of Sterne.[3] He is sympathetic, however, to empiricism and deism, explains the intellectual milieu well enough, and writes appreciatively of Defoe, Swift, and Fielding.

It would be unfair to disparage these introductory volumes. Hettner is at his best when he treats the German Enlightenment and classicism. The German volumes are models of clear exposition, rich documentation, and straightforward criticism. In them he restates the main topics of his early writings, which are more polemical, more contemporaneous, and more critical.

Hettner first wrote a pamphlet, *Gegen die spekulative Aesthetik* (1845), directed against Hegel and Vischer: he repudiates the enterprise of speculative aesthetics in terms of a naturalism derived from Feuerbach. Rather naively he argues that art always falls below nature; that in front of the Medici Venus in Florence our glances will stray to the living girls admiring the statue and that there is no landscape picture that can rival the view of the Bay of Naples.[4] Hettner objects both to the abstract classicism of a Winckelmann, which seems to him divorced from life and history, and to the romantic exaltation of the imagination. He stresses that the language of the poet is not an indifferent, mechanical sign but the very material of poetry. Technique and its stylistic laws are part of artistic creation itself. But strangely enough, Hettner divorces content and style and considers content historical while style is not. Style is the subject of theory, content of history. Every theory thus ends in history. Aesthetics and the history of art make up together a single, organic "science of art."[5]

The radicalism of Hettner's position is much subdued in his next small book, *Die romantische Schule* (1850). At a time when in liberal circles (to which Hettner belonged with all his ardor) romanticism was equated with reaction and obscurantism, Hettner showed that this is true only of its last phase, that the early romantics were closely associated with Goethe and Schiller, and that they all share in the common curse of German literature: the divorce from society, the conflict of poetry and life.[6] There is, Hettner argues, a continuity between German classicism and romanticism: Goethe and Schiller fled to Greece, the romantics to the Middle Ages and the ancient Teutons. Hettner severely criticizes both the German classics and romantics. Goethe and Schiller vacillated between naturalism and idealism. Schiller, though Hettner considers him superior to Goethe in his grasp of antiquity, was in all his later plays obsessed by a futile ambition of resuscitating the ancient tragedy of fate. He was a poet of freedom only in his youth.[7] The romantics were free with a vengeance: they indulged in unfettered subjectivism and irresponsible irony. Hettner hails the beginnings of "historical" poetry, i.e., poetry concerned with a realistic presentation of the forces and interests of history. The later Tieck and Hebbel, whom Hettner had known in Naples in 1845, point in the right direction; but a rebirth of poetry will come only with a "free and great nation."[8] The political hope for a liberal unified Germany animates the early Hettner. He differs from Gervinus in not believing in a contradiction between art and politics, in hoping for an imminent resurrection of art.

His next little book, *Das moderne Drama* (1852), is even more

directly concerned with the present and future. Hettner hoped
that the pamphlet would influence young dramatists. His hope was
realized only much later when the young Ibsen read it with enthusiastic approval.[9] Hettner had discussed the issues with Gottfried
Keller in conversations and letters and felt that he was sketching a
poetics of the drama for the use of his gifted Swiss friend.[10] Like his
whole age, Hettner is greatly concerned with historical tragedy. He
is anxious to show that Shakespeare's history plays must not be taken
as a model: they, at their best—he singles out *Coriolanus*—are
rather psychological tragedies of character. In order to succeed, historical tragedy must not be antiquarian but must be nourished by the
"moods and needs" of our time, by political pathos.[11] The bourgeois
social drama seems to him more genuinely "historical" than historical drama. Even *Romeo and Juliet*, *Othello*, *Timon of Athens*
are bourgeois family tragedies, and the social drama is the drama
of the future, whether it is a drama of conditions, of passion, or of
idea. Among the three types, Hettner puts the last highest: intrigue
and close plotting are inferior to character as sources of tragedy. In
tragedy there must be no chance; its world must be an absolutely
reasonable world of inner necessity. Tragedy is supreme if it is a
tragedy of idea—which Hettner sees realized, though imperfectly,
in Hebbel's best plays.[12] Hettner hopes also for a new comedy that
would be an "idealizing mirror of real world conditions": Aristo-
phanic in content and realistic in form. He even hopes for a musical
drama, though he has misgivings about Wagner, of whom he then
could know only the early operas.[13]

These suggestions and dreams were belied by later developments:
Keller buried his dramatic plans, no new German drama stirred,
and Hettner turned to the *History*, in which he developed the
themes suggested in *The Romantic School*. Whole passages of the
earlier book were incorporated into the *History*. But the *History* is
much more detailed and takes us much further back into the past
(to the end of the Thirty Years' War in 1648). It is also animated by
a different basic conception. German classicism now appears as the
direct continuation of the Enlightenment, as a renaissance of the
Renaissance. Its gospel of humanity seems to Hettner the finest
flower of Western civilization: it has made the Germans "the most
educated and spiritually freest nation of the world." [14] Goethe may
not equal Shakespeare "in firm security and elementary power of

poetic creation, but he surpasses him in depth and width of spiritual meaning, in the sublimity and purity of mental life." [15] These patriotic extravagances and the lavish praise for *Nathan der Weise, Iphigenie, Wilhelm Meister,* and *Hermann und Dorothea* in particular, are happily counterbalanced by a constant sober analysis of ideas and many severely critical discussions of the most famous works of the German classics.

There are two kinds of art that meet Hettner's approval: the first is realistic, psychological art, the loving detail of *Goetz* and *Egmont,* the incomparable vitality of the first part of *Faust,* the peculiarly German style of *Kabale und Liebe.* But this art, Hettner recognizes, has its severe limits: the ideal classical phase of Goethe's writings and Schiller's thought rises higher. *Iphigenie* seems to him perfect: it has the "high ideality of the best Italian Renaissance," [16] as do the *Roman Elegies* and *Hermann und Dorothea.* But the later stage of Goethe's development is condemned as a false classicism. *Die Natürliche Tochter* is not Renaissance but imitative and dead pseudo art. Schiller is also treated from this point of view: the early Schiller, though crude and merely realistic, is admirable; but the later Schiller mistakenly embraced the classical idea of a tragedy of fate. *Wallenstein* is criticized acutely for wavering between a tragedy of character and a tragedy of fate.[17] *Maria Stuart* depicts a judicial murder with no direct relation between guilt and punishment; *Die Jungfrau von Orleans* is similarly vitiated by subjecting the heroine to an arbitrary command, which she violates by committing a sin that is no sin in our eyes. *Wilhelm Tell* disintegrates: there is no necessary relation between Tell's private revenge against Gessler and the Swiss struggle for liberty. Only with *Demetrius* did Schiller return to a genuine tragedy of character [18]—but the play was left a fragment at his death.

Similarly, Hettner criticizes the later Goethe: Hettner has no understanding of allegory and symbolism and thus condemns the second part of *Faust* far too quickly, but he analyzes *Die Wahlverwandtschaften* acutely. Though he considers it the model and the source of the modern social novel, he criticizes it as if it were a tragedy. The conflict between the indissolubility of marriage that appears with its claim of indubitable validity, like the power of fate, on the one hand and the "predestined fatalistic natural magic," [19] the attraction of the elective affinities, on the other, is totally unbelievable, artificially and over-ingeniously contrived.

In such analyses Hettner the critic excels. Hettner the historian regards the setting of the works and lives in a cultural situation but often abandons any attempt to account for men or works causally. Winckelmann seems "fallen from heaven." German "Anacreontic" poetry cannot be explained by cultural history.[20] But international connections are always observed and parallel developments in the other arts and in music are considered. Ideas in aesthetics, philosophy, theology, and science are recounted very fully. It is precisely in its ideological scheme, however, that Hettner's book has aged most. His liberalism is too inflexible to allow him sympathy for anything that does not favor progress toward parliamentary democracy, unorthodox Protestant religiosity, and Kantian idealism: he has no use for materialism, mysticism, or Catholicism. The art criticism that praises only pseudoclassicism, Carstens, Thorwaldsen, and Schinkel[21] may not be disturbing, as there was little else to praise at that time; but in the literary criticism also Hettner's taste is too easily content with the right balance of realism and idealism in the classical phase of Goethe and Schiller.

Whatever the limitations of Hettner's knowledge and sensibility, his *Literaturgeschichte des achtzehnten Jahrhunderts* belongs to the very few great achievements in literary history during the later 19th century: it seems to me superior to Brandes' *Main Currents* or to Taine's *English Literature,* though it must yield to De Sanctis' great *History of Italian Literature.* Hettner, in spite of his generosity with quotations and concrete information, always remains on the level of abstract analysis—even when he psychologizes. For all his shrewdness and moral pathos, he lacks the power of evocation, the sensibility of De Sanctis or even of Taine.

The work of Wilhelm Scherer (1841–86), the most influential German literary historian in the later part of the century, shows very strikingly the change of intellectual climate brought about by the victory of positivism. In aspiration, at least, literary scholarship became an inductive social science governed by rigid determinism, inspired by a search for complete explanation of the poetic process and for general laws of history. Very early (1866) Scherer discussed Buckle, Comte, and Mill.[22] In his posthumous *Poetik* (1888, written

1885) anthropology, psychology, and economic theory are drawn upon. Even the teachings of the economic historian Wilhelm Röscher (1817–94) suggested new terms and problems.[23]

In many scattered writings, often on Goethe, or in discussions of earlier scholarship, Scherer formulated his aims. He wished to prove that "the general lawfulness of nature extends also to poetic productions"—otherwise, "every caprice of the imagination would constitute an exception to the scheme of things." [24] We must, he says, refute the saying *"individuum est ineffabile,"* [25] by employing a deterministic theory of genius similar to Taine's *race, milieu, moment.* Scherer prefers the formula, "Ererbtes, Erlerntes, Erlebtes," [26] where "inheritance" means nationality, family, etc., "learning" the literary tradition, and "experience" the biographical vicissitudes. In practice, Scherer searches for literary sources, analogues, and parallels, and for models in life. Though none of this is new, the careful attention to every possible earlier handling of the same subject and the relentless pursuit of possible suggestions in the biography of a writer are distinct features of his practice. "One cannot go far enough," he asserts, "in the careful and circumspect study of similarities between the life and progress of a poet on the one hand and his works on the other," since "imagination is nothing but the power of memory: its production is essentially reproduction." [27] Beyond the explanation of the individual work and life, there arises in Scherer's mind the hope of establishing laws of literary history, harmonies and recurrencies. He thought he had discovered such a law when he decided that German literature flowered every six hundred years in 600, 1200, and 1800, and that its periods of deepest decline came in exactly 900 and 1500, allowing for a nice symmetrical curve and the cold comfort of a new flowering in 2400.[28] Finally, he envisages an ideal scientific comparative poetics that would start with the mental states of primitive nations and trace the origin of poetic kinds.[29]

Though Scherer's unfinished *Poetik* must be treated with indulgence, it often seems incoherent and gives only elementary answers. Thus the very definition of poetics, "the doctrine of verse and of some uses of prose which are nearly related to those of verse," [30] skirts the crucial problem of the nature of that kinship; and similarly, in dismissing judgment from aesthetics, Scherer does not see that he reintroduces it by the back door when he says, "A poetry of which it can be said that it affected the noblest men of all time is surely more valuable than any other." [31] He discusses the origin of poetry in naturalistic terms—jumping, dancing, singing, laughing, sexual joy—and arrives at the disconcertingly trivial conclusion that "poetry arises from joy and affects the majority of people as pleasurable." [32] The next section on the value of poetry, which starts with amusement, instruction, and other old topics, introduces something new. Poetry is a kind of "merchandise" and has its "exchange value" which is regulated by supply and demand.[33] The poet is concerned with three factors of production: nature, capital, and labor. But the economic terminology merely conceals old problems. We are told, for example, that the poet must look at nature "with the eyes of a poet," without being informed of the nature of his peculiarity. The "capital" on which the poet draws is the literary tradition; "labor" is the process of composition, under which heading we are regaled with information on collaboration among writers, interrupted work, and similar topics.[34] We then move into the sociology of the writer, his provenience, education, the esteem in which he was held, and then into reflections on the public of literature, its differences, and the conditions of pleasing by means of truth and probability. Under "aesthetic helps" toward enjoyment, we hear of the congruence of form and content and of outer and inner form. "Inner form," a term derived from Wilhelm von Humboldt, is emptied of its original Neoplatonic content; in Scherer, it is merely a synonym for "a specific conception of the subject matter" by the poet.[35] Under "themes" we get classifications under such headings as "Botany": Mignon's song "Kennst Du das Land?" is listed under "Botany" apparently because lemons and oranges are mentioned. Finally we arrive at a "doctrine of *motifs*." *Motif* is "an elementary, unitary part of a poetic theme." [36] Scherer rejects the term "idea" because of its Hegelian intellectualist associations and concludes that motifs lead to a survey of human feeling, thinking, and acting. His general doctrine of motifs is a doctrine of ethics. In practice, Scherer classifies motifs by listing human relationships like marriage, unnatural love, friendship, etc. "Patterns of complication" follow—for example, "spatial distance between lovers." Pleasurable, comic, and other effects are classified. The chapter on inner form discusses the difference between objective and subjective choice and treatment of themes, and such distinctions among "objective inner form" as those between naturalism, realism, and idealism. Subjective "inner form" is really "manner" and might be "humorous, satirical, elegiac, or idyllic" according to Schiller's "sentimental" modes. There is a final chapter on external form: kinds, composition, language, and metrics.[37] The whole will strike us as strangely crude and even naive: we see a mind groping in a direction similar to what Dilthey sought about the same time and what Alexander Veselovsky achieved, with incomparably greater learning, in Russia.

Scherer's great achievement as a literary historian, however, belies the low level of theoretical awareness in his *Poetik*. It is precisely the crudity of the *Poetik* and of some of his other theoretical pronouncements that shows the basic conflict in the man and in the time. Scherer tries to acquire the new scientific outlook: he is, no doubt, convinced and even dazzled by the prospect of comparative poetics, laws of history, total deterministic explanation. But, actually, all his roots and all his strength are in the romantic past. Scherer grew out of Germanic philology in the wake of Jakob Grimm: his first book was a monograph on the founder of *Germanistik* (1862). He collaborated with Karl Müllenhof on an edition of German poetry and prose from the 8th to 12th centuries (1864) and produced a large book on the history of the German language (1868).[38] The enormously successful *Geschichte der deutschen Litteratur* (1883) uses the scheme of the flowering and decay of German literature in intervals of 600 years. It attempts, here and there, to trace sources and models: we are told that Orestes is Goethe and Frau von Stein, Iphigenie; that Schiller's Wallenstein is modeled on Goethe and on Karl August, the Duke of Weimar, and that the life course of Faust parallels Goethe's own.[39] But by far the greatest bulk of the text is simply informative description and characterization, a skillful narrative account of the whole course of German literature. The ethos is nationalistic, Prussian, and Protestant (though Scherer was born in an Austrian village). In the early dedication to Müllenhof preceding *Zur Geschichte der deutschen Sprache* (1868), Scherer spoke, in romantic terms, of poetry and science collaborating in a "firm national plan" and of *Germanistik* as a science that aims at defining a "system of national ethics," "a doctrine of national values and duties." [40] The *History* is such an inventory of national values, which are to serve as both artistic and moral models. The congruence of taste and moral approval explains the exaltation of *Hermann und Dorothea* as "the summit of all our modern art." "The Homeric tone is forever linked with the best content of our domestic life," [41] its solidity, its resistance against the foreigner and the Revolution, its reliance on the pristine verities of love and loyalty. Similarly, *Iphigenie* is exalted for its humanity and the healing power of womanhood as well as for its classicism, which to Scherer seems the "drama of Racine raised to a higher level." [42] On the other hand, Scherer disapproves of Grillparzer (on whom he had earlier written a long study [43]) because he preaches resignation, the simple heart and mind. St. Joan, if Grillparzer had treated the subject, would have perished because it is unfeminine to take command of an army. Bancban in *Der treue Diener seines Herrn* is an Austrian bureaucrat of the old school, full of petty scruples, a symbol of servility.[44] This activist nationalism permeates the book, which concludes with an interpretation of the end of the second part of *Faust* as an appeal to social action. The section on modern literature begins with praise of Frederick the Great and ends with Baron von Stein, the organizer of the victory over Napoleon; but the last words voice misgivings that now the nation has gone too far to the extreme of materialism and that it is time to remember the spiritual conquests of the past.[45]

Compared to Hettner and even Gervinus (not to speak of the Schlegels) the decline of critical ability and ambition in Scherer is striking. Many works are described without explicit judgment at all: neither *Egmont* nor the dramas of Schiller give occasion to any analytical criticism. But judgment is not completely absent. The criteria of German classicism are implied or sometimes openly applied in the distinction between naturalism, typical realism, and idealism exemplified in the three stages of Goethe's evolution.[46] Realistic standards are sometimes enforced somewhat inappropriately. Thus Klopstock, we are told, should have studied travel books of Palestine before writing his *Messias*.[47] Heinrich von Kleist is praised for the realism of his characteristic art, his "colossal figures," and even his "objectivity." [48] In discussing *Faust,* Scherer tried to construct an early prose version (a theory refuted later by the discovery of the *Urfaust*) [49] and tortuously defended the conventionality of some of Gretchen's songs. He asks whether "a naive girl can give such a well-ordered survey of the state of her mind" in the monologue at the spinning wheel and feels it necessary, in order to justify "idealized fiction," to tell us that "Gretchen cannot compose verse." [50] While here the assumptions seem crudely naturalistic, in other contexts Scherer can praise *Die Braut von Messina* as "the highest work of pure art" composed by Schiller and single out fairy-tale art such as Raimund's or Chamisso's for special admiration.[51] These are the uncertainties of an ill-defined mixture of classical, realist, and academic taste that allowed him, for example, to couple Eichendorff with the insignificant Wilhelm Müller, to disparage Hölderlin as nebulous and gloomy, and to admire both Geibel and Freytag.[52]

Still, it seems unjust to ascribe to Scherer or the "school of Scherer" (hardly more than a name for quite different scholars) all the sins of dull factualism, parallel hunting, biographical gossip-mongering of German literary scholarship. Neither Scherer, nor his prominent pupils were mere dry-as-dusts. Erich Schmidt (1853–1913), Scherer's successor at the University of Berlin, gave in his inaugural lecture on "Wege und Ziele der deutschen Literatur-geschichte" (1880) a romantic definition of literary history as "the developmental history of the intellectual life of a nation with comparative views of other national literatures," but then, in the new scientific spirit, spoke of "inheritance" and "adaptation" and made a long list of questions on every possible problem from literary sources to aesthetics and inductive poetics.[53] His chief work, a two-volume book on *Lessing* (1884, 1892), is a monumental piece of research written in a precious, allusive style: it continues the tradition established by Haym, though with more emphasis on sources and biographical detail. Another pupil, Richard Moritz Meyer (1860–1916), wrote an ambitious *Die deutsche Litteratur des neunzehnten Jahrhunderts* (1900), conceived as a continuation of Scherer's *History*. Meyer has a gift of witty and often malicious characterization and frequently shows real critical acumen. But the book is vitiated by a mechanical organization by decades, by arbitrary groupings, and by indiscriminate crowding of names. Meyer likes to characterize writers by their physique, the style of their beards, the manner of their walk, and to bring together the most ill-assorted authors under some newly invented label.[54] While Schmidt is elegant and official, Meyer is clever, affected, and often absurd.

The reaction in the 20th century against the factualism, source and parallel hunting, biographical obsession, literary insensibility, and philosophical emptiness of academic scholarship found in Scherer and his school a symbol for a phenomenon that actually extended far beyond the few scholars directly associated with the man, and which had its analogues all over the Western world, including the universities of the United States.

One vehicle of criticism seems a peculiarly German creation of this time: the literary biography in the sense of an evolutionary study of an author's personality and his work. There are no strict parallels in other countries: John Morley's books on *Voltaire* (1872), *Rousseau* (1873), and *Diderot* (1878) would come nearest. But the Germans were first, possibly because they had unrivaled models in Goethe's *Dichtung und Wahrheit* and the whole tradition of the educational novel. Rudolf Haym (1821–1901), an exact contemporary of Hettner, is the first master of literary biography. While Hettner comes from art history and dramaturgy, Haym was involved with politics and philosophy. He is thus less central to our literary concern and belongs rather to intellectual history. But he did write of great literary figures, though his attention is mainly focused on ideas. His dream was to write "a history of the evolution of the German mind in a realistic spirit," [1] realistic meaning here historical, nondeductive, non-Hegelian. His first life, *Wilhelm von Humboldt, Lebensbild und Charakteristik* (1856), defines "characterization" as "essentially historical. An individuality presents itself by developing in front of our eyes. It develops primarily from the core of its own being; but it develops simultaneously with the events of its external life, with the formative influences of the century, in connection with the general historical events and conditions." [2] Humboldt, described and analyzed for the first time as an aesthetician and linguist, emerges mainly as a moral and political model. In a time of reaction an ideal, free, liberal statesman is held up for imitation.

Haym's second book *Hegel und seine Zeit* (1857), signalized the break with the idealistic past most sharply by its ruthless historical criticism of Hegel's philosophy. As Haym later formulated his aim: "What if everywhere the realities were uncovered of which the abstract world of the great thinkers was only a reflection in thoughts? What if one would everywhere destroy the halo of the eternally valid and exchanged it for the knowledge of the temporal-real which lies behind it? What if it were said boldly that Plato got his 'ideas' from the sublime edifices which adorn the Acropolis and that the Kantian categorical imperative is nothing but the generalization of the discipline dominating the state and army of the great Frederick?" [3] The reductionist method which we today associate with Marxism is applied to Hegel. He was a perfect expression of his time; his philosophy is the *summa* of the European *Restauration*.

The *Humboldt* and the *Hegel* are on the fringes of literature. *Die romantische Schule* (1870) is straight literary history built on a series of interlacing biographies of the Schlegels, Tieck, and Novalis, here for the first time studied closely from the documents both as men and thinkers, artists, and critics. In this very same year Wilhelm Dilthey published the first volume (there never was to be a second) of his *Leben Schleiermachers* (1870), which includes a long discussion of the romantic movement overlapping with Haym's. Nothing could be more instructive than to compare the two. Haym himself reviewed the rival book, most generously endorsing its historical, pragmatic, and genetic method as also being his own. But he objects that Dilthey pursues his own ethical and epistemological ideas under the guise of biographical-historical presentation: "the thinker pushes aside the judicious narrator and reporter." [4] Haym had become such a judicious narrator and reporter.

The two-volume *Herder: nach seinem Leben und seinen Werken dargestellt* (1880–85) is a model of quiet scholarship. Haym traces Herder's development, psychologically and intellectually, with incomparable mastery. But there is always a point where even Haym's sympathy fails. He cannot go along with mystical speculations, and he is too overawed by the authority of Kant to see the value of Herder's anti-Kantian arguments. But he does not try to romanticize Herder as many have tried since, and he always keeps a certain distance from the man, as he did from the romantics. Haym remained, as he himself recognized, a rationalist, a Protestant, a Prussian, and, in poetics, an adherent of Goethe and Schiller. The new psychological poetics of Scherer and Dilthey seem to him trivial and questionable. [5] Haym shows that German historicism at that time had its roots still in the idealist classical tradition: his attacks

on Hegel (and on Schelling, the romantic philosophy, Schopenhauer, and Eduard von Hartmann) [6] should not obscure the fact
that Haym (like Hettner) did not become a positivist and relativist
but rather returned to the "historical school," to Goethe, to Kant,
and to Herder as his masters and rejected speculative philosophy
and romantic reaction from the point of view of the German
Enlightenment.

Vischer's voluminous *Aesthetik* marked the end of a period of
speculative poetics. A general reaction against the whole method
set in, induced or paralleled by the change of the philosophical
atmosphere: the turn to positivism or related forms of empiricism.
The poetic theory of the later 19th century was much more modest
in its aspirations. Three authors stand out: Otto Ludwig, Gustav
Freytag, and Friedrich Spielhagen. They all write only about the
problems of single genres, the drama and the novel, and they think
as craftsmen, as practitioners who want to formulate the principles
and even tricks of their trade. Only later in the century two great
scholars attempted to put poetics on an entirely new basis. Wilhelm
Dilthey and Wilhelm Scherer drew on psychology, anthropology,
and sociology to restate the age-old problems in the terms of modern
social science.

Otto Ludwig (1813–65), a dramatist of great reputation in his
time, devoted himself during the last fifteen years of his life to a
study of Shakespeare from which he expected immediate profit for
his own dramatic practice. Discovering the secret of Shakespeare's
form and technique seemed to him the surest means to success as a
dramatist. But ill health and possibly also the overanxious regard
for his theoretical principles foiled Ludwig's ambition. He left a
mass of dramatic fragments and plans and several notebooks filled
with little essays and aphorisms about dramatic theory, Shakespeare,
Schiller, Hebbel, and a few other playwrights. The notebooks were
first published in chronological order as *Shakespearestudien* in
1874, and again, in 1891, rearranged according to themes and
supplemented by *Romanstudien*. These studies (some of them
dating back to the 1850's) can hardly be considered a book. They
repeat themselves, overlap, contradict each other, meander from
one theme to another, but still have so much distinction that they
have been praised as "one of the highest critical achievements of

world literature." [1] A more sober view will recognize the peculiar appeal of these notes. Some of it is personal. Otto Ludwig describes the process of composition in detail: it begins with a mood, usually a musical mood, to which a color—"a deep mild gold yellow or a glowing scarlet"—is added; and then figures in some attitude of making some gesture. "The fable invented itself and its invention was nothing but the rise and completion of a figure and a situation." This "spectrum of colors and forms" [2] has attracted much reverent attention but to my mind belongs to the innumerable accounts of inspiration such as those of Valéry or A. E. Housman, which establish nothing of communicable value. With Ludwig this description of a semiconscious state is coupled with a self-critical insight into his own inability to keep this initial mood. [3] The destructive power of reflection has rarely been observed with such pathetic resignation.

The result of these reflections, Ludwig's dramatic theory, seems far less original than it is usually claimed to be. It is a development of motifs dominant in older German theory: particularly in Lessing, Vischer, and Gervinus, whose book on Shakespeare Ludwig admired extravagantly. [4] For Ludwig, tragedy is a form of *theodicée*—more particularly a defense of a moral world order. It is not a conflict between man and fate, or man and God, but the result of a purely internal process within the hero: by his passion or the excess of his passion, the hero becomes guilty, suffers, and is punished for his guilt. This "ideal nexus," "the inevitable connection between guilt and passion and between suffering and guilt" is tragic. [5] "The causal nexus, the external event is only a symbol of the necessary inner event," so that "once the poet has got the guilt he has got the whole work: it is implied in it as a tree is in its seed." [6] Thus tragedy is tragedy of character: plot is secondary even though it should follow logically from the character. Tragedy is psychologized, individualized but, of course, the soul of the individual must be typical. Also the "causal nexus" must be "of a typical nature": with it "is given wholeness, unity, completeness, concordance, and necessity, which is poetic truth." [7] Ludwig draws the furthest consequences from this view: every tragedy must be an organism, a "world of which the most secret motives lie open before our eyes," in which "we see nothing which could make us doubt the reasonableness of the world order." [8] In Ludwig's eyes tragedy is only a closely motivated study of guilt and punishment, which implies and demands a moral but not a metaphysical world order. Ludwig calls this "realism" and often "poetic" or "artistic realism," [9] rejecting both abstract idealism and empirical, accidental naturalism. He distrusts metaphysics and speculative aesthetics and constantly emphasizes concreteness, passion, and emotion as opposed to theory and argument. He also consistently sees drama as an enactment on the stage and wants the close collaboration of author, actor, and public.[10] Though Ludwig differs here from his predecessors, Gervinus and Vischer, who are much more concerned with "ideas" and treat drama as closet drama, in practice Ludwig is, after all, still moving in the same circle of objectivity, totality, necessity, and moral judgment which is that of the old poetic justice.

The plays of Shakespeare are supposed to confirm these views. Ludwig studies only a few of the major tragedies but wrenches even these into his Procrustean bed. The assumption that every Shakespearean tragedy contains, "so to speak, its own Last Judgment" [11] leads to the most incredible sophistries. "Guilt and punishment are proportioned in every person of every play. How mild is the punishment of Desdemona, of Cordelia for small guilt; how terrible that of Macbeth!" [12] Ludwig, strangely enough, interprets the strangling of Desdemona as a kind of sacrifice. "The deed is without struggle, without the contortion and all the repulsive accompaniment which would be the case in reality," [13] asserts Ludwig, as if Othello did not say expressly, "Down, strumpet! . . . Nay, an you strive," and as if Desdemona did not protest with justice, "A guiltless death I die." [14]

The formula that "every tragedy of Shakespeare shows how a man contracts a suffering which he could have avoided and then struggles with the suffering until his fall" [15] cannot possibly fit *Hamlet*. Ludwig can say that Hamlet shows "how the excess of reflection and the weakening of the power for action by philosophical meditation can ruin a man with the finest gifts, with all the favor of fortune," [16] as if Hamlet were not faced with murder of his father and the marriage of his mother. Here the romantic, intellectual Hamlet is accepted without question: in another context Ludwig oddly denigrates his character. Hamlet seems to him an intriguing, sullen, vain weakling, ruthless toward women, murderous and treacherous when he kills Polonius and lures Rosenkrantz and Guildenstern to their deaths.[17] There are many good psychological remarks in Ludwig's discussions (e.g. on Coriolanus being forced into situations in greatest contrast with his nature),[18] but, on the whole, Ludwig merely presses to an extreme the identification of morality and reality and makes the poet (Shakespeare and any poet) a painter of moral disease and a meticulous judge of crime. The spectator complacently "sees situation and guilt; he can cast the account himself and calculate it from number to number, from position to position." [19] Nothing seems to me more alien to Shakespeare's mind and time.

Ludwig also tries to prove his view negatively by sharply criticizing any drama that does not conform to his image of Shakespeare. Fate, chance, circumstance, forces external to the hero, are condemned as untragic. Schiller in particular is Ludwig's target, because in Schiller there is a divorce between character and fate, and his characters are puppets of historical forces, subject to cruel chance. Ludwig severely criticizes shifting motivations and ambiguous characterization in *Die Räuber* and *Wallenstein* [20] and comments satirically on Schiller's diction: it reminds him of "the fine cloaks they used to put on horses in medieval festivities: one does not see a leg, hardly anything of the neck, just enough to guess what kind of creature is hidden under it." [21] Elsewhere Shakespeare is compared to a gnarled oak, and Schiller to a Christmas tree on which the "sentences" hang loosely like toy ornaments.[22] Similarly, Hebbel is condemned for abstract, contrived art: one sees the purpose everywhere. Drama should render the eternal passions of man: in Hebbel we find rather the citizen of a specific time.[23]

The slighter reflections on the novel parallel the dramatic studies. Again the emphasis is on psychological motivation, poetical realism, and logical composition. Ludwig distinguishes three forms of storytelling. The story proper assumes that the teller himself experienced the subject, at least in part, or received the story from another person. He must take care not to tell things he cannot have experienced or he must explain his knowledge of such matters. The second form is "scenic" telling, in dialogue, where the teller builds his own imaginary theater. He is freer than the teller in the first method since he need not bother overmuch about credibility. But the most common manner is the third, a combination of the two, mixing action and event, the subjective and the objective.[24] Among English authors Dickens, Scott, and George Eliot furnish material for reflections, which are, however, rarely focused on this question of technique that Ludwig must have been one of the first to formulate.

Ludwig disparages Gustav Freytag's (1816–95) *Technik des Dramas* (1863) as superficial,[25] but actually Freytag's conception is not so very different from Ludwig's. They are both derivative from classical German aesthetics and they both repudiate its metaphysics. The moral world order, guilt and punishment are Ludwig's preoccupation. Freytag brushes aside the whole question of the tragic with this outrageously complacent advice: be an "upright man who approaches his subject with a gay heart" and the question of guilt and purgation will take care of itself.[26] But then he expounds the difference between the Greek tragedy of fate and modern psychological tragedy very much as Ludwig discussed it, except that Ludwig would have been incapable of the Philistine optimism of Freytag. "The modern poet," says Freytag, "must give the spectator the proud joy, that the world into which he introduces him corresponds to the ideal demands that the heart and judgment of the hearers raise toward the events of reality." "The unity of the divine and the rational"[27] is assumed without Hegel's very different context. Catharsis—for which Freytag accepts the medical interpretation newly propounded by Jakob Bernays[28]—is dismissed as "pathological": it was necessary for the Greeks but we moderns luckily come away from tragedy elated, in "joyful activity."[29]

Still, the shallowness of these conceptions should not obscure the real merits of Freytag's book. It is mainly a modernization of the *Poetics,* a restatement of the demands for unity, probability, magnitude, movement, and gradation in a play. Freytag describes the structure of drama, its rising and falling curve of tension, in five steps corresponding to the traditional five acts: introduction, gradation, point of culmination, reversal, and catastrophe. The application of such terms as "the exciting moment," "the tragic moment," "the moment of last tension"[30] to different plays of Sophocles, Shakespeare, and Schiller is often ingenious and concrete. But much of the book is trivial practical advice of the order of saying: "allow for cuts, talk to actors, keep your play under 2,000 lines."[31] Freytag never doubted that he had analyzed *the* drama though he had merely restated some principles of the Aristotelian tradition modified by German classicism.

Much more original and surprisingly new for their time were

the reflections on his art of the popular novelist Friedrich Spielhagen (1829–1911). As early as 1863 Spielhagen formulated the
principle of objectivity in the novel [32] as radically as Henry James
did much later. Spielhagen transfers the epic theory of Wilhelm von
Humboldt to the novel. Without objectivity "a work of art ceases
to be a work of art." An objective work of art has no regard for the
public or for the self of the artist: the artist creates a world, a
microcosm, an objectified idea. In a novel, no reference or address to
the reader can be allowed. "Each character presented must explain
himself completely by what he does and says." [33] Spielhagen suggests
that we should experiment with crossing out all the reflections and
discussions of an author, all his explanations of the fable and the
characters, and will then arrive at the distressing conclusion that
there is "no congruence of idea and form" in most novels.[34]
Modern novelists violate this principle: they analyze a historical
situation as if they were writing a doctoral dissertation or insert
moral reflections as if they were composing a sermon. If the author
feels compelled to speak his mind, he should invent a special character involved in the plot. Any kind of interference by the author is
proof that the presentation is incomplete and hence not objective.
A novelist must have contact with his readers only through his
characters. Authors such as Thackeray should write historical
monographs, moral treatises, and articles for humor magazines.[35]
All the later writings of Spielhagen, collected in *Beiträge zur
Theorie und Technik des Romans* (1883), elaborate this original
insight. For example, an article on "Der Ich-roman" (1882) tries
strenuously to vindicate a form which by its very freedom endangers
objectivity. All fiction is a struggle for acceptance by the reader, for
the illusion which, Spielhagen is convinced, can be achieved only
by the complete absence of the author. He does not see (as Henry
James later refused to see) that, for instance, even the most
capricious digressions of Sterne do not damage the objective fictive
existence of Uncle Toby or Walter Shandy. Thackeray creates the
voice and mind of the narrator with whom we can identify ourselves as much or as little as with the "I" of a storyteller speaking
of his own experiences. The act of telling is "epic" in the proper
sense: Spielhagen, Flaubert, and Henry James push the novel
toward the drama.

If we compare the essayists of the time with the massive achieve-ments of a Hettner and Haym or Scherer and Dilthey, they will appear of lighter weight, which is not compensated by the brilliance and taste of a Sainte-Beuve or Arnold. Among them Karl Hille-brand (1829–84) stands out as an attractive figure, unusual in his time and place. The son of a literary historian, Joseph Hillebrand in Giessen, the young Karl took part in the abortive uprising of 1848 and escaped to Paris. There he was Heine's secretary for a time and succeeded in getting a foothold in the French school system. He graduated from the Sorbonne in 1860, won a prize of the Academy of Bordeaux, and became Professor at Douai. He started writing in French: a monograph on the Florentine historian Dino Compagni (1862) was his first book. He translated Otfried Müller's *History of Greek Literature* into French and provided it with a long introduction (1865) on the German historical school.[1] A later long essay on Herder, published in English in the *North American Review* (1872–73), shows his grasp of the origins of the movement.[2] Hillebrand had begun to place articles in the *Revue des Deux Mondes* when the Franco-German war drove him from France. He did not return to Germany but settled in Florence, where he became active as a German essayist: at first with a book on *Frankreich und die Franzosen* (1872) and a similar book on England (1873), then with an anonymous pamphlet against bad taste in the arts, *Briefe eines aesthetischen Ketzers* (1873), and finally with wide-ranging literary and historical articles collected in the seven volumes of *Zeiten, Völker und Menschen* (1874–85). Hillebrand made several trips to England, where he delivered a series of lectures on *German Thought from the Seven Years' War to Goethe's Death* (1879, pub-lished 1880). He edited four volumes of a periodical *Italia* (1874–77) to give Germans information about the newly united country, and late in his life returned to his original love and ambition, France and French history. His *Geschichte Frankreichs von der Thronbesteigung Louis Phillips bis zum Falle Napoleons III* (2 vols., 1877, 1898) was left unfinished.

This biographical and bibliographical account suggests that Hillebrand stood at the crossroads of four nations and at the borderlines of several disciplines: history, literature, politics, and philosophy. His center of interest is not literature in a strict sense;

he is preoccupied with the problem of the differences between the chief European nations. He is a reporter, an analyst and historian of his own age, but also a book reviewer and commentator and essayist on literary figures. He has been compared to Sainte-Beuve but lacks Sainte-Beuve's range, learning, and sensibility, though he shares the interest in persons and the ambition, rare in Germany, of writing easily and fluently, with a sense of form and style. Hillebrand constantly defends "dilettantism," protests against the idolatry of specialized scholarship,—appealing to Sainte-Beuve and Goethe—and praises the individuality and personality that alone survive in literature.[3] He thus welcomed the early writings of Nietzsche, particularly the "Meditation on the use and abuse of history," and wrote that Germans are "unfrocked schoolmasters who get angry at the schoolroom." [4] He deplored the pernicious habit of reading only books about books, and the whole bookish derivative modern civilization. He detested all rationalism, radicalism, utilitarianism: anything that impoverishes the wholeness of man.[5] He was conservative in politics and literature, though he preserved an open mind toward the variety of the world. His outlook is historical without succumbing to relativism. He can keep things sharply separate: he praises Carducci in spite of his Jacobinism; he reviews Settembrini's revolutionary *Ricordanze* with touching enthusiasm.[6] He loves Schopenhauer and Carlyle, Stendhal and Mérimée, but also Goethe and Fielding. His tolerance is part of his cosmopolitanism. The new feverish nationalism, French and German, is distasteful to him. German culture has, for him, its roots in France—in Voltaire, Diderot, and Rousseau—and it achieved with Goethe and Schiller the universal, the generally human and humane which is his own ideal. Hillebrand attacks a doctrinaire nationalist such as Gervinus with some acrimony: Gervinus lacks joy and justice, noble tolerance and humanity; Gervinus describes German literature as if it had evolved by spontaneous generation; he sees only collective forces and slights great men.[7] Sainte-Beuve is the opposite: tolerant, subtle, flexible, sensitive, completely independent. In a fine essay Hillebrand makes, however, several reservations: Sainte-Beuve preserved something of the *carabin,* the student of medicine, a hatred of pretense but also some cynicism, some malice against everything that is noble.[8]

Hillebrand excels in literary portraiture, be it of Petrarch,

Rabelais, Tasso, or Herder. His judgments of modern literature are limited in range and information and often quite mistaken. He is convinced that France in the seventies is decadent and sterile. Surprisingly, he thinks that Mérimée produced "perhaps the most enduring literary works of the century." [9] He considers Flaubert's *Tentation de Saint Antoine* a "deplorable aberration," a delirium tremens, and concludes after a laborious synopsis that its highest wisdom is complete skepticism and eclecticism: *credo quia absurdum*.[10] Even *Madame Bovary* is ranked below Balzac's novels and regarded as an analysis clothed in the form of a novel rather than a proper novel.[11] Hillebrand admires the French critics and historians from whom he had learned his art; but he dislikes French contemporary poetry and drama and detests Zola. The account of English literature is even more fragmentary. In the lectures on *German Thought* he confesses his lack of sympathy for utilitarianism and positivism of all sorts. There is an admiring section on Dickens and Bulwer in the book on England; there are essays on Defoe, Fielding, and Sterne which say little out of the common.[12]

Thus Hillebrand appeals today as a good European, as a cultivated literary portraitist, as an intelligent reporter on the cultural scene, but it seems impossible to resurrect him as an important literary critic.

In retrospect, the years between 1850 and the early 1880's in Germany appear dominated by a view that has been labeled "poetic realism," a term devised by Ludwig for Shakespeare. But actually one cannot speak of a clearly defined realism in Germany in these years. Rather, classicist aesthetics survived in different versions. The poets such as Geibel were academic and derivative. The novelists shared the trend toward realism in the sense of a truthful depiction of reality without giving up the idealizing demands inherited from classicism. Only the importation of Zola and his doctrines and particularly the triumph of Ibsen and later of Hauptmann on the stage brought about a real change. The first performance of *Vor Sonnenaufgang* (1889) may be considered the decisive date for German naturalism.

Hauptmann's play was welcomed as "the fulfillment of Ibsen" by the theatrical critic of the *Vossische Zeitung*, the fine novelist Theodor Fontane (1819–98). He defends the play vigorously against the charge of vulgarity. "It is foolish always to suspect lack of art in naturalistic crudities. On the contrary, properly used, they are proof of highest art."[1] Thus, at the age of 70, Fontane became the champion of the new generation. But his enthusiasm is somewhat deceptive. He had begun his long career as a critic, with a praise of realism. The article "Unsere lyrische und epische Poesie seit 1848" (1853) proclaims realism characteristic of the time. "Realism in art is as old as art itself; even more so: it is art." But clearly, the term here means little more than "the reflection of all real life, all true forces and interests in the medium of art" exclusive only of "the lie, the forced, the foggy and the dead." Fontane affirms his dislike for Teutonic and classical mythology in modern poetry but considers Goethe and Schiller, in their early stages, as "representatives of realism" and praises highly such authors as Freiligrath, Theodor Storm, and Paul Heyse,[2] none of whom seems a realist in an international perspective. Throughout the long critical career of Fontane, the position taken in his youth was hardly modified. He wants and recommends the social novel whose task is "to depict a life, a society, a circle of men which is an undistorted reflection of the kind of life which we lead." It will differ from reality by its "intensity, clarity, comprehensiveness, and finish, and thus by an intensity of feeling which is the transfiguring task of art."[3] Transfiguration is the key word drawn from classical aesthetics which recurs in Fontane's criticism: the ugly can and must be transformed in art. There is no justification for pessimism in the sunny realm of art.[4] Even the demand for a picture of our time admits exceptions. A historical novel is entirely possible if it preserves a continuity with our time, if it is not an antiquarian reconstruction such as Freytag's novel *Die Ahnen,* which is located in dim Teutonic antiquity.[5] Fontane dislikes, however, subjective romanticism. Somewhat testily, he complains that Gottfried Keller "delivers mercilessly the whole of God's world to his Keller-tone," and that he is, at bottom, a fairy-tale teller like Arnim.[6] But he prefers the old romanticism of the Scottish and English ballads, Bürger's *Lenore, Der Erlkönig,* and Walter Scott to anything in Zola, Turgenev, Tolstoy, or Ibsen.[7]

At first, Fontane welcomed the new naturalism: "reportage," documentation, seems to him an enormous step forward in literature, though it is only a first step.[8] The men-characters in *Wilhelm*

Meister strike him as mere ghosts. He would prefer figures where he can "count the buttons on their jacket and the veins on their hands." [9] He praises much in Ibsen and Hauptmann, and even defends the dreary *Familie Selicke* of Holz and Schlaf (1890). But Fontane goes with the naturalists only part of the way. He complains of the spitting and belching in Hauptmann's *Florian Geyer* and, while he recognizes the power of Zola, he is repelled by his vulgarity and pessimism. Even Turgenev disappoints him because he lacks, in *Virgin Soil* and "Mumu," anything reconciling, anything hopeful.[10] Fontane recommends Dickens as an antidote to the Norwegian novelist Kielland, a gloomy fellow who "does not move you, uplift you, cheer you, does not stimulate you to cheerful competition and does not encourage you to see something equally good and beautiful in life." [11] Fontane's temperament is determinedly optimistic, his mind conciliatory, responding to common sense and *juste milieu*. At the most, he builds a fragile bridge to naturalism.

The German naturalist movement is usually supposed to be initiated by *Kritische Waffengänge* (1882), a series of pamphlets by the brothers Heinrich and Julius Hart (1855–1906, 1859–1930). It seems an exceedingly innocuous manifesto today. The brothers dislike prudery and the dominance of women, complain that Goethe and Schiller wrote only for a highly educated public, and propose a popular national art, featuring realism and objectivity in the novel. Naively enough, they expect much from the patronage of Bismarck, and repeat all the commonplaces about the poet as prophet.[12] Karl Bleibtreu (1859–1928) in *Revolution der Literatur* (1886) is much more brash. Zola, he proclaims, "is the only world poet since Lord Byron." [13] Wilhelm Bölsche (1861–1939), a zoologist, in *Die naturwissenschaftlichen Grundlagen der Poesie* (1887) demands a new poetry based on natural science, observation, and psychology. Determinism will, he hopes, encourage poetry. Love should be seen as a biological fact and studied as something normal and natural. The main message of realism is to show that poetry and science are not enemies.[14] Arno Holz (1863–1929) in *Die Kunst: ihr Wesen und ihre Gesetze* (1891) appeals to Comte, Mill, Taine, Buckle, and Spencer. The names of Marx and Engels appear fleetingly, and he attacks Zola elaborately, even in French.[15] After much shouting against Zola's "corner of nature seen through a temperament," he comes up with the "law" that "art has the tendency to become nature again. It will become so according to the conditions of reproduction prevailing and their handling by the artist." [16] This revelation came to him while observing a small boy trying to draw a soldier. The boy was limited by the "conditions of reproduction," the pencil and paper, and by his "handling," his skill, but still he wanted to achieve "nature." Holz, in a diffuse defense of his theory, acknowledged that art actually will never become nature, but prided himself, nevertheless, on having made all former aesthetics obsolete by his discovery.[17] He himself wrote a play, with his friend, Johannes Schlaf, *Die Familie Selicke* (1890), which tries to reproduce speech almost in a phonographic manner, and in *Die Revolution der Lyrik* (1899), which accompanied volumes of his verse, he announced that rhyme was out-of-date, that poetic diction must be colloquial, and that his precursor was Whitman.[18]

The theoretical level of these discussions seems deplorably low. It is a tedious variation of the issues debated elsewhere. The enemies of naturalism complain of photography and pornography, the defenders exalt naturalism as true, scientific, modern, etc. French theories jostle German classical aesthetics, and often a primitive naturalism emerges which reminds one of the *Sturm und Drang*. The theatrical critics who brought about the victory of Ibsen and Hauptmann on the Berlin stage are much subtler observers and analysts. Otto Brahm (1851–1912), the best in a brilliant group, was originally a literary historian, a disciple of Wilhelm Scherer, and wrote first a long piece on Gottfried Keller (1882) in the manner of his teacher. He divides Keller's work into periods, compares the two versions of the *Grüne Heinrich,* and traces sources and models in real life much to the annoyance of the still living author.[19] Brahm then wrote the first scholarly biography of *Heinrich von Kleist* (1884),[20] and finally an extremely detailed life of *Schiller* (2 vols. 1888, 1892) which exalts the early Schiller because "he coincides with the realistic principles of our days." [21] For external reasons Brahm did not get beyond a discussion of *Don Carlos* to the later plays: his sympathy for the classical Schiller was in any case imperfect. Brahm's most important critical role was that of a crusader for Ibsen in many reviews and in an independent essay (1887) which follows Scherer's formula: *Ererbtes, Erlebtes und Erlerntes.*[22] With equal enthusiasm, Brahm took up the cause of

Hauptmann. He formulated the program of the Berlin *Freie Bühne* (1890)—truth, contemporaneity, etc.—and finally took over the stage management, first of that theater and then of the *Deutsche Theater* (1894). Brahm ceased writing criticism in 1892. He had achieved his purpose, the victory of naturalism on the stage, which he saw as a moral institution, as a mirror of the nation, a test of truth.

While the naturalist movement was triumphant on the stage, and Zola and the realistic novel conquered the reading public, critics welcomed and attacked the movement with new weapons and new methods. During these years, for the first time, literature was examined by a psychiatrist and by a Marxist. In his *Entartung* (1892), Max Nordau (1849–1923) anticipates a whole trend of 20th-century criticism: the diagnosis of literature as physical decadence, as neurosis, and even madness. Cesare Lombroso, a psychiatrist in Turin, who had written much earlier the sensational book *Genio e follia* (1864), drew his material from biographies and often from the distant past. Nordau examines the whole literature of the *fin de siècle* with the complacency of the "normal" man who reduces every modern artistic effort, Zola and naturalism, Wagner and Nietzsche, Ibsen and symbolism, to symptoms of egomania and pathological degeneracy. Nordau undoubtedly scores many points; his blunt, sarcastic manner even has a superficial charm; it would be difficult to deny, for example, that he succeeds in exposing improbabilities and scientific ignorance in Ibsen or that, convincingly, he refutes Tolstoy's views on sex.[23] Nietzsche and the symbolists are an easy target for a man of sturdy common sense, logic, and social morals. But the method defeats itself by its sweeping all-inclusiveness, its lack of discrimination between authors, and the humorless insistence with which even such harmless techniques as Rossetti's monotonous refrains are interpreted as symptoms of feeble-minded incoherence.[24] Nordau anticipates the Philistine condemnation of modern art, which in the 20th century was to succeed in enlisting the strong arm of several governments, and the psychographic and psychoanalytical clinical view of art as neurosis. The work of art is reduced to a document for mental ills, and the artist becomes an outcast from human society who should, by right, be confined to an asylum.

The very next year (1893), a book was published that heralded another method of reducing art to a document or symptom. Franz Mehring's *Lessing-Legende* was the first piece of Marxist criticism of any consequence since the pronouncements of the masters. It is an effective attack on the literary historians who made Lessing the mouthpiece and representative of the age of Frederick the Great. Mehring (1846–1916) shows that Lessing hated Frederick and the Prussian monarchy and that it is absurd to ascribe the flowering of German literature in the 18th century to the effects of Prussian ascendancy. Mehring examines political and social conditions of the 18th century in Prussia and Saxony. He gives a sympathetic account of the lonely and struggling Lessing. But the discussion of Lessing's work is perfunctory and shows, in germ, the fatal consequences of economic materialism when applied to imaginative literature or aesthetic ideas. Thus Lessing's *Laokoon* is interpreted as an appeal to the middle classes to abandon descriptive poetry in order to use "stronger and manlier tones." "With the singing about colored Alpine flowers and sacred forest shades the bourgeois humdrum life had been lulled to sleep." [25]

Mehring established himself as the foremost critic of Social Democratic newspapers and indefatigably spread a knowledge of good literature among the working classes. Because Mehring, aged 70 and disgusted with the supine war policy of the Social Democratic party, became one of the founders of the Spartacus League, he is today revered and studied like a Church Father in East Germany. In 1933, however, the eminent Marxist theorist Georg Lukács tried to show how unorthodox a Marxist Mehring was.[26] Mehring, Lukács complained, had even praised Schiller for escaping into the realm of ideals: he had accepted the autonomy of art in a Kantian sense and embraced Darwinian evolutionism without a proper understanding of the workings of dialectics.[27] Recently, Mehring has again been vigorously defended against these charges of "deviation" from the "correct" doctrine.[28] As we have no desire to take sides in the disputes among the Communist schoolmen, it will be sufficient to say that Mehring's criticism ranges from Winckelmann to Hauptmann, with some occasional excursions into other literatures (reviews of Molière, Voltaire, Zola, Dickens, Tolstoy, Ibsen, Gorky) and that it always asks one question: is or is not a work of art favorable to the interests of the working class? Mehring developed the technique of "unmasking," of searching for the class roots of literary movements. Thus "pure art" is only a "reactionary invention directed against the great revolutionary poets of the bourgeoisie who had all been propagandists on behalf of their class." [29] The naturalists, welcomed at first by Mehring, are condemned because "they wanted to remain on the soil of bourgeois society, as if even the most faithful reproduction of the capitalist dirt could open a new period in art!" [30] But Mehring was surprisingly skeptical about the immediate prospects of proletarian literature. *"Inter arma Musae silent,"* he quotes, arguing that just "as the declining bourgeoisie cannot anymore produce great art, so the rising working class cannot yet create it." [31] Mehring's doctrinaire temper is somewhat moderated by historical relativism and by a cultivated, though conventional, taste. Still, Mehring must be one of the first not only to claim Lessing and Schiller for his cause, but to announce hopefully that "the day on which the German people will free itself economically and politically will be a day of rejoicing for Goethe when art will become the common property of the whole nation." [32] Mehring sees the problem of popular art in a mass society and tries to solve it, abstractly, by the hope for a new art in a Utopia, which would, however, preserve the heritage of the past. He genuinely tried to make the German classics acceptable to the proletariat in spite of their different social outlook. He could not foresee the dismal results of Socialist Realism nor the distortions to which the classics would be subjected in its name. His own much more gentle and timid attempts ominously presage the things to come.

14 : WILHELM DILTHEY

WILHELM DILTHEY (1833–1911) was a philosopher who formulated a *Lebensphilosophie* which anticipates some of the insights of Bergson and Existentialism; he was a psychologist who stimulated Gestalt psychology and its theories of types and structures; he was a theorist of historical thought who all his life worked on a comprehensive Critique of Historical Reason trying to establish the independence in methodology of the historical from the natural sciences; he was an extremely prolific and learned historian of ideas and feelings: of philosophy and theology, of religious sentiment, of the concept of man, of theories of education, even of Prussian law. Among his many activities his interest in literature—at least in imaginative literature as we may more strictly define it—was comparatively minor. Still, Dilthey wrote the most important German treatise on poetics in the later half of the 19th century (*Die Einbildungskraft des Dichters, Bausteine für eine Poetik*, 1887),[1] and he wrote extensively on the German poets of the great age. A collection of essays on Lessing, Goethe, Novalis, and Hölderlin, which in earlier versions had appeared in periodicals between 1865 and 1877, published in 1905 under the title *Das Erlebnis und die Dichtung*, first carried his name beyond academic precincts. To these should be added two posthumous collections, *Von deutscher Dichtung und Musik* (1933), which contains a survey of German medieval literature (1907–08), along with essays on Klopstock (1907–08), Schiller (begun 1894, 1904–06), and Jean Paul (1906) ; and *Die grosse Phantasiedichtung* (1954), which prints fragments of a work on Renaissance literature, particularly about Shakespeare (1895), and reprints older essays—for example, a long piece on Dickens (1877). In addition, the early very detailed *Leben Schleiermachers* (1870) discusses the German romantic movement and particularly Friedrich Schlegel. Throughout the ten large volumes of *Gesammelte Schriften* (which do not include the *Schleiermacher* or the three volumes of essays mentioned) there are scattered passages, paragraphs and whole chapters which are of interest to the student of literature.[2] Many of Dilthey's most original and profound philosophical treatises, such as *Beiträge zum Studium der Individualität* (1895–96) and *Das Wesen der Philosophie* (1907) as well as many late fragments and papers about historical consciousness and the types of world views,[3] contain reflections on the relations of literature to philosophy and history, and develop a theory of interpretation which is directly relevant to a study of literature. From Dilthey's writings one can abstract an aesthetics and a poetics and an almost continuous history of German literature from its beginnings to the death of Goethe. There are many less systematic comments on Western literature: particularly on Shakespeare and Dickens, but also on Marlowe, Cervantes, Molière, Voltaire, Rousseau, Balzac, George Sand, and even Alfieri.

Dilthey was a polyhistor of enormous erudition, a philosopher of considerable analytical power and original insight, had a subtle intellect of wide range, but was hardly—as Hofmannsthal's obituary [4] makes him out to be—a Faust or a Lynceus, a man mysterious and passionately dark and angry. His style is often clumsy; his exposition long-winded; his thought groping and obscure—not dark, but sometimes foggy and even fuzzy. For a historian of criticism, the limitations of Dilthey's contribution are apparent at first sight. Dilthey was not a practical critic who judged his contemporaries: he was rather, on the one hand, a historian of literature in a general context of the history of thought, and, on the other, the propounder of a psychological poetics focused on the poet's creative process, the experience behind his work, and the reader's response.

These two sides of Dilthey's interest in literature have strangely little contact with each other. Dilthey was a historian of thought in literature all his life: he always preserved an intense interest in literary history and biography, but only for about a decade (1877–87) was he deeply engaged in a study of poetics, though late in his life he wanted to return to these problems and in 1907–08 drafted some revisions of his earlier views. Two early essays, those on Dickens and Goethe (1877), outline the theory of poetry systematically expounded in the *Bausteine* of 1887. But when Dilthey included the Goethe essay in *Das Erlebnis und die Dichtung* (1905), the psychological terminology of the essay disturbed the unity of the volume, which is not otherwise about poetic theory at all, but about intellectual biography: the religion of Lessing, the *Realpsychologie* of Novalis, and the concept of nature in Hölderlin. Still, there is something profoundly appropriate in that title, *Das Erlebnis und die Dichtung*.

Erlebnis and *Leben* are the key terms of Dilthey's philosophy and aesthetics. We are told many times that "the foundation of all genuine poetry is in *Erlebnis*." [5] *Erlebnis*, in Dilthey, is by no means restricted to specific events. Anything can become an *Erlebnis* to the poet: "the religious, scientific, philosophical movements of the age" for Goethe; [6] the "abstract world of moral principles" for Lessing; [7] "a mood from the world of ideas independent of individual experiences" for Schiller; [8] even "the dead newspaper report under the heading 'From the world of crime,' the dry story of the [medieval] chronicler, or a grotesque legend." [9] An *Erlebnis* may be evoked by "an individual experience, determined from the outside, or by moods arising from within, independently of the external world, or even by a complex of historical or philosophical ideas." [10] "Mephisto, Gretchen, the *motif* of *Elective Affinities* may have flashed on Goethe's mind in casual encounters which meant almost nothing for the edifice of his own life." [11] An *Erlebnis* need not even be a continuous, unified mental event: the sight of a specific picture seen in a gallery on repeated visits also constitutes an *Erlebnis*.[12] Thus neither the content nor the duration of the experience distinguishes the *Erlebnis* from any other kind of experience, but only its relation to the mind. It must be intensely felt; it must not merely be received passively, but transformed actively; it must engage the whole man. It involves the basic unity of what Dilthey calls misleadingly *life*: the total *psyche* (not *bios*), the mental structure which fuses intellect, will, and feeling into one.

But how, we may ask as literary critics confronted with the texts of poems, can we know that a specific work or a specific passage was produced under intense emotional pressure, with the totality of the *psyche* of the poet engaged? How can we reconstruct mental events long past and how can we be sure that a passage which successfully conveys emotion or a totality of emotion and intellect was created in emotion or in a fusion of intellect and emotion? What correlation is there between good art and intense experience, or even between good art and a fusion of ideas and emotion? Some of our worst poetry is agonizingly felt adolescent love poetry and fervently experienced religious hymnology.

Only once, as far as I know, does Dilthey use *Erlebnis* to substantiate a concrete critical value judgment. Goethe is praised as the model of "realism" in the lyric because he started with the individual *Erlebnis* and stayed close to it, whereas Hölderlin "in dithyrambs such as the 'Archipelagus' lost the measure of what moods and images may be connected in an inner process." In reading Hölderlin, "we cannot anymore experience the extensive whole." [13] The word *nacherleben* here merely states that these poems are lacking in a proper unity—a criticism that could have been made in formalistic terms and needs neither an appeal to the putative processes in the author's mind nor to the reader's supposed bafflement.

Dilthey, late in his life when he wrote notes for a revision of the Poetics (1907–08), saw the failure of his psychologistic conception. He gives up the central feature of *Erlebnis,* personal involvement. He speaks of the "disinterestedness" of the poet. "Disinterested means impersonal. Disinterestedness is not merely a matter of the impression, but also of the experience of the creator. . . . In the detachment of the imaginative process from the occasion lies the detachment from the personal." [14] Dilthey now wants to speak of value, purpose, and meaning and not of feelings and emotions. He recognizes now that the work of literature is not "the inner processes within the poet," but rather a "nexus created by him and detachable from them. . . . Thus the subject with which literary history and poetics have to deal primarily, is totally distinct from psychic events in the poet or his readers." [15] No sharper repudiation of the very basis of Dilthey's own early poetics could be imagined. But unfortunately "the system of poetics from a doctrine of meaning" [16] was never carried out.

Dilthey's early poetics (1887) professes to be empirical, descriptive and not prescriptive.[17] It aims at establishing principles, "unalterable norms," and even laws,[18] and hopes to give a causal explanation of the creative process in psychological terms. Other disciplines such as rhetoric or hermeneutics can make only incidental contributions, as they have not yet progressed to causal explanation.[19] Grammar has established such causal nexuses, but they are of no relevance to poetics. Dilthey sees no use in phonetics and does not admit an analogy between the history of language and that of literature. There is no "genealogical sequence of poetic schools"; "the changes which occur with a type or motif, cannot be arranged in fixed series." [20] Dilthey thus rejects, in advance, the enterprise of Veselovsky and the Russian formalists.

What Dilthey can do is to give a psychological description of the process of imagination. He conceives imagination mainly as an image-making power, as "thinking in images." [21] Dreams and hallucinations are parallel activities: the dream is even called "this hidden poet in us": [22] psychiatry is drawn upon to show the relation between poetry and madness.[23] Genius, however, is "not a pathological phenomenon, but the healthy, the perfect man." [24] Genius is characterized by "the great energy of his psychic system," [25] the power of his memory, the liveliness of his feelings and the freedom of his imagery. Dilthey collects testimonies from the poets to show how these images grew out of moods, often musical moods, vague states of feeling, and how clearly the poets have seen their fictional characters, almost as if they had seen them with bodily eyes.

The whole system of poetics is developed from what Dilthey calls "circles of feeling," of which he distinguishes six. The first—"elementary feelings"—arouses immediate pleasure and pain. The second, "contents of sensations," refers to feelings arising from sensuous qualities—for example, the prevalence of soft sounds in a poem by Goethe. The third, "pleasing relations of sensations," refers to symmetry, rhythm, and meter; the fourth, "chains of representations," to any unifying systems of manifolds—for example, wit or the comic, and external form in general; the fifth, "material drives," includes elementary impulses of human existence; while the sixth and last refers to "general qualities of impulses of the will," to man's aspirations for an ideal.[26] The naming of these six classes accomplishes Dilthey's aim: a translation into psychological terms of age-old distinctions within a work of art. The first four circles refer to what is ordinarily called "form," the last two to "content." The classes seem hardly well defined, and one wonders about the certainty with which Dilthey ranked them according to degrees of intensity of our and the poet's feelings: from the mere pleasure in sound to the highest satisfaction of our striving for the ideal.

Dilthey then tries to establish laws according to which, under the

influence of the life of feelings, "representations transform themselves freely beyond the limits of the real." [27] We are told that
images change in three ways: by the exclusion of some of their parts;
or by expansion or contraction, while the intensity of the sensations
of which they consist increases or decreases; or finally by the admission of new parts and links into their inner core. "Exclusion,"
"heightening," "unfolding" [28] are laws of the transformation which
are not only principles of the workings of the imagination but also
principles of style. But if we examine the examples and drop the
psychological terminology, we arrive again at rather commonplace
classifications. "Exclusion" is the selection from reality made by
the poet, "heightening" is idealization or intensification—for
example, in the hyperbolic descriptions of Dickens and Carlyle—
while the "unfolding" of images seems Dilthey's only way of
accounting for what is romantically called "creative imagination,"
i.e. the power of the poet to animate something external or to represent something internal by an external image.

The whole elaborate scheme obscures the central problem: how
can we pass from mental images or feelings to a work of art which,
in literature, is, after all, a linguistic construct? In Dilthey this
passage is accomplished by the assumption that art is expression,
expression of life, of the whole of experience. "Expression springs
from the soul immediately, without reflection," [29] and "what is
experienced, enters completely into the expression." [30] The experience in a work of art is, Dilthey believes, a particularly true expression. "In human society filled with lies [the work of a great poet] is
always true." [31] In art "we enter a realm in which deception ends." [32]
Dilthey assumes—unconvincingly to my mind—that a gesture, a
facial expression, an action is harder to interpret than a work of art,
which would seem the creation most obliquely related to the private
mind of man, steeped as it is in tradition, technique, and craft.
Expression (and art), for Dilthey, contains more of the psychic system than any introspection can yield. "It taps depths which consciousness does not illuminate." [33] Art, in being expression of
experience, is thus hardly distinct from life. There is no problem
raised by the translation of the psychic life into its medium: language. The feelings, representations, and images of the poet develop
immediately into characters and types, actions and ideas.

The type guarantees universality and necessity and thus a relation to social reality and to knowledge. Characters, passions, plots must fulfill a law of probability: everything that disturbs the causal relation must be eliminated if the typical is to be achieved. "Persons [in fiction] act necessarily when the reader or spectator feels that he himself would act that way." [34] The type is not to be confused with the average: it is rather a norm, a standard of value, the ideal.[35] Types are thus means of expressing the meaning of life, the world view of the poet. The typical contains "a guide to seeing." [36] The typical is often considered part of the process of "symbolization." "Symbolization," however, is a term used by Dilthey not in a modern sense but as an alternative for mere expression by signs. Still, on occasion, he sees that the "central ideality of art lies in this symbolization of the inner state by external images, in this animation of the external reality by a projected inner state." [37] Dilthey would recognize that our dreams are impoverished symbols. These symbols appear fully developed in the great fixed symbols of myth, metaphysics, and poetry.[38] Something like Cassirer's philosophy of symbolic forms seems adumbrated, with the same implication that art is a system of symbols parallel to myth, religion, and philosophy, all conceived as diverse means toward a purely relative knowledge.

Another term inherited from German romantic aesthetics which serves to bridge the gap from psychology to form is "inner form." It is a Neoplatonic concept picked up earlier by Shaftesbury and James Harris, and thence by Wilhelm von Humboldt; but it remains as obscure in Dilthey as in his predecessors. Dilthey, for instance, calls the tendency of Goethe's imagination "to raise reality to the poetic," his "inner form," [39] or speaks of "inner form" when he refers to the transformation of images by emphasis, energy, and expansion.[40] Sometimes "inner form" is simply identified with style,[41] which in turn is called obscurely "an inner drawing of lines." [42] Very rarely Dilthey does make remarks which directly refer to observable stylistic traits, in the young Goethe or in Schiller.[43] For the most part "form," in a wide or narrow sense, has disappeared from Dilthey's theory, which assumes, like Croce's, the identity of author's mind, expression, and reader's response.

In practice, as a critic, Dilthey was almost exclusively interested in content: in the power of the poet to present an ideal of life, an interpretation of reality which makes him almost a philosopher and seer. From his earliest writings, such as *Leben Schleiermachers* (1870), to his last, such as *Das Wesen der Philosophie* (1907), he insists that poetry "expresses a general in the presentation of a singular case" and delineates the "life-ideal of an age." [44] Poetry, like all art, is "an organ of the objective understanding of the world," [45] next to science and religion. "The poet is a seer who sees into the meaning of life." [46] "No scientific mind can exhaust, no progress of science can reach what the artist has to say on the meaning of life." [47] Dilthey knows that art "cannot be dissolved into a thought or ideas," but he argues that "by meditation, especially by generalization and the establishment of connections, it can be put into relation with the whole of human existence and thus understood in its essence, i.e., its significance." [48] The poet thus differs from the philosopher by not aiming at analysis or system; he differs by creating from the totality of his powers [49] rather than from the intellect alone and by expressing his intuition "graphically." [50] The whole problem of the nature of art, its medium and form, is concealed or rather evaporated in a single adverb.

What actually interests Dilthey is not what makes literature "graphic" but how he can extract from literature a world view, a wisdom, an ideal of life which is not, of course, purely intellectual and organized systematically, but still is, in practice, a philosophy read off from characters and situations. Dilthey has paid much attention to the historical connections of works of literature with specific philosophies. He has made valuable studies, for instance, of Goethe's knowledge of Spinoza and Shaftesbury.[51] He sees Shakespeare in relation to Montaigne and Seneca and discusses Molière with the early (lost) translation of Lucretius in mind.[52] Besides establishing such historical relationships, Dilthey links up poetry with the main types of philosophy he has devised. There are three of them: positivism (and all forms of naturalism), objective idealism or pantheism, and dualistic idealism, what Dilthey calls "idealism of freedom." Hobbes, Hegel, and Kant would be characteristic representatives of the three types. All writers must belong to one of them, even though implicitly, unconsciously. "Thus Stendhal and Balzac see life as a web of illusions, passions, beauty and corruption, created by Nature itself without purpose, in a dark urge . . . Goethe sees life as a plastic power which unifies the organic systems, the evolution of man and the orders of society, into a value-charged continuity; Corneille and Schiller see it as a theater of heroic action." [53]

In classifying poetry into these types of world view, Dilthey inevitably implicates literature in the whole problem of relativism that vexed him all his life. Most impressively Dilthey stated it in a fictional "dream." He had once fallen asleep in a room with a reproduction of Raphael's "School of Athens" on the wall, and in a dream the Greek sages there depicted came to life, disputed and finally ranged themselves into Dilthey's three groups. Dilthey concludes that "every view of the world is historically conditioned, and hence limited and relative. A terrible anarchy of thought seems to follow." But Dilthey hopes to overcome such consequences precisely by historical consciousness: there is a law in these groupings. Each world view expresses one side of the universe. Each is true, though each is one-sided. "We are not allowed to see these sides simultaneously. We can see the pure light of truth only in its diversely reflected ray." [54] The historical consciousness, Dilthey hopes, will set man free from the chains which even philosophy and science cannot break. "The historical consciousness of the finitude of every historical phenomenon, of every human or social state, of the relativity of every sort of belief, is the last step in the liberation of man. . . . Life becomes free from knowledge by concepts; the mind brushes away all cobwebs of dogmatic thought. Every form of beauty and sanctity, every sacrifice, relived and expounded, opens up perspectives which disclose reality. . . . And in contrast with the relativity, the continuity of the creative force makes itself felt as the central historical fact." [55] But it is hard to see what solution is offered by this pantheistic surrender to life and its diversity: especially as it requires a retreat from the intellect and consciousness. Actually this proposal contradicts another remedy frequently proposed by Dilthey: "a philosophy of philosophy" which makes "philosophy itself the subject of philosophy." [56] The mere increase of our consciousness of the historicity of all human endeavor offers no escape from total skepticism and anarchy of values. How can historical consciousness be said "to heal the wounds which it has inflicted"? [57] How can such a homeopathic cure succeed? Actually, in a speech given on his 70th birthday (1903, the year of the "Dream") Dilthey sadly acknowledged defeat and merely asked "where the means are of overcoming the anarchy of convictions which threatens to destroy us." [58] He promises to search for them further, but he did not find them and could not find them on his terms.

Dilthey, like any human being, had to make choices, and as a philosopher could not simply teeter among three equally "true" world views. He has, I think, definitely chosen objective idealism. He tells us that "only from the point of view of pantheism is an interpretation of the world possible which exhausts its meaning." [59] This commitment is confirmed by Dilthey's constant preference for the whole tradition of German idealism, for Goethe, interpreted in close relation to Spinoza and Shakespeare, for Hegel, shorn of his dialectics and logic, and for Schleiermacher without his dogmatic prejudices. Even the thinkers of the German Enlightenment—Leibniz and Lessing—are seen in terms of an irrationalistic, emotional religion. In his judgments of literature Dilthey often postulates an absolute norm. "There is a core, in which the meaning of life, as the poet wants to represent it, is the same in all ages. Hence the great poets have something eternal." [60] Specifically, a mechanistic determinism is considered unpoetic. "All great and genuine poetry shows common traits. It requires both a consciousness of the freedom and responsibility of our actions and their coherence according to cause and effect. The doctrine that we are determined in our actions from the outside will never arouse a stable conviction in a great poet." [61]

Usually, with Dilthey, relativism is not only psychological, according to eternal types, but also historical. Literature is implicated in the historical process, and thus there is no universally valid technique of poetry and "even the most perfect form will be historically relative." [62] Often social explanations of literary changes and situations are suggested. During the Renaissance "decisive differences in the poetry arose from the economic, social, and political life of the individual states." [63] The low level of German 17th-century literature has social reasons: even strong personalities "lacked the free mobility of feeling arising out of life and society." [64] The flowering of German classicism, its intensive search for an ideal of life, for the destiny of man, is linked with the culture of a middle class excluded from political power, driven inwards, forced to look for intellectual distinction and personal cultivation.[65] But

Dilthey knows that social, political, and economic conditions do not contain the full explanation of intellectual phenomena and that causal explanation fails in the end.[66]

Frequently enough Dilthey, like Hegel, sees literature as part of a general development of the human spirit in which each epoch shows a single unified *Zeitgeist*. "It expresses itself in stone, on canvas, in deeds or in words. It objectifies itself in the constitutions and legislation of the nations." Every age has "its circle, in which the men of the age are enclosed." [67] The succession of ages forms the continuity of historical evolution. Evolution is, with the early Dilthey, a slow transformation, as in Leibniz or Herder. Dilthey spoke even of a necessary order of stylistic forms, assuming for instance that a sublime early style must always precede a florid late one.[68] On occasion, he speaks even of progress in literature: in the sense that the increasing complexity of mental life postulates a more complex art.[69] Only later did he come to recognize that "in creative periods there is a heightening which cannot be derived from earlier stages." [70] The idea of historical evolution did not occupy him, as history was to him psychological and biographical by definition. Even shifts of ideas are implicated in psychological processes, in changes of sentiments that cannot crystallize into forms amenable to a study of evolution as attempted in Hegel, Marx, or Brunetière.

But besides the psychology of imagination and the typology of world views, Dilthey is interested in a third aspect of literary and aesthetic theory: in the response of the reader, in the effect of art. Dilthey assumes the identity of creation and taste,[71] or, at most, would admit that aesthetic impression "is a faded copy of the creative process." [72] He does not doubt that the laws of aesthetic effect are the same as those of creation and that he can establish poetics, so to say, from the other end, the reader's experience. The poetic work is then conceived as an orderly series of pleasurable and painful impressions which have a definite structure, and increase in effect as the quantity of the parts of pleasure are increased.[73] This calculus of pleasures and pains assumes the need of an equilibrium, a final reconciliation. "Every work of art which seeks to evoke permanent satisfaction must conclude with a situation of equilibrium or with a pleasurable state, in any case in a reconciling final state, even if this state is only in an idea that lifts us above life." [74] A lyrical poem tends toward such a state of equilibrium. Tragedy and epic fit into the scheme too. "It has often been demonstrated that Shakespeare's tragedy corresponds to this aesthetic principle, and there is the one advantage in the untechnical structure of *Faust* that it answers completely to this scheme of the feeling process. Also epic poetry . . . must be like a symphony in which one disharmony after another is resolved and the whole at last concludes in mighty harmonious cadences." [75] Dilthey here closely anticipates the theories of I. A. Richards [76]—probably because both seem to derive from Fechner on this point. As in Richards, the function of poetry is often seen as "heightening of our feeling for life." [77] The aim of art is "to preserve, strengthen, and awaken vitality": to make us "enjoy the whole world as an experience." It is "life-feeling radiating into the luminosity of images." [78] In a passage which bears the stamp of the Longinian tradition Dilthey describes this effect of art by concrete examples. "The style of a fresco of Michelangelo or of a fugue by Bach arises from the activity of a great soul and the reception of these works of art communicates to the soul of the enjoyer a specific form of activity in which it broadens, rises, and as it were expands." [79]

Tragedy fulfills a human need for excitement and elation. The tragic is a violent and even painful emotion which we still enjoy as uplifting. Aristotle's purgation, as interpreted by Bernays, seems to Dilthey "worthless." [80] Emotions are not purged but strengthened in tragedy: tragedy frees the mind, "lifts it into the free sphere of the universal." [81] But Dilthey will not admit a theory of tragedy which would go beyond these generalities. The main types of tragedy are historically distinctive: Greek, Shakespearean, Spanish, French, German—and one must not force them into a single pattern.

But the increase of vitality through reconciled opposites is to Dilthey, and here he differs from Richards, only *one* function of poetry. Besides elating us, "art widens the narrow circle of our experience," it expands man's horizon in space and time.[82] This is Dilthey's justification of historical and sociological drama and fiction. This widening of experience implies a deepening of insight. Art becomes knowledge, not rational systematic philosophy, but still knowledge about the meaning of life and a guide to this meaning. Dilthy rejects a value theory that would divorce value from the process of evaluation. Value is to him merely an expression

of feeling.[83] The distribution of values in a work of art is a distribution of our feelings toward it.[84] Thus an understanding of values
in literature is ultimately again a knowledge of feelings, as the
whole process of understanding is *Einfühlung*, empathy. Dilthey
developed an elaborate theory of understanding from the hermeneutics of Schleiermacher, accepting its main features unchanged.
Comprehension, understanding is sharply distinguished from causal
explanation. "Understanding is a process of knowing, an inner
process from signs given externally." [85] It is a "rediscovery of the I
in the Thou." [86] It is a process of identification which assumes the
basic unity of humanity. This process is, however, confined to
mental phenomena. Dilthey repeats Vico's famous doctrine, "Only
what mind has created, mind can understand," [87] in order to defend
the superior certainty of the methods of philology and the moral
sciences against those of the natural sciences. Dilthey criticizes
Boekh's definition of philology ("das Erkennen des Erkannten") as
too intellectualistic. It should be changed to "das Erkennen des
Produzierten," because much human creation can be "understood"
without being "known" intellectually.[88] Comprehension, with
Dilthey, is a circular process—we understand the detail from the
totality, and we understand the totality only from the detail. This
circle, however, is not a vicious circle but the necessary procedure
of all interpretation. It thus requires something of "creative
genius." [89] "Only through inner affinity and sympathy does it attain
a high degree of perfection." [90] It is "an act of divination" which
aims at "understanding the author better than he understood himself." [91] Dilthey defends this seeming paradox, first suggested by
Kant,[92] from a position which makes understanding "something
irrational as life is something irrational." [93] Understanding is
always an understanding of life: of the life of a human being. Thus
biography is to Dilthey "the most philosophical form of history"; [94]
this is even truer of autobiography, which is "the highest and most
instructive form in which the understanding of life comes before
us." [95] Dilthey often says that the work is secondary compared to the
life. The essay on Goethe concludes: "No criticism will succeed in
lowering the life, nature, and development of Goethe to a means
for the understanding of his works." [96]

In the framework of his system Dilthey is unable to make certain
important distinctions. All knowledge is to him physiognomic,

directed to something psychic. The world of logical and mathematical propositions is ignored: Dilthey, as Hodges says rightly,
"is able to side-track the whole of general metaphysics and natural
philosophy," [97] and even within the field of "understanding"
Dilthey cannot make clear distinctions between a spontaneous
gesture, a traditional rite, or a work of literature which is part of a
tradition, acts and reacts to it, uses its inherited devices, crystallizes
a form. It is true that in practice Dilthey's irrationalism is not as
extreme as some of his theories sound. His concept of life is broad
enough to assimilate the intellect; his intuition is not completely
pre-logical or a-logical, as is Bergson's. In spite of all the worship
of "life," Dilthey remained a scholar and preserved an ideal of
systematic scholarship. He never shared Nietzsche's nihilistic view
of the intellect. He is saved from the consequences of Richards'
dualism between intellect and emotion which results in an emotionalism divorced from an object, and he is saved from the intuitional-
ism of Croce, which leads to a critical paralysis. But he is saved, I
think, only at a price of a grandiose confusion: almost everything,
even abstract thought, even the most contrived work of art, is experience, life, living, and expression.

It is thus a little surprising that Dilthey values literary history of
a conventional sort and defends it against complaints "that we read
about books we have not read. As if one could read about the French
Revolution only if one had been an eye-witness." Reports about
books are as much needed as travellers' tales.[98] Dilthey praises comparative literature. "The comparative study of works of art of all
ages and all people must gather the material for an inductive
aesthetics." [99] He criticizes Gervinus' *History of German Literature*
for being too narrowly confined to things German: we need either
"a comparative history of poetry according to themes and forms" or
"a history of intellectual life." [100] Even an understanding of Goethe
and Schiller requires going beyond national frontiers. This recognition of the unity in the Western tradition of literature and thought
was not incompatible in Dilthey's mind with a strong German
nationalism, even in his literary judgments. It may surprise us that
Dilthey can speak of the "Nordic humor" of Dante,[101] can consider
the connection between Spring and the Beloved a "truly Germanic
motif," [102] and makes pantheism or vitalism "the original creed of
Germanic poets and thinkers." [103] He considers "the inwardness of

moral conscience" [104] and the view that evil is ultimately unreal [105] peculiarly German traits. Such pronouncements are the more baffling because Dilthey knew the history of thought and would, even in the very same context in which he has proclaimed pantheism to be particularly German, refer to Plato's *Symposium,* to Dante, and to Giordano Bruno for the doctrine of harmony, and the parallel between microcosm and macrocosm.[106] These confusions are apparently tributes to the time spirit. Dilthey hailed the rise of Imperial Germany, admired Frederick the Great extravagantly, and, though from the Rhineland, came to identify himself politically with Prussia.

The case of nationalism only illustrates the breakdown, in practice, of the theory of empathy, of universal sympathy, and historical relativity, of Erasmian humanism. Criticism as judgment has no place in a theory of types which are all equal, in a doctrine of interpretation as identification, in a concept of art as spontaneous expression. But actually Dilthey did continually judge and rank and choose, even among authors and works. He had a specific taste which was largely German classical, but also found much to admire among the Romantics. *Heinrich von Ofterdingen* seems to him, for instance, the greatest work of German romanticism. No superlatives are enough for Lessing's *Nathan der Weise,* Schiller's *Wallenstein,* and the *Nibelungenlied.*[107] Dilthey was one of the first critics who had a deep admiration for Hölderlin, though his conception of the poet may strike us as a little sentimental and wrongly focused. His essay, of course, was written long before the discovery of many of the late hymns.

Dilthey, at least for a time, was actively interested in contemporary realism. He makes a point of relating his poetics to modern art and chides idealistic aesthetics for its limited view of beauty. "Art is everywhere," and man has taken pleasure at all times in "a faithful reproduction of the real." [108] Dilthey especially admired Balzac and Dickens. Balzac seems to him an analytical mind, a critic who could have worked like Sainte-Beuve or Renan,[109] while Dickens appears as the much greater imaginative, even hallucinatory creator of a poetic world which still is a key to reality.[110] Realism, reality, matter-of-factness are often used as terms of praise; even Wolfram von Eschenbach grasps things in their full reality,[111] and "Nature herself speaks" from Gottfried's *Tristan und Isolde* "pure and true." [112]

It was only very late in life that Dilthey came to recognize theoretically the need of criticism. "According to the principle of the indivisibility of enjoyment and evaluation, literary criticism is inevitably linked with (and immanent in) the hermeneutic process. There is no understanding without a feeling of value . . . but only by comparison can the value be ascertained to be objective and universal." [113] This is a late insight. In the body of his work Dilthey's is a grandiose attempt to reconcile a purely psychological theory of poetics—which must needs appeal to universal human nature—and a theory of interpretation that must assume an identity between men with a concept of historical relativism, a theory of types and world views which leads to skeptical, anarchic, and irrationalistic conclusions. Dilthey tried to build a bridge from the romantic emotionalism and expressionism of Schleiermacher to a new positivistic age. He tried to account for the deep emotion he felt in German music, in Goethe's lyrics, and in Schleiermacher's religious sentiment, for the whole tradition of German *Innerlichkeit* which he admired above all else, by devising a philosophy that would be not a rationalistic system but a kind of emotional thought: "Life" itself in Dilthey's sense. His late struggle to free himself from what I would consider the limitations of the 19th century—its psychologism and historical relativism—failed to bear fruit in any systematic theory, but the urgency with which he faced, in his last stage, the crisis of historicism and of emotional psychologism makes him a figure of peculiar personal poignancy and great historical significance.

His recognition of the impasse to which historical relativism leads and his admission that psychologistic expressions, emotions, experiences need, in poetics, to be replaced by a study of meaning, structures, and values means much to us because Dilthey himself had pushed the older views to their furthest extremes, had thought them through and found them wanting. What he has to say is as relevant as it was sixty years ago.

15: FRIEDRICH NIETZSCHE

FRIEDRICH NIETZSCHE (1844–1900) dominates, at least in retrospect, the later 19th century in Germany. He is the only German literary figure of international significance. Actually his influence in his own time was slight. His first book, *Die Geburt der Tragödie aus dem Geiste der Musik* (1872) excited some, mainly hostile, reaction, and the first of the *Unzeitgemässe Betrachtungen* (1873), an attack on David F. Strauss, made a fleeting impression. But then Nietzsche retired more and more into solitude and isolation. His books sold very slowly, and he could not even find a publisher for the last part of *Zarathustra*. Georg Brandes was the first, in 1888, to lecture and write effectively on Nietzsche; but the period of rising fame began after the mental breakdown, in January 1889. It became a consciously contrived cult with the establishment of the *Nietzsche-Archiv* in Weimar by his sister in 1893: his wasted body, clothed in a white Christ-like garb, was presented for veneration to visitors. Even this early fame was largely a *succès de scandale,* due to the spread of such terms as "superman," "will to power," "immoralism," "beyond good and evil," "the transvaluation of values," "the blond Beast," and "the herd man."

In the 20th century Nietzsche's influence has been immeasurable in Germany and France and, to a lesser degree, in Russia and Italy. The English-speaking world has kept very much aloof. The interest of G. B. Shaw, Havelock Ellis, H. L. Mencken, and a few cultists hardly compares with the force of his impact on Stefan George and his circle, on Thomas Mann, on Rilke, Spengler, Scheler, Klages, and the whole of existentialism or with the impression he made on Gide and Malraux, D'Annunzio, Strindberg, Merezhkovsky, and Ortega y Gasset. A systematic, searching study of his thought has only recently been attempted: and it has led to the most baffling clash of irreconcilable interpretations. Nietzsche conceived as the ancestor of existentialism by Karl Jaspers is a far cry from the rational continuator of the Enlightenment described by Walter Kaufmann. The benign socialist in Charles Andler's six volumes confronts the Fascist obsessed by hatred for humanity depicted by Georg Lukács.[1]

Fortunately we are concerned only with Nietzsche's view of literature, of tragedy in particular, and of literary history. By interpreting him cautiously, taking each argument or assertion in its context, observing the tone and polemical purpose, one can take Nietzsche seriously and still refuse either to reduce him to a capricious paradox-monger or to exalt him to an inspired prophet. Possibly more so than any other writer of such passionate intensity, Nietzsche must be read imaginatively. He must frequently be taken *cum grano salis*, provisionally, as an experimenter with ideas and attitudes. Ultimately, I believe, his thinking, at least in matters of art and literature, will show a remarkable cohesion and consistency in spite of undeniable shifts of emphasis and changes of vocabulary. The originality and truth of many of his insights and judgments cannot be gainsaid merely because he has suffered mental illness or has been exploited by fanatics and cranks or even because, on an honest examination, we can show him to be patently mistaken and often self-contradictory. His is far too searching, far too disquieting, far too critical a mind to be neglected in a history of criticism.

We have to deal with four fairly distinct strands in Nietzsche's thinking: his early speculations on the origin and nature of tragedy; his critique of modern decadence and its symptom, "historicism"; his later aesthetics, which he called "Dionysiac"; and his defense of classicism and the classical tradition in literature.

Nietzsche's first book, *Die Geburt der Tragödie aus dem Geiste der Musik* (1872), is usually interpreted as the discovery of the Dionysiac behind the Apollonian façade of Greek civilization: as overthrow of the classicism of "noble simplicity and quiet grandeur" propounded by Winckelmann and his pupil, Goethe, in favor of a pessimistic, orgiastic, dithyrambic interpretation of Greek religion and tragedy. But this would be a gross oversimplification of Nietzsche's treatise. The Apollonian-Dionysiac contrast is not simply a new typology continuing the many attempts, mainly German, to distinguish the natural from the artificial, the ancient from the modern, the classical from the romantic, the naive from the sentimental, the plastic from the musical, etc., but is part of a metaphysical and historical scheme. Roughly Nietzsche conceives of the "eternal core of the world," "the thing in itself," the "real and Original Being" as suffering and self-contradictory. Sometimes he endows this suffering and self-contradictory being with a personality, as "the genius of the world" or "the primary artist of the world." [2] It seeks relief and redemption by creating the universe: humanity as well as the changing world of time, space, and causality. Thus the whole universe is something like a work of art: its impersonal creator is the original artist who looks at this artificial comedy and finds solace in looking at it. "Only as an aesthetic phenomenon," Nietzsche asserts over and over again, "is existence and the world justified." [3] Apollonian dream and Dionysiac intoxication are "art-drives of nature," and "without mediation of the human artist." The Apollonian dream is a beautiful healing vision, an illusion within an illusion, clearly outlined, sharply individualized, but therefore not fully satisfying. The dreamer is conscious of his dreaming, of engaging in deception; he has not achieved the redemption from the principle of individuality which is the source of all suffering. The Dionysiac "art-drive" is more successful and less precarious because it is related to intoxication, to ecstasy induced by narcotics or spring fever, exemplified in St. Vitus' dancers during the Middle Ages or by the roving bands of Bacchic revelers in Greece. Ecstasy establishes equality among men, makes them members of a higher community. Man becomes a work of art. "The art-power of the whole of nature reveals itself in the throes of ecstasy to the highest satisfaction of the Primordial One." [4] The veil of Maya is at least temporarily torn apart; the original unity is restored.

So far this theory remains outside history and outside art in our sense. Nietzsche, not always clearly distinguishing metaphysics from aesthetics, general art history from Greek events, uses this dichotomy to construct a conjectural scheme of development that embraces, potentially, the whole history of mankind. A dim Dionysiac age of lustful and cruel barbarians remains in the background. The Greeks passed through four art stages of alternating Dionysiac and Apollonian principles: the bronze age of the struggle of the Titans and its austere popular philosophy; the victory of the Apollonian Homeric world, triumphant in its creation of the serene Olympian gods; then a new Dionysiac age; and finally the rigid majesty of Doric art and philosophy. Only after these four stages does Attic tragedy, conceived as a union and fusion of the Apollonian with the Dionysiac principle come into being. It is the synthesis after the preceding oscillations.[5]

Nietzsche is very positive in explaining the birth of tragedy from melody and harmony, which seem to him a Dionysiac world entirely different from rhythm, recognized to have existed before as a thin, monotonous cithara accompaniment of the Apollonian, Homeric epic.[6] Nietzsche believes that music always precedes poetry: as in popular song, where different words may follow the same melody but also, to give his modern example, as Schiller describes his musical moods preceding the composition of a play.[7] Lyric poetry, Nietzsche argues elaborately, is only apparently subjective. The "I" of the lyricist sounds also "from the abyss of being."[8] At this stage of his argument Nietzsche cannot admit subjective art and thus has difficulty explaining the relation of musician and lyric poet, of melody and image. Metaphors such as "melody squirting sparks of images," "a discharge of music in images," "an imitative effulgence of music in images and ideas"[9] do not elucidate the matter: we are simply asked to accept his assertion that there arose in Greece, after the age of Homer, a Dionysiac music that somehow gave birth to the lyric. Language strained to imitate music; it followed music.

Just as unclear is the analogous origin of tragedy. The Greeks, we are told, have seen the horrible truth. They know the wisdom of Silenus, the companion of Dionysus, that it is best "not to have been born, not to be, to be _nothing_. The second best is to die soon."[10] In the chorus of satyrs, however, the Greek has escaped the danger of a Buddhistic denial of the will. Though he is nauseated at the ghastly absurdity of existence, he has discovered a remedy: the healing power of art, the metaphysical solace that life is at bottom "indestructibly joyful and powerful."[11] In the chorus the gulf between man and man disappears, an overwhelming sense of unity leads back into the heart of nature. Nietzsche indignantly rejects the shallow explanations of the chorus as a representative of the people or an ideal spectator or a living wall against reality. The chorus is made up of natural beings, dancing and singing satyrs. The Greek is literally changed, transformed, "bewitched" in becoming a choriast.[12]

The crucial change from the dancing, singing chorus to the actual

drama on the stage is left as much in the dark as the change from
music to poetry. We are told only that the dithyrambic choriast
sees himself as satyr and as satyr he sees the God, Dionysus, i.e., in
his metamorphosis he sees a new vision outside himself, as an
Apollonian completion of his state. Nietzsche assumes that this
vision was originally purely internal, that the chorus spoke of it in
a symbolism of dance, tone, and word, that the God, Dionysus, was
only imagined as present. Original tragedy is thus chorus alone and
not drama.[13] But the next decisive step is once more veiled in
metaphor: "The Dionysiac chorus discharges itself again and again
in an Apollonian world of images." The chorus is the matrix of the
dialogue. "This substratum of tragedy irradiates, in several consecu-
tive discharges, the vision of the drama." [14] Suddenly there is Greek
tragedy, scenic art, with its heroes; and for Nietzsche these heroes
must all be masks of the one God, Dionysus. He discusses, however,
only two tragic protagonists, Prometheus and Oedipus. Aeschylus'
Prometheus is the artist, Sophocles' Oedipus is the saint. Prometheus commits a manly active crime against the gods, which
Nietzsche slyly contrasts with the biblical fall induced by "curiosity,
deception, seduction, concupiscence." [15] Oedipus is a sufferer, a
pattern of nobility, who brings magic blessings even after his death.
Like Prometheus he has been punished for violating the order of
nature: reading the riddle of the Sphinx, killing his father, marry-
ing his mother. Wisdom is a crime against nature. Man suffers for
it like the dismembered Dionysus. Thus tragedy conveys a philosophy: "a recognition of the unity of all being, an insight into
individuation as the prime ground of all evil, a conception of art as
the joyful hope that the curse of individuation may yet be broken,
as an augury of eventual reintegration." [16]

Finally, Nietzsche continues, Greek tragedy died, or rather committed suicide: the myth was replaced by reality. Euripides eliminated the Dionysiac element, introduced optimistic dialectics,
poetic justice, and the *deus ex machina*. The new comedy, with its
bourgeois mediocrity, is merely the last consequence of the process.
Euripides is inspired by Socrates who, in Nietzsche, appears as a
type of the theoretical man, the nonmystic who understands at most
the Aesopian fable, purely allegorical or didactic art. But Socrates,
though the destroyer of Greek tragedy, is, by a dialectic reversal, also
the guarantor of the rebirth of art. The idea that thought will

plumb the abysses of being is a sublime delusion that leads man again to the abyss, to negation, to despair. As the only escape from despair, thought must return to art. "Tragic knowledge needs the protection and healing power of art." [17]

In its original version the treatise concluded with this image of the "music-playing Socrates": [18] the paradoxical reconciliation of art and thought. But Nietzsche then added new chapters which bring the story down to our time and make the practical application. In the modern period the historical scheme appears reversed: the tragic age is only dawning now, after the age of science, and Wagner is its prophet. Nietzsche describes opera as a false recreation of Greek drama: it is contrived, theoretical, born of a desire for the idyllic. The Italian operatic shepherd contrasts neatly with the Greek tragic satyr. In the great tradition of German instrumental music, from Bach to Beethoven, in German philosophy from Kant to Schopenhauer, a tragic world view re-emerges: a new myth is being created. In Greece, Dionysus spoke the language of Apollo; with Wagner, Apollo speaks again the language of Dionysus. The highest aim of tragedy and hence of art is achieved; the myth, the German myth, is reborn. In the dissonances of Wagner's music the Dionysiac rapture, experienced even in the presence of pain, is revived. In Wagner's music-drama and in Greek tragedy the world is justified: "even the ugly and discordant are an aesthetic game which the Will, in its utter exuberance, plays with itself." [19]

The whole intricate scheme can be further clarified by a knowledge of the lectures and fragments that preceded and followed the book and by a study of Nietzsche's relations to the writers and ideas that inspired him. He is obviously a disciple of Schopenhauer, a fervent Wagnerian, and a rebellious classical philologist. The Schopenhauerian influence on the general scheme and the vocabulary is most striking: the will which seeks redemption, the curse of individuation, the solace of art, the central position of music sharply distinguished from the plastic arts and from poetry are all Schopenhauerian. But Nietzsche uses Schopenhauer for different purposes, and transforms and even distorts his teaching by translating it into historical terms. The "Hellenic will" [20] of Nietzsche would be inconceivable to Schopenhauer. The position of music is not the same, after all, since in Nietzsche music is not a direct expression of the will but only a semblance of the will, which is "unaesthetic in itself." [21] Schopenhauer conceives the solace of art quite differently, as a temporary escape from the servitude of will; and tragedy teaches resignation. Even in this early book, Nietzsche interprets art as triumphal ecstasy, as a joyful assertion of existence—achieved, of course, only against despair and nausea at the absurdity of existence.

Nietzsche is at this stage a Wagnerian: he shares Wagner's dreams of a resurrection of Germany by means of his musical drama, a new tragic art. To Nietzsche the composer appears as a new Aeschylus; his plans for a new theater promise a national art. Nietzsche absorbed Wagner's views from personal contacts but also read his writings: *Das Kunstwerk der Zukunft* (1849), *Oper und Drama* (1851), and particularly the treatise on *Beethoven* (1870) which, in contrast to the revolutionary, anarchic, Feuerbachian early writings, was permeated by Schopenhauerian aesthetics and metaphysics. It would be difficult to isolate Wagner's contribution to Nietzsche's thought, but clearly the criticism of opera as a "caricature of ancient music-drama" [22] is Wagnerian, and even the interpretation of Greek tragedy owes something to Wagner. Still, their common sources are so numerous that one cannot be sure whether the strange concept of Oedipus is derived from *Oper und Drama*,[23] and whether the whole interpretation of Greek tragedy and myth is necessarily Wagnerian. Such an alliterative formula as "Wahn, Wille, Wehe," which presumably means that Will overcomes Sorrow by the Illusion of Art is surely Wagnerian. A lecture, "Das griechische Musikdrama" (1870), and a lecture course on *Oedipus Rex* (summer 1870) are quite explicit in their defense of the art work of the future and are ample proof of the original Wagnerian motivation behind the *Birth of Tragedy*.[24]

Nietzsche was a trained classical philologist who had studied under Ritschl in Bonn and Leipzig, and had early produced sufficiently impressive specialized studies (on Theognis, on the sources of Diogenes Laertius) to become Professor at the University of Basel at the age of 24.[25] His conception of Greek religion and tragedy was nourished by a whole tradition of German classical scholarship, which could be called "romantic" in the sense that it was suggested by remarks of Friedrich Schlegel and developed by Schelling.[26] Creuzer had studied the ancient Dionysiac mysteries, the Orphic myths, the whole Asiatic substratum of Greek religion in his *Symbolik und Mythologie* (1810–12), and Friedrich Gottlieb

Welcker and Anselm Feuerbach had elaborated the interpretation of Greek tragedy as rising from the dithyramb.[27] But Nietzsche's book did not and could not convince the classical philologist then or today. The criticism of the young Ulrich von Wilamowitz-Möllendorf, in his pamphlet *Zukunftsphilologie!* (1872), though captious in detail and blind to the main argument, is well-founded: there is nothing to Nietzsche's view that Euripides depended on Socrates or that the tragic heroes are different masks of Dionysus. "Who," he asks, "in the *Choephoroi,* the *Suppliants,* the *Eumenides,* the *Persians,* who in *Ajax, Electra, Philoctetes* is the tragic avatar of Dionysus Zagreus?"[28] In conclusion, Wilamowitz-Möllendorf arrogantly demanded that Nietzsche step down from his chair of classical philology. Actually, the profession succeeded in boycotting Nietzsche: he had few advanced pupils and finally gave up his position. (Other reasons were his health and the fact that he had moved away from philological concerns.) Still, a lecture course on Greek literature (1874–76) shows that, within the Academy, Nietzsche studied his subject with wide-ranging knowledge and considerable originality.[29] Oddly enough, Nietzsche there describes the effect of tragedy in traditional idealistic terms: "Man catches a glimpse of a totally transfigured order of things: guilt, fate, and the fall of the hero are only means toward that glance into the transfigured world."[30]

The Birth of Tragedy has weaknesses that Nietzsche himself stated sharply in a late preface (1886): the imagery is "frantic and confused"[31] and the involvement in the Wagnerian project distorts the perspective for contemporary ends. Nietzsche himself was disillusioned when he saw what actually happened at Bayreuth. But the shortcomings should not be allowed to obscure the greatness or the influence of *The Birth of Tragedy.* The reorientation of Greek studies toward the history of religion and myth had many sources and supporters (among them Nietzsche's old friend and defender, Erwin Rohde, who in his *Psyche* (1894) cautiously refrained from mentioning Nietzsche); but Nietzsche gave it a formula and a slogan. His concept of tragedy was intended as a rejection of Aristotle's purgation of pity and fear and of the interpretation of tragedy by Lessing, Schiller, and Hegel as a vindication of a higher moral order, a *theodicée*.[32] It provided a focus for the later accounts of tragedy in terms of myth and ritual—of suffering rather than action, lyric rather than epic, music rather than sculpture, feeling rather than form. But in a sense Nietzsche himself conceived of tragedy as *théodicée*: God is called the Primal One, the world genius, but tragedy still provides metaphysical comfort and belief in an eternal life, though this life may be impersonal and aimless.

When Nietzsche abandoned his belief in Schopenhauer and turned against Wagner, he gave vent for a time to a general disillusionment with art. He tells us, in 1878, that the "intuitions" of art into the unity of all being are quite unfounded. He even envisages the time when art will become superfluous and die out.[33] But, in general, Nietzsche is preoccupied in these years with a skeptical analysis of the artist as a human type. The artist, we are told, is a "retarded being who has not got further than games which befit youth and childhood."[34] Artists are men of the moment, sensual, and stubborn, who take revenge in their work for some inner desecration. They are vain and weak, "unbridled" though not deeply passionate. They are often sick. They seek honors, and power. They exploit their experiences shamelessly. They flatter their public. They are servile "valets of some morality" who take their cue from the rich and from men of leisure. They love acting, a role, a mask, hide-and-seek, mimicry.[35] In short, as Zarathustra tells us, "the poets lie too much." "There are so many things between heaven and earth which only the poets have been dreaming up."[36] But with his usual honesty, Nietzsche immediately turns this condemnation of the artist as "deceiver" against himself: he himself is "only a fool, only a poet, excluded from all truth." There is no truth and art is a lie. "God is dead."[37]

But the moment Nietzsche reached the bottom of his nihilism and confessed defeat, he began to return to his earlier acceptance of the illusion and consolation of art and to glorify it as necessary and joyful. Throughout the "skeptical" period he had admitted some modest values of art. He protests, for instance, that poets are not "fantastic economists" who should paint a social utopia. Poets point to the future only in the sense that they elaborate the image of man.[38] Art must beautify: it should hide everything that is ugly or transmute it.[39] Traditional motifs of aesthetics—illusion, idealization, creation of ideal types of men, even poetic wisdom—are common in Nietzsche's reflections, but only in the last years is art again exalted in tones that remind us of *The Birth of Tragedy*. Art is, then, the great "stimulant of life," a "tonic," the "Yea-saying, blessing, deification of existence." [40] Art, we are told, is more "divine" than truth: more "valuable" than truth, valuable for life and living.[41] Art is power, "intoxication," domination, idealization in violation of reality: it is our "compulsion to transform the real into the perfect." [42] Art is "the will to defeat the flux of Becoming, as eternizing." [43] Nietzsche still exposes the artist who creates from baseness or weakness, but glorifies the true artist among the strong, superior men. He now believes in a continuity of body and mind, a total unity of man, and can accept and even exalt the lowly origins of art. While in *The Birth of Tragedy* he had clung to the view of Kant and Schopenhauer that art is "disinterested contemplation," he now dismisses this view as the "emasculation" of art and frankly asserts the physical and even sexual sources of art. "The peculiar sweetness and fullness" of the aesthetic state of mind has its source in "sensuality": it is not canceled but only transfigured in art.[44]

Tragedy reappears with a changed emphasis but substantially as it was conceived in *The Birth of Tragedy*. However, Nietzsche rejects or ignores his earlier view of a reconciliation of Apollo and Dionysus. Tragedy and all true art is Dionysiac. Dionysus has absorbed Apollo, has become a symbol of affirmation, of a joyful fatalism. Dionysus dismembered is a promise of life: it will be reborn eternally and return from destruction.[45] The "pessimism of power" ends with what Nietzsche himself surprisingly calls "a *theodicée*, an absolute yea-saying to the world." [46] Art is the great counterforce to the denial of life; art is anti-Christian, anti-Buddhist, anti-nihilist. Art is "the redemption of the man of truth, . . . of the man of action, . . . and of the man of suffering as a way to states of mind where suffering is willed, transfigured, deified, where suffering is a form of the great ecstasy." [47]

It seems a strange conclusion: the artist becomes the prophet of the doctrine of Eternal Recurrence, Dionysus becomes Nietzsche himself. An exalted stoicism harnesses the supreme illusion of art to the *amor fati*. But one wonders whether Nietzsche, who has rejected any distinction between a real and an apparent world and must reject the supernatural, has any right to such a concept as "redemption." It can only mean a psychological state of joy and contentment if art is an illusion—a willed illusion desirable because it is biologically and psychologically beneficial. Art is a self-delusion, a

contrived myth like the doctrine of Eternal Recurrence. Deprived
of its religious phraseology of "redemption," "justification," and
"theodicée," which can have only metaphorical meaning in
Nietzsche's scheme, his late aesthetics amounts to a desperate illusionism. Art serves life even at the expense of truth: "art is a setting-
right of things, interested in the highest degree and interested ruth-
lessly, an essential falsification . . . The aesthetic spectator allows
a violation," enjoys a violation of reality.[48] We achieve in art "the
joy of being in *our* world, of being free from the anxiety of the
alien." [49] Art is an imposition of order over contraries. In beauty
"contrasts are tamed, the highest sign of power thus manifest-
ing itself in the conquest of opposites." [50] We may welcome this
apology for difficult, arbitrary, purely subjective art, but must
realize that for Nietzsche "harmony" should "ring out of every
discord," [51] and that art is to serve life: life conceived as health,
strength, and courage. The new art, in Nietzsche's suggestion,
would be a "mocking, light, volatile, divinely unconcerned, divinely
artificial art: an art for artists, only for artists," "a buoyant, dancing,
laughing, childish, and joyous art." The artist would reach the
summit of greatness when he would be able to see himself and his
art below himself, when he could laugh at himself.[52] Something like
romantic irony, even divine buffoonery is Nietzsche's ideal.

If we examine Nietzsche's literary taste, however, the extremism
of these theories seems considerably moderated. Nietzsche himself
composed "Dionysus dithyrambs" inspired by the free rhythms of
Goethe, Hölderlin, and Heine. *Also sprach Zarathustra* is permeated
by biblical pathos and parody. But in general, Nietzsche's own art of
prose is trained on that of the great essayists: on Montaigne, the
tradition of the French moralists, Schopenhauer, and Emerson.[53]
Clarity, wit, balance, order—in short, the classical virtues—are its
ideal. Classical standards rather than any Dionysiac exuberance are
asserted and implied throughout Nietzsche's judgments on literature and in the whole scheme of literary history that he has in
mind. Nietzsche's analysis of decadence, which he sees anticipated
in the baroque and in romanticism, and his preferences in modern
literature have had a great influence on later German literary criticism. Even very casual pronouncements have contributed to a
"transvaluation" of German literature, to a profound change of
taste. But one cannot, in an international perspective, speak of a

radical break with the past. With a wider horizon than that of his provincial German contemporaries, Nietzsche simply and more selectively reasserts the European classical tradition.

Medieval literature he ignores, if we except some jibes at Dante and some final praise which seems to approve the cruelty of the *Inferno*.[54] The Renaissance he always exalts as the time of the reawakening of the classical ideal, as the last great age, but largely in a general cultural sense. Nietzsche admires the strong universal Renaissance man as Burckhardt did and seems little concerned with the literature of the time in any country. He dislikes *Don Quixote* as "a most harmful book," as a ridicule of all heroic aspirations; [55] and Shakespeare seems to him always unclassical: a "Spanish-Moorish-Saxon synthesis of taste," a "mine full of an immensity of gold, lead and rubble." [56] This judgment is not substantially modified by Nietzsche's admiration for Shakespeare's Brutus, who could kill his friend on principle, or for Shakespeare's supposed self-contempt in creating the poet Cinna.[57] Nietzsche's attitude toward Shakespeare responds in part to the way Shakespeare had been used by the Germans to disparage French classical drama, but his views also correspond to the basic tendencies of his taste.

Nietzsche recognizes a "baroque" stage in art after the Renaissance. He conceives of it, I believe for the first time, as a recurrent, rhetorical, dramatic, theatrical phenomenon at the decline of great art. He speaks of the baroque style of the Greek dithyramb and of the baroque phase of Greek eloquence.[58] But his enthusiasm is absorbed by the French classical tradition, a taste which in Germany at that time was quite singular. He sides with Molière, Corneille, and Racine "not without anger against such a wild genius as Shakespeare." [59] He very early defended the unities and other formal restrictions as a beneficial discipline, such as that which counterpoint provides in music.[60] The French of the great age seem to him comparable to the Greeks in their self-confidence, their will to form themselves, their acceptance of happiness as the aim of life.[61] When Nietzsche dedicated *Menschliches Allzumenschliches* (1878) to the memory of Voltaire, he thought of Voltaire as a liberator in the struggle against theology and the Church but also as the last "perfecter of courtly taste," the last of the great dramatists who achieved Greek serenity.[62]

Yet one wonders how much Nietzsche knew or cared for the

actual French classical writers. He read the moralists, no doubt, but hardly the poets and playwrights, if one can judge from his papers. He admired Montaigne and the whole line: La Rochefoucauld, La Bruyère, Fontenelle, Vauvenargues, Chamfort. They seemed to him nearer antiquity than any other group of six authors in any nation. They contain, he asserts, blithely affronting a German prejudice, "more genuine thoughts than all the books of the German philosophers combined." [63] He had a great admiration for Pascal and something like a strange feeling of pity for him: "the ruin of Pascal, who thought his reason was ruined by Original Sin, when it was only ruined by Christianity." [64] But the interest in the great Frenchmen was strictly ethical and psychological: sympathy for their skepticism and stoicism, their hedonism, or simply for their probing of man's egotism and vanity. He admired their way of writing, imitated their aphoristic forms (which he knew also from Lichtenberg and Emerson), but hardly cared for anything that could be called literary classicism.

It is different with German classicism, where he has aesthetic standards in mind. Nietzsche agrees with Sainte-Beuve that there are no German classics. [65] He discusses the great names with ruthless severity. Lessing seems to him a critical talent with only an artistic "side-drive" whose intellectual significance far exceeds any single one of his works. He has the French virtue of order but a disagreeable manner: a mixture of quarrelsomeness and bitterness. His universality is no virtue but rather a sign of the cramped German conditions. Still, he remains an exception to clumsy German taste: Lessing loved "free thinking, the flight from Germany." [66] Herder is discussed by Nietzsche as a failure in life and literature: there is something "wounded and unfree" in him; he always missed his rewards. His style crackles, sputters, and smokes; "he wanted the great flame but it never broke through." [67]

Schiller he consistently disparages as a man of the theater whose plays are "displaced popular eloquence," full of commonplaces and monotonous pathos. Nietzsche dismisses even Schiller's expository prose and his pretensions to learning. It is a sure sign of obsolescence that Schiller has dropped from the hands of youth into the hands of boys. [68] But Nietzsche often reminds us that we should pity these Germans for their cramped, hunted life, for the narrowness of their surroundings, the whole contrast between the sorry reality and their soaring ideals. It is "soft, kind hearted, silvery-glittering idealism," " 'beautiful' in a bad fuzzy taste." [69]

Nietzsche exempts only Goethe, in whom he sees the classical man who "disciplined himself to wholeness, who created himself," who achieved style and dignity.[70] Nietzsche brings many charges against Goethe: he jeers at the Faust-Gretchen story, complains of the formlessness of *Faust*, considers Goethe epic rather than lyric or dramatic, calls his prose style a "mixture of stiffness and daintiness," and even chides him for his fumblings as painter and scientist.[71] Increasingly, however, Goethe becomes the unique German, a "European event" and thus, in Germany, "an incident without consequences." [72] Goethe at the end assumes the features of Nietzsche and the God with whom in the last stage he identifies himself: Dionysus. Goethe is a "freed spirit who stands with a joyful and confident fatalism in the midst of the universe, in the faith that only the individual is worth rejection, that everything is redeemed and affirmed in the whole—he does not deny any more . . . Such faith is the highest of all possible faiths. I have baptized it with the name of Dionysus." [73]

Goethe, exalted even beyond the Olympian, appears always as the foil for romanticism and decadence. Rousseau, the ancestor of romanticism, is contrasted with Goethe: he returned to nature *in impuris naturalibus* while Goethe raised himself to the true naturalness of the Renaissance.[74] Rousseau is the plebeian, Goethe the aristocrat; Rousseau is sick, Goethe is supremely healthy. Rousseau is a lying feminine sentimentalist who absurdly enough believes in the goodness of man, while Goethe is a clear-eyed masculine skeptic.[75] Only once, rather early, Nietzsche gave a sympathetic account of Rousseau's anxiety, his call for "sacred nature," his self-contempt.[76] Surprisingly, there is one obvious Rousseauist who earns Nietzsche's approval: Laurence Sterne. As Nietzsche characterizes him in two brilliant pages, he seems to embody everything that Nietzsche condemned: his rejection (Nietzsche calls it superiority) of "discipline, coherence, character, steadiness of aims, clarity of disposition, simplicity, dignity in gait and mien." But he admires Sterne as the "freest writer of all time," for his "squirrel soul" [77]— a double-edged metaphor suggesting the lightness and mobility that Nietzsche often admired (his praise of Bizet is the best-known instance) at the expense of other qualities.

Nietzsche sees romanticism in the terms of Goethe's saying: the classical is healthy, the romantic is diseased. Its sources are discontent with reality, hunger rather than thankfulness and abundance, the desire for revenge, and romantic pessimism, which Nietzsche sharply distinguishes from his own dionysiac pessimism.[78] When Nietzsche speaks of romanticism, he usually has Wagner (and sometimes Schopenhauer) in mind, and the strictly literary movement is rarely discussed concretely. Nietzsche complains, however, of the cult of feeling and the disparagement of the intellect by the German romantics, of the general anti-Enlightenment prejudice of the Germans. He deplores the lowering of myth to fairy tale and speaks of fantastic philosophies and "the carnival of all Gods and myths" during the romantic age.[79] Hölderlin (the favorite poet of Nietzsche's youth), Kleist, and sometimes Leopardi and Shelley are pitied for their false idealism and exaggerated delicacy: "I am hard enough," he can say in an ugly mood," to laugh at their perdition." [80] Jean Paul is called "a comfortable good man but still a curse—a curse in a dressing-gown." [81] But then Nietzsche can, on occasion, recognize the merits of the German romantic movement as a "scholarly movement" for its "historiography, its understanding of origin and evolution, its feeling for the past." [82] He exempts only two romantic poets from his general condemnation: Byron and Heine. He prefers *Manfred* to *Faust*,[83] and Heine is praised as second only to Goethe. He is the first artist of the German language, free in his divine malice; he gave Nietzsche the highest idea of lyric poetry.[84]

The later 19th century marks only a further stage of romantic decadence. Nietzsche drew from Bourget his definition of decadence as the anarchy of atoms, the "disintegration" of the will,[85] but he had described the symptoms many times before under different names, such as the modern "counterfeiting" in the arts or the movement of "nihilism" to which romanticism, decadent art, and Wagner were a preparation.[86] The diagnosis is made in general cultural terms and is rarely restricted to literature. But it encompasses the two extremes of literary theories and movements: naturalism and aestheticism. Nietzsche always condemns naturalism as weakness, submission, and fatalism or as a symptom of insecurity betrayed by its enthusiasm for little firm facts; "a kind of 'fait-alism' which is now ruling in France." [87] Naturalistic objectivity seems to

Nietzsche a misunderstanding, a sign of self-contempt, a flight to brute matter, a self-negation. There is no thing in itself: what is achieved is only science or photography, not art.[88] At the other pole, the art-for-art's-sake doctrine seems to Nietzsche only "decorated skepticism and paralysis of the will." He twists the antididacticism of the doctrine to mean "rather no purpose than a moral purpose." [89] But art had at that time a supreme purpose for Nietzsche: the celebration of life.

Nietzsche rarely comments on "decadent" writers in any detail. Wagner, whom he analyzes with ruthless malice, is actually his prime example. The jibes at Zola ("the delight in stinking"), the Goncourts, and Renan are epigrams, not criticism.[90] The remarks on Baudelaire, the typical decadent corrupted by Wagner, or on Flaubert, who became "creative out of hatred for life," betray a modicum of admiration.[91] Nietzsche read Sainte-Beuve assiduously but remained unsympathetic: he is spineless, neutral, feminine, Jesuitical in spite of his professed enmity to Jesuits, a "genius of malice," "a critic without standards," and "a historian without philosophy," hiding behind a mask of objectivity.[92] Otherwise Nietzsche admired much French 19th-century literature that might be classed as romantic or decadent as long as it appealed to his intelligence and interest in psychological probing. Stendhal particularly is praised as the "last great psychologist," as a "strange Epicurean," even as the "discoverer" of the "European soul." [93] Nietzsche admired Taine, with whom he corresponded briefly, as the "first living historian." Taine, Nietzsche notes, wants to be objective and positive but actually has a predilection for "strong expressive types." Unfortunately he has been corrupted by Hegelianism.[94] Nietzsche constantly praises contemporary French culture as the only one existing in his time. He wishes, of course, to spite the Germans and actually saw the 1871 victory as a catastrophe for the permanent values of German civilization.

Nietzsche is always determinedly anti-English: the English utilitarian or Christian moralistic tradition repelled him, and one feels that he read very little outside of books on science and travel. In addition to the praise of Sterne and Byron there are a few jibes at Carlyle. He "deafens something in himself with the *fortissimo* of his worship for men of strong faith: he needs noise." His peculiarity is "the constant passionate insincerity toward himself." [95] George

Eliot seems to Nietzsche a frightening proof that in England one must atone for a little emancipation from theology by becoming a moral fanatic. John Stuart Mill, in a famous paragraph of epigrams on great men, is "defined" as "insulting clarity." [96]

Contacts with other literatures were casual and occurred only in the last years. Nietzsche discovered Dostoevsky early in 1887 (he must have read the *Memoirs from the Dead House, The Insulted and the Injured, Notes from Underground,* and possibly *The Idiot*) , and later spoke of him as "the only psychologist from whom I had something to learn," as one of "the most fortunate events in my life, even more so than the discovery of Stendhal." He is impressed by the psychology of the criminal and the analysis of resentment: but he knows that Dostoevsky must be classed as decadent, as creating from want and not abundance in his sense.[97] It seems unlikely that Nietzsche could have understood the religious and political position of Dostoevsky: he is to him another psychologist, another unmasker.

Not surprisingly, Nietzsche was delighted with the attention of Brandes, who brought about a brief epistolary contact between Nietzsche and Strindberg.[98] Ibsen seems to Nietzsche "a typical old spinster" who "wants to poison both good conscience and nature in sexual love." [99]

Nietzsche's criticism of 19th-century literature is only part and parcel of a general criticism of the modern mind. Since culture is a "unity of artistic style in all the expressions of the life of a nation," [100] the lack of style, the masquerade of the 19th century is, in Nietzsche's view, a symptom of decadence, of loss of vitality and of power to assimilate the past. "Historicism," a term used by Feuerbach in 1837 for the excess of the historical sense, is Nietzsche's particular target and is a problem which is still with us, even in the very different situation of present-day American literary scholarship. Nietzsche has in mind primarily Germany, and his criticism is colored by his preoccupation with the overbearing conceit of the German 19th-century scholar and by his deep disillusionment with the Germany of the Bismarck era. In his early years, in *The Birth of Tragedy,* Nietzsche constantly speaks, often in bombastic tones, of "German Genius," the "German spirit," the "pure and strong core of German nature." [101] Indeed, even after he had turned against Schopenhauer and Wagner, in the moments of deepest disgust with his nation, one feels Nietzsche's concern for its rebirth. Although Nietzsche contemns the faith in progress and prophesies, often with terrifying precision, the horrors of the crisis humanity will face in the near future, he is not a prophet of the inevitable decline of the West or of Germany or even of historiography and philology. His analysis always suggested a remedy or possibly several remedies.

The famous second *Unzeitgemässe Betrachtung,* "On the Use and Abuse of History" (1874), has usually been understood as an exposure of the evils of the historical sense from a pragmatic point of view. Too much history hurts life; history should serve life.[102] The *Meditation* begins with a look at a herd of animals happy in their ignorance of the past, in their power of forgetting (or rather inability of remembering) contrasted with the burden of history carried by modern man and particularly the educated German. Nietzsche vividly describes the "walking encyclopedias" produced by German education, the way they are early "blinded by too bright, too sudden, and too frequently changing light." The young man is whipped through millennia, chased through galleries, dragged to concerts. He loses all power of admiration, becomes blasé, or nauseated; in history he is taught to comprehend everything and so he learns to admire only power and success—any success; in matters of art he is without taste, or rather subject to other men's tastes. He is a modern barbarian, an educated Philistine.[103]

His teacher is no better. Nietzsche had inherited a conception of philology devoted to the ideals of Greek *paideia.* The philologist used to be an educator, *the* educator of Germany; but now, Nietzsche sees he has become a scholar, an "objective" scholar. Antiquity means nothing to him: he studies comparative philology with Greek and Latin as a mere pretext for an introduction to Indo-Germanic linguistics.[104] He learns something that does not concern him; he studies a classical author even though he might just as well have studied an English or Turkish writer. He plays his sterile games, fleeing from boredom; he becomes a "specialist" who has grown a "hunchback," since every mastery of a craft has to be paid for. The Alexandrian man, the "librarian" is another symptom of decadence.[105]

But it would be an error to think of Nietzsche simply as an enemy of the historical outlook and of philology. Actually Nietzsche can be described as primarily a philosopher of history. Certainly he believes in the primacy of becoming over being, in growth and evolution, and explicitly recognizes that "philosophy is the most general form of history: an attempt to describe somehow the Heraclitan Becoming." [106] Nietzsche often claimed that the evolutionary point of view—which he conceived in Hegelian and Lamarckian and not Darwinian terms—is the peculiar achievement of German thought and is basic to his own.[107] But in the second *Meditation,* he disconcertingly shifts his view of the study and writing of history. He distinguishes three kinds of history: "monumental," antiquarian, and critical. Each is judged very equitably both in respect to utility for the present and as an abstract ideal of truth. "Monumental" history (which might better be called "exemplary" [108]) upholds the past as an inspiration for the present; it assumes a continuity among the great men of all ages and their power as models, but it runs into the danger of transforming the past into a "mythic fiction" and thus of paralyzing the present, justifying the slogan "Let the dead bury the living." [109] Nietzsche recognizes that the second type, antiquarian history, is usually considered the only expression of genuine historical sense. Antiquarianism has its preservative and conservative function but leads to the danger of accepting everything old and past as equally worthy of worship. It degenerates into the "repulsive spectacle of blind collectors' mania." [110] The function of the third type, critical history, is purely negative (though beneficial), since "every past is worthy to be condemned," but condemned, after all, at the expense of justice and truth.[111] Nietzsche seems always fearful that the past might "suffer," and he celebrates "justice" as one of the highest human virtues.[112] But then, with a sudden change of front, the whole ideal of truth and of scholarship is attacked, not in the name of life or happiness (which is the standard at the beginning of the *Meditation*), but in the name of what he calls the "superhistorical," in the name of art and religion.[113] History "changed into a work of art, becomes a pure work of art," [114] seems to return to the "monumental" history which Nietzsche himself has seen as not devoid of danger. But actually Nietzsche recommends a "new history" that will use all three types—"monumental," antiquarian, and critical— but use them in the service of genuine culture: a "concord of life, thought, appearance, and will." [115] He never ceased to admire the right historical sense, "the ability to guess quickly at the ranking of value judgments" [116] in the past without surrendering personality and concern for the present and future. Nietzsche even welcomes the critic if properly purged of his snooping curiosity for the lives of great men and his mania for sterile comparisons. Such a critic is not a skeptic but has "a certainty of standards, a conscious unity of method, sophisticated courage, loneliness, and the ability to account for himself." [117] Also the good philologist has his place. Though Nietzsche often looked back on his own activity as an aberration, he never ceased to value the philological virtues: honesty, intellectual conscience, close attention. The philologist knows the art of right reading. He teaches us "to take time, to become quiet—to become slow—as a goldsmiths' art and connoisseurship of the word." [118]

Nietzsche rarely lives up to his ideal of the historian, the critic, and the philologist. He cares for other things and is not immune to what he himself describes as the false presumption of many a critic: "This work delights me: how could it not be beautiful?" [119] He uses the past too often for his polemical purposes and often looks for ancestry *a posteriori*.[120] He sometimes capriciously singles out writers for praise without giving any reasons for his choice. Why are there only four great prose writers in the 19th century: Leopardi, Mérimée, Emerson, and Landor? [121] Nietzsche never mentions Landor in any other connection. Why should the treasury of German prose, besides Goethe and Eckermann's *Conversations* ("the best German book") contain only Lichtenberg's *Aphorisms,* the first book of Jung-Stilling's autobiography, Adalbert Stifter's *Nachsommer,* and Gottfried Keller's *Leute von Seldwyla?* [122] We know that Nietzsche enjoyed the placid novel by Stifter. He indulged himself occasionally, found pleasure in the idyllic, the *Biedermeier,* or, as with Sterne, the eccentric and bizarre.

As a critic Nietzsche rarely reads slowly or pays close attention to the text, though he himself frequently reflected on style and the art of writing—on the importance of tempo, for instance, knowing well that his own style was *presto*.[123] Only once did Nietzsche analyze style in detail: in the devastating attack on David F. Strauss' late book, *Der alte und der neue Glaube* (1872) . He exposes confused images, obscure abbreviations, crudities, and pretensions, though his strictures seem sometimes too closely modeled on Schopenhauer's rationalistic assumptions about correct German style.[124]

Nietzsche always disparaged system, even the desire for system, as "lack of integrity." [125] He wanted mobility, freedom, dancing, stepping from summit to summit, flying. But there is more coherence to his views, including those on literature, than is usually admitted. The concept of tragedy, though the emphasis shifts, remains substantially the same: it is the exaltation of life in spite of its horror. The criticism of the 19th century and its art—its excessive historicism, naturalism, and false aestheticism—is coherent with Nietzsche's general scheme of history. These are faults consistently traced back to romanticism and the baroque and even to the decadent Hellenism of Alexandria. Clearly the exaltation of classicism is difficult to reconcile with the original and central preoccupation of tragic art as a dionysiac intoxication. The admiration for French tragedy, for the most Olympian side of Goethe, or the serenely *Biedermeier* Stifter does not harmonize well with the admiration for Aeschylus and Pindar—seen, as they are, as lyric, orgiastic, tumultuous singers of life's glories. There is something deliberately contrived in Nietzsche's idolization of classicism, in his admiration of the "grand style" as the "expression of the will to power itself," in his praise of "convention" and "tyranny of arbitrary laws," of "coldness, lucidity, hardness, and, above all, logic" in art.[126] The exaltation of an ideal of rational control in the name of an irrational will to power is an extreme paradox. It seems a defiance of his own instinctive taste, a polemical weapon in the struggle against the 19th century, against decadence. Nietzsche's criticism is held together by the criterion of effort, will, self-mastery, just as his philosophy of the *amor fati* and the Eternal Recurrence is a desperate imposition of order on flux and anarchy. Zarathustra's "dancing star over the chaos" [127] is a fit image for Nietzsche's forced reconciliation of the Dionysiac and the classical. This personal, psychological solution may have solved the conflict in his mind but does not offer a resolution that would satisfy the theorist. Dionysiac tragedy, intellectual classicism, Sternian humor, and physiological aesthetics remain unreconciled.

WHEN GEORG BRANDES (1842–1927) came to New York in June 1914 to lecture on Shakespeare, police had to disperse a crowd of a thousand persons who could not gain admittance to the Comedy rmany and France and 1e United States. One taken him is deserved, nality and substance. 1 literature at Oxford, o Brandes: he's just a not know what poetry rationalism, progress, tzsche had put it more en he called him "ein

ovedstrømninger i det rst in Danish between *gen der Literatur des* vols. 1872–76) , were a ation in Denmark and 901–05, while a French 1 the French romantic , German, and English literature in the first half of the 19th century according to a scheme derived from the assumptions of European liberalism. The central topic is the reaction against the 18th century and the overcoming of that reaction. The Revolution is the thesis, the *Restauration* the antithesis, and the Liberal movement the synthesis that preserved and superseded, in good Hegelian fashion, the values of the romantic reaction.[5] The six acts of the drama correspond to Brandes' six volumes: three on French, two on German, and one on English literature. The first volume (1872) , on French *Emi-*

grants' Literature, presents the reaction against the Revolution still strongly mixed with revolutionary elements: Madame de Staël is its heroine. The second volume (1873), *The Romantic School in Germany*, gives an unsympathetic picture of the rising tide of reaction, which culminates in *The Reaction in France* after the Restauration to which Brandes devotes his third volume (1874). In the fourth, called *Naturalism in England* (1875), Byron marks the point of reversal, symbolically in the year of his death (1824), the exact middle of the great drama. The next group, described in the fifth volume (1882), *The Romantic School in France*, just before the July Revolution, marks the triumph of Liberalism; and the sixth group, *Young Germany*, described in a later, final volume (1890), brings the movement to a victorious conclusion, preparing the way for what Brandes called "the biblical year of rejoicing" (1848).[6] Nothing is said about Italy or Russia, but the application to Denmark is constantly in Brandes' mind.[7] The whole country has missed the boat of progress: it is still stagnating in the backwaters of reaction.

Brandes calls his scheme "psychological" because he conceived of "psychology" as "national psychology" and wants to think of literature constantly as the expression of men, as a part of life.[8] But basically his scheme is still the old romantic concept of history as the history of the national mind or minds: a history of ideas, mainly political and religious, as it was practiced by Hettner or Gervinus. Literature is judged by asking whether it "put problems to debate,"[9] whether it contributes to progress, to political liberalization, to religious free thought and to sympathy for modern science and its deterministic and evolutionary doctrines. Brandes is perfectly sure of his standards of judgment: literature must be judged by its *Tendenz*, which is the "spirit of the century," which in its turn is "the lifeblood of genuine poetry."[10] Political reaction is wrong; so is obscurantism, and any revealed religion. Feuerbach, Brandes believed, has settled for good the problem of theology: God is an invention of man. Theology is anthropology or psychology. Science has solved all other mysteries: belief in the freedom of will is as obsolete as belief in werewolves.[11] The straight march of progress is assumed at every point. For instance, speaking of Scott, Brandes deplores that "seen from the pinnacle of our time" Scott had not yet achieved "the liberation of personality from tradition."

His reputation has declined quite justly because he "remained untouched by the evolution of the whole of modern science." [12] Chateaubriand is commiserated with for not "having experienced 19th-century science" and hence "a new faith." Even in purely literary matters a steady progress is implied when we are told that we shall meet Nodier "at a higher stage of the evolution of French literature," or when Mérimée is assumed to represent progress as a scholar and writer when compared with Stendhal.[13]

Brandes conceived of criticism as exhortation and propaganda. "Criticism moves mountains: mountains which are called belief in authority, prejudice, and dead traditions." [14] He always asks one question: did the writer contribute to the victory of liberalism, agnosticism, and the scientific outlook? Was he "progressive"? As with present-day Marxists (who hold, of course, a different creed), there is, in Brandes, an inherent unresolved contradiction between the fervently held creed with which everything is judged and the pretention to scientific objectivity. He uses the well-worn image of the literary historian as a "botanist" who is just as concerned with nettles as with roses,[15] but does not tell us that he considers nettles obnoxious and wants to weed them out. Brandes is thus no follower of Taine, in spite of his professions of indebtedness and his genuine admiration for the man and his work.[16] There is no real attempt to explain literature in terms of *milieu, moment,* and *race.* There is no literary sociology in Brandes, but literature is treated, in De Bonald's words, as "the expression of society." A great writer must be permeated with the spirit of his time; he must be, or is assumed to be, representative. Occasionally Brandes makes rather naive correlations between literature and society. We are told, for instance, that there was "no poetry in France during the Empire" because epics and tragedies were being acted out in life.[17] But mostly Brandes provides simply a political history as background, dwelling at length on events often entirely unrelated to concrete literary works or figures: we hear, for instance, much about the Irish rebellions in 1782 and 1799, or are provided with a fairly detailed account of the events in Berlin in 1848. At times we are given mere sketches of thinkers and their ideas—for example, of De Bonald's treatise on divorce, or of public figures who are assumed to be characteristic of the time or its mood. There is a whole chapter on Madame de Krüdener and another on Charlotte Stieglitz, who committed suicide in order to stimulate her husband to write great poetry out of suffering.[18] In imaginative literature Brandes looks mainly for types: Werther is a great symbol in which "the passions, desires, and sorrows of a whole era found expression." The next modern type was Chateaubriand's René, in whom the "poetry of desire" was replaced by the "poetry of disillusion." René "is a melancholiac and misanthropist. He forms the transition from Goethe's Werther to Byron's Giaour and Corsair." Constant's Adolphe is the next variation of the basic type. Balzac then discovered a new female type, *la femme de trente ans,* which rules over the whole of the modern French stage.[19] Danish literature, Brandes laments, has no types, certainly nothing to compare to Nathan the Wise, Faust, Prometheus, or Marquis Posa. Oehlenschläger's heroes are "abstract and ideal": they "mirror their age only imperfectly." They could not, as Brandes imagines, do anything like Posa running his sword through Phillip II, Prometheus rising from his rock and purging Olympus, or Faust subduing the earth with the help of steam, electricity, and methodical research.[20]

With such ideas in mind we can predict the judgments on writers pretty easily. The volume on the German romantics is completely negative, though Brandes describes many writers with some care, often translating very closely and for long stretches from Haym and Goedeke.[21] Brandes is particularly upset by the romantic disruption of illusion, the interest in the division of personality and the "nature and night side of man." He wants "striving, will, decision" which make man a whole.[22] The Reaction in France excites his indignation and distaste: he is amusingly satirical about Madame de Krüdener standing next to Tsar Alexander reviewing 150,000 Russian troops on the Champs des Vertus, or about Lamartine's highflown mixture of religiosity and eroticism.[23] In the English volume the emphasis on naturalism gives a completely distorted picture of the visionary company of the great romantic poets. "Naturalism" is a term that covers Wordsworth's love of nature, Keats' sensualism, and Byron's revolutionary liberalism. Comprehensibly, Wordsworth and Coleridge are played down: oddly enough, Wordsworth's love of nature is considered only a stage in his development, and "Heart Leap Well" is singled out as his best poem.[24] Coleridge's poetry is disparaged: there is nothing of interest in "Christabel," and "The Ancient Mariner" has no poetic core.

Brandes grants Coleridge's poetry only "sweetness: each verse has the taste and the weight of a honeydrop." [25] The philosopher and critic is hardly mentioned. Keats is a sensualist and aesthete who is given less attention than Tom Moore. Moore glorified Irish nationalism and was an erotic poet, "one of the greatest, certainly the most musical that ever lived." [26] Landor's politics finds Brandes' approval, and Shelley is exalted for his "radical naturalism." He is the greatest lyrical poet of the English and of the whole century. His life had "a greater and more lasting importance for the liberation of the human spirit" than everything that happened in France in August 1792 (the month of Shelley's birth) .[27] Byron, we are told, took over his intellectual heritage. The volume concludes with a hymn on Byron, the man and the poet, which will seem today completely out of focus not only because Brandes dismisses the incest as gross calumny but because he can see Byron as the beginning of the modern spirit in poetry. *Cain,* we are told, effected a revolution in European poetry. *Don Juan* is the greatest poem of the century, the only one that can stand comparison with *Faust*. French romanticism and German liberalism derive directly from Byron's naturalism.[28]

The romantic group in France is Brandes' greatest love: "Without exaggeration it is the greatest literary school that this century has seen." [29] Brandes can reconcile his aversion for German romanticism with his boundless admiration for the French not only by the obvious political distinction, but by emphasizing the traditional character of the French. "All French romantics are classicists. Mérimée, Gautier, George Sand, even Hugo, are classicists." [30] George Sand is "a female genius, so important, so comprehensive that never before a woman possessed such rich creative power." [31] In Balzac, Brandes admires not only the founder of the modern novel and the scientific observer of reality, but the visionary,[32] and Mérimée and Gautier seem to him major writers who each achieved perfection.

Brandes has fewer illusions about the poetic values of German liberal literature. But he is greatly interested in Börne, also as a converted Jew, and he must be one of the most fervent admirers of Heine on record. The account of Heine's poetry and prose surpasses most of Brandes' earlier essays in analytical and critical power: he gives close readings of individual poems, sensitively developing the implications of a passage; [33] he can criticize the early poetry for its sentimentality and conventionality, and he praises the last poems addressed to Mouche, as they deserve to be praised. Brandes draws elaborate parallels to Rembrandt for Heine's attempts to achieve chiaroscuro and to Aristophanes for comic imagination, and he makes much of Heine's discovery of the sea as a theme of nature poetry hitherto missing in Germany. Heine is to him "the wittiest man who ever lived," and at the same time the finest lyrical poet, comparable only to Shelley; and, needless to say, Heine was a good fighter for the liberation of humanity, in spite of some back-slidings.[34]

The volume on the French romantics contains appreciative pages on Sainte-Beuve as the founder of modern criticism. Sainte-Beuve knew how to explain the genesis of a work, and to discover "the man behind the paper." He rightly chose as motto for his writings the words of Sénac de Meilhan: "Nous sommes mobiles et nous jugeons des êtres mobiles." [35]

This could have been Brandes' motto also, for it is ultimately an injustice to pin him down to the ideological scheme of the *Main Currents,* a panoramic set of lectures often heavily dependent on secondary sources, indulging in glib comparisons and easy categorizations. The better Brandes is elsewhere. Brandes, we must not forget, has his roots in the Danish soil and is at his best as a critic of his native literature, in which he developed his art of portraiture before the lecture series. There, we see also that he had a well-defined taste and sense of beauty which often clashes with the ideology.

His first book, *Aesthetiske Studier* (1868), shows him a close student of Hegel and of F. T. Vischer, whom he opposes from a point of view that can be called Herbartian formalism. The essay on "The Idea of Fate in Ancient Tragedy" (1863) argues in a scholastic manner that tragic guilt is neither metaphysical nor ethical, but must be conceived as purely aesthetic; and another study on "The Theory of the Comic" (1866) develops the old idea of contradiction: the laughable must be illuminated by the idea of poetry to become comic. But the book contains also studies of Ibsen, against whose raw ugliness and moral harshness Brandes felt still much resistance.

The turn toward a positivistic point of view came with Brandes' two stays in Paris: in 1867 when he heard Taine lecture at the Ecole des Beaux Arts and in 1870, when he saw him frequently and met also Renan and Chasles. But the book *Den franske Aesthetik i vore Dage* (1870), written before his second stay, is by no means an uncritical exposition of Taine. It gives up speculative aesthetics in the Hegelian sense but makes many reservations against Taine's method. Brandes sees that Taine considers art as "psychology, as historical material. The work of art is a monument or a curiosity and never a revelation of beauty." He invokes Herbartian aesthetics in protest: Taine, he sees, is unable to distinguish between the beautiful and the ugly. "One feels how much they need in France the still unknown Herbartian aesthetics of measure." [36] But Brandes recognized his own lack of clarity on these issues. A book published simultaneously with the volume of French aesthetics, *Critiker og Portraiter* (1870), contains mostly theatrical criticism and essays on Andersen, Mérimée and the piece on Sainte-Beuve used so much later in the lecture series. Brandes advanced in both directions simultaneously: in adopting the historistic method for which he had criticized Taine and in developing his taste for portraiture and individual psychology.

The book on *Søren Kierkegaard* (1877) not only has a great historical merit but in German translation (1879) made Kierkegaard first known outside Denmark, and even in his homeland it was the first serious study. But it is also Brandes' first and most delicate psychological portrait, written with deep sympathy and penetration. The way Brandes traces the disguises of the unhappy love affair with Regina Olsen through Kierkegaard's writings—for example, in the interpretation of Antigone or the sacrifice of Isaac— is most ingenious and convincing. But of course Brandes' psychology has a reductive result: he cannot understand Kierkegaard's religion or philosophy.[37] On the plane of ideas he sympathizes only with Kierkegaard's anticlericalism and with his fierce individualism. Kierkegaard, according to Brandes, discovered "the America of personality, of great passions and great independence," but it was his "incurable folly" to insist on calling it "the India" of tradition and orthodoxy. Kierkegaard is often criticized for not sharing Brandes' outlook: he "cannot and will not understand that the history of modern literature is identical with the liberation from the moral and religious conceptions of the tradition." [38] This is a good description of Brandes' *Main Currents*: it is entirely alien to the ethos of Kierkegaard, who still appealed to something deep within Brandes. Kierkegaard helped Brandes to become the fervent expounder of Ibsen and the main architect of Ibsen's international fame.

Brandes' criticism accompanied all of Ibsen's writing life. The essays of 1867 were the very first study of Ibsen's development. Brandes is still cool, though he admires Ibsen's character as "something combative, rebellious, violent, and melancholy" and sees the relationship to Kierkegaard. But *Brand* is criticized for "lack of motivation"; the principal figures seem to him "incarnate ideas" rather than living human beings; *Peer Gynt* is even called "neither beautiful nor true" because of Ibsen's contempt for humanity and his self-hatred.[39] But the second monograph (1882) benefited enormously not only from Brandes' personal contact with Ibsen but from the changed perspective on Ibsen's new plays. Now Brandes can define and defend Ibsen's pessimism as different from Schopenhauer's and Flaubert's, can describe his politics concretely and demonstrate the conflict between "an inborn tendency to mysticism, and an equally strong tendency toward hard, dry rationality." Brandes feels that, after *Ghosts,* Ibsen "in proportion as he has become more modern has become a greater artist." [40] The third set of articles (1898) treats Ibsen as an established classic. Brandes studies the very earliest plays for anticipations of the later Ibsen and traces the continuity and relationship of different stage characters through the plays. "Hedda [Gabler] is one of Ibsen's old, romantic, legendary figures, an amazon in a modern riding habit. Jörgen Tesman is Bengt or Gunnar in the guise of the scientific lecturer of the present day." [41] But Brandes is acutely uncomfortable with Ibsen's improbabilities and symbols. The whole business of the lost and burnt manuscript in *Hedda Gabler* is suspect, and the *Master Builder* has to be conceived as acted out in a world of magic. One must not break the spell with a breath of everyday common sense. But this is what Brandes does when he suggests that "it is no criterion whatever of a master builder's greatness whether or not he turns giddy when climbing a church spire." [42] Brandes' whole conception turns round the idea that "realism and symbolism have thriven very well together" in Ibsen's later work, but obviously Brandes would have preferred that Ibsen had stayed with realism.[43]

This preference comes out clearly in Brandes' many essays on recent French and Russian literature. He expounds Flaubert, Zola, and Maupassant with sympathy and skill: but he cares only for Flaubert's *Madame Bovary* and *L'Education sentimentale* and not for the historical fantasies. He likes Zola the realist but smiles at the inflated rhetoric and symbolism of the later novels.[44] Brandes is completely puzzled by Mallarmé and dislikes most of Verlaine, particularly the religious poetry. "French poetry at the end of the nineteenth century," he concludes, "is the most obscure poetry in all history." [45]

Similarly, in Russian literature all Brandes' sympathies go to the realist tradition, particularly to Turgenev and the early Tolstoy. Brandes rejects the Tolstoy after the conversion; *The Kreutzer Sonata* offends his good sense, and he suspects insincerity behind Tolstoy's asceticism: the muzhik in the Russian blouse driving a wooden plough had himself painted by Ilya Repin.[46] Brandes was, after de Vogüé, one of the first Western critics to discuss Dostoevsky. But his conception goes hardly further than de Vogüé's, as a letter to Nietzsche phrased it bluntly: "He was a great poet but a repulsive fellow, completely Christian in his feelings and at the same time *sadique*. His morality was what you baptized slave morality." [47] Of all Russian writers Brandes admired Lermontov most. *The Hero of Our Time* was a favorite of his youth. Lermontov's liberalism, his defiance of conventions, and his romantic pessimism spoke to Brandes' deepest sympathies. Pushkin, on the other hand, left him cold. He seemed an inferior Byron. *Boris Godunov* is far below Mérimée's *Les Débuts d'un aventurier,* which treats the same story of the Pretender.[48]

In 1887 Brandes had discovered Nietzsche: he entered into correspondence with him and gave the first public lectures on him in Copenhagen. He drew from them an essay on "aristocratic radicalism," a phrase that Nietzsche himself accepted as "the cleverest word which he had read about himself." [49] The treatise was the first serious laudatory consideration given to Nietzsche's philosophy: it will strike us today as remaining on the surface of Nietzsche's thought, concentrating as it does on the *Genealogie der Moral* and on Nietzsche's psychology and immoralism. But Brandes does make some obvious and correct comparisons: with Schopenhauer, Eduard von Hartmann, Dühring, Rée, and, surprisingly, Kierkegaard, whom he recommended to Nietzsche; and he does make some judgments that seem to hold even today. Brandes, for example, cannot share Nietzsche's own preference for *Also Sprach Zarathustra*.[50] Nietzsche suffered his mental breakdown too soon to draw the full benefits of Brandes' proselytism: but Brandes put him in touch with Strindberg, another of Brandes' new protégés, on whom he wrote with somewhat condescending sympathy: admiringly, but with the attitude of a father toward a wayward child.[51]

Partly under the influence of Nietzsche and in the changed atmosphere of the *fin de siècle,* Brandes turned more and more to a worship of great men, supermen, Caesars, and away from his earlier, optimistic liberalism. Literary biography is the main form he cultivated in later life. The large book on *William Shakespeare* (2 vols. 1895–96; English translation, 1898) was his major widely known achievement. It is now unduly neglected, though it is by no means mere fanciful speculation, as Frank Harris' *The Man Shakespeare,* but contains some well digested history, literary history, and simple exposition and criticism. This summary of Shakespeare lore obscures somewhat Brandes' central aim: to refute the idea of Shakespeare's impersonality. "It is the author's opinion that, given the possession of forty-five important works by any man, it is entirely our own fault if we know nothing whatever about him. The poet has incorporated his whole individuality in these writings, and there, if we can read aright, we shall find him." [52] Brandes is aware of the problem of what "reading aright" means: he knows that it is "unreasonable to attribute conscious and deliberate autobiographical import to speeches torn from their context in different plays," but in practice he does, as does any other biographical interpreter of Shakespeare, play it by ear. He catches (like Dowden) the accent of Shakespeare in Biron, and is confident that Jaques' voice is Shakespeare's. "Hamlet springs from within, has its origin in an overmastering sensation in the poet's soul." Shakespeare, he knows, has "lived through Hamlet's experiences," [53] a statement that is true and trite if taken as referring to Shakespeare's imagination, but surely unverifiable and unilluminating if it assumes, as Brandes does, that there must be empirical grounds for Hamlet's sentiments of humiliation, disillusionment, and thirst for revenge. How does Brandes know that Shakespeare met Iago in his own life, that Arthur's entreaties to spare his young life in *King John* are Shakespeare's prayers for his sick child, or that the death of Shakespeare's mother inspired the character of Volumnia in *Coriolanus*?[54] Brandes accepts the Pembroke–Mary Fitton–Chapman theory about the Sonnets when he affirms that "Shakespeare does here enter the confessional." But it seems plain bad taste for him to say, in reference to Cleopatra, that Shakespeare "was a gentleman, a landed proprietor and tithe-farmer; but in him still lived the artist-Bohemian, fitted to mate with the gypsy queen."[55] The most personal voice, the one that appeals most strongly to Brandes, is that of Troilus in his contempt for women and of Timon of Athens in his hatred for the human race in general. Brandes senses there "the Anglo-Saxon vein in which flows the life blood of Swift's, Hogarth's, and even some of Byron's principal works":[56] the English spleen, which refutes the Merrie England myth. The admiration for Imogen, "the most adorable woman Shakespeare has ever drawn," arouses speculations about her model in real life. *Cymbeline* puzzled Brandes enough to ask, "What did Shakespeare mean by this play?" and to become aware that he never answered this question directly; but always wanted to find out "what impelled [Shakespeare] to write it." He solves the riddle by interpreting the play as an allegory of "the ethics of intention." "All the good characters commit acts of deception in violence and falsehoods, or even live their whole life under false colors, without in the least derogating from their moral worth. They touch evil without defilement." Brandes is sure that "purely personal impressions"[57] have taught this to Shakespeare. He overcame his contempt of humanity and saw human worth in the mere existence of goodness and beauty. In substance, Brandes offers another version of the change from the dark bitter period of the tragicomedies to the hopeful serenity of the last plays.

It is most obvious that such a preoccupation with Shakespeare's presumed ethical development is alien to aesthetic considerations when Brandes disparages plays that do not lend themselves to this approach. In *Richard II* he sees "the hand of the beginner in the way in which the poet there leaves characters and events to speak for themselves without any attempt to range them in a general scheme of perspective. He conceals himself too entirely behind his work."[58] Even more damaging is Brandes' confession that *Macbeth* seems to him "one of Shakespeare's less interesting efforts; not from the artistic, but from a purely human point of view. It is a rich, highly moral melodrama, but only at occasional points in it do I feel the beating of Shakespeare's heart." [59] But the "beating of Shakespeare's heart" is clearly not a criterion that makes for good literary criticism.

Brandes' late books—on *Goethe* (1914–15), and on *Voltaire* (1916–17)—keep the same pattern: the combination of history, biography, and literary criticism dominated by psychological standards of sincerity. The *Voltaire* book shows Brandes' complete identification with the rationalist and secular outlook (it made him write a book on Jesus that dissolves Him conveniently into mere myth). Brandes, for instance, assumes without question that Voltaire has refuted Pascal, and he does not see the flaws in Voltaire's character or the limits of his mind and art.[60] This lack of distance is the more surprising because Brandes had just written a long book on Goethe that emphasizes Goethe's life as a model of self-culture free from supernatural ties, and still shows understanding for reaches of the mind and soul entirely inaccessible to Voltaire. There is a lively appreciation of *Westöstlicher Divan* and even of the second part of *Faust*, which is seen in terms of impressionism. The praise of *Die Natürliche Tochter* is unusual, and the genuine appreciation of Goethe's lyrics and ballads shows that there is a vein of feeling for poetry in Brandes that goes beyond the taste for Byron, Heine, and Musset. The Goethe book is often fragmentary, disorganized, and scrappy, but it makes an effort to show Goethe's development without paying attention to distinctions of genres and kinds. Goethe's work in natural science (interpreted too rigidly as anticipating Darwin) is shown as part of his concern for life, growth, and personal evolution.[61] Much is perceptive, but the focus is again elsewhere than in literature. Brandes says himself programmatically: "Literary history used to treat of books. The writer of these lines has the weakness and strength to be more interested in men than in books and to like looking into a man through the book." [62]

Brandes thus cannot be dismissed as a mere ideologist. His enormous energy and curiosity made him an important intermediary among several literatures. For his own country he became the pioneer of a new era. But even if he is taken outside of his historical context, we must, I think, grant him an original, effervescent sensi-

bility, an insight into psychology, and a power of marshaling currents and movements, which, as he knew very well, is an art.[63] Purely
as a critic he must appear as a follower of Sainte-Beuve rather than
Taine: a Sainte-Beuve of wider horizon but much less subtlety and
finesse.

AN "AESTHETIC MOVEMENT" in England is said to have originated with Ruskin and to have been killed by the trial of Oscar Wilde (1895). But it seems misleading to speak of a coherent "movement." Ruskin himself, as we have seen, was primarily a moralist.[1] The Pre-Raphaelite Brotherhood is supposed to be another source of the aesthetic movement in English criticism. The Brotherhood, founded in 1848, was dissolved in 1850 shortly after the failure of *The Germ,* which ran for only four numbers (January to April 1850). In retrospect its members tried to claim the original Brotherhood for their own later views and to rewrite its history. Holman Hunt interpreted its doctrine as pure naturalism and minimized the role of the brothers Rossetti, while William Michael Rossetti in his many publications emphasized the share of his brother and the "medievalism" of his ideals.[2]

An examination of the innocuous little magazine shows that both tendencies were present. F. G. Stephens formulated the naturalistic program: "the object we have proposed to ourselves in writing on Art, has been an endeavour to encourage and enforce an entire adherence to the simplicity of nature . . . Truth in every particular ought to be the aim of the artist." [3] Dante Gabriel Rossetti introduced the medievalism. His story, "Hand and Soul," tells of an imaginary Florentine painter, Chiaro dell' Erma, to whom an apparition, his own soul, gives the solemn advice to paint her as she is. "Set thine hand and thy soul to serve man with God." The ineffectiveness of art in the world is incidentally illustrated in an episode of the story. Chiaro dell' Erma sees the warring factions of Florence unconcernedly spill blood on his frescoes of an allegory of Peace.[4] This is hardly aestheticism, though it sets the tone for Rossetti's later concept of art as an almost sacramental ritual and anticipates his feeling for the isolation of the artist in this world. Rossetti was not a literary critic, but from numerous pronouncements we know that he admired Smart's "Song to David," idolized Chatterton as "great as any English poet whatever," and extravagantly praised the forgotten Charles Wells, the author of a drama, *Joseph and His Brethren*. "The mighty Wells! What has it profited him to have been born the greatest English poet since Shakespeare." [5] The common denominator of these opinions is the kinship Rossetti felt with the outsiders, the resentment against the lack of recognition and the prudish criticism of his own work. Robert Buchanan's "Fleshly School of Poetry" (1871) charged Rossetti with "animalism," with "wheeling his nuptial couch out into the public streets." [6] Much of what is considered "aestheticism" in England is simply the defense of the artist against the arrogant moral pretensions of his critics, who forbade the treatment of whole areas of human experience and feelings. Rossetti's later concept of art is the same as that implied in "Hand and Soul": it is a secular service at the altar of Love, an induction into the final mystery of life.

ALGERNON SWINBURNE (1837-1909)

Only Swinburne propounded a definite creed of "art for art's sake." The crucial passage in his book on *William Blake* (1868) says: "Art for art's sake first of all, and afterwards we may suppose all the rest shall be added to her (or if not she need hardly be overmuch concerned) ; but from the man who falls to artistic work with a moral purpose, shall be taken away even that which he has." Swinburne appeals to "a living critic of incomparably delicate insight and subtly good sense, himself 'impeccable' as an artist." The term "l'hérésie de l'enseignement" Swinburne retranslates into English as "the great moral heresy" without apparently knowing its source in Poe's "heresy of the Didactic." [1] Thus Baudelaire and also Gautier, whose *Mademoiselle de Maupin* Swinburne elsewhere calls "the most perfect and exquisite book of modern times," [2] are the acknowledged inspirers and authorities for Swinburne's creed. The tone is new: what in others before Swinburne was apology—or, at most, apologetics—becomes proud assertion and a claim to superiority. Swinburne rejects not only Puritanism as an enemy of art but also the attempt to set art "to grind moral corn in the Philistine mills." "Let us hear no more of the moral mission of earnest art" is his uncompromising conclusion.[3] This ringing pronouncement does not, however, define Swinburne's position accurately. Swinburne's adherence to the art-for-art's-sake point of view was very ambiguous from the beginning. In 1862 he defended Meredith's *Modern Love* with the argument that a poet need not express convictions, and he mildly chided even Hugo for the blatant social purpose of *Les Misérables*.[4] The praise of *Fleurs du Mal* (1862) indignantly rejects didactic prescription—"the poet's business is presumably to write good verses, and by no means to redeem the age and remould society"—but ends by finding "a distinct and vivid background of morality" to every single poem in the collection. "Like a medieval preacher, when [Baudelaire] has drawn the heathen love, he puts sin on its right hand, and death on its left." [5] When *Poems and Ballads* (1866) aroused the indignation of many reviewers and John Morley spoke of "a mind all aflame with the feverish carnality of a schoolboy," [6] Swinburne wrote a pamphlet in his own defense, *Notes on Poems and Reviews* (1866). There he protests against the standard of the nursery and the schoolroom, the question "whether this book or that can be read aloud by her mother to a young girl." But on the actual issue Swinburne retreats, not quite candidly, behind the defense that "the book is dramatic, many-faced, multifarious; and no utterance of enjoyment or despair, belief or unbelief, can properly be assumed as the assertion of the author's personal feeling or faith." [7] In 1868 when the book on Blake was published, Swinburne's enthusiasm for Italian liberalism dominated his thought. He had already literally gone down on his knees before Mazzini and kissed his hand. He had written the "Ode on the Insurrection in Candia" (1867), and shortly afterward *Songs before Sunrise* (1869) glorified the cause of the Italian republic. In 1872 Swinburne explicitly modified his theoretical view. "The well-known formula of art for art's sake . . . has like other doctrines a true side to it and an untrue. Taken as an affirmative, it is a precious and everlasting truth. No work of art has any worth or life in it that is not done on the absolute terms of art." Swinburne quotes the crucial passage from his *Blake* book and reaffirms his preference for Goethe to Körner and Sappho to Tyrtaeus. "We admit then that the worth of a poem has properly nothing to do with its moral meaning or design . . . but on the other hand we refuse to admit that art of the highest kind may not ally itself with moral or religious passion, with the ethics or the politics of a nation or an age." [8] Later Swinburne even pretended not to know "the imaginary creatures who affirm that poetry must never be moral or didactic." [9] One can interpret this as a retreat from an overexposed position, but it would be a mistake to accuse Swinburne of abandoning his basic views.

Only in the book on Blake does Swinburne flaunt the art-for-art's-sake doctrine in its purity, and only there does he argue for the divorce of form and content. "Strip the sentiments and re-clothe them in bad verse, what residue will be left of the slightest importance to art? Invert them, retaining the matter or form (supposing this feasible, which it might be), and art has lost nothing. Save the shape, and art will take care of the soul for you." [10] But he soon saw that this is an impossible experiment and recognized a "twin-born music of co-equal thought and word without which there is no high poetry possible." [11] He even came to doubt that "beauty and power of expression can accord with emptiness or sterility of matter." [12] Swinburne held fast to his objections against Victorian restrictions and the folly of judging poetry merely by its doctrinal content, by the justice of its criticism of life. It is absurd to put, for instance, "the national devotion and patriotic fire of King Henry V" above "the pointless and aimless beauty of A Midsummer Night's Dream," [13] but Swinburne came to see also the error of the opposite view that a poet may have "verbal harmony and nothing else." He acknowledged the argument for totality and organicity: "The test of true and great poetry is just this: that it will endure, if need be, such a process of analysis or anatomy; that thus tried as in fire and decomposed as in a crucible, it comes out . . . in solid and flawless unity, whole and indissoluble." [14]

Unfortunately, Swinburne as a practicing critic could not always apply his theoretical insight. A concrete "process of analysis or anatomy" eludes him because he is content with gestures toward the final ineffability of poetry. No definition of poetry is possible, he believed. "The test of the highest poetry is that it eludes all tests." [15] This conviction allows him, quite rightly, to reject the reliance on metrical tables and statistics in the study of Shakespeare's development and to prefer his own ear to the "five fingers" of Furnivall and Fleay. But he drew the premature conclusion that he should trust "his own instinct . . . that last resource and ultimate reason of all critics, in every case and on every question," and that the attraction of criticism is merely "the noble pleasure of praising." [16]

He surely indulged in this pleasure on a grand scale, though he also cultivated the less noble pleasure of vituperation. Swinburne's criticism suffers from two extremes: the superlatives of praise which he heaped on Hugo, Shelley, and the Elizabethan dramatists and the extravagant abuse with which he regaled his enemies and dislikes. Some of the praise is so hyperbolic and repetitious that it defeats its purposes: Hugo, within a few pages, is called "the greatest tragic and dramatic poet born since the age of Shakespeare," "the greatest man born since the death of Shakespeare," "incomparably and immeasurably the greatest poet of his age and one great among the greatest of all time," "the greatest Frenchman of all time," "the spiritual sovereign of the nineteenth century," while, in the same few pages, *La Légende des siècles* is called "the greatest book published in the nineteenth century" and *Les Misérables* "the greatest epic and dramatic work of fiction ever created or conceived." [17] The vituperation of such diverse authors as Euripides, Musset, Heine, Carlyle, and Emerson ("the gap-toothed ape"), or the witticisms about J. A. Symonds, George Eliot, and G. H. Lewes,[18] may often be amusing in their violence but ultimately bore and repel by their lack of measure, their injustice and verbal extravagance.

Between these two uncritical extremes Swinburne plays the game of comparison and rankings. It is a legitimate game, and no critic should avoid judgment, or comparative judgment, but Swinburne often judges without proper argument, so arbitrarily and with so little recourse to clear criteria that the ranking loses all interest except as it gratifies our curiosity about the poet's opinions. The essay "Wordsworth and Byron" (1884) does stand out as an attempt to argue a comparative judgment. Stung by Arnold's ranking of the romantic poets, Wordsworth and Byron ahead of Shelley and Keats, Swinburne launched into an all-out attack on Byron as a poet—though in an introduction to *Selections* from Byron (1866) he had praised the poet and the man very generously.[19] Now Swinburne asserts that Byron is a third-rate poet whose works are a "chaos of false images," who has "neither a note of real music nor a gleam of real imagination," who cannot create a character and writes halting bad verse. Swinburne grants him greatness as a "Bernesque writer," and admits that Byron "wrote from his heart when he wrote of politics"; he admires "the forcible and fervent eloquence" of "The Isles of Greece"; but he constantly denies Byron credit for genuine poetry. Swinburne's judgment is vitiated by quibbling over some of Byron's similes and by silence on Byron's finest satirical work. It abandons its claim to purely aesthetic judgment by abusing the man for his vanity, his lack of chivalric feeling, and his inborn vulgarity.[20]

Swinburne exalts Shelley far above Wordsworth and Keats. "At the sound of the Ode to the West Wind, the stars of Wordsworth's heaven grow fainter in our eyes, and the nightingale of Keats' gardens falls silent in our ears." Shelley's "incomparable transfusion from notes into words of the spirit of a skylark's song" puts to rout "the dissonant doggrel [sic] of Wordsworth's halting lines to a skylark." Arnold's emphasis on the pastoral Wordsworth is mistaken. "He is rather with Milton and Pindar than with Cowper and Burns." Wordsworth is "the heroic poet of his age" in his *Sonnets* and he is the poet of meditation and sympathy. Swinburne does not care much for *The Prelude* or even for the "Ode: Intimations of Immortality." He admires most the "Ode to Duty," the "Feast at Brougham Castle," "Resolution and Independence," and "Tintern Abbey"; but he denounces *The Borderers* as the "hysterical and spasmodic eccentricity of moral and imaginative perversion" and is so harshly critical of many other poems that one wonders how he can come up with the final judgment that Wordsworth belongs to the poets just below the greatest—Virgil, Chaucer, and Spenser.[21]

Swinburne is always looking for "pure poetry," which he analyzes into only two components, "imagination" and "harmony." These we may interpret as visual imagery and verbal music. Shelley's poetry realizes both ideals. For Swinburne, of course, Shelley's greatness was enhanced by his political and religious views and the feeling Swinburne had for a fellow aristocrat cast out by his society. Coleridge as a poet follows closely after Shelley, though Swinburne thinks Shelley was as far superior to Coleridge morally as Milton to Dryden, or Sophocles to Horace.[22] He dismisses Coleridge's philosophy as "a holy and pestilential jungle" and considers only "The Ancient Mariner," "Kubla Khan," and "Christabel" great and pure poems. The superlatives rain on them abundantly: "Kubla Khan" is "the most wonderful of all poems," "The Ancient Mariner" is "beyond question one of the supreme triumphs of poetry." But the whole conception of Coleridge as a "footless bird of paradise" and the reverse of Antaeus ("the contact of earth took all strength out of him") misinterprets the man and distorts even the three great poems. Coleridge for Swinburne is "the greatest dreamer of dreams" whose "sensuous fluctuation of soul . . . had absorbed all emotion of love or faith, all heroic beauty of moral passion," the qualities that Swinburne recognizes in Dante, Shelley, Milton and Hugo.[23]

If we accept this standard of "pure poetry," the thrill of the visual flash and the musical phrase, and admit Swinburne's skill in anthologizing and appreciating such poetic moments, we still have trouble accounting for many of his judgments. One can see why he would downgrade Chaucer on the grounds that "pure or mere narrative is a form essentially and avowedly inferior to the lyrical or the dramatic form of poetry" (though we may wonder precisely who "avows" the doctrine),[24] but it is difficult to see why Swinburne should complain about Spenser's shortcomings of "inborn sense of rule and outline," and of "the luminous and fluid nebulosity of Spenser's cloudy and flowery fairyland."[25] Clearly Swinburne cannot care greatly for Dryden and Pope, but why should he disparage Gray in order to exalt Collins for his "incomparable and infallible eye for landscape"—which he then recklessly compares to Corot, Millet, Millais, and Courbet?[26]

William Blake (1868) is Swinburne's most satisfactory single book of criticism precisely because it is nourished by many interests: the fondness for the magic of Blake's lyrics, which Swinburne tries to reproduce in one of his most admired purple passages;[27] the sympathy for the isolated artist devoted to his craft; and the passionate agreement with which Swinburne interpreted Blake's revolutionary views on morals, Christianity, and politics. Swinburne, one must recognize, was the first man to launch into the prophetic books and the doctrines of Blake with any kind of perspective and perception. He often gave up in bafflement at Blake's "insane cosmogony, blatant mythology, and sonorous aberration of thoughts and theories," at the "sands and shallows of prophetic speech."[28] He fastened on "The Marriage of Heaven and Hell," hardly more than a scrapbook of Blake's philosophy, as "the greatest of all his books: a work indeed which we rank as about the greatest produced by the eighteenth century in the line of high poetry and spiritual speculation," [29] and concluded by linking Blake and Whitman as "passionate preachers of sexual and political freedom." [30] But Swinburne does not assimilate Blake to his own 19th-century atheism and liberalism, as he is often alleged to do. He sees that Blake "was possessed by a fervor and fury of belief," that "no artist of equal power had ever a keener and deeper regard for the meaning and teaching—what one may call the moral—of art." [31] Though Swinburne had neither the patience nor the tools to unravel Blake's symbolism, he recognizes the central importance of his mysticism and mythology and makes a sustained effort to explain, if not the details, then the general position of Blake in intellectual history. Blake scholarship, in new editions and commentaries and such systematic interpretations as Northrop Frye's, has gone far beyond Swinburne's pioneering effort; but Swinburne's great merits should be recognized and the book must be singled out from the large body of his criticism because it engages facts and texts concretely and is least encumbered by the windy declamations that spoil many later essays.

Swinburne rarely discusses the admired romantic poets in any detail. However, as a textual critic he also studied Shelley, commenting sensitively and sensibly on some of the cruxes posed by William Michael Rossetti. [32] But there is no detailed criticism of the poems. The praise of Keats and the extravagant admiration for Landor remain curiously general and abstract. The criticism of Tennyson is, for Swinburne, surprisingly ideological and even moralistic. Swinburne recognizes his greatness and singles out "Rizpah" for lavish praise; against Taine's famous comparison, he exalts Tennyson over Musset; but he sneers at the *Idylls of the King*. Tennyson "reduced" Arthur to a wittol, Guinevere to a woman of intrigue, and Launcelot to a "corespondent." Vivien is "about the most base and repulsive person ever set forth in serious literature." [33] The attitude toward Browning is much more favorable; in the little book on George Chapman (1875) Swinburne digresses to defend obscurity in Browning, arguing that it is rather the opposite, an excess of brilliance and subtlety, "a faculty of spiritual illumination." Browning is "hard—not obscure." The point of the defense is, however, somewhat double-edged. Browning, we feel, is put into his place—outside of proper poetry. He is an analyst, a psychologist, not really, Swinburne implies, a competitor of Swinburne. [34]

Even more ambivalent is Swinburne's attitude toward Arnold. As an undergraduate Swinburne had attacked Arnold's comparative disparagement of the Elizabethan Age.[35] But the review of Arnold's *New Poems* (1867) is almost wholly panegyric. Arnold is treated as a reborn Greek. "Everywhere is the one ruling and royal quality of classic work, an assured and equal excellence of touch."[36] Only Arnold's criticism of French literature excites some polite dissent. But later, partly because of genuine disagreement with his ranking of the romantic poets and partly because Swinburne took offense at Arnold's reference to him as "a sort of pseudo-Shelley,"[37] his comments become harsher and harsher. Swinburne retaliates by calling him "a sort of pseudo-Wordsworth" and asking, "Take his teachers and his models from him and what is left?"[38] Arnold is called "the most brilliant and the most harebrained of all eccentric dealers in self-willed and intemperate paradox," and is compared to Rymer and Emerson as "one of the worst critics."

No such distance or disagreement divided Swinburne from Rossetti. Swinburne's review of Rossetti's *Poems* (1870) goes through the whole collection, praising each poem in glowing terms, ranking them carefully, distributing superlatives with some odd, almost scholastic discrimination: "The Song of the Bower" is the "noblest song of all"; "The Burden of Nineveh," "the greatest of his poems"; "Sister Helen," "the greatest ballad in modern English"; "Troy Town" and "Eden Bower," "the master-pieces of Mr. Rossetti's magnificent lyrical faculty." The praise culminates in the assertion of a complete unity of form and content. The "golden affluence of images and jewel-coloured words never once disguises the firm outline, the justice and chastity of the form." Strangely enough, Swinburne even claims that Rossetti's poems are "not over pictorial and his pictures over poetical." Rossetti ranks beside Tennyson, Browning, Arnold, and Morris.[39]

The notorious change in Swinburne's view of Whitman is due in part to external causes, but it is not illogical. The early praise in the Blake book is for Whitman the heretic; the admiration in *Under the Microscope* (1872) is more measured. Swinburne rightly selects "Out of the Cradle Endlessly Rocking" and "When Lilacs Bloomed" for special praise but is disturbed by Whitman's doctrinaire views of Europe and free verse. He knows now (and the future confirmed his insight) that Whitman is not "the founder of a future school of poetry." [40] But the late piece "Whitmania" (1887) shows Swinburne's annoyance all too picturesquely. Still, even the ridicule of Whitman's Eve as a "drunken apple-woman indecently sprawling in the slush and garbage of the gutter amid the rotten refuse of her overturned fruit-stall" should not disguise Swinburne's genuine objections to Whitman's "chaotic jargon" and his lack of lyrical charm.[41]

Swinburne's voluminous criticism of the English dramatists (I do not say dramatic criticism) is greatly inferior to his discriminations among the poets and their poems. Swinburne aimed at a history of the English drama from Marlowe to Shirley and had actually read and discussed almost every playwright down to Robert Davenport, John Day, and Thomas Nabbes. He lacks, however, any interest in the stage, and the technique and structure of drama. Unlike his admired model Lamb, he does not confine himself to praising passages, scenes, and characters but indulges in dogmatic and often entirely unfounded assertions and speculations about authorship, collaboration, and attributions—all on the single authority of his ear: his feeling for difference or agreement of style. But he discusses all his authors with such awestruck admiration and applies such superlatives that hardly any concession is made to those who see the crudities and improvisations of Elizabethan drama.

A Study of Shakespeare (1880), in spite of its high pitch, is comparatively sober and disappointingly unoriginal. It aims to trace "the progress and development of style, the outer and inner changes of manner as of matter, of method as of design," dividing Shakespeare's production into the three familiar periods and characterizing the plays in the most general terms.[42] Where Swinburne comes down to specific criticism, he embraces moral criteria of poetic justice with strange rigidity. He is shocked by the conclusion of *Measure for Measure,* by the "fetid fun and rancid ribaldry of Pandarus and Tersites," by the "hysterics" of Troilus and "the harlotries" of Cressida which "remove both alike beyond the outer pale of all rational and manly sympathy." [43] Many plays are discussed only in terms of the characters. For the character of Hamlet, Swinburne objects both to Goethean "half-heartedness" and Coleridgean "doubt," and points to the expedition to England as proof of Hamlet's courage.[44] Oddly enough, Swinburne, who is not ordinarily devoid of historical sense or knowledge, lapses into extravagant claims for Shakespeare's political and social modernity. He calls "social revolution" the "key-note of the creed and the watchword of the gospel according to Shakespeare," speaks of Shakespeare, because of *Julius Caesar,* as "at least potentially republican," and, on the strength of *King Lear,* "a spiritual if not a political democrat and socialist." [45]

In the non-Shakespearian drama, Swinburne's taste runs to the tragic sublime, to the macabre and the horrible, to Webster, Tourneur, and Marston. He puts Webster next to Aeschylus, Dante, and Shakespeare. "No poet is morally nobler" than Webster, and "he never condescends to the vulgar shock of ignoble or brutal horror" [46]—as if Webster had not written, or Swinburne read, the madmen scene in the *Duchess of Malfi.* The extravagant praise of the Jacobean and Caroline melodrama of blood and thunder contrasts with the comparative coolness with which Swinburne regards Jonson, Dekker, and Massinger, though he treats the latter as giants before the flood. The book on *Ben Jonson* (1889) comes to the odd conclusion that a "single leaf of his *Discoveries*" is "worth all the lyrics, tragedies, elegies, and epigrams put together," though the *Discoveries* are in great part only a patchwork of translations from Seneca, Quintilian, and other ancient authors.[47] The lyrics of Ben Jonson are considered inferior to Herrick's in magic, and only the great comedies, *Volpone, Every Man in His Humour,* and *The Alchemist* are praised according to their deserts.[48]

Novelists are also treated with this central concern for the imaginative and "sublime" at the expense of realism, plausibility, and wisdom. Swinburne's hero among the novelists is Dickens, "the greatest Englishman of his generation," whom he loves as a great imaginative genius. In ranking the novels, Swinburne praises *Barnaby Rudge* extravagantly and calls even *The Tale of Two Cities* "a faultless work of tragic and creative art." He admires *Great Expectations, Martin Chuzzlewit,* and *David Copperfield* as the greatest masterpieces; he considers *Dombey and Son* a "comparative failure" and *Little Dorrit* "the least satisfactory" novel. Swinburne appreciates the "bitter and burning pathos" [49] of Dickens, the side that to us may seem the most perishable. With Dickens, Swinburne ranks the Brontë sisters. Charlotte is called "a woman of the first order of genius" and Rochester as well as Paul Emanuel are extolled as "creations." *Wuthering Heights* is a "genuine tragedy," "a poem in the fullest and most positive sense of the term." [50] The booklet on *Charlotte Brontë* (1877) was written to contrast the "creative" Brontës with the "constructive" George Eliot, to compare "genius" with "intellect." Swinburne condemned *Daniel Deronda* as "waxwork" and preferred Reade's *Cloister and the Hearth* to *Romola*.[51] It is only consistent with Swinburne's taste that he should exalt the novels of Victor Hugo and attack Zola as "a dealer in coloured photographs of unmentionable subjects." [52] Though much has been made of the influence of de Sade on Swinburne's sensibility, he actually saw through de Sade as soon as he read him: he found *Justine* "flat, flaccid, impotent, misshapen," even ludicrous, a mere "juggler's show," and de Sade a "typical monk, alternately bestial and spiritual." [53] Nobody today will object to Swinburne's admiration for *Cousine Bette* (or rather for Madame Marneffe). In 1859 he declared *Madame Bovary* "one of the most perfect and complete books I know." [54]

The limitations and failings of Swinburne's taste are obvious, yet he was a genuine critic who succeeded in defining and upholding a specific coherent taste for the imaginative sublime and the moment of poetic magic. The hectic splutter of his eloquence, the hollow declamations and recurrent, precious or pompous metaphors,[55] his alliterations, and even the shrill hyperboles of praise and abuse should not disguise the hard core of an aesthetic structure. It was a simple system, in part derived from Baudelaire and Gautier, in part from Leigh Hunt and Lamb, but Swinburne was, in effect, the first in England to apply purely imaginative standards to the whole range of literature without too many concessions to purely moralistic, realistic, or philosophical standards. Leigh Hunt and Charles Lamb are his nearest predecessors, but they are thinner, more genteel, and far less discriminating. His closest ally and rival was Walter Pater, who was two years younger than Swinburne and became famous only with his book on the Renaissance in 1873.

WALTER PATER (1839–1894)

Today Pater is under a cloud. He is no longer widely read, and he is dismissed as an "impressionistic" critic. T. S. Eliot gives him as the example of a type of criticism which he calls "etiolated." "This is not worth much consideration, because it only appeals to minds so enfeebled or lazy as to be afraid of approaching a genuine work of art face to face." [1] Eliot must be thinking of the famous passage on Mona Lisa, which has become the stock warning against "creative" criticism. The young smiling woman with a widow's veil is transformed into a *femme fatale,* "older than the rocks among which she sits; like the vampire, she has been dead many times." [2] In addition a passage from the Conclusion to *The Renaissance* is remembered: "To burn always with this hard, gemlike flame, to maintain this ecstacy, is success in life." [3] It is often quoted as the summary of Pater's philosophy, an aesthetic hedonism or hedonistic aestheticism. Today few want to burn with such a gemlike flame, and those few are usually very young indeed.

But these two passages—too well known for the good of Pater's reputation—are not really representative either of his method or his philosophy. The Mona Lisa passage is quite isolated in Pater's work. It is a tour de force modeled, it has been shown, on such poems as Gautier's "Caerulei Oculi" or Swinburne's "Cleopatra" or on Swinburne's "Notes on Designs of the Old Masters in Florence," describing Michelangelo's female heads.[4] Nowhere else in Pater is there such a revery quite out of touch with the work of art itself. The fantasy contains, one should admit, one of Pater's and Gautier's favorite ideas: the hypothesis of the multiplicity of individuals in one individual, "the idea of humanity summing up in itself all modes of thought and life." [5] If we look for other examples of a metaphorical method of criticism, even on a small scale, we are hard put to find many in Pater's writings. I have noticed only four which are at all conspicuous. Morris' poem "The Defense of Guenevere" is described in an early essay, "Aesthetic Poetry" (1868), as "a thing tormented and awry with passion, like the body of Guenevere defending herself from the charge of adultery." [6] In the sonnets of Michelangelo, we are told, there is "a cry of distress," "but as a mere residue, a trace of the bracing chalybeate salt, just discernible, in the song which rises like a clear, sweet spring from a charmed space in his life." [7] The concluding paragraph of the essay on Lamb, the originator of the method,[8] compares him elaborately to the London of sixty-five years before.[9] The *Bacchae* of Euripides is described as "excited, troubled, disturbing—a spotted or dappled thing, like the oddly dappled fawn-skins of its own masquerade." [10] These are

little marginal fancies or rhetorical flourishes, but one would give
an entirely false impression of Pater's mind and method if one
advanced them as typical.

Rather, Pater's theory of criticism stresses not only personal
impression but the duty of the critic to grasp the individuality, the
unique quality of a work of art. Pater never advocates the impressionistic theory of the "adventures of the soul among masterpieces,"
the "speaking of myself on occasion of Shakespeare," as it was
formulated by Anatole France. Pater quotes Arnold, "To see the
object as in itself it really is," and modifies that only by adding that
the "first step in criticism" is "to know one's impression as it really
is, to discriminate it, to realize it distinctly." [11] He paraphrases
Goethe when he asks, "What is this song or picture, this engaging
personality in life or in a book to *me*? Does it give me pleasure?" [12]
But this personal pleasure is merely the first step, the prerequisite of
criticism. The critic must go beyond it: penetrate "through the
given literary or artistic product, into the mental and inner condition of the producer, shaping his work." [13] Moreover, he must know
how to communicate this insight to others. In practice, Pater looks
for the "formula," [14] the "virtue," the "active principle," [15] the
"motive" [16] in a work—terms substantially the same as Taine's
"master-faculty" or Croce's "dominant sentiment." The "formula"
for Mérimée is "the enthusiastic amateur of rude, crude, naked
force in men and women wherever it could be found; himself carry-
ing ever, as a mask, the conventional attire of the modern world." [17]
The "motive" of all Michelangelo's work is "this creation of life—
life coming always as a relief or recovery, and always in strong contrast with the rough-hewn mass in which it is kindled." [18] The
"virtue," the "active principle" in Wordsworth is "that strange,
mystical sense of a life in natural things, and of man's life as a part
of nature." [19]

The whole essay on Wordsworth circles around this one problem:
how to define this "intimate consciousness of the expression of
natural things," [20] his sense for "particular spots of time," [21] his
"recognition of local sanctities." [22] "By raising nature to the level
of human thought he gives it power and expression: he subdues
man to the level of nature, and gives him thereby a certain breadth
and coolness and solemnity." [23] Pater puts Wordsworth in a framework of intellectual history: he speaks of the survival of ancient

animism; [24] he draws the parallel with pantheism in France which from Rousseau to Hugo sought the "expressiveness of outward things." [25] When he writes on the *Intimations Ode,* he alludes to the Platonic doctrine of reminiscence [26] and elsewhere quotes the anticipation of mood and doctrine in Henry Vaughan's "The Retreat." [27] He speaks of Wordsworth's drawing on old speculations about the *anima mundi,* the one universal spirit.[28] He is certain that Wordsworth felt, as Pater probably did too, that "the actual world would, as it were, dissolve and detach itself, flake by flake," that "he himself seemed to be the creator, and when he would the destroyer, of the world in which he lived—that old isolating thought of many a brain-sick mystic of ancient and modern times." [29] Pater, in short, attempts to define the mood, the temper, the dominant quality of Wordsworth's personality and work, what he once calls "the fine mountain atmosphere of mind." [30] He uses the traditional methods of 19th-century criticism: historical, when he suggests the intellectual affinities; descriptive, evocative, when he recalls "the biblical depth and solemnity which hangs over this strange, new, passionate, pastoral world"; [31] and evaluative, when he discriminates between the good and the inferior in Wordsworth. As to method, there is nothing new except insight and finesse, nor is there anything subjective in it except sympathy.[32] It is a "portrait" as good as anything in Sainte-Beuve.

Pater's essays vary greatly in quality. Some are only book reports or exercises in translation from the French which should never have been reprinted (the colorless piece on Octave Feuillet's *La Morte* was even included in *Appreciations*). Others are small noncommittal reviews written to recommend (rather tepidly) the publication of a friend or disciple: George Moore, Edmund Gosse, George Saintsbury, Arthur Symons, Oscar Wilde. But if we make the necessary discriminations, we are left with a handful of subtle studies, models of the art of the essayist and portraitist. The essays concerned with English literature treat of Shakespeare, the romantics and the Pre-Raphaelites. It is true that of the three essays on Shakespeare only one is really distinguished. The piece on *Love's Labour's Lost* tries to convey a sense of Shakespeare's joy in verbal artistry. "Shakespeare's English Kings" pursues the theme of the sad fortune of English kings as "conspicuous examples of the ordinary human condition." [33] But the essay on *Measure for Measure* takes an original view of the play. Contrary to the usual complaints about its "painfulness," Pater sees the play as the "central expression of Shakespeare's moral judgments," [34] of his "finer justice," of his tolerance and insight into man's fatal subservience to circumstance and temptation. In substance, he anticipates the view of Wilson Knight and F. R. Leavis, though he makes concessions to the view that Shakespeare did not properly assimilate the old story. The preoccupation with the moral issues of the play, "those peculiar valuations of action and its effect which poetry actually requires," [35] supplies a ready refutation of the common cliché about Pater's amoral aestheticism.

The essay on Sir Thomas Browne is largely narrative and descriptive but conveys a clear image of Browne's mentality, though Pater was, I think, mistaken in saying that "Browne, in spite of his profession of boisterous doubt, had no difficulties with religion." [36]

The companion piece to the Wordsworth essay, that on Coleridge, suffers somewhat from being pieced together from two parts: an older essay on "Coleridge's Writings," [37] from which Pater dropped the passages on the theology,[38] and a much later piece on the poetry.[39] Pater's discussion of Coleridge's philosophy and criticism is unsympathetic because he objects to Coleridge's search for the absolute and is suspicious of German metaphysical aesthetics. In the section on poetry, Pater oddly enough ignores *Kubla Khan* and does not get beyond rather random comments on *The Ancient Mariner* and *Christabel*. His essay on Lamb is more unified and superior in perceptiveness and sympathy both for the criticism (which seems to Pater the "very quintessence of criticism") [40] and for the general mood of the essays of Elia: the enchantment of distance, the poetry of things, the dark undercurrent of tragedy.

The Pre-Raphaelites were obviously near to Pater's mind and heart: his early essay on William Morris (1868) describes very well Morris' "sense of death," [41] though it argues obscurely for the "charming anachronisms" of Morris' *Death of Jason,* the Greek legend told as if it were by Chaucer. The superior essay on Rossetti defines well the fusion of the "material and the spiritual," [42] his knowing, like Dante, "no region of spirit which shall not be sensuous also, or material." [43] But one is less convinced by Pater's praise for his "quality of sincerity," [44] by which he means unconventionality, novelty, and originality.

Though ostensibly art criticism, *The Renaissance* (1873) [45] is really a very literary book. Pater's conception of the Renaissance is substantially that of Burckhardt (and Michelet). It is the age that makes the discovery of man, of his body and his senses; the age that accomplishes the revelation of antiquity. Pater makes much of the traces of paganism in the Middle Ages, the medieval Renaissance, with its spirit of rebellion and revolt, "its worship of the body." [46] Still, in the first essay, "Two Early French Stories," he can do little beyond producing the passage from *Aucassin and Nicolette* where, to be with his mistress, Aucassin is ready to start for hell rather than heaven. In the next essay Pater picks Pico della Mirandola as an example of the desire for the reconciliation of paganism and Christianity, the syncretism of the Florentine Platonic Academy. He emphasizes again the Platonic tradition in Michelangelo's poetry, which he contrasts with Dante's as being based on "principles diametrically opposite." [47] Michelangelo appears as the "spiritualist," Dante as the "materialist" in the sense that he believes in the literal resurrection of the body.[48] Michelangelo is pronounced neither baroque nor a precursor of the baroque (though Pater does not yet use these terms), but a kind of survivor in the new and incomprehensible world of the Counter Reformation. Italy is the center of the Renaissance, but with the exception of the sonnets of Michelangelo no Italian literature is discussed in Pater's highly selective series of studies.

The French Renaissance is the "aftermath, a wonderful later growth." [49] Ronsard and Du Bellay are characterized, one-sidedly, as having "elegance, the aerial touch, the perfect manner." [50] Pater, in this context, seems to depend on Sainte-Beuve, the early *Tableau de la poésie au XVIe siècle* (1828) and the very late essays on Du Bellay,[51] which Pater quotes. This view of Ronsard, the stress on "his exquisite faintness, a certain tenuity and caducity," [52] is repeated in the fictional evocation of the elderly man retired to a convent, in *Gaston de Latour*. Ronsard's feeling for nature is described as if it were Wordsworth's. "The rain, the first streak of dawn, the very sullenness of the sky, had a power, only to be described by saying that they seemed to be *moral facts*." [53]

Obviously one must not treat Pater's fiction precisely as criticism, but it is difficult not to touch on it, as whole chapters of *Marius the Epicurean* and *Gaston de Latour* are concerned with works of literature: with Apuleius' *Golden Ass,* the *Pervigilium Veneris,* the *Meditations* of Marcus Aurelius, Ronsard's poetry, the *Essays* of Montaigne, and the philosophy of Giordano Bruno. These discussions have a strange ambiguity, a double focus as it were. Pater does not describe *The Golden Ass* as a book; he traces the aesthetic and moral experience of his hero, and Marius, though ostensibly a Roman of the later Empire, is a thinly veiled Walter Pater passing through the same or analogous experiences. The *Golden Ass* is, in *Marius,* not just a particular book but a representative of all or any finely wrought art: it is something like Gautier's *Mademoiselle de Maupin.* It illustrates what Pater calls, with deliberate anachronism, "Euphuism"; it shows "jeweller's work," "curious felicity," the art of concealing art, the "labor of the file," [54] the worship of the word that was Pater's. Although Pater alludes to "an unmistakably real feeling for asses" [55] and translates the whole of the episode "The story of Psyche and Cupid," he loses sight of the text of the *Golden Ass.* Similarly Ronsard in *Gaston de Latour,* while a fictional figure with definite traits of the historical man, functions also as the representative of youth's enthusiasm for contemporary poetry, for "modernity," and of Pater's own enthusiasm for nature poetry of a kind found in Wordsworth, Keats, Tennyson, and the Pre-Raphaelites: poetry that reproduces "the exact pressure of the jay at the window; you could count the petals,—of the exact natural number; no expression could be too faithful to the precise texture of things . . . the visible was more visible than ever before, just because soul had come to its surface." [56]

The book on the Renaissance concludes with an essay on Winckelmann (1867), who in Pater's mind "really belongs in spirit to an earlier age." By his "Hellenism, his life-long struggle to attain the Greek spirit, he is in sympathy with the humanists of a previous century. He is the last fruit of the Renaissance." [57] Winckelmann is seen in the light of Goethe's memorial tract and of Hegel's aesthetics; his life is told in the terms of Otto Jahn's short biography.[58] But the analysis of Winckelmann's position is rather vague and shows little knowledge of its complexities: this early essay, with its many close parallels to Hegel,[59] is still not quite emancipated from its sources, still impersonally reproductive in spite of Pater's marked sympathy for its hero.

"The aim of a right criticism is to place Winckelmann in an intellectual perspective, of which Goethe is the foreground," [60] says Pater, and thus implies that the Renaissance actually ends with Goethe. Goethe is for Pater not only the last of the classics, but the first of the romantics. He represents their union, "the union of the Romantic spirit, in its adventure, its variety, its profound subjectivity of the soul, with Hellenism, in its transparency, its rationality, its desire of beauty—that marriage of Faust and Helena, of which the art of the nineteenth century is the child, the beautiful lad Euphorion." [61] Pater, oddly enough if one considers chronology, speaks of the romantic school in Germany as "that movement which culminated in Goethe's *Goetz von Berlichingen,*" or couples the names of Goethe and Tieck as examples of romanticism. [62]

Pater looks at German romanticism through the eyes of Madame de Staël and Heine. He does not seem to know any of the texts, with the exception of one passage from Novalis, [63] and he thought that "neither Germany with its Goethe and Tieck, nor England, with its Byron and Scott, is nearly so representative of the romantic temper as France, with Murger, and Gautier, and Victor Hugo." [64] Pater admired Hugo greatly, alluding to several of his novels [65] and comparing him with Michelangelo and Blake. [66] It is obvious that he is deeply read in Gautier. [67] He wrote a laudatory essay on Mérimée that shows some uneasiness about Mérimée's "exaggerated art: intense, unrelieved, an art of fierce colours. Terror without pity." [68] Pater's admiration for the weird and macabre Gothic extends from *Wuthering Heights* [69] to Wilhelm Meinhold's vulgar, sensational novels, [70] which Rossetti had made known in England. [71] Pater's taste defines itself clearly as late romantic, a taste that does not exclude an appreciation for the ancients and the Renaissance.

Theoretically, Pater was less interested in the national variety of the romantic schools than in romanticism as an eternal, ever-recurring type. In the postscript to *Appreciations* he defines romanticism: "It is the addition of strangeness to beauty which constitutes the romantic character of art." [72] Poe had quoted Bacon, in speaking of Ligeia: "There is no exquisite beauty without some strangeness," and Baudelaire had said: "Le beau est toujours bizarre." [73] But Pater is the first to add "strangeness" to a definition of romanticism. He enumerates other traits, such as curiosity, the new, the contemporaneous, the grotesque, and these he contrasts with the classical qualities of measure, purity, temperance, as he found them stated in Sainte-Beuve's famous lecture. Pater defines romanticism so broadly, as "a spirit which shows itself at all times, in various degrees, in individual workmen and their work," [74] that he can speak of the *Odyssey* as being "more romantic than Sophocles." [75] The term—like all such terms when they divide the whole world into two camps—has lost all precision and hence all usefulness.

Only now can we return to the passage about "burning with this hard, gemlike flame." Pater in the second edition of the *Renaissance* (1877) suppressed the Conclusion, because it was misunderstood as the advocacy of vulgar hedonism. He had been ridiculed under the name of Mr. Rose in W. H. Mallock's satirical novel, *The New Republic*,[76] and therefore thought it necessary to define and defend his position in many passages of *Marius the Epicurean* [77] before he again reprinted the Conclusion in later editions (3d ed. 1888). In *Marius* Pater tells us that hedonism means "Be perfect in regard to what is here and now," and not "let us eat and drink, for tomorrow we die." [78] It is culture, *paideia*, "an expansion and refinement of the power of reception," [79] "not pleasure, but fulness of life, and insight as conducting to that fulness." [80] The association with the Epicurean style, the attempt of enemies "to see the severe and laborious youth [Marius] in the vulgar company of Lais" [81] is a gross libel. I find no difficulty in recognizing the high-mindedness of Pater's ideal and in admitting that the pleasures he recommended are intellectual and aesthetic. In our context we need not argue the sufficiency of his doctrine as a rule of life. The point important for criticism is Pater's central experience of time. To him "our existence is but the sharp apex of the present moment between two hypothetical eternities." [82] "All that is actual is a single moment, gone while we try to apprehend it." [83] Such a feeling for "the perpetual flux," the *panta rhei* of Heraclitus,[84] is the corollary of Pater's almost solipsistic sense of man's confinement within "the narrow chamber of the individual mind," "that thick wall of personality through which no real voice has ever pierced on its way to us." Man is a "solitary prisoner" with his own "dream of a world." [85] This basic conception—no doubt a psychological *datum* of the retiring, shy, and unloving man—must lead him to a theory that sees the highest possible value in the individual moment of aesthetic experience. "Art comes proposing to us frankly to give nothing but the highest quality to your moments as they pass, and simply for those moments' sake." [86] This highest quality concentrated in a moment, is, however, inconsistently interpreted as oriented toward an outward reality. Art, in these moments, presents us with the concrete variety of the world. This hedonism is a form of empiricism and sensationalism. Pater condemns philosophical and aesthetic abstractions and the world of Platonic ideas. "Who would change the colour or curve of a rose leaf . . . for that colourless, formless, intangible being—Plato put so high?" [87] Hence the "first condition of the poetic way of seeing and presenting things is particularization." [88] Poetry should be as "veritable, as intimately near, as corporeal, as the new faces of the hour, the flowers of the actual season." [89] Poetry is thus concrete and sensuous, almost imagistically so. But poetry in this moment must be also intense and hence charged with emotion, with personal emotion. Pater thus values— side by side with a poetry of images—the personal lyric. As emphatically as Leopardi, John Stuart Mill, and Poe, Pater declares lyrical poetry to be "the highest and most complete form of poetry." [90] Lyrical poetry, "which in spite of a complex structure often preserves the unity of a single passionate ejaculation, would rank higher than dramatic poetry." A play "attains artistic perfection just in proportion as it approaches that unity of lyrical effect, as if a song or ballad were still lying at the root of it." [91] *Richard the Second,* like a musical composition, possesses "a certain concentration of all its parts, a simple continuity," and *Romeo and Juliet* approaches to "something like the unity of a lyrical ballad, a song, a single strain of music." [92] Unity of impression follows from lyrical intensity as a criterion of good art. Pater can praise a poem of Browning [93] for the "clear ring of a central motive. We receive from it the impression of one imaginative tone, of a single creative act." [94] *Measure for Measure* is even considered as having "almost the unity of a single scene." [95] But precisely because their unity is a unity of impression, a lyrical moment, Pater refuses to follow Coleridge into identifying unity with organism. The organic analogy "expresses truly the sense of self-delighting, independent life which the finished work of art gives us: it hardly figures the process by which such a work is produced." [96]

If art is lyrical, emotional, intense, it must be "sincere." Pater often uses this term, as do other English critics, as a vague term of praise for successful art, for the tone of conviction in Browne,[97] or even for "the grandeur of literary workmanship," the great style of Rossetti.[98] But often sincerity means something more concrete to him, "that perfect fidelity to one's own inward presentation, to the precise features of the picture within, without which any profound poetry is impossible." [99] It thus is a term for faithfulness to the inner vision, for the success of the transformation of the intuition into expression. Often it is another term for personality, the "impress of a personal quality, a profound expressiveness, what the French call *intimité,* by which is meant some subtler sense of originality. . . . It is what we call *expression,* carried to its highest intensity of degree. . . . It is the quality which alone makes work in the imaginative order really worth having at all." [100] Pater finds such personality even in the pale terra-cotta reliefs of Luca della Robbia, and he "longs to penetrate into the lives" of the Florentine sculptors of the 15th century "who have given expression to so much power and sweetness." [101] But in spite of this statement and although the life of Winckelmann attracts him, Pater is not primarily interested in biography. He has to make some defense for the "loss of absolute sincerity" which Winckelmann suffered when he became a convert to Roman Catholicism in order to go to Rome.[102] But his guess that there is "something of self-portraiture" in Shakespeare's Mercutio and Biron [103] is a quite isolated remark in Pater's work.

Still, Pater, with his lyrical pathos, must reject the theory of impersonality in art and especially as he meets it in Flaubert. "Impersonality in art, the literary idea of Gustave Flaubert, is perhaps no more possible than realism. The artist *will* be felt. His subjectivity must and will colour the incidents, as his very bodily eye selects the aspects of things." [104] Pater is deeply impressed by the objectivity of Flaubert and Mérimée, and temperamentally he is given to hiding his own personality. But he sees that Mérimée's "superb self-effacement, his impersonality, is itself an effective personal trait." [105]

Pater's preference for concrete, intense, sincere, personal poetry manages to include the criterion of unity, and unity (while it is not organic unity) is the fusion of matter and form. "The ideal of all art is . . . the point where it is impossible to distinguish form from the substance or matter." [106] Art is a constant effort to obliterate the distinction between form and matter, as "the matter is nothing without the form, the spirit, of the handling." [107] This is also the meaning of Pater's much misinterpreted dictum that "all art constantly aspires towards the condition of music." [108] This does not mean that all art should become music, or even like music. Music is the "typically perfect art . . . precisely because in music it is impossible to distinguish the form from the substance or matter." [109] Good poetry should aspire to such an identity, but with its own means, and the arts should and will remain separate, since "each art has its peculiar beauty, untranslatable into the forms of any other." [110] Still, in one context, Pater recommends what he calls, using a Hegelian term, an *Andersstreben,* "a partial alienation of each art from its limitations through which the arts are able, not indeed to supply the place of each other, but reciprocally to lend each other new forces." [111] Pater's endorsement of the union of the arts is thus very partial: even the frequent parallelisms between the arts, acknowledged by him, are drawn only as a "great stimulus to the intellect," [112] not as literal truths, and, in a concrete question, he can appeal to arguments drawn from Lessing's *Laokoon* for the distinction between poetry and painting.[113]

So far Pater's concept of poetry and art is consistently romantic, lyrical, pastoral. Romantic also is the great role Pater ascribes to imagination. The office of imagination is "to condense the impressions of natural things into human form," [114] to achieve "the complete infusion of the figure into the thought," [115] to be as it is in Coleridge, a "unifying or identifying power." [116] Pater, however, ascribes no significance to Coleridge's distinction between imagination and fancy: this reduces itself to a difference "between the lower and higher degrees of intensity in the poet's conception of his subject." [117] Romantic also (though hardly reconcilable with his emphasis on the intense moment) is Pater's acceptance of the idea of an ideal world of poetry, "a new order of phenomena, a creation of a new ideal" [118] which we are to contemplate (and not merely enjoy), "behold for the mere joy of beholding." [119] This ideal world is often thought of as a "refuge," "a sort of cloistral refuge from a certain vulgarity in the actual world," and even compared, in its uses, to a religious "retreat," [120] or called "a refuge into a world slightly better—better conceived, or better finished—than the real one." [121] The ivory tower—the dream world of the poet, the theme of escape—is prominent in Pater.

But these romantic motifs are crossed and modified or even contradicted by Pater's intellectualistic strain: by his sense of art as craft and labor. He thought of "severe intellectual meditation" as the "salt of poetry" [122] and argued that "without a precise acquaintance with the creative intelligence itself, its structure and capacities . . . no poetry can be masterly." [123] He can even say that "the philosophical critic" (and here Pater himself is the philosophical critic) "will value, even in works of imagination seemingly the most intuitive, the power of understanding in them, their logical process of construction, the spectacle of a supreme intellectual dexterity which they afford." [124] Pater protests that with Schelling and Coleridge the artist "has become almost a mechanical agent: instead of the most luminous and self-possessed phase of consciousness, the associative act in art or poetry is made to look like some blindly organic process of assimilation." [125] Pater sees the particular task of his time as that of doing "consciously what has been done hitherto for the most part unconsciously, to write the English language as the Latins wrote theirs, as the French write, as scholars should write." [126] Only in the case of Wordsworth would he grant that the "old fancy which made the poet's art an enthusiasm, a form of divine possession, seems almost literally true." [127] But just this feeling that "the larger part was *given* passively" [128] explains the unevenness, the fitfulness, of Wordsworth's achievement.

On the question of style, however, Pater is not entirely on the side of labor and the search for the right word. The famous essay "On Style" (1889) consists of two rather abruptly joined parts: a defense of what could be called "ornate," "imaginative" prose, "the special art of the modern world," [129] and a discussion of Flaubert's views of style for which Pater draws not only on the *Correspondance* but also on Maupassant's Preface to *Lettres de G. Flaubert à G. Sand* (1884) . Pater first defends a personal style aimed at transcribing not "the world, not mere fact, but the sense of it." [130] The beauties of such a style will be not exclusively "pedestrian." "It will exert all the varied charms of poetry, down to the rhythm which as in Cicero, or Michelet, or Newman, at their best, gives its musical value to every syllable." [131] The names mentioned are extremely diverse, and neither Cicero nor Michelet conform to Pater's own ideal style. Pater seems to have learned something from Newman but even more from Ruskin and De Quincey. In vocabulary, he recommends a sensible eclecticism which will not be afraid to assimilate the phraseology of pictorial art, of German metaphysics, or of modern science, but this eclectic vocabulary must be used with restraint, with an economy of means, a sense of difficulty overcome.[132] His recommendation of a highly imaginative, rhythmic, personal prose drawing on a varied modern vocabulary is modified by his insistence on the classical virtue of restraint and a polished style achieved by intellectual labor. "In truth all art does but consist in the removal of surplusage." [133] This is a rule that would make havoc of many of those Pater would consider to be the greatest stylists. Pater's recommendation that a conscientious writer "be fully aware not only of all latent figurative texture in speech, but of the vague, lazy, half-forgotten personification" [134] and his conviction that in prose "structure is all important," that "mind is a necessity in style" are consistent with his stress on consciousness and labor. "Insight, foresight, retrospect," "design," "a true composition and not mere loose accretion," "constructive intelligence which is one of the forms of the imagination" [135] are variations on the same theme. But suddenly Pater sees the insufficiency of his intellectual criterion and begins to speak of "soul in style." He finds it in theological writings as diverse as the English Bible, the Prayer Book, Swedenborg's visions and the *Tracts of the Times*. Each of these writings has a "unity of atmosphere" rather than of design.[136]

The essay switches then to an exposition of Flaubert's theory of style. Pater obviously admires Flaubert's "martyrdom" and toil and agrees with the doctrine of *le mot juste*. He sympathizes with Flaubert's struggle against "facile poetry, facile art—art facile and flimsy," [137] though he does look for a moment in another direction to recognize the "charm of ease." [138] "Scott's facility, Flaubert's deeply pondered evocation of 'the phrase,' are equally good art." [139] This concession to a taste opposite from his own is wrung from him reluctantly, with a hidden envy for the easygoing master. On the question of the impersonal style, however, Pater had to decide against Flaubert. Style *is* the man; the "essence of all good style is expressiveness." [140] Expressiveness must not, however, be confused with subjectivity, with "the mere caprice, of the individual, which must soon transform [style] into mannerism." [141] The subjectivity must not only be faithful to the inner vision but widen it into something objective.

The essay concludes with a sudden *salto mortale*. Pater now draws a distinction between good and great art not according to form but according to matter:

> Thackeray's *Esmond,* surely, is greater art than *Vanity Fair,* by the greater dignity of its interests. It is on the quality of the matter it informs or controls, its compass, its variety, its alliance to great ends, or the depth of the note of revolt, or the largeness of hope in it, that the greatness of literary art depends, as the *Divine Comedy, Paradise Lost, Les Misérables, The English Bible,* are great art. Given the conditions I have tried to explain as constituting good art;—then, if it be devoted further to the increase of men's happiness, to the redemption of the oppressed, or the enlargement of our sympathies with each other, or to such presentment of new or old truth about ourselves and our relation to the world as may ennoble and fortify us in our sojourn here, or immediately, as with Dante, to the glory of God, it will be also great art; if, over and above those qualities I summed up as mind and soul—that colour and mystic perfume, and that reasonable structure, it has something of the soul of humanity in it, and finds its logical, its architectural place, in the great structure of human life.[142]

There could not be a fuller and more explicit revocation of Pater's earlier aestheticism. It is a recantation at the expense of any unified, coherent view of art. It gives up the earlier insight into the unity of matter and form, divides and distinguishes them again, and either introduces a double standard of judgment or shifts the burden of criticism to the subject matter. Pater ends in a dichotomy destructive of his own insights into the nature of art. It reminds one of the distinction drawn years later by T. S. Eliot between art and great art, the latter to be judged by its conformity to orthodoxy and tradition, and of Tolstoy's distinction between good universal art and the highest art flowing from the love of God. *Les Misérables* appears on both Pater's and Tolstoy's lists among the great works of literature, and Pater's phrases about "the increase of men's happiness, the redemption of the oppressed, the enlargement of our sympathies with each other, the soul of humanity" imply that he had now accepted art as an agency of sympathy and even of humanitarianism. He had returned to the Church. In his last days he wrote an essay on Pascal, who interested him "as precisely an inversion of what is called the aesthetic life." [143]

It is true, however, that even in his last stage Pater preserved the fundamental critical insight of his time, the historical sense. In fact he seems to have accepted Christianity and specifically the Anglican Church out of this sense of history. He criticizes Amiel in 1886 for "shrinking from the concrete," for "his fear of the actual, in this case the Church of history." [144] "By failure, as we think, of that historic sense, of which he could speak so well, he got not further than the glacial condition of rationalistic Geneva." [145] The implication that Pater himself had reached a warmer place seems obvious. But Pater had come a long way before he could apply the historical sense to the purposes of apologetics. The late religious moment of Pater's career is hardly represented in his literary criticism. To analyze the concept of history in Pater we need to turn back to the earlier phases.

In his very first essay, he had criticized Coleridge for "the dulness of his historical sense," [146] for getting involved in difficulties "which fade away before the modern or relative spirit, which, in the moral world as in the physical traces everywhere change, growth, development." [147] "Truth is a thing fugitive, relative, full of fine gradations." Coleridge was mistaken when he "tried to fix it in absolute formulas." [148] Relativism applies also to art. "All beauty is relative." [149] Everything changes and passes, develops and progresses. Pater was pleased with the Darwinian theory. "The idea of development," he says approvingly, "is at last invading . . . all the products of mind, the very mind itself, the abstract reason; our certainty, for instance, that two and two make four. Gradually, we have come to think, or to feel, that primary certitude. Political constitutions, again, as we now see so clearly, are 'not made,' cannot be made, but 'grow.' Races, laws, arts, have their origins and end, are themselves ripples only on the great river of organic life; and language is changing on our very lips." [150] The evolutionary theory—Hegelian and Darwinian—confirms the old Heracliteanism, the *panta rhei*,[151] Pater's fundamental experience of the flux of time. What to him personally was a tragic experience of the transience of all things he accepts as part of a cosmic scheme in which he, as a good Victorian, still sees "the dominant undercurrent of progress in things." [152]

Pater inherits from German historicism the belief and emphasis on *Zeitgeist*. The artist is "a child of his time." [153] There is a genius of an age, and art and literature "must follow the subtle movements of that nimbly shifting Time-Spirit or Zeitgeist." [154] In every age "there is a peculiar *ensemble* of conditions which determines a common character in every product of that age, in business and art, in fashion and speculation, in religion and manners, in men's very faces . . . nothing man has projected from himself is really intelligible except at its own date, and from its proper point of view in the never-resting 'secular process.' " [155] No wonder he can say of the historical spirit that "the scholar is nothing without it." [156]

At other times, however, Pater will argue against the purely "historical," antiquarian view in favor of an "individual," present-day relativism. Speaking of Du Bellay, he says that if a poet's work is to have "an aesthetic as distinct from an historical value, it is not enough for a poet to have been the true child of his age, to have conformed to its aesthetic conditions, and by so conforming to have charmed and stimulated that age; it is necessary that there should be perceptible in his work something individual, inventive, unique, the impress there of the writer's own temper and personality." [157] Here Pater does not appeal to any absolute standard; he rather abandons the criterion of historical success or representativeness in favor of personal impression and pleasure.

At other times it is with a somewhat different accent that he rejects the view that modern man can somehow transform himself in order to become an ancient in imagination. "Such an antiquarianism," he feels, "is a waste of power. The composite experience of all the ages is part of each of us; to deduct from that experience, to obliterate any part of it, to come face to face with the people of a past age, as if the Middle Ages, the Renaissance, the eighteenth century had not been, is as impossible as to become a little child, or enter again into the womb and be born." [158] What has been called historical reconstructionism is rejected in favor of a fuller, wider universal historicism.

In the early essay on Winckelmann, Pater had still accepted "a standard of taste, an element of permanence, fixed in Greece." [159] When in that essay he reproduced Hegel's scheme of evolution in the arts—the triad of symbolical, classical, and romantic art—he shared Hegel's (and Winckelmann's and Goethe's) view that classical art is exempt from time and sets an absolute standard. But the view that the classical tradition is "the orthodoxy of taste" [160] did not last. Pater's later Hellenism is a historical Hellenism, which sees Greece as a past stage of human culture that cannot be revived today. Though in his actual critical practice his preferences for the Greeks, for the Renaissance, and for the romantics are so strong that they exclude any interest in the genuinely medieval, the baroque, or the neoclassical, in his theorizing Pater accepts the full consequence of historicism. "All periods, types, schools of taste are in themselves equal." [161] He proclaims for his own time the role of "eclecticism," [162] as he had, in *The Renaissance,* admired the syncretism of Christianity and paganism propounded by Pico della Mirandola. What Pater wants for himself and his time is humanism, "the belief that nothing which has ever interested living men and women can wholly lose its vitality," [163] a feeling for the totality of the past, which is still alive in us:

> For in truth we come into the world, each one of us, 'not in nakedness,' but by the natural course of organic development clothed far more completely than even Pythagoras supposed in a vesture of the past, nay, fatally shrouded, it might seem, in those laws or tricks of heredity which we mistake for our volitions; in the language which is more than one half of our thoughts; in the moral and mental habits, the customs, the literature, the very houses, which we did not make for ourselves; in the vesture of a past, which is (so science would assure us) not ours, but of the race, the species: that *Zeit-geist,* or abstract secular process.[164]

Pater found another image in Bunyan's *Pilgrim's Progress* for this living past. He speaks of the *House Beautiful* "which the creative minds of all generations—the artists and those who have treated life in the spirit of art—are always building together." In it the oppositions between styles and types, classical and romantic, cease. "The Interpreter of the *House Beautiful,* the true aesthetic critic, uses these divisions, only so far as they enable him to enter into the peculiarities of the objects with which he has to do." [165] In our age "we must try to unite as many diverse elements as may be." "The individual writer or artist, certainly, is to be estimated by the number of graces he combines, and his power of interpenetrating them in a given work . . . The legitimate contention is, not of one age or school of literary art against another, but of all successive schools alike, against the stupidity which is dead to the substance, and the vulgarity which is dead to form." [166]

Ernst Robert Curtius has called these words

> a landmark in the history of literary criticism: they signify a breakthrough to a new freedom. The tyranny of Standard Classicism is surmounted. Obedience to the rules and imitation of model authors no longer bestows any right to a good grade. Only the creative minds count. The concept of tradition is not abandoned in consequence, it is transformed. A community of the great authors throughout the centuries must be maintained if a kingdom of the mind is to exist at all. But it can only be the community of creative minds. This is a new kind of selection—a canon if you like, but bound only by the idea of beauty, concerning which we know that its forms change and are renewed. That is why the House Beautiful is never finished and closed. It continues to be built, it remains open.[167]

But it seems to me that Pater's House Beautiful has not escaped, and none of Pater's work has escaped the limitations of 19th-century aestheticism, its hectic cult of Beauty (a very narrow and exclusive type of beauty), its Alexandrian eclecticism, which made it impossible for the age to create a style of its own and which encouraged a historical masquerade. Historicism had to be transcended, as it has been during more recent years in Eliot's concept of tradition or in Malraux's imaginary museum.

WE CAN SPEAK of the pervasive influence of Swinburne and Pater in their time. But as soon as we examine critics closely and analyze their intellectual positions with care, we recognize how various the Victorian critics were, how sharply they asserted their individuality, and how distinctly they used and combined ideas of the most various provenience. It will be best to discuss them independently of each other.

JOHN ADDINGTON SYMONDS (1840–1893)

In extensive critical and historical works John Addington Symonds achieved an apparently easy symbiosis of the most diverse elements of thought. They have the impress of a personality that has attracted psychological biographers as recently as Van Wyck Brooks. But even the sympathetic Brooks had to confess an "ultimate defect of power; and also a defect of coherence" [1] that made Symonds recede into a limbo of semi-oblivion. But the neglect is not altogether deserved and seems mainly due to secondary causes—the prolixity of much of his writings and the present-day reaction against his preoccupation with the evolutionary explanation of the process of literature. Still, there is a valuable core of critical thought in Symonds.

The view that Symonds is a follower of Pater or an "aesthete" is quite mistaken. Symonds definitely rejected the art-for-art's-sake point of view. "Art," he tells us, "exists for humanity." [2] Pater's style had "a peculiarly disagreeable effect upon my nerves (like the presence of a civet cat) " or like getting lost "in a sugar-cane plantation." Symonds' admiration for Swinburne did not extend to his criticism. The reasoning of the book on Blake he characterized as "insolent, irrational, and paradoxical—the feeling bad (as bad as the taste) ." [3] There are, however, passages of precious metaphorical writing in Symonds which sound like Swinburne or Pater. There is, for example, a florid address to "this country-lass—the bride-elect of Shakspere's genius." [4] There is a passage about the "Muse of Tourneur" who "wears no evergreens of singing, nay, no yew-boughs even, on her forehead. Her dusty eyes sparkle with sharp metallic scintillations." [5] There is an odd comparison of *The Yorkshire Tragedy* with an asp, "short, ash-coloured, poison-fanged, blunt-headed, abrupt in movement, hissing and wriggling through the sands of human misery." [6] But such purple patches, which seem to us precious and irrelevant, are exceptions almost as rare as they are in Pater.

The bulk of Symonds' work is intellectual and rational in style and even scientific in pretension. Symonds expounds a cosmic evolutionism, a modernized Hegelianism. As early as 1867 he proposed to do a version of Hegel's *Aesthetics* and prophesied (with an unfortunate degree of accuracy) that he would "end with being what the French call a *polygraphe féconde*—a Jack of all trades, aesthetical, and a humbug who has gorged and disgorged Hegel." [7] But he seems to have studied the text of Hegel's *Aesthetics* not until 1875, admiring it but complaining that it did not train the taste.[8] Clearly, Hegelianism and a cosmic pantheism, nourished by Wordsworth, Goethe, and Whitman, are the philosophical background for Symonds' evolutionary theory of the history of art and literature. The theory is expounded best in the essay "On the Application of Evolutionary Principles to Art and Literature" in *Essays Speculative and Suggestive* (1890), but was sketched in outlines in his diary in 1865 [9] and animated all of Symonds' histories: *Studies of the Greek Poets* (2 vols. 1873, 1876), *The Renaissance in Italy* (7 vols. 1875–86), and *Shakspere's Predecessors in the English Drama* (1884). This last book was actually Symonds' first: he worked at it in the sixties and published two long chapters in 1865 and 1867.[10]

Long before Brunetière, Symonds conceived of the evolution of art, or rather of a specific artform in one nation and one period, as a life-cycle comparable to that of a living individual, running a well-defined, unalterable, and irreversible course through birth, adolescence, maturity, decline, and death. Symonds argues that "criticism has hitherto neglected the real issues of what is meant by development in art and literature." "We are indeed familiar with phrases like 'rise and decline,' 'flourishing period,' 'infancy of art.'

But the inevitable progression from the embryo through ascending stages, of growth and maturity by declining stages to decrepitude and dissolution has not been sufficiently insisted on." [11] Symonds recognizes that his scheme "shifts the centre of gravity from men as personalities to men as exponents of their race and age." He describes the process constantly in deliberately impersonal terms. "The form appears to emerge spontaneously from the spirit of the nation as a whole," and "individual genius is incapable of altering the sequence." [12]

Symonds' prime example is the history of Elizabethan drama. The whole volume on *Shakspere's Predecessors in the English Drama* is devoted to this proposition. The miracle play—a type common to all European nations—is conceived as reaching a state of dissolution. From it "certain episodes detached themselves." "Comedy found its germ in the lighter scenes." [13] The morality play contributed to the dissolution of the ancient structure of the drama. The romantic drama emerged, passed with "astonishing speed to fixity in Marlowe, to perfection in Shakespeare, to over-ripeness in Beaumont and Fletcher, to decadence in Davenant." [14] Exactly the same process is illustrated by the course of Attic drama from Aeschylus to Euripides, by Greek sculpture, by Gothic architecture, by Italian painting from Giotto to the last Mannerists in Bologna, and by Italian romantic poetry. Italian romance "originated with obscure street-singers of Roland, to which Boccaccio contributed form, which Pulci and Boiardo had developed . . . which Ariosto had perfected, which Tasso attempted to handle, in a novel spirit, and from which Marino wrung the very last drops of life-sap." [15] The history of all the arts thus yields the confirmation of a single process, of one ever-recurring pattern.

Symonds admits only one alternative—the idea of the "hybrid" or "hybridization." Hybrids do not obey the same "laws of evolutionary progress as the specific art-growths of a single race and a continuous era." They lack "evolutionary energy," are almost invariably "stationary." [16] Roman art is Symonds' prime example, but "rare" Ben Jonson is also a literary hybrid, a cross between romantic drama and humanism,[17] and the 19th century is the age of hybrids *par excellence.* The novel is "no less certainly a hybridisable genus than the Orchis." It has become "a mongrel of many types." [18] In an elaborate comparison of Victorian poetry with Elizabethan,

Symonds comes to the conclusion that "no type, like the drama of the sixteenth century, has controlled its movements," that "we cannot regard it as a totality composed of many parts, progressing through several stages of development." Victorian poetry is in large measure the criticism of all existing literatures. The genius of the age is scientific, not artistic. "In such an age poetry must perforce be an auxiliary to science," a mere reflection of the "revolution of thought which history, philosophy, and criticism are effecting." [19]

Symonds recognizes that this evolutionary scheme raises the question of criticism in its most acute form. If we are in truth confronted with an inevitable cycle, criticism ceases to have any judicial function. "It is as absurd to blame Thespis because he was uncouth, as to blame a stalk because it is stalky, as unscientific to condemn Chaeremon because he left nothing after him, as it is to condemn a husk because it is husky." [20] The analogy with a plant must lead to universal tolerance. It is impossible to criticize youth for being young, or old age for being close to death. Symonds' ideal is criticism as science or, at least, scientific; he comments favorably on Taine and Hennequin.[21] But it seems to me greatly to Symonds' credit that he was not satisfied with a criticism that would merely place a work in the evolutionary scheme. He pleads as a first step that "this toleration and acceptance of unavoidable change need not imply want of discriminate perception. We can apply the evolutionary canon in all strictness without ignoring that manhood is preferable to senile decrepitude, that Pheidias surpasses the sculptors of Antinous, that one Madonna of Gian Bellini is worth all the pictures of the younger Palma." [22] He cannot see, at this stage of the argument, that such judgments about youth and age are actually judgments of taste, that the taste that condemns the baroque as decadent is based not on an objective fact, such as physical decline, but on an act of aesthetic judgment. But Symonds sees, at least, that "not in evolution but in man's soul, his intellectual and moral nature, must be sought those abiding relations which constitute sound art, and are the test of right aesthetic judgment." The critic, therefore, cannot be confined by history. "He must divert his mind from what is transient and ephemeral, must fasten upon abiding relations, *bleibende Verhältnisse.*" [23]

There are three types of critics: the judge, the showman, and the natural historian of art and literature. The judge is the old neoclassical critic who judges by principles and by decisions of his predecessors—Aristotle, Longinus, Horace, Aristarchus, Boileau. The showman is the romantic critic who judges by his own preference and proclivities, points out beauties, and reproduces masterpieces with engaging rhetoric or by eloquently exhibiting his own sensibilities in animated prose.[24] The scientific analyst is the morphological historian who provides the skeleton frame for all of Symonds' histories. But this scientific analyst, who seems to represent the highest type of criticism, does not finally satisfy Symonds' demands: the true critic must combine all three types in himself. "He cannot abnegate the right to judge—he cannot divest himself of subjective tastes which colour his judgment: but it is his supreme duty to train his faculty of judgment and to temper his subjectivity by the study of things in their historical connections."[25] Ultimately Symonds admits that "criticism is not of the same nature as science." It can only be exercised in a scientific spirit. We need guard against "subjective fancies, paradoxes of opinions, and over-subtleties of ingenuity."[26] Our subjectivity is a perpetual source of danger, but mere knowledge of objective fact, mere learning, does not supply the critical faculty. Common sense, prudence, shrewdness, the power of weighing evidence are the main qualities of the critic, and "sense, in the region of criticism, is equivalent to imagination." What we are finally left with is the "trained perception in a man endowed with common sense and sound imagination" and the "consensus of wise men," which is needed to establish "taste."[27] The consensus of such verdicts eventually forms that voice of the people which, according to the old proverb, is the voice of God.[28]

Symonds, in his practice, tried to live up to the demands of his excellent theory of criticism. He wanted to do all three things: to judge, to appreciate, and to trace the evolution of art. He was attracted mainly by two modern literatures: Italian, from Dante to Tasso, and Elizabethan. The books on Shelley and Whitman are peripheral. *Shelley* (1878) is an undistinguished biography written before Dowden's. Only the epilogue contains criticism: praise for the poet of "ideality, freedom and spiritual audacity," and some blame of "haste, incoherence, verbal carelessness, incompleteness, a want of narrative force, and a weak hold on objective realities."[29] *Walt Whitman: A Study* (1893) is the late payment of a debt of gratitude. Symonds felt that at the lowest point of his life, in a

Slough of Despond induced by the crisis of his lifelong illness, pulmonary tuberculosis, Whitman's "almost brutal optimism" saved him from despair and added "conviction, courage, self-reliance to his sense of the Cosmic enthusiasm." [30] Whitman's religion "shone upon me, when my life was broken, when I was weak, sickly, poor, and of no account: and I have ever lived thenceforward in the light and warmth of it." [31] Symonds' interest in Whitman is almost wholly ideological. Whitman confirmed his evolutionary pantheism and raised the question of homosexuality, which disturbed Symonds deeply.[32] Symonds elicited from Whitman the well-known letter boasting of six illegitimate children which convinced him that "what Whitman calls the 'adhesiveness' of comradeship is meant to have no inblending with the 'amativeness' of sexual love." [33]

Symonds' literary enthusiasm went out very early to the Italians, to Dante and his forerunners, to Petrarch, Boccaccio, Poliziano, Ariosto, and Michelangelo, all of whom Symonds translated with skill and understanding and interpreted with imaginative sympathy. His first full-length book, *An Introduction to the Study of Dante* (1872) has the expository skill, the luminosity of description, and the power of evocation of almost all his later books, but it has also the basic defects: the burden of elementary information and the disturbing unoriginality of the central critical conception. At times Symonds does little more than embroider on the lecture on Dante in Carlyle's *Of Heroes and Hero-worship*. He plays variations on Dante's piercing into the deep, his symmetry, his intensity, his earnestness, his representativeness, preferring, like Carlyle, the later *cantiche*. The dependence goes so far that Symonds reproduces Carlyle's image of Francesca da Rimini as "a thing woven as out of rainbows on a ground of eternal black." [34]

This descriptive and compilatory procedure mars also the volumes devoted to literature of *The Renaissance in Italy*. Volumes 4 and 5 (1881) of the seven-volume work are a history of Italian literature from its beginnings to the end of the Renaissance, and the second volume of *The Catholic Reaction* (1886) —the seventh and last of the series—is half-concerned with literature, with Tasso, Bruno, Sarpi, Marino, Chiabrera, and Tassoni. These volumes thus constitute by far the largest history in English of Italian literature of the great centuries. It would be unjust to deny that Symonds gives abundant information, many excellent translations and aptly chosen quotations, and often lively evocative accounts of the main works. The over-all scheme of the usual evolutionary cycle is not rigidly imposed on every detail. The detail is drawn from the texts themselves and from a study of Italian scholarship, from Bartoli, Rajna, Villari, and many other sources. The scholarship of the Italians is used diligently, though not always with discrimination or insight into the issues. Symonds, who worked under difficult conditions, mainly in the Engadin, could only rarely descend to Italy to use the libraries for any length of time and hardly engaged in firsthand research. On the other hand, he also lacked De Sanctis' bold power of historical schematization and direct critical presentation. When Symonds raises serious critical questions, he often has recourse to De Sanctis, though he refers to him expressly in only a few instances, more often alludes to him, and sometimes reproduces him—even in particular phrases—without proper acknowledgment.[35] But the influence of De Sanctis, though undeniable, is not strong enough or pervasive enough to describe Symonds' work as an adaptation of De Sanctis. Symonds can use with equal ease the scheme of the three peoples in Florence from Carducci's lectures on the *Development of the National Literature*.[36] He assimilates so much material from other sources, expounds so much, and describes so many texts that the specific features of De Sanctis' historical scheme and critical insights are obliterated. Symonds' book has aged far more rapidly than De Sanctis'—it lacks the focus and style achieved by De Sanctis and achieved by Symonds himself in his *Shakspere's Predecessors in the English Drama* (1884).

In *Shakspere's Predecessors* Symonds succeeds in combining his evolutionary scheme with exposition, evocation, and criticism of his texts. Since nature does not proceed by leaps and bounds, the scheme requires emphasis on the regularity of progression, on the gradualness of transitions.[37] It requires emphasis on the independence of Elizabethan drama from foreign interference.[38] Symonds makes every effort to define the peculiar contribution of each author to the evolution of Elizabethan drama and to argue his general thesis that Shakespeare inherited a fixed dramatic form, that Shakespeare became possible through the preparatory work of his predecessors.[39] Symonds easily blends this evolutionary scheme with a stress on English nationality and the romantic nature of Elizabethan drama and with a view of the Renaissance that seems to be colored by Taine's flushed pictures of the English noble savage.[40] Symonds draws from Taine the emphasis on the Nordic character of English literature: there is a "deep, Teutonic meditative melancholy" in Elizabethan drama. Comedy in England precedes tragedy because the Northern nations incline naturally to "grotesqueness," and Faust is well suited to the English because he is Northern, Teutonic, and even "of Beowulf's posterity." [41]

Fortunately, neither the evolutionary scheme nor the racial theory can corrupt Symonds' taste and insight into historical relationships. In spite of all the stress on the indigenous development and the peculiarly national character of the Elizabethan drama, Symonds sees correctly that the secular drama was, after all, not a lineal successor of the liturgical drama—that the decisive event was the contact with Italian culture.[42] He draws the parallel to the Italian *farsa* even too closely. He elaborately traces the Continental analogues to Euphuism, conscious even of the direct influence of Guevara.[43] He suggests the similarity between Nashe and Aretino, recognizes the influence of *versi sciolti* on English blank verse, and knows, of course, of Italian Renaissance tragedy, comedy, and masques as models for the Elizabethan types.[44] He classifies, describes, and evaluates the pre-Shakespearean drama with his eye on the object: suggesting, for instance, three stages of Elizabethan realism, analyzing the style of Lyly in some detail, and defining the leading motive of Marlowe as *L'Amour de l'Impossible*.[45] We may feel that Symonds sees Marlowe's plays too much as reflections of the poet's personal dreams, but one cannot deny that Symonds raises pertinent questions about the plays. Thus he asks about the end of *Faustus* whether Marlowe was, after all, an "ill-contented, heartsick atheist." [46] *Shakspere's Predecessors in the English Drama* is Symonds' best book: it reflects the peculiar combination of scientific evolutionism with evocative description and good appreciative criticism; it is one of the few great achievements of English literary historiography in the 19th century.

OSCAR WILDE (1854-1900)

In the terrible accusing letter to Lord Alfred Douglas known as *De Profundis* (1897), Wilde speaks of himself as a "man who stood in symbolic relations to the art and culture of his age." "I made art a philosophy and philosophy an art . . . I treated art as the supreme reality and life as a mere mode of fiction; I awoke the imagination of my century so that it created myth and legend around me." Wilde felt that he had become the martyr of aestheticism, the scapegoat of a society enraged by the worship of beauty and art for art's sake. But in the same letter he recognized that "everything about my tragedy has been hideous, mean, repellent, lacking in style," and that "the one disgraceful, unpardonable, and to all time contemptible action of my life was to allow myself to appeal to Society for help and protection." [1] Today, with the transcript of Wilde's trials in print and a knowledge of Wilde's last years in Paris, we can say that Wilde was condemned for violating a paragraph of the criminal code and that he brought about his imprisonment by the reckless suit he initiated and by the almost suicidal resignation which came over him when he could have escaped. Wilde, one could argue, was not a martyr of art and the aesthetic life at all, unless one deliberately confuses art with sexual deviation. The Philistine enemies of the artists welcomed this confusion, but the cause for the genuine freedom of the artist was hurt rather than helped by Wilde's sordid tragedy.

Still, this myth or legend gives to Wilde's ideas on art and literature a historical position which they may not deserve in a history of criticism, apart from the personality and the pitiful fate of the man. Obviously Wilde's ideas are anything but new and can be easily traced to their sources in Pater, Swinburne, Arnold, Gautier, Baudelaire, and Poe.[2] There is no need to cite Wilde's fervent acknowledgments to his Oxford masters or to refer to his laudatory reviews of *Appreciations* and *Imaginary Portraits*.[3] The admiration for Pater colors all of Wilde's critical work: but the relationship is surely seen falsely if one speaks of plagiarism or even of imitation. Wilde's early lectures in the United States (1882) were those of an avowed propagandist of a creed, of a missionary to the heathens. "The English Renaissance in Art," delivered first in New York, is an exuberant statement of hope and a profession of allegiance to the great men at home. Wilde traces the aesthetic movement from Keats and Shelley, through Ruskin and the pre-Raphaelites, to Morris and Pater. Quotations from Goethe, Heine, Baudelaire, and Gautier buttress the argument. We are supposed to recognize the paraphrases of Pater, the canonical texts about self-development, the distinction between art and morals, the search for "experience itself rather than the fruits of experience." Insolently or naively, Wilde, in the costume of a dandy, asks his American audience for help in creating a "beautiful national life" defiant of Victorian ugliness and English commercialism.[4]

For two years (1887–89) Wilde was the editor of *The Woman's World,* for which he wrote many articles on home decoration, dress-reform, tapestry, embroidery, lace, and bookbinding and reviewed many totally forgotten novels, mostly by women, with kindness and wit. It is journalism—often charming and gracious work—which could be ignored as ephemeral.

Even Wilde's later volume of dialogues and essays, *Intentions* (1890), merely restates with greater brilliance and wit the main ideas he had absorbed from Pater. The continuity from the early reviews to the mature work is uninterrupted. Whole passages are taken over verbatim.[5] We might feel tempted to dismiss Wilde as a figure in social history, a propagandist for the ideas of his predecessors.

Still, there are valid reasons for a deeper interest in Wilde's critical thought. We must take him seriously, if not literally, when he claims that "the way of paradoxes is the way of truth. To test Reality we must see it on the tight-rope. When the Verities become acrobats we can judge them." [6] The very extremism of his formulas, the scintillating wit, the inverting of commonplaces, the studied anticlimaxes shock us into an awareness of issues often hidden by reasonable argumentation conscientiously weighing the pros and cons. Yet, paradox and acrobatic juggling are double-edged devices: they may become automatic and even mechanical and thus obscure the truth of many individual ideas. There is, however, solid brain-work under the glittering surface of Wilde's prose, an ingenious play of mind, and a quick grasp of many verities. The difficulty is that he disconcertingly shifts between three often divergent views: panaestheticism, the autonomy of art, and a decorative formalism. He does not hold his vision steady.

Sometimes Wilde propounds a view that can be labeled "pan-aestheticism": Art embraces all life, art is the standard of life, and life is to be lived for the sake of art. It differs profoundly from the art-for-art's-sake view that asserts the complete autonomy of art, protests against interference in its realm, and retires to the ivory tower. The former point of view—which he sees anticipated by the Greeks, by Goethe, and by Pater—is rather the opposite: the conquest of life and reality by art. Wilde exalts "aesthetics as higher than ethics" [7] and imposes artistic criteria even on government. In the essay "The Soul of Man under Socialism" (1890) he argues that the ideal self-development of man is likely to be achieved under socialism. But Wilde's socialism has little to do with Marxism: it is rather anarchism, extreme individualism that is "socialist" only because Wilde welcomes the abolition of private property and the withering away of the state. "The form of government that is most suitable to the artist is no government at all." [8] Wilde's Utopia still is a collective Utopia, since he wants *all* life and *all* its manifestations to be beautiful. Ruskin and Morris loom behind him. Furniture, dress, buildings, towns, should be beautified. A pre-Raphaelite medievalism agrees easily with a New Hellenism. The actual political and social changes that could bring about such an idyll are not envisaged concretely—even less so than by Ruskin and Morris. There is no radical change in Wilde's ideals when, in prison, he added Jesus Christ as a model for life. Christ is seen through Renan's *La Vie de Jésus*: as a romantic temperament, as the "palpitating centre of romance." Christ said that we should live "flower-like lives" and preached the "importance of living completely for the moment." Wilde can go so far as to say about Christ that "he is just like a work of art." [9] Wilde's ideal remains a variation of hedonism, though sorrow, sympathy, and even martyrdom are now included as part of man's schooling. The extreme individualism remains the same. It is an almost hallucinatory idealism, a desperate sense of the unreality of the world, of man's imprisonment within his senses. Logically it leads to the exaltation of the life of contemplation, to quietism, to the philosophy of Taoism, which Wilde had come to know from a translation of the sayings of Chuang-tzu.

If man is trapped in his ego, the view that life and nature imitate art will be less paradoxical than it seems. Beauty is purely subjective and relative. The artist projects himself, creates his world. The best-known passages in the "Decay of Lying" wittily state what are, after all, empirical truths. Life imitates art in the sense that "a great artist invents a type, and Life tries to copy it." Only after Rossetti painted them does one see women with long ivory throats, strange square-cut jaws, and loosened shadowy hair. "The world has become sad because a puppet [Hamlet] was once melancholy." "Young men have committed suicide because Rolla did so." Women have lived the life of a heroine in a magazine serial. And similarly nature imitates art. "Where, if not from the Impressionists, do we get those wonderful brown fogs that come creeping down our streets, blurring the gas-lamps and changing the houses into monstrous shadows?" Nature is our creation. Things are because we see them, and what we see and how we see it depends on the arts that have influenced us. "To look at a thing is very different from seeing a thing. One does not see anything until one sees its beauty." Surely it is not merely a witticism to say that "sunsets are quite old-fashioned," or that nature shows us "a very second-rate Turner, a Turner of a bad period." [10] Less paradoxically, Wilde can see the profound effect of art on life: its disturbing mission and disintegrating force against the monotony of type, the slavery of custom, the tyranny of habit.[11] "Literature always anticipates life. It does not copy it, but moulds it to its purpose." "Life is terribly deficient in form" [12] and art is here to correct it: a view which is only an overstatement of old classical ideas on the function of art as idealization.

This panaestheticism, however, is not held by Wilde as consistently as the legend assumes. He defends the dominance of art over morals only half-heartedly and even shamefacedly. The flippant praise of Wainewright, the poisoner, in "Pen, Pencil and Poison" cannot be taken seriously. *The Picture of Dorian Gray* presents rather an allegory of moral corruption and its punishment than a defense of the aesthetic life. Even the imitation of art by life and nature is upheld only as a paradoxical formula for the influence of art on life and our mode of seeing nature: not as an actual advocacy of art doing violence to nature and transforming life. Rather, most frequently, Wilde upholds the autonomy of art, the apartness of art from life, nature, and morals. It is the paradox of Victorian aestheticism that Ruskin and Morris wanted to revolutionize society and all the things in it and that finally they and their followers succeeded only in establishing a new decorative style: the Oxford Museum, the Kelmscott Press, the Morris chair, the stained-glass windows in Exeter College. Similarly, Wilde most often shuts out the world and plays with decorative arabesques. Art for art's sake means largely a defense of art against the demands of the moralist, a rejection of all censorship by the state or the public, an assertion of the proud independence of art and its right to any and all subject matter. What sounds like the most imperialist claim for art, in practice, often shrinks to a defense of its inviolate corner in life. "Art has no influence upon action. It annihilates the desire to act. It is superbly sterile," says Lord Henry.[13]

Still, as a theorist of art Wilde shows an extraordinarily clear grasp of the main tenets of the great idealist tradition. He knows that art achieves its perfection in the unity of form and content. "Form and substance cannot be separated in a work of art: they are always one. But for the purposes of analysis, and setting the wholeness of aesthetic impression aside for the moment, intellectually we can so separate them." [14] "Every work of art is the conversion of an idea into an image." In art "the outward is rendered expressive of the inward: the soul made incarnate: the body instinct with spirit." [15] Wilde thus sees clearly the falsity of two rival theories: realism and romantic emotionalism. Realism seems to Wilde "a complete failure" as a method. He protests that "the modern novelist presents us with dull facts under the guise of fiction. He has his tedious *'document humain,'* his miserable little *'coin de la création,'* into which he peers with his microscope." [16] Wilde detests Zola and his imitators, and he has his misgivings about psychological realism. He does not care for Henry James, "his mean motives and imperceptible 'points of view.'" The "realism of Paris filters through the refining influence of Boston"—analysis, not action, psychology rather than passion, vivisection, explanation rather than imagination.[17] Against the naturalists and realists Wilde upholds Balzac for his "imaginative reality," and, in spite of some damaging witticisms, he admires Meredith and Browning.[18] *La Peau de Chagrin* was in Wilde's mind when he wrote *The Picture of Dorian Gray.* The new romance of Stevenson, the "poisonous" book of Huysmans, *À Rebours,* and the early plays of Maeterlinck influenced his own practice.

But this new romanticism ought to be, in aim at least, objective and contrived rather than effusive. Wilde asserts that "all bad poetry springs from genuine feeling." "Style, not sincerity, is the essential" and "insincerity is a method to multiply our personalities." [19] Wilde writes an essay called "The Truth of Masks" and feels that "a mask tells us more than a face." He defends Chatterton: all art is to a certain degree "a form of acting, an attempt to realize one's own personality on some imaginative plane out of the reach of the trammeling accidents and limitations of real life." [20] He says the same when he calls "technique really personality" [21] and recognizes the intentional fallacy. "In art good intentions are not of the smallest value. All bad art is the result of good intentions." What counts are only "realized creations." [22] In his finest moments Wilde grasps the dialectics of art: the union of content and form, technique and personality, the subjective and the objective, the conscious and the unconscious, and sees that only in art criticism can we "realize Hegel's system of contraries." [23]

Wilde frequently lapses from such a grasp of art into what one must call a false formalism. Instead of the unity of form and content, an empty decorative form is exalted. Instead of seeing the proper balance of the conscious and unconscious in creation, he can recommend mere craftsmanship, virtuosity, and sheer contrivance. Instead of recognizing the transforming and idealizing power of art, he can divorce it completely from reality, society, and history. Finally, in his best-known essay, "The Critic as Artist," Wilde propounds a theory of criticism that goes beyond the demands of sympathy, to ask for a criticism that would be a second creation. Criticism in Wilde ceases to have a necessary relation to its object; it becomes autobiography, caprice, willful fantasy.

In his discussion of painting, Wilde often conceives of form as entirely apart from content. He can defend painting without overt subject matter and nonimitative, decorative art. Analogously he can depreciate subject in literature not only as immaterial but as indifferent morally, forgetting his best insights into the unity of form and content. "The highest art rejects the burden of the human spirit, and gains more from a new medium or a fresh material than she does from any enthusiasm for art, or from any lofty passion, or from any great awakening of the human consciousness." [24] "Virtue and wickedness are to him simply what colours on his palette are to the painter." "Vice and virtue are to the artist materials for an art." [25] "The real artist is he who proceeds, not from feeling to form, but from form to thought and passion." "He gains his inspiration from form, and from form purely." "Form is the beginning of things." "Form, which is the birth of passion, is also the death of pain." [26] What matters is workmanship, technique, craft. Wilde was deeply impressed by Poe's "Philosophy of Composition" [27] and rightly declares all fine imaginative work self-conscious and deliberate: but he consistently underrates the role of the unconscious. In some moods he can see art as part of history and society, in others he can deny the relation: art is remote from its age. "A true artist takes no notice of the public." He cannot "live with the people." "Art is not symbolic of any age." "In no case does it reproduce its age. To pass from the art of a time to the time itself is the great mistake that all historians commit." [28]

In his theory of criticism Wilde went farthest in the direction of irresponsible subjectivity. In "The Critic as Artist" he argues for creative criticism: criticism is itself an art which need not bother with a standard of resemblance. Criticism is creation within a creation: it has "least reference to any standard external to itself, and is, in fact, its own reason for existing, and, as the Greeks would put it, in itself, and to itself, an end." The highest criticism really is the record of one's own soul. It is the only civilized form of autobiography. The critic's sole aim is to chronicle his own impressions. Arnold's phrase about "seeing the object as in itself it really is" errs seriously because criticism is purely subjective. Criticism treats the work of art simply as a starting point for a new creation, for "the meaning of any beautiful created thing is, at least, as much in the soul of him who looks at it, as it was in his soul who wrought it." To the critic the work of art is simply a suggestion for new work of his own, that need not necessarily bear any obvious resemblance to the thing it criticizes. A little later Wilde's mouthpiece concedes that "some resemblance, no doubt, the creative work of the critic will have to the work that has stirred him to creation, but it will be such resemblance as exists between Nature and the work of the decorative artist." The aim of the critic is not elucidation: "He may seek rather to deepen its mystery, to raise round it, and round its maker, that mist of wonder which is dear to both gods and worshippers alike." [29] Pater's Mona Lisa passage is an admired model. Wilde saw his own essays as works of art; they were dialogues and hence dramatic fictions. His novel *The Picture of Dorian Gray* is also criticism, and "The Portrait of Mr. W. H." is both fiction and criticism.

But Wilde's obliteration of the difference between creation and criticism is untenable and inconsistent. It is not clear how such criticism could or should replace creation as he prophesies. In effect, the plea for creative criticism often amounts to an advocacy of reasonable and modest things: of fidelity to our impressions, of a recognition that the meaning of a work of art is inexhaustible, and an enmity to false objectivity, colorless tolerance, and provincial complacency. Wilde pleads for the temperament of the critic, against the superstition of objectivity. "A critic cannot be fair in the ordinary sense of the word. The man who sees both sides of a question is a man who sees absolutely nothing at all. It is only an auctioneer who can equally and impartially admire all schools of Art." Wilde rightly sees the dialectics of subjectivity and objectivity: "It is only by intensifying his own personality that the critic can interpret the personality and work of others." [30] The purely subjective caprice implied in several of these statements is actually abandoned: a standard of empathy and even historical imagination is postulated in most other contexts. In praising Pater's *Appreciations* Wilde sounds like T. S. Eliot speaking of tradition: "To realize the nineteenth century one must realize every century that preceded it, and that has contributed to its making. To know anything about oneself, one must know all about others. . . . The true critic is he who bears within himself the dreams and ideas and feelings of myriad generations, and to whom no form of thought is alien, no emotional impulse obscure." [31] Criticism can help us to leave the age in which we were born and to pass into other ages. Criticism makes us cosmopolitan, will annihilate race prejudices, by insisting on the unity of the human mind in the variety of its forms. If imaginative sympathy is the secret of creation, then it must also be the secret of criticism. [32] Identification of the two must be the solution because Wilde cannot accept the alternative: the conception of criticism as aesthetics, as a branch of philosophy, as theory. He distrusts abstractions, because he always believes in art as pleasure, impression, sensation, concrete image, and because he cannot isolate thought from sensation, criticism from creation.

Wilde's views thus shift and oscillate between the three positions: panaestheticism, a grasp of the central idealist tradition in aesthetics, and capricious impressionism. The studied flippancy, the forced overstatement, the polemical violence of many formulations also obscure these basic inconsistencies. But precisely the way Wilde juggled his terms, advanced and retreated from sense to nonsense, from paradox to commonplace, gives him range and scope and makes him the representative figure of the English aesthetic movement.

GEORGE SAINTSBURY (1845-1933)

Saintsbury became by far the most influential academic literary historian and critic of the early 20th century. His reputation has declined in the decades since his death, but recently an eminent English professor, James Sutherland, could argue that he is among the four most characteristically English critics, with Dryden, Johnson, and Hazlitt,[1] and a biographical memoir asserts, apparently without fear of contradiction, that "among critics *per se* it is with Sainte-Beuve, and no other that he must be matched."[2] But I am not aware of any extended consideration of Saintsbury's work. What has been written about Saintsbury is either general appreciation by grateful pupils and admirers, who founded Saintsbury clubs even during his lifetime and hailed him as "King Saintsbury,"[3] or exasperated dismissals by specialists irritated by his errors and his manner. The sheer bulk and scope of his writings have prevented an adequate discussion. A complete bibliography of Saintsbury's writings buried in the files of periodicals (much of it political journalism and book-reviewing between 1875 and the end of the 19th century) would run to several thousand items. According to his own estimate, a reprint of his works would fill over 100 large volumes.

George Bateman Saintsbury established himself as the authoritative historian in his time of French, English, and general literature. The relevant works are: *A Short History of French Literature* (1882), *A Short History of English Literature* (1898), his editorship and the three contributions to *Periods of European Literature* (*The Flourishing of Romance and the Rise of Allegory,* 1897, *The Earlier Renaissance,* 1901, *The Later Nineteenth Century,* 1907), and several more detailed treatments of periods of English literature (*A History of Elizabethan Literature,* 1887, *A History of Nineteenth Century Literature, 1780–1895,* 1896, *The Peace of the Augustans,* 1916). These surveys are supplemented, fortified, and actually far surpassed by Saintsbury's later histories of genres and devices: *A History of Criticism and Literary Taste in Europe* (3 vols. 1901, 1902, 1904), *A History of English Prose Rhythm* (1912), *The English Novel* (1913), and *A History of the French Novel* (2 vols.

1917, 1919) . To this enormous work of literary history-writing we must add many volumes of essays which contain Saintsbury's early work, the two series of *Essays in English Literature 1780–1860*, (1890, 1895) , *Essays on French Novelists* (1895) , *Miscellaneous Essays* (1892), and *Corrected Impressions* (1895), as well as several monographs: *John Dryden* (1881), *Walter Scott* (1897), *Matthew Arnold* (1899), *A Consideration of Thackeray* (1931). It would be impossible to list here the introductions to anthologies, editions, translations, the many addresses, and the numerous contributions to the *Encyclopaedia Britannica* [4] and the *Cambridge History of English Literature*.

Saintsbury's enormous reading, the almost universal scope of his subject matter, the zest and zeal of his exposition, the audacity with which he handles the most ambitious and unattempted arguments should be recognized as a great achievement. Not much need be made of the lapses in accuracy and the lacunae in information inevitable in a work produced at such speed and with such amazing facility. It is best not to probe too closely into anything he wrote of Russian, Scandinavian, or even modern German and Italian literature. He wrote on such topics only because the scope of his surveys demanded that he do so. The frequent errors of dates and titles and his almost total neglect of "secondary literature" of a technical kind cannot surprise us. He could not have done what he did, nor have done it on such a scale, without exposing himself to criticism.[5]

In spite of its variety and scope, Saintsbury's work is held together by a few simple principles. He has two very different sets of critical standards: one for poetry and one for the novel. The drama (including Shakespeare) is either assimilated to poetry or dismissed. Saintsbury considers drama only "accidentally literary" and "not, in absolute necessity or theory, a part of literature at all." He took little pleasure in the theater and confesses, late in his life, that "I should not be sorry if I never passed through its doors again . . . The better the play is as literature, the more I wish that I might be left to read in comfort and see it acted with my mind's eye only." [6]

Saintsbury's theory of poetry is akin to Swinburne's and Pater's and their sources: Baudelaire, and possibly Leigh Hunt, De Quincey, Hazlitt, and Lamb. Here he is a radical formalist. He constantly asserts that in poetry "the so-called 'formal' part is of the essence," that subject does not matter much, "though it is all important in prose." [7] He resolutely divorces form from content, manner from matter, and often roundly condemns the subject matter while loudly praising the form. Thus he speaks of the "rubbish and, what is worse, the mischievous rubbish of the meaning of Morris' 'political poems,'" but asserts that this is not the concern of the *literary* critic. He proposes a strange mental experiment: "It must be a singularly feeble intellect and taste that cannot perform an easy dichotomy of metre and meaning. . . . You pour the poison or the ditchwater out; you keep and marvel at, the golden cup. You can refill it, as far as meaning goes at your pleasure with the greatest things." [8] Saintsbury occasionally seems to believe that poetry is pure sound. He tells a story from the *Life* of Tennyson of a "hearer who knew no English, but knew Tennyson to be a poet by the hearing," and calls it "probable and valuable, or rather invaluable, for it points to the best, if not the only true, criterion of poetry." [9] He thus justifies his own interest in prosody, without regard to meaning, and in "style" in his special sense of "the choice and arrangement of language with only a subordinate regard to the meaning to be conveyed." [10] Usually Saintsbury recognizes that form is not completely independent of the subject. But subject in poetry, he argues, is unimportant because it is always the same, a limited repertory of commonplaces: love and life, man's fate, the inevitability of death, the beauties of nature. "The human intellect and the human temper," Saintsbury believes, "reduce themselves to few varieties." [11] Philosophy amounts to a recognition of *vanitas vanitatum*. Saintsbury, in spite of his bounce and breeziness, is at bottom a melancholy pessimist who admires *Ecclesiastes* as "one of the very greatest books in the world's literature" and is profoundly moved by the "abysmal sadness" of Lucretius.[12] At the same time he feels completely secure in High Church Anglicanism and Tory politics of the extreme Right. The dichotomy between variable form and monotonous content necessarily stunts his insight into the world of intellect and thought and his interest in intellectual history. "Human nature in general is always the same; that which hath been shall be, and the dreams of new worlds and new societies are the most fatuous of vain imaginations." [13] This antihistorical creed goes badly with Saintsbury's great historical learning and tolerance.

In poetry Saintsbury looks always for the "poetic moment," the "single-instant pleasure of image and phrase and musical accompaniment of sound." [14] What matters are "beautiful words," though Saintsbury "does not know and does not believe that anyone knows—however much he may juggle with terms—why certain words arranged in certain order stir one like the face of the sea, or like the face of a girl, while other arrangements leave one absolutely indifferent or excite boredom or dislike." [15] Poetry is ultimately inexplicable, unaccountable, and momentary. That is why he prefers the "multiple, atomic, myrioramic style" of a Tennyson to the "old substantive or structural kind," why he considers Shelley the greatest of lyrical poets and Poe a poet of the very first order.[16] "Perhaps the best and certainly the most compendious definition of poetry" is its success in "making the common as though it were not common." [17] He chides the French for lacking "a sense of the vague, of imagination which goes to make the very highest poetry" and can approve of a saying of John Wilson that "it is not necessary that we should understand fine poetry in order to feel and enjoy it, any more than fine music." The essence of poetry is "in form and colour, suggestion of sound rather than in precise expression and sense." [18]

For a time, in essays on Dante, Milton, and Shakespeare, Saintsbury discussed the "grand style" in an effort to make his poetic theory more precise. But the "grand style" is merely another term for the poetic moment, that "perfection of expression in every direction and kind" which "transmutes the subject and transports the hearer or reader." It is as mysterious as poetry. "You cannot tell how it arises . . . it is truest, precisely because it is the most irresponsible, of the winds of the spirit." [19] In Shakespeare it includes anything which can be picked out as striking, beautiful, and grand: all the *Sonnets* and all the poems, even *Venus and Adonis,* which might seem to us burlesque and sensual rather than grand. In Shakespeare the grand style is ubiquitous though intermittent; in Dante it is "pervading everything and affecting grotesque, extravagance, pedantry"; in Milton it is affectation, though "affectation transcendentalized and sublimed." [20] The "grand style" seems quite unnecessary as a term: we are where we were before. Poetry "communicates an experience of half-sensual, half-intellectual pleasure." "*Why* it does this no mortal can say." [21]

Though Saintsbury wrote the first universal *History of Criticism,* there is, it seems, little room for criticism in his scheme. He comes

very near the view that taste is completely personal—as unarguable
as the taste in wine or food which he often uses for comparison.
Saintsbury appeals to the image of the hydrometer: in poetry we are
ourselves the hydrometer and "consequently it is exceedingly difficult to refer matters to any common standard." "This is this to me
and that to thee." [22] The reader and the critic decide that a "thing
is either poetry or it is not," and there is an end of it.[23] In constant
variations Saintsbury defends this retreat to the fortress of personal
pleasure, the unpredictability and inexplicable impact of literature.
He has no use for the attempts to make criticism science or philosophy. He rejects all theories of causal explanation, all social or
political determinism. He laughs that in his youth everything used
to be explained by association while today everything is explained
"by selection and heredity, evolution and crossing." [24] He disbe-
lieves in "any easily calculable *ratio* of connection between national
and literary idiosyncracy, between political and literary events,"
and constantly denies that politics mean anything to literature
except some excitement in the air or that there is any explanation
for the flowering of a particular literature or genre at a particular
time.[25] Things literary "move in an orbit of their own" in which
there are no predictable laws, continuities, or regularities. There is
no decadence, "no death, no cessation in literature. Here the sadness and decay of certain periods is mere fiction." [26] In Saintsbury's
favorite quotation, "the wind of the spirit blows where it lists" and
"mocks all attempts to foretell the times and seasons of its blowing
or to discover the causes why it has blown." [27]

Still, the critic can improve his own sensibility. Though his
standard of poetry is obscurely personal and criticism seems to end
with a "catalogue of likes and dislikes," Saintsbury sometimes objects to "arbitrary enjoyment and liking" or "mere caprice." Criticism is "an endless process of correcting impressions—or at least of
checking and auditing them till we are sure that they are genuine,
co-ordinated, and (with the real if not the apparent consistency)
consistent." [28] Certain tools for the critic help in elaborating this
consistent taste and certain signs warn against aberrations and
temptations. Saintsbury demands, first of all, catholicity of knowledge and taste. "The study of widely differing periods, forms,
manners, of literature itself" leads to universal tolerance.[29] He constantly rejects the view that there is "something insincere, unnat-

ural, impossible almost in a liking for opposites and things different from each other. I have never been able to share the notion myself or to know why I may not admire A, because I admire B." [30] Complacently, Saintsbury proclaims himself a "critical Pangloss" who has "hardly the slightest desire to alter . . . the literary course of .the world," an optimist in literature (though not, we have seen, in life) who takes a "certain critical delight in reading even the worst books," [31] a veritable library cormorant, a *helluo librorum* who welcomes and accepts almost everything with "an enormous fatalism." [32]

Still, this universal reading cannot be merely passive: it must lead to "comparison" which for Saintsbury is "the one gate and highway to really universal criticism of literature, . . . the strongest, the safest, the best engine of literary criticism altogether." [33] We must cultivate "the constant habit of looking at everything and every writer in conjunction with their analogues and their opposites in the same and other literatures." Saintsbury summarizes his creed in the Conclusion of the *History of Criticism*: the critic "must read, and, as far as possible, read everything—that is the first and great commandment . . . Secondly, he must constantly compare books, authors, literatures indeed, to see in what each differs from each, but never in order to dislike one because it is not the other. Thirdly, he must, as far as he possibly can, divest himself of any idea of what a book *ought to be,* until he has seen what it is." [34] Saintsbury's ultimate critical goal is "an art of appreciation—a reasoned valuing and analysing of the sources of literary charm." He sometimes adds, however, the necessity of judging and ranking the "reasonable distribution of [literary work] into good, not so good, and bad." [35] The final judgment will always be "enthusiastic appreciation," a criticism of beauties, since negative and positive judgments are set off as

> utterly different in weight and scope. The negative is final as regards the individual; he has a right to dislike if he does dislike, though there may be subsequent questions as to his competence. But it is not in the least final as to the work in question. It is (let it be granted) not good for *him*; it does not follow that it is not good in itself. Now the affirmative carries with it results of a very different character. *This* is final in regard to

the work as well as to the reader. That which should be delectable has delighted in one proven and existing case: and nothing—not the crash of the world—can alter the fact. It has achieved—though the value of the achievement in different cases may be different.[36]

In this late passage a recognition of objective value is implied: Saintsbury seems to have abandoned his total impressionism but does not pursue the matter and does not see the consequences of his own position.

Saintsbury believes that all this—universal reading, comparison, appreciation, ranking, and judging—can be accomplished without any recourse to theory. He not only condemns neoclassical rigidity, rules and regulations, principles of kinds, and decorum, but argues in the *History of Criticism* in favor of complete freedom. He not only exalts Longinus' *On the Sublime* as "the greatest critical book of the world" because it takes "the true and only test of literary greatness" to be "the 'transport,' the absorption of the reader," but also avows that there can and should be "critical reading, without theory or with theory postponed."[37] He exposes throughout the *History* "the error of wool-gathering after abstract questions of the nature and justification of poetry, of the *a priori* rules suitable for poetic forms, of Unities, and so forth," the whole "Laputan *meteorosophia* of theories of poetry."[38] This antitheoretical argument becomes particularly violent when Saintsbury, in his historical context, is compelled to deal with the rise of aesthetics. "Literary criticism," he asserts, "has not much more to do with aesthetics than architecture has to do with physics and geology—than the art of the wine-taster or the tea-taster has to do with the study of the papillae of the tongue and the theory of the nervous system generally."[39]

When the first two volumes of the *History of Criticism* were censured by Croce and Spingarn [40] for neglecting theory and aesthetics, Saintsbury defended himself merely by reasserting his position and defining, too modestly, his own aim. He wanted to give a "simple survey of the actual critical opinions," an "atlas of the actual facts." "The complement of Theory I do not pretend to supply, and I cannot see that anybody has a right to demand it."[41] Croce easily replied that there are no "actual facts" in criticism and quoted *Bouvard et Pécuchet,* whose two doubtful heroes thought it sad that the "historians who pretend only to narrate, actually make choices." [42] But one should recognize that the issue is by no means as clear-cut as the contrast between facts and philosophy would indicate. Saintsbury stumbled into a defense of mere facts; much later he complained that he was not, as Croce charged, "barren of philosophy," but had studied the subject in Oxford, had taken a fancy to scholasticism, and wanted to write a book about it.[43] In practice, Saintsbury surely has a theory and principles of selection, and in the *History of Criticism* is not concerned merely with specific critical opinions. He does not worry about general aesthetics and ignores the implications of literary theories in philosophical attitudes and points of view; but he does constantly discuss theory of literature, poetics, rhetoric, and metrics, and generalizes very freely about periods, trends, schools, and movements in literary history.

The main objection to Saintsbury's work is not his neglect of philosophy or abstract theory or even the extreme individualism of his taste, but the poverty and haziness of his concepts and criteria of genres, devices, style, composition—of all the tools of analysis on the level with which he is professedly concerned. The blatant reliance on moods, whims, and crotchets vitiates such enormous, grandly conceived projects as *The History of English Prosody, The History of English Prose Rhythm,* and, to a lesser extent, *The History of the French Novel.*

The History of English Prosody has no clearly defined premises. Saintsbury speaks for instance, of "longs" and "shorts" but cannot make up his mind whether these terms refer to distinctions in duration or stress. He declares even that "shorts" and "longs" may as well have been called "abracadabra" and "abraxas," though at a later point he admits that his book " (as far as it is not a pure record of the facts) is written against the heresy of making stress the sole and single secret of meter." [44] Saintsbury's convictions on metrical theory are all negative. He rejects the musical prosody of Sidney Lanier and William Thomson as well as the phonetic methods of Verrier, because they have "nothing, or next to nothing to do with those on which we are engaged" but deal with the "raw material only." [45] He objects to Edwin Guest's old *History of English Rhythms* (1838) for denying the foot and worshiping the old Germanic accent. He sees nothing in the concept of counterpoint in metrics, of "an antinomy or antimachy of accent and quantity, of thought-movements and rhythms of language and verse." [46] With these exclusions he is reduced to juggling scansions, agreeing with Swinburne that English is "a language to which all variations and combinations of anapaestic, iambic, or trochaic meter are as natural and pliable as the dactylic and spondaic forms of verse are unnatural and abhorrent." [47] Nothing can be done, even by Saintsbury, with such a loose net of questions except to comment on a series of discontinuous scansions by introducing all kinds of extraneous considerations, which make these three volumes a disguised history of English poetry with special reference to versification, stanza forms, and metrical theories.

The History of Prose Rhythm is equally arbitrary in "granting length sometimes to stress, sometimes to positions and sometimes to other causes still." Saintsbury emphasizes that prose-rhythm consists in "variety" and "divergence" but leaves its essence as obscure as that of meter.[48] If Saintsbury's principle of "variety" were correct, there would be no rhythm at all. But doubtless he was only warning us against the danger of having prose rhythm fall into exact metrical patterns. He can do little more than display hundreds of examples of scansion which assume some meaning only from his marginal comments on style and general tone—matters loosely related to the central topic of prose rhythm.

The History of the French Novel, Saintsbury's last extended work, is greatly superior because in writing of the novel he moves beyond his basic poetic theories of the charm of the moment, the glow of individual words, and the sheer music of meter. *The History of the French Novel* is only the highpoint of his voluminous writings on the novel, which from the very beginning of his career applied standards totally different from those with which he judged poetry. "The novel is while the poem is not, mainly and firstly a criticism of life." [49] Saintsbury even admitted that "some of the greatest novels of the world, are, as no one of the greatest poems of the world is, or could possibly be, written anything but well." The novel has "four wheels": "Plot, Character, Description, and Dialogue: Style being a sort of fifth." [50] Saintsbury ordinarily disapproved of ideological intrusions in fiction. "The novel has nothing to do with any beliefs, with any convictions, with any thoughts in the strict sense, except as mere garnishings. Its substance must always be life not thought, conduct not belief, the passions not the intellect, manners and morals not creeds and theories." [51] "The hand of any *purpose*," he repeats in the *History of the French Novel*, "Religious, Scientific, Political, what not, is apt to mummify story." [52] But he is no longer sure that "story" means romance, adventure, and plot. In his earlier writings on the novel Saintsbury had usually sided with the romance, which is "of its nature eternal," while the novel of manners seemed to him "of its nature transitory and parasitic on the romance." [53] He therefore argued against naturalism both in theory and in practice and welcomed enthusiastically the revival of romance late in the 19th century, when Robert Louis Stevenson seemed to promise a return to the adventure story. Saintsbury's enthusiasm for *Morte d'Arthur,* chivalric romances, pastorals, and historical novels à la Dumas père could not be greater. But in some early essays and in the *History of the French Novel* he admits the ideal of realism as "a completed picture of real human life" [54] and contrary to his old rejection of any kind of progress in literature tries to trace the advance of realism from the *fabliaux,* which deserve "the immense praise of having deliberately introduced ordinary life," through the 17th and 18th centuries to Stendhal and Balzac.[55] He even pays some attention to technical matters in the novel, to the relation of *récit* and dialogue, though on the whole he is again unable to analyze what he professes to be concerned with— plot, character, description, dialogue.

The odd result of this inability to use any tools of analysis is that Saintsbury's *History of the French Novel* contains much moralistic comment about the characters in the novels treated as figures in real life and often in deliberately comic or violent terms. Saintsbury would "very much like to have shot Julien Sorel" (in a proper duel, of course). He tells us: "I don't want to meet anybody in (Maupassant's) *Bel-Ami;* in fact, I would much rather not." He calls Emma Bovary "scum of womanhood," and Blanche Amory in Thackeray's *Pendennis* "extremely nice—one would not, I think, marry her except in polygamous and cloistral countries, but that is about all that can be said against her." [56] Saintsbury is indignant about Choderlos de Laclos' *Liaisons dangereuses,* which he calls "prosaic and suburban," though he is not otherwise squeamish and prudish in a Victorian way. He admires Diderot's *La Religieuse* and many things in Crebillon and Restif de la Bretonne.[57] *The History of the French Novel* has been almost completely neglected, even in England, though it contains much knowledge, truthful observation, good description, and some sensitive criticism. The fault is largely Saintsbury's. Like all of his longer histories, the book goes to pieces: it dissolves into an agreeable commentary of an enormously well-read man, sitting in his library, pulling books from his shelves, commenting on this or that passage or character, ranking and grading the books, haphazardly comparing them with others, suggesting historical relationships, and actually stimulating interest, conveying something of his own zest, luring the reader to share in his own enjoyment. Tastes will differ as to the allusive, whimsical style, the funny ferocities, and personal remarks: requesting, for instance, the British Museum to give him one of its three copies of Capriano's *Della Vera Poetica* (Venice, 1555), or pretending that he cannot recognize the gate of Trinity College, Cambridge ("I cannot tell, I am an Oxford man").[58] One doubts whether the frequent comparisons with wine and food mean very much. "Charles de Bernard may but stand to Balzac and George Sand as champagne stands to Romanee Conti and to Chateau Yquem," tells us little even if we knew as much about wine as the author of the *Cellar Book* did.[59] Still, Saintsbury achieves his purpose: even in the dull and dreary stretches on ancient or neoclassical criticism and the 17th-century French novel the personality of the speaker, his particular voice, comes through. The image of a fatherly authority, of an omniscient reader, a somewhat crotchety but amiable connoisseur, and a John Bullish, no-nonsense Englishman is established. All this may not have furthered the cause of criticism in the abstract, but it secured Saintsbury a place among the English essayists and the taste-makers.

In spite of his professions of complete catholicity, Saintsbury's taste has well-defined limitations and preferences. There never was so resolutely bookish a critic: he does not care for drama, for painting, or even for music. Poetry, the novel, and criticism are his concern. To list his enthusiasms would be to list almost all of Western literary history. But one should recognize that Saintsbury, for his time, had some unusual preferences: he began in 1875 with an article on Baudelaire that praises the poet as "the most original, and within his limits, the most remarkable of modern French poets" and dismisses the charge of immorality by "deprecating entirely the introduction of such questions into matters of literature." Saintsbury shrewdly observes that "you may write about murder as often as you like, and no one will accuse you of having committed that crime. You may depict an interesting brigand without being considered a thief. Not in either case will you be thought an inciter to either offence. But so soon as you approach the other deadly sin of Luxury in any one of its forms, instantly it appears self-evident that you not only take pleasure in those who do these things but also do them yourself." [60] The actual analysis of Baudelaire's writings falls short of doing more than quoting and selecting, mainly from the *Poems in Prose*. The essay, courageous and lively as it was, also established the pattern of Saintsbury's shortcomings.

Saintsbury's taste for what today would be called baroque is much more clearly defined. In an introduction to an edition of the *Poems* (1896) he concretely describes Donne's "spiritualized worldliness and sensuality . . . the strange regions where sensuality, philosophy and devotion meet," [61] and the characterization of Donne in the *Short History of English Literature* (1898) resumes the theme. "Behind every image, every ostensible thought of his, there are vistas and backgrounds of other thoughts dimly vanishing, with glimmers in them here and there, into the depths of the final enigmas of life and soul. Passion and meditation, the two avenues into this region of doubt and dread, are tried by Donne." [62] The comment on the other metaphysical poets is equally appreciative and well-phrased, and with his edition of the *Minor Poets of the Caroline Period* (3 vols. 1905–21) Saintsbury made accessible a body of difficult and extravagant texts totally condemned by conventional 19th-century taste.

It will be shorter to list some of Saintsbury's exclusions from his Noah's Ark. They are largely confined to modern realism and naturalism, particularly outside of England. He detests the Goncourts but more rationally depreciates Zola.[63] The condemnations of Ibsen and the Russians are quite sweeping and undiscriminating. He recommends "hanging" for Nekrasov, tells us that Dostoevsky is "such as one could have done without," and asserts that Tolstoy's novels are "hardly works of art at all," though he makes an exception for "The Death of Ivan Ilyich." [64] At the same time, he praises Thackeray as "the greatest master of artistic realism," professes not to know "a greater novel than *Esmond*," and does not find any *longeurs* in *The Newcomes*.[65]

Saintsbury does not succeed in strictly separating his artistic judgment from ideological or national prejudices and in achieving his ideal of universal learning and personal impression. But one should recognize his great merits as a mapmaker in the *History of Criticism* and as a lively commentator and surveyor of modern literary history, at least of England and France. His influence in the English-speaking academic world has been enormous. His insistence on comparison, on the broad map of Western literatures, on the comparative isolation of literary history from social history, on the necessity of judging is wholly admirable. On the other hand, he strengthened unfortunate tendencies in English criticism of the time: the contempt for theory, the pose of dilettantism, the indulgence in moral, political, religious, and national prejudice. He helped to bring about the situation that reached its nadir before the advent of T. S. Eliot: the loss of standards, coherence, penetration, and critical tools.

GEORGE BERNARD SHAW (1856–1950)

At first sight, George Bernard Shaw will appear as the anti-Victorian critic; the enemy of hypocrisy and smugness, the self-proclaimed destroyer of *bourgeois* values. He has even been considered the first Marxist critic, a claim easily disposed of, as Franz Mehring in Germany preceded him. Actually Shaw comes by his Marxist reputation in criticism cheaply. The one book that could be considered to exemplify it, *The Perfect Wagnerite* (1898), is a preposterous allegorical reading of *Der Ring des Nibelungen*. Alberich is a capitalist hoarder and exploiter and Siegfried "a totally unmoral person, a born anarchist, the ideal of Bakoonin [sic], an anticipation of the 'overman' of Nietzsche."[1] When the allegory breaks down, Shaw simply declares that drama changes into opera and that the story cannot be taken seriously any more. He probably would not himself want his theory taken seriously: it served to shock the Wagnerian public then flocking to Bayreuth in religious adoration and to remind them that Wagner actually took part in the 1848 revolution.

Shaw's literary criticism before *The Perfect Wagnerite* must, however, be taken seriously, but not for its social interpretation of literature. He does not even try to apply a sociological (not to speak of Marxist) method to the theater and drama. He is a straightforward ideologist and didacticist. In spite of his professed break with tradition Shaw belongs to the Victorian propounders of realism, common sense, and optimism, and the enemies of romanticism and pessimism. His theatrical criticism as drama critic of *The Saturday Review* (1895–98) has much in common with that of George Henry Lewes, who wrote theatrical reviews for *The Leader* between 1850 and 1854.[2] Shaw himself acknowledged that Lewes "in some respects anticipated me": certainly Lewes has something of the "vulgarity and impudence" used by Shaw, and he has the same distaste for the Elizabethan dramatists as Shaw.[3]

Shaw's activity as a drama critic was preceded by his advocacy of Ibsen. *The Quintessence of Ibsenism* (1891) was in its time an important pamphlet defending Ibsen's message and attacking the social conventions and hypocrisies of the time, but it disappoints as literary criticism. The plays are retold purely for their message, as if they were little Shavian fables: there is no suggestion of the complexities of *The Wild Duck* in Shaw's summary, and *Little Eyolf* is grossly distorted to serve Shaw's purpose. Allmers, we are told by Shaw, is a "male sultana," his relation to Asta gives him "blessed comfort and relief," and much is made, quite falsely, of the wealth of Allmer's wife.[4] The "new element" in Ibsen is seen as a "tragedy that stripped the soul naked instead of bedizening it in heroic trappings": an antitragic unmasking and Ibsen's main innovation is simply the introduction of discussion on the stage.[5] Action and plot are minimized, situations are familiar, violence is avoided. One might think that Shaw is describing his own plays: hardly anything is conveyed of Ibsen's own individual characteristics. It seems odd that a pamphlet mostly devoted to the discussion of the woman's question should be considered a "work of genius."[6]

Shaw conceived of the theater (like Schiller) as "a moral institution," "as important as the Church in the Middle Ages," as "a factory of thought, a prompter of conscience, an elucidator of social conduct, an armory against despair and dullness, and a temple of the Ascent of Man."[7] Shaw had to review the English stage in the 1890's, a period in which it was barely emerging from the dreary wastes of the 19th century. He was confronted with an endless procession of French or French-imitated melodramas, drawing-room comedies, and farces, and with the feeble attempts of Henry Arthur Jones and Arthur Wing Pinero to smuggle some social problems on the stage, without disturbing the waters too much. Besides, there was Shakespeare, produced in utmost splendor by great showmen with little regard for the text. It is difficult to judge criticism of acting and production without visual evidence, and the nature of the plays and the productions reviewed is so ephemeral that even Shaw's continuous shrewdness, vivacity, and wit cannot hold attention today. Shaw has easy game with the bulk of these plays: he can be very funny about sentimentalities, improbabilities, and absurdities. He disposes of his competitors, praises a fellow dramatist like Wilde with some detachment, and harasses, hectors, ridicules, or rages at the great actors and actresses of the time: Eleanora Duse, Sarah Bernhardt, Henry Irving, etc. He fulfilled his function as "the policeman of dramatic art." [8]

The standards applied to plays are simple. Is the play like real life? Does it convey sensible, progressive ideas? The classics also must be judged this way. Thus Shaw's notorious criticism of Shakespeare exactly conforms with his other judgments. Shakespeare's plays are, no doubt, often highly improbable, unrealistic, melodramatic in their plots; the characters indulge in rhetoric and even bombast and in elaborate horseplay or badinage. Shakespeare does not preach the emancipation of women, the revolt of the masses, or hatred of war. He does not believe in progress. But Shaw, goaded by the bardolatry of the time and the new exaltation of Shakespeare's contemporaries by Swinburne and others, goes to absurd lengths in his condemnation of Shakespeare. Much, no doubt, is written purely for effect. Shaw could stand on his head for a very long time: Max Beerbohm discovered after years that "the dear fellow had not moved." [9] But there is some truth in the old observation that one sees the world in a different light through one's legs, and certainly Shaw managed to see Shakespeare, and make others see Shakespeare, with different eyes. He may dismiss Shakespeare's contemporaries too rashly, though Webster may deserve the label of the "Tussaud laureate" and Beaumont and Fletcher may have "no real power or seriousness." [10] But it is another matter to call Ben Jonson "a brutish pedant" and to trounce Marlowe for the "resourceless tum-tum of his mighty line" or his "vulgar and wooden humor." [11] One can understand the view that *Cymbeline* is "stagey trash of the lowest dramatic order," "vulgar, foolish, offensive, indecent," full of "monstruous rhetorical fustian," [12] that *Othello* is pure melodrama and Iago is a "hopeless mess of motives." [13] Julius Caesar may be travestied as a "silly braggart," [14] Richard III may be a "prince of Punches," [15] and it may even be true that "there is not a breath of medieval atmosphere in Shakespeare's histories." [16] But surely Shaw is completely mistaken in his view of Shakespeare as "a vulgar pessimist." He asserts that Shakespeare's characters "have no religion, no politics, no hope, no convictions of any sort." [17] In constant variations we are told that Shakespeare "understood nothing and believed nothing," or, somewhat contradictorily, that he was "a thoroughly respectable snob." [18] Shaw reacted against the sentimental exaltation of Shakespeare to a philosopher and abstract moralist, but he shows his unhistorical incomprehension of Shakespeare's actual, ascertainable thoughts and attitudes in such sweeping generalizations. Still, Shaw is not completely blind to Shakespeare's greatness: individual discussions of plays, such as perceptive comments on Forbes Robertson's Hamlet [19] or his preference for the so-called problem plays,[20] show his lifelong concern for the greatest of all English poets. But mostly Shaw tries to put all of Shakespeare's greatness into his linguistic skill and verbal music, or at most into his comic power. In a letter to V. C. Chertkov, Shaw voiced his disagreement with parts of Tolstoy's attack on Shakespeare: "I have endeavored to open the eyes of Englishmen to the emptiness of Shakespeare's philosophy, to the superficiality and unoriginality of his moral views, to his weakness and confusion as a thinker, to his snobbery, to his vulgar prejudices, to his ignorance, to every aspect of his undeserved reputation as a great philosopher." But he would not deny "his humor, his gaiety, his capacity to create characters more real for us than actual living people, his tenderness, but chiefly his unusual powers as a musician of words." [21] When in 1929 he asked the famous question "Better than Shakespeare?" he answered it in the negative. "No man will ever write a better tragedy than *Lear* . . . I do not profess to write better plays." [22]

In taking his farewell as dramatic critic Shaw said complacently, "I am an extraordinarily witty, brilliant and clever man." [23] But wit, brilliance, and cleverness, which nobody will deny him, is insufficient for an understanding of poetry. Shaw had little use for poetry. When asked to write about Keats, he could only apologize: "I find myself with nothing to say except that you cannot write about Keats," though Shaw did quote the stanzas from *Isabella* on the two wealthy, cruel brothers as containing "all the Factory Commission Reports that Marx read." [24] It fits with Shaw's view of poetry that he should praise Poe's poetry, since he likes beautiful sound, and that he should reduce Shelley to a revolutionary.[25] Shaw has no great interest in the problems of the novel, which, he declares surprisingly, "raises no question of technique." [26] Discussing novelists, he never gets beyond their ideology: he cared for Butler's *Way of All Flesh,* for George Eliot, and for Dickens, though with many reservations. With his knowledge of music, he chides Dickens for his Philistinism and provincialism: "For him the great synthetic ideals do not exist, any more than the great preludes and toccatas of Bach, the symphonies of Beethoven, the paintings of Giotto and Mantegna, Velasquez and Rembrandt. Instead of being heir to all the ages, he came into a comparatively small and smutty literary property bequeathed by Smollett and Fielding." [27] Shaw had access to German music and to contemporary biology and sociology beyond the reach of Dickens. But his experience of literature seems almost as limited. There is no evidence of any concern with foreign literatures or the remoter past nor with actual modernist art: his view of poetry suffers from the divorce of content and form, the lack of awareness for evil and tragedy, the whole narrow ideology of enlightenment, which may be irrationalistic in its reliance on instinct but is deeply insensitive to the inner life of man, and thus to the essence of poetry and art.

Not only in France but all over the Western world 20th-century conceptions of poetry are dominated by the doctrines enunciated in the French symbolist movement. This influence is in part due simply to the poetic achievement of Baudelaire, Rimbaud, Mallarmé and their followers: Claudel and Valéry in France, George and Rilke in Germany, Blok and Ivanov in Russia, Ungaretti and Montale in Italy, Rubén Darío and Machado in the Spanish-speaking world, Yeats and Eliot in English. Moreover, the general concept of "symbol" in literature, though old enough, struck the wide Western public only in its French formulations. The term is highly ambiguous and shifting even today: in phrases such as "symbolic logic" or "mathematical symbol" it is used in a sense contrary to that of "poetic symbol." The use of the word in literature has more and more departed from that of a mere sign or allegory and has become a term inclusive of image and metaphor, a substitute for the "concrete universal," a name for the basic instrument of all art.

Strangely enough, Jean Moréas, a French poet of Greek extraction, the man who proclaimed the existence of the symbolist movement in a manifesto published in *Le Figaro littéraire* (18 September 1886), very soon abandoned the slogan and made himself the head of another group, "L'Ecole romane." The 1886 manifesto declaims pompously on the inevitability of change and the necessity of literary evolution, annexes Baudelaire as the "true precursor of the present movement" and vaguely defines its aim: "symbolic poetry seeks to clothe the Idea in a sensuous form." [1] What was then a name for one of the numerous schools, movements, coteries, and cliques of the Paris of the eighties became through channels that have not been clearly traced [2] the victorious slogan for almost all modern poetry and much modern fiction. Its application has also been pushed back into the past: attempts have been made to show that

English romantic poetry is symbolist or that American literature of the mid-19th century is symbolist rather than romantic.[3] Both the term and the concept, as well as the poetic practice, can, however, be found at least as early as Goethe in Germany. German romantic aestheticians—Schelling, August Wilhelm Schlegel, and Solger—developed a theory of symbolism which, in various forms, reappeared in Coleridge, Carlyle, and Emerson and also, intermittently and casually, in France: in passages that can be quoted from Madame de Staël, Sainte-Beuve, and Pierre Leroux.[4]

In a history of criticism it seems more profitable to examine the complete doctrines of particular critics than to trace the shifting meaning of an omnipresent term or even to expound the welter of pronouncements during the eighties and nineties by various adherents, popularizers, and enemies—pronouncements that were never sufficiently coherent or backed by concrete analysis to constitute any real contribution to critical theory. Only two writers, Baudelaire and Mallarmé, meet the test of coherence and originality.

CHARLES BAUDELAIRE (1821–1867)

Charles Baudelaire should not, of course, be labeled a symbolist. Chronologically he precedes the movement by so many years (he began to write art criticism in 1845 and produced his most important literary criticism from 1857 to 1861) that he can be considered only a "precursor," a term that hardly fits a man whose critical power and original sensibility are such that he has been considered one of the greatest critics of the century. His main critical achievement was in art, but he was, though hardly a systematic theorist, an important general aesthetician and a literary critic of great distinction. But neither the aesthetics nor the criticism of Baudelaire quite lives up to the novelty and originality of his sensibility that made him the *magnus parens* of modern poetry. Because of his poetry, his aesthetics and his criticism have increasingly attracted close attention: but the aesthetics and the criticism do not really, except in rare passages, rationalize the implied poetics of his actual achievement. Baudelaire's aesthetics instead plays an important historical role transmitting romantic motifs to the later 19th century—that is, "romantic" not in the French sense of emotionalism, nature worship, and the exaltation of the ego but rather the German and

English romantic doctrine of creative imagination, a rhetoric of metamorphoses, and the central role of the symbol. Many elaborate investigations and conflicting arguments have been carried on to trace the exact sources of Baudelaire's conceptions, but they flowed so plentifully in his time that it seems impossible to pin them down with certainty. There seems little likelihood that Baudelaire had a close acquaintance with the mystical antecedents of these theories in Swedenborg and Saint-Martin. Had he known nothing but the "philosophical novels" of Balzac, the tales of E. T. A. Hoffmann, the visions of De Quincey, the feuilletons of Heine, and the talk of Delacroix, he would have had access to most of these ideas, even before he read and translated Poe, or met with a passage in Mrs. Catherine Crowe's *Night Side of Nature*.[1]

At first sight, his relations to Poe seem to be the most important aspect of Baudelaire's critical position. Baudelaire not only translated "The Philosophy of Composition" but reproduced "The Poetic Principle" in an article on Poe (1856) and in an essay on Gautier three years later quoted it as if he were quoting his own words. He clearly agrees with Poe on some main points of aesthetics: the assertion of the autonomy of art and dislike of didacticism, the distrust of inspiration, the stress on the role of the intellect in the creative process, and the cult of beauty, especially strange and sad beauty. When Baudelaire praised Emma Bovary for "that double character of calculation and dreaming which makes up a perfect being,"[2] he was describing his own ideal of poetry and the central dualism in Poe's theory.

Many passages could be quoted to show that Baudelaire asserts the autonomy of art, and condemns didacticism, philosophical poetry, and political tendentiousness in literature. Only at an early stage had he referred contemptuously to the "puerile utopia of the school of *art for art,* which by excluding morals, and often even passion, was necessarily sterile."[3] But later Baudelaire constantly protested against the "didactic heresy," taking Poe's term and developing the theme that "poetry has no other aim than itself," that the "more art frees itself from the didactic the more it soars toward pure and disinterested beauty."[4] As early as 1846 Baudelaire had condemned philosophical poetry as "a false genre,"[5] and again and again he deplored the view that poetry should express ideas drawn from a world so strange to art as science or politics.[6]

Baudelaire also distrusted inspiration. He counseled young writers that "daily work serves inspiration" [7] and ridiculed the view that inspiration is enough and takes the place of everything else.[8] Later he often reverted to this theme. He complains of the absolute confidence of youth in genius and inspiration. "Youth concludes that it need not submit to any exercise. It does not know that a man of genius . . . must, like an apprenticed acrobat, risk his bones a thousand times in private before he walks the rope in public; that inspiration, in short, is only the reward of daily exercise." [9] Baudelaire laughs at "those theories which promote laziness and allow the poet to consider himself a talkative, light, irresponsible, uncatchable bird." [10]

Finally, as in Poe, the doctrine of pure art and the belief in the dominance of the intellect in the creative process are combined with a cult of beauty: supernatural, "supernal," or, at least, strange, sad, and disconcerting beauty. Baudelaire quotes Poe on beauty, paraphrasing even the passage on the "glories beyond the grave," [11] and often refers to the element of strangeness in beauty. Beauty in Poe and Baudelaire is not simply disproportion but something "ardent and sad, something slightly vague, giving free rein to conjecture." [12]

However, Baudelaire's firm hold on the autonomy of art, its distinction from philosophy, science, politics, and especially morals, though reinforced by Poe's influence, had already been achieved in contact with the whole art-for-art's-sake movement and with such men as Delacroix and Gautier. Similarly, Baudelaire had rejected the romantic trust in inspiration long before he knew Poe. If we examine the three main motifs clearly related to Poe's doctrines— the rejection of didacticism, the emphasis on the intellect in creation, and the cult of strange beauty—we can easily see that Baudelaire modifies Poe's formulas significantly. While rejecting didacticism, he solves the relation of art and morals in a way different from that of Poe, who on occasion admitted a subordinate moral purpose. Baudelaire simply declares that art as such is moral. "Is art useful? Yes. Why? Because it is art. . . . I defy anybody to find a single work of imagination which unites all the conditions of the Beautiful and is still a pernicious work." [13] Speaking of Hugo, he argues that "the poet is a moralist without wanting to be one, through the abundance and fullness of his nature." [14] In a similar way, he defends the morality of *Madame Bovary* by asserting that the "logic of the work suffices for all demands of morality." [15] The solution is, one must admit, somewhat complacent and glib: it really camouflages what Baudelaire said bluntly in praising De Quincey's *Confessions of an English Opium Eater*: "the Beautiful is more noble than the True." [16]

Baudelaire only partly accepts Poe's deliberate calculation and is especially skeptical of the account of the composition of "The Raven." He notes "the tone of light impertinence" and the "affectation in hiding spontaneity and simulating cold-bloodedness and deliberation." He approves of "The Philosophy of Composition" as polemics, an antidote against "the lovers of chance, the fatalists of inspiration." [17] But even this partial endorsement and Baudelaire's frequent resolutions, in his diaries and letters, to work and to *will* to work on his poetry should not obscure one fact: Baudelaire actually sought and at times captured "certain almost supernatural states of the soul [in which] the profundity of life reveals itself, completely, in any spectacle, however ordinary it may be, upon which one gazes." [18] Off and on, both in *Paradis artificiels* and outside its context, he asserted that there are "moments of existence immensely enhanced," "miraculous moments," "feast-days of the brain," "fine days of the soul." [19] There is a lost paradise, an Eden that the poet tries to recapture and can recapture. Imagination is also memory, and genius is one's childhood found again by will power, or simply "childhood clearly formulated." [20] There is in Baudelaire, at least, an aspiration toward mysticism, a belief that art, at its highest, is vision, ecstacy, and thus inspiration—an almost Wordsworthian quest for "spots of time." As in Poe, there is a gulf between the stress on deliberation, calculation, work, and will and the longing for supernatural beauty, for a paradise of childhood achieved and achievable only in moments of rapture. But usually Baudelaire differs from Poe (and himself in certain moments) by interpreting beauty not as some ethereal ideal but as something human, even evil, satanic, bizarre, and grotesque. Baudelaire's doctrine is, in part, an aesthetic of the ugly, a belief in the artist's power of overcoming any and all obstacles, of eliciting "flowers" from evil.[21] But it is more than that: he has a genuine grasp of creative imagination, of the dialectics of subject and object, of a rhetoric of transformation by art which is based on a theory of universal analogies, correspondences, and symbols.

It seems unnecessary, however, to speak of an actual "mysticism" or even occultism in Baudelaire. He probably passed through such a stage, and the poem *Correspondances,* if taken literally as a profession of Swedenborgian faith, would represent it. But, on the whole, Baudelaire holds rather a philosophical and ultimately aesthetic version of this creed, as it is found in Schelling or E. T. A. Hoffmann. The evidence is conflicting on this point. Speaking of Hugo, Baudelaire refers to the sources of the theory—analogy in Fourier, correspondence in Swedenborg, the physiognomy of Lavater—and continues:

> We arrive at that truth that everything is hieroglyphic, and we know that the symbols are only relatively obscure according to the purity, the good will, and the inborn clearsightedness of souls. Now what is a poet if not a translator, a decipherer? In excellent poets there is not a single metaphor, comparison, or epithet which could not be a mathematically exact adaptation to the present circumstance, because these comparisons, metaphors, and epithets are drawn from the inexhaustible fund of *universal analogy.*[22]

Here the process of poetry is conceived of as comparatively passive: as far as the deciphering of any difficult language can be called passive. Still, the universe appears as some kind of riddle in ciphers, as a given task confronting the poet, and the terms suggest the mystic tradition of the *signatura rerum,* the "hieroglyphics" inscribed in nature, and other old metaphors such as an alphabet or a dictionary of nature.[23] Baudelaire even introduces the term "correspondence" into Poe when he paraphrases him on the "immortal instinct of beauty which makes us consider the earth and its sights as a sketch, a correspondence of the Heavens," though Poe's text contains nothing about "correspondence." [24] But elsewhere Baudelaire does not seem to believe literally in a universe of correspondences. He can say that "imagination is the most scientific of faculties because it alone comprehends universal analogy, or what in a mystical religion is called *correspondence.*" [25] The distance from the occult use is even clearer in the discussion of Gautier. Gautier is praised for "an immense inborn intelligence of universal *correspondence* and symbolism, the repertory of all metaphor" which allows him to "define the mysterious attitude which the objects of creation have before the eyes of man." [26] The artist, we understand, plays on "the immense keyboard of the correspondences," [27] or "the entire visible universe appears as but a storehouse of images and signs to which the imagination will give a relative place and value; it is a sort of pasturage which the imagination must digest and transform." [28]

At times, one must admit, Baudelaire saw the poet as confronted with a given universe of analogies and symbols, a nature obscurely challenging man to read its riddles; usually, and this point of view seems to me more sane and profound, he thought of the poet as overcoming and transforming nature, as being a creator, as endowed with imagination. Baudelaire endorses Heine's profession of "supernaturalism," which he quotes to the effect that "the artist cannot find all his forms in nature but that the most remarkable forms are revealed to him in the soul, like the innate symbolism of innate ideas." [29] Baudelaire here seems to agree with an ultimately Neoplatonic trust in an inner model, in the vision of "the artist who dominates the model as the creator dominates His creation." [30] Such supernaturalism in practice means aversion to the theories of naturalism and realism that were flourishing at that time. Baudelaire constantly attacked the doctrine of copying nature as being the enemy of art, and he ridiculed the new vogue of photography.[31] But Baudelaire's antinaturalism is not only an instinct of taste, a dislike for the drab and the literal, but also a protest against the "silly cult of nature." [32] In contradiction to the world of hieroglyphics, which is somehow divine and good, nature for Baudelaire is usually evil, fallen, and can be only a counselor to crime.[33] We all know of Baudelaire's defense of makeup and fashion and of his dandyism. The artist must overcome nature. His "first business is to protest against nature by putting man in her place." [34]

Baudelaire angrily rejects the term "realism"—"a disgusting insult thrown into the face of all analysts, a vague and elastic word which means for the vulgar not a new method of creation but the minute description of inessentials." [35] There are, he says, two kinds of artists. The realists, whom he prefers to call "positivists," say, " 'I want to represent things as they are, or rather as they would be, supposing I did not exist.' The universe without man. The other, however—the imaginative artist—says: 'I want to illuminate things with my mind and to project their reflection upon other minds.' " [36]

Imagination is thus the instrument of the soul "to throw a magic and supernatural light upon the natural darkness of things." "The more positive and solid the *thing* appears to be, the more subtle and laborious is the work of the imagination." [37] Sometimes reverting to the idea of a universe of riddles, Baudelaire still asserts that "the imagination is a quasi divine faculty which perceives at once, beyond the methods of philosophy, the intimate and secret relations of things, the correspondences and analogies." [38] He endorses an even bolder claim by quoting Mrs. Catherine Crowe, the compiler of *The Night Side of Nature* (1848), a weird collection of anecdotes about ghosts, hallucinations, and premonitions. In the passage quoted by Baudelaire Mrs. Crowe uses Coleridge's distinction that there is "a *constructive* imagination, which is a much higher function [than fancy], and which, inasmuch as man is made in the likeness of God, bears a distant relation to that sublime power by which the Creator projects, creates and upholds his universe." [39] Baudelaire assigns to imagination a role in prehistory. "Imagination taught man the moral meaning of color, of contour, of sound, and of scent. In the beginning of the world it created analogy and metaphor. It decomposes all creation." [40] "Imagination is the queen of truth, and the *possible* is one of the provinces of truth." [41] The realm of the possible is another metaphor for the ideal symbolic make-believe world of art. "A good picture [or, one may presume, a poem] which is a faithful equivalent of the dream which has begotten it, must be brought into being like a world." [42] The highest design, "the noblest and the strangest, can afford to neglect nature because it realizes another nature analogous to the mind and the temperament of the artist." [43] Baudelaire's concept of the imagination is obviously continuous with the ancient views of poetry that creates another cosmos, a world of the possible on the analogue of God's own creation. Sometimes Baudelaire implies that the otherness of this world of art is only that of a dream, of an escape from this sordid world into a land of imagination. Sometimes he suggests that it may be the lost Paradise of childhood innocence or a world that has a claim to metaphysical meaning or has "a positive relation with the infinite," [44] as Baudelaire says in a romantic phrase. A painting of Delacroix, he can say, retains "the stamp and temper of its conception. It is the infinite within the finite"—a literal quotation from Schelling. "It is a dream and by this word I do not mean the riotous Bedlams of the night, but rather the vision which comes from intense meditation." [45] The terms are various—another world, the "possible," the "infinite within the finite," "the constructive imagination," the dream which is meditation—but they all aim at the same basic idea: that art is another cosmos which transforms and hence humanizes nature.

In the panegyric of Hugo (which is a hymn to poets in general) Baudelaire tries to relate this humanizing, animating function of the poet to his theory of the unity of the senses. "The music of Victor Hugo's verses adapts itself to the profound harmonies of nature; a sculptor, he carves out the immemorial shape of things in his stanzas; a painter, he lights them up in their particular color. And, as if they had come directly from nature, the three impressions penetrate the brain of the reader simultaneously. From this triple impression the spirit of things results." He thus evokes a somewhat monstrous ideal that the poet is musical, sculptural, and pictur-esque at the same time, but hardly defends it rationally. Actually Baudelaire thought of Hugo's art mainly as simple anthropomorph-ism and even as mere empathy with the world of nature, including inanimate nature, "not only the form of a being external to man, vegetable, or mineral, but also its physiognomy, its look, its sadness, its tenderness, its bounding joy, its repulsive hate, its enchantment, or its horror: in other words, all that is human in anything what-soever, and also all that is divine, sacred, or diabolic." [46] By his creation the artist abolishes the gulf between subject and object, man and nature. At the moment of his finest insight Baudelaire sees these dialectics. Art is "to create a suggestive magic containing at one and the same time the object and the subject, the external world and the artist himself." [47]

With this general view of supernaturalism and creative imagina-tion Baudelaire must emphasize the power of the artist over his subject matter, the role of form and style and even convention, the role of poetic language and all poetic devices such as metaphor and symbol, and the transformation of theme into myth. But he does so only intermittently, no doubt first because the occult view of nature as a tapestry of symbols militates against a view of free creation, and also, possibly, because in painting at least he could not quite free himself from the presuppositions of realism. He can, for instance, say that "the right way to know if a picture is melodious is to look at it from far enough away to make it impossible to understand its subject or to distinguish its lines. If it is melodious, it already has a meaning." [48] Since "melody" here means "the unity of color," something like an abstract color design seems to be recommended— a painting without subject or, at least, without recognizable or material subject. Elsewhere Baudelaire expressly speaks of line and color as "absolutely independent of the subject of the picture." [49] But he also says that "the subject makes for the artist a part of his genius" [50] and criticizes subjects as not being "worthy" of a specific artist.[51] As a critic of painting Baudelaire is constantly concerned with subject matter in its human and psychological meaning. He came before the rise of impressionism: Delacroix is to him the greatest modern painter; he admires but dislikes Ingres and is cool to Corot and Millet. He knew only the early Manet, whom he liked as a person and thought well of as a painter but whom he coupled with the conventional Legros.[52] His love for Constantin Guys, the "painter of modern life," his interest in caricaturists from Hogarth to Daumier are due, in part, to Baudelaire's cult of modernity, his faith in "the ephemeral and fleeting beauty of present-day life." [53] For he believes (oddly enough in view of his general outlook) that "almost all our originality comes from the stamp that *time* imprints on our perceptions." [54] Baudelaire tries to distinguish between eternal beauty and an element of the transitory, between absolute and particular beauty, always defending "the heroism of modern life," [55] the attraction of the surface of metropolitan life, because he distrusts all classicism and antiquarianism.

Baudelaire values highly the role of form as a stimulus to the imagination. In defending the sonnet and its Pythagorean beauty, he asserts:

> Because form is constraining, the idea wells forth all the more intensely. Everything is appropriate for the sonnet: buffoonery, gallantries, passion, revery, philosophical meditation. In it is to be found the beauty of a well-worked metal and mineral. Have you noticed that a bit of sky, seen through a skylight or from between two chimneys, two rocks, or through an arcade, gives a more profound idea of infinity than a great panorama seen from the top of a mountain? [56]

Similarly, "systems of rhetoric or prosody are no arbitrarily invented tyrannies but rather collections of rules demanded by the very constitution of the spiritual being. And systems of prosody and rhetoric have never prevented originality from emerging clearly." [57] But while Baudelaire recognizes the stimulating power of a form such as a sonnet or a metrical convention, he usually uses "style" in a deprecatory sense. Style is an "alien poetry usually borrowed from the past" instead of being "the naturally poetic quality of the subject which must be extracted so that it may become more visible." [58] Ingres and Millet are criticized for having "style": a distortion or pretense rather than proper creation. Baudelaire thus holds fast to a middle position that allows him to reject both academic formalism and photographic naturalism. Art is not "idealization" because nature, while evil, must not be "purified" by abstraction or sentimentalization: rather, nature is taken up into the permanence of art, metamorphosed, symbolized, but not evaporated. This is, at least, the novelty of Baudelaire's poetic sensibility: his power over the ugly and the evil. "The horrible, artistically expressed, becomes beauty, and pain, rhythmic and cadenced, fills the mind with calm joy." [59] At times this power is conceived of as a momentary escape or mere illusion. "The intoxication of art hides the terrors of the abyss: for genius can play comedy on the edge of the tomb." [60] The clown condemned to death never shows a trace of his imminent fate in the superb performance of his act.

Thus irony is another fundamental requirement of art,[61] next to supernaturalism. Superiority over one's fellow men is the essence of laughter and the superiority over nature is the essence of the grotesque. The grotesque culminates in the absolute comic, which Baudelaire admires in Hoffmann's most fantastic stories.[62] There the artist is himself and someone else at one and the same time; he is an actor, superior to his own self and to the world. He is double, *homo duplex*.[63] This stage of superiority and irony, so similar to the romantic irony of Friedrich Schlegel or Solger, is, strangely enough, identical with the "poetic beatitude" Baudelaire had described as a "state where the poets are at the same time cause and effect, subject and object, magnetizer and somnambulist." [64]

These speculations about the metaphysical role of art were far less influential than certain remarks that Baudelaire made about poetic devices. The latter were isolated, undeveloped, and casual, but seminal for French symbolism. In his criticism, Baudelaire paid little attention to language, but in speaking of Gautier he said: "There is something sacred in a word, in the *Word,* which prohibits us from making it a game of chance. To manage a language knowingly is to practice a kind of evocatory sorcery." [65] Magic, evocation, hatred of the chance and contingent were to become Mallarmé's preoccupation.

Nor is the term "symbol" or the concept of "myth" at all prominent in Baudelaire. "Symbol" occurs rather casually in the context of the theory of correspondences and universal analogy, and is in Baudelaire's use interchangeable with allegory, cipher, hieroglyphic, and even emblem.[66] Mythology to Baudelaire is "a dictionary of living hieroglyphs, of the hieroglyphs known by everyone." [67] Only when Baudelaire discusses Wagner does he quote his defense of the myth [68] with approbation and sees then in *Lohengrin* an analogy to the Psyche story—without asserting, however, any literary derivation. The similarity of the two stories is "the sign of a single origin, the proof of an irrefutable common parentage, but on the condition that we seek this origin only in the absolute principle and the common origin of all beings." "Myth is a tree which grows everywhere, in every climate, under every sun, spontaneously." [69] But there is no evidence that Baudelaire saw myth as the center of poetry or of his own poetry, however clearly he may have seen its universality and its universal appeal and admired its use by Wagner.

The sonnet *Correspondances,* hardly a critical text, seems to have served as the starting point for the interest in synesthesia that has become a hallmark of symbolism. Rimbaud's sonnet *Les Voyelles,* in which vowels are arbitrarily identified with specific colors, became the focal point of an enormous debate. Its participants, however, rarely show any knowledge of the all-pervasive presence of synesthetic metaphor—even in antiquity, and certainly in baroque and romantic poetry—or any awareness of the complex issues involved: the supposed original community of the senses, the presence of synesthesia in all language, the synesthetic elements in cosmological speculations, or the distinction between the physiological compulsive type of synesthesia and the much more common analogies between the senses that have become a conventional rhetorical figure.[70] Baudelaire himself quoted a passage from E. T. A.

Hoffmann [71] that definitely asserted an experience of compulsive synesthesia, but he could also have noticed inter-sense metaphors in Heine, Nerval, Poe and many others. There is no evidence that Baudelaire himself confused the senses or compulsively asserted their identity. In the sonnet *Correspondances* he proclaimed an occult theory; in his poetry he uses synesthesia as merely another analogy in the great dictionary of symbolism, just as he constantly used comparisons between the arts, characterizing pictures in musical terms or musical compositions in visual images without confusing the arts or even advocating their fusion. Though Baudelaire draws parallels between the arts freely and a poem of Gautier, for instance, can remind him of a symphony of Beethoven,[72] he constantly asserts that "the encroachment of one art upon another" is a vice [73] and that "every art must be sufficient to itself and at the same time stay within its providential limits." [74] At most, Baudelaire recognizes that the tendency toward a fusion of the arts is a symptom of his age, which seems to him decadent. "The arts aspire if not to take another's place, at least reciprocally to lend each other new powers." [75] Baudelaire understood that Wagner wanted to develop each art in its own terms in order to produce the synthetic art of the music drama, which is not a confusion of the arts but their collaboration in a common aim. When, in the article on Wagner, Baudelaire quotes his own sonnet *Correspondances,* he does so to justify his verbal depiction of the *Lohengrin* overture in analogues of light and lightness and whiteness. But there is no confusion of the senses in him; there is only an art of translation, a rhetoric of analogizing in which the metaphors, alternating among the senses, play only a minor role. The false idea that this single device is central to symbolism and its interpretation as a clinical trait of the poets have made symbolism suspect as decadent and pathological.

The main source for this view is the letter of Rimbaud in which he proposed, at the age of sixteen, that the "poet should make himself a *seer* by a long, immense, and deliberate *disorder* of *all the senses.* All forms of love, suffering, madness; he searches himself, he exhausts within himself all the poisons so as to retain only their essences. Unspeakable torment in which he needs all faith, all superhuman power, where he becomes among all the great diseased, the great criminal, the great damned,—and the supreme wise man—for he arrives at the *unknown.*" [76] The confusion of the senses, possibly by stimulants like alcohol, is a means, like love and suffering, toward the achievement of a vision and a wisdom which Rimbaud thought of as hallucination and even supernatural illumination. In *A Season in Hell* Rimbaud expounds his "alchemy of the word."

> I invented the color of vowels . . . *A* black, *E* white, *I* red, *O* blue, *U* green . . . I defined the form and movement of every consonant, and, with instinctive rhythms, I prided myself on inventing a poetic language which would be, some day, accessible to all the senses. I reserved the right of translation. It was at first an experiment. I wrote of silences, of nights, I recorded the inexpressible.

The line between deliberate metaphorical substitution and actual hallucination is even less clear when he says:

> I saw frankly a mosque in place of a factory, a school of drummers made by angels, carriages on the highways of the sky, a drawing-room at the bottom of a lake; monsters, mysteries; the title of a vaudeville would spread terror before me. Then I explained my magic sophisms with the hallucination of the word. I came to regard the disorder of my mind as sacred.[77]

One need not emphasize the violent bravado of these passages nor minimize their interest for the poetic practice of Rimbaud to see that their magic claims hardly constitute a literary theory. Still, bold experimentation with the poet's self, even at the expense of suffering and madness, and the claim of supernatural illumination fit well into the tradition of romantic mysticism, in which the magic of the word achieves an illumination that is as obscure as the words themselves.

Compared to Rimbaud's irrational boastings, Baudelaire's literary criticism is a model of sober sense and fine sensibility. It is guided by his theory of the imagination and analogy though often only remotely so. Baudelaire's criticism defines his own historical position in the tradition of French poetry without being historical in its method. It is occasional, completely confined to its own time, both in its self-conscious "modernity," which still rejects progress in the arts, and also in its individualism, which sees that the artist "stems only from himself" and rarely has any forerunner.[78]

Baudelaire's discovery of Poe is obviously one of his main critical achievements. One knows how far he went in identifying himself with Poe: how much he characterized Poe in terms of himself, a man in conflict with his society, a *poète maudit,* who used alcohol (as Baudelaire for a time used opium) to stimulate his work.[79] His sociological misinterpretation of Poe (which is due in part to his use of suspect sources) is understandable. It seems more difficult to explain his exaltation of Poe's intellect, the seriousness with which he takes Poe's supposed mysticism, and his praise of "profound and plaintive poetry, transparent and correct like a crystal jewel—his admirable pure and bizarre style, compact as the meshes of mail."[80] A deficiency in Baudelaire's knowledge of English must have contributed to this overrating of a shoddy craftsman, but one must simply recognize his genuine attraction to Poe's poetic theories and the themes and motifs which, however melodramatic, appealed to the caverns of his soul. Baudelaire's misjudgment of Poe's poetic and intellectual rank seems to me, however, undeniable; it is a feature of his critical sense that can be explained but not defended.

Outside of Poe, Baudelaire discussed no foreign writer, if one ignores the spotty praise of E. T. A. Hoffmann and the wavering comments on Heine.[81] Instead, his reviewing allowed him to define his taste in relation to the immediate history of French literature. The attitude toward the romanticism of his youth is necessarily ambivalent. Baudelaire recognizes that "Victor Hugo, Sainte-Beuve, Alfred de Vigny had rejuvenated, nay, had resuscitated French poetry, which had been dead since Corneille"; that romanticism "recalled us to the truth of the image"; that "it destroyed the academic *clichés*"; that it let "prevail the glory of pure art." [82] In romanticism he singles out the satanic, demonic tendency of modern art, the line of Beethoven, Maturin, Poe, Byron, Musset—as he makes up an oddly incongruous pedigree. He sees in it "a celestial or infernal grace to which we owe eternal stigmata," and the "most recent, the most modern expression of beauty." [83] But he can also emphasize another aspect of romanticism, "intimacy, spirituality, color, aspiration toward the infinite." [84] Among the romantics, Baudelaire admired Chateaubriand the most: "the great gentleman of the decadences who wants to return to savage life." [85] He also admired the early poetry of Sainte-Beuve, *Joseph Delorme,* which is

"The Flowers of Evil of yesterday," [86] and Pétrus Borel, who appealed to him as a kindred *poète maudit,* for his pessimism and dilettantism.[87]

Baudelaire wrote at length only on two older poets: Hugo and Gautier. Both relations were personal, and his criticism is colored by literary politics. His view of Hugo shifts from the highest admiration to exasperated pronouncements about Hugo's "stupidity." Basically, one can see that Baudelaire admired Hugo as a great poet, but he could not sympathize with his ideas and temperament. Very early he had compared Delacroix with Hugo much to the disadvantage of the latter. Hugo is really not a romantic if romanticism means intimacy and spirituality. He is a correct workman rather than a creator. "In all his pictures, both lyric and dramatic, Victor Hugo reveals a system of uniform alignment and contrasts. With him even eccentricity takes symmetrical forms. . . . He is a composer of decadence or transition, who handles his tools with a truly admirable and curious dexterity. M. Hugo was a natural academician even before he was born." [88] Baudelaire finds him "too material, too attentive to the surfaces of nature," too much a painter-poet.[89] Later, in slightly different terms, he repeats that Hugo is a "great sculptural poet whose eye is closed to spirituality." [90] In his long essay he expounds the aesthetic of correspondences, which he rightly sees exemplified in Hugo. He characterizes well "the turbulences, accumulations and collapses of verses, the masses of stormy images"; he complains that the public "ignores the mysterious, shadowy, the most charming parts of Hugo"; he calls him the "king of landscape painters"; and he lauds the *Légende des siècles* as "the only epic poem which could be created by a man of his time for the readers of his time." [91] Grandeur, universality, the excessive, and the immense are some of the attributes singled out for praise, but even here, at a time when Baudelaire wanted to please Hugo, the fundamental lack of sympathy is obvious. The opening statement of the main article, which says that Hugo is "always master of himself, supported by an abridged wisdom consisting of several irrefutable axioms," [92] seems a scarcely disguised complaint against his platitudes. Occasionally Baudelaire criticizes Hugo for his didacticism and social sentimentality. The late review of *Les Misérables* is, on the surface, oddly noncommittal about this "book of charity," but it concludes with Baudelaire's boldly asserting his own sense of man's fall and original sin against Hugo's entire trust in the natural goodness of man.[93] In private, Baudelaire even condemned the book as "unclean and inept" and complained of Hugo's "seeing nothing but his own navel." [94] The antagonism became sharper, no doubt, for political reasons: it comes into the open when Baudelaire, in an anonymous letter to the editor of *Figaro* on 14 April 1864, protests against the taking of Shakespeare's birthday celebration as an excuse for an antigovernment demonstration and makes sharp comments on Hugo's book about Shakespeare. "God, in a spirit of an impenetrable mystification, amalgamated foolishness and genius" in Hugo.[95] The meetings with Hugo and his family in Brussels did not improve matters: Baudelaire writes that all three Hugos— mother and sons—"are as foolish and as stupid as their father," and reflected, even before Hugo had arrived in Brussels, that "one can be both a genius and a boor—just as one can possess a special talent and be a fool at the same time." [96] Baudelaire was dazzled by the genius of the most famous poet of his time: but he consistently felt it to be devoid of true spirituality and inwardness, devoid of real intelligence.

No such ambivalence marks his attitude toward Gautier. The dedication of *Les Fleurs du mal* to the "impeccable poet, the perfect magician of French letters, my dearest and most honored master and friend," [97] and the two highly laudatory articles celebrating Gautier's aristocratic disdain for the crowd, his devotion to beauty and art free of didacticism and sloppy sentiment, his worship of the word, of perfection, and of difficulties overcome, his melancholy, outweighed by "consolation through the arts, through all the picturesque objects which delight the eyes and amuse the mind," [98] form a single paean of enthusiastic praise for a kindred, older fellow artist. The letter to Hugo avowing "confidentially" that Baudelaire "knows the gaps of his [Gautier's] astonishing mind" [99] must be dismissed as a piece of backstage diplomacy. Baudelaire's public comments are so high-pitched in their claim for Gautier's greatness and perfection and brush aside the obvious objections to his lack of humanity so cavalierly that one cannot help feeling that Baudelaire was genuinely insensitive to the limitations of this glossily picturesque but empty and monotonous virtuoso.

He is far more critical of Banville. In an early article, without mentioning his name, he attacks Banville together with the whole "pagan school"—presumably Ménard and Leconte de Lisle—for blaspheming Christianity. The whole effort to reverse the wheel of history, the attempts of these poets to produce *pastiches* of antiquity, to be "plastic," to admire "form" at any price, seem to him futile.[100] In a later essay he praises Banville as a lyrical poet, lyrical meaning in Baudelaire's terminology "longing for the Lost Eden." While one must remember that the article was an introduction to a selection in Crépet's *French Poets,* the tone of its conclusion, proclaiming Banville "a true classic," is sincerely laudatory, even though it contains Baudelaire's essential reservations: Banville ignores the satanic trends in modern poetry, he lacks dissonance and irony, "he expresses nothing but the beautiful, the joyous, the grand, the rhythmic." [101]

The cult of beauty, of pagan antiquity, the sheer artistry and craft of Banville did not satisfy Baudelaire, but neither did it offend him. Sentimental, egotistic emotionalism repelled him strongly. "The apes of sentiment are, in general, bad artists." [102] "The cry of feeling is always absurd"; the "poetry of the heart" that ascribes infallibility to passion is an aberration in aesthetics.[103] He remembers "in regard to sentiment, the heart, and other female sloppiness, the profound saying of Leconte de Lisle: 'all elegiacs are scoundrels.' " [104] He condemns Lamartine, Béranger, and especially Musset, "the master of fops," "a bad poet" whose books can be found in prostitutes' bedrooms, "a languorous undertaker's man," "feminine and without doctrine." [105] George Sand, "stupid, heavy, garrulous, a slut," "a foolish creature," [106] is Baudelaire's pet aversion. Neither the neopagan *Parnasse* nor sentimental romanticism—thus Baudelaire defines his own position in the French tradition; but he makes two uncritical exceptions: he accepts Gautier, who is surely open to the criticism directed against the pagan school, and he has a weak spot for Mme Marceline Desbordes-Valmore, whom he characterized sympathetically, condoning her sentimental vagueness.[107]

Surprisingly, Baudelaire's best criticism is devoted to the novel. The draft of an essay on Choderlos de Laclos, who at that time had no critical attention, shows remarkable insight into his "Racinian analysis." [108] The comments, casual as they are, on Balzac as a visionary, "a passionate visionary" rather than an observer,[109] are perceptive in their rejection of the label "realism." And the essay on *Madame Bovary* is a triumph of sympathetic imagination at a time when Flaubert was being badly misinterpreted. Baudelaire sees that the book is a "wager": a tour de force to prove that a work of art can be written on the tritest of subjects, adultery, "the most exhausted barrel organ." [110] Baudelaire defends the implied morality, the high objectivity of the book, but sees also that Emma has something of the author. Flaubert infused a man's blood into the veins of his creature, gave her imagination, the sudden energy of action, an immoderate taste for seduction and domination, made her a dandy and even a hysterical poet. Baudelaire goes too far in seeing her as a great woman pursuing the Ideal: he overstates a genuine insight at a time when Emma was being disparaged as ridiculous and weak. He overstates again when he sees a close parallel between *Madame Bovary* and the fragments of *The Temptation of Saint Anthony* that he had read in the serial installments. "It would have been easy," he says, "to find under the minute texture of *Madame Bovary* the high capacities for irony and lyricism which so sharply light up *The Temptation of Saint Anthony*." He sees in both works "that suffering, subterranean and rebel faculty" which Flaubert tried to hide in *Madame Bovary* but gave free rein to in *The Temptation*. Baudelaire finds *The Temptation* "evidently more interesting for poets and philosophers." [111]

But the review of *Madame Bovary* is the only first-rate piece of strictly literary criticism in Baudelaire. This small showing is due simply to the narrow range, to the occasional character of Baudelaire's reviewing, to the diplomacy and topicality of his work, but also to Baudelaire's failure to find a proper relation to criticism or to formulate an adequate theory of criticism. Baudelaire knew that "all the great poets become naturally, fatally critics. I pity poets who are guided only by instinct; I believe they are incomplete . . . It is impossible that a poet should not contain a critic . . . I consider the poet the best of all critics. Diderot, Goethe, Shakespeare were all creators, all admirable critics." [112] The inclusion of the name of Shakespeare shows, however, that Baudelaire thought here of criticism not in the sense of theory or the judgment of other writers but simply as self-criticism, as consciousness, as the "calculus" he always exalted against mere inspiration. Sometimes he recognizes that criticism touches metaphysics, requires a sense of variety within unity, a sense of the various aspects of the absolute. [113] But more frequently Baudelaire voices suspicion of system, "a kind of damnation" which ever forces the critic to invent a new one, and expresses a sense of the final inadequacy of all criticism. "There is always something new in the manifold productions of art which will eternally escape the rule and the analyses of the school." [114] At one point Baudelaire formulates his ideal of sympathetic criticism when he demands of the critic: "In order to present the work well, you must *enter into the skin* of the created being, become deeply imbued with the feelings which he expresses, and feel them so thoroughly, that it seems to you as if it were your own work." [115] But for the most part, in his literary criticism, Baudelaire did not make any effort to attain either aesthetic coherence or a sympathetic "entering into the skin." He contented himself with fulfilling his early demands:

> The best criticism is that which is most amusing and poetic: not a cold, mathematical criticism, which, on the pretext of explaining everything, has neither love nor hate, and voluntarily strips itself of every shred of temperament . . . To be just, that is to say, to justify its existence, criticism should be partial, passionate, and political, that is to say, written from an exclusive point of view, but a point of view that opens up the widest horizon.[116]

This is a good ideal for a poet and creative artist: actually in his art criticism and in many scattered reflections on aesthetics Baudelaire went much further in the direction of a coherent theory. But his strictly literary criticism remained "partial, passionate, and political."

STÉPHANE MALLARMÉ (1842–1898)

Stéphane Mallarmé fixed the idea of pure, obscure, and hermetic poetry firmly in the public mind—less by his theories than by his own austere and difficult work and by his personal example as a High Priest of poetry. Mallarmé's thoughts on aesthetics are scattered through his precious and often willfully vague and involved essays, first collected in *Divagations* (1897) , but were often more clearly expressed in letters and interviews. They can be expounded as a system of ideas that is far more coherent and consistent than the often oblique and highly metaphorical formulations might suggest.

As a theorist Mallarmé derives from Poe and Baudelaire but radically differs from them on central points. He worships Poe as his "great master," [1] "the noblest poetic soul that ever lived," [2] "the spiritual prince of this age." [3] He translates the poems, which he considers almost all "masterpieces," [4] and in poetic theory adopts from Poe an emphasis on calculation and effect, an enmity to romantic inspiration, and the worship of work and craft. "The philosophy of composition" seems to him "a very new theory of poetry," which he defends against the charge of "mystification." Poe's pages, even if they were written after the poem and even if they had no "anecdotal basis," would still be "sincere." Poe taught him that "all chance must be banished from a modern work and that it can be only pretended"; and that "the eternal stroke of the wing does not exclude a lucid glance at the space devoured by its flight." [5] Mallarmé protests against the common conception that the ideal poet is "a great epileptic whom one depicts unkempt, with haggard eyes, haphazardly pouring forth his facile and incoherent verses in one stream under the inspiration of I know not what talkative Muse." Rather, he is "a serious thinker who conceives strongly and who surrounds his conceptions with bold and slowly chiseled images." [6] In Mallarmé, as in Poe, the concept of poetry as a calculus of effects is combined with an aspiration toward pure beauty, but Mallarmé's ideal is far from the sentimental, ethereal, "supernal" beauty of Poe: it is something much more austere, icy, frozen, and at the same time frighteningly, dazzlingly dark and even hollow.

The link with Baudelaire's aesthetics is far more tenuous than with Poe's. Mallarmé shares with Baudelaire the views common to Poe but does not believe in the creative imagination, in the mastery and assimilation of reality, in that identification of subject and object which is the central, ultimately romantic core of Baudelaire's aesthetics. Though Mallarmé occasionally speaks of correspondences and analogies and certainly uses the method in his poems, he neither shares Baudelaire's general philosophy of a universe of symbols or hieroglyphics nor is particularly concerned with a rhetoric of metamorphoses. The passage on the "Word which prohibits us from making it a game of chance," on language as "evocatory sorcery," [7] though isolated in Baudelaire's writings, suggests much more clearly Mallarmé's chief concerns than the rest of Baudelaire's aesthetic thought.

In truth, independent of Poe or Baudelaire, Mallarmé develops several other old ideas to their logical or illogical extremes. He is, as far as I know, the first writer who is radically discontent with the ordinary language of communication and attempts to construe an entirely separate poetic language. *Il Trobar clos* and Góngora (whom he did not know) attempted something similar, and even Collins thought of the poet mainly as an inventor of diction. Gerard Manley Hopkins, almost contemporaneously, elaborated his personal poetic language. But in Mallarmé the proposal is far more radical. The language of communication, in its "crude, immediate use" is set off from the "essential language" of poetry,[8] not merely, and certainly not primarily (though Mallarmé has been accused of so doing), because of snobbery, aristocratic disdain for the common herd, or even a desire for poetic experimentation, but because of a radical discontent with language as such. Sarcastically, Mallarmé suggests that "an adequate exchange of human thoughts might well be achieved through the silent exchange of money," [9] since our commercial civilization needs no thinking. But also the narrative, didactic, descriptive use of everyday language, which he identifies with its journalistic use, utilitarian reportage, is condemned as unfit material for poetry. All historical languages are deficient because they do not reach Mallarmé's ideal: language as "real language, language as magic, words as things." "The diversity of the languages of this earth prevents anyone from uttering words which otherwise, if minted only once, would be Truth itself incarnate. This is clearly nature's law . . . to the effect that we have no sufficient reasons for equating ourselves with God." [10] Presumably God alone knows the truth, and real words would speak absolute truth. On occasion Mallarmé toys with the project of a new universal language, which Leibniz had dreamed of and which the mathematical logicians have since devised in their own fashion; but in practice Mallarmé as a poet proposes, rather, a transformation of the French language into a special poetic idiom. He described and exploited systematically most of the traditional devices for separating poetic language from ordinary speech.

Mallarmé believed in a fixed relation of sound and sense that the poet has to discover and use. Sound symbolism seemed to him a "future science," which he himself tried to investigate in his oddly amateurish *Les Mots anglais* (1877). Thus "sneer" and "snake" share *Sn,* which is a "sinister diagram," while "fly" and "flow" have something soaring and fluid.[11] In his *Traité du verbe* (1887), for which Mallarmé wrote some introductory remarks, René Ghil developed, in a mechanical fashion, a scheme of sound-symbolism which he called "poetic instrumentation." Maurice Grammont, in *Le Vers français* (1913), tabulated systematically the sound-symbolism of French; but even he did not escape the extreme subjectivity of interpretation and association that Mallarmé wished in theory to exclude. Moreover, Mallarmé believed in synesthesia as embedded in the language. He complains, for example, that in French "jour" has a dark vowel and "nuit" a light one, though it should be the other way around.[12] Sound patterns, alliterations, rhyme make up one level of poetic devices. The other is formed, of course, by meter, which through its rhythmic spell achieves the isolation of the word from ordinary speech, draws something like a magic circle around the poem, and "atones for the defects of language."[13] Meter has a blending power over the words of which it is composed. Verse "becomes a new element, in itself and by itself one, and devouring its own words."[14] Thus "words reflect each other until they no longer seem to have any color of their own but seem to be only the transitions on a scale."[15]

Mallarmé conceives this sound-stratum of poetry as achieving the effects of music, but, in contrast to many of his contemporaries who loudly proclaimed "De la musique avant toute chose," he did not confuse the sounds of poetry with the sounds of music and did not want to have poetry become music. Though he writes in a letter, "Je fais de la musique,"[16] he still understands that music in poetry is vain unless language confers sense on sound. He claims that the word achieves the same immediate approach to the soul as strings or brass, "though they exult to any height."[17] Music, in Mallarmé, is music in the Greek sense, the rhythm of the Idea, "the totality of relations existing in the whole,"[18] something more divine than a symphony. "Poetry, near the Idea, is Music, at its best—it does not admit inferiority."[19] While Mallarmé admires Wagner highly, he is far from subordinating poetry to music (as he means it) or aiming at a synthesis similar to that of the composer. Rather, he annexes Wagner to poetry.

> In the case of Wagner I do not perceive theater in the strictest sense of the word (without any doubt, there is much more of the dramatic in Greece or in Shakespeare). His is rather a vision of myth which lives for itself beneath a veil of sounds and mingles with them. His scores, moreover, compared with those of a Beethoven or a Bach, are not merely musical. Something more special, something more complex is involved: namely Fiction, or Poetry, which lies at the crossroads of the other arts, stems from them, and yet dominates them.[20]

Poetry, in Mallarmé's eyes, is clearly the highest art.

But even more than by an organization of sound, Mallarmé wants to achieve this poetic language by a change in the meaning of words: through their use in their etymological meaning, with denotations unusual in ordinary speech (these he sometimes seems to have derived from an examination of Littré);[21] through the inclusion of neologisms, whose meaning can be guessed, or occasional archaisms; and mainly through the development of a new syntax that violates the ordinary relations of the structure of the French sentence and the established uses and distributions of the French parts of speech. It has been argued that Mallarmé was influenced by English syntax, but surely little clarity is gained by transcribing Mallarmé's constructions faithfully into English. Far more is derived from Latin than from English, and his syntax, on the whole, is neither English nor French, but personal.[22]

In a late stage of his career, as further devices to break with convention, Mallarmé added the graphic picture on the printed page, and even the physical makeup of the book. This again resumes an old idea: there was the graphic poetry of the Greek anthology, the Persian pattern poems, the "Altar" and the "Churchfloor" of George Herbert. Since Mallarmé, graphic arrangements have been used by Apollinaire, E. E. Cummings, and many other modern poets. In Mallarmé's *Le Coup de dés* the theme of the constellation of stars is suggested by graphic means, but the arrangement of the lines and words on the page mostly suggests hierarchies of importance, emphasis and de-emphasis, and, in the blank spaces, intervals, pauses, and silences. The model of a musical score is obviously in Mallarmé's mind. The layout of the page, visible at a glance, is intended to remove poetry from time, to achieve something similar to the static effect of a picture. Even the makeup of the book—the way it is folded, its format—is to share in the effect of the work of art. This turn toward the written picture (*l'écriture*) shows Mallarmé's growing distrust of the sound element in poetry, the complete abandonment of his ambition to rival music, the retirement into solitary and silent reading. The change is paralleled by Mallarmé's abandonment of regular meter and his use of *vers libre,* which he had until then considered loose and capricious and whose invention he had announced to his English audience with the horrified phrase: "On a touché au vers." [23]

But all this is only a descriptive account of what Mallarmé meant by the famous line in "Le Tombeau d'Edgar Poe":

Donner un sens plus pur aux mots de la tribu.

His real originality appears only when we understand the justification for the whole enterprise of a special poetic language so far removed from that of ordinary communication. The aim is first of all negative: it is to keep out reality, to exclude society, nature, and the person of the artist himself. The implied antinaturalism needs no elaboration. Mallarmé's art cannot be descriptive: the poet must not name an object, only suggest and evoke, and hence Mallarmé constantly uses ellipsis and periphrasis. Art is not, and must not be, personal or lyrical. "The pure work presupposes the disappearance of the poet as a speaker. The initiative will be taken óver by the words." [24] The poet is a priest, devoted to his art, serving it humbly, ascetically, in profound solitude, without hope of personal gain or glory. At the moment of writing *Hérodiade,* Mallarmé wrote to a friend: "I am impersonal now, not the Stéphane you once knew, but one of the ways the Spiritual Universe has found to see itself, to unfold itself through what used to be me." [25] The disappearance of the poet seems to him to be "without question *the* discovery of modern poetry." [26] Poet and man are entirely distinct in Mallarmé. He criticizes Taine for the view that "an artist is simply a powerful man." Rather, he believes, that "it is perfectly possible to have a human temperament quite distinct from the literary. . . . When the artist sits down to write, he makes himself. Taine does not

believe, for example, that a writer can change his manner completely. As a matter of fact, he can. I have seen it in my own case." [27]
He had changed from the early Parnassian and Baudelairian styles
to the conciseness and complexity of his mature verse.

The aristocratic contempt for the Philistine is quite blatant in
the early writings. The paper "L'Art pour tous" (1862) boldly
proclaims the need of "mystery in art," deplores the fact that poetry
is taught at school, and asserts that persons who would not dare to
pronounce on a technical aspect of painting or music have their
opinion about poetry merely because they use the language. Actually, poetry is accessible only to the very few. "Man can be democratic; the artist divides himself and must remain aristocratic." The
hope of popularizing art seems to Mallarmé a blasphemy; the idea
of a workers' poet is merely grotesque, if not pitiful. Corneille,
Molière, and Racine are not popular despite appearances. "Their
names are popular, perhaps; but their verses are not." He concludes
with an exhortation in a tone like Nietzsche's: "Let the masses read
works on moral conduct, but, please, don't let them ruin our poetry.
Oh, poets! you have always been proud: now be more than proud,
be scornful!" [28]

Later Mallarmé made several proposals as to how art could escape
isolation and become collective, even national and popular. In an
essay on Richard Wagner, "Rêverie d'un poète français" (1885),
Mallarmé admires Wagner's synthesis between the intimate drama
and ideal music, his success in enthroning Myth on the stage, though
he voices misgivings as to whether something similar can be created
in France. The French spirit "shrinks back from the Myth; therein
it agrees with Art in its integrity, which is invention"—presumably
because free Imagination cannot be content with reproducing a
traditional myth. The French may accept a Fable instead of a
Myth or possibly one myth, free of individuality, instead of many
myths. A type, a hero without a name, somebody like Hamlet or his
Igitur, may emerge. A theater, a ritual under the auspices of the
City, is vaguely envisaged, but on the very same page doubt seems
to be thrown not only on the necessity of real actors but on any kind
of externalization. "Does a gesture of our soul, do symbols in preparation or in flower need any place for their development other than
the fictitious stage of vision which flashes in the sight of the audience?" [29] Something like a *monodrame* or possibly an ode distri-

buted among voices is occasionally hinted at. Later, in the essay *Catholicisme* (1895), a liturgical art, similar to the Mass seems suggested: a Passion play, organized by the four seasons, which would "convey the authenticity of the words and the triumphant light of Country, or Honor and Peace." He invokes the example of Old Church music, of *a capella* choirs, of organ music, but a postscript (which he later withdrew) insists that the intention is strictly secular: Mallarmé would rather have the ludicrous reputation of being anticlerical than be confused with the mystics of the New Catholic vogue.[30]

All these proposals for a social art remain disconcertingly vague. His belief that "poetry should be for the supreme pomp and circumstance of a constituted society in which Glory should have its place"[31] is quite theoretical, as unreal as his pathetically frustrated attempts, described in a sketch *Conflict*, to find an intimate relationship with working people. In practice, Mallarmé realizes that "this society . . . does not allow the poet to live," that he is "a man who seeks out solitude in order to sculpture his own tomb," that he "is on strike against society."[32] The only art possible for Mallarmé is a solitary austere art, culminating in the "architectural, premeditated" work, a divine and intricate organism which Mallarmé calls the Book.[33] But it would be an error to think of this book as merely the cherished possession of a bibliophile. The Book appeals to Mallarmé precisely because it is the best insurance of immortality, the most secure assertion of the permanence of art. The Book is reproducible almost illimitably: it will, like the Bible, make poetry, his poetry, universal, enduring, indestructible, immortal. All the elaborate devices of sound and shifts of verbal meaning, the whole special language of poetry, serve to achieve the elimination of chance and of contingency which afflict all ordinary language. A structure is erected that is to be coherent, like a system of number symbols where not one iota could be changed without toppling the edifice. Logically there can be only one such Book, as there could be only one universal language.[34] Such a book (for which Mallarmé's own writings were only sketches) would simply exist, independent of the mind of the author or reader.[35] It would be like language creating itself. The Word in Mallarmé was not at the beginning but will be at the end.

Recently, late notes and jottings made by Mallarmé in prepara-

tion for the Book have been published.[36] They suggest that he
envisaged his Book more concretely than the printed hints have
hitherto revealed. He thought of it as containing no less than 20
volumes apparently of 480, 384, or 320 pages each, to be read aloud
to a select group of 24 auditors over a period of 5 years by the author,
whose task would be that of an "interpreter" or "operator." Mallarmé worked out even the financial details: there would be a fee of
500 francs, to be returned when 480,000 copies of the Book had
been sold to the unprivileged masses. Each copy would yield a profit
of one franc, thus bringing in 480,000 francs—no small sum at the
end of the 19th century. The public reading of the manuscript
would be held in a small apartment; though limited, it would still
satisfy Mallarmé's desire for some kind of reconciliation between
the printed book and the intimate theater. The reading would not
be mere recitation. There would be interpretations and, particularly, constant reshuffling of the sheets of the volumes so that they
would assume new meanings in new contexts. "The volume, in spite
of its fixed impression, becomes mobile by this manipulation—
from death it springs to life." [37] But in spite of these disconcerting,
mechanical speculations, which include even a plan to have adver-
tisements on the blank pages or spaces,[38] the notes are extremely
vague as to the actual text of "The Book"; it is not even clear
whether it was to be in verse or in prose, and the hints at its themes
or "myths" are disappointingly sketchy: a grotesque situation of an
invitation by a lady to a visitor who is not allowed to eat and, confronted with the risk of death by hunger, is compelled to eat the
lady; a man confronted with two women on a beach; a man alive
in his tomb dying of hunger. It would be unfair to judge these
jottings as a finished work, but it is difficult to believe that Mallarmé
could have seriously considered the whole scheme of readings and
enormous printings. (A certain playful, melancholic irony arouses
sympathy but hardly convinces one of the feasibility of the plan.)
The hints at the actual contents, fragmentary as they are, pathetic
in their incompleteness and vagueness, suggest that Mallarmé could
not solve the ambitious problem of the "canonical" book, of the
Bible demanded by his theory. He seems to have had a strong desire
for what he calls "proof" or "confirmation," a sense that what he had
written was not merely an arbitrary, subjective invention but precisely that one Book which is reality and real language. However, he

could not advance beyond seeing the problem and suggesting that it might be solved by public approval and recognition,[39] for obviously the whole idea of a single book, a "real" language, is a mistake. It runs counter to the diversity of reality as evolved in history. It is a desperate and heroic cast of the dice, which, however, will never abolish chance.

His Book was to give "an orphic explanation of the earth"; [40] it was to be a book of magic, trying to suggest or to evoke the central mystery, the inexpressible, the Idea, Silence, Nothingness. All these terms are used almost interchangeably, but it seems to me no really obscure problem is raised by what has been extolled as Mallarmé's negative aesthetics. There is, no doubt, a psychological basis for his feeling of sterility, impotence, and final silence. He has described, in many letters, especially from Tournon, the way he agonized over his work, possibly more than any other writer. He was a perfectionist, with a lofty ideal of what poetry should be, a meticulous craftsman who proposed something by its very nature impossible of fulfillment: a book to end all books. "All earthly existence exists to be contained in a book . . . a hymn, all harmony and joy, an immaculate grouping . . . of universal relationships": [41] in short, a magic abstract of the universe. But whatever the psychological difficulties, there seems little that calls for awestruck contemplation in Mallarmé's central paradox. Like many poets before him, he wants to express the mystery of the universe but feels that this mystery is not only insoluble and immensely dark but also hollow, empty, silent, Nothingness itself. Very early, Mallarmé abandoned religion and seems, like many atheists, to have vacillated between materialism or agnosticism and some kind of occultism. It seems unlikely that he had more than a bowing acquaintance with Plato or Hegel, with whom he has been associated. Nor need one mention Freemasonry, Buddhism, or Schopenhauer and Schelling (or their intermediary, Wagner) , as others have done.[42] Nothing more is required, at least to explain Mallarmé's poetic theories, than the atmosphere of 19th-century atheistic pessimism and some knowledge of the general ideas of the Neoplatonic tradition in aesthetics. Art searches for the Absolute but despairs of ever reaching it: the essence of the world is Nothingness, Nirvana, and the poet can do nothing but speak of this Nothingness, this Silence.

Mallarmé is no mystic in the sense of any claim of contact with the supernatural. Even the depersonalization he requires is not mystical. It is a surrender of personality for the purpose of adequately mirroring the universe and its riddle. Impersonality is objectivity, truth. Art reaches for the Idea, which is ultimately inexpressible, because so generalized as to be devoid of any concrete traits. Mallarmé calls the French spirit "strictly imaginative and abstract and therefore poetic." [43] The general term "flower" is to him poetic precisely because it suggests "the one, absent from all bouquets." [44] Hence art is both abstract and obscure. It can only hint at the mystery. Art must "evoke, in a deliberate shadow, the object which is silenced, be allusive, never direct." [45] The word "symbol," which Mallarmé uses sparingly, would be one device to achieve this effect. Without using the word, he says that art is "to institute an exact relation between images; and then a third aspect, clear and fusible, will break from it and be presented to divination." [46] The enmity toward description, toward the ideal of Parnassian poetry, finds support in a Poe-like emphasis on effect. We "renounce that erroneous aesthetic" which would have the poet "fill the delicate pages of his book with the actual and palpable wood of trees, rather than with the forest's shuddering or the silent scattering of thunder through the foliage." [47] Here is implied an impressionism and of course an illusionism still based, after all, on earthly objects. But usually Mallarmé exalts an abstract art in a tone of desperate pride: "Poetry . . . is the expression of the mysterious meaning of the various aspects of our existence. It therefore gives true value to our life on earth and is the duty of our soul." [48] "Literature exists and, if you will, it alone exists, to the exclusion of everything else." [49] This paradox becomes clearer when we read a letter that rehearses the skeptical creed that "we are all only empty forms of matter—empty and yet sublime, because we have invented God and our own souls." The poet plunges nonetheless "desperately into dreams which he knows do not exist, singing all the while of our Soul and of all similar and heavenly impressions stored up in us since the earliest times, and, in the face of Nothingness which is the truth, proclaiming this glorious lie." [50] This is not just the pride of a poet, but a genuine belief that everything perishes but the work of art, the perfect work of art, and especially the least destructible of all, the work of poetry: the Book. In the famous lines of "Toast funèbre," addressed to the dead Gautier,

> Duty imposed by the gardens of this star,
> Survived far the honor of the calm disaster
> By a solemn agitation in the air of words
> Drunken purple and great clear chalice,
> Which, rain and diamonds, his diaphanous look
> (Remaining) there on the flowers, of which none fades,
> Isolates in the hour and the day's luminosity! [51]

Art theory has here reached an extreme that fittingly concludes this account of 19th-century criticism. Art alone survives in the universe, and not only art but poetry in particular. Man's main vocation is to be an artist, a poet, in order to save something from the wreckage of time. The work or, in Mallarmé's term, the Book is suspended over the Void, the silent Godless Nothingness. Poetry is resolutely cut off from concrete reality, from its old concern with the imitation of nature, from the expression of the personality of the poet, from any rhetoric of emotion, and becomes only a Sign, signifying Nothing.

The contrast to Tolstoy or Zola could not be more extreme. In Mallarmé poetry absorbs all reality and becomes the only reality; in Zola and Tolstoy and many others art is identified with life and becomes superfluous and finally useless. Clearly, the task of a new era would be a reassertion of the balance: a recognition of the independence and autonomy of art but also of its meaningful relation to the reality of nature, man, and society.

POSTSCRIPT

LOOKING BACK at the long road we have traveled, recalling the variety of doctrines and opinions we have expounded, imagining the gallery of intellectual portraits we have drawn, we might well examine, or rather re-examine, our method of telling the story of 19th-century criticism. Is it correct to say that we have written a history? A history of criticism, we may have to conclude, cannot be narrative history in the way that a history of political or personal events can be. It is rather a description, analysis, and judgment of books or, more accurately, theories, doctrines, and opinions expounded in many books. Have they a history beyond the chronological order of exposition and the differences and changes of setting in which they were pronounced?

Clearly, critics wrote and still write in a concrete social, political, and literary-historical setting; often they argue for a specific purpose at a specific moment of time. Some attempts have been made here to point out these relations. We might, for example, be struck by the contrast between a critic like De Sanctis, who was fully and enthusiastically involved in the concerns of his society and rose to play a great social role in the victory of the Italian unification movement, and a critic like Flaubert, who despised the society of his time and wrote criticism only in letters to friends. The general 19th-century conflict between bourgeois and bohemian can be illustrated also in literary criticism. Something has been said to suggest the close relationship between much criticism and the political issues of the time. The liberal fervor of Young Germany or the Russian Radical critics or Georg Brandes, with their belief in progress and democracy, can be contrasted with the French conservative and Catholic critics who looked back to the 17th century, to monarchy, authority, and tradition. A good deal of attention has been paid to the relation of criticism to philosophy. The change from the idealistic Hegelian atmosphere of the early 19th century to the prevalence of empirical, positivistic or materialistic allegiances and terminologies is too obvious to be missed. The profound impact of science, or rather the model of scientific method, on criticism has been described in discussing Taine's triad of *milieu–race–moment*, the evolutionism of Brunetière, and the scientific pretensions of Zola's theories. Criticism is closely related to historiography, cultural and, in particular, literary; and in literary history, which we treated as a kind of subtheme of our book, we saw the same changes toward the scientific ideal, toward objective factualism. Criticism, no doubt, is involved in all the other activities of man: critics are after all men living in their time, sharing or opposing its creeds and convictions, political, religious, philosophical, and so on. All this is true, and something has been done to indicate these truths.

But can a history of criticism be written in terms of these relationships? And can they be considered determining causes? Can one establish, as political historians on occasion claim they can, causalities in the history of criticism? I do not believe we can do so or have ever succeeded in doing so. Rather, this history conceives of criticism as what has strikingly been called "an essentially contested concept" which is continually debated in history and will be debated for a long time to come. The problems of criticism are permanent problems in the sense that they are with us even today and that they were set early in history with the emergence of the arts and our growing awareness of the nature of the arts. There seems to be no convincing reason to reduce this debate to merely a reflection of the social, political, philosophical, or even literary-historical conditions of a time. Criticism is not completely involved *in* history; rather, it has its own history, which is comparatively independent of its relations to other endeavors of mankind. But can this debate then be described simply by acknowledging its lack of resolution or by exhibiting its endless variety? Could it be handled neutrally, impartially? I do not believe so. Sides have to be taken: the interlocutors have to be interrupted, perhaps rudely; questioned in turn; and called to account by the historian. Some of them, or even many of them, were never allowed to speak; others were permitted to display all their arguments at leisure; others could hardly put in a word. I would have abdicated the function of a historian if I had simply described book after book and expounded systems in chronological order. History, we have to recognize, cannot be written without a sense of direction, a feeling for the future. We must know where it is tending; we require some ideal, some standard, and some hindsight. As E. H. Carr notes, "History properly so called can be written only by those who find and accept a sense of direction in history itself." Direction also implies a desire for change, but change is impossible without knowledge and knowledge includes a knowledge of history.

Obviously I constantly keep in mind an ideal of criticism that can be briefly outlined—though I hope it emerges from the history itself. Criticism aims at a theory of literature, at a formulation of criteria, and standards of description, classification, interpretation, and finally judgment. It is thus an intellectual discipline, a branch of knowledge, a rational pursuit. If we want to arrive at a coherent theory of literature, we must do what all other disciplines do: isolate our object, establish our subject matter, distinguish the study of literature from other related pursuits. It seems obvious that the work of literature is the central subject matter of a theory of literature and not the biography or psychology of the author, or the social background, or the affective response of the reader. Such an ideal has to be guarded against two misunderstandings: that literary theory is not concerned with the individual work of art and that it wants to become a science, to establish universal laws by methods of quantification. On the contrary, literary theory can thrive only in contact with works of art which initially at least demand sensitivity, enjoyment, and involvement. Literary theory will remain a humanistic discipline concerned with value which will remain, also, value for oneself. In literary study there is an interplay between the intense contemplation of the object and the desire to organize our experience into a network and even system of concepts. The individual and the general must be kept in balance.

The very same problem is raised by writing a history of criticism. While theories of literature serve as guideposts, while we must try to discern trends and study the struggle of diverse *isms,* we must never consider critics merely as "cases." They are individuals and develop their sensibilities, formulate their literary opinions, and combine or invent theories in specific, personal ways. There must be both portraiture of critics and tracings of trends and concepts, both analysis and synthesis.

A sense of this ideal of criticism has allowed us to orient ourselves in the variety of 19th-century trends. We can evaluate all of them from this point of view. The prevalent conceptions of criticism as imitating the methodology of science, the belief in deterministic causality or in the evolution of literature as biological evolution, to be found in Taine and Brunetière, all ignore or minimize the autonomy of art. On the other hand, we cannot be satisfied with impressionism as propounded by Anatole France and Lemaître, for it leads to anarchy and antirationalism. We cannot accept realism and naturalism, as they confuse life and art and propound the ideal of art mirroring reality instead of creating a new reality of art. Didacticism, moralism, political ideology of the type we found in Brandes or the Russian radicals will distort the meaning of literature. Classicism, the norm of beauty as it is upheld by Nisard and, in a different form, modeled rather on the Goethean ideal, in Arnold's humanism, will impose a narrow ideal of beauty strongly tinged with moral nobility. Symbolism, which had grasped a central procedure of art, slid, with Mallarmé, into claims that would make poetry and language a brand of magic, while aestheticism with its formula of defiance in "art for art's sake," impoverished the meaning of literature by retreating into an ivory tower and denying the social role of literature.

The 20th century will grow out of the 19th. Some points of view will survive unchanged or developed into more radical forms. Naturalism lingers on; symbolism will be more fully defined by Yeats and Valéry. Nineteenth-century classicism will be restated by the American neohumanists and preached again by many French critics. The imitation of scientific methodology will re-emerge with different allegiances: for example, in Marxist criticism, which appeals to the economic interpretation of history, and in I. A. Richards when he appeals to neurology and behaviorist psychology to interpret poetry as a kind of mental therapy. Impressionism will again run riot, and art for art's sake develop into a formalism that is technological in its purity, in Russia. But new motifs emerge in the 20th century which have little preparation in the 19th. Though Freud defined psychoanalysis late in the 19th century, its effect is felt only in the 20th and is, I think, never foreshadowed in 19th-century criticism in spite of attempts to find forerunners in the psychologists concerned with the irrational. While the scientific study of myth and ritual had begun in the 19th century, its application to literature as a structure of myths is an innovation of the 20th century. The feelings formulated by existentialism are, no doubt, age-old, but the interpretation of literature in terms of the poet's attitude to time, space, and being was attempted only later in the 20th. It will be the task of our last volume to describe, interpret, and evaluate these developments. But the past survives within the present; the present is comprehensible in terms of the past, and the past only in terms of the present.

BIBLIOGRAPHIES AND NOTES

On realism, for a survey of theories and literature, see my "The Concept of Realism in Literary Scholarship," *Neophilologus, 44* (1960), 1–20, reprinted in *Concepts of Criticism* (New Haven, 1963), pp. 222–55. See also the anthology edited by George J. Becker, *Documents of Literary Realism*, Princeton, 1963.

On French discussions see Emile Bouvier, *La Bataille réaliste (1844–1857)*, Paris, 1914; Bernard Weinberg, *French Realism: The Critical Reaction, 1830–1870*, New York, 1937 (thorough examination of all evidence); F. W. J. Hemmings, "The Origin of the Terms *Naturalisme, Naturaliste,*" *French Studies, 8* (1954), 109–21; and Harry Levin, *The Gates of Horn: A Study of Five French Realists,* New York, 1963 (pays attention to criticism).

On Balzac as critic:

Geneviève Delattre, *Les Opinions littéraires de Balzac,* Paris, 1961 (a complete description). Geoffroy Atkinson, *Les Idées de Balzac,* Geneva, 1950 (Vol. 5 contains chapters on aesthetics and literary criticism). The best general book on Balzac's mind is Ernst Robert Curtius, *Balzac,* 1923, new ed. Bern, 1951. Two striking views of Balzac's criticism: Georg Lukács, "Balzac als Kritiker Stendhals" (1935), in *Balzac und der französische Realismus* (Berlin, 1952), pp. 66–87. René Etiemble, "Balzac critique," in *Hygiène des lettres* (Paris, 1952), *1,* 23–40.

On Flaubert:

I quote, as *Co., Correspondance: Nouvelle Edition Augmentée,* Conard ed., 9 vols. Paris, 1926–33. I have used the translations in *Letters,* ed. Richard Rumbold, trans. J. M. Cohen, New York, 1951; and in *The Selected Letters,* trans. Francis Steegmuller, New York, 1957. Two large French thèses, E. L. Ferrère, *L'Esthétique de Gustave Flaubert* (Paris, 1913), and Hélène Frejlich, *Flaubert d'après sa correspondance* (Paris, 1933), are useful but diffuse. Marianne Bonwit, *Gustave Flaubert et le principe d'impassibilité,* University of California Publications in Modern Philology, 33 (Berkeley, 1950), makes an important point. Albert Thibaudet, *Gustave Flaubert* (Paris, 1935), is still the most perceptive critical book.

On Maupassant:

Maupassant's critical writings are collected as *Chroniques, Etudes, Correspondance,* ed. René Dumesnil, Paris, 1938. The Preface to *Pierre et Jean,* "Etude sur le roman," is quoted from *Une Vie: Pierre et Jean,* ed. R. Dumesnil (Paris, 1935), pp. 269–83. There is a good survey in Helmut Kessler, "Zu den literaturaesthetischen Anschauungen Guy de Maupassants," *Archiv für das Studium der neueren Sprachen, 199,* Year *114* (1962), 1–16.

On Zola:

I quote *Les Œuvres complètes,* ed. Maurice Le Blond, Paris, 1929. F. W. J. Hemmings, *Emile Zola* (Oxford, 1953), is the best monograph. See also Henri Mitterand, *Zola Journaliste,* Paris, 1962; and Angus Wilson, *Emile Zola,* New York, 1952. F. Doucet, *L'Esthétique de Zola et son application à la critique* (The Hague, 1923), is a careful study.

Details of Zola's criticism discussed in: Jean Triomphe, "Zola collaborateur du *Messager de l'Europe,*" *Revue de Littérature Comparée, 17* (1937), 754–65; L. W. Tancock, "Some Early Critical Work of Emile Zola: *Livres d'aujourd'hui et de demain,*" *Modern Language Review, 42* (1947), 43–57; G. Robert, "Trois Textes inédits d'Emile Zola," *Revue des Sciences Humaines, 51* (1948), 181–207; George Heard Hamilton, *Manet and His Critics,* New Haven, 1954; and F. W. J. Hemmings, "Zola's Apprenticeship to Journalism (1865–70)," *PMLA, 71* (1956), 340–54.

On Lemaître and France:

I quote Lemaître, *Les Contemporains,* 8 vols. Paris, 1903–18; and Anatole France, *La Vie littéraire,* 2 vols., from *Œuvres complètes illustrés,* Paris, 1950. There are chapters on Lemaître in three mediocre surveys: Georges Renard, *Les Princes de la jeune critique,* Paris, 1890; Ernest Tissot, *Les Evolutions de la critique française,* Paris, 1890; and Alexandre Belis, *La Critique française à la fin du XIXᵉ siècle,* Paris, 1926. Belis also has a chapter on Anatole France. Anette Antoniu, *Anatole France, critique littéraire* (Nancy, 1929), is a careful thesis. Maurice Kahn, *Anatole France et Emile Zola* (Paris, 1927), corrects a common misconception.

NOTES: FRENCH CRITICISM

1. Cf. my paper "The Concept of Realism in Literary Scholarship" in *Concepts of Criticism* (New Haven, 1963), pp. 222–55.
2. In "Vom Ich in der Philosophie," *Sämmtliche Werke* (Stuttgart, 1856), Abtheilung 1, *1,* 213: "Der reine Realismus setzt das Daseins des Nicht-Ichs überhaupt."

3. Friedrich Schlegel, *Literary Notebooks 1797–1801,* ed. Hans Eichner (Toronto, 1957), p. 60: "Dieser Realismus ist in seinem Wesen gegründet." Page 65: "Es fehlt ihm an Stoff, an Realismus, an Philosophie."

4. April 27, 1798. "Der Realism [sic] kann keinen Poeten machen."

5. *Seine prosaischen Jugendschriften,* ed. J. Minor, Vienna, 1882. 2, 299: "Es giebt keinen wahren Realismus als den der Poesie."

6. Quoted from E. B. O. Borgerhoff, "*Réalisme* and Kindred Words," *PMLA, 53* (1938), 837–43: "Cette doctrine littéraire qui gagne tous les jours du terrain et qui condurait à une fidèle imitation non pas des chefs-d'œuvre de l'art mais des originaux que nous offre la nature, pourrait fort bien s'appeler le réalisme: ce serait suivant quelques apparences la littérature du XIXᵉ siècle, la littérature du vrai."

7. "Moralité de la poésie," *Revue des Deux Mondes,* 4th ser. *1* (1835), 259: "Quel écusson était placé à la porte du château, quelle devise était inscrite sur l'étendard, quelles couleurs portées par l'amoureux baron."

8. "Revue littéraire du mois," *Revue des Deux Mondes, 4* (1 November 1834), 339; "avec une exagération de réalisme, qu'il a emprunté à la manière de M. Hugo."

9. "M. H. de Balzac" in *Semaine* (4 October 1846), quoted by Weinberg, *French Realism,* p. 70.

10. *Histoire de la peinture flamande et hollandaise,* Paris, 1846. On the role of Dutch painting in rise of realistic theories, see Peter Demetz, "Dutch Painting and the Theory of the Realistic Novel," *Comparative Literature, 15* (1963), 97–115.

11. 25 February 1851, in *Le Messager de l'Assemblée,* quoted in Bouvier, *La Bataille réaliste.* Page 238: "Les bourgeois sont ainsi."

12. Champfleury knew a Swiss writer, Max Büchon, and learned from him about the Swiss peasant novel; see "La littérature en Suisse" (1853) in *Le Réalisme* (Paris, 1857), pp. 224–54. A later note (1857) expresses disappointment with Gotthelf as absolutely lacking in art (p. 255).

13. *Le Réalisme,* p. 234: "Chasse l'auteur de son livre autant qu'il est possible."

14. "Lettre à M. Veuillot," *Figaro* (10 July 1856), quoted by Bouvier, p. 305: "L'idéal pour un romancier impersonnel est d'être un protée, souple, changeant, multiforme, tout à la fois victime et bourreau, juge et accusé, qui sait tour à tour prendre le rôle du prêtre, du magistrat, le sabre du militaire, la charrue du laboureur, la naïveté du peuple, la sottise du petit bourgeois."

15. *Le Réalisme,* p. 5: "un mot de transition qui ne durera guère plus de trente ans." Page 3: "Je n'aime pas les écoles, je n'aime pas les drapeaux, je n'aime pas les systèmes."

16. *Le Réalisme,* "Lettre à Madame Sand," p. 272: "Le titre de réaliste m'a été imposé comme on a imposé aux hommes de 1830 le titre de romantiques. Les titres, en aucun temps, n'ont donné une juste idée des choses; s'il en était autrement, les œuvres seraient superflues." More on Courbet in George Boas, ed. *Courbet and the Naturalist Movement,* Baltimore, 1938.

BALZAC

1. *Œuvres complètes,* ed. Marcel Bouteron and H. Lognon (Paris, 1912), *1, XXIX:* "l'histoire oubliée par tant d'historiens, celle des mœurs." Page *XXVIII:* "Imprimait alors une allure gigantesque à un genre de composition injustement appelé secondaire." Page XXXVI: "Sa géographie comme il a sa généalogie et ses familles, ses personnes et ses faits."

2. *Œuvres complètes, 38,* 219, 220, 255. Page 351: "L'artiste commande à des siècles entiers; il change la face des choses." Page 355: "un miroir où l'univers tout entier vient se réfléchir."

3. See Pierre Laubriet, *Un Catéchisme esthétique: Le Chef-d'œuvre inconnu de Balzac* (Paris, 1961), for comparison of two versions and interpretation.

4. *Œuvres, 23, 283. Les Paysans:* "Les mutations du goût, les bizarreries de la vogue, et les transformations de l'esprit humain."

5. *Œuvres complètes,* review of Auguste Borget, "La Chine et les Chinois" (1846). *40, 545:* "L'infertilité de ce que nous appelons le *Beau.* Le Beau ne peut avoir qu'une ligne. L'art grec était réduit à la répétition d'idées, en définitive très pauvres, n'en déplaise aux Classiques. La théorie chinoise a vu, quelque mille ans avant les Sarrasins et le Moyen-Âge, les immenses ressources que présente le *Laid,* mot si niaisement jeté à la face des romantiques, et dont je me sers par opposition à ce mot le *Beau.* Le Beau n'a qu'une statue, il n'a qu'une temple, il n'a qu'un livre, il n'a qu'une pièce: *l'Iliade* a été recommencée trois fois, on a perpétuellement copié les mêmes statues grecques, on a reconstruit le même temple à satiété, la même tragédie a marché sur la scène avec les mêmes mythologies, à donner des nausées. Au contraire, le poème de l'Arioste, le roman du trouvère, la pièce hispano-anglaise, la cathédrale et la maison du Moyen-Âge sont l'infini dans l'art."

6. *Œuvres, 10,* 214–15: *La Muse du département:* "toute une science, elle exige une compréhension complète des œuvres, une vue lucide sur les tendances d'une époque, l'adoption d'un système, une foi dans certains principes."

7. Lukács, p. 66: "ausserordentlich tiefe Kritik." Page 87: "Eines der grossen Ereignisse in der Geschichte der Weltliteratur." Etiemble, p. 25, considers Balzac the only French critic in 1830.

8. *Œuvres complètes, 40, 374: "Le Prince* moderne."

9. 20 October 1840. Correct text in Paul Arbelet, "La Véritable Lettre de Stendhal à Balzac," *Revue d'Histoire Littéraire de la France, 24* (1917), 548–59. Page 552: "Pour prendre le ton, je lisais chaque matin deux ou trois pages du Code civil."

10. *Œuvres, 40,* 371–72. "Littérature des Idées," "Littérature des Images," "Eclecticisme littéraire."

FLAUBERT

1. In *Le Correspondant,* 25 June 1857, reprinted in *Nouvelles Causeries du samedi* (Paris, 1859), pp. 299–326. "L'auteur a si bien réussi . . . à rendre son œuvre impersonelle, qu'on ne sait pas, après avoir lu, de quel côté il penche."

2. "Nouvelles diverses," in *Réalisme* (15 March 1857), No. 5, p. 79.

3. *Causeries du lundi, 13,* 363: "M. Gustave Flaubert tient la plume comme d'autres le scalpel. Anatomistes et physiologistes, je vous retrouve partout!"

4. *Co., 4, 52* (7 April 1854): "Mon Dieu! Que de mal! Que d'échignements et de découragements."

5. *Co., 2,* 394 (24 April 1852): "J'aime mon travail d'un amour frénétique et perverti, comme un ascète le cilice qui lui gratte le ventre."

6. *Co., 2,* 339 (12 January 1852): "les affres de l'Art." Henry James, *Essays in London and Elsewhere* (New York, 1893), p. 139.

7. Preface to *Pierre et Jean* in *Une Vie: Pierre et Jean,* p. 277: "quel vilain mot!"

8. *Co., 3,* 61–62 (9 December 1852): "L'auteur, dans son œuvre, doit être comme Dieu dans l'univers, présent partout, et visible nulle part. L'art étant une seconde nature, le créateur de cette nature-là doit agir par des procédés analogues. Que l'on sente dans tous les atomes, à tous les aspects, une impassibilité cachée et infinie."

9. *Co., 7,* 280 (20 December 1875): "L'artiste ne doit pas plus apparaître dans son œuvre que Dieu dans la nature. L'homme n'est rien, l'œuvre tout." *5,* 253 (5–6 December 1886): "un romancier n'a pas le droit d'exprimer son opinion sur quoi que ce soit. Est-ce que le bon Dieu l'a jamais dite, son opinion?"

10. *Co., 3,* 183 (26–27 April 1853): "A l'heure qu'il est, je crois même qu'un penseur (et qu'est-ce que l'artiste si ce n'est un triple penseur?)

ne doit avoir ni religion, ni patrie, ni même aucune conviction sociale."

11. *Co.*, 7, 285 (6 February 1876): "Le lecteur est un imbécile ou le livre est faux au point de vue de l'exactitude."

12. Jean-Paul Sartre, *Situations II* (Paris, 1948), p. 13: "Je tiens Flaubert et Goncourt pour responsables de la répression qui suivit la Commune parce qu'ils n'ont pas écrit une ligne pour l'empêcher."

13. *Essays in London*, pp. 149–50.

14. *Co.*, *3*, 344 (16 September 1853): "Une tout autre chose et d'un ordre inférieur. J'ai pleuré à des mélodrames qui ne valaient pas quartre sous et Goethe ne m'a jamais mouillé l'œil, si ce n'est d'admiration."

15. *Co.*, *4*, 164 (18 March 1857): "L'illusion . . . vient . . . de l'impersonnalité de l'œuvre . . . une histoire totalement inventée."

16. *Co.*, *1*, 254 (15 August 1846): "J'ai écrit des pages fort tendres sans amour, et des pages bouillantes sans aucun feu dans le sang."

17. *Co.*, 2, 268–69 (15 December 1850): "Tu peindras le vin, l'amour, les femmes, la gloire, à condition, mon bonhomme, que tu ne seras ni ivrogne, ni amant, ni mari, ni tourlourou. Mêlé à la vie, on la voit mal; on en souffre ou on en jouit trop. L'artiste, selon moi, est une monstruosité, quelque chose hors nature."

18. It appears first in R. Descharmes, *Flaubert avant 1857* (Paris, 1909), pp. 347–48, in a note reported secondhand as said to Mlle Amélie Bosquet.

19. *Co.*, *3*, 276 (12 July 1853): "La vulgarité de mon sujet me donne parfois des nausées." *3*, 345 (21–22 September 1853): "un milieu aussi fétide." *3*, 166 (13–14 April 1853): "J'en ai presque envie de vomir physiquement." *4*, 168 (30 March 1857): "Une femme de fausse poésie et de faux sentiments."

20. *Co.*, 2, 432 (10 June 1852): "un tour de force prodigieux." *5* (3 January 1854): "une œuvre surtout de critique, ou plutôt d'anatomie." *3*, 180 (22 April 1853): "Une œuvre d'une rude volonté." *3*, 201 (21–22 May 1853): "Une chose voulue, factice."

21. *Co.*, *3*, 249 (25–26 June 1853): "Yvetot donc vaut Constantinople . . . L'artiste doit tout élever."

22. *Co.*, *8*, 225 (February–March 1879): "Le Gange n'est pas plus poétique que la Bièvre, mais la Bièvre ne l'est pas plus que le Gange. Prenez garde, nous allons retomber, comme au temps de la tragédie classique, dans l'aristocratie des sujets et dans la préciocité des mots. On trouvera que les expressions canailles font bon effet dans le style, tout comme autrefois on vous l'enjolivait avec des termes choisis."

23. *Co.*, *3*, 320 (26 August 1853): "Rien de ce qui est de ma personne ne me tente." Page 322: "Homère, Rabelais, Michel-Ange, Shakespeare, Goethe m'apparaissent *impitoyables*."

24. *Co., 3*, 405 (23 December 1853): "Aujourd'hui par exemple, homme et femme tout ensemble, amant et maîtresse à la fois, je me suis promené à cheval dans une forêt, par un après-midi d'automne, sous des feuilles jaunes, et j'étais les chevaux, les feuilles, le vent, les paroles qu'ils se disaient et le soleil rouge qui faisait s'entre-fermer leurs paupières noyées d'amour."

25. *Extraits,* ed. G. Bollème (Paris, 1963), p. 238 (November 1866): "Quand j'écrivais l'empoisonnement de Mme Bovary j'avais si bien le goût d'arsenic dans la bouche, j'étais si bien empoisonné moi-même que je me suis donné deux indigestions coup sur coup,—deux indigestions réelles car j'ai vomi tout mon dîner." Taine quoted this passage, with some changes in *De l'Intelligence, 1,* 190.

26. *Co., 1,* 321 (18 September 1846): "Il n'y a pas de belles pensées sans belles formes, et réciproquement . . . l'Idée n'existe qu'en vertu de sa forme."

27. *Co., 2,* 339 (14 January 1852): "Ces distinctions de la pensée et du style sont un sophisme."

28. *Co., 3,* 141 (27 March 1853): "La forme est un manteau. Mais non! La forme est la chair même de la pensée, comme la pensée en est l'âme, la vie." *7, 290* (March 1876): "Deux entités qui n'existent jamais l'une sans l'autre."

29. *Co., 2,* 345 (16 January 1852): "Ce qui me semble beau, ce que je voudrais faire, c'est un livre sur rien, un livre sans attache extérieure, qui se tiendrait de lui-même par la force interne de son style, comme la terre sans être soutenue se tient en l'air, un livre qui n'aurait presque pas de sujet ou du moins où le sujet serait presque invisible, si cela se peut. Les œuvres les plus belles sont celles où il y a le moins de matière. . . . Il n'y a ni beaux ni vilains sujets."

30. *Co., 2,* 282 (24 December 1850): "On a beau dire, l'Art n'est pas un mensonge."

31. *Co., 7,* 294 (3 April 1876): "Eh bien. Je me demande si un livre, indépendamment de ce qu'il dit, ne peut pas produire le même effet. Dans la précision des assemblages, la rareté des éléments, le poli de la surface, l'harmonie de l'ensemble, n'y a-t-il pas une vertu intrinsèque, une espèce de force divine, quelque chose d'éternel comme un principe? (Je parle en platonicien.)"

32. *Co., 4,* 134 (October–November 1856): "On me croit épris du réel, tandis que je l'exècre; car c'est en haine du réalisme que j'ai enterpris ce roman."

33. *Co., 7,* 285 (6 February 1876): "J'exècre ce qu'on est convenu d'appeler le réalisme, bien qu'on m'en fasse un des pontifes."

34. *Co. 7,* 377 (25 December 1876): "Pourquoi a-t-on délaissé ce bon

Champfleury avec le 'Réalisme,' qui est une ineptie de même calibre, ou plutôt la même ineptie?"

35. *Co.*, *7*, 359 (8 December 1877): "La Réalité, selon moi, ne doit être qu'un tremplin. Nos amis sont persuadés qu'à elle seule elle constitue tout l'État. Ce Matérialisme m'indigne, et, presque tous les lundis, j'ai un accès d'irritation en lisant les feuilletons de ce brave Zola. Après les Réalistes, nous avons les Naturalistes et les Impressionnistes. Quel progrès! Tas de farceurs, qui veulent se faire accroire et nous faire accroire qu'ils ont découvert la Méditerranée."

36. *Co.*, *9*, 22 (18 April 1880): "Un colosse qui a les pieds malpropres, mais c'est un colosse."

37. *Co. 3*, 367–68 (12 October 1853): "Mon *Histoire du sentiment poétique en France.* Il faut faire de la critique comme on fait de l'histoire naturelle, avec absence d'idée morale. Il ne s'agit pas de déclamer sur telle ou telle forme, mais bien d'exposer en quoi elle consiste, comment elle se rattache à une autre et par quoi elle vit."

38. *Co.*, *6*, 8 (2 February 1869): "Quand sera-t-on artiste, rien qu'-artiste, mais bien artiste? Où connaissez-vous une critique qui s'inquiète de l'œuvre *en soi,* d'une façon intense? On analyse très finement le milieu où elle s'est produite et les causes qui l'ont amenée: mais la poétique *insciente*? d'où elle résulte? sa composition, son style? le point de vue de l'auteur? Jamais!"

39. *Co.*, *5*, 160 (October 1864): "Il y a autre chose dans l'Art que le milieu où il s'exerce et les antécédents physiologiques de l'ouvrier. Avec ce système-là, on explique la série, le groupe, mais jamais l'individualité, le fait spécial qui fait qu'on est *celui-là.* Cette méthode amène forcément à ne faire aucun cas du *talent.* Le chef-d'œuvre n'a plus de signification que comme document historique."

40. *Co.*, *3*, 336–37 (7 September 1853): "La critique esthétique est restée en retard de la critique historique et scientifique: on n'avait point de base. La connaissance qui leur manque à tous, c'est l'*anatomie du style.*"

41. *Co.*, *3*, 360 (30 September 1853): "Ils pouvaient peut-être connaître l'anatomie d'une phrase, mais certes ils n'entendaient goutte à la physiologie du style."

42. *Première Éducation sentimentale* (Paris, 1910), p. 259: "Chaque œuvre d'art a sa poétique spéciale en vertu de la quelle elle est faite et elle subsiste." Cf. *Co.*, *4*, 23 (29 January 1854): "Chaque œuvre à faire a sa poétique en soi, *qu'il faut trouver.*"

43. *Co.*, *2*, 469 (July 1852): "La consistance du vers. Une bonne phrase de prose doit être comme un bon vers, *inchangeable,* aussi rhythmée, aussi sonore."

44. "Apropos du style de Flaubert," in *Chroniques,* Paris, 1927.

45. *Co., 3,* 136–37 (27 March 1853): "Cette harmonie de choses disparates. . . . Jaffa où, en entrant, je humais à la fois l'odeur des citronniers et celle des cadavres; le cimetière défoncé laissait voir les squelettes à demi pourris, tandis que les arbustes verts balançaient au-dessus de nos têtes leurs fruits dorés. Ne sens-tu pas combien cette poésie est complète, et que c'est la grande synthèse?"

46. "The Metaphysical Poets" in *Selected Essays* (London, 1932), p. 273.

MAUPASSANT

1. *Chroniques,* p. 108: "Une révolution dans les lettres."

2. *Une Vie: Pierre et Jean,* p. 275: "La photographie banale de la vie . . . la vision plus complète, plus saisissante, plus probante que la réalité même." Page 276: "Sensation profonde de la vérité . . . l'illusion complète du vrai . . . Illusionnistes . . . Nos yeux, nos oreilles, notre odorat, notre goût différents créent autant de vérités qu'il y a hommes sur la terre . . . Les grands artistes sont ceux qui imposent à l'humanité leur illusion particulière." Page 281: "Pour décrire un feu qui flambe et un arbre dans une plaine, demeurons en face de ce feu et de cet arbre jusqu'à ce qu'ils ne ressemblent plus, pour nous, à aucun autre arbre et à aucun autre feu." Page 282: "En quoi un cheval de fiacre ni ressemble pas aux cinquante autres qui le suivent et le précèdent." Page 271: "Un critique ne devrait être qu'un analyste sans tendances, sans préférences, sans passions, et, comme un expert en tableaux, n'apprécier que la valeur artiste de l'objet d'art qu'on lui soumet."

ZOLA

1. Hemmings, *Zola,* p. 109. Angus Wilson, *Zola,* pp. 25, 30.

2. *Le Roman expérimental,* p. 33: "Puisque la médicine, qui était un art, devient une science, pourquoi la littérature elle-même ne deviendrait-elle pas une science, grâce à la méthode experimentale?"

3. *Ibid.,* p. 38: "Une enquête générale sur la nature et sur l'homme."

4. *Ibid.,* p. 35: "La méthode n'est qu'un outil." Page 36: "Il reste le génie, l'idée *a priori.*"

5. *Une Campagne,* p. 105: "Le mot naturalisme, qui se trouve dans Montaigne, avec le sens que nous lui donnons aujourd'hui. On l'emploie en Russie depuis trente ans, on le trouve dans vingt critiques en France, et particulièrement chez M. Taine."

6. *Sämtliche Werke,* ed. Güntter-Witkowski (Leipzig, 1909–11), *20,* 254: "Alles ist nur ein Symbol des Wirklichen."

7. *Sobranie sochinenii,* ed. Golovenchenko (Moscow, 1948), *3,* 775, 776, 789.

8. *Nouveaux Essais de critique et d'histoire* (Paris, 1865), p. 118: "L'idéal manque au naturaliste; il manque encore plus au naturaliste Balzac"; p. 120: "L'objet propre du naturaliste"; p. 133: "Ce sont, en effet, les héros du naturaliste et du rude artiste que rien ne dégoûte."

9. *Légende des siècles,* ed. R. Berret (Paris, 1921), *1,* 15–16: "Il n'est pas défendu au poète et au philosophe d'essayer sur les faits sociaux ce que le naturaliste essaie sur les faits zoologiques: la reconstruction du monstre d'après l'empreinte de l'ongle ou d'alvéole de la dent."

10. *L'Evénement* (22 July 1866): "Aujourd'hui en critique littéraire et artistique, il nous faut imiter les naturalistes, nous avons charge de retrouver les hommes sous les œuvres, de rétablir les sociétés dans leur vie réelle, à l'aide d'un livre ou d'un tableau." Quoted by J. W. J. Hemmings, "The Origin of the Terms *Naturalisme, Naturaliste,*" *French Studies,* 8 (1954), 109–21.

11. Preface (Paris, 1868), p. iii: "J'ai simplement fait sur deux corps vivants le travail analytique que les chirurgiens font sur des cadavres." Page ix: "Le groupe d'écrivains naturalistes auquel j'ai l'honneur d'appartenir."

12. *Une Campagne,* p. ix: "La méthode est restée la même, et le but, et la foi" (1882).

13. *Mes Haines,* p. 24: "Une œuvre d'art est un coin de la création vu à travers un tempérament."

14. *Le Roman expérimental,* p. 102: "un procès-verbal," "un lambeau d'existence." Page 209: "Les documents humains."

15. *Les Romanciers naturalistes,* p. 298: "On gagne l'immortalité, en mettant debout des créatures vivantes, en créant un monde à son image."

16. *Mes Haines,* p. 11: "Je n'ai guère souci de beauté ni de perfection. Je me moque des grands siècles. Je n'ai souci que de vie, de lutte, de fièvre. Je suis à l'aise parmi notre génération."

17. Feuilleton on *Macbeth,* in *Bien Public* (14 January 1878), quoted in Flaubert, *Lettres inédites à Tourgueneff* (Monaco, 1946), pp. 156–57. On Goethe, *Une Campagne,* pp. 61 ff.

18. In *L'Événement Illustré* (4 July 1867): "Notre plus grand romancier . . . Stendhal étudiat les hommes comme des insectes étranges, qui vivent et meurent, poussés par des forces fatales; son humanité ne sympathisait pas avec celle de ses héros, il se contentait de faire son travail de dissection exposant simplement les résultats de ce travail." Quoted by Hemmings, "Zola's Apprenticeship," *PMLA, 71* (1956), 351.

19. *Les Romanciers naturalistes,* p. 103: "Il est compliqué comme

une machine dont on finit par ne plus voir clairement la fonction."
Page 91: "Julien me cause les mêmes surprises que d'Artagnan." Page
104: "Il est notre père à tous comme Balzac. Il apporté l'analyse, il a
été unique et exquis, mais il a manqué de la bonhomie des romanciers
puissants. La vie est plus simple."

20. *Une campagne*, p. 104: "Le père du naturalisme." *Mes Haines*,
pp. 145–46.

21. In *Le Rappel* (13 May 1870), quoted by Henri Mitterand, *Zola
Journaliste* (Paris, 1962), pp. 110–13. "Balzac est à nous; Balzac, le
royaliste et le catholique, a travaillé pour la République, pour les
sociétés et les religions libres de l'avenir."

22. *Les Romanciers*, p. 55: "L'inconscience venait surtout de son
manque de sens critique." Page 62: "Il a écrit l'œuvre la plus révolu-
tionnaire, une œuvre où, sur les ruines d'une société pourrie, la démo-
cratie grandit et s'affirme." Page 63: "Balzac, bon gré, mal gré, a conclu
pour le peuple contre le roi, et pour la science contre la foi."

23. *Une Campagne*, p. 104: "Il a pu professer ouvertement des opinions catholiques et monarchiques, toute son œuvre n'en est pas moins
scientifique et démocratique, dans les sens large du mot."

24. *Les Romanciers naturalistes*, p. 47: "Comment le génie d'un
homme peut aller contre les convictions de cet homme."

25. See this *History*, Vol. 3, 237–8.

26. *Mélanges*, p. 107: "Son horreur secrète pour les choses, les livres
et les hommes bruyants."

27. *Documents littéraires*, p. 220: "La jolie médisance, la politesse
parfaite, toute pleine de sous-entendus méchants, le continuel sourire
déguisant la sévérité des jugements."

28. *Le Roman expérimental*, p. 180: "Le chef de notre critique."

29. In letter 25 July 1866, quoted by Hemmings, *PMLA*, p. 349.

30. *Mes Haines*, p. 159: "L'amour de la puissance, de l'éclat ... des
aspirations passionnées vers la force et la vie libre." Page 171: "de raide
et de tendu dans le système, de généralisé et d'inorganique."

31. *Une Campagne*, p. 197: "La robe du professeur ... un académicien timoré, un trembleur de la philosophie, un équilibriste de la
critique."

32. *Le Roman expérimental*, p. 115: "La dernière citadelle de la
convention." Page 108: "un joujou curieux, amusant." Page 119: "Ou
le théâtre sera naturaliste, ou il ne sera pas."

33. *Mes Haines*, p. 84: "Un voile entre les objets et nos yeux."

34. *Une Campagne*, p. 35: "Cet incroyable galimatias." Page 40:
"colossal et vide."

35. *Documents*, p. 141: "Que des mots mis côte à côte."

36. *Roman expérimental*, p. 87: "Faire la musique, pendant que nous travaillerons."

37. "Proudhon et Courbet" in *Mes Haines*, pp. 21–34. Page 31: "Faiseurs de la chair."

38. *Mes Haines*, p. 253: "La nature telle qu'elle est." Page 259: "quelques raideurs élégantes qui surprennent." Pages 267–69: "Ce corps nu indécent; cela devrait être."

39. For comment see George Heard Hamilton, *Manet and His Critics*, New Haven, 1954; and John Rewald, *The Ordeal of Paul Cézanne*, London, 1950.

40. *L'Evénement* (25 August 1866), quoted in Hemmings, *PMLA*, p. 348: "un chimiste-poète, un mécanicien-peintre."

41. *Le Roman*, p. 101: "Un artist parfait". *Les Romanciers*, pp. 161, 156: "les évolutions en littérature."

42. *Une Campagne*, p. 315.

43. *Ibid.*, pp. 262, 264. A funeral speech in *Mélanges*, pp. 284–89.

44. *Une Campagne*, p. 205: "Il raffine trop, il tourmente et travaille trop ses phrases comme des bijoux."

45. For details see the pamphlet *Pernicious Literature*, which reprints the Debate in the House of Commons, in Becker, *Documents*, pp. 382 ff.

46. On the front page of *Le Figaro* (18 August 1887): "Manifeste de Cinq contre *La Terre*." See Becker, pp. 344–49.

47. *Là Bas* (Paris, 1891), p. 2: "l'éloge de la force brutale . . . l'apothéose du coffre fort, l'américanisme nouveau des mœurs."

48. *Le Roman russe* (Paris, 1886), p. xxxiv: "Sans foi, sans émotion, sans charité," p. XLII: "Détachés personnellement du dogme chrétien, ils en gardent la forte trempe, cloches du temple qui sonnent toujours les choses divines, alors mêmes qu'on les affecte à des usages profanes."

49. *Ibid.*, pp. 255, 263, 265–66. Page 268: "Le Jérémie du bagne ou le Shakspeare de la maison des fous."

50. *Ibid.*, p. 280: "Le propagateur de nihilisme." Page 282: "L'esprit d'un chimiste anglais dans l'âme d'un bouddhiste hindou."

LEMAÎTRE

1. *Les Contemporains*, 2, 84: "Les œuvres défilent devant le miroir de notre esprit; mais, comme le défilé est long, le miroir se modifie dans l'intervalle, et, quand par hasard la même œuvre revient, elle n'y projette plus la même image."

2. *Ibid.*, p. 85: "Définir l'impression que fait sur nous, à un moment donné, telle œuvre d'art où l'écrivain a lui-même noté l'impression qu'il recevait du monde à une certaine heure."

3. *Ibid., 3,* 341: "Une représentation du monde aussi personnelle, aussi relative, aussi vaine et, par suite, aussi intéressante que celles qui constituent les autres genres littéraires."

4. *Ibid., 3,* 342: "L'art de jouir des livres et d'enrichir et d'affiner par eux ses impressions."

5. *Ibid., 2,* 85: "On juge bon ce qu'on aime."

6. *Ibid., 1,* 164: "L'imagination sympathique." Page 130: "L'âme moderne semble faite de plusieurs âmes, contient, si l'on peut dire, celles des siècles écoulés."

7. *La Comédie après Molière et le théâtre de Dancourt,* Paris, 1882. *Corneille et la poétique d'Aristote,* Paris, 1888.

8. *Les Contemporains, 1,* 239: "Et est-ce ma faute, à moi, si j'aime mieux relire un chapitre de M. Renan qu'un sermon de Bossuet, le *Nabab* que la *Princesse de Clèves* et telle comédie de Meilhac et Halévy qu'une comédie même de Molière?"

9. *Ibid., 3,* 220: "Une des plus futiles entre les occupations humaines." Page 221: "Amusant leur intelligence par des difficultés faciles" (a quotation from Flaubert's *Madame Bovary* about Binet turning his napkin rings). Page 222: "L'erudit méprise au fond les poètes, les romanciers, les critiques, les journalistes . . . la philologie l'empêche de comprendre la littérature." Page 221: "Les trois quarts des textes du moyen âge . . . distillent un insupportable ennui," p. 225.

10. *Ibid., 4,* 20: "La recherche la plus puérile des opinions singulières."

11. *Ibid., 1,* 284: "Une épopée pessimiste de l'animalité humaine."

12. *Ibid., 6,* 268: "Le chauvinisme littéraire." Page 230: "Une impression contrôlée et éclairée par des impressions antécédentes."

FRANCE

1. *La Vie littéraire, 1,* 5–6: "le bon critique est ceci qui raconte les aventures de son âme au milieu des chefs-œuvres. Il n'y a pas plus de critique objective qu'il n'y a d'art objectif, et tous ceux qui se flattent de mettre autre chose qu'eux-mêmes dans leur œuvre sont dupes de la plus fallacieuse illusion. La vérité est qu'on ne sort jamais de soi-même. C'est une de nos plus grandes misères. Que ne donnerions-nous pas pour voir, pendant une minute, le ciel et la terre, avec l'œil à facettes d'une mouche, ou pour comprendre la nature avec le cerveau rude et simple d'un orang-outang? Mais cela nous est bien défendu. Nous ne pouvons pas, ainsi que Tirésias, être homme et nous souvenir d'avoir été femme. Nous sommes enfermés dans notre personne comme dans une prison perpétuelle...Pour être franc, le critique devrait dire:—Messieurs, je vais parler de moi à propos de Shakespeare, à propose de Racine, ou de Pascal, ou de Goethe."

2. *Ibid.*, 2, 385: "L'esthétique ne repose sur rien de solide. C'est un château en l'air."

3. W. G. C. Bijvanck, *Un Hollandais à Paris en 1891*, Paris, 1892. Preface by A. France, p. XIII: "Nous n'en savons pas plus long aujourd'hui sur les lois de l'art que les troglodytes de la Vézère qui dessinaient à la pointe du silex le mammouth et le renne sur l'os et l'ivoire."

4. *La Vie littéraire*, *1*, 332: "Tout livre a autant d'exemplaires différents qu'il a de lecteurs et qu'un poème, comme un paysage, se transforme dans tous les yeux qui le voient, dans toutes les âmes qui conçoivent."

5. *Le Temps*, 6 November 1892 (uncollected article). "Le plaisir qu'une œuvre donne, est la seule mesure de son mérite . . . C'est la cause de l'éternelle diversité de nos jugements." Quoted in Antonui, *France*, p. 136.

6. *La Vie littéraire*, 2, 386. "L'opinion presque générale . . . favorise certaines œuvres. Mais c'est en vertu d'un préjugé, et nullement par choix et par l'effet d'une préférence spontanée."

7. *Ibid.*, 2, 12.

8. *Ibid.*, 2, 388: "Ossian, quand on le croyait ancien, semblait l'égal d'Homère. On le méprise depuis qu'on sait que c'est Mac-Pherson."

9. *Ibid.*, 2, 9: "S'il on doute, il faut se taire."

10. *Ibid.*, 2, 383: "Je ne saurais pas manœuvrer les machines à battre dans lesquelles d'habiles gens mettent la moisson littéraire pour en séparer le grain de la balle . . . contes de lettres."

11. *Ibid.*, *1*, 362.

12. *Ibid.*, *1*, 517.

13. *Ibid.*, *1*, 210: "Il n'y a pas de goût, et je finis par croire que le manque de goût est ce péché mystérieux dont parle l'Ecriture, le plus grand des péchés, le seul qui ne sera pas pardonné."

14. *Ibid.*, 2, 355.

15. *Ibid.*, *1*, 213: *1*, 508: "Talent vigoureux . . . grossier." For the whole relationship see Maurice Kahn, *Anatole France et Emile Zola* (Paris, 1927), who shows convincingly that France did not change his mind about Zola's art because of the Dreyfus affair.

16. *Ibid.*, *1*, 511: "Il faut être léger pour voler à travers les âges."

17. *Ibid.*, 2, 34: "Un très mauvais chrétien"; p. 39: "Homme détestable. Mais c'est un poète, et par là il est divin."

18. *Les Contemporains*, 4, 279 ff. Page 288: "L'énormité de cette discovenance du fond et de la forme."

19. *La Vie littéraire*, *1*, 355: "Rude et bon, enthousiaste et laborieux, théoricien médiocre, excellent ouvrier et grand honnête homme."

BIBLIOGRAPHY: HIPPOLYTE TAINE

I quote the writings thus:

La Fontaine et ses fables (Paris, 1853); new revised ed. 1861; 31st ed. as *Laf.*

Essai sur Tite Live (1856); 6th ed. 1896, as *Livy.*

Les Philosophes classiques du XIX⁰ siècle en France (1857); 10th ed. 1910, as *Phil. cl.*

Essais de critique et d'histoire (1858); 5th ed. 1887, as *Essais.*

Histoire de la littérature anglaise (1864); 2d ed. 5 vols. 1866, as *Hla.*

Nouveaux Essais de critique et d'histoire (1865), as *Nouveaux.*

The essay on Stendhal (1864) can be found only in the 12th ed. (1923), quoted as *Nouveaux,* 12th ed.

Derniers Essais de critique et d'histoire (1894); 3rd ed. 1903, as *Derniers.*

Philosophie de l'art (1865), as *Ph.a.*

Voyage en Italie, 2 vols. 1866.

De l'Idéal dans l'art (1867), as *Idéal.*

Philosophie de l'art dans les Pays-Bas (1869), as *Pays-Bas.*

De l'Intelligence (1870); 4th ed. 2 vols. 1900, as *Inte.*

Notes sur l'Angleterre (1871); 2d ed. 1872, as *Notes.*

Les Origines de la France contemporaine (1875–93); 36th ed. 11 vols. 1947, as *Ori.*

Derniers Essais de critique et l'histoire (1894); 3d ed. 1903, as *Derniers.*

I use, with changes, the English translation by H. Van Laun of *History of English Literature,* 3d ed. 2 vols. Edinburgh, 1872; and by John Durand of *Lectures on Art,* first series, New York, 1875.

The only biography is still *H. Taine: Sa Vie et sa Correspondance,* 2d ed. 4 vols. 1902 (ed. by his widow).

Books:

André Chevrillon, *Taine: Formation de sa pensée,* 25th ed. 1932 (draws on unpublished materials; partly biographical, excellent).

Otto Engel, *Der Einfluss Hegels auf die Bildung der Gedankenwelt H. Taines,* Stuttgart, 1920 (a thesis confined to the early writings).

Alvin A. Eustis, *Hippolyte Taine and the Classical Genius,* Berkeley, Calif., 1951 (a good essay on Taine's anti-classicism).

Victor Giraud, *Essai sur Taine: son Œuvre et son Influence,* 6th ed. 1912 (the first full study, still one of the best; contains extracts from Taine's scattered uncollected articles and reviews in appendix).

Victor Giraud, *Hippolyte Taine: Etudes et Documents,* Paris, 1928 (contains 4 essays by Giraud and further unreprinted extracts and papers).

Sholom J. Kahn, *Science and Aesthetic Judgment: A Study in Taine's Critical Method,* New York, 1953 (contains an acute discussion of the problem defined in title using Taine as springboard).

Paul Lacombe, *La Psychologie des individus et des sociétés chez Taine historien des littératures,* Paris, 1906 (a page-by-page destructive analysis of the introduction to the *History of English Literature* from a sociological point of view).

F. C. Roe, *Taine et Angleterre,* Paris, 1923 (much more narrow in scope than the title indicates; only on Taine's contacts with contemporary England and on his reception in England).

D. D. Rosca, *L'Influence de Hegel sur Taine théoricien de la connaissance et de l'art,* Paris, 1928 (an excellent book, though it pushes the thesis too far; the title indicates that the influence on the philosophy of history is not discussed).

K. de Schaepdryver, *Hippolyte Taine: Essai sur l'unité de sa pensée,* Paris, 1938 (an Amsterdam thesis, pursues the theme of Taine's pessimism throughout his writings).

Articles:

Irving Babbitt, in *The Masters of Modern French Criticism* (Cambridge, Mass., 1912), pp. 218–56.

P. Bourget, "M. Taine," in *Essais de psychologie contemporaine* (7th ed. Paris, 1891), pp. 176–210.

F. Brunetière, three articles: the section in *L'Evolution des genres,* Vol. 1. *L'Evolution de la critique* (3d ed. 1898), pp. 245–78. *Discours de Combat,* Nouvelle Série (1912), pp. 209–53. And a posthumous sketch in V. Giraud, *Etudes et Documents* (see above), pp. 279–99.

Ernst Cassirer, "Naturalistische und humanistische Begründung der Kulturgeschichte," *Göteborgs Kungl. Vetenskaps-och Vitterhets-Samhäller Handlingar,* 5th foldjen. Ser. A, Vol. 7, 1939; and the chapter "Positivism and its Ideal of Historical Knowledge: Taine," in *The Problem of Knowledge: Philosophy, Science and History since Hegel* (New Haven, 1950), pp. 243–55 (disappointing).

Edouard Droz, "Taine: Histoire de la littérature anglaise," *Revue des Cours et des Conférences,* 4th année, 2ème série (1896), pp. 120–32, 217–28, 321–34, 411–25, 471–79, 519–27, 569–76, 610–22, 698–710, 754–65, 791–808 (detailed hostile comment).

Emile Faguet, in *Politiques et moralistes du dix-neuvième siècle,* 3ème série (1900), pp. 237–314 (Taine as positivist).

Eduard Fueter, in *Geschichte der neueren Historiographie* (3d ed. Munich, 1936), pp. 582–90 (good comment on historian).

V. Hommay, "L'Idée de nécessité dans la philosophie de M. Taine," *Revue Philosophique, 24* (1887), 394–408 (excellent essay on the concept of necessity and its source in Spinoza).

Iredell Jenkins, "H. Taine and the Background of Modern Aesthetics," *Modern Schoolman, 20* (1943), 141–56 (makes Taine the first aesthetician who turned from an Aristotelian imitation theory to an expressionist concept!).

Viktor Klemperer, "Taine und Renan," in *Die französische Literatur von Napoleon bis zur Gegenwart,* Teil 2 (Leipzig, 1926), 1–58 (makes excellent observations).

Harry Levin, "Literature as an Institution," *Accent, 6* (1946), 159–68, reprinted in *Criticism,* ed. M. Schorer et al. (New York, 1948), pp. 546–53; and in *Literary Opinion in America,* ed. M. D. Zabel (New York, 1951), pp. 655–66 (opens with a brilliant section on "The Contribution of Taine").

Gabriel Monod, in *Les Maîtres de l'histoire: Renan, Taine, Michelet* (Paris, 1894), pp. 51–173 (an early, partly biographical account).

Winthrop H. Rice, "The Meaning of Taine's Moment," *Romanic Review, 30* (1939), 273–79 (*moment* is superfluous).

Sainte-Beuve, C. A., on Taine's early writings, two causeries (9 and 16 March 1857) in *Causeries du lundi, 13,* 249–84. Review of *Histoire de littérature anglaise,* in *Nouveaux Lundis, 8,* 66–137. First published 30 May, 6 and 11 June 1864.

Leslie Stephen, "Taine's History of English Literature," *Fortnightly Review, 20* (1873), 693–714, reprinted in *Men, Books and Mountains* (Minneapolis, 1957), pp. 81–111.

Martha Wolfenstein, "The Social Background of Taine's Philosophy of Art," *Journal of the History of Ideas, 5* (1944), 332–58 (contains good criticism from vaguely Marxist point of view).

Emile Zola, "M. H. Taine Artiste," in *Mes Haines* (new ed. 1907), pp. 201–32 (elaborates contrast of sick spirit and joy in flesh and brutal force).

NOTES: HIPPOLYTE TAINE

1. *Hla., 1,* xxix: "la vitesse acquise." Page xxxiv: "l'impulsion déjà acquise."

2. Rice, "The Meaning of Taine's *Moment,*" *Romanic Review, 30* (1939), 273–79.

3. Six letters by Taine to Brandes can be found in *Correspondance de Georg Brandes,* ed. P. Krüger (Copenhagen, 1952), *1,* 1–21. A letter by Gosse to F. C. Roe disclaiming interest in Taine (1924) is in Evan

Charteris, *The Life and Letters of Sir Edmund Gosse* (London, 1931), p. 477. On Parrington, see the obituary by E. H. Eby prefixed to *The Beginnings of Critical Realism in America* (New York, 1930), p. VII, dealing with Parrington's discovery of Taine.

4. See the bibliography, above.

5. *Hla., 1*, xxxiv: "si ces forces pouvaient être mesurées et chiffrées, on en déduirait comme d'une formule les propriétés de la civilisation future ... et lorsque nous avons considéré la race, le milieu, le moment ... nous avons épuisé non seulement toutes les causes réelles, mais encore toutes les causes possibles du mouvement."

6. Cf. *Hla., 5*, 276.

7. Giraud, *Essai*, pp. 236–37: "une personne morale."

8. *Hla., 1*, xxv.

9. *Laf.*, p. 343: "Une race se rencontre ayant reçu son caractère du climat, du sol, des aliments, et des grands événements qu'elle a subis à son origine."

10. *Essais*, p. 109: "en combinant les qualitiés des cinq ou six races qui ont fourni leurs ancêtres." But late in life Taine made much of Napoleon's Italian forebears in order to characterize him as a 19th-century *condottiere* (*Ori., 9*, 5 ff., 26).

11. *Hla., 2*, 365, 367 313; *5*, 251; *4*, 326, 341, 81; *3*, 234, 245; *5*, 64; *4*, 443; *2*, 111.

12. *Ibid., 4*, 445–46.

13. *Ibid., 4*, 432: "la grande idée anglaise ... la persuasion que l'homme est avant tout une personne morale et libre." *4*, 467, or *5*, 153.

14. *Essais*, p. 316: "une race légère et sociable."

15. *Laf.*, p. 17: "Le besoin de rire est le trait national." See also *Hla., 1*, 95.

16. *Hla., 1*, 80: "esprit facile, abondant, curieux ... tel est le génie de la race."

17. *Hla., 1*, 85–86: "Quand le Français conçoit un événement ou un objet, il le conçoit vite et *distinctement* ... Les mouvements de son intelligence sont adroits et prompts comme ceux de ses membres; du premier coup, et sans effort, il met la main sur son idée. Mais il ne met la main que sur elle ... Il est privé, ou, si vous l'aimez mieux, il est exempt de ces soudaines demi-visions, qui, secouant l'homme, lui ouvrent en un instant les grandes profondeurs et les lointaines perspectives. C'est l'ébranlement intérieur qui suscite les images; n'étant point ébranlé, il n'imagine pas. Il n'est ému qu'à fleur de peau; la grande sympathie lui manque ... C'est pourquoi nulle race en Europe n'est moins poétique." Cf. *Ori., 1*, 305 f.

18. *Vie, 4,* 133–34: "Il est rhétoricien et bavard."

19. Giraud, *Etudes,* p. 247: "ni la folie ni le génie de l'imagination."

20. *Ori., 10,* 137 n.: "la sotte vanité."

21. Cf. *Laf.* 11 ff. and *Hla., 1,* 91–96. In the *History* the characterization of the French spirit applies indiscriminately to the Normans. The common denominator is presumably the Old French spirit, whether Norman or Gallic.

22. *Pays-Bas,* 2: "La race avec ses qualités fondamentales et indélébiles, telles qu'elles persistent à travers toutes les circonstances et dans tous les climats ... le peuple lui-même avec ses qualités originelles ... transformées par son milieu et son histoire."

23. *Hla., 1,* xxx.

24. *Hla., 1,* xxxiii: "le caractère sociable et l'esprit de conversation innés en France rencontrèrent les habitudes de salon et le moment de l'analyse oratoire."

25. See Leo Spitzer, "*Milieu* and *ambiance*," in *Essays in Historical Semantics* (New York, 1947), esp. pp. 210–13.

26. *Vie,* 2, 345, 352.

27. *Ph.a.,* p. 77: "L'œuvre d'art est déterminée par un ensemble qui est l'état général de l'esprit et des mœurs environnantes." Cf. p. 98.

28. *Ori., 1,* 276–77.

29. *Vie,* 2, 305: "L'assimilation des recherches historiques et psychologiques aux recherches physiologiques et chimiques."

30. *Vie,* 2, 183: "Je fais de la physiologie en matières morales, rien de plus. J'ai emprunté à la philosophie et aux sciences positives des méthodes qui m'ont semblé puissantes, et je les ai appliquées dans les sciences psychologiques."

31. *Ph.a.,* p. 22, pp. 15–17.

32. *Hla., 1,* xv: "Le vice et la vertu sont des produits comme le vitriol et le sucre."

33. In a letter to *Journal des Débats* (19 December 1872), *Vie, 3,* 213–15.

34. *Ph.a.,* pp. 55–56: "On pourrait dire qu'en ce pays, l'eau fait l'herbe, qui fait le bétail, qui fait le fromage, le beurre et la viande, qui, tous ensemble avec la bière, font l'habitant. En effet, de cette grasse vie et de l'organisation physique imbibée d'air humide, vous voyez naître le tempérament flamand, le naturel flegmatique, les habitudes régulières, la tranquillité d'esprit et de nerfs, la capacité de prendre la vie raisonnablement et sagement, le contentement continu, le goût du bien-être, partant le règne de la propreté et la perfection du confortable."

35. *Hla., 1,* 4: "il n'y a de place ici que pour les pensées sinistres ou mélancoliques."

36. *Hla., 1,* 157–58: "ce que le climat impose à l'homme d'incommodités et ce qu'il en exige de résistances est infini. De là la mélancolie et l'idée du devoir."

37. *Laf.,* pp. 4–5: "tout y était sur un petit modèle, en proportions commodes . . . Il n'a ni excès ni contrastes."

38. *Laf.,* p. 8: "l'homme prend et garde l'empreinte du sol et du ciel."

39. There is an odd passage on the dry climate of the United States in *Pays-Bas,* p. 31.

40. *Hla., 1,* 101: "la littérature s'accommode toujours au goût de ceux qui peuvent la goûter et la payer."

41. *Hla., 3,* 38 f.

42. *Nouveaux Essais,* pp. 108–09.

43. *Hla., 5,* 460 f.

44. *Hla., 3,* 178: "le pire des publics, débauché et frivole, dépourvu d'un goût personnel."

45. *Hla., 3,* 178–79: "Le personnage qui pleure sur la scène ne fait que renouveler nos propres larmes; notre intérêt n'est que de la sympathie, et le drame est comme une conscience extérieure."

46. *Vie, 2,* 197.

47. *Vie, 2,* 344: "je suis si peu matérialiste qu'à mes yeux le monde physique n'est qu'une apparence."

48. A. Chevrillon, *Taine,* p. 224 n.

49. Article in *Journal des Débats* (6 July 1864). See Giraud, *Essai,* p. 232, and Rosca, *L'Influence,* p. 262 n.: "Entre les mauvais écrivains, il est probablement un des pires . . . il est entièrement étranger aux spéculations métaphysiques, à la culture littéraire, à la critique historique, au sentiment psychologique."

50. *Hla., 5,* 369 ff.

51. *Derniers,* p. 199.

52. *Hla., 5,* 406: "de connaissances absolues et infinies." *5,* 415: "la métaphysique . . . est possible."

53. *Inte., 2,* 462: "l'existence elle-même est explicable." Cf. *Vie, 1,* 47.

54. *Phil. cl.,* p. 370: "l'axiome éternel . . . formule créatrice."

55. We have over 200 pp. of notes, *Vie, 1,* 145, 162, 180, 209, 217. Charles Bénard, the translator (or rather free adapter) of the *Aesthetic,* was one of Taine's teachers at the Lycée Bourbon. Cf. *Vie, 1,* 19.

56. *Vie, 1,* 179, 270, 274.

57. *Vie, 1,* 154: "Hegel est un Spinoza multiplié par Aristote."

58. *Vie, 2,* 258: "qui s'est le plus rapproché de la vérité."

59. E.g. the preface to *Phil. cl.*, p. x; in the *Mill* essay, *Hla.*, *5*, 412, 416; and at the end of *Inte.*, *2*, 462 f.

60. *Derniers*, p. 198: "à concevoir les époques historiques comme des moments, à chercher les causes intérieures, le développement spontané, le devenir incessant des choses."

61. *Hla.*, *4*, 211; *3*, 142.

62. *Hla.*, *2*, 302: "Tout grand changement a sa racine dans l'âme."

63. Chevrillon, p. 378, quoting an unpublished note: "comme cause de l'état social l'état psychologique."

64. *Hla.*, *1*, xvi.

65. *Hla.*, *1*, 369: "les causes des événements sont des lois innées dans les choses."

66. *Essais*, xiv–xv: "Entre une charmille de Versailles, un raisonnement philosophique et théologique de Malebranche, un précepte de versification chez Boileau, une loi de Colbert sur les hypothèques, un compliment d'antichambre à Marly, une sentence de Bossuet sur la royauté de Dieu, la distance semble infinie et infranchissable."

67. *Hla.*, *1*, 231.

68. *Hla.*, *4*, 211.

69. *Vie*, *2*, 221. Cf. *Graindorge*, p. 147, and *Voyage en Italie*, *1*, 72–73.

70. A fact Taine recognizes himself: *Hla.*, *4*, 421.

71. *Laf.*, p. 319: "l'art de transformer les idées générales en petits faits sensibles."

72. *Vie*, *2*, 47: "une idée générale devenant la plus particulière possible."

73. *Hla.*, *1*, xlvii: "si elles fournissent des documents, c'est qu'elles sont des monuments."

74. E.g. *Hla.*, *2*, 517.

75. *Nouveaux*, p. 255: "une correspondance exacte entre la manière de sentir publique et sa manière de sentir privée. Son esprit est comme l'abrégé de l'esprit des autres."

76. *Laf.*, p. 64: "en abrégé tout le siècle."

77. *Laf.*, p. 343: "Plus il pénètre dans son art, plus il a pénétré dans le génie de son siècle et de sa race."

78. *Hla.*, *1*, xlvi. Once a mysterious M. Weber was listed with Sainte-Beuve, Renan, Carlyle, and Macaulay. (Essay on De Sacy [1858] in *Derniers*, 2d ed. 1896, p. 20). Taine probably referred to Albrecht Weber (1825–1901), the indologist whose *Vorlesungen über indische Literaturgeschichte* (1852) might have interested him in connection with his reading on Buddhism. Or it could be Karl Julius Weber (1767–1832), the author of *Democritos* (1832–40), a miscellany then well-known; or even Georg Weber (1808–88), the author of an *All-*

gemeine Weltgeschichte (15 vols. 1857–80), which might have impressed Taine with its references to literature and culture. Taine was obviously anxious to include a German in his list.

79. *Hla.*, *5*, 300: "un révélateur de l'infini, comme un représentant de son siècle, de sa nation, de son âge; vous reconnaissez ici toutes les formules germaniques. Elles signifient qu l'artiste démêle et exprime mieux que personne les traits saillants et durables du monde qui l'entoure, en sorte qu'on peut extraire de son œuvre une théorie de l'homme et de la nature, en même temps qu'une peinture de sa race et de son temps." Taine says that Carlyle's method was taken from Hegel and Goethe, but Carlyle knew nothing of Hegel; see "Carlyle and the Philosophy of History," in my *Confrontations* (Princeton, 1965), p. 103.

80. *Ori.*, *1*, 311.

81. *Hla.*, *4*, 294, 301.

82. *Ph.a.*, p. 22: "des sympathies pour toutes les formes de l'art et pour toutes les écoles . . . comme autant de manifestations de l'esprit humain."

83. *Ibid.*, pp. 21, 22: "la science ne proscrit ni ne pardonne; elle constate et elle explique . . . elle fait comme la botanique qui étudie, avec un intérêt égal, tantôt l'oranger et le laurier, tantôt le sapin et le bouleau."

84. *Idéal*, p. 3, 15.

85. *Laf.*, p. 344.

86. *Idéal*, pp. 33–55.

87. *Ibid.*, p. 83: "Plus l'artiste est grand, plus il manifeste profondément le tempérament de sa race."

88. *Hla.*, *2*, 12. Taine ascribes the play to Middleton, referring to Philarète Chasles.

89. *Essais*, p. 203. Hence one understands Taine's low opinion of philology; it comes out almost crudely in the attack on Cousin, whose editorial labors are disparaged. (Some of these were extremely valuable, e.g. his book on the manuscript of Pascal's *Pensées*.) Philology is described as a "dark, narrow, bottomless cellar" (*Phil. cl.*, p. 194) without air and light; and even later Taine comments with some puzzlement on its attractions (*Nouveaux Essais*, p. 190).

90. *Derniers*, p. 2: "ni les livres ni les tableaux n'avaient menti; les personnages de Lope, de Calderon, de Murillo et de Zurbaran couraient les rues."

91. See Foulché-Delbosc, "Mme d'Aulnoy et l'Espagne," in *Revue Hispanique*, 67 (1926), pp. 1–151.

92. *Hla.*, *1*, xlvi: "je donnerais cinquante volumes de chartes et cent volumes de pièces diplomatiques pour les mémoires de Cellini, pour

les lettres de Saint Paul, pour les propos de table de Luther ou les comédies d'Aristophane."

93. *Hla.*, *1*, xlvii: "c'est en représentant la façon d'être de toute une nation et de tout un siècle qu'un écrivain rallie autour de lui les sympathies de tout un siècle et de toute une nation."

94. *Idéal*, p. 59: "quelque fragment de l'homme universel."

95. *Ph.a.*, p. 158: "le personnage régnant . . . le modèle."

96. *Hla.*, *1*, 242: "il y a une correspondance fixe entre ce que l'homme admire et ce que l'homme est."

97. In *Rêveries littéraires, morales, et fantastiques* (Brussels, 1832), pp. 41–58.

98. *Idéal*, p. 96.

99. *Hla.*, *4*, 384: "Partout où est la vie, même bestiale ou maniaque, est la beauté."

100. *Nouveaux*, p. 152: "J'aime mieux en rase campagne rencontrer un mouton qu'un lion; mais derrière une grille, j'aime mieux voir un lion qu'un mouton. L'art est justement cette sorte de grille."

101. *Nouveaux*, p. 152: "en ôtant la terreur, il conserve l'intérêt . . . nous pouvons contempler les superbes passions . . . Cela nous tire hors de nous-mêmes . . . Notre âme grandit par spectacle."

102. *Idéal*, pp. 101, 104–05.

103. *Idéal*, pp. 107–08: "Plus haut encore et dans un ciel supérieur sont . . . les sauveurs et les dieux . . . de la Grèce . . . (ou) de la Judée et du christianisme représentés dans les Psaumes, dans les Evangiles, dans l'Apocalypse, et dans cette chaîne continue de confidences poétiques dont les derniers et les plus purs anneaux sont les *Fioretti* et l'*Imitation*."

104. *Idéal*, pp. 106–07.

105. *Idéal*, p. 103: "elles manifestent mieux que les autres les caractères importants, les forces élémentaires, les couches profondes de la nature humaine."

106. *Ph. cl.*, p. 150: "la beauté morale . . . un maître de vertu."

107. *Vie*, *2*, 122: "L'artiste n'a pour but que de produire le beau."

108. *Vie*, *2*, 344–45. *Nouveaux*, p. 40.

109. *Hla.*, *5*, 155: "un juge entre des justes et des pêcheurs."

110. *Hla.*, *5*, 70.

111. *Hla.*, *2*, 420. Taine refers to Shakespeare with Coleridge's term "myriad-minded" (*Laf.*, p. 66).

112. *Hla.*, *5*, 118: "jouit par contemplation de la grandeur d'un sentiment nuisible ou du mécanisme ordonné d'un caractère pernicieux."

113. *Nouveaux*, 12th ed., pp. 240, 246–47.

114. *Derniers*, pp. 225–26: "il s'efface . . . il ne se fait pas lui-même le cicerone de ses trésors."

115. *Hla.*, 5, 127: "l'art s'est amoindri, la poésie a disparu."

116. *Vie*, 3, 177: "il y a un grand principe de Gautier et de Stendhal que je crois vrai: ne pas faire étalage de ses sentiments sur le papier . . . il est indécent de donner son cœur en spectacle; il vaut mieux être accusé de n'en avoir pas."

117. *Hla.*, 5, 142–43: "L'essence de l'homme se trouve cachée bien loin au-dessous de ces étiquettes morales."

118. *Hla.*, 5, 156: "Que Pierre ou Paul soit un coquin, peu nous importe, c'était l'affaire des contemporains."

119. *Ph.a.*, p. 51: "le caractère capital, quelque qualité saillante et principale, un point de vue important, une manière d'être essentielle de l'objet."

120. *Nouveaux Lundis* (3d ed. 1879), 8, 88.

121. *Vie*, 2, 308: "Je n'ai jamais eu l'intention de déduire l'individu, de démontrer qu'un Shakespeare, un Swift devaient apparaître en tel temps, en tel pays."

122. *Vie*, 2, 261: "mon idée fondamentale a été qu'il faut reproduire l'émotion, la passion particulière à l'homme qu'on décrit . . . bref le peindre à la façon des artistes et en même temps les construire à la façon des raisonneurs."

123. *Hla.*, 5, 156: "je calcule le jeu de ses moteurs, je ressens avec elle les coups des obstacles, je vois d'avance la courbe que son mouve-ment va décrire; je n'éprouve pour elle ni aversion ne dégoût; j'ai laissé ces sentiments à la porte de l'histoire, et je goûte le plaisir très-profond et très-pur de voir agir une âme selon une loi définie, dans un milieu fixé, avec toute la variété des passions humaines."

124. *Hla.*, 5, 4–5: "Le génie d'un homme ressemble à une horloge: il a sa structure, et parmi toutes ses pièces un grand ressort. Démêlez ce ressort, montrez comment il communique le mouvement aux autres, suivez ce mouvement de pièce en pièce jusqu'à l'aiguille où il aboutit."

125. *Essais*, pp. xxvi–xxvii.

126. *Vie*, 4, 109.

127. *Ori.*, 7, 330: "Le gorille féroce et lubrique."

128. *Essais*, p. ix: "état psychologique, dominateur et persistant."

129. *Nouveaux*, 12th ed., p. 225: "sensible qu'à une couleur."

130. III, 2, "Du Repentir." Montaigne, *Essais*, ed. Maurice Rat (Paris, 1948), 3, 25.

131. See Maynard Mack's ed. of *Pope's Essay on Man* (London, 1950), pp. xxxvi, 71 n.

132. *Hla.*, 2, 158: "A proprement parler, l'homme est fou, comme le

corps est malade, par nature; la raison comme la santé n'est en nous qu'une réussite momentanée et un bel accident."

133. *Hla.,* 2, 159: "vie d'insensé, qui par intervalles simule la raison, mais qui véritablement est 'de la même substance que ses songes!' "

134. *Hla.,* 2, 259: "L'homme est une machine nerveuse, gouvernée par un tempérament, disposée aux hallucinations, emportée par des passions sans frein, déraisonnable par essence, mélange de l'animal et du poète, ayant la verve pour esprit, la sensibilité pour vertu, l'imagination pour ressort et pour guide, et conduite au hasard, par les circonstances les plus déterminées et les plus complexes, à la douleur, au crime, à la démence et à la mort."

135. *Hla.,* 2, 194: "délivrée des entraves de la raison et de la morale."

136. *Nouveaux,* p. 151 n.

137. *Vie, 4,* 311.

138. *Hla.,* 5, 4: "Quarante volumes suffisent, et au delà, pour bien connaître un homme . . . son talent est dans ses livres."

139. *Hla., 4,* 176 ff.

140. *Hla., 4,* 185: "En vérité, je voudrais admirer les œuvres d'imagination de Pope; je ne saurais."

141. *Hla.,* 2, 516: "en prêtant à Satan son âme républicaine."

142. *Hla.,* 2, 258: "Hamlet, c'est Shakspeare."

143. *Hla.,* 2, 270: "masque transparent, derrière lequel on voit la figure du poète."

144. *Etudes sur Shakespeare* (1852), Chasles, in turn, drew the theory from Armitage Brown's *Shakespeare's Autobiographical Poems* (1838). See M. H. Abrams, *The Mirror and the Lamp* (New York, 1953), pp. 246 ff.

145. *Hla.,* 2, 176.

146. In *Ariosto, Shakespeare e Corneille* (3d ed. Bari, 1944), p. 84: "si finisce col non sapere più se ci sfilino dinanzi poeti o assassini, contrasti ed armonie artistiche o risse a colpi di pugnale."

147. *Hla.,* 2, 187: "la métaphore n'est pas le caprice de sa volonté, mais la forme de sa pensée. Au plus fort de sa passion, il imagine encore. Quand Hamlet, désespéré, se rappelle la noble figure de son père, il aperçoit les tableaux mythologiques dont le goût du temps remplissait les rues. Il le compare au héraut Mercure, 'nouvellement descendu sur une colline qui baise le ciel.' Cette apparition charmante, au milieu d'une sanglante invective, prouve que le peintre subsiste sous le poète. Involontairement et hors de propos, il vient d'écarter le masque tragique qui couvrait son visage, et le lecteur, derrière les traits contractés de ce masque terrible, découvre un sourire gracieux et inspiré qu'il n'attendait pas".

148. *Ph.a.*, p. 62.

149. *Hla.*, *4*, 179: "il faut une source pleine d'idées vives et de passions franches pour faire un vrai poète."

150. *Hla.*, *1*, 51: "on n'est puissant dans les œuvres de l'esprit que par la sincérité du sentiment personnel et original."

151. *Hla.*, *4*, 318: "Après tout, cet homme est convaincu."

152. *Hla.*, *1*, 277: "il pense moins souvent à bien aimer qu'à bien écrire."

153. *Laf.*, p. 69: "des bouts de paysages, des gestes, des figures comiques, touchantes, et tout cela comme dans un rêve. Pendant ce temps, sa main écrit des lignes non finies, terminées par des syllables pareilles; et il se trouve que ces lignes sont la même chose que ce rêve; ses phrases n'ont fait que noter des émotions."

154. *Ori.*, *1*, 305: "le cri involontaire de la sensation vive, la confidence solitaire de l'âme trop pleine."

155. *Hla.*, *1*, 355: "la sensation de l'ensemble. Ils comprennent les proportions, les attaches et les contrastes; ils *composent*." Cf. *1*, 215.

156. *Idéal*, p. 142: "justement une suite d'événements et un ordre de situations arrangés pour manifester des caractères."

157. *Hla.*, *4*, 267: "A ce moment, la forme semble s'anéantir et disparaître; j'ose dire que ceci est le grand trait de la poésie moderne."

158. *Phil. cl.*, p. 81: "C'est au style qu'on juge un esprit."

159. *Essais*, pp. 248–50.

160. *Nouveaux*, pp. 59–60.

161. *Ibid.*, pp. 98 ff.

162. *Ibid.*, 12th ed., p. 254.

163. *Vie*, 2, 44–45.

164. *Ori.*, *1*, 300: "la raison raisonnante."

165. *Nouveaux*, pp. 264–65.

166. *Phil., cl.*, p. 110.

167. *Essais*, p. 265: "si éloignés des nôtres, que nous avons peine à les comprendre. Ils sont comme des parfums trop fins: nous ne les sentons plus; tant de délicatesse nous semble de la froideur ou de la fadeur."

168. *Essais*, p. 262.

169. *Laf.*, p. 42 n.; *Hla.*, *5*, 466 ff.

170. On Flaubert, see *Vie*, 2, 157, 229–36, and *Inte.*, *1*, 90. In a letter to Zola quoted by John C. Lapp, in "Taine et Zola: autour d'une correspondance," *Revue des Sciences Humaines*, new ser., fasc. 87 (July–September 1957), 319–26, esp. 320, 325: "cauchemars . . . un peu de pitié pour la pauvre humanité."

171. Taine's knowledge and interest in German literature (as op-

posed to scholarship and philosophy) were very limited and his sympathy very imperfect. Still, he planned a book on German literature since the middle of the 18th century and made an exploratory journey in 1870. But the outbreak of the Franco-Prussian War made him abandon the project, for he knew that he could not preserve impartiality and felt that other tasks had become more urgent (see *Vie*, 2, 354 ff.; 3, 48). He greatly admired Goethe's *Iphigenie* as "le plus pure chef-d'œuvre de l'art moderne" (*Essais*, 401). He evoked its "serene and immortal beauty" in an essay, "Sainte-Odile et Iphigénie en Tauride" (1868). He praised Heine quite extravagantly as "the greatest German poet since Goethe and, possibly, the most intense poet since Dante" (letter to Georg Brandes, 4 November 1890, in Brandes, *Correspondance, 1,* 19). But he judged severely most of Goethe's other writings as forced and ill-written and considered Kleist a third-rate writer without style (*Vie*, 2, 367; *4,* 110–11; Brandes, *Correspondance, 1,* 13). Obviously German literature did not live up to his concept of Nordic spontaneity. Its history seems to him "un contre-sens continu: fabriquer un art au moyen d'une esthétique préconçue" (*Vie,* 2, 372).

172. *Essais,* p. 306: "cet homme passionné, concentré, intérieur."

173. *Hla., 4,* 350: "un scalde transporté dans le monde moderne."

174. *Hla., 2,* 42: "la confession intime de Marlowe, comme aussi celle de Byron et des vieux rois de la mer. Le paganisme du Nord."

175. *Hla., 2,* 353: "une anxieuse idée du ténébreux au-delà."

176. *Hla., 3,* 196: "l'âge de l'imagination et de l'invention solitaire qui convient à leur race, pour l'âge de la raison et de la conversation mondaine, qui ne convient pas à leur race."

177. No Frenchwoman would have accepted the dedication of the *Rape of the Lock, Hla., 4,* 192–93.

178. *Hla., 4,* 165: "parce qu'ils sont pour nous insipides et lourds que le goût d'un Anglais s'en accommode."

179. *Hla., 4,* 81: "ce grand et malheureux génie, le plus grand de l'âge classique."

180. Taine has similarly assimilated English humor to his dominant idea of English gloom. The English humorists are either ignored (Lamb), or disparaged (Sterne) or transformed. There is not a word about *Pickwick Papers* in the essay on Dickens; Thackeray appears as a bitter cynic indulging in his anger at mankind; a list of humorists includes Swift, Arbuthnot's *John Bull,* but also Courier, Voltaire, and Montesquieu (*Vie 4,* 249). In Taine "humor" really means savage, acid satire.

181. *Hla., 5,* 262: "les simples savants, les vulgarisateurs, les orateurs, les écrivains, en général les siècles classiques et les races latines . . . les

poètes, les prophètes, ordinairement les inventeurs, en général les siècles romantiques et les races germaniques."

182. See *Nouveaux*, p. 93.

183. *Ibid.*, p. 103: "a de mauvaises manières; il est grossier et charlatan."

184. *Ibid.*, pp. 118–19: "La vraie noblesse lui manque; les choses délicates lui échappent; ses mains d'anatomiste souillent les créatures pudiques; il enlaidit la laideur."

185. *Hla.*, *1*, 258: "l'affreuse nuit."

186. *Hla.*, *2*, 4: "sur un fumier." Cf. *Nouveaux*, pp. 196–99.

187. *Hla.*, *1*, 225.

188. *Hla.*, *3*, 310–11.

189. See *Hla.*, *4*, 180–82.

190. *Nouveaux*, pp. 249–50.

191. *Hla.*, *2*, 489: "J'écoute, et j'entends un ménage anglais, deux raisonneurs du temps, le colonel Hutchinson et sa femme. Bon Dieu! habillez-les bien vite."

192. *Hla.*, *2*, 490: "Adam a passé par l'Angleterre avant d'entrer dans le paradis terrestre. Il y a appris la *respectability* et il y a étudié la tirade morale."

193. *Hla.*, *2*, 494: "mange comme un fermier du Lincolnshire."

194. *Hla.*, *2*, 503, n. 2.

195. *Hla.*, *2*, 497.

196. *Hla.*, *2*, 500.

197. *Hla.*, *3*, 99 f.

198. *Hla.*, *3*, 47: "vraiment anglais, c'est-à-dire énergique et sombre."

199. *Hla.*, *4*, 387–88: "Dans quelle médiocrité et quelle platitude recule auprès de lui le Faust de Goëthe! . . . Est-ce là un héros? . . . Sa plus forte action est de séduire une grisette et d'aller danser la nuit en mauvaise compagnie, deux exploits que tous les étudiants ont accomplis . . . A côté de lui, quel homme que Manfred!"

200. *Laf.*, pp. 75–76: "La Fontaine est moraliste, et non pamphlétaire; il a représenté les rois, et non le roi. Mais il avait des yeux et des oreilles, et faut-il croire qu'il ne s'en soit jamais servi? On copie ses contemporains en dépit de soi-même."

201. *Nouveaux*, p. 63: "un homme d'affaires endetté."

202. *Hla.*, *4*, 329, 386.

203. *Hla.*, *4*, 322; but cf. a laudatory letter in *Vie*, *2*, 210.

204. But see *Hla.*, *4*, 286–87, 290.

205. *Hla.*, *4*, 311.

206. *Hla.*, *4*, 335, 359, etc.

207. *Notes*, p. 361.

208. *Hla.*, *5*, 131 ff.

BIBLIOGRAPHY: FRENCH LITERARY HISTORY

For a study of Brunetière's theoretical pronouncements on evolution and his attempts to show its workings, the following books and articles are most important:

L'Evolution des genres dans l'histoire de la littérature. Tome *1, L'Evolution de la critique depuis la Renaissance jusqu'à nos jours,* 1890; lectures at *Ecole normale,* 1889 *(EG).*

Les Epoques du théâtre français, 1636–1850, Conférences de l'Odéon, 1892 (given 1891–92).

L'Evolution de la poésie lyrique en France aux dix-neuvième siècle, 2 vols. 1894; given at the Sorbonne, 1893 *(EPL).*

"La doctrine évolutive et l'histoire de la littérature," in *Etudes critiques sur l'histoire de la littérature française (EC), 6* . . . (1899, dated February 1898), 1–36 *(EC).*

"L'Evolution d'un genre: La tragédie," *ibid., 7* (article dated November 1901), 151–200.

"L'Evolution d'un poète: Victor Hugo," *ibid.* (dated 1902), pp. 201–21.

See also:

Le Roman naturaliste, 1883; I use the 6th revised ed. 1896 *(RN).*

Honoré de Balzac, 1906.

Manuel de l'histoire de la littérature française, 1898, and many collections of essays, especially:

Etudes critiques sur l'histoire de la littérature française, 8 vols. 1880–1907 *(EC);* Vol. 9 (1925) contains the Encyclopaedia article on criticism.

Histoire et littérature, 3 vols. 1884–86 *(HL).*

Questions de critique, 1889 *(QC).*

Nouvelles questions de critique, 1890 *(NQC).*

Essais sur la littérature contemporaine, 1892 *(ELC).*

Nouveaux Essais sur la littérature contemporaine, 1895 *(NELC).*

Discours de combat, 3 vols. 1899–1907.

Variétés littéraires, 1904.

Sur les Chemins de la croyance, 1904.

Etudes sur le XVIIIᵉ siècle, 1911 (fragment of book on Voltaire).

Bossuet, 1913.

Lectures: *Histoire de la littérature française classique,* 4 vols. 1905–17.

Comment on Brunetière, Books:

E. R. Curtius, *Ferdinand Brunetière,* Strasbourg, 1914 (still best).

John Clark, *La Pensée de Ferdinand Brunetière,* Paris, 1954 (emphasis on evolution of his general thought).

Victor Giraud, *Brunetière*, Paris, 1932 (thin).

Elton Hocking, *Ferdinand Brunetière: The Evolution of a Critic*, Madison, Wis., 1936 (solid, but unperceptive).

Comment, Articles:

Irving Babbitt, in *Masters of Modern French Criticism* (Boston, 1912), pp. 298–337.

Anatole France, preface to *La Vie littéraire*, 3d series.

Alfredo Galletti, "Critica letteraria e critica scientifica in Francia nel sec. XIX," in *Studi di Filologia moderna II* (1909), pp. 201–28 (good).

Jules Lemaître, "Ferdinand Brunetière," in *Les Contemporains, 1* (1885), 217–48; a small piece in *6* (1893), 314–18, see also the preface, directed against Brunetière.

I am not aware of any study of Lanson.

There are chapters on Faguet in Alexandre Belis, *La Critique française à la fin du XIXe siècle*, Paris, 1926: and in Maurice Wilmotte, *Trois Semeurs d'idées*, Paris, 1907.

FRENCH LITERARY HISTORY

BRUNETIÈRE

1. *HL, 1*, 31–54, "Théorie du lieu commun."
2. *RN*, p. 156.
3. *RN*, p. 158: "l'expression d'une correspondance intime entre les sentiments et les sensations des personnages qui sont en scène. Et pourquoi ne le dirions-nous pas, en termes presque métaphysiques? elle ne sert pas seulement à marquer le rapport secret de l'être humain et de son milieu, mais elle l'unit, ou mieux encore, elle le réunit à ce milieu même."
4. *RN*, p. 162: "de fondre et de confondre plus intimement encore l'histoire de l'être humain et la description du milieu où les circonstances l'ont placé."
5. *RN*, pp. 165–66.
6. *RN*, p. 175: "ce sont les moyens eux-mêmes du romantisme qui servaient d'instruments à cette dérision du romantisme."
7. *RN*, p. 193: "le sentiment est encore engagé dans la sensation, où la volonté se confond avec le désir."
8. *RN*, p. 171.
9. *RN*, pp. 36–37, 44.
10. *ELC*, p. 137.
11. *ELC*, p. 143: "distinguent, divisent, et séparent . . . le symbole . . . l'unit, le joint ensemble, et n'en fait qu'une seule et même chose."

12. *ELC*, pp. 143, 145, etc.

13. *ELC*, p. 141.

14. *EPL*, 2, 247, 253.

15. *NQC*, pp. 307 ff., 329. *EPL*, 2, 244.

16. *ELC*, p. 217: "le roi des mystificateurs." *QC*, pp. 253–74.

17. *EPL*, 2, 230 ff.

18. *EC*, *9*, 50: "C'est qu'en effet les œuvres de la littérature et de l'art peuvent bien être des signes, mais elles sont d'abord des œuvres de littérature ou d'art, qui doivent donc être considérées comme telles . . . En même temps qu'un témoignage de l'âme du poète, un poème est un poème, et si c'est ce que la critique oublie quand elle prétend s'abstenir de juger, elle n'est plus la critique, mais l'histoire ou la psychologie."

19. *EC*, *9*, 32–34.

20. *EC*, *9*, 34. *NELC*, pp. 1–30.

21. "Le Mouvement littéraire au XIX⁰ siècle" (1889), in *NQC*, pp. 153–253. "Le Cosmopolitisme et la littérature nationale" (1895), in *EC*, 7, 289–316. "La littérature européenne" (1900), in *Variétés littéraires* (1904), pp. 1–51.

22. *EC*, *9*, 49.

23. *QC*, p. 321: "compose parfaitement ses phrases et ses paragraphes, médiocrement ses chapitres, et mal ses livres." Quotations from E. Hennequin, *La Critique scientifique* (Paris, 1888), p. 73.

24. Anatole France, *La Vie Littéraire, 1* (Paris, 1950), 5–6. For full text see above, p. 483. n. 1.

25. *ELC*, pp. 7–8: "et nous le sommes surtout par le pouvoir que nous avons de sortir de nous-mêmes pour nous chercher, nous retrouver, et nous reconnaître chez les autres . . . La duperie . . . c'est de croire et d'enseigner que nous ne pouvons pas sortir de nous-mêmes, quand au contraire la vie ne s'emploie qu'à cela . . . il n'y aurait autrement ni société, ni langage, ni littérature, ni art."

26. *ELC*, p. 9: "ni M. France, ni M. Lemaître, ni M. Desjardins ne l'ont eux-mêmes jamais essayé, ne l'essaieront jamais."

27. *ELC*, p. 4: "Elle dispense . . . d'étudier les livres dont on parle et les sujets dont ils traitent."

28. *EC*, *4*, 28: "Un effort commun." Compare Eliot's "the common pursuit."

29. *Sur les Chemins de la croyance* (1904), p. 12: "Les opinions ne sont pas libres . . . On ne l'est pas (libre) . . . d'avoir une opinion, son opinion et, comme on dit, son goût: il y a toujours un critérium, un fondement objectif du jugement critique. Et on peut d'ailleurs se tromper dans l'application de ce critérium, ce qui est l'une des origines de la diversité des opinions parmi les hommes. On peut ne pas savoir où

est ce critérium, auquel cas, l'obligation qui s'impose à nous . . . est donc alors de le chercher. Mais qu'il existe, voilà ce qui n'est pas douteux!" :

30. *NQC*, p. 281: "On rit plus . . . au *Voyage de M. Perrichon* qu'au *Misanthrope.*"

31. *EPL, 1*, 25: "Nous pouvons sortir de nous-mêmes; nous pouvons nous élever au-dessus de nos goûts; nous le devons même."

32. *HL, 3*, 96–97: "Le commencement de la critique est de juger d'abord, pour les approuver ensuite, mais plus souvent pour y contredire, nos impressions personelles."

33. "L'Expression dans les beaux-arts," in *Revue des Deux Mondes*, 54th year, 3d period, Vol. 61 (1884), 224: "il se peut que nous n'ayons pas le droit de prendre du plaisir, et, réciproquement, si certaines œuvres nous déplaisent, il se peut que nous ayons tort."

34. *EC, 9*, 62: "Toute 'critique' en effet, qui n'est pas l'application d'une 'esthétique' n'est pas de la critique."

35. *EG*, p. 121: "Ils ne visent pas au même but, quoiqu'on en puisse dire; ils n'emploient pas les mêmes moyens; et, ne s'adressant pas aux mêmes sens, ils n'opèrent point les mêmes effets."

36. *EC, 3*, 104: "Car tout genre a ses lois, et qui sont déterminées par sa nature même."

37. "La Poésie intime," *Revue des Deux Mondes*, 45th year, 3d period, *10* (1875), 685.

38. *Balzac*, pp. iv–v.

39. *EC, 9*, 62–63.

40. *EG*, p. xii.

41. *Manuel*, p. iv.

42. *EC, 3*, 4: "L'histoire d'une littérature . . . en elle-même et d'abord le principe suffisant de son développement."

43. *EC, 6*, 15: "une filiation des œuvres; et en tout temps, en littérature comme en art, ce qui pèse du poids le plus lourd sur le présent, c'est le passé."

44. *EG*, p. 262: "La grande action qui opère, c'est celle des œuvres sur les œuvres."

45. *Manuel*, p. iii: "La Pléiade du seizième siècle a voulu faire 'autre chose' que l'école de Clément Marot. Racine dans son *Andromaque*, a voulu faire 'autre chose' que Corneille dans son *Pertharite;* et Diderot dans son *Père de Famille* a voulu faire 'autre chose' que Molière dans son *Tartuffe*. Les romantiques en notre temps ont voulu faire 'autre chose' que les classiques."

46. *EG*, 22: "il introduit ainsi dans l'histoire de la littérature et de l'art quelque chose qui n'y existait pas avant lui, qui n'y existerait pas sans lui, qui continuera d'y exister après lui."

47. *EPL*, 2, 288: "Disposition nouvelle d'éléments identiques; 'changement de front,' si je puis ainsi dire; modification des rapports que soutenaient ensemble les parties d'un même tout, c'est uniquement ce que signifie le mot d'*évolution;* il ne veut pas dire autre chose."

48. *EG*, p. 262: "Voulez-vous savoir la vraie cause . . . de la tragédie de Voltaire? Cherchez-la d'abord dans l'individualité de Voltaire, et surtout dans la nécessité qui pesait sur lui, tout en suivant les traces de Racine et de Quinault, de faire pourtant autre chose qu'eux."

49. *Manuel,* p. v.

50. *Manuel,* pp. i–ii.

51. *EG,* p. 23: "un genre naît, grandit, atteint sa perfection, décline, et enfin neurt."

52. *EC, 7,* 198–99.

53. Sainte-Beuve, *Causeries du lundi, 5,* 384: "les genres ne meurent pas; ils peuvent s'éclipser, se laisser dominer par d'autres plus en vogue; mais ils durent, ils se perpétuent, et ils sont là en réserve pour offrir aux talents nouveaux, quand il s'en présente, des cadres et des points d'appui tout préparés."

54. *EC, 7,* 201 ff.

55. *EC, 7,* 220.

56. *EG,* pp. 5 ff.

57. *EG,* pp. 27 ff.

58. *EG,* p. 27: "des pertes successives de la comédie, comédie de caractère, comédie de mœurs, comédie d'intrigue."

59. *Balzac,* p. 17: "des genres ou des espèces dont la fortune et l'existence même sont liées aux circonstances, à un moment précis de leur évolution, et qui meurent de leur victoire."

60. *EG,* p. 25.

LANSON

1. *Manuel bibliographique de la littérature française moderne: XVIᵉ, XVIIᵉ, XVIIIᵉ et XIXᵉ siècles,* new ed. Paris, 1921. Voltaire, *Lettres philosophiques,* 2d ed. 2 vols. Paris, 1915–17. Lamartine, *Méditations poétiques,* 2 vols. Paris, 1915.

2. *Méthodes de l'histoire littéraire* (Paris, 1925), p. 33: "La saine discipline des méthodes exactes." Page 33: "La curiosité désintéressée, la probité sévère, la patience laborieuse, la soumission au fait." Page 35: "réduire au minimum indispensable et légitime la part du sentiment personnel dans notre connaissance."

3. See *Troi Mois d'enseignement aux États-Unis,* Paris, 1912.

4. *Histoire,* 4th ed. (1896), quoted. *Avant-Propos,* p. vii: "la description des individualités."

5. *Ibid.,* p. vi: "L'étude de l'Histoire littéraire est destinée à rem-

placer en grande partie la lecture directe des œuvres de l'esprit humain." Lanson quotes *L'Avenir de la science* (1890, written in 1848).

6. *Ibid.*, p. xi: "le monument littéraire du document historique ou philologique."

7. *Ibid.*, pp. 884, 1036, 951.

8. *Ibid.*, p. 25: "sèche et rude . . . raide et pauvre."

9. *Ibid.*, pp. 41, 45.

10. *Ibid.*, p. 133: "Un fatras, un chaos."

11. *Ibid.*, p. 171: "l'absolue sincérité." Page 173: "nous, honnêtes gens, paisibles bourgeois."

12. *Ibid.*, pp. 7–8, 78. Page 51: "Ces grandes amours n'étaient pas faites pour nos Français."

13. *Ibid.*, p. 105: "une forme de l'esprit de la race." Page 369: "une forme nécessaire de l'esprit français."

14. *Ibid.*, p. 501: "un rationalisme positiviste se combine avec la recherche d'une forme esthétique, et qui pose ces trois termes comme identiques ou inséparables . . . la doctrine littéraire la plus appropriée aux qualités et aux besoins permanents de notre esprit."

15. *Ibid.*, pp. 538, 544.

16. See the lecture course "Origines et premières manifestations de l'esprit philosophique dans la littérature française de 1675 à 1748," in *Revue des cours et conférences, 16* (1907–08), *17* (1908–09), *18* (1909–10).

17. *Histoire*, p. 1043: "le bas romantisme, prétentieusement brutal, macabre, immoral, artificiel, pour ahurir le bon bourgeois."

18. *Ibid.*, p. 1092: "de bien mince valeur."

19. *Histoire* (17th ed. 1922), p. 1129: "un artiste incomplet, qui n'est pas arrivé à s'exprimer." Page 1130 n. on Rimbaud.

20. *Ibid.*, p. 1146.

21. *Ibid.*, p. 1145 n.: "Un bel artiste, si grec dans sa prose si française."

22. *Ibid.*, p. 1182: "la France éternelle." Page 1177: "la victoire de l'esprit latin sur l'esprit germanique."

23. *Ibid.*, p. 1026: "le vrai catéchisme du Français." *Histoire* (4th ed.), p. 1009: "un des deux ou trois écrivains supérieurs de notre siècle."

24. Quoted by Joseph Bédier, *Hommage à Gaston Paris* (Paris, 1904), p. 10: "Nous nous attachons moins à apprécier et à faire apprécier le moyen âge qu'à le connaître et à le comprendre."

25. See, e.g., his review of L. Léger, *Chants héroiques et chansons populaires des Slaves de Bohême,* in *Revue Critique, 1* (1866), 2nde semestre, pp. 312–22, arguing that recognition of the Czech MSS as forgeries is good, as "la vérité ne peut jamais être dangereuse."

26. A self-characterization in L. Petit de Julleville, *Histoire de la langue et de la littérature française* (Paris, 1897), *8,* 420: "Ce qu'il se refuse, probablement parce qu'il lui manque, c'est l'art de combiner

les ensembles, de dégager l'esprit général d'un siècle, de suivre les lignes sinueuses des filiations et des influences, en un mot c'est l'art des idées générales en littérature, et 'l'esprit des lois' littéraires."

27. *Flaubert* (Paris, 1899), p. 68.

28. *Politiques et moralistes du dix-neuvième siècle* (Paris, 1899), *3*, 204: "Travail et art; science, non pas, ou pas encore, et sans doute jamais."

29. *Flaubert*, pp. 138–44: "Ce qui est resté du réaliste dans le romantique et du romantique dans le réaliste."

30. *Ibid.*, pp. 77–78.

31. In *La Revue des Revues*, 1 September 1910. See André Gide, "Baudelaire et M. Faguet," in *Nouveaux Prétextes* (Paris, 1911), pp. 134–55.

32. *Dix-huitième siècle* (Paris, 1890), p. v: "singulièrement pâle entre l'âge qui le précède et celui qui le suit." Page vi: "ni chrétien ni français." Page x: "tout neuf, tout primitif et comme tout brut." Page xl: "un siècle enfant, ou, si l'on veut, adolescent."

33. *Ibid.*, p. 180: "son manque de profondeur, et d'imagination, et de sensibilité."

34. *Ibid.*, p. 224: "demi-artiste, demi-penseur."

35. *Ibid.*, pp. 286 f.

36. *Vie de Rousseau* (1911); *Les Amies de Rousseau, Rousseau artiste, Rousseau contre Molière, Rousseau penseur*—all in 1912.

37. E.g. the chapters on Bertaut, Racan, and Maynard in Vol. 1 and particularly Volume 3, called *Précieux et Burlesques*.

38. *Le Théâtre en Angleterre depuis la conquète jusqu'aux prédécesseurs immédiats de Shakespeare*, Paris, 1878. *Le Roman au temps de Shakespeare*, Paris, 1887. *Shakespeare en France sous l'ancien régime*, Paris, 1898.

39. 2, xiii: "Mais, en réalité, en quoi cela contribue-t-il à la moindre explication de son génie?" Page xvi: "il n'y a pas, il ne saurait y avoir de critique scientifique, au moins en ce qui regarde la fleur du génie, la saveur propre d'une œuvre."

40. Page 131: "Il descend en droite ligne de nos trouvères et il a tout d'eux sauf la langue."

41. *Ibid.*, p. 277: "s'est posé en professeur de morale." Cf. p. 279.

42. *Ibid.*, pp. 509, 432: "un excès de lyrisme."

43. *Ibid.*, pp. 55–65.

44. On the history of the term see F. Baldensperger, "Littérature comparée: le mot et la chose," *Revue de Littérature Comparée*, *1* (1921), 1–29. Max Koch's *Zeitschrift für vergleichende Literaturgeschichte* continued publication till 1910. On Posnett, see p. 143.

45. Page 9: "d'une révolte contre le despotisme du joug français."

46. See my "The Crisis of Comparative Literature" in *Concepts of Criticism* (New Haven, 1963), pp. 282–95.

BIBLIOGRAPHY: MINOR FRENCH CRITICS

On Barbey d'Aurevilly: Giselle Corbière-Gille, *Barbey d'Aurevilly Critique littéraire*, Geneva, 1962; a systematic survey. Jacques Petit, *Barbey d'Aurevilly Critique*, Annales littéraires de l'Université de Besançon. No. 53, Paris, 1963. Chronological account of polemics, personal relations, etc. Bibliographies in both.

On Edmond Scherer: no modern monograph. Cf. Arnold, in *Mixed Essays;* the chapter in Babbitt; and Saintsbury's introduction to his translation of *Essays on English Literature,* London, 1891. Napoléon Tremblay, *La Critique littéraire d'Edmond Scherer,* partial printing of Brown University diss., 1932; has valuable bibliography but slight text. John G. Clark, "Edmond Scherer et la littérature anglaise," *Revue de Littérature Comparée, 28* (1954), 282–98.

On Emile Montégut: A. Laborde-Milâa, *Emile Montégut,* Paris, 1922. Pierre Alexis Muenier, *Emile Montégut,* Paris, 1925; and *Bibliographie méthodique et critique des œuvres d'Emile Montégut,* Paris, 1925; the older book is better but less fully documented. Reino Virtanen, "Emile Montégut as a Critic of American Literature," *PMLA, 63* (1948), 1265–75. Richard M. Chadbourne, "Emile Montégut and French Romanticism," *PMLA, 74* (1959), 553–67; perceptive.

On Bourget: I quote *Essais de psychologie contemporaine* (Paris, 1883) and *Nouveaux essais de psychologie contemporaine* (Paris, 1885), as Essais 1 and 2. There are three monographs which comment on the criticism:

Albert Feuillerat, *Paul Bourget,* Paris, 1937; mainly a sensitive psychological biography.

J.-L. Austin, *Paul Bourget: Sa Vie et son œuvre jusqu'en 1889,* Paris, 1940; rather schematic.

Michel Mansuy, *Un Moderne: Paul Bourget de l'Enfance au Disciple,* Paris, 1960; immensely detailed, bibliography.

There are chapters in Tissot and Renard.

On Hennequin:

There are no reprints.

Ernest Tissot, *Les Evolutions de la critique française* (Paris, 1890), has a chapter, pp. 325–58.

Edouard Rod, "Emile Hennequin et la critique scientifique" in *La Nouvelle Revue,* 10th year, 55 (1888), 364–83; also in *Nouvelles Etudes sur le XIXᵉ siècle,* Paris, 1898.

Ferdinand Brunetière, in *Questions de critique,* 1889.

NOTES: MINOR FRENCH CRITICS
BARBEY D'AUREVILLY

1. Paris, 1880, p. 16: "Le serpent . . . le limaçon."

2. *Lettres à Trebutien* (Paris, 1927), *4*, 186: "cet onagre suivi de trompettes." *Dernières polémiques* (Paris, 1891), p. 43: "Un poète prussien." *Le Roman contemporain* (Paris, 1902), p. 231: "Tailler . . . dans l'excrément humain."

3. *Littérature étrangère* (Paris, 1890), pp. 145, 227, 325: "La tristesse de l'aigle, dans son aire, n'est pas celle du pingouin, et Leopardi n'est qu'un pingouin."

4. *Les Critiques ou les juges jugés* (Paris, 1885), pp. 43 ff., 57, 60, 62.

5. Cf. *Les Poètes* (2d ser. Paris, 1889), pp. 33-49, 141–55, 271–85. On Vigny, *Les Poètes* (1st ser. Paris, 1862), pp. 49–61, 345–60. On Guérin, *Poésie et poètes* (Paris, 1906), pp. 153–67.

6. *Romanciers d'hier et d'avant-hier* (Paris, 1904), pp. 17–61; cf. *Pensées et maximes de Balzac,* ed. Barbey d'Aurevilly (Paris, 1909), preface. On Stendhal see *Romanciers d'hier,* pp. 1–16, article dating from 1853.

7. *Les Romanciers* (1st ser. Paris, 1865), pp. 61–76, on *Madame Bovary. Le Roman contemporain* (Paris, 1902), pp. 91–105, on *Education sentimentale. Ibid.,* pp. 106–23, on *Tentation de Saint-Antoine.*

8. *Les Poètes* (1st ser. Paris, 1862), pp. 371–82: "Dante athée et moderne." Also in *Poésie et poètes* (Paris, 1906).

SCHERER

1. *Etudes sur la littérature contemporaine* (Paris, 1886), *4*, 282: "Il m'en a donné le sentiment, il m'en a révélé la nature." Page 286: "Le terrible est-il épuisé, on arrive au dégoûtant. On peint les choses immondes. On s'y acharne, on s'y vautre. Mais cette pourriture elle-même pourrit; cette décomposition engendre une décomposition encore plus fétide, jusqu' à ce qu'enfin il reste un je ne sais quoi qui n'a de nom en aucune langue. Voilà Baudelaire."

2. *Ibid.,* *8,* 86: "une fumisterie . . . l'esthétique de la débauche, le poème du mauvais lieu."

3. *Ibid.,* *7,* 186: "Le Balzac du caboulot." Page 172: "cette horrible certitude."

4. *Ibid., 1,* 184: "Le génie le plus stérile de notre littérature."

5. *Ibid., 1,* 123: "La vanité de Chateaubriand a une âcreté brûlante qui la rend malfaisante et terrible."

6. *Ibid.*, *8*, 51–72: "Une hérésie littéraire." Page 57: "Un maniaque à enfermer dans une maison de santé."

7. *Ibid.*, *6*, 295–351. Page 351: "Goethe n'a pas de naïveté, pas de feu, pas d'invention; il manque de la fibre dramatique et n'est point créateur."

8. *Ibid.*, *6*, 151–94. Page 192: "Un poème faux, un poème grotesque, un poème ennyeux."

9. *Ibid.*, *6*, 128: "Une des superstitions françaises."

10. *Ibid.*, *7*, 66: "Prophète et bouffon."

11. *Ibid.*, *7*, 5: "Ses affectations de profondeur . . . ces poses étudiées d'un charlatanisme."

12. *Ibid.*, *6*, 195–221. Page 212: "L'ironie tempérée d'une sorte de mélancolie."

13. *Ibid.*, *7*, 5: "La clarté limpide et la bonne grace."

14. *Ibid.*, *7*, 38, 48: "Une science supérieure, une gnose à laquelle ne saurait atteindre le raisonnement."

15. *Ibid.*, *1*, 17–27; *8*, 187–242. Page 187: "Les romans les plus parfaits qu'on eût encore vus." Page 242: "La personnalité littéraire la plus considérable qui ait paru depuis la mort de Goethe." On *Daniel Deronda*, see *5*, 287–304, esp. 293–94.

16. *Ibid.*, *1*, 278: "Ni la force poétique et l'originalité des Anglais ni la science et la puissance spéculative des Allemands."

17. *Ibid.*, *1*, 177; *8*, 65; *10*, 154: "Je ne me souviens pas avoir jamais rencontré . . . un Anglais ou un Allemand qui sentît Racine."

18. On Lamartine, *Ibid.*, *7*, 39. On Amiel, *8*, 135–53.

19. *Ibid.*, *2*, 105–06. The little book on Diderot (1880) is full of prudish reservations but is fundamentally admiring.

20. *Ibid.*, *4*, 97–112. Page 97: "Décidément le premier de nos critiques modernes." *1*, 343–45: "Equité . . . point de rancunes . . . souplesse." Page 339, on the religious phase.

21. *Ibid.*, *4*, 255–61; *6*, 11–35; *7*, 230–47; *4*, 263–74. *4*, 270: "Ne renfermera ni un mot d'art ni un mot de philosophie."

22. *Ibid.*, *4*, 64–65: "Le sentiment du développement." On Nisard, *1*, 171–86. On Saintsbury, *10*, 137–57.

23. *Ibid.*, *1*, 322: "Comprendre, c'est sortir de soi pour se transporter autant que possible au sein des réalités."

24. *Ibid.*, *1*, 178: "Nous devons réagir contre ces sensations, chercher à les dominer, nous efforcer de considérer les choses dans leur essence même, c'est-à-dire dans leur nécessité."

25. *Ibid.*, *8*, vi, vii: "Je trouve mon plaisir dans Racine aussi bien que dans Shakespeare, sans même éprouver le besoin d'instituer entre eux une comparaison."

26. *Ibid.*, *10*, 328, 334–35.

27. *Ibid.*, *6*, 154: "De . . . l'analyse du caractère de l'écrivain et l'étude de son siècle, sort spontanément l'intelligence de son œuvre. Au lieu d'une appréciation personelle et arbitraire, portée par le premier venu, nous voyons cette œuvre se juger elle-même en quelque sorte, et prendre le rang qui lui appartient parmi les productions de l'esprit humain."

MONTÉGUT

1. Hector Talvart in *Mélanges à Jean Bonnerot offerts* (Paris, 1954), p. 484: "Le seul grand essayiste du XIX siècle."

2. *Essais sur la littérature anglaise* (Paris, 1883), p. 71: "Dureté brillante." Page 101: "Taciturne et libre." Page 105: "Chaucer n'est qu'un Français, qui s'exprime en langue anglaise." Page 111: "Lord Byron rejoint directement à travers les siècles les vieux poètes saxons et scandinaves primitifs."

3. *Ibid.*, p. 203: "Le drame n'était pas le moule nécessaire de son génie." Page 201: "Infidèles non pas aux lois de l'art et de la poésie . . . mais infidèles aux lois particulièrement constitutives du théâtre et du genre dramatique."

4. *Heures de lecture d'un critique* (Paris, 1891), pp. 80, 84. Page 120: "Un véritable hérétique dissimulé sous les formes les plus scrupuleuses de l'orthodoxie classique."

5. "Un penseur et poète americain: Ralph Waldo Emerson," *Revue des Deux Mondes, 19* (1 August 1847), 462–93. The essay is reprinted as an introduction to Montégut's translation of *Essais* (Paris, 1851). "Thomas Carlyle, sa vie et ses écrits," *Revue des Deux Mondes,* N.S. *19* (15 April 1849), 278–314.

6. *Ecrivains modernes de l'Angleterre,* 3 vols. (Paris, 1885). On realism, see *1*, 19 ff., in the first article on George Eliot, 1859.

7. *Dramaturges et romanciers* (Paris, 1890), p. 28: "Elle n'a ni été un grand romancier, ni un grand écrivain dramatique, ni un véritable poète."

8. *Ibid.*, p. 182, and *Nos Morts contemporains* (Paris, 1884), *2*, 199, in the essay on Saint-René Taillandier (1880).

9. *Nos Morts contemporains, 2*, 32.

10. *Poètes et artistes de l'Italie* (Paris, 1881), pp. 23–51.

11. *Mélanges critiques* (Paris, 1887), p. 233: "La plus grande imagination de ce temps-ci."

12. *Ibid.*, p. 90.

13. *Dramaturges et romanciers*, pp. 263–64: "La sentimentalité sensuelle."

14. *Types littéraires et fantaisies esthétiques* (Paris, 1882), p. 81: "Un personnage historique et qui a réellement vécu."

15. *Ibid.*, p. 118: "A la fois méditatif et énergique, mâle et irrésolu, mélancolique et brutal."

16. *Ibid.*, pp. 130–31, 133, 135, 147–48.

17. "Un roman socialiste en Amérique," *Revue des Deux Mondes, 16* (1 December 1852), 809–41, and "Un romancier pessimiste en Amérique," *Revue des Deux Mondes, 28* (1 August 1860), 668–703. Henry James, in *Hawthorne* (1876) comments on Montégut: Ithaca, N.Y., 1956 reprint, pp. 22, 47–48, 81.

18. *Nos Morts contemporains* (Paris, 1883), *1*, 335, 343, 345.

BOURGET

1. *Essais 1*, 280: "d'agir à la fois et de se regarder agir, de sentir et de se regarder sentir."

2. *Ibid., 1*, 25: "l'unité du livre se décompose pour laisser la place à l'indépendance de la page, où la page se décompose pour laisser la place à l'indépendance de la phrase et la phrase pour laisser la place à l'indépendance du mot."

3. *Ibid., 1*, 149: "Emma et Frédéric ont lu des romans et des poètes; Salammbô s'est repue des légendes sacrées que lui récitait Schahabarim. . . . l'abus du cerveau est la grande maladie."

4. *Ibid., 1*, 162: "associations d'idées qui marchent."

5. *Ibid., 1*, 61: "l'extrême civilisation a peu à peu aboli la faculté de créer, pour y substituer celle de comprendre."

6. *Ibid., 2*, 265: "trop-plein de cette vie intérieure."

7. *Ibid., 2*, 290: "L'analyse tue la spontanéité. Le grain moulu en farine ne saurait plus ni germer ni lever."

8. *Ibid., 2*, 62: "Nous sommes malades d'un excès de pensée critique, malades de trop de littérature, malades de trop de science."

9. See below, p. 350.

HENNEQUIN

1. See my "Modern Czech Criticism and Literary Scholarship," in *Essays on Czech Literature* (The Hague, 1963), pp. 179 ff.

2. *La Critique scientifique,* (Paris, 1888). Pages 39–40: "L'art est la création en nos cœurs d'une puissante vie sans acte et sans douleur."

3. *Ibid.*, pp. 96, 105, 108. Page 118: "De [Flaubert] ou de Corneille lequel des deux représente les caractères physiques et pittoresques de Rouen?"

4. *Ibid.*, p. 129: "L'œuvre d'art est l'expression des facultés, de l'idéal, de l'organisme intérieur de ceux qu'elle émeut."

5. *Ibid.*, p. 135: "Il réalisera la vérité subjective, dont it rend les idées, dont il ne contredit pas l'imagination."

6. *Ibid.*, pp. 147, 160, 162, 194. Pages 204–05: "Il tend à maintenir l'homme dans la pratique de ces inclinations ataviques." Page 207: "Les Etats les plus policés sont les plus faciles à conquerir."

7. *Ecrivains francisés* (Paris, 1889), p. 290–94. Pages 297–98: "Les catégories supérieures des lecteurs de Dickens, dans la bourgeoisie, aisée et éclairée, particulièrement dans la bourgeoisie protestante."

8. *Ibid.*, pp. 263–67.

9. *Ibid.*, p. 127. Page 117: "Un mécanisme d'acier." Page 128: "métallique," "machinal."

10. *Ibid.*, pp. 71, 78, 84. Page 66: "Un des nôtres."

11. *Ibid.*, pp. 251–52.

12. *Ibid.*, pp. 20, 36, 38, 13.

13. *Ibid.*, pp. 91, 94, 100. Page 116: "L'élégiaque du réalisme."

14. *Ibid.*, p. 165: "Où les rues, les maisons et les êtres, d'abord stables ou marchants, vacillent tout à coup et planent, ombres ou noirs profils de songes. Et jamais ce miracle ne s'opère qu'un souffle d'autre monde volatilise toute cette matière en indécis mirage."

15. *Ibid.*, pp. 164, 171. Page 181: "Le manque de proportion . . . entre la sensibilité et le raisonnement."

16. *Ibid.*, p. 183: "La folie, l'idiotie, l'imbécillité, la candeur des idiots et la bonté des criminels."

17. *Ibid.*, pp. 200–01, 214, 220–21.

18. *Ibid.*, p. 218: "Le lecteur de Tolstoï se sent aus cours même de l'œuvre vaguement mais sûrement repoussé du spectacle même qu'elle présente. Sans cesse l'écrivain semble se ceindre pour le grand effort d'enserrer son immense sujet, et sans cesse il défaille, se détourne et se détache, comme insouciant de l'œuvre entreprise; les scènes s'equissent inachevées, marquées à peine par quelques traits, les grandes crises des personnages s'accusent en mots confus et vagues; les descriptions des actes principaux, entamées avec une fiévreuse ardeur, faiblissent en phrases brouillées; une lassitude immense se trahit aux exposés d'idées, grisaille les psychologies, émousse les dialogues, estompe les physionomies."

19. *Ibid.*, p. 219: "La vague et menaçante présence d'un nihilisme transcendant." Pages 229–30: "au point de toucher à l'irrationalité aigüe des pires fous."

20. *Quelques écrivains français* (Paris, 1890), pp. 9, 60. Page 19: "Enormes cubes d'un miroitant granit."

21. *Ibid.*, pp. 71, 75, 84, 92, 101. Page 96: "gigantesques abstractions."
Page 103: "Le don suprême de la vie."

22. *Ibid.*, pp. 111, 116, 120. Page 127: "Il explique le rictus des
cadavres par la joie des morts de rentrer dans le grand tout, et la position des yeux des crapauds par leur désir de voir le ciel bleu."

23. *La Critique scientifique*, pp. 22, 211.

BIBLIOGRAPHY: FRANCESCO DE SANCTIS

I quote from the edition in the Scrittori d'Italia series (Laterza, Bari)
thus:

Storia della letteratura italiana, ed. B. Croce (4th ed. 2 vols. 1949), as *Sto.*
Saggi critici, ed. L. Russo (3 vols. 1952), as *S.C.*
La Letteratura italiana nel secolo XIX:
  Vol. 1, *Alessandro Manzoni,* ed. L. Blasucci (1953), as *Manz.*
  Vol. 2, *La Scuola liberale e la scuola democratica,* ed. F. Catalano
    (1953), as *Scuola.*
  Vol. 3, *Giacomo Leopardi,* ed. W. Binni (1953), as *Leop.*
Saggio critico sul Petrarca, ed. E. Bonora (1954), as *Pet.*
La Poesia cavalleresca e scritti vari, ed. M. Petrini (1954), as *Poesia.*
Lezioni sulla Divina Commedia, ed. M. Manfredi (1955) as *Lez.*
Memorie, Lezioni e scritti giovanili, Vol. 1: *La Giovinezza e studi heg-
eliani,* ed. F. Brunetti (1962), as *Gio.*

There is a rival edition, *Opere di Francesco De Sanctis,* ed. Carlo
Muscetta, Turin, 1953 ff., projected at 21 volumes, of which 11 had
appeared by 1961. Each volume has a long Marxist-slanted introduction
by Muscetta, N. Sapegno, and others.

I quote *Teoria e storia della letteratura,* ed. B. Croce (2 vols. Bari,
1926), as *Teoria.*

Translations
  History of Italian literature, trans. Joan Redfern, 2 vols. New York
1931; reprinted 1959. Brief foreword by Croce.
  De Sanctis on Dante, ed. J. Rossi and A. Galpern, Madison, Wisc.,
1957.

Comment
  Attisani, Adelchi, "L'estetica di F. De Sanctis e dell' idealismo itali-
ano," in *Momenti e problemi di storia dell' estetica* (Milan, 1959–61),
pp. 1430–1580.
  Binni, Walter, ed., *I Classici italiani nella storia della critica,* 2 vols.
Florence, 1954–55. Special sections on De Sanctis.
  Binni, Walter, "Amore del concreto e situazione nella prima critica

desanctisiana," in *Critici e poeti dal Cinquecento al Novecento* (Florence, 1951), pp. 99–116.

Biondolillo, F., *La Critica di Francesco De Sanctis* (Naples, 1936). Thin.

Borgese, G. A., "De Sanctis," in *Studi di letterature moderne* (Milan, 1915), pp. 3–19. Short, high praise.

———, "Francesco De Sanctis," in *Storia della critica romantica in Italia* (Florence, 1949; original ed. 1905), pp. 331–42. The concluding chapter interprets De Sanctis as the culminating point of romantic criticism.

Breglio, Louis A., *Francesco De Sanctis: Life and Criticism*, New York, 1940. Informative, descriptive.

Cantimori, Delio, "De Sanctis e il 'Rinascimento,' " *Società, 9* (1953), 58–78.

Cesareo, G. A., "L'Estetica di F. De Sanctis," in *Saggio su l'arte creatrice* (2d ed. Bologna, 1921), pp. 305–42. Vaguely Crocean.

Cione, Edmondo, *L'Estetica di F. De Sanctis* (2d ed. Milan, 1945). Fullest and best Crocean exposition.

Contini, Gianfranco, Introduction to *Scelta di Scritti Critici di Francesco De Sanctis* (Turin, 1948), pp. 11–43. Excellent. Emphasis on "situation" and interest in style.

Croce, Benedetto:

1. "Le Lezioni sulla letteratura italiana del secolo XIX" (1896), in *Una Famiglia di patrioti ed altri saggi storici e critici* (3d ed. Bari, 1949), pp. 163–71.

2. "Francesco De Sanctis e i suoi critici recenti" (1898), *ibid.*, pp. 123–239.

3. "Gli 'Scritti Vari' " (1898), *ibid.*, pp. 173–89.

4. "Francesco De Sanctis" (1902), in *Estetica* (8th ed. Paris, 1945), pp. 400–12.

5. "De Sanctis e Schopenhauer" (1902), in *Saggio sullo Hegel* (4th ed., Bari, 1948), pp. 354–68.

6. "Per la nuova edizione del' 'Saggio sul Petrarca' " (1907), in *Una famiglia, op. cit.*, pp. 241–52.

7. "Francesco De Sanctis" (1911), in *La Letteratura della nuova Italia* (5th ed. Vol. 1, Bari, 1947), pp. 357–78.

8. "Come fu scritta la 'Storia della letteratura italiana' " (1912), in *Una Famiglia, op. cit.*, pp. 267–76.

9. "De Sanctis e l'Hegelismo" (1912) in *Saggio sullo Hegel* (4th ed. Bari, 1948), pp. 369–95.

10. "Il De Sanctis e il pensiero tedesco" (1912), in *Una Famiglia, op. cit.*, pp. 277–86.

11. "Le Lezioni del De Sanctis nella sua prima scuola e la sua filosofia" (1913), *ibid.*, pp. 287–92.

12. "Il Giudizio del De Sanctis sul Metastasio," in *La Letteratura italiana del settecento* (Bari, 1949), pp. 15–23.

13. "Il Posto del De Sanctis nella storia della critica d'arte" (1950), in *Indagini su Hegel* (Bari, 1952), pp. 216–21.

14. "La Determinatezza dell'espressione poetica," in *Letture di poeti* (Bari, 1950), pp. 298–300. Comments on Ugolino essay.

Debenedetti, Giacomo, "Commemorazione del Francesco De Sanctis," in *Saggi critici,* new series (Roma 1945), pp. 3–23.

Formigari, Francesco, "Il concetto dell'arte nella critica letteraria di Francesco De Sanctis," *Giornale Critico della Filosofia, 3* (1922), 33–57, 126–52. Gentile's point of view.

Fubini, Mario, "Francesco De Sanctis et la critique littéraire," in *Cahiers d'histoire mondiale, 7* (1963), 342–62. Italian version in *Romanticismo italiano* (3rd ed. Bari, 1965), pp. 249–77.

———, "Il Giudizio del De Sanctis sul Metastasio e una questione di storia letteraria," ibid., pp. 235–44.

———, "Racine et la critique italienne," in *Dal Muratori al Baretti* (2d ed. Bari, 1954), pp. 397–448. Contains discussion of the essay on *Phèdre.*

Galletti, Alfredo, "Il Romanticismo tedesco e la storia letteraria in Italia," *Nuova Antologia, 268* (1916), 135–53.

Gaspary, Adolf, "Francesco De Sanctis," *Archiv für das Studium der neueren Sprachen, 53* (1874), 129–40, and *54* (1874), 1–38.

Gerratana, Valentino, "Introduzione all'estetica desanctisiana," *Società, 9* (1953), 22–57. Marxist interpretation.

Getto, Giovanni, "La Storia della letteratura del De Sanctis," in *Storia delle storie letterarie* (Milan, 1942), pp. 305–52.

Holliger, Max, *Francesco De Sanctis: Sein Weltbild and seine Aesthetik,* Basil diss., Freiburg in Switzerland, 1949. Emphasis on ethos.

Lombardo, Agostino, "De Sanctis e Shakespeare," in *English Miscellany, 7* (1956), 91–146.

Neri, Ferdinando, "Francesco De Sanctis e la critica francese," in *Storia e poesia* (Turin, 1944), pp. 223–90.

Orsini, Napoleone, "De Sanctis, Hegel e la 'situazione poetica,'" *Civiltà Moderna, 14* (1942), 138–40.

Parente, A., "L'Estetica di Francesco De Sanctis e i suoi limiti," *La Nuova Italia, 7* (1936), 207–12. Crocean.

———, "Pensieri di Francesco De Sanctis intorno alla musica," *La Rassegna Musicale, 7* (1934), 169–85.

Petronio, G., "De Sanctis e Quinet," *Romana, 3* (1939), 321–45.

Raya, Gino, *Francesco De Sanctis*, 1st ed. Palermo, 1935; 2d ed. Milan, 1952.

Rossi, Joseph, "De Sanctis' Criticism: Its Principles and Method," *PMLA, 54* (1939), 526–64. Informative, Crocean.

Russo, Luigi, "La 'Storia' del De Sanctis," in *Problemi di metodo critico* (Bari, 1950), pp. 184–208.

Sapegno, Natalino, "De Sanctis e Leopardi," *Società, 9* (1953), 79–87.

Schalk, Fritz, "Einleitung" to German translation (by Lili Sertorius) of *Geschichte der italienischen Literatur* (2 vols. Stuttgart, 1941), *1,* ix–xxx. On Hegel and De Sanctis.

Toffanin, Giuseppe, "De Sanctis e il Rinascimento," *La Rinascita, 4* (1941), 169–205. Violently polemical. Reprinted in *La Religione degli Umanisti* (Bologna, 1950), pp. 183–220.

NOTES: FRANCESCO DE SANCTIS

1. Cf., e.g., *Saggi e scritti critici e vari* (8 vols. La Universale Barion, Milan, 1936–38), with notes assuming total ignorance of history and literature.

2. *Estetica* (8th ed. Bari, 1946), p. 411: "Come critico e storico della letteratura, egli non ha pari."

3. *Studi di letterature moderne* (Milan, 1915), p. 3: "Il capolavoro della cultura nostra nel secolo XIX."

4. See the bibliography, above, under Contini, Gerratana, Muscetta, Sapegno.

5. Vol. 3, p. 390. Saintsbury could not have read the *History of Italian Literature* when he wrote: "They complain of the *History of Italian Literature* that, good as it is, it is too much of a bundle of Essays."

6. See Bibliography under Gaspary and Orsini.

7. *Essais critiques, 8,* 65.

8. See Bibliography, under Breglio.

9. De Sanctis often addresses the poets he discusses, or his audience, and makes statements like "Il nostro Alfieri è un uomo che al solo nominarlo ci sentiamo superbi di essere italiani" (*S.C., 1,* 153). Some lectures are printed with insertions about the reactions of the audience: vivi applausi, ilarità, benessimo, etc. See, e.g., *S.C., 3,* 277 ff.: "Zola e l'*Assommoir*."

10. Cf. *Gio.,* p. 113; *S.C., 3,* 296, 298.

11. *S.C.,* 2, *176*: "La letteratura, che ha in sé stessa il suo fine e il suo valore, e vuol essere giudicata secondo criteri propri, dedotti dalla sua natura."

12. *S.C., 1,* 210: "Il sentimento non è in sé stesso estetico . . . Il

dolore, l'amore, ecc . . . dove non abbia la forza di trasformarsi ed idealizzarsi, può, nella sua espressione, essere eloquente, non artistico. Non solo il sentimento non è il sostanziale dell'arte, ma, perché, sia capace di suscitare la facoltá estetica, dee tenersi in una giusta misura. Il sentimento non deve intorbidare l'anima, toglierle ogni arbitrio di sé, ogni serenità, turbare l'armonia interiore."

13. *S.C.*, 2, 4: "La moralità non è consequenza dell'arte, ma il presupposto, l'antecedente." ˙

14. *Sto.*, *1*, 63: "al ragionamento, alla forma dottrinale, che è la negazione dell'arte."

15. *Lez.*, p. 339: "Il pensiero in quanto pensiero è fuori dell'arte."

16. *Manz.*, p. 38.

17. *Manz.*, p. 36: "Ma a patto che sia reale artistico, e non naturale e non storico."

18. *Scuola*, p. 424: "L'interesse storico non ha niente a vedere con la poesia, la quale anche cose straordinarie e fuori natura può rappresentare, purché le rappresenti con tale colorito da non lasciarci tempo per difenderci dall'entusiasmo e domandarci:—E vero?"

19. *Manz.*, p. 36: "Un'ombra, una immagine, una parvenza del reale." *Pet.*, p. 232: "Realtà innalzata ad illusione."

20. *Gio.*, p. 153. *Sto.*, 2, 201. *S.C.*, *3*, 283.

21. *S.C.*, *1*, 238, 266. *Pet.*, p. 24–25.

22. *S.C.*, *3*, 268.

23. *Pet.*, p. 91. *S.C.*, 2, 268–69.

24. *Manz.*, p. 59: "Questo processo interiore costituisce ciò che in linguaggio scientifico dicesi 'forma', da non confondersi con simile parola adoperata da' retori a significare le sue apparenze piú grossolane." The phrasing of this passage is odd: the claim to "scientific language" and the remark that a "similar" word is used by rhetoricians though De Sanctis must have known that it is the same.

25. *Gio.*, pp. 154–5: "Incoscienza e spontaneità."

26. *Sto.*, 2, 230: "Individua."

27. *S.C.*, 2, 93: "La poesia . . . dee calare in terra e prender corpo."

28. *Sto.*, *1*, 67: "Paganizzare."

29. *S.C.*, *1*, 88: "Ci dee essere il tale magistrato, il tale prete, il tale soldato: in questo 'tale' è tutto il segreto della creazione artistica."

30. *Gio.*, p. 172: "Dire che Achille è il tipo della forza e del corragio, e che Tersite è il tipo della debolezza e della vigliaccheria, è inesatto, potendo queste qualità avere infinite espressioni negl'individui. Achille è Achille, e Tersite è Tersite."

31. *Lez.*, p. 354: "La sua culla."

32. *Lez.*, p. 350.

33. *Sto.*, *1*, 166: "Non ci è compenetrazione dei due termini. Il pen-

siero non è calato nell'immagine; il figurato non è calato nella figura."

34. *Lez.*, p. 353: "L'allegoria muore e la poesia nasce."

35. *S.C.*, 2, 172: "Altro è dire e altro è fare."

36. *Sto.*, 1, 169: "Distinguere il mondo intenzionale e il mondo effettivo, ciò che il poeta ha voluto e ciò che ha fatto."

37. *Manz.*, p. 41: "Il metodo piú sicuro e concludente è di guardare il libro in sé, e non nelle intenzioni dell'Autore." But De Sanctis recognizes here that it is not superfluous to study the intentions of an author; it is not yet criticism but a preparation for it. Willy nilly, something of the intentional world always penetrates into the book and underlies it, as a motive or obstacle.

38. *S.C.*, 1, 306–07: "Non falsi o distrugga l'ingenuitá de' miei sentimenti. . . . Siccome la poetica non può tener luogo del genio, cosí la critica non può tener luogo del gusto; ed il gusto è il genio del critico. Si dice che il poeta nasce; anche il critico nasce; anche nel critico ci è una parte geniale, che gli dee dar la natura."

39. *Pet.*, p. 7: "Può ricrearlo, dargli la seconda vita, può dire con l'orgoglio di Fichte:—Io creo Dio!"

40. *S.C.*, 2, 90: "di rifare quello che ha fatto il poeta, rifarlo a suo modo e con altri mezzi."

41. *S.C.*, 1, 125: "La critica é la coscienza o l'occhio della poesia, la stessa opera spontanea del genio riprodotta come opera riflessa dal gusto. Ella non deve dissolvere l'universo poetico; dee mostrarmi la stessa unità divenuta ragione, coscienza di sé stessa . . . La critica . . . è la stessa concezione poetica guardata da un altro punto . . . la creazione ripensata o riflessa."

42. *Leop.*, 283–84: "Poiché la critica non crea, ricrea; deve riprodurre." *S.C.*, 2, 20. *Sto.*, 2, 309: "Una scienza superiore." *S.C.*, 2, 72: "Una forma che molto si avvicina all'arte: la scienza vi sta come un sottointeso."

43. *S.C.*, 2, 69: "Il critico raccoglie quelle poche sillabe, ed indovina la parola tutta intera . . . entrambi non riproducono semplicemente il mondo poetico, ma lo integrano, empiono le lacune."

44. *S.C.*, 2, 81: "Poi che il critico ha acquistata una chiara coscienza del mondo poetico, può determinarlo, assegnandogli il suo posto ed attribuendogli il suo valore. E ciò che si dice propriamente *giudicare o criticare*."

45. *Pet.*, p. 10: "Valore intrinseco . . . non ciò che esso ha di commune col secolo, con la scuola, co' predecessori, ma in ciò che ha di proprio e incomunicabile."

46. *Pet.*, pp. 19–20: "Perché non ci è il piú o il meno vivo, c'è il vivo e il morto; ci è il poeta e c'è il non poeta, il cervello eunuco."

47. This must be emphasized against recent attempts of Italian

Marxists to make De Sanctis a materialist. Art with De Sanctis is not a mirror of the social development, inferior to reality. Art must not produce types as Marxist criticism demands. What is in common to Marxism and De Sanctis is easily explained by the common ancestry in Hegelianism and a common interest in 19th-century realism.

48. *S.C.*, *3*, 288: "Tutto è materia di arte."

49. *Sto.*, *1*, 184: "Niente è nella natura che non possa esser nell'arte."

50. *S.C.*, *2*, 268–69 n.

51. *Sto.*, *1*, 185: "Il bello non è che se stesso: il brutto è se stesso e il suo contrario." De Sanctis might have known Karl Rosenkranz's *Aesthetik des Hässlichen* (1853) or the extensive discussions in F. T. Vischer's *Aesthetik* (Reutlingen, 1846–57), e.g. *1*, 336 ff.; *2*, 14, 17; and *3*, 1187–1910.

52. *Pet.*, p. 20: "La Taida . . . è piú viva e piú poetica di Beatrice, quando è pura allegoria . . . Iago . . . una delle piú belle creature del mondo poetico."

53. *Sto.*, *1*, 185. *S.C.*, *2*, 246. See the odd reflections on Francesca da Rimini: "La poesia della donna è d'esser vinta . . . La donna depravata dalla passione è un essere contro natura, perciò straniero a noi e di nessuno interesse."

54. *S.C.*, *2*, 268 n.: "Tal contenuto, tal forma."

55. *Pet.*, 91: "In poesia non ci è propriamente né contenuto, né forma, ma che, come in natura, l'uno è l'altro. Il gran poeta è colui che uccide la forma, di modo que questa sia esso medesimo il contenuto."

56. *S.C.*, *2*, 268: "Il contenuto non è dunque trascurato. Apparisce due volte nella nuova critica; la prima, come naturale o astratto, qual era; la seconda, come forma, qual è divenuto."

57. *S.C.*, *2*, 286: "Un fondo astratto e pedantesco, che resiste a tutti gli sforzi della fantasia."

58. *Sto.*, *2*, 392: "Il contenuto politico e morale non è qui semplice stimolo e occasione alla formazione artistica, ma è la sostanza, e invade e guasta il lavoro dell'arte."

59. *S.C.*, *3*, 124: "Si pone non come arte, giá formato e trasfigurato, ma come staccato dall'arte, anteriore e superiore all'arte."

60. *Scuola*, p. 6: "Ma quando esiste il contenuto, picchia e ripicchia a lungo andare si fa la via, si crea la forma sua."

61. *Pet.*, p. 49: "Un puro gioco di forme."

62. *S.C.*, *2*, 355: "Questa disarmonia tra il contenuto e la forma."

63. *S.C.*, *3*, 216: "Onde nasce l'interna scissura della sua forma poetica, il carattere drammatico della sua lirica, riso e lacrima, vita e morte."

64. *Sto.*, *1*, 177: "Perché un argumento non è tabula rasa, dove si puó scrivere il genio; ma è marmo giá incavato e lineato, che ha in sé

il suo concetto e le leggi del suo sviluppo. La piú grande qualitá del genio è d'intendere il suo argumento."

65. *S.C.*, 2, 89: "E una materia condizionata e determinata, contenente giá in sé virtualmente la sua poetica, cioè le sue leggi organiche, il suo concetto, le sue parti, la sua forma, il suo stile."

66. *S.C.*, *1*, 91: "Non ha considerato seriamente il suo argumento."

67. *Manz.*, p. 27: "La materia . . . in una posizione concreta e determinata, acquista un carattere, diviene una 'situazione'."

68. *Gio.*, p. 134: "All'unità del disegno, all'ossatura e al congegno delle parti." Page 128: "che determina il suo comparire, cioé il suo stile."

69. Cf. *S.C.*, *1*, 137.

70. *Pet.*, pp. 101–02: "Le poesie che non vengono dall'animo, dal di dentro, ma sono un prodotto meccanico e artificiale, non hanno situazione, e perciò non hanno forma, nel senso elevato di questa parola."

71. *S.C.*, *1*, 29: "La situazione è qui dunque inestetica, ovvero incapace di rappresentazione."

72 *S.C.*, *3*, 106: "Una vera situazione lirica, cioè a dire l'anima in una condizione determinata, che le mette in moto il suo mondo interiore."

73. *Vorlesungen über Ästhetik*, ed. Glockner, *1*, 245, 268 f., 271–72; on lyrical situation, *3*, 431.

74. See the Bibliography, under Contini. On "situation" see also Binni and Orsini.

75. *S.C.*, *1*, 257: "Il puro ideale (il perfetto) cioè a dire l'astratto . . . il morto ideale." *Manz.*, p. 65 and passim.

76. *S.C.*, *3*, 268: "Il vivo sentimento dell'ideale umano e la potente immaginazione costruttrice e rappresentatrice."

77. *Manz.*, p. 66.

78. *S.C.*, *1*, 227: "Cosí, alzando a significazione generale i loro affetti, poterono amendue fondere in una sola personalità ciò che la loro anima avea di più proprio ed intimo e ciò che il concetto ha di piú estrinseco ed astratto."

79. *S.C.*, *1*, 202: "Il campo proprio del poeta è l'immagine."

80. *Sto.*, *1*, 64–65: The distinction comes from Schelling, Jean Paul, A. W. Schlegel, and Hegel. In Coleridge the terms are reversed. See above in this *History*, 2, 164.

81. *Sto.*, *1*, 69: "Questa immagine spiritualizzata . . . quella mezza realtá."

82. *Sto.*, *1*, 299: "Ci è l'immagine, manca il fantasma, que' sottintesi e que' chiaroscuri, che ti dánno il sentimento e la musica delle cose."

83. *S.C.*, *1*, 33: "Egli non ha l'intuizione immediata e diretta del fantasma."

84. *S.C.*, *1*, 34: "In luogo di dire alla sua creatura:—Sorgi e cammina:—lasciandole tutta la sua libertá di persona . . . l'autore dice:— Tu sei la mia fattura; tu mi appartieni."

85. *Sto.*, *1*, 416: "In questo sorriso, in questa presenza e coscienza del reale tra le piú geniali creazioni è il lato negativo dell'arte, il germe della dissoluzione e della morte."

86. *S.C.*, *1*, 248: "L'umore è una forma artistica, che ha, per suo significato, la *distruzione del limite, con la coscienza di essa distruzione* . . . il sentimento che niente vi è di vero e di serio, che ciascuna opinione vale l'altra."

87. On "sarcasm" cf. F. T. Vischer, *Aesthetik* (Reutlingen, 1846), *1*, 438–39: "Vernichtender Hohn." *Sto.*, *1*, 205: "La porta per la quale volgiamo le spalle al comico e rientriamo nella grande poesia."

88. *S.C.*, *2*, 184: "L'epopea trae la sua vita dall'intimo della nazione."

89. *S.C.*, *3*, 44: "L'epica primitiva e integra, dove non è ancora penetrata la lirica e il dramma."

90. *Manz.*, p. 15.

91. *S.C.*, *2*, 306: "C'è lí dentro la stoffa ancora epica del'uomo, non ancora drammatica. Manca l'eloquenza, manca la vita interna dell'anima."

92. *S.C.*, *1*, 23: "Ma senza la umana libertá, non che il dramma, la poesia è distrutta."

93. *S.C.*, *3*, 26: "Personaggio assolutamente prosaico."

94. *S.C.*, *3*, 285: "L'arte muore in un accento lirico, in un sospiro musicale. Lirica, musica, sono le ultime forme dell'arte."

95. *Pet.*, *p.* 88: "Il poema d'un quarto d'ora . . . puó meglio rappresentare il simultaneo che il successivo."

96. *S.C.*, *2*, 302. *Pet.*, p. 93. *Scuola*, pp. 449–50. *Sto.*, *2*, 401.

97. *Sto.*, *1*, 344: "Sarebbe insopportabile questo mondo e profondamente disgustoso, se l'arte non vi avesse profuse tutte le sue veneri, inviluppando la sua nuditá in quelle ampie forme latine, come in un velo agitato da venti lascivi."

98. *Manz.*, p. 85: "Non è costruito 'a priori' . . . l'è consequenza di un dato modo di concepire, di sentire e d'immaginare."

99. *Sto.*, *2*, 384: "Un fenomeno arbitrario e isolato . . . l'intima connessione che è tra quello stile e tutto il congegno della composizione."

100. *Gio.*, p. 128: "L'espressione, questa prende la sua sostanza e il suo carattere dalla cosa che si vuole esprimere."

101. *Pet.*, p. 91: "La forma è specchio che ti faccia passare immediatamente all'immagine, sí che tu non t'accorga che di mezzo ci sia il vetro."

102. *Poesia,* p. 94: "Questa trasparenza della forma consiste nel suo annullamento, quando diviene una semplice trasmissione e non attira l'occhio per sé. Come uno specchio in cui non vi fermate al vetro . . . E la limpidezza. Acqua limpida è quella che lascia vedere il fondo come se non esistesse. La forma limpida lascia uscir fuori di sé l'oggetto senza attirar l'attenzione del lettore."

103. *S.C.*, *3*, 296: "Il motto di una arte seria è questo: Poco parlare noi, e far molto parlare le cose, sunt lacrimae rerum!"

104. *S.C.*, *1*, 240: "Dimentichi la parola . . . la parola non è per lui altro che un istrumento . . . mezzo diafano entro il quale si reflette il pensiero in tutta la sua limpidezza ed evidenza."

105. *S.C.*, *2*, 268 n.: "La formola eccesiva."

106. *S.C.*, *3*, 117: "L'uccello canta per cantare, ottimamente. Ma l'uccello cantando esprime tutto sé, i suoi istinti, i suoi bisogni, la sua natura. Anche l'uomo cantando esprime tutto sé. Non gli basta essere artista, dee essere uomo."

107. *Sto.*, *2*, 134: "Chi voglia conoscer bene addentro i misteri di quella corruttela italiana."

108. *Sto.*, *1*, 332: "Questa società tal quale, sorpresa calda calda nell'atto della vita, è trasportata nel *Decamerone.*"

109. *Sto.*, *2*, 371: "L'arte non è un capriccio individuale . . . L'arte, come religione e filosofia, come istituzioni politiche ed amministrative, è un fatto sociale, un risultato della coltura e della vita nazionale."

110. *Sto.*, *1*, 441.

111. *Pet.*, p. 23: "Il principio direttivo . . . la successiva riabilitazione della materia, un graduale avvicinarsi alla natura ed al reale."

112. *Sto.*, *1*, 275: "La bella unitá di Dante, che vedeva la vita nell'armonia dell'intelletto e dell'atto mediante l'amore."

113. *Sto.*, *1*, 64: "La fede . . . la condizione preliminare e necessaria della poesia."

114. *Sto.*, *1*, 169: "Era poeta e si ribella all'allegoria."

115. *Sto.*, *1*, 175: "Questo mondo artistico, uscito da una contraddizione tra l'intenzione del poeta e la sua opera, non è compiutamente armonico, non è schietta poesia."

116. *Sto.*, *1*, 210: "Queste grandi figure, lá sul loro piedistallo rigide ed epiche come statue, attendono l'artista che le prenda per mano e le gitti nel tumulto della vita, e le faccia esseri drammatici. E l'artista non fu un italiano: fu Shakespeare."

117. *Sto.*, *1*, 212–13: "Innanzi all porta del purgatorio scompare il diavolo e muore la carne, e con la carne gran parte di poesia se ne va."

118. *Sto.*, *1*, 234: "Siamo all'ultima dissoluzione della forma. Corpulenta e materiale nell'*Inferno,* pittorica e fantastica nel *Purgatorio,*

qui è lirica e musicale: immediata parvenza dello spirito, assoluta luce senza contenuto, fascia e cerchio dello spirito, non esso spirito."

119. *Sto., 1*, 254: "All' 'alta fantasia' manca la possa; e insieme con la fantasia muore la poesia."

120. *Sto., 1*, 263: "L'uomo è trovato."

121. *Sto., 1*, 267: "Il reale comparisce la prima volta nell'arte."

122. *Sto., 1*, 269: "L'alba della realtá."

123. *Pet., p.* 228: "Non è un'aspirazione, ma un ostacolo che egli non può vincere."

124. *Pet.,* p. 66: "Confesso che non saprei rispondere a queste e simili domande, per la semplice ragione che non lo so, e che il Petrarca non me ne ha fatto confidenza."

125. *Sto., 1*, 279–80: "Dante, che dovea essere il principio di tutta una letteratura, ne fu la fine. Il suo mondo, cosí perfetto al di fuori, è al di dentro scisso e fiacco: è contemplazione d'artista, non piú fede e sentimento."

126. *Sto., 1*, 282.

127. *Sto., 1*, 329: "L'anticommedia."

128. *Sto., 1*, 345.

129. *Sto., 1*, 327: "Avventure," "casi straordinari."

130. *Sto., 1*, 334–35: "Il motivo comico non esce dal mondo morale, ma dal mondo intellettuale . . . Si vede la coltura in quel suo primo fiorire mostrar coscienza di sé, volgendo in gioco l'ignoranza e la malizia delle classi inferiori."

131. *Sto., 2*, 79: "Ci era lo scrittore, non ci era l'uomo."

132. *Sto., 1*, 358: "Ne nasce l'indifferenza del contenuto. Ciò che importa non è cosa s'ha a dire, ma come s'ha a dire."

133. *Sto., 1*, 357: "Non viene dal popolo e non cala nel popolo."

134. *Sto., 2*, 36: "Lo spirito è giá adulto, materialista e realista, incredulo, ironico, e si trastulla a spese della sua immaginazione."

135. Cf. *S.C., 2,* 174 ff.

136. *Sto., 2*, 30: "Non hai il sentimento della patria, della famiglia, dell'umanitá, e neppure dell'amore, dell'onore."

137. *Sto., 2*, 163: "La sua serietá è come la sua religione, superficiale e letteraria . . . cerca l'epico, e trova il lirico; cerca il vero o il reale, e genera il fantastico; cerca la storia, e s'incontra con la sua anima."

138. *Sto., 2*, 179: "Il cadavere."

139. *Sto., 2*, 67, 75, 104. Cf. the lecture on Machiavelli, *S.C., 2,* 309 ff.

140. *S.C., 3,* 1 ff.

141. *Sto., 2*, 233: "Un metodo organico."

142. *Sto., 2*, 310.

143. *Sto.,* 2, 191: "Vuoto di passione e di azione e vuoto di coscienza."

144. *Sto.,* 2, 331–51. See also the somewhat different article on Metastasio (1871) reprinted in *Poesia,* pp. 192–215, and for comment the bibliography under Croce (no. 12) and Fubini.

145. *S.C., 3,* 122: "E nella musica avea trovata la sua tomba la vecchia letteratura."

146. *Scuola,* p. 182: "Ecco dove era la nostra genialitá!"

147. *Sto.,* 2, 365.

148. *Sto.,* 2, 374: "Un mondo interiore della coscienza . . . la sincerità e la forza delle convinzioni."

149. *Sto.,* 2, 377–78: "Rinasce l'uomo . . . la sostanza dell'arte è il contenuto, e l'artista è per lui l'uomo nella sua integrità che esprime tutto se stesso: il patriota, il credente, il filosofo, l'amante, l'amico. La poesia ripiglia il suo antico significato, ed è voce del mondo interiore . . . la forma . . . diviene essa medesima l'idea, armonia tra l'idea e l'espressione."

150. *S.C., 3,* 112–39, esp. 138: "In lui l'uomo valeva piú che l'artista."

151. *Sto.,* 2, 389: "Manca a lui la scienza della vita."

152. See *S.C., 1,* 100–03, 144–62, 187–99.

153. *S.C., 3,* 102: "La resurrezione di un mondo interiore in un popolo oscillante tra l'ipocrisia e la negazione."

154. *S.C., 3,* 95: "Senti una sola corda; manca l'orchestra; manca sopratutto la grazia, la delicatezza, la soavitá, quella certa interna misura e pacatezza, dov'è il segreto della vita." Page 106: "Una lezione con accessori poetici."

155. *Manz.,* p. 10: "Libertá, uguaglianza, fratellanza, vangelizzata."

156. *Manz.,* p. 33: "Quel suo mondo ideale inviluppato in un mondo storico, che gli dá tutta l'illusione di una esistenza piena e concreta, diviene il vero centro vivente, l'unitá di tutto il lavoro."

157. *Manz.,* pp. 52–53: "Il piú puro e insieme il piú moderno di tutti gl'ideali, non dirò della reazione, ma della restaurazione europea."

158. *Manz.,* pp. 61, 65.

159. *Sto.,* 2, 433–34.

160. *S.C., 2,* 115–60: For the curious story of Schopenhauer's misinterpretation of the essay as praise, see the Bibliography under Croce (no. 5).

161. *S.C., 2,* 159–60: "Non crede al progresso, e te lo fa desiderare; non crede alla libertá, e te la fa amare. Chiama illusioni l'amore, la gloria, la virtú, e te ne accende in petto un desiderio inesausto . . . É scettico, e ti fa credente . . . e mentre chiama larva ed errore tutta la vita, non sai come, ti senti stringere piú saldamente a tutto ciò che

nella vita è nobile e grande." The translation in the text is that of Geoffrey L. Bickersteth, in *The Poems of Giacomo Leopardi* (Cambridge, 1923), pp. 131–32.

162. *Leop.*, p. 99: "Questo dualismo è la forza dinamica della poesia leopardiana, la leva che la mette in moto e ne fa un organismo originale."

163. *Leop.*, p. 92: "Di una bonomia quasi fanciullesca nella sua profonditá."

164. See *S.C.*, *1*, 25–43, on Guerrazzi; *1*, 44–70, on Padre Bresciani; *1*, 71–99, on Prati; *2*, 189–215, again on Prati.

165. *S.C.*, *3*, 234–276: "Studio sopra E. Zola" (1878). *3*, 277–99, on l'*Assommoir* (1879).

166. "L'Ideale" (1877), in *Poesia*, pp. 308–13; *Pet.* 23–25, a note, added in 1883; and "Il Darwinismo nell'arte" (1883), conclusion, *S.C.*, *3*, 325.

167. *S.C.*, *3*, 299: "Per una razza fantastica, amica delle frasi e della pompa, educata nell'arcadia e nella rettorica."

168. *Sto.*, *2*, 437: "Giá vediamo in questo secolo disegnarsi il nuovo secolo. E questa volta non dobbiamo trovarci alla coda, non a' secondi posti."

169. *Sto.*, *1*, 364: "Quel mondo spensierato e sensuale non ti potea dare che l'idillico e il comico."

170. *Sto.*, *2*, 166: "Nessuna cosa vale tanto a mostrare il fondo frivolo e scarso della vita italiana quanto questi sforzi impotenti del Tasso a raggiungere una serietá . . . Volere o non volere, rimane ariostesco."

171. *Sto.*, *2*, 206: "Il corruttore del suo secolo. Piuttosto è lecito di dire che il secolo corruppe lui o, per dire con piú esattezza, non ci fu corrotti né corruttori. Il secolo era quello, e non potea esser altro; era una consequenza necessaria di non meno necessarie premesse. E Marino fu l'ingegno del secolo, il secolo stesso nella maggior forza e chiarezza della sua espressione."

172. *Sto.*, *2*, 283: "L'intelletto spinto sino alla sua ultima depravazione . . . Furono effetto e causa . . . Perciò furono un progresso, un naturale portato della storia."

173. *Manz.*, p. 4: "Era un serio movimento dello spirito, secondo le eterne leggi della storia."

174. *Sto.*, *2*, 164: "Giudice inappellabile di poesia."

175. *Sto.*, *2*, 338: "Nessun poeta è stato cosí popolare come il Metastasio, nessuno è penetrato cosí intimamente nello spirito delle moltitudini. Ci è dunque ne' suoi drammi un valore assoluto, superiore alle occasioni, resistente alla stessa critica dissolvente del secolo decimonono."

176. *Sto.*, 2, 349.

177. *S.C.*, *1*, 189: "Una letteratura popolare cavata dall'intimo della nazione."

178. *Sto.*, 2, 15: "Ludovico e Dante furono i due vessilliferi di opposta civiltá . . . le sintesi in cui compí e si chiuse il tempo loro."

179. *S.C.*, *1*, 190, 197–98.

180. For further comment on the concept of Renaissance and music see the Bibliography under Cantimori, Parente, and Toffanin.

181. *Sto.*, 2, 191, 194–95.

182. See the Bibliography under Binni.

183. *S.C.*, 2, 278–79: "Quando su ciascuna epoca, su ciascuno scrittore importante ci sará tale monografia o studio o saggio, che dica l'ultima parola e sciolga tutte le quistioni."

184. See the list in the back of Croce's ed. of *Sto.*, 2, 453–57.

185. *S.C.*, 2, 279: "Non sappiamo ancora cosa è la letteratura e cosa è la forma."

186. *Pet.*, p. 8: "Una storia della critica è uno de' lavori importanti che restano ancora a fare."

187. *S.C.*, 2, 280: "Anche de' criterii critici che hanno guidato i nostri scrittori e artisti manca una storia. Ogni scrittore ha la sua estetica in capo, un certo suo modo di concepire l'arte, e le sue predilezioni nel metodo e nell'esecuzione."

188. *Gio.*, p. 177: "La storia, come la natura, non procede per salti: gradazioni progressive generano da ultimo il gran poeta, che dá a tutta la serie la forma definitiva. Così Dante è il gran poeta delle visioni religiose; Petrarca è il gran poeta dei trovatori; Ariosto dié l'ultima mano alla serie cavalleresca."

189. *Poesia*, p. 3: "Una vera progressione."

190. Letter to Camillo de Meis (1869): "Il Reale poetico, che io chiamo la Forma, la Ragione vivente, è colta nell'atto della vita, la Ragione-Storia."

191. *S.C.*, *3*, 45–46. Cf. *S.C.*, 2, 256 and 307, and *Sto.*, *1*, 210, quoted in n. 116.

192. *Sto.*, *1*, 230: "La stoffa da cui dovea sorgere piú tardi il dramma spagnuolo."

193. *Sto.*, 2, 164: "Un presentimento di una nuova poesia . . . che . . . si chiamerá un giorno *I promessi sposi*."

194. For fuller discussion see the Bibliography under Neri and Petronio.

195. On the history of the translation see B. Croce in *La Critica*, *10* (1912), 146–47.

196. *Lez.*, p. 340: "La sua maggior gloria è di avere altamente pro-

clamata la contemporaneitá de' due termini nello spirito del poeta, e di aver posta l'eccellenza dell'arte nell'unitá personale, in cui l'idea stia involuta e come smemorata . . . Nessuno piú di lui ti parla d'individuo e d'incarnazione, sente che lá è il vero; ma, in grazia del sistema, questo suo individuo libero e poetico è nel fatto un individuo-manifestazione, o per dirla col linguaggio in moda, un velo trasparente dell'idea; sicché il principale, l'importante è sempre la cosa manifestata."

197. *Lez.*, pp. 341–42: "Un velo del generale, la sua forma è l'apparenza dell'idea . . . Il contenuto, il significato interiore, l'idea, il concetto, ecco la calamità del critico hegeliano."

198. On Vischer and De Sanctis, see Croce (No. 9). *Pet.*, p. 236: "Niente mi pareva piú inestetico che l'*Estetica* di Vischer." De Sanctis probably refers to its clumsy form—divisions, paragraphs—rather than to its doctrine.

199. *Gio.*, p. 176: "Che cercava nell'arte le idee e i tipi."

200. *Manz.*, p. 19. *S.C.*, 2, 237. *S.C.*, 2, 6 n.: "Fondatore di una nuova critica." *Scuola*, pp. 14, 416.

201. *S.C.*, 2, 10 ff.

202. Cf. *Teoria*, *1*, 105–08, dating from 1842.

203. *Gio.*, p. 179: "Fanatici panegirici." Cf. *S.C.*, *1*, 194, 230.

204. *Teoria*, 2, 73. *Leop.* 282.

205. *S.C.*, *1*, 107–08, 110.

206. *S.C.*, *1*, 130. *S.C.*, 2, 6 n., 73.

207. *S.C.*, *1*, 110, 253–67.

208. *S.C.*, *1*, 134: "Io odio la critica a paralleli." Cf. *S.C.*, *1*, 141, 262; 2, 3. Also *Gio.*, p. 141.

209. *S.C.*, *1*, 139–40. *S.C.*, *1*, 175: "Un letterato, secondo il senso antico di questa parola: ciò che a lui importa principalmente, è la rettorica, l'arte di ben dire."

210. *S.C.*, *3*, 172.

211. *Leop.*, p. 286: "Manchevole e mediocre." Cf. *Leop.*, p. 15, and *S.C.*, 2, 342.

212. *Pet.*, p. 9: "E l'autore isolato dalla sua opera e studiato ne' fatti della sua vita, ne' suoi difetti, nelle sue virtú, nelle sue qualitá . . . ne può nascere un giudizio piú o meno esatto dell'uomo, non del suo lavoro."

213. *S.C.*, 2, 12: "Una tragedia può avere tutti questi caratteri, ed essere mediocrissima."

214. *S.C.*, 2, 246–47, 252–53, 255.

215. *S.C.*, 2, 294: "*Come avesse l'inferno in gran despitto.*" *Inferno*, Canto 10, line 36.

216. *S.C.*, *3*, 38.

217. *Inferno*, Canto 33, line 75. Note that Croce (no. 14) strongly disapproves of De Sanctis' admission of ambiguity.

218. *S.C.*, *3*, 43–44.

219. *S.C.*, *1*, 116: "Perchè . . . non è commosso ancora da quello che dice."

BIBLIOGRAPHY: ITALIAN CRITICISM AFTER DE SANCTIS

Luigi Tonelli, *La Critica letteraria italiana negli ultimi cinquant' anni* (Bari, 1914), surveys this time. A briefer sketch: Aldo Borlenghi, "La Critica letteraria da De Sanctis a oggi," in Vol. 2 of *Orientamenti culturali: La Letteratura italiana. Le Correnti* (Milan, 1956), pp. 932–1051. Binni, quoted above (p. 512), is also most useful. An anthology of texts: Giorgio Pullini, *Le Poetiche dell' Ottocento*, Padua, 1959.

On the historical school see B. Croce, "La Critica erudita della letteratura e i suoi avversarii" (1911), in *La Letteratura della nuova Italia* (Bari, 1949), *3*, 373–91; Luigi Russo, "Allesandro d'Ancona e la scuola storica italiana," in *Annali della R. Scuola Normale Superiore di Pisa*, 3d ser. 5 (1936), 1–16.

On Torraca: Carlo Giordano, "Da Francesco De Sanctis a Francesco Torraca," in *Studi in onore di Francesco Torraca* (Naples, 1922), pp. 1–176 (with bibliography).

Carducci is quoted from *Opere*, Edizione nazionale (30 vols. Bologna, 1935–40), as EN, and *Lettere*, 20 vols. 1938–57.

On Carducci's criticism see Foscarina Trabaudi Foscarini, *Della Critica letteraria di Giosuè Carducci*, Bologna, 1911, undistinguished; Daniele Mattalia, *L'Opera critica di Giosuè Carducci*, Genova, 1934, schematic. See review by Mario Fubini in *Giornale storico della letteratura italiana*, *104* (1934), 117–24. Important chapters in general books: Alfredo Galletti, *Carducci: il poeta, il critico, il maestro*. Milan, 1929, 1948 (2d ed.); Natale Busetto, *Giosuè Carducci: l'uomo, il poeta, il critico e il prosatore*, Padua, 1958, a careful survey; Luigi Russo, *Carducci senza retorica*, Bari, 1957. The chapter on the critic in *La Critica letteraria contemporanea* (Bari, 1942), *1*, 12–47. On sources see Gabriel Mauguin, *Carducci et la France*, Paris, 1914.

Articles: e.g. Benedetto Croce, "Carducci pensatore e critico," in *La Letteratura della nuova Italia*, 2, 91–115; also in G. *Carducci*, Bari, 1920. Attilio Momigliano, "Carducci critico," in *Studi di Poesia*, Bari, 1938; and G. Contini, "Presentazione" of the reprint of Carducci's ed. of Petrarch's *Rime*, Florence, 1957.

On Graf: B. Croce in *La Letteratura della nuova Italia*, 2, 203–19.

On Capuana: G. Trombatore, "Luigi Capuana critico," *Belfagor*, 4 (1949), 410–24.

NOTES: ITALIAN CRITICISM AFTER DE SANCTIS

1. Vol. 1, p. 2: "Sintesi più o meno geniali, in cui, più assai che allo studio diretto dei fatti, si badò ad alcuni preconcetti estetici, politici, filosofici, con l'aiuto de' quali si pretese d'interpretare e ordinare fatti male sceverati e mal noti, ossia di ricostruire sistematicamente la storia." Page 3: "studio diretto dei monumento . . . che rifugga da ogni costruzione sistematica."

2. See Vittorio Santoli, "Gli studi di letteratura populare" in C. Antoni and R. Mattioli, *Cinquant'anni di vita intellettuale Italiana, 1896–1946* (Naples, 1950), 2, 115–36. D'Ancona wrote an essay, "La Poesia popolare italiana," in *Rivista di Firenze*, 4 (1858), 108–34, and 5 (1859), 3–22, long before Ermolao Rubieri's *Storia della poesia popolare italiana* (Florence, 1877), a highly romantic book, and Costantino Nigra, *Canti popolari del Piemonte* (Torino, 1888), the most important collection.

3. *I Precursori di Dante* (Florence, 1874), *Scritti danteschi* (Florence, 1912), reprints an essay on *La Beatrice* (Pisa, 1865), which argues convincingly for her historical reality.

4. Giorgio Pasquali in introduction to reprint of *Vergilio nel Medio Evo*, 2 vols. Florence, 1937.

5. *Le Fonti dell'Orlando Furioso* (2d ed. Florence, 1900), p. 609: "Creatori nel senso assoluto della parola non ne esistono. I prodotti della fantasia non si sottraggono alle leggi universali della natura. Anche qui il nuovo, considerato da vicino, non è altro che la metamorfosi del vecchio; ogni forma presuppone una catena di forme anteriori; gl'incrementi possono essere più o meno rapidi, ma sono sempre graduati." Page 612: "Conchiudo che se Messer Lodovico avesse inventato da sé moltissimo che ebbe da altri, alla corona della sua gloria se ne aggiungerebbe più che una foglia d'alloro."

6. There is a complete edition of *Opere di Francesco D'Ovidio*, 18 vols. Rome, Caserta, Naples, 1923. On Tasso, "Il carattere, gli amori e le sventure di Torquato Tasso" in Vol. 11, Rome, 1926.

7. Vol. 1, p. 170: "Questa repugnanza d'Italia ad ogni lavoro leggendario, ad ogni elaborazione poetica della saga." Croce in "La critica erudita . . ." in *La Letteratura della Nuova Italia*, (5th ed. Bari, 1949),

3, 393, quotes Bartoli: "Il realismo è la caratteristica dell'arte italiana; fuori del suo grembo non c'è salute."

8. "De Sanctis conferenziere e insegnante" (1903) in *Opere complete,* Vol. 14, *Rimpianti vecchi e nuovi,* Caserta, 1930. Cf. "Critica storica e critica estetica," originally Preface to *Saggi critici,* 1878. In *Varietà critiche, Opere complete,* Vol. 12, Caserta, 1929.

9. *Saggi e rassegne* (Livorno, 1885), there "Per Francesco De Sanctis." Also *Per Francesco De Sanctis* (Naples, 1910), which contains "Francesco De Sanctis e la sua seconda scuola" (1902).

10. *Per F. De Sanctis,* p. 113: "Il fine supremo della critica è quello di esaminare l'opera d'arte in sè stessa, in ciò, che ha di proprio, e per cui solo è viva." *Saggi e rassegne,* p. 85: "Uno è il còmpito suo, quello di dare vita a' suoi fantasmi, i quali egli non può, si è vero artista, costruirli *a priori,* alla stregua di preconcetti."

11. On Verga see *Saggi e rassegne,* pp. 217 ff., and *Scritti critici* (Naples, 1907), pp. 381 ff.

12. E.g. *Il Teatro italiano dei secoli XIII, XIV, e XV,* Florence, 1885. *Studi su lirica italiana del Duecento.* Bologna, 1902; the ed. of *Divina Commedia.* 3 vols. Milano, 1905–07; *Studi danteschi,* Naples, 1912.

13. "Donne reali e donne ideali," in *Discussioni e ricerche letterarie* (Livorno, 1888), pp. 289–348. Cf. Rodolfo Renier, *Il Tipo estetico della Donna nel Medio evo,* Ancona, 1885.

14. *Discussioni,* pp. 345, 419, etc.

15. "Del valore dell'arte forestiera per gl'Italiani," in *Studi letterari e bizzarrie satiriche,* ed. B. Croce (Bari, 1907), pp. 1–27.

16. *Studi letterari,* pp. 28–118. Page 82: "Intuizione, Immaginativa, Caratterizzativa."

17. *Fame usurpate,* 3d ed., ed. B. Croce (Bari, 1912), esp. p. 145. Pages 226–27: "Il Fausto del Goethe è la più contentabile persona che immaginarsi possa, vera figura comica." Also pp. 210, 229, 138–39.

18. "Versificatore e poeta," in *Studi letterari,* p. 349.

19. "I vizi di Dante" (1883) in *Studi letterari,* and *Studi danteschi,* Florence, 1891.

1. EN, *20,* 203. Or one may refer to the rhetoric about Italy's sacrifices for Europe, "Cara e santa patria!" (EN, *7,* 161) or the stuff about Dante, the lark, and the eagle, etc., EN, *7,* 327–28.

2. "Di alcune poesie popolari bolognesi del secolo XIII inedite," EN, *8,* 155–343. "Della varia fortuna di Dante," EN, *10,* 255–420. Preface to ed. of *Rime* in EN, *11,* 125–84, and "Sul testo e sui commentatori del Canzioniere," *ibid.,* pp. 273–309.

3. *Lettere*, 5, 65 (27 December 1866): "Il mio genere . . . la critica storica," EN, *24*, 196–97: "Il disinteressato conforto dello scoprire un fatto o un monumento ancor nuovo della nostra storia . . . sano e piene di visioni da quanto l'aria e l'orror sacro delle vecchie foreste."

4. EN, *25*, 92: "Alzare col metodo storico più severo la storia letteraria al grado della storia naturale" (1878). EN, *28*, 324: "Giudizio? E troppo superbo vocabolo per me. Io combatto, ammiro, commento; non giudico" (1896). Similarly EN, *20*, 83; *13*, 327.

5. EN, *7*, 393: "L'emanazione morale della civiltà, la spirituale irradiazione dei popoli." Similarly, EN, *24*, 313.

6. See Maugain, *Carducci*. This is an old-fashioned, mechanical study, but it shows convincingly that Carducci often paraphrased or simply translated Guingené, Fauriel, Quinet, Ozanam, and J. P. Charpentier (*Histoire de la Renaissance des lettres en Europe au XVe siècle*, Paris, 1843). The similarities between De Sanctis' chapter and Carducci's speech on Boccaccio ("Ai parentali de Giovanni Boccaccio," 1875, in EN, *11*, 313–34), pointed out by Croce (in "Il De Sanctis e il Carducci," in *Una Famiglia de patrioti*, 3d ed., Bari, 1949, pp. 253–66) are explicable by the common source in Quinet. Cf. Carlo Pellegrini, "E. Quinet e la letteratura italiana" in *Raccolta di studi di storia e di critica letteraria dedicata a F. Flamini*, Pisa, 1918, pp. 25–48. The thesis of Mattalia (*loc. cit.*) which traces the main ideas to Gioberti and the argument in Galletti (*loc. cit.*) that they come eventually from the German Romantics are no doubt true on the level of general concepts, but the dependence on French sources is quite specific and immediate.

7. EN, *7*, 72: "Il popolo vecchio, il popolo nuovo, il popolo minuto, o la plebe."

8. EN, *7*, 69: "La fantasia religiosa etrusca, l'intelletto sociale romano, il sentimento individuale germanico, lo spirito leggiadro provenzale e francese, l'istinto pratico e progressivo dei comuni lombardi."

9. EN, *7*, 327 (1888).

10. EN, *7*, 23–24.

11. EN, *7*, 3–5, 104. Cf. EN, *12*, 140.

12. EN, *20*, 110: Pieno di preoccupazioni e di pregiudizi (pregiudizi, intendiamoci, filosofici, estetici, critici, ecc., che sono i peggio, perchè più abbracciati e seguitati)." There are many openly or covertly disparaging remarks on De Sanctis in Carducci's letters and writings; e.g. in *Lettere*, 5, 225 (4 June 1868), Carducci calls De Sanctis' *Saggio sul Petrarca* "un lavoro di fantasia." See also EN, *7*, 131–32, against De Sanctis' concept of the Renaissance; EN, *20*, 115, 152 in defense of Monti, etc.

13. EN, *12*, 142–43: "Il movimento erudito del secolo XV non fosse
. . . fuori della tradizione nazionale."

14. EN, *5*, 303: "indigena e nazionale"; similarly *5*, 510. EN, *7*, 139:
"Una, classica, italiana . . . individuale e d'impronta toscana . . .
parziale e federale."

15. EN, *10*, 196–97.

16. EN, *6*, 484; *23*, 134 364. *Lettere 4*, 35 (28 March 1864).

17. EN, *25*, 404–05; *26*, 177; *7*, 408 ("eternal classicism").

18. EN, *17*, 1 ff. esp. 272 ff.

19. *Poeti erotici del secolo XVIII*, Florence, 1868; *Lirici del secolo
XVIII*, Florence, 1871. The introductions in EN, *15*. See also there,
"Dello svolgimento dell'ode in Italia" (1902), pp. 3–81.

20. On Foscolo: "Adolescenza e gioventù di Ugo Foscolo," EN, *18*,
151–83 (1882); on Monti: EN, *18*, 123–50; on Metastasio: EN, *15*,
239–67 (1882).

21. EN, *20*, 103–75 (1898).

22. EN, *20*, 341; *Lettere*, 2, 251 (3 May 1861).

23. *Lettere, 4*, 125 (19 November 1864): "Anche, in critica, io sono
un po' *fatalista* . . . Io amo, per esempio, i latinisti del quattrocento:
prediligo gli accademici del cinquecento; mi diverto un buggerio co'
secentisti; mi consolo con gli arcadi: mi svagono gl'infranciosati . . .
il bello per me è relativo e morale di per se stesso."

24. EN, *7*, 14; *23*, 29–30. Here the dislike of Calderón is strengthened
by the distaste for the Schlegels on whom Carducci accepts Heine's
views.

25. See "A proposito di alcuni giudizi su Alessandro Manzoni"
(1873), EN, *20*, 299–375. Cf. EN, *20*, 390: "Una certa aria deprimente"
in *Promessi sposi*.

26. EN, *25*, 231. On Stendhal, EN, *24*, 282: "Scrivere falso e affet-
tato."

27. EN, *24*, 384: "Né favola né scienza . . . né epopea né storia."
Cf. *7*, 416.

28. *Lettere, 1*, 61–62, 11 September 1853: "Abbrucio di uno spregio
grandissimo, immenso, sovrumano per tutto quel che è forestiero." Or
EN, *5*, 30–31.

29. EN, *25*, 373–74

30. On Heine, see the preface to Chiarini's translation of *Atta Troll*,
EN, *23*, 93–137. On a translation of Goethe's dramas, EN, *26*, 41 ff. On
the influence of German metrics see F. D'Ovidio, "La Versificazione
delle *Odi barbare*," in *Opere*, *9*, part 1, Naples, 1932. *Lettere*, 7, 104
(17 February 1872), speaks of Platen as "grande artista e poeta."

31. Preface to *Prometheus*, 1894. EN, *25*, 358–59. *Lettere, 12*, 204

(14 February 1880): "Sono poeti oggi molto più di noi: molto più veri poeti, massime gl'inglesi."

32. Parini in EN, *16* and *17*; Poliziano in EN, *12*, Dante in EN, *10*, Tasso in EN, *14*, 139–275; Foscolo in EN, *18*.

33. See *Lettere, 8*, 293 (4 October 1873). EN, *23*, 71. Carducci quotes or uses Sainte-Beuve in writing on Littré (EN, *23*, 269–90) and Barbier (*28*, 293–309) and in sketching a history of the *mal du siècle* on the occasion of Leopardi, EN, *20*, 1 ff., but I cannot see that he follows him as a critic.

1. E.g. *Studi e ritratti letterari* (Livorno, 1900), collecting essays printed in the 1880's. Also *Ombre e figure,* Rome, 1883; *Donne e poeti,* Rome, 1885.

2. Livorno, 1896. Pages 334–36: "La critica d'arte ha qualche cosa di essenzialmente soggettivo, la quale in ultima analisi si riduce a questo che dove uno dice: mi piace, un altro dice: non mi piace."

3. "Primo Centenario di P. B. Shelley" and other essays in *Saggi critici di letteratura inglese,* Florence, 1897 (preface by G. Carducci).

4. *Studi sul Petrarca,* Naples, 1878. *Studi sul Leopardi,* 2 vols. Florence, 1902, 1904.

5. *Studi di letterature straniere* (2d ed. Florence, 1907; 1st ed. 1893), p. 98: "Spontaneità e riflessione . . . l'eroe posto in azione e l'eroe descritto." E. M. Tillyard in his *Milton* makes similar distinctions.

6. *Studi di letteratura italiana* (2d ed. Florence, 1906; 1st ed. 1889–94), p. 232: "Il pregio estetico dell opera, ma nel tempo stesso riconosce l'importanza del contenuto." Page 237: "poesia naturale, ciò che chiamai poesia naturale dell'idea."

7. *La Critica letteraria,* Rome, 1894; reprinted in *Primi Saggi* (Bari, 1919), pp. 75–125.

8. Croce's severe judgment in *La Letteratura della nuova Italia* (5th ed. Bari, 1948), *2,* 210–19.

9. *Di una trattazione scientifica della Storia letteraria, Prolusione,* Turin, 1877; "Questioni di critica," in *Atti della R. Accademia delle Scienze di Torino, 24* (1889).

10. *Foscolo, Manzoni, Leopardi* (Turin, 1920), p. 278: "attitudine sensorie."

11. "Amleto, indole del personaggio e del dramma," in *Studi drammatici* (Turin, 1878), esp. p. 64. There also a descriptive essay on Marlowe's *Faustus* and a long piece on Italian 16th-century comedy: Bibbiena's *La Calandria,* Machiavelli's *La Mandragola,* Bruno's *Il Candelaio.*

12. In D'Ovidio's *Opere,* see n. 49. G. Chiarini, *Vita di Giosuè Carducci,* Florence, 1903.

13. *Cronache letterarie* (Catania, 1899), p. 247: "Strenuo campione del naturalismo in Italia."

14. *Il Teatro italiano contemporaneo,* Palermo, 1872; *Studi sulla letteratura contemporanea,* 2 vols. Milan, 1880–82; *Cronache letterarie,* Catania, 1899.

15. *Studi sulla letteratura contemporanea, 1,* 63: "La sensazione non rimane in lui il semplice stato di sensazione ma s'innalza, si purifica, diventa sentimento, poesia." *Ibid.,* 2, 124: "L'immensa tristezza."

16. *Studi, 1,* is prefaced by a quotation from De Sanctis: "tal contenuto, tal forma"; p. 55, 303: "Arte innanzi vuol dire forma," vol. 2, 132, 188; *Cronache, loc. cit.,* p. 251, in *Gli 'Ismi' contemporanei,* Catania, 1898, p. 26, etc.

17. *Gli 'Ismi' contemporanei,* p. 46: "Il tipo è cosa astratta: è l'usuraio, ma non è Shylock; è il sospettoso, ma non è Otello; è l'esitante, il chimerizzante, ma non è Amleto."

18. Unfavorable reviews of D'Annunzio, e.g. of *La Città morta* in *Cronache letterarie,* of *Giovanni Episcopo* in *Gli 'Ismi'.* The polemics against cosmopolitanism mainly in *Gli 'Ismi'.*

19. Preface to "L'Amante di Gramigna," in *Vita dei Campi* (1880), in *Tutte le Novelle,* Milan, 1955. *1,* 169: "la mano dell'artista rimarrà assolutamente invisibile . . . l'opera d'arte sembrera essersi fatta da sè, aver maturato ed esser sorta spontanea come un fatto naturale, senza serbare alcun punto di contatto col suo autore."

20. A letter to Capuana, 25 February 1881: "artificio voluto e cercato anch'esso, per evitare, perdonami il bisticcio, ogni artificio letteraria, per darvi l'illusione completa della realtà." Quoted in Pullini, *Le Poetiche dell'Ottocento,* p. 246.

21. "Dal tuo al mio" (1906), in *Tutte le novelle,* 2, 389: "in pro degli umili e dei diseredati . . . senza bisogno di predicar l'odio e di negare la patria in nome dell'umanità."

BIBLIOGRAPHY: ENGLISH CRITICISM

On English literary historiography see this *History, 3,* 87 ff. There are no reprints of E. S. Dallas. Comment:

    Saintsbury, *A History of Criticism* (3 vols. Edinburgh, 1901–04), *3,* pp. 511–13.

    John Drinkwater, *The Eighteen-Sixties* (Cambridge, 1932), pp. 201–23.

Michael Roberts, "The Dream and the Poem," *TLS* (18 January 1936), pp. 41–42; interesting.

Francis X. Roellinger, "E. S. Dallas: A Mid-Victorian Critic of Individualism," *Philological Quarterly*, 20 (1941), 611–21.

———, "E. S. Dallas on Imagination," *Studies in Philology, 38* (1941), 552–64.

Alba H. Warren, *English Poetic Theory* (Princeton, 1950), pp. 126–51.

For Realism see Richard Stang, *The Theory of the Novel in England 1850–1870*, London, 1959.

On G. H. Lewes, see:

Morris Greenhut, "Lewes as a Critic of the Novel," *Studies in Philology, 45* (1948), 491–511.

———, "G. H. Lewes and the Classical Tradition of English Criticism," *Review of English Studies*, 25 (1948), 126–37.

Gordon S. Haight, "Dickens and G. H. Lewes," *PMLA, 71* (1956), 166–79.

George H. Ford, *Dickens and His Readers* (Princeton, 1955), esp. pp. 149 ff.

There is recent collection of *Essays of George Eliot*. ed. Thomas Pinney. New York, 1963. On George Eliot: Richard Stang, "The Literary Criticism of George Eliot," *PMLA, 72* (1957), 952–61.

Browning's *Essay on Shelley* is reprinted with Peacock's *Four Ages of Poetry: Shelley's Defence of Poetry*, ed. H. F. B. Brett-Smith, Boston, 1921.

On Hopkins see:

M. G. Lloyd Thomas, "Hopkins as Critic," *Essays and Studies by Members of the English Association, 32* (1946), 61–73.

Harold Whitehall, "Sprung Rhythm" in *G. M. Hopkins by the Kenyon Critics* (Norfolk, Conn., 1946), pp. 28–54.

Selma Jeanne Cohen, "The Poetic Theory of G. M. Hopkins," *Philological Quarterly*, 26 (1947), 1–20.

John K. Mathison, "The Poetic Theory of G. M. Hopkins," *ibid.*, pp. 21–35.

Sister Marcella Marie Holloway, *The Prosodic Theory of G. M. Hopkins*, Washington, D.C., 1947.

NOTES: ENGLISH CRITICISM

1. Cf. Alba H. Warren, Jr., *English Poetic Theory 1825–1865*, Princeton, 1950.

2. Cf. Klaus Dockhorn, *Der deutsche Historismus in England*, Göttingen, 1950.

3. *The "Co." of Pigsbrook & Co.* (London, 1881), p. 4.

4. *Mr. Swinburne's 'Flat Burglary' on Shakspere* (London, 1879), p. 4.

5. *Collected Papers: Historical, Literary, Travel and Miscellaneous* (5 vols. Cambridge, 1921), *5*, 300.

6. Cf., e.g., *Characteristics* (2d ed. Edinburgh, 1881), pp. 1, 276.

7. "Byron," in *Critical Miscellanies, 1* (London, 1886), 209–10.

8. "On the Study of Literature" (1887), in *Studies in Literature* (London, 1891), pp. 219–20.

9. *Shakspere* (14th ed. London, 1909), pp. 44, 46 n., 49.

10. More on these issues in my *Concepts of Criticism* (New Haven, 1963), pp. 43, 47–48, and below, pp. 278–80.

11. Preface.

12. A letter to F. C. Roe, 19 March 1924, in Evan Charteris, *The Life and Letters of Sir Edmund Gosse* (London, 1931), p. 477.

13. *British Novelists and their Styles* (Cambridge, 1859), pp. 35–36. "How Literature May Illustrate History" (1871), in *The Three Devils: Luther's, Milton's and Goethe's, and Other Essays* (London, 1874), pp. 304–05.

14. *English Writers: The Writers before Chaucer* (London, 1864), preface. Henry S. Solly, *The Life of Henry Morley* (London, 1898), pp. 288–89, 330

15. Cf. O. Elton, "The Meaning of Literary History," in *Modern Studies* (London, 1907), pp. 138–48.

16. See the dedication to *Poetics*, London, 1852; and *The Gay Science* (London, 1866), *1*, 333, and 2, 14.

17. *Poetics*, p. 135. *Gay Science, 1*, 30.

18. See *Lectures on Metaphysics and Logic*, ed. H. L. Mansel and J. Veitch (Edinburgh and London, 1859–60), *1*, 338 ff.

19. On Jean Paul see *Gay Science, 1*, 81, 157–58, 191.

20. For Ruskin see, e.g., *Poetics*, p. 251; *Gay Science, 1*, 28, 51, 118–19, 170, 193, 243, 252, 282; 2, 73, 172. On Arnold, *ibid., 1*, 29, 38, 65, 67; 2, 114, 247.

21. *Gay Science, 1*, 6, 91, 115, 172, 311.

22. *Ibid.*, 2, 193.

23. *Poetics*, p. 291.

24. *Gay Science*, 2, pp. 33 ff., 65 ff., 109 ff., esp. 52 ff.

25. *Ibid., 1*, 229.

26. *Ibid., 1*, 316.

27. *Poetics*, p. 64.

28. *Ibid.*, p. 50.

29. *Ibid.*, pp. 147–48.

30. *Gay Science, 1,* 329.

31. *Ibid., 1,* 323.

32. *Ibid., 1,* 318.

33. Cf. this *History,* 2, 103–04.

34. *Poetics,* pp. 82, 91.

35. *Ibid.,* p. 99.

36. *Gay Science, 1,* 273–74.

37. *Ibid., 1,* 281–83.

38. *Ibid., 1,* 285–86.

39. *Ibid., 1,* 291.

40. *Ibid., 1,* 292, 294.

41. *Poetics,* p. 251.

42. *Gay Science,* 2, 220.

43. *Ibid.,* 2, 287, 323.

44. Michael Roberts in *TLS* (18 January 1936), p. 42.

45. *Principles of Success,* ed. Albert S. Cook (San Francisco, 1885), p. 5; also ed. T. S. Knowlson, London, 1898. Originally in *Fortnightly Review,* 1865.

46. "The Philosophy of Art: Hegel's Aesthetic," *British and Foreign Review, 13* (1842), 1–49.

47. "Augustus Wilhelm Schlegel," *Foreign Quarterly Review, 32* (1843), 87–99, esp. 88, 90.

48. "Lessing," *Edinburgh Review, 82* (1845), 451–70.

49. Above, n. 47: pp. 88, 90.

50. Above, n. 48: pp. 453, 463.

51. "The Errors and Abuses of English Criticism," *Westminster Review, 38* (1842), 466–86, esp. 481.

52. John Foster, George Henry Lewes, *Dramatic Essays,* ed. W. Archer and Robert W. Lowe (London, 1896), reprints essays from *The Leader* (1850–54).

53. "Realism in Art: Recent German Fiction," *Westminster Review, 70* (1858), 488–518, esp. 493.

54. "Victor Hugo's New Novel," *Fortnightly Review, 5* (1866), 30–46. "Recent Novels: French and English," *Fraser's Magazine, 36* (1847), 686–95.

55. "Dickens in Relation to Criticism," *Fortnightly Review, 17* (1872), 141–54.

56. *Principles of Success,* p. 39.

57. *"See-saw:* A Novel, by Francesco Abati," *Fortnightly Review, 3* (1865–66), 784. "Victor Hugo's New Novel," *Fortnightly Review, 5* (1866), 46.

58. *Essays,* ed. Pinney, pp. 137, 192, 359, 366–67.

59. *Adam Bede,* Ch. XVII; cf. the ed. of Gordon S. Haight (New York, 1948), pp. 180, 182.

60. *Essays,* ed. Pinney, pp. 270–71.

61. *Ibid.,* pp. 300–24 (October 1856).

62. *The George Eliot Letters,* ed. Gordon S. Haight (7 vols. New Haven, 1954–55), *4, 300.*

63. *Essays,* ed. Pinney, pp. 147, 129.

64. *Letters, 5,* 459.

65. "Belles Lettres and Art," *Westminster Review, 66* (1856), 260.

66. *Essays,* ed. Pinney, p. 446.

67. *Ibid.,* p. 435. The manuscript is in the Yale University Library.

68. Westminster, 1897, pp. 8, 82, 83. First published in *The New Quarterly Magazine,* 1877.

69. Peacock's *Four Ages,* etc., ed. Brett-Smith, pp. 65, 82.

70. *Further Letters of G. M. Hopkins,* ed. C. C. Abbott (London, 1938), p. 225. *Letters of G. M. Hopkins to Robert Bridges,* ed. C. C. Abbott (London, 1935), p. 66. See the fine essay by Austin Warren, "Instress of Inscape," in *G. M. Hopkins by the Kenyon Critics,* pp. 76–77.

71. *Further Letters,* pp. 69–71.

72. See the Bibliography under Whitehall and Holloway.

73. Coventry Patmore, *Essay on English Metrical Law,* ed. Sister Mary Augustine Roth, Washington, D.C., 1961.

BIBLIOGRAPHY: ARNOLD, BAGEHOT, AND STEPHEN

On Arnold: I quote the early writings from the still incomplete new edition of *The Complete Prose Works of Matthew Arnold,* ed. R. H. Super, Ann Arbor, Mich., 1960–: Vol. 1, *On the Classical Tradition* (1960), as S, *1,* and Vol. 3, *Lectures and Essays in Criticism* (1962), as S, *3.* The edition contains valuable textual and explanatory notes.

The later writings I quote from the old Macmillan editions: *Mixed Essays: Irish Essays* (London, 1894), as *Mix.; Discourses in America* (London, 1885), as *Dis. A.;* and the second series of *Essays in Criticism* (London, 1888), as 2 *E.* Scattered essays in Edward J. O'Brien, ed., *Essays in Criticism: Third Series,* Boston, 1910; Kenneth Allott, ed., *Five Uncollected Essays,* Liverpool, 1953; Fraser Neiman, ed., *Essays, Letters, and Reviews,* Cambridge, Mass., 1960. *Letters of an Old Playgoer,* ed. Brander Matthews, exist in a small edition, New York, 1919. It is worth looking at Arnold's anthologies of Wordsworth and Byron (London 1879, 1881).

There is an unsatisfactory collection of Arnold's *Letters, 1848–1888,* ed. G. W. E. Russell, 2 vols. London, 1895. The most important find since then is *The Letters of Matthew Arnold to Arthur Hugh Clough.* ed. Howard F. Lowry (London, 1932), quoted as Lowry. The correspondence with Sainte-Beuve has to be pieced together from L. Bonnerot, *Matthew Arnold* (Paris, 1947), appendix, pp. 517–39; A. F. Powell, "Sainte-Beuve and Matthew Arnold," *French Quarterly, 3* (1921), 151–55; and Arnold Whitridge, "Matthew Arnold and Sainte-Beuve," *PMLA, 52* (1938), 303–13.

The Note-books of Matthew Arnold, ed. Howard F. Lowry, Karl Young, and Waldo H. Dunn (Oxford, 1952) is a disappointing commonplace book of interest largely to the student of the sources of some of Arnold's favorite quotations.

Of books on Arnold: G. Saintsbury's *Matthew Arnold* (Edinburgh, 1899), Lionel Trilling's *Matthew Arnold* (New York, 1939, new ed. 1949) and L. Bonnerot, *Matthew Arnold, poète: Essai de biographie psychologique* (Paris, 1947; 585 pp., excellent bibliography) are most rewarding for the student of criticism. Stuart P. Sherman, *Matthew Arnold, How to Know Him* (New York, 1917), is negligible. Frederic E. Faverty, *Matthew Arnold: The Ethnologist* (Evanston, Ill., 1951) studies his race theories, and E. K. Brown, *Matthew Arnold: A Study in Conflict* (Chicago, 1948), pursues the theme of the conflict between disinterestedness and practical interests. Paul Furrer, *Der Einfluss Sainte-Beuve's auf die Kritik Matthew Arnold's,* is a small, mediocre Zurich diss. (1920). John Dover Wilson, *Leslie Stephen and Matthew Arnold as Critics of Wordsworth* (Cambridge, 1939), is a lecture defending Stephen. John S. Eels, Jr., *The Touchstones of Matthew Arnold* (New York, 1955) is an elaborate analysis of the eleven passages selected by Arnold.

Three recent books discuss Arnold and Romanticism: William A. Jamison, *Arnold and the Romantics,* Copenhagen, 1958; D. J. James, *Matthew Arnold and the Decline of English Romanticism,* Oxford, 1961 (sharply critical from a point of view which could be called visionary Christianity); and Leon Gottfried, *Matthew Arnold and the Romantics,* London, 1963 (greatly superior to Jamison).

F. J. W. Harding, *Matthew Arnold the Critic and France,* Geneva, 1964 (not used).

Of the many articles the following offer some interest:

A. C. Bradley, "Shelley and Arnold's Critique of his Poetry," *A Miscellany* (London, 1929), pp. 139–62.

E. K. Brown, "Matthew Arnold and the Elizabethans," *University of Toronto Quarterly, 1* (1932), 333–51.

Robert H. Donovan, "The Method of Arnold's *Essays in Criticism,*" in *PMLA, 71* (1956), 922–31.

T. S. Eliot, "Arnold and Pater," in *Selected Essays* (London, 1932), pp. 379–91.

T. S. Eliot, "Matthew Arnold," a chapter in *The Use of Poetry and the Use of Criticism* (London, 1933), pp. 103–20. Important.

Oliver Elton, a chapter in *A Survey of English Literature, 1830–1880* (2 vols. London, 1920), *1*, 254–78.

Walther Fischer, "Matthew Arnold und Deutschland," in *Germanisch-romanische Monatsschrift,* new series, *4* (1954), 119–37.

H. W. Garrod, "Matthew Arnold as Critic," in *Poetry and the Criticism of Life* (Oxford, 1931), pp. 67–84.

H. J. C. Grierson, "Lord Byron: Arnold and Swinburne," in *The Background of English Literature* (London, 1934), pp. 68–114.

Walter J. Hipple, Jr., "Matthew Arnold Dialectician," *University of Toronto Quarterly, 32* (1962), 1–26.

John Holloway, "Matthew Arnold and the Modern Dilemma," in *Essays in Criticism, 1* (1951), 1–16.

John V. Kelleher, "Matthew Arnold and the Celtic Revival," in *Perspectives of Criticism,* ed. Harry Levin (Cambridge, Mass., 1950), pp. 197–221.

F. R. Leavis, "Matthew Arnold," in *The Importance of Scrutiny,* ed. E. Bentley (New York, 1948), pp. 88–98. Originally as "Arnold as a Critic," in *Scrutiny, 7* (1938), 319–32. Excellent.

J. B. Orrick, "Matthew Arnold and Goethe," in *Publications of the English Goethe Society,* new series, *4,* London, 1928.

T. S. Omond, "Arnold and Homer," *Essays and Studies by Members of the English Association, 3* (1912), 71–91. Slight.

David Perkins, "Arnold and the Function of Literature," *ELH, 18* (1951), 287–309.

Sir Walter Raleigh, in *Some Authors* (Oxford, 1923), pp. 300–10.

R. H. Super, "Arnold's Oxford Lectures on Poetry," in *Modern Language Notes, 70* (1955), 581–84.

A. C. Swinburne, "Wordsworth and Byron," in *Miscellanies* (London, 1886), pp. 63–156.

Geoffrey Tillotson, "Matthew Arnold; The Critic and the Advocate," and "Matthew Arnold and Eighteenth Century Poetry," both in *Criticism and the Nineteenth Century* (London, 1951), pp. 42–46, 61–91.

Helen C. White, "Matthew Arnold and Goethe," *PMLA, 36* (1921), 436–53.

On Bagehot: Bagehot's essays are quoted from *Literary Studies,* ed. Richard Holt Hutton (3 vols. New York, 1905), as *LS.*

There is an able monograph by William Irvine, *Walter Bagehot,* London, 1939.

Norman St. John-Stevas, *Walter Bagehot: A Study of His Life and*

Thought (Bloomington, Ind., 1959), contains only a short perfunctory section on the critic (pp. 31–37).

On Stephen:

Hours in a Library (3 vols. London, 1909; originally, 1874, 1876, 1907), quoted as *HL*.

History of English Thought in the Eighteenth Century, 2 vols. London, 1876; London, 1927, reprint quoted.

Samuel Johnson, London, 1878.

Alexander Pope, London, 1880.

Swift, London, 1882.

George Eliot, London, 1902.

English Literature and Society in the Eighteenth Century, Ford Lectures (1903), London, 1904.

Studies of a Biographer, 4 vols. London, 1899–1902.

Men, Books, and Mountains. Essays. Collected, and with an Introduction by S. O. A. Ullmann, Minneapolis, 1956. Contains bibliography of articles and 3 literary essays hitherto unreprinted.

Comment:

Noel Gilroy Annan, *Leslie Stephen: His Thought and Character in Relation to His Time*, Cambridge, Mas., 1952. Has excellent chapter on criticism.

Q. D. Leavis, "Leslie Stephen, Cambridge Critic," *Scrutiny*, 7 (1939), 404–15.

Desmond MacCarthy, *Leslie Stephen*, The Leslie Stephen Lecture for 1937, Cambridge, 1937.

Frederic William Maitland, *The Life and Letters of Leslie Stephen*, London, 1906.

NOTES: ARNOLD

1. *2 E*, pp. 1–3.
2. See E. K. Brown, *Matthew Arnold: A Study in Conflict*, Chicago, 1948.
3. S, *1*, 140.
4. S, *1*, 199.
5. S, *1*, 140.
6. S, *3*, 282.
7. S, *3*, 268.
8. S, *3*, 283–84.
9. S, *3*, 283.
10. S, *3*, 227.
11. S, *3*, 261.

12. Allott, *Five Uncollected Essays,* p. 74.

13. S, *3*, 243.

14. S, *1*, 172.

15. 2 *E*, pp. 6–7.

16. 2 *E*, p. 11.

17. *Mix.,* pp. 191–92.

18. S, *1*, 127, 128.

19. S, *1*, 31.

20. S, *1*, 30.

21. S, *1*, 33–34.

22. S, *1*, 35.

23. S, *1*, 36.

24. Letter to Thomas Arnold the Younger (28 December 1857), in Robert Lidell Lowe, "Two Arnold Letters," *Modern Philology, 52* (1955), 262–64.

25. S, *3*, 121.

26. S, *3*, 240.

27. *Dis. A.,* pp. 47–48.

28. As in n. 24, above.

29. S, *3*, 262.

30. S, *3*, 122.

31. S, *3*, 263.

32. *Mix.,* p. 212.

33. *Mix.,* p. 233.

34. Lowry, p. 65.

35. S, *3*, 260.

36. S, *3*, 247.

37. Lowry, p. 95.

38. *Dis. A.,* pp. 43 ff.

39. S, *3*, 353.

40. S, *3*, 361.

41. S, *3*, 370.

42. See John V. Kelleher, "Matthew Arnold and the Celtic Revival," in *Perspectives of Criticism*, ed. H. Levin (Cambridge, Mass., 1950), pp. 197–222.

43. *Culture and Anarchy,* p. 34.

44. *Dis. A.,* p. 135.

45. S, *3*, 231.

46. S, *3*, 261.

47. S, *3*, 107.

48. S, *3*, 269.

49. S, *3*, 261.

50. S, *3*, 253.

51. Lowry, p. 131.

52. Lowry, p. 11.

53. *Dis. A.,* pp. 168, 162, cf. 198.

54. See *Unpublished Letters,* ed. A. Whitridge (New Haven, 1923), p. 52; and *Letters, 1,* 200.

55. S, *1,* 204.

56. Lowry, p. 154.

57. Lowry, p. 147.

58. *Letters, 1,* 196.

59. *Letters, 2,* 164.

60. Letter to Davies (3 April 1872), in *From a Victorian Post-Bag* (London, 1926), pp. 76–77, repeating Arnold's view of Thackeray after his death.

61. Lowry, p. 132; cf. *Letters, 1,* 213.

62. *Letters, 1,* 29.

63. 2 *E,* p. 186.

64. 2 *E,* pp. 5, 146–47, 186.

65. 2 *E,* p. 143.

66. 2 *E,* pp. 148–49.

67. *Mix.,* pp. 151–52.

68. 2 *E,* p. 191.

69. 2 *E,* pp. 21, 33, 41, 48, 52, 81, 246.

70. 2 *E,* pp. 33, 81, 246.

71. 2 *E,* p. 28.

72. 2 *E,* p. 192.

73. S, *3,* 208.

74. S, *1,* 2.

75. S, *1,* 4.

76. S, *3,* 110.

77. *Mix.,* p. 435.

78. 2 *E,* p. 128.

79. 2 *E,* pp. 106–07.

80. S, *3,* 33.

81. Lowry, p. 63.

82. S, *1,* 211. 2 *E,* pp. 140–41.

83. 2 *E,* pp. 142–43.

84. *Dis. A.,* p. 154.

85. S, *3,* 345.

86. S, *3,* 230–31.

87. 2 *E,* p. 95.

88. 2 *E,* p. 42.

89. 2 *E,* p. 97.

90. 2 *E,* pp. 44–45.

91. *Letters,* 2, 184 (November 1880).

92. 2, *E,* p. 276; cf. *Letters of an Old Playgoer,* pp. 36–37.

93. 2 *E,* p. 260.

94. S, *1,* 7.

95. S, *1,* 40–41.

96. *Mix.,* pp. 438–39.

97. *Mix.,* p. 445.

98. *Mix.,* pp. 441–42.

99. S, *3,* 239.

100. "Homeric Translation in Theory and Practice," reprinted in M. Arnold, *On Translating Homer* (London, n. d.), p. 115.

101. S, *1,* 187.

102. 2 *E,* p. 62.

103. 2 *E,* pp. 156–57.

104. S, *3,* 232.

105. S, *3,* 181.

106. Lowry, p. 100.

107. 2 *E,* p. 114.

108. S, *3,* 234.

109. S, *1,* 188.

110. S, *1,* 190.

111. S, *1,* 189.

112. S, *1,* 188.

113. 2 *E,* p. 159.

114. Lowry, p. 99.

115. S, *1,* 208.

116. S, *1,* 5.

117. *Mix.,* p. 241.

118. *Dis. A.,* p. 134.

119. *Ibid.* A phrase from Leonardo da Vinci's Notebooks, picked up from Charles Clement, *Michel-Ange, Léonard de Vinci,* etc., Paris, 1867. See *Note-Books,* p. 446.

120. 2 *E,* p. 63.

121. 2 *E,* p. 120.

122. *Mix.,* p. 232.

123. *Dis. A.,* p. 154.

124. 2 *E,* p. 168.

125. 2 *E,* p. 170.

126. 2 *E,* p. 259. The criticism is not justified, as Arnold does not perceive the compositional principle of Tolstoy's novel: the moral and

social contrast between the Anna Vronsky and the Kitty Levin stories
and the elaborate tying together of the Anna story by the motif of the
guard killed by the train.

127. 2 *E*, p. 17.

128. 2 *E*, p. 19.

129. 2 *E*, p. 17.

130. John S. Eels, Jr., *The Touchstones of Matthew Arnold*, New
York, 1955.

131. F. R. Leavis, "Arnold as a Critic," in *The Importance of Scrutiny,* ed. Bentley, p. 95.

132. See *The Touchstones of Poetry, selected from the Writings of
Matthew Arnold and John Ruskin* (San Francisco, 1887).

133. Cf. *Experiments in Education* (Ithaca, N.Y., 1943), p. 130.

134. *Paradiso 3*, 85. Eliot, *Selected Essays* (London, 1932), p. 256.

135. 2 *E*, pp. 40–41.

136. 2 *E*, p. 32.

137. 2 *E*, pp. 97–98.

138. S, *3*, 124.

139. Paris, 1862, p. 214. Identified by L. Bonnerot, *Matthew Arnold*,
p. 355 n. The usual ascription to Hugo is wrong.

140. Act 1, sc. 2, lines 304–05.

141. 3:35; see S, *3*, 362.

142. *Défense de la poésie française* (London, 1912), pp. 22–23.

143. Phillipians 4:7; II Corinthians 1:7.

144. *Five Uncollected Essays*, p. 79.

145. S, *1*, 59.

146. *Note-Books*, pp. 5–8, 459.

147. S, *3*, 83.

148. S, *3*, 189, 208.

149. In *Causeries du Lundi, 14*, 195–217.

150. S, *3*, 108.

151. S, *3*, 132.

152. In "Noch ein Wort für junge Dichter," in *Werke, 38, 325*, quoted
by Arnold, S, *3*, 109.

153. S, *3*, 132.

154. S, *3*, 376.

155. S, *3*, 119.

156. 29 September 1854, in Bonnerot, *Matthew Arnold*, pp. 521–22.

157. Letter to Grant Duff (14 May 1863), *Letters*, 2, 193.

158. S, *3*, 110.

159. According to Arnold, this was why Goethe was so impressed by
Spinoza, S, *3*, 176.

160. S, *1*, 8.

161. *Mix.*, p. 234.

162. 2 *E*, 155.

163. *Mix.*, p. 218.

164. *Letters of an Old Playgoer*, pp. 51–53.

165. The high tribute of the *Encyclopaedia Britannica* article, in 1886, does not change the fact of Arnold's emancipation from Sainte-Beuve's tutelage.

166. 2 *E*, p. 309.

167. 2 *E*, p. 312.

168. 2 *E*, p. 237.

169. 2 *E*, p. 252, repeated from the Byron essay, *ibid.*, p. 234.

170. Russian literature was obviously very new to him, as he can say, almost 50 years after the death of Pushkin, that "the Russians have not yet had a great poet" (2 *E*, p. 257).

171. S, *3*, 121 ff., 132.

172. *Wordsworthiana*, ed. W. Knight (London, 1887), p. 125.

173. See J. D. Wilson, *Leslie Stephen and Arnold* (Cambridge, 1939), pp. 24–25.

174. S, *3*, 262.

175. See Markham L. Peacock, *The Critical Opinions of William Wordsworth* (Baltimore, 1950), pp. 264–66.

176. 2 *E*, pp. 177–78.

177. 2 *E*, p. 238.

178. Arnold misuses the quotation. Goethe was speaking not of Byron's poetry and its reflective parts, but of Byron's wild surmises on the sources of *Faust*. See Eckermann, ed. H. H. Houben (Leipzig, 1948), p. 111, 2 *E*, p. 185.

179. S, *3*, 132.

180. 2 *E*, p. 169.

181. 2 *E*, p. 103.

182. 2, *E*, p. 105.

183. 2 *E*, p. 112.

184. 2 *E*, p. 113.

185. 2 *E*, p. 115.

186. 2 *E*, p. 119.

187. 2 *E*, p. 120.

188. S, *3*, 34.

189. 2 *E*, p. 165.

190. 2 *E*, p. 196.

191. S, *3*, 34 n.

192. 2 *E*, p. 246.

BAGEHOT

1. Oliver Elton, *A Survey of English Literature, 1830–1880* (2 vols. London, 1920), *1*, 104.
2. William Irvine, in the Bibliography, above.
3. *LS, 2*, 150.
4. *LS, 1*, 85.
5. *LS, 2*, 113, 97, 89, 105.
6. *LS, 1*, 126, 125.
7. *LS, 2*, 101, 142, 160.
8. *LS, 2*, 316, 323.
9. *LS, 2*, 285, 295, 303, 304.
10. *LS, 1*, 5.
11. *LS, 2*, 277.
12. *LS, 2*, 80, 57.
13. Bagehot quarreled with H. C. Robinson for "urging that Hazlitt was a much greater writer than Charles Lamb—a harmless opinion which I still hold" (*LS, 3*, 250). Bagehot refers to Hazlitt's "soreness of mind" (*LS, 1*, 61) and quotes him frequently.
14. *LS, 2*, 56, 59, 80.
15. *LS, 2*, 184.
16. *LS, 1*, 297, 291–92.
17. *LS, 1*, 172.
18. *LS, 1*, 33, 130.
19. *LS, 1*, 283, 299.
20. *LS, 1*, 31.
21. *LS, 1*, 124, 128.
22. *LS, 2*, 201.
23. *LS, 2*, 329, 331, 332, 333.
24. *LS, 2*, 335, 336.
25. *LS, 1*, 22, 23, 24.
26. *LS, 2*, 61.
27. *LS, 1*, 38, 42–43, 48, 54, 55, 64, 73, 86.
28. *LS, 2*, 149, 364–65.

STEPHEN

1. Desmond MacCarthy, *Leslie Stephen*. The Leslie Stephen Lecture for 1937. Cambridge, 1937.
2. Leavis, *Scrutiny*, 7, 404–15.
3. Annan, *Leslie Stephen*, p. 256.
4. *Studies of a Biographer*, 2, 79.

5. *HL, 2, 250.*

6. *HL, 2, 253.*

7. *HL, 2, 256.*

8. *Studies of a Biographer, 2, 90.*

9. *HL, 2, 187.*

10. *HL, 2, 159.*

11. *HL, 2, 173.*

12. *HL, 2, 254–55.*

13. *HL, 2, 3.*

14. *HL, 3, 6.*

15. *HL, 1, 98.*

16. *HL, 3, 110.*

17. *HL, 3, 334;* cf. *ibid.,* p. 61.

18. *Alexander Pope,* pp. 131–32.

19. *HL, 1,* 8 ff.

20. *HL, 1,* 64 f.

21. *HL, 2, 144.*

22. *History of English Thought in the Eighteenth Century, 2,* 330.

23. *English Literature and Society in the Eighteenth Century,* p. 14.

24. Frederic William Maitland, *The Life and Letters of Leslie Stephen* (London, 1906), p. 283.

25. *HL, 2, 26.*

26. *Studies of a Biographer, 2,* 137.

27. *Men, Books, and Mountains,* p. 22.

28. *Ibid.,* p. 232.

29. *Ibid.,* p. 217.

30. *English Literature and Society in the Eighteenth Century,* p. 6.

31. *Men, Books, and Mountains,* p. 231.

32. *HL, 3,* 143.

33. *HL, 3,* 197.

BIBLIOGRAPHY: AMERICAN CRITICISM

On Whitman: I quote from the *Complete Writings*, ed. R. M. Bucke, T. B. Harned, and Horace L. Traubel (10 vols. New York, 1902), as *W*.

The Gathering of the Forces, ed. C. Rogers and J. Black, 2 vols. New York, 1920.

I quote the preface to the 1st edition of *Leaves of Grass* (not in *W*) from Clarence A. Brown, ed., *The Achievement of American Criticism* (New York, 1956), pp. 336–51, as Brown.

The literature is surveyed in Willard Thorp's chapter in *Eight American Authors: A Review of Research and Criticism*, ed. Floyd Stovall (New York, 1956), pp. 271–318.

There is an excellent chapter on Whitman in Norman Foerster, *American Criticism*, Boston, 1928. Maurice O. Johnson, "Walt Whitman as a Critic of Literature," *University of Nebraska Studies in Languages, Literature, and Criticism, 16*, 73 pp., is useful. Roger Asselineau, "A Poet's Dilemma: Walt Whitman's Attitude to Literary History and Literary Criticism," in Leon Edel, ed., *Literary History and Literary Criticism: Acta of the Ninth Congress of the International Federation for Modern Languages and Literature* (New York, 1965), pp. 50–61.

Much can be learned of the many general treatments of Whitman's philosophy, language, reading, etc. in monographs, e.g. the chapter in F. O. Matthiessen, *The American Renaissance*, New York, 1941; Newton Arvin, *Whitman*, New York, 1938; Gay Wilson Allen, *Walt Whitman Handbook*, Chicago, 1946; Roger Asselineau, *L'Evolution de Walt Whitman*, Paris, 1953; English trans., 2 vols. Cambridge, Mass., 1960–62.

On German sources see, besides Henry A. Pochmann, *German Culture in America*, Madison, Wisc., 1957. Mody C. Boatright, "Whitman and Hegel," *University of Texas Studies in English, 9* (1929), 134–50. W. B. Fulghum, "Whitman's Debt to Joseph Gostwick," *American Literature, 12* (1941), 491–96. Olive W. Parsons, "Whitman the Non-Hegelian," *PMLA, 58* (1943), 1073–93. Sister Mary Eleanor, "Hedge's *Prose Writers of Germany* as a Source of Whitman's Knowledge of German Philosophy," *Modern Language Notes, 61* (1946), 381–88.

On Lowell: I quote the Riverside edition of the *Writings* (11 vols. Boston, 1892) as *W*.

The Round Table, Boston, 1913; and *The Function of the Poet and other Essays.* ed. Albert Mordell, Boston, 1920.

Joseph J. Reilly, *James Russell Lowell as a Critic* (New York, 1915) is an elaborate attack.

Norman Foerster's chapter in *American Criticism* (reprinted also as introduction to James Russell Lowell, *Representative Selections,* ed. H. H. Clark and N. Foerster, New York, 1947) is the best defense.

Other comment besides that in biographies of F. Greenslet, Horace Sendder, R. C. Beatty, Leon Howard, etc.:

J. M. Robertson, "Lowell as a Critic," *North American Review, 209* (1919), 246–62.

Harry H. Clark, "Lowell's Criticism of Romantic Literature," *PMLA, 41* (1926), 209–28.

Austin Warren, "Lowell on Thoreau," *Studies in Philology, 27* (1930), 442–61.

George Wurfl, *Lowell's Debt to Goethe*, State College, Pennsylvania, 1936.

Richard D. Altick, "Was Lowell an Historical Critic?" *American Literature, 14* (1942), 250–59.

On Howells: There is no collected edition.

I quote *Modern Italian Poets: Essays and Versions*, New York, 1887.

Criticism and Fiction, New York, 1893, 1st ed. 1891.

My Literary Passions, New York, 1895.

Heroines of Fiction, 2 vols. New York, 1901.

Recent reprints:

Prefaces to Contemporaries (1882–1920), ed. G. Arms, W. M. Gibson and F. C. Marston, Jr., Gainsville, Florida, 1957.

Criticism and Fiction, and Other Essays, ed. C. M. Kirk and R. Kirk, New York, 1959. Reprinted as *European and American Masters*, New York, 1963.

For list of Howells' numerous uncollected articles see William M. Gibson and George Arms, "A Bibliography of W. D. Howells," *Bulletin of the New York Public Library, 50* (1946), 671–98, 857–68, 909–28; *51* (1947), 48–56, 91–105, 213–48, 341–45, 384–88, 431–57, 486–512.

Most books on Howells contain comment on his criticism, e.g. Delmar G. Cooke, *William Dean Howells*, New York, 1922; Oscar W. Firkins, *William Dean Howells*, Cambridge, Mass., 1924; and Everett Carter, *Howells and the Age of Realism*, Philadelphia, 1954, *The Road to Realism: The Early Years, 1837–85, of W. D. Howells*, Syracuse, 1956, and *The Realist at War: The Mature Years, 1885–1920, of W. D. Howells*, Syracuse, 1958.

Royal A. Gettmann, *Turgenev in England and America* (Urbana, Ill., 1941), pp. 51–61, and Stanley T. Williams, *The Spanish Background of American Literature* (2 vols. New Haven, Conn., 1955), 2, 240–67, are important for my purposes.

Claudio Gorlier, "William Dean Howells e le definizioni del realismo," in *Studi Americani*, ed. A. Lombardo (Rome, 1956), 2, 83–126.

Donald Pizer, "The Evolutionary Foundation of W. D. Howells' *Criticism and Fiction*," *Philological Quarterly, 40* (1961), 91–103.

James L. Woodress, Jr., *Howells and Italy*, Durham, N. C., 1952.

NOTES: AMERICAN CRITICISM

1. See Perry Miller, *The Raven and the Whale: The War of Words and Wits in the Era of Poe and Melville*, New York, 1956.

2. A phrase used by Charles Eliot Norton in his review of Whitman's *Leaves of Grass*, in *Putnam's* (September 1855), quoted from Miller, p. 334.

WHITMAN

1. Cf. G. W. Allen, "Walt Whitman and Jules Michelet," *Etudes Anglaises, 1* (1937), 230–37; and Esther Shephard, *Walt Whitman's Pose* (New York, 1938), on George Sand.

2. *W, 5,* 189–90, 201.

3. Birds of Passage: "With Antecedents," *W, 1,* 294.

4. *Rivulets of Prose,* ed. C. Wells and A. F. Goldsmith (New York, 1928), p. 223.

5. Second ed. of *Leaves of Grass* (Brooklyn, August 1856), p. 346.

6. *W, 5,* 26, 37–8.

7. *W, 5,* 8. J. T. Trowbridge, *My Own Story* (Boston, 1903), p. 367.

8. *W, 5,* 266–68. *Uncollected Poetry and Prose,* ed. E. Holloway (2 vols. Garden City, N.Y., 1921), *2,* 53.

9. *W, 5,* 270. A letter (25 February 1887) in William Sloane Kennedy, *Reminiscences of Walt Whitman* (London, 1896), p. 76.

10. Letter by W. J. O'Connor to R. M. Bucke, 23 February 1883, in R. M. Bucke, *Walt Whitman* (Philadelphia, 1883), p. 82. Clifton J. Furness, *Walt Whitman's Workshop* (Cambridge, Mass., 1928), p. 236. Cf. poem "The Base of All Metaphysic": "And now gentlemen . . . ," p. 149.

11. Advertisement, p. 4 (John Burrough's "Note") in *As a Strong Bird on Pinions Free,* Washington, 1872.

12. *W, 9,* 172.

13. *W, 4,* 311 n.

14. *W, 9,* 170, 184; *4,* 322 n.

15. *W, 9,* 181–82.

16. "Roaming in Thought over the Universe," *W, 2,* 35.

17. See the bibliography, above.

18. *W, 5,* 134. Brown, p. 337.

19. *W, 5,* 201. Brown p. 343.

20. *W, 9,* 21; *3,* 45.

21. *W, 9,* 11–12.

22. *W, 3,* 49.

23. *W, 4,* 270.

24. *W, 5,* 276–77.

25. *W, 5,* 209.

26. *W, 5,* 275–76.

27. *W, 5,* 229; *6,* 295; *5,* 210.

28. *W, 4,* 323–24.

29. *The Gathering of the Forces* (26 April 1847), *2,* 264.

30. *W, 9,* 112.

31. H. Traubel, *With Walt Whitman in Camden* (New York, 1914), *3*, 400.

32. *The Gathering of the Forces* (7 December 1846), 2, 282–83.

33. *W, 9, 97*.

34. *W, 6, 137*, "Boz and Democracy" (1842), in *Rivulets of Prose*, p. 23.

35. *W, 5, 212–13*.

36. *W, 3, 66; 9, 120–21*.

37. *W, 6, 102, 104* ff., 124 etc. On Ossian, see *W, 9, 94–95*, 188.

38. *W, 6, 183*. Cf. poem "Old Chants," "An ancient song . . ."

39. *W, 5, 58*.

40. *W, 5, 274*.

41. *W, 6, 102*.

42. Cf. Roger Asselineau, "Un inédit de Walt Whitman; 'Taine's History of English Literature,'" *Etudes Anglaises, 10* (1957) 128–38. Horace Traubel reports (*With Walt Whitman in Camden, 21 January to 7 April 1889*, ed. Scully Bradley, Philadelphia, 1953, p. 109) that Whitman called Taine's *History of English Literature* "one of the greatest books of our time: most genuine, most subtle, most profound."

43. *W, 9, 127*.

44. *W, 5, 56–57*.

45. *W, 5, 60*.

46. *W, 5, 116*.

47. *W, 5, 95–96* n.

48. *The American Primer*, ed. H. Traubel (Boston, 1914), p. viii.

49. Ibid., pp. 4, 8, 34. For date, see p. 11, where Whitman speaks of 80 years since the Declaration of Independence.

50. *W, 6, 149–50*.

51. *W, 9, 33–34*.

52. *W, 9, 39*.

53. Brown, p. 342.

54. Ibid., p. 340.

55. *W, 5, 271–72*.

56. *W, 5, 202*.

57. See D. S. Mirsky, "Walt Whitman: Poet of American Democracy," in *Critics Group Dialectics*, No. 1, New York, 1937.

LOWELL

1. Whitman, *Complete Writings, 3*, 55–56. Brown, *Achievement of American Criticism*, p. 340.

2. See "The Study of Modern Languages" (1889), his Presidential Address to the then recently (1883) founded Modern Language Associa-

tion of America. Lowell even then saw the dangers of philological learning for the study of literature (*W, 11*, 157–58).

3. Saintsbury, *A History of Criticism* (3 vols. Edinburgh, 1901–04), *3*, 636.

4. See J. Reilly, N. Foerster, and H. Clark in the bibliography, above.

5. *W, 3*, 29–30.

6. *W, 3*, 114; cf. *11*, 147.

7. *W, 4*, 402.

8. *Round Table*, 53.

9. *W, 11*, 150.

10. *Round Table*, 118.

11. *W, 4*, 261.

12. *W, 4*, 298.

13. *W, 2*, 138.

14. *W, 3*, 34.

15. *Round Table*, 19.

16. E.g. *W, 3*, 31–32; *Function of the Poet*, 75–76; *W, 3*, 322, 324; *6*, 71.

17. *W, 3*, 97; *2*, 136.

18. *W, 3*, 6.

19. *W, 3*, 31; cf. *11*, 144.

20. Foerster, p. 147.

21. *W, 3*, 365.

22. *W, 3*, 293. A metrical point in the last stanza of *Troilus* is raised in *W, 3*, 342–43.

23. *W, 4*, 174.

24. By Adolf Stahr. Next to nothing is said of Lessing's criticism or of the plays except some complaint about the dullness of *Nathan* (*W, 2*, 227).

25. *W, 4*, 27. Cf. Frederick A. Pottle, *The Idiom of Poetry* (Ithaca, N.Y., 1936), for a modern restatement of this view.

26. *W, 4*, 27–28, 36, 46, 48, 53.

27. *W, 4*, 49–50. This contradicts a passage in the Dryden essay (*W, 3*, 177) where Pope is described as "watching his chance, to squirt vitriol from behind a corner," a view grotesquely exaggerated in Lytton Strachey's essay (*Pope*, Cambridge, 1925).

28. *W, 2*, 250. *Function of the Poet*, p. 71. *W, 2*, 249.

29. *W, 2*, 253.

30. *W, 2*, 92 n. 2, 229.

31. *W, 1*, 378, 381. Cf. the older review in *Round Table*, pp. 43–64.

32. On Donne, see *W, 2*, 160; *3*, 35, 171; *6*, 108.

33. *W, 2*, 261.

34. *W*, *2*, 241, 270.

35. *W*, *4*, 411–12.

36. *W*, *4*, 407–08. J. K. Stephen's "The Two Voices" in *Lapsus Calami and Other Verses*, London, 1896, 1st ed. 1891.

37. *W*, *4*, 401.

38. *W*, *6*, 99–114.

39. *W*, *4*, 405, 415.

HOWELLS

1. In C. A. Brown, *The Achievement of American Criticism* (New York, 1954), p. 307.

2. *Ibid.*, p. 292.

3. "The Confidence Man" (1857), ch. XXXIII, in Brown, p. 304.

4. See, e.g., A. J. Salvan, *Zola aux Etats-Unis*, Brown University Studies, *8*, Providence, R. I., 1943.

5. *Criticism and Fiction* is made up of passages from articles in a series "The Editor's Study" begun in 1886 in *Harper's*. For details see Carter, *Howells and the Age of Realism*, pp. 185–90.

6. See, e.g., p. 97 ("a very clever and brilliant Italian"), and pp. 131–35, 188, 257–58, 273–74.

7. Preface to Carlo Goldoni, *Memoirs* (Boston, 1877), p. 6.

8. "*Edelweiss* by Berthold Auerbach," *Atlantic*, *23* (1869), 762.

9. "*Liza* by Ivan Turgenieff," *Atlantic*, *31* (1873), 239; *33* (1874), 745; and *Munsey's Magazine*, *17* (1897), 19. From Gettmann, pp. 55–57.

10. "Henry James, Jr.," *Century Magazine*, *25* (1882), 26.

11. *Ibid.*, pp. 27–28.

12. *Criticism and Fiction*, pp. 8, 9, 15, 128–29, 150, 157, 188.

13. *My Literary Passions*, pp. 254, 258. *Prefaces*, pp. 4, 42.

14. *My Literary Passions*, pp. 256–57. *Prefaces*, p. 6.

15. A lecture "Novel Writing and Novel-Reading" (1899), published from MS by William M. Gibson in *Howells and James: A Double Billing* (New York, 1958), pp. 8, 9, 10, 15, 20, 22, 23, 24.

16. *Heroines of Fiction*, *1*, 2–3, 5, 12.

17. *Ibid.*, *1*, 162.

18. *Ibid.*, *1*, 229; *2*, 209.

19. *Prefaces*, pp. 98, 93. (Originally in the *North American Review*, 1902.)

20. *Ibid.*, 98. "Criticism no longer assumes to ascertain an author's place in literature. It is very well satisfied if it can say something suggestive concerning the nature and quality of his work, and it tries to say this with as little of the old air of finality as it can manage to hide its poverty in." (From "Emile Zola," 1902.)

21. See *Prefaces,* pp. 35, 62, 149.

22. *The House by the Medlar-Tree,* New York, 1890; in *Prefaces,*
p. 19.

23. *Criticism and Fiction,* pp. 58–72.

24. Galdós (1896); in *Prefaces,* p. 53. *The Shadow of the Cathedral,*
New York, 1919; in *Prefaces.* pp.. 173, 181. On the whole relationship
with Spain, cf. Stanley T. Williams, 2, 240–67.

25. *Harper's,* 72 (1886), 812.

BIBLIOGRAPHY: HENRY JAMES

I quote the essays:

French Poets and Novelists (London, 1878) as *FPN.* The 1884
   reprint is used.

Hawthorne (London, 1879) as *Ha.* The reprint from Ithaca, N.Y.,
   1956, is used.

Partial Portraits (London, 1888) as *PP.* The 1919 reprint is used.

Essays in London and Elsewhere (New York, 1893) as *EL.*

Views and Reviews, intro. by Le Roy Phillips (Boston, 1908) as *VR.*

Notes on Novelists with Some Other Notes (New York, 1914) as
   NN. The 1916 reprint is used.

Notes and Reviews, preface by Pierre de Chaignon La Rose
   (Dunster House, Cambridge, Mass., 1921) as *NR.*

The Art of the Novel Critical Prefaces, intro. by Richard P.
   Blackmur (New York, 1934) as *AN.*

The Scenic Art: Notes on Acting and the Drama, ed. Allan Wade,
   New Brunswick, N. J., 1948.

The Future of the Novel: Essays on the Art of Fiction, ed. Leon
   Edel (New York, 1956) as *FN.*

The American Essays, ed. Leon Edel (New York, 1956) as *AE.*

The Painter's Eye: Notes and Essays on the Pictorial Arts, ed.
   John L. Sweeney, Cambridge, Mass., 1956.

*Literary Reviews and Essays, on American, English, and French
   Literature,* ed. Albert Mordell (New York, 1957) as *LRE.*

French Writers and American Women: Essays, ed. Peter Buitenhuis,
   Branford, Conn., 1960. Contains a few unprinted pieces.

Letters and Notebooks:

The Letters, ed. Percy Lubbock, 2 vols. New York, 1920.

The Notebooks, ed. F. O. Matthiessen and K. Murdock, New York,
   1947.

The Selected Letters, ed. Leon Edel (New York, 1955) as *SL.* Contains many new letters.

Comment on James's criticism:

T. S. Eliot, "On Henry James" (1918), in *The Question of Henry James,* ed. F. W. Dupee, New York, 1945.

Marie-Reine Garnier, *Henry James et la France,* Paris, 1927. Contains a compilation of James's opinions on French writers.

Morris Roberts, *Henry James's Criticism,* Cambridge, Mass., 1929. Still the best general account.

Cornelia Pulsifer Kelley, *The Early Development of Henry James,* University of Illinois Studies in Language and Literature, 15 (1930). Discusses early criticism.

Leon Edel, *The Prefaces of Henry James,* Paris, 1931.

Van Wyck Brooks, "Henry James as a Reviewer," in *Sketches in Criticism* (New York, 1932), pp. 190–96.

R. P. Blackmur's introduction to *Art of the Novel.* See above. Excellent.

Laurence Barrett, "Young Henry James Critic," in *American Literature, 20* (1948–49), 385–400.

R. W. Short, "Some Critical Terms of Henry James," *PMLA, 65* (1950), 667–80. Useful.

Agostino Lombardo, *Introduzione a le Prefazioni di Henry James,* Venice, 1956.

F. R. Leavis, "James as Critic," in Henry James, *Selected Literary Criticism,* ed. M. Shapira (New York, 1964), pp. xiii–xxiii.

The chapters on James in De Mille's *Literary Criticism in America* (New York, 1931), pp. 158–81, are perfunctory; that in Bernard Smith, *Forces in American Criticism* (New York, 1939), pp. 202–20, makes James out to be an aesthete.

Le Roy Phillips, *A Bibliography of the Writings of Henry James* (rev. ed. New York, 1930), was most helpful in locating the many scattered reviews and introductions. It is superseded by Leon Edel and Dan H. Laurence, *A Bibliography of Henry James,* New York, 1957, rev. ed. 1961.

NOTES: HENRY JAMES

1. "On Henry James" (1918), in *The Question of Henry James,* ed. F. W. Dupee (New York, 1945), pp. 109–110.

2. London, 1921, pp. 186–187.

3. Cambridge, Mass., 1929, p. 120.

4. Introduction to *AN,* pp. vii–viii.

5. To T. S. Perry, 20 September 1867, *SL,* pp. 22–23.

6. *AE,* pp. 275–76.

7. *EL*, p. 74.

8. *NR*, pp. 103–04.

9. *Nation, 4* (4 June 1868), 454–55. Reprinted in *LRE*, pp. 78–79.

10. *Nation, 20* (18 February 1875), 117–18; in *LRE*, pp. 79, 82–83.

11. *Ibid.* (15 April 1875), 261–62; in *LRE*, pp. 86–87.

12. Review of Correspondence (1878) in the *North American Review, 130* (January 1880), 56–57.

13. *NR*, pp. 102, 105.

14. Review of *Etudes critiques de littérature*, in *Nation, 22* (6 April 1876), 233; in *LRE*, pp. 118, 121.

15. *NR*, p. 106.

16. Review of *History of English Literature*, in *Atlantic Monthly, 29* (April 1872), 469–72; in *LRE*, pp. 63, 65, 67.

17. See review of *Notes sur l'Angleterre*, in *Nation, 14* (25 January 1872), 58–60; in *LRE*, p. 60.

18. *FN*, p. 115. See also *FPN*, p. 67, and *NN*, p. 128.

19. Review of *History of English Literature*, p. 470; in *LRE*, pp. 63–64.

20. Review of *Dallas Galbraith* (by Mrs. R. H. Davis); in *Nation*, VII, 330–31 (22 October 1868).

21. *PP*, pp. 395–96.

22. *FN*, p. 97.

23. *AN*, p. 155.

24. *VR*, p. 94.

25. *NN*, p. 259. Similarly *AN*, p. 201; *AE*, p. 206.

26. *PP*, pp. 137–38.

27. *AE*, p. 228.

28. *VR*, p. 227.

29. *AE*, p. 116.

30. *FPN*, p. 201.

31. *FPN*, p. 38.

32. *FPN*, p. 35.

33. *FPN*, p. 44.

34. *FPN*, pp. 55–56.

35. *FPN*, p. 54.

36. *NR*, pp. 132–33.

37. *VR*, p. 58–59.

38. To E. Gosse (13 December 1894), *SL*, p. 146.

39. To Gosse, (8 April 1895), *SL*, p. 147.

40. *NN*, p. 246.

41. *NN*, p. 283.

42. *NN*, p. 293.

43. *PP,* p. 378, or p. 227.
44. *PP,* p. 402.
45. *AN,* p. 312.
46. *FPN,* p. 184.
47. *NR,* pp. 23, 32.
48. *NN,* pp. 320–24.
49. *NN,* p. 342.
50. *Ha,* pp. 106–07. See also *AN,* p. 230.
51. *NN,* p. 275.
52. *AN,* p. 120.
53. *NN,* p. 275.
54. *NN,* p. 193.
55. *AN,* p. 123.
56. *VR,* p. 4.
57. *NR,* p. 199.
58. It "has little to do with nature and nothing to do with history of morality," *VR,* p. 188.
59. *AN,* p. 254.
60. *AN,* p. 175. The theory of Edmund Wilson (*The Triple Thinkers,* New York, 1948, pp. 88 ff.) that the ghosts are a hallucination of the governess is also refuted by the evidence of the *Notebooks,* ed. F. O. Matthiessen and K. Murdock (New York, 1947), pp. 178–79.
61. *NR,* pp. 34–35.
62. *The Scenic Art: Notes on Acting and the Drama,* ed. Allan Wade (New Brunswick, N. J., 1948), pp. 322–24.
63. *AN,* pp. 32–34.
64. *Ha,* p. 90.
65. *Ha,* p. 131.
66. *PP,* p. 387.
67. *NN,* p. 151.
68. *VR,* pp. 153–61.
69. *PP,* p. 116; cf. p. 379.
70. *AE,* p. 230.
71. Letter, 5 October 1901, *SL,* pp. 202–03.
72. *PP,* p. 390.
73. *NN,* p. 316.
74. *Ha,* p. 2.
75. *Ha,* p. 34.
76. *NN,* p. 151.
77. *NN,* p. 436.
78. *FN,* p. 33.
79. *FPN,* p. 243.

80. *PP*, p. 238.
81. 20 January 1909, *SL*, p. 134.
82. *NN*, p. 296.
83. *NN*, p. 309.
84. *NN*, p. 313.
85. *PP*, pp. 284, 287.
86. *FPN*, p. 64.
87. *FPN*, p. 89.
88. *EL*, p. 159.
89. *EL*, p. 183.
90. *EL*, p. 157.
91. *EL*, p. 155.
92. *EL*, p. 157.
93. *PP*, p. 255.
94. *EL*, pp. 208–09.
95. *EL*, p. 184.
96. *FPN*, p. 221.
97. *VR*, p. 37.
98. *PP*, p. 50.
99. See Marius Bewley, *The Complex Fate* (London, 1952), for the best discussion of Hawthorne's influence.
100. *Ha*, p. 46.
101. *Ha*, p. 50.
102. *PP*, pp. 406–07.
103. *NN*, p. 36.
104. *FN*, p. 101.
105. *AN*, p. 111.
106. *FN*, p. 104.
107. *FPN*, pp. 19–20.
108. *EL*, pp. 63–64.
109. *AE*, pp. 136–37.
110. *AN*, p. 111.
111. *VR*, p. 228.
112. *FN*, p. 232.
113. *PP*, p. 116.
114. *PP*, p. 379.
115. *NR*, p. 21.
116. *AN*, p. 321.
117. *VR*, pp. 180–82.
118. *EL*, p. 241.
119. *VR*, p. 29.
120. *AN*, p. 157.

121. *AN*, p. 110.
122. *AN*, p. 115.
123. *FN*, pp. 122–23.
124. *NN*, pp. 352–53.
125. *AN*, p. 298.
126. *FN*, p. 121.
127. *EL*, p. 197.
128. *PP*, p. 269.
129. *NN*, p. 279.
130. *FPN*, p. 139.
131. *VR*, p. 135.
132. *AN*, p. 130.
133. *AN*, p. 147.
134. *AN*, p. 317.
135. *AN*, p. 296.
136. *AN*, p. 329.
137. *AN*, p. 300.
138. *AN*, p. 62.
139. *AN*, p. 71.
140. *AN*, p. 67.
141. *NN*, pp. 83–87.
142. *NN*, p. 345.
143. *SL*, pp. 157–58.
144. *NN*, pp. 349, 355.
145. *AN*, p. 12.
146. *PP*, pp. 317–18.
147. *PP*, pp. 51–52.
148. *NN*, pp. 83–84.
149. *PP*, pp. 105–06.
150. *PP*, p. 392.
151. *NR*, p. 19.
152. *NR*, p. 22.
153. In the *Pall Mall Gazette;* see *SL*, p. 74.
154. *PP*, pp. 401–02.
155. *PP*, p. 393.
156. *FN*, p. 120.
157. *AN*, p. 45.
158. *NR*, p. 25.
159. *SL*, p. 210.
160. *SL*, p. 168.
161. *FN*, p. 228.
162. To Hugh Walpole (19 May 1912), *SL*, p. 171.

163. *PP*, p. 395.

164. *FPN*, p. 215.

165. *FN*, p. 229.

166. *AN*, pp. 115–16.

167. *NN*, p. 80.

168. *SL*, p. 171.

169. *NN*, p. 361.

170. *SL*, p. 107.

171. *AE*, p. 155.

172. *AN*, p. 52.

173. *FPN*, pp. 75–80.

174. *FPN*, p. 180.

175. *PP*, p. 32.

176. *PP*, pp. 139–140. *NN*, p. 255.

177. *NN*, p. 219.

178. *NN*, p. 100.

179. *AN*, p. 84.

180. *AN*, p. 219.

181. *VR*, p. 135.

182. *PP*, p. 392.

183. *NN*, p. 93.

184. *VR*, p. 8.

185. *VR*, p. 96.

186. *AN*, p. 84.

187. *PP*, pp. 65 ff.

188. *NN*, p. 329.

189. *NN*, pp. 394–95.

190. *NN*, p. 118.

191. *FPN*, p. 43.

192. *NR*, p. 154.

193. *FPN*, pp. 249–50.

194. *NR*, pp. 225–26.

195. *SL*, p. 206.

196. *EL*, p. 126.

197. *EL*, p. 146.

198. *EL*, p. 159.

199. *EL*, pp. 149–50.

200. *AE*, pp. 200–01.

201. See letter to W. Roughhead (30 September 1914), *SL*, p. 220.

202. *North American Review*, *101* (July 1865), 281–85; in *LRE*, p. 271.

203. See *Nation*, *17* (30 October 1873), 292–94; in *LRE*, p. 117.

BIBLIOGRAPHY:
THE RUSSIAN RADICAL CRITICS

I. Chernyshevsky is quoted from *Izbrannye sochineniya*, Moscow and Leningrad, 1950. Where this edition fails, I have recourse to the published volumes of *Polnoe sobranie sochinenii*, ed. V. Ya. Kirpotin et al., 15 vols. (Vols. 1–4, 9–10, 13–14 accessible) Moscow, 1939–51. There is an anonymous English translation of *Selected Philosophical Essays*, Moscow, 1953. Introduction by M. Grigoryan.

Dobrolyubov is quoted from *Izbrannye sochineniya*, ed. A. Lavretsky, Moscow and Leningrad, 1947. When this fails, I quote *Pervoe polnoe sobranie sochinenii*, ed. M. K. Lemke, 4 vols. St. Petersburg, 1911. There is a good English translation by J. Fineberg, *Selected Philosophical Essays*, Moscow, 1948.

Pisarev is quoted from F. Pavlenkov's 4th ed., *Sochineniya. Polnoe sobranie*, 6 vols. St. Petersburg, 1907–17. I had no access to *Izbrannye sochineniya* ed. V. Kirpotin, (2 vols. Moscow, 1934–35), but have seen *Izbrannye filosofiskie i obshchestvenno-politicheskie stati*, ed. V. S. Krushkov, 1949. *Selected Philosophical, Social and Political Essays* (Moscow, 1958) is an inadequate English selection.

II. From the large literature, besides the general books on Russian criticism quoted in the section on Belinsky (this *History*, *3*, 243–264), mainly devoted to biography and politics, these were most useful for my limited purposes:

On Chernyshevsky: *N. G. Chernyshevsky: 1828–1928*, ed. S. Z. Katzenbogen, Saratov, 1928. M. Rozental', *Filosofickie vzglyady N. G. Chernyshevskogo*, Moscow, 1948. B. I. Bursov, *Chernyshevsky kak literaturny kritik*, Moscow and Leningrad, 1951. Georg Lukács, "Einführung in die Ästhetik Tschernyschewskijs," in *Beiträge zur Geschichte der Ästhetik* (Berlin, 1954), pp. 135–90. G. O. Berliner, "Chernyshevsky i Gogol," in V. V. Gippius, ed., *N. V. Gogol': materialy i issledovanya, Literaturny archiv* (Moscow, 1936), *2*, 472–533. Gleb Struve, "*Monologue intérieur:* The Origins of the Formula and the First Statement of Its Possibilities," *PMLA*, *69* (1954), 1101–11. Charles Corbet, "Čérnyševskij esthéticien et critique," *Revue des Etudes Slaves*, *24* (1948), 107–28.

On Dobrolyubov: Valeryan Polyansky, *N. A. Dobrolyubov. Mirovozzrenie i literaturno-kriticheskaya deyatelnost*, Moscow, 1935. Charles Corbet, "Principes esthétiques et réalités sentimentales dans la critique de Dobroljubov," *Revue des Etudes Slaves*, *29* (1952), 34–54, and "Dobroljubov als Literaturkritiker," *Zeitschrift für slavische Philologie*, *24* (1956), 156–73.

On Pisarev: Armand Coquart, *Dmitri Pisarev (1840–1868) et l'idé-ologie du nihilisme russe,* Paris, 1946. A. A. Plotkin, *Pisarev i lite-raturno-obshchestvennoe dvizhenie shestidesyatykh godov.* Leningrad, 1945.

CHERNYSHEVSKY

1. The overwhelming circumstantial evidence for suicide is assembled by Armand Coquart in his *D. Pisarev* (Paris, 1946), pp. 380 ff.

2. *Polnoe sobranie, 4,* 765: "Не книгами, не журналами, не газетами пробуждается дух нации, — он пробуждается событиями."

3. *Ibid., 4,* 767, 770.

4. *Izbrannye sochineniya,* p. 422-l.

5. *Ibid.,* pp. 431-l, 432-l.

6. *Ibid.,* p. 435-r.

7. *Ibid.,* p. 437-r.

8. *Ibid.,* p. 438-l.

9. *Ibid.,* pp. 438-r, 440-r, 441-r, 443-r, 449-r: "Бо́льшая полнота подробностей, или то, что в плохих произведениях приобретает имя 'реторического распространения' . . . Наука и искусство (поэзия)—'Handbuch' для начинающего изучать жизнь."

10. *Ibid.,* p. 415-r.

11. *Ibid.,* p. 409.

12. *Ibid.,* p. 434.

13. *Ibid.,* pp. 428-l, 428-r.

14. Mainly from Eduard Müller's *Geschichte der Theorie der Kunst bei den Alten,* 2 vols. 1834–37.

15. *Izbrannye,* p. 474: "Без истории предмета нет теории предмета; но и без теории предмета нет даже мысли об его истории. . ."

16. *Ibid.,* p. 478: "Сиденье на завалине (у поселян), или вокруг самовара (у горожан) больше развило и нашем народе хорошего расположения духа и доброго расположения к людям, нежели все произведения живописи, начиная с лубочных картин до 'Последнего дня Помпеи.' " The allusion is to a picture by K. Bryulov exhibited in 1834.

17. *Ibid.,* p. 485: "Едва ли есть драматическое произведение, сюжет которого не мог бы так же хорошо (или еще лучше) быть рассказан в эпической форме."

18. *Ibid.,* p. 616.

19. *Ibid.,* p. 679: "Литература у нас пока сосредоточивает почти всю умственную жизнь народа . . ."

20. *Polnoe sobranie, 2* (1855), 424–517, and *4* (1857), 626–63.

21. *Polnoe*, *2*, 475; and *Izbrannye*, p. 518: "Он первый возвел у нас литературу в достоинство национального дела . . . Пушкин, не будучи по преимуществу ни мыслителем, ни ученым, был человеком необыкновенного ума и человек чрезвычайно образованный . . . хотя в его произведениях не должно искать главнейшим образом глубокого содержания, ясно сознанного и последовательного, зато каждая страница его кипит умом и жизнью образованной мысли."

22. *Izbrannyie*, pp. 517–18: "Критического направления."

23. *Ibid.*, p. 515 n.

24. *Polnoe*, *4*, 633: "Виновать ли он в этой тесноте своего горизонта?"

25. *Izbrannye*, p. 677: "О так называемом чистом искусстве."

26. *Ibid.*, p. 678: "Поэзия есть жизнь, действие, борьба, страсть."

27. *Ibid.*, pp. 491 ff.

28. *Ibid.*, p. 743: "Русский человек на 'Rendez-vous' . . . Но сцена, сделанная нашим Ромео Асе, как мы заметили, — только симптом болезни, которая точно таким же пошлым образом портит все наши дела. . . ."

29. *Ibid.*: "Бог с ними, с эротическими вопросами, — не до них читателю нашего времени, занятому вопросами об административных и судебных улучшениях, о финансовых преобразованиях, об освобождении крестьян."

30. *Ibid.*, pp. 705–6: "Занимают . . . графа Толстого всего более — сам психический процесс, его формы, его законы, диалектика души . . . Это изображение внутреннего монолога." As far as I know, the only earlier occurrence of the term is in Alexandre Dumas' *Trente Ans après*, in 1845. Cf. W. L. Schwarz, "The Interior Monologue in 1845," *Modern Language Notes*, *63* (1948), 409–10.

31. *Ibid.*, p. 707.

32. *Ibid.*, pp. 709 ff.

DOBROLYUBOV

1. Chernyshevsky himself refers to Danzel-Guhrauer and to F. C. Schlosser's *Geschichte des achtzehnten Jahrhunderts* (8 vols. 1843–52) as to his sources, see, e. g., *Polnoe sobranie*, *4*, 52 n.; cf. 49, 73 n. Much is translated from Karl Lessing's life of his brother and from Lessing's writings. Cf. V. Kaplinsky, "Lessing Chernyshevskogo," in S. Z. Katsenbogen, ed., *Nikolay Chernyshevsky 1828–1928. Neizdannye texty, materialy i stati* (Saratov, 1928), pp. 151–74.

2. Dobrolyubov, *Izbrannye sochineniya*, pp. 20–1, 24.

3. *Ibid.*, p. 27: "Спокойная обдуманность, хладнокровное соображение мнений разных сторон."

4. *Ibid.*, p. 166-r: "Литература только воспроизводит жизнь и никогда не дает того, чего нет в действительности."

5. *Ibid.*, pp. 333, 350–r: "Главное, следите за непрерывным, стройным, могучим, ничем несдержимым течением жизни . . ."

6. *Ibid.*, pp. 20. 27.

7. *Ibid.*, p. 219-l: "Что падает, что побеждает, что начинает водворяться и преобладать в нравственной жизни общества, — на это у нас нет другого показателя, кроме литературы."

8. Review of A. Pleshcheyev's stories, "Good Intentions and Action" (Blagonamerennost i deyatelnost, 1860) in *Pervoe polnoe sobranie*, ed. Lemke, 4, 233: "Для ускорения и большей полноты сознательной работы общества."

9. *Izbrannye*, p. 292: "Таким образом, вообще говоря, литература представляет собою силу служебную, которой значение состоит в пропаганде, а достоинство определяется тем, что и как она пропагандирует."

10. *Polnoe*, 7, 272: "Могут выражаться в административной деятельности."

11. *Ibid.*, 7, 316, and 3, 343: "При известной степени развития народа литература становится одною из сил, движущих общество . . . твердит обществу о честной и полезной деятельности, она все поет ту же песню: Встань, проснись, подымись. На себя погляди!"

12. *Izbrannye*, p. 52-r: "Предупредить жизни литература не может, но предупредить формальное, официальное проявление интересов, выработавшихся в жизни, она должна. Пока еще известная идея находится в умах, пока еще она только должна осуществиться в будущем, тут-то литература и должна схватить ее, тут-то и должно начаться литературное обсуждение предмета с разных сторон и в видах различных интересов. Но уж когда идея перешла в дело, сформировалась и решилась окончательно, тогда литературе нечего делать: разве только один раз (не больше) похвалить то, что сделано.

13. *Ibid.*, pp. 29–30, 31: "Всего ближе, разумеется, было выразиться в литературе интересам и мнениям тех, в чьих руках было книжное дело, и тех, в ком оно находило хоть маленькую поддержку и опору."

14. *Ibid.*, p. 35-l.

15. *Ibid.*, p. 36-r.

16. *Ibid.*, p. 41-r: "Ломоносов сделался . . . но уже никак не

человеком, сочувствующим тому классу народа, из которого вышел он.''

17. *Ibid.*, p. 46: ''Чуждая упорной деятельности мысли . . .''
18. *Ibid.*, p. 52.
19. *Ibid.*, p. 28-г: ''Массе народа чужды наши интересы, непонятны наши страдания, забавны наши восторги.''
20. *Ibid.*, p. 119-г: ''Мы не видим из комедии, как рос и воспитывался Большов, какие влияния на него действовали с молоду.''
21. *Ibid.*, p. 107-г: ''Но если *естественность* требует отсутствия *логической последовательности?*''
22. *Ibid.*, p. 287-г.
23. *Ibid.*, p. 290-г.
24. *Ibid.*, p. 285-г.
25. *Ibid.*, p. 335.
26. *Ibid.*, p. 330.
27. *Ibid.*, p. 328-l.
28. *Ibid.*, p. 326-г.
29. *Ibid.*, pp. 324, 329.
30. *Ibid.*, pp. 329, 331: ''Покамест литература имеет хоть малейшую возможность хоть издалека прислушиваться к общественным интересам и хоть неясным, кротким лепетом выразить свое к ним участие,—неужели думаете вы возбудить в ком-нибудь интерес даже самыми блестящими эстетическими этюдами.''
31. *Ibid.*, p. 20.
32. *Polnoe sobranie, 5*, 537.
33. *Izbrannye*, p. 323.
34. *Ibid.*, p. 282-l.
35. *Ibid.*, p. 168-г.
36. *Ibid.*, p. 104-l.
37. *Ibid.*, p. 130-г: ''В этих образах поэт может, даже неприметно для самого себя, уловить и выразить их внутренний смысл гораздо прежде, нежели определит его рассудком. Иногда художник может и вовсе не дойти до смысла того, что он сам же изображает; но критика и существует затем, чтобы разъяснить смысл, скрытый в созданиях художника . . .''
38. *Ibid.*, p. 136–7.
39. See this *History*, *2*, 27. An essay of Charles Nodier, ''Des Types en littérature'' (Brussels, 1832), is relevant. In *Reveries littéraires, morales, et fantastiques. Oeuvres, 5*, 41–58.
40. *Izbrannye*, p. 104-г: ''Образы, созданные художником, собирая в себе, как в фокусе, факты действительной жизни, весьма много способствуют составлению и распространению между людьми правильных понятий о вещах.''

41. *Ibid.*, p. 79-l.
42. *Ibid.*, p. 92-l: "Обломовка есть наша прямая родина . . . В каждом из нас сидит значительная часть Обломова . . ."
43. *Ibid.*, p. 91-r: "Но теперь уж все этих герои . . . потеряли прежнее значение, перестали сбивать нас с толку своей загадочностью и таинственным разладом."
44. *Ibid.*, p. 93-l: "Но все-таки он противен в своей ничтожности."
45. *Ibid.*, p. 103-l.
46. *Ibid.*, pp. 117-r, 123-r: "Низости и преступления не лежат в природе человека."
47. *Ibid.*, p. 316-l: "Служит представителем великой народной идеи . . . Вот высота, до которой доходит наша народная жизнь в своем развитии . . ."
48. *Ibid.*, pp. 321-l, 315-l , 303, 292: "Страшный вызов самодурной силе . . . Новое движение народной жизни, о котором мы говорили выше и отражение которого нашли в характере Катерины . . ."
49. *Ibid.*, p. 322: "Искусство опять сделано орудием какой-то посторонней идеи! . . . Русская жизнь и русская сила вызваны художником в 'Грозе'. . ."
50. *Ibid.*, p. 233-l.
51. *Ibid.*, p. 231-l.
52. *Ibid.*, p. 242-r: "Но мы все-таки думаем . . . что недалеко время, когда этим идеям можно будет проявиться на деле . . . Нужен человек, как Инсаров,—но русский Инсаров . . . Придет же он наконец, этот день!"
53. *Ibid.*, p. 341-r.
54. *Ibid.*, p. 328-l: "Художник—не пластинка для фотографии . . . Художник дополняет отрывочность схваченного момента своим творческим чувством . . . создает одно стройное целое . . . находит живую связь . . . сливает и переработывает . . . разнообразные и противоречивые стороны живой действительности . . . что так должно быть, что иначе и быть не может . . ."
55. *Ibid.*, p. 333-l.

PISAREV

1. *Rusko a Evropa* (Prague, 1921), 2, 112–14.
2. One should note that Pisarev translated and digested R. Haym's book on Humboldt as a student and must have read, at least in Haym's digest, Humboldt's fiercely individualistic "Versuch die Grenzen der Wirksamkeit des Staats zu bestimmen" (1792), first published in full in 1851; see Coquart, p. 84 n.

3. *Izbrannye*, ed. Kruzhkov, p. 632.

4. *Soch.* ed. Pavlenkov, *5*, 86.

5. P, *4*, 508–9.

6. P, *4*, 96.

7. P, *5*, 77.

8. P, *5*, 81.

9. P, *4*, 115.

10. *Izbrannye*, ed. Kirpotin, *2*, 92.

11. P, *1*, 459.

12. P, *4*, 501: "Всякий вполне здоровый и нормально развившийся человек прекрасен."

13. P, *4*, 514.

14. P, *4*, 516.

15. P, *4*, 107.

16. P, *4*, 499.

17. P, *4*, 120.

18. P, *3*, 269: "Ни один действительно умный и даровитый человек нашего поколения не истратит своей жизни на пронизывание чувствительных сердец убийственными ямбами и анапестами."

19. P, *4*, 280.

20. P, *3*, 269.

21. *Izbrannye*, ed. Kirpotin, *1*, 492: "Ученое путешествие на берега Тигра для чтения гвоздеобразных надписей—дело очень похвальное, но оно произведет слабое впечатление на черствую душу лапотника, не умеющего разбирать печатные буквы собственного языка."

22. P, *4*, 371.

23. P, *4*, 61.

24. P, *4*, 68. "Реалист—мыслящий работник . . ."

25. P, *4*, 117: "Вторым средством . . . является влияние литературы. Задавать обществу психологические задачи, показывать ему столкновение между различными страстями, характерами и положениями, наводить его на размышления о причинах этих столкновений и о средствах устранить подобные неприятности . . ."

26. P, *4*, 118.

27. P, *4*, 98–9: "Рыцарь духа." "Die Ritter vom Geist," title of a novel by Gutzkow.

28. P, *3*, 269.

29. P, *4*, 119.

30. Stanitsky's (i.e. Mme Panaeva's) *A Woman's Fate*.

31. P, *4*, 192: "Я говорю совершенно искренно, что желал бы лучше быть русским сапожником или булочником, чем русским Рафаэлем или Гриммом."

32. P, *5*, 15, 34.
33. P, *5*, 43: "С онегинским типом мы не связаны решительно ничем."
34. P, *5*, 85: "Пушкин пользуется своей художественной виртуозностью, как средством посвятить всю читающую Россию в печальные тайны своей внутренней пустоты, своей духовной нищеты и своего умственного бессилия."
35. P, *5*, 126, and 55: "Совершенно неспособного анализировать и понимать великие общественные и философские вопросы."
36. In Pavlenkov's edition the essay is dated 1862, but there seems no reason to give it an earlier date than 1867, the date of its publication. See the argument in A. A. Plotkin's *Pisarev*, p. 324 n.
37. Pisarev, *Izbrannye*, ed. Kruzhkov, p. 595: "Перед вами стоит живописец. На палитре его горят краски невиданной яркости. Он взмахнул кистью, и через две минуты вам улыбается с полотна или даже просто со стены прелестная женская физиономия. Ещё две минуты, и вместо этой физиономии на вас смотрят демонически-страстные глаза безобразного сатира; ещё несколько ударов кисти, и сатир превратился в развесистое дерево; потом пропало дерево, и явилась фарфоровая башня, а под ней китаец на каком-то фантастическом драконе; потом всё замазано чёрной краской, и сам художник оглядывается и смотрит на вас с презрительно-грустной улыбкой."
38. *Ibid.*, p. 590.
39. *Ibid.*, pp. 609, 622.
40. *Ibid.*, pp. 624, 629: "Когда художник поёт, как соловей, безо всякой тенденции, тогда Гейне находит в его произведениях запах свежего сена. Когда художник становится на всю жизнь под знамя одной, строго определённой идеи, тогда Гейне кричит, что мир затоплен волнами румфордова супа."
41. *Ibid.*, p. 602.
42. *Ibid.*, p. 613.
43. P, *1*, 457.
44. P, *1*, 497.
45. P, *1*, 180.
46. P, *1*, 522, 525.
47. P, *2*, 408, 413–14.
48. P, *2*, 418.
49. P, *2*, 409.
50. P, *2*, 415–16.
51. P, *2*, 396.
52. P, *2*, 397–8.
53. P, *2*, 419.

54. P, *2*, 412–13.
55. Turgenev's letters on Bazarov to K. K. Sluchovsky, 14 April 1862, and to Dostoevsky, 22 April 1862, in *Pervoe sobranie pisem* (St. Petersburg, 1884), pp. 104 ff. Pisarev's article on Bazarov appeared in the March 1862 number of *Ruskoe Slovo*. See Coquart, p. 136 n.
56. Letter, 18 May 1867, first printed in *Raduga. Almanakh Pushkinskogo Doma*, 1922. "Что же сделалось с этой каланчой? Куда она девалась? . . . Неужели же вы думаете, что первый и последний Базаров действительно умер в 1859 году от пореза пальца?"
57. P, *3*, 271.
58. P, *3*, 307: "Русская Офелия, Катерина, совершив множество глупостей, бросается в воду и делает таким образом последнюю и величайшую нелепость."
59. *Izbrannye*, ed. Kruzhkov, p. 647. The article, first printed with the title "A New Type" in 1865, and reprinted as "The Thinking Proletariat" (1867), was not allowed in Pavlenkov's edition.
60. P, *5*, 311–12.
61. A letter by Pisarev's mother, to Dostoevsky (1878) printed in *Krasny Arkhiv*, *5* (1924), 249. Quoted by Coquart, p. 357.
62. P, *6*, 343.
63. P, *6*, 350, 375.
64. P, *6*, 352.
65. P, *6*, 354.
66. P, *6*, 382.
67. P, *6*, 392.
68. P, *4*, 243–6.
69. P, *6*, 479.
70. P, *6*, 510.
71. Printed in *Zvenya*, *6* (1936), 649–84, ed. E. Kazanovich.
72. I paraphrase the words of F. O. Matthiessen, who cannot be suspected of a lack of sympathy for the social role of art. See his review of Granville Hicks' *The Great Tradition*, in *The Responsibilities of the Critic* (New York, 1952), pp. 189 ff.

BIBLIOGRAPHY:
THE RUSSIAN CONSERVATIVE CRITICS

On Grigoriev: I quote *Sochineniya*, ed. N. N. Strakhov (St. Petersburg, 1876), Vol. 1 (no more published) as *S*.

I use also *Sobranie sochinenii*, ed. V. Th. Savodnik, 14 pamphlets, Moscow, 1915.

I have seen *Polnoe sobranie sochinenii i pisem*, ed. V. Spiridinov (Petrograd, 1918), only one volume published.

Letters are quoted from *A. A. Grigoriev. Materialy dlya biografii*, ed. Vlad. Knyazhnin, Petrograd, 1917.

On Grigoriev see:

Leonid Grossman, *Tri Sovremmenika, Tyutchev–Dostoevsky–Apollon Grigoriev*, Moscow, 1922.

V. Friche, in *Ocherki po istorii russkoy kritiki*, ed. A. Lunacharsky and Val. Polyansky (Moscow, 1929), *1*, 305–20, makes him representative of the Russian merchant class.

U. A. Gural'nik in *Istoriya russkoy kritiki*, ed. B. P. Gorodetsky, A. Lavretsky, and B. S. Mellakh (Moscow, 1958), *1*, 470–87. Marxist.

Ralph E. Matlaw, introduction to *My Literary and Moral Wanderings* (New York, 1962), esp. pp. xxvii–xl. Good.

On Dostoevsky: I quote the Paris YMCA ed., 1925, and when this fails, the Tomashevsky-Khalabaev ed., *Polnoe sobranie*, 13 vols. Moscow, 1926–30. I use the English translations in the text freely.

Occasional writings, ed. David Magarshack, New York, 1963.

The Diary of a Writer, trans. Boris Brasol, 2 vols. New York, 1949. A clumsy and faulty translation.

Dostoevsky: A Collection of Critical Essays, ed. René Wellek, Englewood Cliffs, N. J., 1962. The introduction on the history of Dostoevsky criticism surveys the literature.

On Dostoevsky as critic see:

J. J. Lapshin, *Estetika Dostoevskago*, Berlin, 1923.

L. Grossman, *Poetika Dostoevskogo* (Moscow, 1925), has little on criticism.

A chapter in Reinhard Lauth, *Die Philosophie Dostojewskis*, Munich, 1950.

J. Van der Eng, *Dostoevskij Romancier* (The Hague, 1957), contains some discussion of criticism.

A chapter in V. Zenkovskij, *Aus der Geschichte der ästhetischen Ideen in Russland im 19. und 20. Jahrhundert*, The Hague, 1958.

The chapter by G. M. Fridlender in *Istoriya russkoy kritiki* (2 vols. Moscow, 1958), *2*, 269–87, is useful.

Robert L. Jackson, "Dostoevsky's Critique of the Aesthetics of Dobroliubov," *Slavic Review*, 23 (1964), 258–74, is a sample chapter of a full study of Dostoevsky's aesthetics and criticism.

On Strakhov: I quote K. N. Strakhov, *Kriticheskiya stati o I. S. Turgeneve i L. N. Tolstom (1862–1885)*, 3d ed. St. Petersburg, 1895.

Borba s zapadom v nashei literature, 3 vols. St. Petersburg, 1882, 1883, 1896.

Iz istorii literaturnago nigilizma, 1861–65, St. Petersburg, 1890.

Bednost nashei literatury, St. Petersburg, 1868.

The Correspondence with Tolstoy in *Tolstovsky Muzei,* Vol. 2, St. Petersburg, 1914.

On Strakhov see V. V. Rozanov, *Literaturnye izganniki,* Vol. 1 (St. Petersburg, 1913), pp. 1–435. With letters.

On Potebnya and Veselovsky:

Alexander Potebnya wrote *Iz lekcii po teorii slovesnosti,* Kharkov, 1894; *Iz zapisok po teorii slovesnosti,* Kharkov, 1905; and *Yazyk i mysl',* 3d ed. Kharkov, 1926.

There is an unfinished edition of Alexander Veselovsky's works: *Sobranie sochinenii,* St. Petersburg, 1919–38, only 8 vols. published—1, 2, 3–6, 8, 16.

Selections: *Izbrannye stati* (Leningrad, 1939) and *Istoricheskaya poetika* (Leningrad, 1940) both contain long introductions by V. Zhirmunsky.

B. M. Engelgardt, *Alexandr Nikolaevich Veselovsky,* Petrograd, 1924 is a good study by a foremost Formalist.

In English: Victor Erlich, in *Russian Formalism: History: Doctrine* (The Hague, 1955), discusses both Potebnya and Veselovsky.

There is a short account of Veselovsky by Erlich in *Yearbook of Comparative and General Literature* (ed. W. P. Friederich), Chapel Hill, N.C., 8 (1959), 33–6.

On Tolstoy: I quote *Polnoe sobranie sochinenii* (the so-called Jubilee ed. in 90 volumes, 1928–57) as *PSS.*

Letters, reminiscences, etc., however, are quoted from the convenient collection *Lev Tolstoy ob iskusstve i literature,* ed. K. N. Lomunov, with long introductions, 2 vols. Moscow, 1958.

I quote the English translations of Aylmer Maude, *What Is Art and Essays on Art* (as *WA*), Oxford, 1930, and *Recollections and Essays,* Oxford, 1937.

Special studies in Russian:

P. N. Sakulin, ed., *Estetika Lva Tolstogo. Sbornik statei,* Moscow, 1929.

K. N. Lomunov, "Tolstoy v borbe protiv dekadentskogo iskusstva," in *Lev N. Tolstoy, Sbornik statei i materialov,* ed. D. D. Blagoy, K. N. Lomunov, and I. N. Uspensky, Moscow, 1951.

In English see: G. Wilson Knight, *Shakespeare and Tolstoy,* Oxford, 1934; and H. W. Garrod, *Tolstoy's Theory of Art,* Oxford, 1935 (a lecture).

George Orwell, "Lear, Tolstoy and the Fool" (1947), reprinted in *Inside the Whale and Other Essays* (Harmondsworth, 1962), pp. 101–20.

NOTES:
THE RUSSIAN CONSERVATIVE CRITICS
GRIGORIEV

1. Grossman, p. 61: "В русской критике первенство его вне всякого сомнения."
2. *Geschichte der russischen Literatur* (Stuttgart, 1962), p. 99.
3. *S*, p. 209: "Платон нового мира." *S*, p. 210: "Величайший из мирских мыслителей."
4. *S*, p. 640.
5. *S*, p. 142: "Искусство есть идеальное выражение жизни."
6. *S*, p. 224: "Везде, где была жизнь, была и поэзия." Cf. *S*, p. 257.
7. *S*, p. 187: "Бессознательность придает произведениям творчества их неисследимую глубину."
8. *S*, p. 192: "Никакое явление словесности не может почти никогда быть рассматриваемо в одной его замкнутой отдельности."
9. *S*, p. 334: "Искусство как синтетическое, цельное, непосредственное, пожалуй, интуитивное разумение жизни."
10. *S*, pp. 307, 335: "веяние."
11. *S*, pp. 204, 306.
12. *S*, pp. 196–7.
13. *S*, p. 576: "Не имеет критериума, вечного идеала." "Индифферентизм и фатализм."
14. *S*, p. 223.
15. *S*, p. 208.
16. *S*, pp. 207, 228: "Рабское служение жизни."
17. *S*, p. 214: "Верить в историю, значит, верить в вечную и непеременную правду."
18. *S*, p. 219: "Чувство органической связи между явлениями жизни, чувство цельности и единства жизни."
19. *S*, pp. 224, 212.
20. *S*, p. 224: "Развитие идеала."
21. Letter to A. Maikov, 9 January 1859, in *A. A. Grigoriev*, ed. Vlad. Knyazhnin, p. 217: "Мечты о новом искусстве—судороги истощенного германо-романского мира в его добросовестнейших представителях Занде, Листе и т. п. Они не видят и не могут видеть того, что жизнь истощилась, и новая начинается." "Не

новое искусство, а Гомеровское, Дантовское, Шекспировское искусство нового мира.''

22. *S*, p. 210: ''Народам и лицам возвращается—их цельное само-ответственное значение, что разбит кумир отвлеченного духа человечества и его развития.''

23. *S*, p. 187: ''Тип, каков бы он ни был, есть уже прекрасное.''

24. *S*, p. 413: ''Все новое вносится в жизнь только искусством: оно одно воплощает в созданиях своих то, что́ невидимо присутствует в воздухе эпохи. Больше еще: искусство часто заранее чувствует приближающееся будущее, как птицы заранее чувствуют вёдро или ненастье.''

25. *Sämtliche Werke*, *1*, III, 628. Cf. this *History*, *2*, 76.

26. *S*, pp. 544–79, 619–24, etc.

27. *S*, pp. 244, 248, 252, 254, etc.

28. *Sobranie sochinenii*, ed. Savodnik, Vypusk 8. "N. V. Gogol i ego perepiska s druzyami," first in *Moskovsky Gorodskoy Listok*, 1847. An appendix: three letters by Grigoriev to Gogol.

29. *S*, pp. 14, 17, 30.

30. *S*, pp. 327–8.

31. *Sobranie sochinenii*, ed. Savodnik, Vypusk 4, pp. 4–5: ''быт''

32. *S*, pp. 9, 162.

33. *S*, pp. 44, 62, 454–6, etc. ''Темное царство.''

34. *S*, p. 425: ''Новый, живой тип, положительный.''

35. *S*, p. 411: ''Он родился, а не сочинился.''

36. *Sobranie sochinenii*, ed. Savodnik, Vypusk 12. Cf. Letter to N. N. Strakhov, 19 October 1861, in *A. A. Grigoriev*. ed. Knyazhnin, p. 284.

37. A note on Grigoriev's views of Dostoevsky in Grossman, pp. 336–7. Grigoriev reviewed *Poor People* in *Finsky Vestnik* in 1846.

DOSTOEVSKY

1. *Idiot*, *1*, 6; *2*, 239: ''Мир спасет красота.''

2. *Dnevnik Pisatelya za 1873 god*, pp. 84–85: ''Искусство есть такая же потребность для человека, как есть и пить. Потребность красоты и творчества, воплощающего ее,—неразлучна с человеком, и без нее человек, может быть, не захотел бы жить на свете. Человек жаждет ее, находит и принимает красоту без всяких условий.'' ''Она есть гармония, в ней залог успокоения; она воплощает человеку и человечеству его идеалы.'' Magarshack, *Occasional Writings*, p. 125.

3. *Bratya Karamazovy*, Part I, Book II, ch. 3; *1*, 143.

4. *Dnevnik Pisatelya za 1873 god*, p. 290: ''Но для повество-

вателя, для поэта могут быть и другие задачи, кроме бытовой стороны; есть общие, вечные и, кажется, вовеки неиследимые глубины духа и характера человеческого." Brasol, *Diary*, p.91.

5. *Dnevnik Pisatelya za 1873 god*, p. 281: "Надо изображать действительность как она есть, говорят они, тогда как такой действительности совсем нет, да и никогда на земле не бывало, потому что сущность вещей человеку недоступна, а воспринимает он природу, так, как отражается она в его идее, пройдя через его чувства; стало быть, надо дать поболее ходу идее и не бояться идеального." Cf. Brasol, p. 83.

6. See letter to Turgenev, 23 December 1863. *Pisma*, ed. Dolinin (4 vols. Moscow, 1930), *1*, 343: "Копирование действительного факта." "Поэтическая правда."

7. *Polnoe sobranie*, *13*, 523–4.

8. *Dnevnik Pisatelya za 1873 god*, p. 298. Brasol, pp. 96, 314, 111.

9. Letter to Strakhov, 26 February 1869. *Pisma*, *2*, 170: "Мелочь и низменность воззрения и проникновения в действительность."

10. See Jury Nikolsky, *Turgenev i Dostoevsky*, (*Istoriya odnoy vrazhdy*) (Sofia, 1921); and I. S. Zilberstein, *Istoriya odnoy vrazhdy*. *F. M. Dostoevsky i I. S. Turgenev*, Leningrad, 1928.

11. Cf. the last pages of *A Raw Youth*.

12. *Dnevnik Pisatelya za 1877 god*, pp. 276–91, 304–11. Brasol, pp. 777–9, 783–5.

13. *Dnevnik Pisatelya za 1873 god*, p. 91: "Мы связаны . . . и с историческим прошедшим и с общечеловечностью." Cf. *Occasional Writings*, p. 131.

14. *Ibid.*, p. 90: "Искусство не всегда верно действительности." *Occasional Writings*, p. 129.

15. Letter to A. N. Maykov, 11–23 December 1868. *Pisma*, *2*, 150: "Совершенно другие я понятия имею о действительности и реализме, чем наши реалисты и критики. Мой идеализм—реальнее ихнего. Господи! Порассказать толково то, что мы все, русские, пережили в последние 10 лет в нашем духовном развитии—да разве не закричат реалисты что это фантазия! между тем это исконный, настоящий реализм! Это-то и есть реализм, только глубже, а у них мелко плавает." Letter to N. N. Strakhov, 26 February–10 March 1869. *Pisma*, *2*, 169: "У меня свой особенный взгляд на действительность в искусстве и то что большинство называет почти фантастическим и исключительным, то для меня иногда составляет самую сущность действительного. Обыденность явлений и казенный взгляд на них по моему не есть еще реализм, а даже напротив."

16. N. N. Strakhov, *Biografiya, pisma i zametki iz zapisnoy knizhki*

F. M. Dostoevskogo (St. Petersburg, 1883), p. 373: "Меня зовут психологом: неправда, я лишь реалист в высшем смысле, т. е. изображаю все глубины души человеческой."

17. *Polnoe sobranie*, *13*, 328: "Внушите себе за правило, что яблоко натуральное можно съесть, а яблоко нарисованное нельзя съесть. Следственно, искусство вздор, роскошь и может служить только для забавы детей." "Сапоги во всяком случае лучше Пушкина." English trans. by Ralph E. Matlaw in *Notes from Underground and The Grand Inquisitor* (New York, 1960), pp. 218–19.

18. *Dnevnik Pisatelya za 1873 god*, p. 57: "Все же вытребованное, все вымученное спокон веку до наших времен не удавалось и вместо пользы приносило один только вред." *Occasional Writings*, p. 96.

19. *Ibid.*, p. 83: "В сущности вы презираете поэзию и художественность; вам нужно прежде всего дело, вы люди деловые." *Occasional Writings*, p. 123.

20. *Ibid.*, p. 84: "Органическое целое." "У искусства собственная, органическая жизнь." *Occasional Writings*, p. 124.

21. *Ibid.*, p. 86: "Как вы определите, вымеряете и взвесите—какую пользу принесла всему человечеству Илиада?" "Может быть, Лаура-то у Клавира и окажется на что-нибудь полезна?" *Occasional Writings*, p. 126.

22. *Dnevnik Pisatelya za 1877 god*, p. 510: "Говорю теперь не как литературный критик." Brasol, p. 967. *Dnevnik*, p. 523: "*Дон Жуана*" вы бы никогда не узнали, что это написал не испанец." Brasol, p. 977.

STRAKHOV

1. *Dnevnik pisatelya za 1877 god*, p. 270: "Литературной критики у меня не будет." Brasol, p. 779.

2. Letter, 28 November 1883, in *Tolstovsky Muzei*, Tom II. *Perepiska L. N. Tolstogo s N. N. Strakhovym* (St. Petersburg, 1914), pp. 307–8: "Ни хорошим, ни счастливым человеком. Он был зол, завистлив, развратен." "Лица, наиболее на него похожие—это герой *Записок из Подполья*, Свидригайлов в *Прест. и Нак.* и Ставрогин в *Бесах.*" For a sensible discussion of Strakhov's allegation see A. Yarmolinsky, *Dostoevsky: His Life and Art* (New York, 1957), pp. 299–301.

3. *Kriticheskie stati ob I. S. Turgeneve i L. N. Tolstom.* (*1862–1885*) (3d ed. St. Petersburg, 1895), p. 434: "Раскаявшийся нигилизм."

4. *Ibid.*, p. 296: "Лучший наш критик."

5. Best in *Iz istorii literaturnogo nigilizma 1861–1865* (St. Petersburg, 1890), pp. 11 ff.

6. *Ibid.*, pp. 19–20. The article dates from 1873.

7. *Kriticheskie stati*, p. 150: "Поэт часто не знает, что он хочет сказать."

8. *Ibid.*, pp. 19–20, 33, 38, 42–43, etc.

9. *Ibid.*, pp. 446, 175.

10. *Ibid.*, pp. 247, 279, 312, 344, 353, 372.

11. *Ibid.*, pp. 447–8, 453, 477 f.

12. Letter to N. N. Strakhov, 28 February 1869, in *Pisma*, 2, 167: "Единственного представителя нашей теперешней критики, которому принадлежит будущее." "Бесконечная, непосредственная симпатия к Льву Толстому."

13. *Tri rechi v pamyat Dostoevskogo*, in *Sobranie sochinenii* (St. Petersburg, n. d.), *3*, 169–205.

14. *Legenda o Velikom Inkvizitore F. M. Dostoevskogo*, first in *Russky Vestnik*, 1890. In book form, St. Petersburg, 1894.

15. "Zhestokii talant," first in *Otechestvennye zapiski*, 1882. In *Sochineniya*, *5* (1897), 7.

POTEBNYA AND VESELOVSKY

1. *Mysl i Yazyk* (4th ed. Odessa, 1922), pp. 144 ff.

2. *Boccaccio. Ego streda i sverstniki*, 2 vols. St. Petersburg, 1893–94.

3. E.g. "Iz vvedenia v istoricheskuyu poetiku" (1894) and "Tri glavy iz istoricheskoy poetiki" (1899) in *Sobranie sochinenii*, Vol. 1, St. Petersburg, 1913.

4. "Psykhologicheskii parallelism i ego formy v otrazheniyakh poeticheskago stila" (1898), *ibid.*, pp. 130–225.

5. "Poetika syuzhetov" (1897–1906), in *Sobranie sochinenii*, Vol. 2, St. Petersburg, 1913.

6. *V. A. Zhukovsky, poeziya chuvstva*, St. Petersburg, 1904.

TOLSTOY

1. Henri Peyre, *Writers and Their Critics* (Ithaca, N. Y., 1944), p. 166.

2. *PSS*, *30*, 28: "Сотни тысяч людей с молодых лет посвящают все свои жизни на то, чтобы выучиться очень быстро вертеть ногами (танцоры); другие (музыканты) на то, чтобы выучиться очень быстро перебирать клавиши или струны; третьи (живописцы) на то, чтобы уметь рисовать красками и писать всё, что они увидят; четвертые на то, чтобы уметь перевернуть всякую фразу на всякие лады и ко всякому слову подыскать рифму. И такие люди, часто очень добрые, умные, способные

на всякий полезный труд, дичают в этих искоючительных, одуряющих занятиях и становятся тупыми ко всем серьезным явлениям жизни, односторонними и вполне довольными собой специалистами, умеющими только вертеть ногами, языком или пальцами." *WA*, p. 74.

3. *PSS*, *30*, 65: "Вызвать в себе раз испытанное чувство и, вызвав его в себе, посредством движений, линий, красок, звуков, образов, выраженых словами, передать это чувство так, чтобы другие испытали то же чувство,—в этом состоит деятельность искусства. Искусство есть деятельность человеческая, состоящая в том, что один человек сознательно известными внешними знаками передает другим испытываемые им чувства, а другие люди заражаются этими чувствами и переживают их." *WA*, p. 123.

4. *L'Esthétique* (Paris, 1878), p. vii: "L'Artiste vraiment ému n'a doue qu'à s'abandonner à son émotion pour que son émotion devienne contagieuse."

5. *Ibid.*, p. 389: "L'art, c'est moins l'émotion communiquée, que l'intervention de la personnalité humaine dans cette émotion même."

6. *PSS*, *30*, 66: "Искусство не есть, как это говорят метафизики, проявление какой-то таинственной идеи, красоты, Бога; не есть, как это говорят эстетики-физиологи, игра, в которой человек выпускает излишек накопившейся энергии; не есть проявление эмоций внешними знаками; не есть производство приятных предметов, главное—не есть наслаждение, а есть необходимое для жизни и для движения к благу отдельного человека и человечества средство общения людей, соединяющее их в одних и тех же чувствах." *WA*, p. 123.

7. See this *History*, 2, 141–2, for further quotations and comment.

8. *PSS*, *30*, 78: "Полудикий рабовладельческий народец, очень хорошо изображавший наготу человеческого тела и строивший приятные на вид здания." *WA*, p. 140.

9. *PSS*, *30*, 71; *WA*, pp. 130–1.

10. *PSS*, *30*, 84: "И потому, если искусство есть важное дело, духовное благо, необходимое для всех людей, как религия (как это любят говорить поклонники искусства), то оно должно быть доступно всем людям. Если же оно не может сделаться искусством всего народа, то одно из двух: или искусство не есть то важное дело, каким его выставляют, или то искусство, которое мы называем искусством, не есть важное дело." *WA*, p. 148.

11. *PSS*, *30*, 87: "К чувству гордости, половой похоти и к чувству тоски жизни." *WA*, p. 152.

12. *PSS*, *30*, 96; *WA*, p. 163.
13. *PSS*, *30*, 107: "Единственное преимущество того искусства, которое я признаю перед декадентским, состоит в том, что это, мною признаваемое, искусство понятно несколько большему числу людей, чем теперешнее." *WA*, p. 175.
14. *PSS*, *30*, 108: "Сказать, что произведение искусства хорошо, но непонятно, всё равно, что сказать про какую-нибудь пищу, что она очень хороша, но люди не могут есть ее." *WA*, p. 176. *PSS*, *30*, 109: "Великие предметы искусства только потому и велики, что они доступны и понятны всем." *WA*, p. 177. *PSS*, *30*, 109: "Искусство действует на людей независимо от их степени развития и образования." *WA*, p. 178.
15. *PSS*, *30*, 123: "Художник, если он настоящий художник, передал в своем произведении другим людям то чувство, которое он пережил: что же тут объяснять?" *WA*, p. 194.
16. *PSS*, *30*, 149: "Настоящее произведение искусства делает то, что в сознании воспринимающего уничтожается разделение между ним и художником, и не только между ним и художником, но и между ним и всеми людьми, которые воспринимают то же произведение искусства. В этом-то освобождении личности от своего отделения от других людей, от своего одиночества, в этом-то слиянии личности с другими и заключается главная привлекательная сила и свойство искусства." *WA*, p. 228.
17. *PSS*, *30*, 149: "Особенность того чувства, которое передается; ясность передачи этого чувства и искренность художника, т. е. большей или меньшей силы, с которой художник сам испытывает чувство, которое передает. Чем особеннее передаваемое чувство, тем оно сильнее действует на воспринимающего." *WA*, pp. 228–9.
18. *PSS*, *30*, 116: "Лишено главного свойства произведения искусства—цельности, органичности, того, чтобы форма и содержание составляли одно неразрывное целое, выражающее чувство, которое испытал художник." *WA*, p. 186.
19. *PSS*, *30*, 117: "Только смешанное чувство страдания за другого и радости за себя, что я не страдаю,—подобное тому, которое мы испытываем при виде казни или которое римляне испытывали в своих цирках." *WA*, p. 188.
20. *PSS*, *30*, 158: "Чувства, вытекающие из сознания сыновности Богу и братства людей." *WA*, p. 240.
21. *PSS*, *30*, 160: "Образцы высшего, вытекающего из любви к Богу и ближнему, религиозного искусства, в области словесности я указал бы на 'Разбойников' Шиллера; из новейших—на 'Les pauvres gens' V. Hugo и его 'Misérables', на повести,

рассказы, романы Диккенса: 'Tale of two cities', 'Chimes' и др., на 'Хижину дяди Тома', на Достоевского, преимущественно его 'Мертвый дом', на 'Адам Бид' Джоржа Эллиота.'' *WA*, p. 242.

22. *PSS*, *30*, 161, 108, 163n; *WA*, pp. 243, 177, 246 n.

23. *PSS*, *30*, 194–5: ''Искусство, настоящее искусство, с помощью науки руководимое религией, должно сделать то, чтобы то мирное сожительство людей, которое соблюдается теперь внешними мерами,—судами, полицией, благотворительными учреждениями, инспекциями работ и т.п.,—достигалось свободной и радостной деятельностью людей. Искусство должно устранять насилие. Искусство должно сделать то, чтобы чувства братства и любви к ближним, доступные теперь только лучшим людям общества, стали привычными чувствами, инстинктом всех людей. Задача христианского искусства—осуществление братского единения людей.'' *WA*, pp. 286–8.

24. *PSS*, *46*, 71: ''У народа есть своя литература—прекрасная, неподражаемая. Нет потребности в высшей литературе, и нет ее.''

25. *PSS*, *8*, 114: ''Кто это сказал, почему, чем это доказано? Это только изворот, лазейка из безвыходного положения, в которое привела нас ложность направления, исключительная принадлежность нашего искусства одному классу. Почему красота солнца, красота человеческого лица, красота звуков народной песни, красота поступка любви и самоотвержения доступны всякому и не требуют подготовки?''

26. *PSS*, *35*, 239, 246, 267 f., 272. Cf. *Recollections and Essays*, trans. Aylmer Maude (Oxford, 1937), pp. 338, 349, 377 f., 382.

27. *PSS*, *30*, 4: ''Нравственного отношения автора к предмету.'' *WA*, p. 21; *PSS*, *30*, 7; *WA*, p. 24; *PSS*, *30*, 9; *WA*, p. 26; *PSS*, *30*, 18: ''Но Мопассан был талант, т.е. видел вещи в их сущности, и потому невольно открывал истину.'' *WA*, p. 38; *PSS*, *30*, 21: ''Он хотел восхвалять любовь, но чем больше узнавал, тем больше проклинал ее.'' *WA*, p. 41.

28. *Ob iskusstve*, 2, 161: ''Он хотел свалить Душечку, и обратил на нее усиленное внимание поэта и вознес ее.'' *WA*, p. 327.

29. *Ibid.*, 2, 357, 359: ''Ницше совершенно сумасшедший . . . безнравственная, грубая, напыщенная, бессвязная болтовня Ницше.''

30. *Ibid.*, 2, 213: ''Его драмы я тоже все читал, и его поэма 'Бранд', . . . все выдуманы, фальшивы и даже очень дурно написаны в том смысле, что все характеры не верны и не выдержаны.''

31. To Dušan Makovický, 20 May 1908, quoted in K. N. Lomunov,

"Tolstoy v borbe protiv dekadentskogo iskusstva," in *Lev Tolstoy. Sbornik* (Moscow, 1951), p. 67: "Совершенное сумасшедствие, набор слов."

32. *Ob iskusstve*, 2, 363, 365, 370, 148, 175, etc.
33. *Ibid.*, 2, 145: "Но ваши пьесы еще хуже."
34. *Ibid.*, 2, 199: "Это возмутительная гадость."
35. *Ibid.*, 2, 469: "Последний, долженствующий быть самым трогательным, эпизод рассказа состоит в том, что Юлиан ложится на одну постель с прокаженным и согревает его своим телом. Прокаженный этот—Христос, который уносит с собой Юлиана на небо. Все это описано с большим мастерством, но я всегда остаюсь совершенно холоден при чтении этого рассказа. Я чувствую, что автор сам не сделал бы и даже не желал бы сделать того, что сделал его герой, и потому и мне не хочется этого сделать, и я не испытывал никакого волнения при чтении этого удивительного подвига."

BIBLIOGRAPHY: GERMAN CRITICISM

There is no general book. The 4th volume of Bruno Marckwardt's *Geschichte der deutschen Poetik* (Berlin, 1959) covers our period. The book is instructive but excessively schematic and very provincial. For an anthology see Hans Mayer, *Meisterwerke deutscher Literaturkritik* (Berlin, 1959), Vol. 2, which does not include Nietzsche, Dilthey, and Hillebrand. There is something in Erich Rothacker, *Einleitung in die Geisteswissenschaften,* 2d ed. Tübingen, 1930; in Vol. 2 of K. G. Just, "Essay," in *Deutsche Philologie im Aufriss* (Berlin, 1955), and in Fritz Martini, *Deutsche Literatur im bürgerlichen Realismus, 1848–1898,* Stuttgart, 1962; and his "Zur Theorie des Romans im deutschen Realismus," *Festschrift für Eduard Berend* (Weimar, 1959), pp. 272–96.

Hettner: see Ernst Glaser-Gerhard, *Hermann Hettner und Gottfried Keller,* Weida i. Thüringen, 1929; Rudolf Unger, "Hermann Hettner," in *Aufsätze zur Literatur- und Geistesgeschichte* (Berlin, 1929), pp. 163–73; and Jürgen Jahn, "Einleitung," *Schriften zur Literatur,* Berlin, 1959 (Marxist slant).

On Scherer, see Rothacker, pp. 207–53, for an excellent discussion. Wilhelm Dilthey, "Wilhelm Scherer zum persönlichen Gedächtnis," in *Deutsche Rundschau, 49* (1886), 132–46. Peter Salm, "The Literary Theories of Scherer, Walzel and Staiger," Yale diss., 1959.

Haym: *Kritische Schriften,* ed. E. Howald, Zurich, 1963. Hans Rosenberg, *Rudolf Haym und die Anfänge des klassischen Liberalismus,* Munich, 1933 (mainly political, up to 1850). Wolfgang Harich, *Rudolf Haym und sein Herderbuch,* Berlin, 1955 (Marxist).

Ludwig: I quote *Gesammelte Schriften,* ed. Adolf Stern, 6 vols. Leipzig, 1891. On Ludwig:

Kurt Adams, *Otto Ludwigs Theorie des Dramas,* Greifswald, 1912.

Léon Mis, *Les Etudes sur Shakespeare d'Otto Ludwig,* Lille, 1922. Contains MS material.

Gaston Raphael, "Les *Shakespearestudien* d'Otto Ludwig et le *Shakespeare* de Gervinus," in *Mélanges offerts à Charles Andler* (Paris, 1924), pp. 291–310.

Walter Silz, "Otto Ludwig and the Process of Poetic Creation," *PMLA, 60* (1945), 860–78.

Alfred Schwarz, "Otto Ludwig's Shakespearean Criticism," in *Perspectives of Criticism,* ed. Harry Levin (Cambridge, Mass., 1950), pp. 85–102.

Spielhagen: Winfried Hellmann, "Objektivität, Subjektivität und Erzählkunst, Zur Romantheorie Friedrich Spielhagens," in *Wesen und Wirklichkeit des Menschen, Festschrift für Helmuth Plessner,* ed. K. Ziegler (Gottingen, 1957), pp. 340–97. H. H. Hughes, "Wilhelm von Humboldt's Influence on Spielhagen's Esthetics," *Germanic Review, 5* (1930), 213 ff.

Hillebrand:

Heinrich Homberger, "Karl Hillebrand," in Hillebrand, *Zeiten, Völker und Menschen,* (4th ed. 7 vols. Strasbourg, 1898), *1,* 415–62.

Hermann Uhde-Bernays, "Nachwort," in Karl Hillebrand, *Unbekannte Essays* (Bern, 1955), pp. 283–373.

Wolfram Mauser, *Karl Hillebrand, Leben, Werk, Wirkung,* in *Gesetz und Wandel,* Innsbrucker literarhistorische Arbeiten, ed. K. K. Klein and E. Thurnher, Vol. 1, Dornbirn, 1960.

Theodor Fontane is quoted from *Schriften zur Literatur,* ed. Hans-Heinrich Reuter, Berlin, 1960 (Marxist introduction). On Fontane, see Bertha E. Trebein, *Theodor Fontane as a Critic of Drama,* New York, 1916. Joachim Biener, *Fontane als Literaturkritiker,* in Vol. 4 of *Wir Diskutieren: Eine Schriftenreihe,* ed. Fritz Zschech, Rudolstadt. 1956 (Marxist).

On naturalism see Walter Linden, ed., *Naturalismus,* Leipzig, 1936 (an anthology, part of *Deutsche Literatur in Entwicklungsreihen).* Helmut Kasten, *Die Idee der Dichtung und des Dichters in den literarische Theorien des sogennanten "Deutschen Naturalismus,"* Königsberg diss., 1938.

Brahm: *Kritiken und Essays.* ed. F. Martini, Zurich, 1964. Oskar Koplowitz, *Otto Brahm als Theaterkritiker,* Zurich, 1936. Basler *Bei-*

träge zur deutschen Literatur und Geistesgeschichte, ed. F. Zinkernagel, Vol. 3. Maxim Newmark, *Otto Brahm: The Man and the Critic,* New York, 1937.

Nordau: G. B. Shaw, *The Sanity of Art* (1895), reprinted in Vol. 19 of *The Collected Works,* Ayot St. Lawrence Edition, New York, 1931.

Mehring: *Gesammelte Schriften,* ed. Th. Höhle, H. Koch, and J. Schleifstein, 14 vols. Berlin, 1961–65; still incomplete.

Georg Lukács, *Beiträge zur Geschichte der Asthetik* (Berlin, 1954), pp. 318–403 (dates from 1933; Marxist).

Peter Demetz, *Marx, Engels und die Dichter* (Stuttgart, 1959), pp. 238–49.

Hans Koch, *Franz Mehrings Beitrag zur marxistischen Literaturtheorie,* Berlin, 1959 (Full bibliography of articles; Marxist).

NOTES: GERMAN CRITICISM

1. *Literaturgeschichte des achtzehnten Jahrhunderts* (Braunschweig, 1856–70, 2, 129: "In England und Deutschland liest und kennt man sie nicht mehr, aber man schmäht sie." Page 130: "Ein unverwüstlicher Kern von Wahrheit, hochherzige Begeisterung und Thatkraft."

2. *Ibid.,* 2, 515: "Man sollte daher endlich einmal aufhören, immer nur von dem auflösenden, zersetzenden, verneinenden Wesen, von der Leichtfertigkeit und Frechheit der französischen Aufklärer zu sprechen."

3. *Ibid., 1,* 232: "Äusserst flach und trocken verständig." On Sterne, pp. 478–90.

4. *Schriften zur Literatur* (Berlin, 1959), p. 33.

5. *Ibid.,* pp. 21, 41, 47, 49: "Kunstwissenschaft."

6. *Ibid.,* p. 63.

7. *Ibid.,* pp. 64, 102, 108.

8. *Ibid.,* pp. 156, 163, 165: "Eine grosse und freie Nation."

9. See R. Woerner, *Henrik Ibsen* (2 vols. Munich, 1900–10), *1,* 52, 107; 2, 93.

10. See Ernst Glaser-Gerhard, bibliography, above, and the same author's, "Briefe von und an Gottfried Keller: Aus Hermann Hettners Nachlass," *Euphorion, 28* (1927), 411–70.

11. *Schriften zur Literatur,* pp. 194–95: "Stimmungen und Bedürfnisse."

12. *Ibid.,* pp. 209, 225, 237.

13. *Ibid.,* p. 241: "Die verklärende Spiegelung der realen Weltverhältnisse." On Wagner, p. 264.

14. *Literaturgeschichte* (in n. 1, above), *4,* 486: "Das gebildeste und geistig freieste Volk der Erde."

15. *Ibid.*, *5*, 15: "An fester Sicherheit und elementarer Kraft des dichterischen Gestaltens; aber an Tiefe und Weite des geistigen Gehalts, an Hoheit und Reinheit des Seelenlebens überragt er ihn."

16. *Ibid.*, *6*, 76; "Die hohe Idealität der besten italienischen Renaissance."

17. *Ibid.*, *6*, 287, 248.

18. *Ibid.*, *6*, 301, 308–09, 326, 333.

19. *Ibid.*, *6*, 536–38: "Prädestinierte fatalistische Naturverzauberung."

20. *Ibid.*, *4*, 402: "Vom Himmel gefallen." Also *4*, 107–08.

21. Special chapter on art in *6*, 457–86.

22. *Kleine Schriften* (2 vols. Berlin, 1893), *1*, 169–75.

23. On Roscher, *ibid.*, and *Poetik* (Berlin, 1888), pp. 121 ff.

24. *Aufsätze über Goethe* (Berlin, 1886), p. 127: "Ob die allgemeine Gesetzlichkeit der Natur sich auch auf die poetischen Productionen erstreckt, oder ob für die Willkür der Phantasie eine Ausnahmsstelle im Weltplan offen gehalten ist."

25. *Kleine Schriften*, *1*, 109: "Den Satz *individuum est ineffabile* so viel als möglich, wenn auch nur immer annähernd, zu widerlegen." Said about Lachmann, but obviously Scherer's own ideal.

26. *Aufsätze über Goethe*, p. 15.

27. *Ibid.*, p. 128: "Man kann in sorgfältiger und besonnener Aufsuchung von Ähnlichkeiten in dem Leben und der Bildung eines Dichters einerseits und in seinen Werken andererseits gar nicht weit genug gehen. . . . Die Kraft der Phantasie ist nichts anderes als die Kraft des Gedächtnisses . . . Die Production der Phantasie ist im wesentlichen Reproduction."

28. *Kleine Schriften*, *1*, 675. *Geschichte der deutschen Litteratur* (5th ed. Berlin, 1889), pp. 18–20.

29. *Kleine Schriften*, *1*, 189.

30. *Poetik*, p. 32: "Die Lehre von der gebundenen Rede; ausserdem aber von einigen Anwendungen der ungebundenen, welche mit den Anwendungen der gebundenen in naher Verwandtschaft stehen."

31. *Ibid.*, p. 64: "Eine Poesie, von der gesagt werden kann, dass sie auf die edelsten Menschen aller Zeiten gewirkt hat, is gewiss werthvoller als eine andere."

32. *Ibid.*, p. 113: "Die Poesie entspringt aus der Heiterkeit und wirkt auf die Mehrzahl der Menschen als Vergnügen."

33. *Ibid.*, p. 121: "Waare," "Tauschwerth."

34. *Ibid.*, pp. 150, 157, etc. Page 148: "Natur, Kapital, Arbeit."

35. *Ibid.*, p. 199: "Die aesthetischen Hilfen." Page 204: "Innere Form? Die specifische Auffassung des Gegenstandes durch den Dichter."

36. *Ibid.*, p. 205: "Die Stoffe." Page 209: "Botanik. Mignons "Kennst Du das Land?" Page 212: "Allgemeine Motivenlehre. . . . Ein elementarer, in sich einheitlicher Theil eines poetischen Stoffes."

37. *Ibid.*, pp. 214–15, 228, 230–32, 235 ff. Page 216: "Figuren der Verwicklung." Page 233: "Manier."

38. *Denkmäler deutscher Poesie und Prosa aus dem VIII–XII Jahrhundert.* Berlin, 1864. *Zur Geschichte der deutschen Sprache,* Berlin, 1868.

39. *Geschichte, der deutscher Literatur,* pp. 536–37, 591, 718–19.

40. *Zur Geschichte der deutschen Sprache,* pp. v–ix. "Ein fester nationale Lebensplan. . . . Ein System der nationalen Ethik . . . Eine nationale Güter- und Pflichtenlehre."

41. *Geschichte der deutschen Literatur,* p. 576: "Der Gipfel unserer ganzen neueren Kunst . . . Der homerische Ton ist für immer verbunden mit dem besten Gehalt unseres häuslichen Lebens."

42. *Ibid.*, p. 539: "Er erhob die Dramatik Racines auf eine höhere Stufe."

43. *Vorträge und Aufsätze zur Geschichte des geistigen Lebens in Deutschland und Oesterreich* (Berlin, 1874), pp. 193–308.

44. *Geschichte der deutschen Literatur,* pp. 697–98. *Vorträge und Aufsätze,* p. 252: "Ein österreichischer Bureaukrat der alten Schule voll kleinlicher Bedenklichkeit."

45. *Geschichte,* pp. 394, 418, 518, 718–20.

46. *Ibid.*, pp. 534–35, 712–13.

47. *Ibid.*, p. 424.

48. *Ibid.*, p. 693: "Colossalische Figuren."

49. See *Aus Goethes Frühzeit* (Strasbourg, 1879), esp. p. 99: "Der prosaische Faust (1772)."

50. *Aufsätze über Goethe,* p. 307: "Kann ein naives Mädchen eine so wohlgegliederte Uebersicht von dem Zustand ihres Innern geben? . . . Gretchen selbst kann doch nicht dichten!" Page 308: "Idealistische Fictionen."

51. *Geschichte,* pp. 699, 679. Page 608: "Das höchste Werk reiner Kunst."

52. *Ibid.*, p. 655. On Hölderlin see *Vorträge und Aufsätze,* pp. 346–55. The remarks in *Geschichte* are more favorable (pp. 644–45, 669). On Freytag see *Kleine Schriften,* 2, 3–39. On Geibel, *Rede auf Geibel,* Berlin, 1884.

53. *Charakteristiken* (Berlin, 1902), *1*, 466: "Entwicklungsgeschichte des geistigen Lebens eines Volkes mit vergleichenden Ausblicken auf die andern Nationallitteraturen." "Vererbung." "Anpassung."

54. Berlin, 1900; e.g. pp. 801–02 on Sudermann at Lake Como. Page

690 on Scherer. Page 416, Keller, "der kleine Mann mit den kurzen Beinen." Page 548 on the beards of Jordan and Hamerling.

1. Rudolf Haym, *Aus meinem Leben* (Berlin, 1902), p. 218: "Eine Geschichte der Entwicklung des deutschen Geistes im realistischen Sinne."

2. *Wilhelm von Humboldt* (Berlin, 1856), p. vi: "Wesentlich historisch. Ein Individuum stellt sich nur dar, indem es sich vor unsren Augen entwickelt. Es entwickelt sich vor Allem aus dem Kern seines eignen Wesens; es entwickelt sich zugleich mit den Schicksalen des äusseren Lebens, an den Bildungseinflüssen des Jahrhunderts, im Zusammenhang mit den allgemeinen geschichtlichen Ereignissen und Verhältnissen."

3. *Aus meinem Leben*, p. 255: "Wie, wenn überall die Realitäten aufgedeckt würden, deren gedankenhaftes Spiegelbild nur die Abstraktionswelt der grossen Denker gewesen sei? wenn man überall den Nimbus des Ewig-Gültigen zerstörte und ihn gegen die Erkenntniss des Zeitlich-Wirklichen, das dahinter stecke, vertauschte, wenn es ausgesprochen würde, dass Platon seine 'Ideen' den hohen Werken abgeschaut habe, die die Akropolis schmückten, oder dass der Kantsche kategorische Imperativ nichts anderes als die Verallgemeinerung der im Staat und Heer des grossen Friedrich herrschenden Zucht sei?"

4. *Gesammelte Aufsätze* (Berlin, 1903), pp. 355–407. Page 362: "Der Selbstdenker schiebt oft zu sehr den urteilenden Erzähler, den Berichterstatter bei Seite."

5. *Ausgewählter Briefwechsel*, ed. Hans Rosenberg (Stuttgart, 1930), pp. 355, 350.

6. See elaborate unfavorable analyses of Schopenhauer and Hartmann (1864 and 1873) in *Gesammelte Aufsätze*, pp. 239–354, 461–592. Rejections of French positivism in *Briefwechsel*, pp. 182, 184–85, 212.

1. Arthur Eloesser, in *Ludwigs Werke* (Berlin, 1908), *4*, 15: "Eine der höchsten kritischen Leistungen der Weltliteratur."

2. *Gesammelte Schriften, 6*, 215, 219: "Ein tiefes, mildes Goldgelb, oder ein glühendes Karmosin." "Das Farben- und Formenspektrum." "Die Fabel erfand sich, und ihre Erfindung war nichts andres, als das Entstehen und Fertigwerden der Gestalt und Stellung."

3. *Ibid., 6*, 221: "Gefahren der Reflexion."

4. Letter to Berthold Auerbach (1860), in *Gesammelte Schriften, 6*, 446. See article by Gaston Raphael in bibliography, above.

5. *Gesammelte Schriften, 5*, 163: "Der immer notwendige Nexus von Schuld aus Leidenschaft und von Leiden aus Schuld."

6. *Ibid.*, "Die äussere Begebenheit ist nur ein Symbol der notwendig

innern." Also 5, 424: "Hat der Dichter die Schuld, so hat er das ganze Werk, es liegt darin, wie der Baum in seinem Samen."

7. *Ibid.*, 5, 68: "Auch der Kausalnexus muss durchaus typischer Natur sein . . . Ist die Geschlossenheit, Ganzheit, Einheit, Vollständigkeit, Übereinstimmung und Notwendigkeit, d. i. die poetische Wahrheit gesetzt."

8. *Ibid.*, 5, 80: "Eine Welt, deren geheimste Motive uns vor den Augen liegen . . . wir sehen nichts, was uns an der Vernünftigkeit der Weltordnung zweifeln machen könnte."

9. *Ibid.*, 5, 458–62: "Poetischer Realismus, künstlerischer Realismus."

10. See especially "Die dramatische Aufgaben der Zeit: mein Wille und Weg" (1858–59), a long piece destined for *Die Grenzboten*, 5, 35–61; cf. 5, 158, 162 etc.

11. *Ibid.*, 5, 83: "Sozusagen ein jüngster Tag."

12. *Ibid.*, 5, 104–05: "Schuld und Strafe proportioniert Shakespeare in jeder Person jedes Stückes. Wie gelind ist die Strafe der Desdemona, der Cordelia für geringe Schuld; wie furchtbar die Macbeths."

13. *Ibid.*, 5, 227: "Die That selbst ohne das Wehren, das Winden and all den widerlichen Beisatz, den solcher Fall in der Wirklichkeit hat."

14. *Othello*, V, 2, lines 79, 81, 120.

15. *Gesammelte Schriften*, 5, 124: "In jeder Trägodie, wie sich ein Mensch, ein Leiden zuzieht, das er vermeiden konnte, und mit diesem Leiden nun kämpft bis zu seinem Untergange."

16. *Ibid.*, 5, 165–66: "Wie das Übermass von Reflexion und die Abschwächung der Thatkraft durch philosophisches Grübeln den Menschen zu Grunde richten kann bei den schönsten Naturanlagen, bei aller Gunst des Glückes."

17. *Ibid.*, 5, 249.

18. *Ibid.*, 5, 69–70.

19. *Ibid.*, 5, 171: "Er sieht Situation und Schuld, er kann den Rechnungsansatz selbst machen und nachrechnen von Ziffer zu Ziffer, von Position zu Position."

20. *Ibid.*, 5, 257, 96, 303; 6, 415–16.

21. *Ibid.*, 5, 132: "Die Prachtmantel, die den Pferden bei mittelalterliche Festen umgehängt wurden; man sieht kein Bein, vom Halse kaum etwas, kaum genug, um zu erraten, welche Art Geschöpf eigentlich darunter steckt."

22. *Ibid.*, 5, 323.

23. *Ibid.*, 6, 217, 94.

24. *Ibid.*, 6, 202–06: "Formen der Erzählung." "Die szenische Erzählung."

25. *Ibid., 6, 320.*

26. *Die Technik des Dramas* (3d ed. Leipzig, 1876), p. 75: "Ein tüchtiger Mann . . . mit fröhlichem Herzen an einen Stoff gehen."

27. *Ibid.*, p. 79: "Der moderne Dichter hat dem Zuschauer die stolze Freude zu bereiten, dass die Welt, in welche er ihn einführt, durchaus den idealen Forderungen entspricht, welche Gemüth und Urtheil der Hörer gegenüber den Ereignissen der Wirklichkeit erheben." "Die Einheit des Göttlichen und Vernünftigen."

28. *Grundzüge der verlorenen Abhandlung des Aristoteles über Wirkung der Tragödie*, Breslau, 1857.

29. *Technik des Dramas*, p. 81: "Fröhliche Rührigkeit."

30. *Ibid.*, p. 105: "Das erregende Moment." Page 112: "Das tragische Moment," Page 116: "Das Moment der letzten Spannung."

31. *Ibid.*, pp. 301, 305.

32. "Über die Objektivität im Roman," in *Vermischte Schriften* (Berlin, 1864), pp. 174–91.

33. *Ibid.*, p. 174: "Aufhört ein Kunstwerk zu sein." Pages 176, 179: "Jeder der vorgeführten Charaktere muss durch das, was er thut und sagt, sich selbst vollkommen erklären."

34. *Ibid.*, p. 179: "Die Kongruenz zwischen Idee und Form."

35. *Ibid.*, pp. 187, 192, 196–97.

1. Ottfried Müller, *Histoire de la littérature grecque*, Paris 1865. Hillebrand's introduction, translated into German, is in *Unbekannte Essays*, ed. Hermann Uhde-Bernays (Bern, 1955), pp. 184–241.

2. *North American Review*, July 1872, October 1872, April 1873. Also in *Unbekannte Essays*, pp. 82–183.

3. *Zeiten, Völker und Menschen* (7 vols. Strasbourg, 1874–85), *2*, 443–45.

4. *Ibid., 2*, 300–26: "Über historisches Wissen und historischen Sinn." Page 309: "Wir sind . . . entkuttete Schulmeister; daher unsere Wuth gegen die Schulstube."

5. *Ibid., 2*, 324; *3*, 303–04. etc. See, e.g. the unfriendly view of Guizot in *5*, 48–72.

6. *Ibid., 2*, 90–108; *6*, 173–216.

7. *Ibid., 2*, 197–280, esp. 218, 228, 256.

8. *Ibid., 6*, 1–47, esp. 15, 31, 37.

9. *Ibid., 6*, 20: "Die vielleicht bleibendsten Schriftwerke des Jahrhunderts."

10. *Ibid., 2*, 165–83, esp. 167, "Die bedauerliche Verirrung," and 170.

11. *Ibid., 1*, 175–76.

12. *Ibid., 3*, 128–81, 341 ff., and esp. 416–17.

1. *Schriften zur Literatur* (Berlin, 1960), p. 207: "Die Erfüllung Ibsens." Page 206: "Es ist töricht, in naturalistischen Derbheiten immer Kunstlosigkeit zu vermuten. Im Gegenteil, richtig angewandt . . . sind sie ein Beweis höchster Kunst."

2. *Ibid.,* pp. 10, 12 ff. Page 4: "Der Realismus in der Kunst ist so alt als die Kunst selbst, ja, noch mehr; er ist die Kunst." Page 9: "Die Widerspiegelung alles wirklichen Lebens, aller wahren Kräfte und Interessen im Elemente der Kunst . . . Die Lüge, das Forcierte, das Nebelhafte, das Abgestorbene." Page 6: "Vertreter des Realismus."

3. *Ibid.,* p. 109: "Ein Leben, eine Gesellschaft, einen Kreis von Menschen zu schildern, der ein unverzerrtes Widerspiel *des* Lebens ist, das wir führen. . . . Jener Intensität, Klarheit, Übersichtlichkeit und Abrundung und infolge davon jener Gefühlsintensität, die die verklärende Aufgabe der Kunst ist."

4. *Ibid.,* pp. 364, 113.

5. *Ibid.,* pp. 80 ff.

6. *Ibid.,* p. 98: "Erbarmungslos überliefert er die ganze Gotteswelt seinem Keller-Ton." Also pp. 93, 95.

7. *Ibid.,* pp. 217, 64–65, 83, 330–31.

8. *Ibid.,* p. 112.

9. *Ibid.,* p. 76: "Die Knöpfe des Rockes und die Venen der Hand zählen."

10. *Ibid.,* pp. 213 ff., 367, 358, 90–92, 346–47.

11. *Ibid.,* p. 116: "Man wird nicht gerührt, nicht erhoben, nicht erfreut, nicht angestachelt zu schönem Wetteifer oder aufgefordert, ein gleich Gutes und Schönes zu sehen."

12. "Offener Brief an den Fürsten Bismarck," in *Naturalismus,* ed. W. Linden (Leipzig, 1936), pp. 28–32.

13. *Naturalismus,* p. 59: "Zola ist der einzige Weltdichter seit Lord Byron."

14. *Ibid.,* pp. 64, 66.

15. Berlin, 1891, pp. 89, 96, 108, 119. The open letter to Zola in French is on pp. 129–49.

16. *Ibid.,* p. 58: "un coin de la nature vu à travers un témperament." Page 117: "Die Kunst hat die Tendenz, wieder die Natur zu sein. Sie wird sie nach Massgabe ihrer jedweiligen Reproductionsbedingungen und deren Handhabung."

17. *Ibid.,* pp. 108 ff.; Neue Folge, Berlin 1892, pp. 90–91. Also *1*, 118.

18. Holz reprinted his theoretical pronouncements in considerably revised form in Vol. 10 of *Das Werk* (Berlin, 1925) as *Die neμe Wortkunst.* Cf. pp. 494, 498–99, 538–39 for quotations from *Die Revolution der Lyrik* (1899), which I could not see in original edition.

19. First in *Deutsche Rundschau* (1882), also as a pamphlet (Leipzig, n.d.) and in *Kritische Schriften,* ed. Paul Schlenther (2 vols. Berlin, 1913–15), 2, 135–235. For Keller's reactions see Emil Ermatinger, *Gottfried Kellers Leben, Briefe und Tagebücher* (3 vols. Stuttgart, 1915–16), *3, 327, 342* f., 346 f., 390, 400 ff., 404, 428, 434, 447, 474, 480.

20. Berlin, 1884. Brahm revised the book considerably in the 2d. ed. Berlin, 1911.

21. Berlin, 1888. *1,* preface: "Wo er mit dem realistischen Prinzip unserer Tage zusammentrifft."

22. *Henrik Ibsen,* Berlin, 1887. The reviews are collected in *Kritische Schriften,* ed. Paul Schlenther, *1,* Berlin, 1913.

23. 2 vols. Berlin, 1892. Cf. 2, 161 ff.; *1,* 263.

24. *Ibid., 1,* 147. Comment on "Troy Town."

25. Stuttgart, 1893, p. 325: "Kräftigere und männlichere Töne" . . . "Mit dem Ansingen der farbigen Alpenkräuter und der heiligen Waldesschatten wurde der bürgerliche Schlendrian erst recht eingelullt."

26. See the bibliography, above.

27. On Schiller (1905) reprinted in *Gesammelte Schriften und Aufsätze* (Berlin, 1929), *1,* 117–276, esp. 266. On Kant see, e.g., *Beiträge zur Literaturgeschichte,* ed. W. Heist (Berlin, 1948), pp. 60–65.

28. See Hans Koch, quoted in the bibliography, above.

29. *Geschichte der deutschen Sozialdemokratie* (Stuttgart, 1897–98), *2,* 543: "Nur eine reaktionäre Erfindung, gerichtet gegen die grossen revolutionären Dichter des Bürgertums, die alle 'tendenziös' im Sinne ihrer Klasse gewesen sind."

30. *Ibid., 2,* 544–45: "Auf dem Boden der bürgerlichen Gesellschaft wollten sie bleiben, als ob mit der möglichst naturgetreuen Wiedergabe des kapitalistischen Schmutzes eine neue Ära der Kunst eröffnet werden könnte!"

31. *Gesammelte Schriften, 2,* 299: "Wenn die absteigende Bürgerklasse keine grosse Kunst mehr schaffen kann, so kann die aufsteigende Arbeiterklasse noch keine grosse Kunst schaffen."

32. "Goethe und die Gegenwart" (1899) in *Die Neue Zeit* Vol. 17, Pt. 2, pp. 676: "Der Tag, an dem das deutsche Volk sich ökonomisch und politisch befreit, wird Goethes Jubeltag werden, weil an ihm die Kunst zum Gemeingut des ganzen Volkes werden wird."

BIBLIOGRAPHY: WILHELM DILTHEY

I quote *Gesammelte Schriften,* 11 vols., but no volume 10 (Leipzig, 1922–36), as *GS.* Besides, I quote *Leben Schleiermachers,* ed. Hermann Mulert (2d ed. Berlin, 1922) as *LS; Das Erlebnis und die Dichtung* (9th ed. Leipzig, 1924) as *ED; Von deutscher Dichtung und Musik* (Leipzig, 1933) as *DD;* and *Die grosse Phantasiedichtung* (Göttingen, 1954) as *GP.* There are letters in *Der junge Dilthey: Ein Lebensbild in Briefen und Tagebüchern 1852–1897,* ed. Clara Misch, Leipzig, 1933; and *Briefwechsel zwischen Wilhelm Dilthey und dem Grafen Paul Yorck v. Wartenburg, 1877–1897,* Halle, 1923.

In English there is a good, largely expository book by H. A. Hodges, *The Philosophy of Wilhelm Dilthey* (London, 1952), which supersedes the same author's earlier *Wilhelm Dilthey: An Introduction,* London, 1944, 2d ed. 1949. There is a translation of *Das Wesen der Philosophie* as *The Essence of Philosophy* by S. A. Emery and W. T. Emery, Chapel Hill, 1954. See also R. G. Collingwood, *The Idea of History* (Oxford, 1946), pp. 171–76 (hostile), and Hajo Holborn, "Wilhelm Dilthey and the Critique of Historical Reason," *Journal of the History of Ideas, 11* (1950), 93–118 (sympathetic).

In German, Georg Misch's introduction to Vol. 5 of *Gesammelte Schriften* (117 pp.) and Otto Friedrich Bollnow, *Dilthey: Eine Einführung in seine Philosophie* (Leipzig, 1936, 2d ed. Stuttgart, 1955) stand out. There is good general comment in Erich Rothacker, *Einleitung in die Geisteswissenschaften* (2d ed. Tübingen, 1930), pp. 253–77. I found most of the German dissertations useless for my purposes. Anneliese Liebe, *Die Ästhetik Wilhelm Diltheys* (Halle, 1938), is quite uncritical; Heinz Nicolai, *Wilhelm Dilthey und das Problem der dichterischen Phantasie* (Munich, 1934), contains some useful criticism from the point of view of Gestalt psychology.

In Italian there is a fervid book by Lorenzo Giusso, *Wilhelm Dilthey e la filosofia come visione della vita* (Naples, 1930), and a critical essay by Carlo Antoni, in *Dallo Storicismo alla sociologia* (Florence, 1940, 2d ed. 1951), pp. 3–38, English trans., Detroit, 1959; W. Kluback, *Wilhelm Dilthey's Philosophy of History* (New York, 1956), translates Antoni without acknowledgment.

Ortega y Gasset wrote an essay, "Guillermo Dilthey y la Idea de la Vita" (1933), in *Obras completas, 6,* Madrid, 1946–47, English trans. by Hélène Weyl in *Concord and Liberty,* New York, 1946.

Since this chapter was written, Kurt Müller-Vollmer, *Towards a Phenomenological Theory of Literature: A Study of Wilhelm Dilthey's Poetik* (The Hague, 1963) was published. He takes issue with some of my interpretations published in a much abbreviated version as "Wilhelm Dilthey's Poetics and Literary Theory," in *Wächter und Hüter: Festschrift für Hermann J. Weigand,* ed. K. Reichardt, C. Faber du Faur, and H. Bluhm (New Haven, 1957), pp. 121–32. I am not convinced by Müller-Vollmer's arguments for a complete consistency and continuity of Dilthey's thinking on poetry.

NOTES: WILHELM DILTHEY

1. *GS, 6,* 103–241.

2. A paper on "Leibniz and his Age" in Vol. 3 contains a sketch of German 17th-century literature (1902); the long essay on Frederick the Great (1901) discusses German literature of the Enlightenment, and there is an essay on Carlyle (1890) in Vol. 4 which analyzes *Sartor Resartus.*

3. Vols. 5, 7, 8, or 11 respectively.

4. Reprinted in *DD,* viii–x.

5. *GS, 6,* 128: "Die Unterlage aller wahren Poesie ist sonach Erlebnis, lebendige Erfahrung."

6. *ED,* p. 239: "Die religiösen, die wissenschaftlichen, die philosophichen Bewegungen der Zeit."

7. *ED,* p. 65: "Die abstrakte Welt der moralischen Prinzipien."

8. *ED,* p. 442: "Wenn in Schillers philosophischen Gedichten aus der Welt der Ideen eine Stimmung kommt, unabhängig vom einzelnem Erlebnis."

9. *GS, 6,* 130: "Die tote Notiz eines Zeitungsblattes, under der Rubrik 'aus der Verbrecherwelt,' der dürre Bericht des Chronisten oder die groteske Sage (wird) zum Erlebnis."

10. *ED,* p. 444: "durch ein Einzelerlebnis, das von aussen bestimmt ist, oder durch Stimmungen, die von innen unabhängig von der äusseren Welt aufsteigen, oder auch durch eine Ideenmasse, sei sie geschichtlich oder philosophisch."

11. *ED,* p. 264: "Mephisto, Gretchen, das Motiv der Wahlverwandtschaften können Goethe in flüchtigen Lebensbegegnungen aufgeblitzt sein, welche für den Aufbau seines eigenen Lebens so gut wie nichts bedeuteten."

12. *GS, 6,* 316.

13. *ED,* p. 447: "Hölderlin dagegen verlor in Dithyramben wie 'der Archipelagus' den Massstab für das was in einem inneren Vorgang . . . von Stimmungen und Anschauungen verknüpft sein kann. Wir vermögen dann nicht mehr das umfangreiche Ganze nachzuerleben."

14. *GS, 6,* 317: "Uninteressiert heisst unpersönlich. . . . Also ist Uninteressiertheit nicht nur eine Eigenschaft des Eindrucks, sondern auch im Erlebnis des Schaffenden. . . . In der Loslösung des Phantasievorgangs von der Gelegenheit liegt Loslösung vom Persönlichen."

15. *GS, 7,* 85: "Dieses sind nicht die inneren Vorgänge in dem Dichter, sondern ein von diesen geschaffener, aber von ihnen ablösbarer Zusammenhang. . . . So ist der Gegenstand mit dem die Literaturgeschichte oder die Poetik zunächst zu tun hat, ganz unterschieden von psychischen Vorgängen im Dichter oder seinen Lesern."

16. *GS, 6,* 319: "Zusammenhang der Poetik von der Bedeutungslehre aus."

17. *GS, 6,* 107, 123, 127.

18. *GS, 6,* 196: "Unveränderliche Normen." Cf. *6,* 157.

19. *GS, 6,* 123–24.

20. *GS, 6,* 124: "Eine genealogische Gliederung der dichterischen Schulen. . . . Sie [die Poetik] vermag auch nicht die Veränderungen, die mit einem Typus oder einem Motiv vor sich gehen, in feste Reihen zu bringen."

21. *ED,* p. 183: "Ein Denken in Bildern."

22. *GS, 6,* 179: "Der Traum, dieser verborgene Poet in uns."

23. *GS, 6,* 90–102, a speech (1886), "Dichterische Einbildungskraft und Wahnsinn." Cf. p. 138.

24. *GS, 6,* 94: "Das Genie ist keine pathologische Erscheinung, sondern der gesunde, der vollkommene Mensch."

25. *GS, 6,* 94: "Grosse Energie des seelischen Zusammenhanges."

26. *GS, 6,* 150–55.

27. *GS, 6,* 163: "Die Gesetze, nach denen sich unter dem Einfluss des Gefühlslebens die Vorstellungen frei über die Grenzen des Wirklichen hinaus umwandeln."

28. *GS, 6,* 172–74.

29. *GS, 7,* 328–29: "Denn der Ausdruck quillt aus der Seele unmittelbar, ohne Reflexion."

30. *ED,* p. 236: "Das Erlebte geht hier voll und ganz in den Ausdruck ein."

31. *GS, 5,* 320: "In dieser von Lüge erfüllten menschlichen Gesellschaft ist ein solches Werk immer wahr [i.e. das Werk eines grossen Dichters]."

32. *GS, 7,* 207: "Wir treten in ein Gebiet, in dem die Täuschung endet."

33. *GS, 7,* 206: "Es hebt aus Tiefen, die das Bewusstsein nicht erhellt."

34. *GS, 6,* 187: "Die Personen handeln notwendig, wenn der Leser oder Zuschauer fühlt, dass er auch so handeln würde."

35. *GS, 5,* 279–80.

36. *GS, 5,* 279: "Eine Anleitung, zu sehen."

37. *GS, 6,* 100: "Die kernhafte Idealität des Kunstwerks liegt in dieser Symbolisierung eines ergreifenden innerern Zustandes durch Aussenbilder, in dieser Belebung äusserer Wirklichkeit durch einen hineingesehenen inneren Zustand."

38. *GS, 6,* 101.

39. *ED,* p.254: "Die erlebte Wirklichkeit in das Poetische zu erheben."

40. *GS, 6,* 201.

41. *GS, 6*, 228.

42. *GS, 6*, 271: "Eine innere Linienführung."

43. *ED*, pp. 189–90, 368.

44. *LS*, p. 194: "Auch die Dichtung spricht ein Allgemeines aus . . . in der Vorstellung *eines* Falles. . . . Was sie dann ausdrückt, ist das Lebensideal einer Epoche."

45. *ED*, p. 260: "Organ eines objektiven Weltverständnisses." Cf. 5, 274, 394.

46. *GS, 5*, 394: "Ein Seher, der den Sinn des Lebens erschaut."

47. *GS, 5*, 274: "Kein wissenschaftlicher Kopf kann je erschöpfen, und kein Fortschritt der Wissenschaft kann erreichen, was der Künstler über den Inhalt des Lebens zu sagen hat."

48. *GS, 6*, 131: "Es kann nie in Gedanken oder Idee aufgelöst werden; aber es kann nun durch Nachdenklichkeit, insbesondere durch Verallgemeinerung und Herstellung der Beziehungen, mit dem Ganzen des menschlichen Daseins in Verhältnis gesetzt und so in seinem Wesen, d. h. seiner Bedeutung verstanden werden."

49. *GS, 5*, 396.

50. *GS, 5*, 17: "Anschaulich."

51. "Aus der Zeit der Spinoza-studien Goethes" (1894), in *GS*, 2, 391–415.

52. *GP*, pp. 56–57, 72, 83.

53. *GS, 8*, 93: "So sehen Stendhal und Balzac im Leben ein aus der Nature selbst absichtslos, in dunklem Trieb geschaffenes Gewebe von Illusionen, Leidenschaften, Schönheit und Verderben . . . Goethe sieht in ihm eine gestaltende Kraft, welche die organischen Gebilde, die Entwicklung der Menschen, wie die Ordnungen der Gesellschaft in einem wertvollen Zusammenhang vereinigt; Corneille und Schiller sehen in ihm den Schauplatz heroischen Handelns."

54. *GS, 8*, 222: "Jede Weltanschauung ist historisch bedingt, sonach begrenzt, relativ. Eine furchtbare Anarchie des Denkens scheint hieraus hervorzugehen. . . . Es ist uns versagt, diese Seiten zusammenzuschauen. Das reine Licht der Wahrheit ist nur in verschieden gebrochenem Strahl für uns zu erblicken."

55. *GS, 7*, 290–91: "Das historische Bewusstsein von der Endlichkeit jeder geschichtlichen Erscheinung, jedes menschlichen oder gesellschaftlichen Zustandes, von der Relativität jeder Art von Glauben ist der letzte Schritt zur Befreiung des Menschen. . . . Das Leben wird frei vom Erkennen durch Begriffe; der Geist wird souverän allen Spinngeweben dogmatischen Denkens gegenüber. Jede Schönheit, jede Heiligkeit, jedes Opfer, nacherlebt und ausgelegt, eröffnet Perspektiven, die eine Realität aufschliessen. Und der Relativität gegenüber macht

sich die Kontinuität der schaffenden Kraft als die kernhafte historische Tatsache geltend."

56. *GS, 8,* 232: "Wir müssen die Philosophie selbst zum Gegenstand der Philosophie machen." For "Philosophie der Philosophie," see *GS, 8,* 204 ff.

57. *GS, 6,* 303: "Die Wunden heilen die sie geschlagen hat." This is said here of the comparative study of religions, but, as other contexts show, is true of all relativistic historicism. Cf. *GS, 8,* 232: "Das Messer des historischen Relativismus, welches alle Metaphysik und Religion gleichsam zerschnitten hat, muss auch die Heilung herbeiführen."

58. *GS, 5,* 9: "Wo sind die Mittel, die Anarchie der Überzeugungen, die hereinzubrechen droht, zu überwinden?"

59. *GS, 4,* 260: "Nur auf dem Standpunkt des Pantheismus ist eine Interpretation der Welt möglich, welche ihren Sinn vollständig erschöpft."

60. *GS, 6,* 241: "Es gibt einen Kern, in welchem die Bedeutung des Lebens, wie sie der Dichter darstellen möchte, für alle Zeiten dieselbe ist. Daher haben die grossen Dichter etwas Ewiges."

61. *GS, 6,* 232: "alle grosse und wahre Poesie [zeigt] gemeinsame Züge. Sie bedarf ebensowohl des Bewusstseins von der Freiheit und Verantwortlichkeit unserer Handlungen als dessen von dem Zusammenhang derselben nach Ursache und Wirkung. Die Lehre, dass wir in unseren Handlungen von aussen mechanisch bestimmt seien, wird nie bei einem grossen Dichter dauernde Überzeugung hervorrufen."

62. *GS, 6,* 202–03, 238: "Die geschichtliche Relativität auch der vollkommensten Form."

63. *GP,* p. 8: "Aus dem wirtschaftlichen, sozialen und politischen Leben in den einzelnen Staaten sind dann auch entscheidende Unterschiede ihrer Dichtung hervorgegangen."

64. *GS, 3,* 47: "mangelte die aus Leben und Gesellschaft entspringende freie Beweglichkeit des Gefühls."

65. *GS, 5,* 15.

66. *ED,* pp. 270–71.

67. *GS, 7,* 186: "Sie drückt sich aus in Stein, auf Leinwand, in Taten oder Worten. Sie objektiviert sich in Verfassung und Gesetzgebung der Nationen. . . . der Kreis, in welchem die Menschen dieses Zeitalters eingeschlossen sind."

68. *GS, 6,* 235–36.

69. *GS, 6,* 177. Cf. pp. 237 ff.

70. *GS, 5,* 224: "In den grossen schöpferischen Perioden tritt eine Steigerung ein, welche aus den früheren Stufen nicht abgeleitet werden kann."

71. *GS, 6,* 271.

72. *GS, 6,* 191: "Das abgeblasste Abbild jenes schöpferischen Vorganges."

73. *GS, 6,* 192–94.

74. *GS, 6,* 162–63: "Jedes Dichtwerk, das nicht nur vorübergehende Empfindungen ausdrücken, sondern eine andauernde Befriedigung hervorbringen will, [muss] in der Gleichgewichtslage oder in einem Lustzustande, jedenfalss also in einem versöhnenden Endzustande schliessen, läge auch dieser Endzustand nur in dem Gedanken, der über das Leben erhebt."

75. *GS, 6,* 163: "Von der Tragödie Shakespeares ist oft genug gründlich gezeigt worden, dass sie diesem ästhetischen Prinzip entspricht, und es ist in dem so untechnischen Bau des Faust doch ein einziger Vorteil, dass er ganz und voll diesem Schema des Gefühlsvorgangs entsprechend verläuft. Auch die epische Dichtung. . . . muss einer Sinfonie gleichen, in welcher eine Disharmonie nach der anderen sich auflöst und schliesslich in mächtigen harmonischen Akkorden das Ganze ausklingt."

76. This is pointed out and discussed by H. A. Hodges, *The Philosophy of Wilhelm Dilthey,* (London, 1952), p. 107.

77. *ED,* p. 197. "Es erhöht sein Daseinsgefühl."

78. *GS, 6,* 131: "Die Funktion der Poesie ist . . . dass sie diese Lebendigkeit in uns erhält, stärkt und wachruft. . . . die ganze Welt als Erlebnis zu geniessen. . . . Lebensgefühl ausstrahlend in der Helle des Bildes."

79. *GS, 5,* 186: "Der Styl eines Fresko von Michelangelo oder einer Fuge von Bach entspringt aus der Handlung einer grossen Seele, und die Auffassung dieser Kunstwerke teilt der Seele des Geniessenden eine bestimmte Form von Handlung mit, in welcher sie sich erweitert, steigert und gleichsam ausdehnt."

80. *GP,* 143–44: "Wertlos."

81. *GP,* p. 146: "in die freie Sphäre des Allgemeinen erhebt."

82. *GS, 5,* 275–76: "Erweitert den engen Umkreis von Erleben."

83. *GS, 6,* 100.

84. *GP,* p. 88.

85. *GS, 7,* 309: "Den Vorgang, in dem wir aus Zeichen, die von aussen gegeben sind, inneres erkennen, nennen wir Verstehen." Cf. *GS, 5,* 318, 332.

86. *GS, 7,* 191: "Das Verstehen ist ein Wiederfinden des Ich im Du."

87. *GS, 7,* 148: "Nur was der Geist geschaffen hat, versteht er."

88. *GS, 5,* 336.

89. *GS, 6,* 335–36: "Schöpferische Genialität."

90. *GS, 5,* 278: "Immer etwas Genialisches, d.h. sie erlangt erst durch

innere Verwandtschaft und Sympathie einen hohen Grad von Vollendung."

91. *GS, 7,* 217: "einen Autor besser zu verstehen als er sich selbst verstand." Cf. *GS, 5,* 335.

92. Dilthey ascribes the saying to Schleiermacher (*GS, 7,* 217), but F. O. Bollnow traces it to Kant. See "Was heisst einen Schriftsteller besser verstehen als er sich selbst verstanden hat?" in *Deutsche Vierteljahrschrift für Literaturwissenschaft und Geistesgeschichte, 18* (1940), 117–39.

93. *GS, 7,* 218: "So ist in allem Verstehen ein Irrationales, wie das Leben ein solches ist."

94. *GS, 5,* 225: "Die am meisten philosophische Form der Historie."

95. *GS, 7,* 199: "Die Selbstbiographie ist die höchste und am meisten instruktive Form, in welcher uns das Verstehen des Lebens entgegentritt."

96. *ED,* p. 267: "Kein Scheltwort [wird] Leben, Natur und Entwickelung Goethes zu Mitteln, seine Werke zu verstehen, herabzudrücken imstande sein."

97. *Philosophy of Wilhelm Dilthey,* p. 62.

98. *GS, 11,* 196: "Pedanten haben sich darüber ereifert, dass wir Heutige in ihr *über* Schriftsteller lesen, anstatt den Schriftsteller *selber.* . . . Als ob man nur das Recht hätte, eine Geschichte der französischen Revolution zu lesen . . . wenn man sie gesehen hat."

99. *GP,* p. 255: "Das vergleichende Studium des Kunstwerke aller Zeiten und Völker . . . das Material für eine induktive Ästhetik."

100. *GS, 11,* 198: "Allgemeine vergleichende Geschichte der Poesie nach ihren Stoffen und Formen. . . . Geschichte des geistigen Lebens."

101. *GP,* p. 112: "Der nordische Humor."

102. *ED,* p. 373: "Das schöne echt germanische Motiv."

103. *DD,* p. 334: "Der ursprüngliche Glaube germanischer Dichter und Denker."

104. *GP,* p. 116.

105. *ED,* p. 64: "Der eigenste Grundzug der deutschen Denkart, die Innerlichkeit des moralischen Bewusstseins."

106. *DD,* p. 335.

107. *ED,* p. 337. *ED,* pp. 125–26, 141, 383, 399, 152, 164, etc.

108. *GP,* p. 302: "Die Kunst its überall . . . Freude an der treuen Abbildung eines Wirklichen."

109. *GP,* p. 241.

110. *GP,* p. 303.

111. *DD,* p. 119.

112. *DD,* p. 140.

113. *GS, 5,* 336: "Nach dem Prinzip der Unabtrennbarkeit von Auf-
fassen und Wertgeben ist mit dem hermeneutischen Prozess die literarische Kritik notwendig verbunden, ihm immanent. Es gibt kein Verstehen ohne Wertgefühl—aber nur durch Vergleichung wird der Wert
objektiv und allgemeingültig festgestellt."

BIBLIOGRAPHY: FRIEDRICH NIETZSCHE

I quote from *Werke,* 19 vols. (Leipzig, 1903–19), as *W.* There is a useful *Nietzsche-Register,* ed. Richard Oehler (Leipzig, 1926), referring to
this standard edition. Note that the arrangement of MSS of the 1880's
under *Wille zur Macht* (in Vols. 15 and 16) is arbitrary. Cf. *Nietzsches
Werke,* ed. Karl Schlechta, 3 vols. Munich, 1954–56.

Among the hundreds of books on Nietzsche are Charles Andler,
Nietzsche: Sa vie et sa pensée, 6 vols., Paris, 1920–31; Ernst Bertram,
Nietzsche: Versuch einer Mythologie, Berlin, 1922; Karl Jaspers, *Nietzsche: Einführung in das Verständnis seines Philosophierens,* Berlin,
1936; Walter A. Kaufmann, *Nietzsche: Philosopher, Psychologist, Anti-
Christ,* Princeton, 1950. These stand out, though bafflingly diverse in
method and results.

On aesthetics, see Julius Zeitler, *Nietzsches Ästhetik,* Leipzig, 1900
(inadequate); Benno Filser, *Die Ästhetik Nietzsche's in der Geburt der
Tragödie,* Munich diss., Passau, 1915; and Georg Lukács, "Nietzsche als
Vorläufer der faschistischen Ästhetik," in *Beiträge zur Geschichte der
Ästhetik* (Berlin, 1954), pp. 286–317 (Marxist, violently polemical).

On literary criticism see Ingeborg Beithan (Mrs. Heinrich Henel),
Friedrich Nietzsche als Umwerter der deutschen Literatur, Heidelberg,
1933 (valuable); W. D. Williams, *Nietzsche and the French,* Oxford,
1952 (useful); and Elizabeth Welt, "Friedrich Nietzsche's Literary Criticism and its European Background," unpublished Yale diss., 1957.
Other topics:

Karl Joël, *Nietzsche und die Romantik,* Jena, 1905, 2d ed. 1923.

Ernst Howald, *Friedrich Nietzsche und die klassische Philologie,*
Gotha, 1920.

Ernst Bertram, "Nietzsches Goethebild," in *Festschrift für Berthold
Litzmann,* ed. Carl Enders (Bonn, 1920), pp. 318–61.

Gerhard Haeuptner, *Die Geschichtsansicht des jungen Nietzsche,*
Stuttgart, 1936.

Alfred von Martin, *Nietzsche und Burckhardt,* 3d ed. Basel, 1945.

Erich Heller, "Burckhardt and Nietzsche" and "Nietzsche and
Goethe," in *The Disinherited Mind* (Cambridge, Eng., 1952), pp.
53–69, 73–95.

Maria Bindschedler, *Nietzsche und die poetische Lüge,* Basel, 1954. Stanley Hubbard, *Nietzsche und Emerson,* Basel, 1958. Cf. my review in *Erasmus,* 13 (1960), 134–36.

NOTES: FRIEDRICH NIETZSCHE

1. See the bibliography, above.

2. *W, 1,* 58: "Der ewige Kern der Dinge, das Ding an sich" *W, 1,* 34: "Das Wahrhaft-Seiende und Ur-Eine . . . Das ewig Leidende und Widerspruchsvolle." Cf. *1,* 49: "Der Urwiderspruch und Urschmerz im Herzen des Ur-Einen." *1,* 42: "Weltgenius." *1,* 45: "Urkünstler der Welt."

3. *W, 1,* 168. Page 45: "Nur als ästhetisches Phänomen ist das Dasein und die Welt ewig gerechtfertigt." Cf. *1,* 8, 18.

4. *W, 1,* 25–26: "Kunsttriebe der Natur . . . ohne Vermittelung des menschlichen Künstlers." *1,* 24–25: "Die Kunstgewalt der ganzen Natur, zur höchsten Wonne-befriedigung des Ur-Einen, offenbart sich hier unter den Schauern des Rausches."

5. *W, 1,* 24, 26, 38.

6. *W, 1,* 28.

7. *W, 1,* 40.

8. *W, 1,* 41: "Aus dem Abgrunde des Seins."

9. *W, 1,* 46: "Bilderfunken um sich aussprüht." *1,* 48: "Entladung der Musik in Bildern." *1,* 48: "Die nachahmende Effulguration der Musik in Bildern und Begriffen."

10. *W, 1,* 31: "Nicht geboren zu sein, nicht zu sein, nichts zu sein . . . Das Zweitbeste . . . ist—bald zu sterben."

11. *W, 1,* 55: "Unzerstörbar mächtig und lustvoll."

12. The theories of the chorus are those of A. W. Schlegel and Schiller (in the preface to *Bride of Messina*). *W, 1,* 58: "verzaubert."

13. *W, 1,* 50, 52, etc.

14. *W, 1,* 61–62: "Der dionysische Chor entladet sich immer von neuem wieder in einer apollinischen Bilderwelt. . . . In mehreren aufeinander folgenden Entladungen strahlt dieser Urgrund der Tragödie jene Vision des Dramas aus."

15. *W, 1,* 70: "Die Neugierde, die lügnerische Vorspiegelung, die Verführbarkeit, die Lüsternheit."

16. *W, 1,* 74: "Die Grunderkenntniss von der Einheit alles Vorhandenen, die Betrachtung der Individuation als des Urgrundes des Übels, die Kunst als die freudige Hoffnung, dass der Bann der Individuation zu zerbrechen sei, als die Ahnung einer wiederhergestellten Einheit."

17. *W, 1,* 77, 78, 86, 97, 100, 108: "Die tragische Erkenntniss . . . braucht als Schutz und Heilmittel die Kunst."

18. *W, 1*, 109: "Der musik-treibende Sokrates." End of section 15.

19. *W, 1*, 130 ff., 138, 140, 153, 168: "Selbst das Hässliche und Disharmonische [ist] ein künstlerisches Spiel, welches der Wille, in der ewigen Fülle seiner Lust, mit sich selbst spielt."

20. *W, 1*, 20, 32, 33.

21. *W, 1*, 48: "Der Wille ist das an sich Unästhetische."

22. *W, 9*, 34: "Das Zerrbild des antiken Musikdramas."

23. Richard Wagner, *Gesammelte Schriften und Dichtungen* (Leipzig, 1872), *4*, 69 ff., on Oedipus.

24. *W, 9*, 140; *W 9*, 33–52; *17*, 291–326.

25. Howald, *Nietzsche*, p. 7 (and see n. 33 on p. 40) considers Nietzsche's philological attainments "average," his conclusions "incorrect."

26. F. Schlegel, *Prosaische Jugendschriften* ed. J. Minor (2 vols. Vienna, 1882), *1*, 140, 241 ff. Schelling, *Sämtliche Werke* (Stuttgart, 1856–61), Abt. II, Vol 4, p. 25, *Philosophie der Offenbarung*, speaks of Apollonian ecstasy differing from Dionysiac by being "zugleich trunken und nüchtern." See Otto Kein, *Das Apollinische und Dionysische bei Nietzsche und Schelling* (Berlin, 1935), p. 13.

27. See W. Rehm, *Griechentum und Goethezeit*, 3d ed. Bern, 1952. W. Rehm, *Götterstille und Göttertrauer*, Bern, 1951. For a modern view see Walter F. Otto, *Dionysus: Mythos und Kultus*, Frankfurt am Main, 1933.

28. Ulrich von Wilamowitz-Möllendorf, *Zukunftsphilologie!* (Berlin, 1872), p. 23: "Wer ist darin [den Choephoren], wer ist in Schutzflehenden Eumeniden Persern, wer ist in Aiax Elektra Philoktetes tragischer avatâra des Dionysos Zagreus?"

29. *W, 18*, 1–198, first published in 1907. This course, which has received no attention, contains interesting reflections on the Greek public, the rise of the reading public, the social provenience of Greek writers, and a decided rejection of Friedrich Schlegel's view of the evolution of genres in Greece. "History is irrational, unpredictable" (p. 169); decay is usual, great artists are exceptions.

30. *W, 18*, 42: "Dem Menschen . . . geht momentan eine ganz verklärte Ordnung der Dinge auf; Schuld, Schicksal, Untergang des Helden sind nur Mittel, um jenen Blick in die verklärte Welt zu tun."

31. *W, 1*, 4: "Bilderwütig und bilderwirrig."

32. E.g. *W, 1*, 156; *2*, 192–93; *5*, 110 (where, oddly enough, Aristotle is interpreted as wanting tragedy to excite pity and fear); *8*, 222; *9*, 45, 267, etc.

33. *W, 2*, 134: "Ahnungen"; *2*, 221.

34. *W, 2*, 166: "Ein zurückbleibendes Wesen, weil er beim Spiel stehen bleibt, welches zur Jugend und Kindheit gehört."

35. *W*, 7, 257; 2, 192 "zügellos"; *3*, 171–72; *18*, 147; 7, 108; *18*, 145; *5*, 35 "Kammerdiener irgendeiner Moral"; *5*, 118; *5*, 311–12.

36. *W*, *6*, 125: "Die Dichter lügen zuviel." *6*, 188: "Ach, es giebt so viel Dinge zwischen Himmel und Erde, von denen sich nur die Dichter etwas haben träumen lassen."

37. *W*, *3*, 105: "Betrüger." *6*, 437: "Dass ich verbannt sei von aller Wahrheit, Nur Narr! Nur Dichter!" *5*, 163: "Gott ist tot." *5*, 271; *6*, 12, and *passim*.

38. *W*, *3*, 57: "phantastische Nationalökonomen . . . an dem schönen Menschenbilde weiterdichten."

39. *W*, *3*, 95: "Alles Hässliche verbergen oder umdeuten."

40. *W*, *16*, 272: "das grosse Stimulans des Lebens." *16*, 268: "Ein tonicum." *16*, 247: "Bejahung, Segnung, Vergöttlichung des Daseins."

41. *W*, *16*, 273: "Göttlicher . . . mehr wert."

42. *W*, 8, 122–23: "Rausch . . . Das Verwandeln-müssen ins Vollkommene."

43. *W*, *16*, 101: "Kunst als Wille zur Überwindung des Werdens, als Verewigen."

44. *W*, 7, 53: "Die Entmännlichung der Kunst." 7, 418: "Jene eigentümliche Süssigkeit und Fülle . . . Aufgehoben . . . Transfiguriert." Nietzsche was the first (in 1878) to use the term "sublimation" in the current sense. Love is "sublimierte Geschlechtlichkeit" (*W*, *3*, 52).

45. *W*, 8, 172; *16*, 391 ff.

46. *W*, *16*, 392, 372: "Dieser Pessimismus der Stärke endet mit einer Theodiceen, d. h. mit einem absoluten Ja-sagen zu der Welt."

47. *W*, *16*, 272: "Kunst ist die Erlösung des Erkennenden . . . des Handelnden . . . des Leidenden,—als Weg zu Zuständen, wo das Leiden gewollt, verklärt, vergöttlicht wird, wo das Leiden eine Form der grossen Entzückung ist."

48. *W*, *14*, 135: "Eine im höchsten Grade interessierte, und rücksichtslos interessierte Zurechtmachung der Dinge . . . eine wesentliche Fälschung . . . der aesthetische Zuschauer gestattet ein Überwältigen."

49. *W*, *14*, 134: "Das Entzücken, jetzt in unserer Welt zu sein, die Angst vor dem Fremden loszusein!"

50. *W*, *16*, 230: "Gegensätze sind gebändigt, das höchste Zeichen von Macht, nämlich über Entgegengesetztes."

51. *W*, *16*, 270: "Die überwältigenden Künstler, welche einen Consonanz-Ton aus jedem Conflikte erklingen lassen."

52. *W*, 5, 10: "Eine spöttische, leichte, flüchtige, göttlich unbehelligte, göttlich künstliche Kunst . . . eine Kunst für Künstler, nur für Künstler." 5, 143: "Eine übermütige, schwebende, tanzende, spottende, kindische und selige Kunst."

53. The relation between Emerson and Nietzsche has been studied by Hubbard, *Nietzsche und Emerson,* and by Eduard Baumgarten, "Mitteilungen und Bemerkungen über den Einfluss Emersons auf Nietzsche," *Jahrbuch für Amerikastudien,* ed. W. Fischer (Heidelberg, 1956), *1,* 93–152, but the attempt to establish a "radical and pervasive influence" (Baumgarten, p. 94) seems to me quite mistaken. Some compositions of the 17-year-old Nietzsche show his influence on the concept of fate, and later Nietzsche annotated and excerpted some of Emerson's *Essays,* often with approval. Still, the profound difference between Emerson, an optimistic Neoplatonist, and Nietzsche seems unbridgeable. See my review of Hubbard in *Erasmus, 13* (1960), 134–36.

54. *W, 8,* 117: "Dante—oder die Hyäne, die in Gräbern dichtet"; *16,* 269, where the *Divina Commedia* (surely only the *Inferno?*) is considered as showing the joy in tragedy characteristic of strong periods and characters.

55. *W, 9,* 445. *10,* 481: "Eins der schädlichsten Bücher."

56. *W, 7,* 178: "Spanisch-maurisch-sächsische Geschmacks-Synthesis." *3,* 84: "Ein Bergwerk voll einer Unermässlichkeit an Gold Blei und Geröll."

57. *W, 5,* 128–29.

58. *W, 3,* 76–78; *16,* 260; *3,* 72; *11,* 105. On the history of the term baroque see my "The Concept of Baroque in Literary Scholarship," *Journal for Aesthetics, 5* (1946), 77–109, reprinted in *Concepts of Criticism,* New Haven, 1963. I overlooked Nietzsche.

59. *W, 15,* 34: "nicht ohne Ingrimm gegen ein wüstes Genie wie Shakespeare."

60. *W, 2,* 201.

61. *W, 15,* 208–09.

62. *W, 2,* 202, 432–33. *5,* 136: "Vollender des höfischen Geschmacks."

63. *W, 3,* 310: "Mehr wirkliche Gedanken als alle Bücher deutscher Philosophen zusammengenommen."

64. *W, 8,* 220: "Die Verderbnis Pascal's, der an die Verderbnis seiner Vernunft durch die Erbsünde glaubte, während sie nur durch sein Christentum verdorben war."

65. *W, 3,* 265.

66. *W, 11,* 109–110; *3,* 255; *1,* 207. *1,* 83: "Nebentrieb." *7,* 47: "Die Freigeisterei, die Flucht aus Deutschland."

67. *W, 3,* 260–61: "Etwas Wundes und Unfreies . . . Er wünschte die grosse Flamme, und diese brach nie hervor."

68. *W, 8,* 27; *9,* 248; *3,* 263, 266. *1,* 540: "Versetzte Volks-Beredsamkeit."

69. *W, 1,* 207. *4,* 180: "Ein weicher, gutartiger, silbern glitzernder

Idealismus . . . schön nach einem schlechten verschwommenen Geschmack."

70. *W, 8,* 163: "Er disciplinierte sich zur Ganzheit, er schuf sich." Cf. *10,* 279.

71. *W, 3,* 264; *2,* 203; *1,* 502; *3,* 127; *7,* 47: "Eine Mischung aus Steifheit und Zierlichkeit."

72. *W, 8,* 162: "Ein europäisches Ereignis." *3,* 265: "Ein Zwischenfàll ohne Folgen."

73. *W, 8,* 163: "Ein solcher freigewordner Geist steht mit einem freudigen und vertrauenden Fatalismus mitten im All, im Glauben, dass nur das Einzelne verwerflich ist, dass im Ganzen sich Alles erlöst und bejaht—er verneint nicht mehr . . . Aber ein solcher Glaube ist der höchste aller möglichen Glauben: ich habe ihn auf den Namen des Dionysos getauft."

74. *W, 8,* 117. *8,* 162: "Ein Hinaufkommen zur Natürlichkeit."

75. *W, 15* 213–16, cf. 209.

76. *W, 1,* 424–25: "Die heilige Natur."

77. *W, 3,* 62–65: "Zucht, Geschlossenheit, Charakter, Beständigkeit der Absichten, Überschaulichkeit, Schlichtheit, Haltung in Gang und Miene. . . . Der freieste Schriftsteller aller Zeiten. . . . seine Eichhorn-Seele."

78. *W, 5,* 324–27.

79. *W, 4,* 189–90; *10,* 464. *1,* 190: "Der Carneval aller Götter und Mythen."

80. A letter dated 19 October 1861 (when Nietzsche was 15), defending Hölderlin, his "Lieblingsdichter," in *Werke,* ed. K. Schlechta (Munich, 1956), *3,* 95–98. *W, 14,* 249–50: "Ich bin hart genug, um über deren Zugrundegehn zu lachen."

81. *W, 3,* 254: "Ein Verhängnis—ein Verhängnis im Schlafrock."

82. *W, 10,* 464: "Eine Gelehrten-Bewegung." *4,* 190: "Die Historie, das Verständnis des Ursprungs, und der Entwicklung, die Mitempfindung für das Vergangne."

83. *W, 15,* 35–36.

84. *W, 15,* 35; *14,* 173; but note the earlier condemnation of his prose, in *10,* 264.

85. *W, 8,* 23. Nietzsche draws on Paul Bourget's "La Théorie de la décadence," in *Essais de psychologie contemporaine,* Paris, 1883.

86. *W, 15,* 143. *16,* 248–49: "Falschmünzerei."

87. *W, 8,* 122. *14,* 183: "Eine Art von '*fait-alisme,*' welcher jetzt über Frankreich herrscht."

88. *W, 14,* 197–98.

89. *W, 7,* 154: "Nur aufgeputzte Skepsis und Willenslähmung." *8,* 135: "Lieber gar keinen Zweck als einen moralischen Zweck."

90. *W*, *8*, 117–18; *7*, 74–75; *16*, 247. *8*, 117: "Die Freude zu stinken."

91. *W*, *15*, 38; *14*, 181. *8*, 194–95: "Der Hass gegen das Leben . . . schöpferisch."

92. Ida Rothpelz, the later Mrs. Overbeck, who had translated Sainte-Beuve read French with Nietzsche in Basel (Williams, *Nietzsche and the French*, p. 8). *W*, *14*, 179–80; *7*, 74. *8*, 118–19: "Ein Genie der médisance . . . Kritiker ohne Massstab . . . Historiker ohne Philosophie."

93. *W*, *7*, 60: "Dieser letzte grosse Psycholog." 226: "ein wunderlicher Epikureer . . . Entdecker dieser (europäischen) Seele."

94. *W*, *15*, 34. *14*, 179: "Der erste lebende Historiker Europa's"; *14*, 182: "starke, expressive, Typen." There are three letters by Taine, acknowledging the receipt of Nietzsche's books, rather cautiously, in *H. Taine: Sa Vie et sa correspondance* (Paris 1907), *4*, 220, 241, 276. Nietzsche's letters in *Gesammelte Briefe* (5 vols. Berlin, 1905), *3*, pp. 195–206.

95. *W*, *8*, 126–27: "Carlyle betäubt Etwas in sich durch das *fortissimo* seiner Verehrung für Menschen starken Glaubens . . . er bedarf des Lärms . . . Eine beständige leidenschaftliche Unredlichkeit gegen sich." Elsewhere Carlyle is called "ein alter anmaasslicher Wirr- und Murrkopf" (*W*, *4*, 249); and in the well-known list of "Meine Unmöglichen" (*8*, 117) he is defined as "Pessimismus als zurückgetretenes Mittagessen."

96. *W*, *8*, 120–21, 117: "Die beleidigende Klarheit."

97. *W*, *8*, 158: "Der einzige Psychologe . . . von dem ich Etwas zu lernen hatte: er gehört zu den schönsten Glücksfällen meines Lebens, mehr selbst noch als die Entdeckung Stendhal's." Cf. *8*, 48–49, 255; *14*, 371; *15*, 313; *16*, 188, 222. Thomas Mann is quite mistaken when he considers "The Pale Criminal" in *Zarathustra* (1883) a portrait of Dostoevsky, or when he derives the doctrine of Eternal Recurrence from the Devil's conversation with Ivan in *The Brothers Karamazov* ("Nietzsches Philosophie," in *Neue Studien*, Stockholm, 1948, pp. 78, 89). *The Brothers* was not even translated at that time.

98. G. Brandes, *F. Nietzsche* (London, 1914), contains translation of correspondence (pp. 62–97). Karl Strecker, *Nietzsche und Strindberg mit ihrem Briefwechsel* (Munich, 1921), contains 4 letters and 2 notes by Nietzsche.

99. *W*, *15*, 59: "Eine typische alte Jungfer . . . das gute Gewissen, die Natur in der Geschlechtsliebe zu vergiften."

100. *W*, *1*, 314, 183: "Einheit des künstlerischen Stiles in allen Lebensäusserungen eines Volkes."

101. *W*, *1*, 170: "Deutscher Genius, deutscher Geist." *7*, 164: "Der reine und kräftige Kern des deutschen Wesens."

102. *W*, *1*, 279–80.

103. *W, 1,* 354–55, 356, cf. *7,* 176–78; *15,* 103. *1,* 186: "Bildungs-philister" (1873). *1,* 313: "Wandelnde Encyklopädien." *1,* 343: "Allzu helles, allzu plötzliches, allzu wechselndes Licht. '

104. *W, 9,* 344–45; *16,* 301; *9,* 363–64.

105. *W, 16,* 301; *1,* 325; *1,* 456–57. *5,* 318–20: "Jeder Specialist hat seinen Buckel."

106. *W, 13,* 23: "Philosophie . . . die allgemeinste Form der His-torie . . . Versuch das heraklitische Werden irgendwie zu beschreiben."

107. *W, 5,* 300–01; *7,* 210; *13,* 10.

108. A suggestion of Karl Hillebrand, who reviewed the *Meditation.* See *Zeiten, Völker und Menschen* (Strasbourg, 1892), 2, 312.

109. *W, 1,* 299: "mythische Fiction." *1,* 302: "Lasst die Toten die Lebendigen begraben."

110. *W, 1,* 306: "Das widrige Schauspiel einer blinden Sammelwut."

111. *W, 1,* 307–08: "Jede Vergangenheit aber ist wert, verurteilt zu werden."

112. *W, 1,* 357. *1,* 305: "Die Vergangenheit selbst leidet."

113. *W, 1,* 379.

114. *W, 1,* 339: "Zum Kunstwerk umgebildet, reines Kunstgebilde."

115. *W, 1,* 382, 384: "Eine Einhelligkeit zwischen Leben, Denken, Scheinen und Wollen."

116. *W, 7,* 176–77: "Die Fähigkeit, die Rangordnung von Wert-schätzungen schnell zu erraten."

117. *W, 1,* 326. *7,* 159: "Die Sicherheit der Wertmaasse, die bewusste Handhabung einer Einheit von Methode, den gewitzten Muth, das Alleinstehn und Sich-verantworten-können."

118. *W, 2,* 252. *4,* 10: "Sich Zeit lassen, still werden, langsam werden—, als eine Goldschmiedekunst und -Kennerschaft des Wortes."

119. *W, 7,* 159: "Jenes Werk entzückt mich: wie sollte es nicht schön sein?"

120. *W, 1,* 309.

121. *W, 5,* 124.

122. *W, 3,* 257.

123. *W, 7,* 47–48. Cf. *3,* 252.

124. *W, 1,* 259 ff.

125. *W, 8,* 64: "Ein Mangel an Rechtschaffenheit." Cf. *14,* 313.

126. *W, 16,* 237–38. *15,* 389: "Der grosse Stil . . . Ausdruck des 'Willens zur Macht' selbst." *7,* 117: "Tyrannei solcher Willkür-Gesetze." *16,* 265: "Kälte, Lucidität, Härte . . . Logik vor Allem."

127. *W, 6,* 19: "Man muss noch Chaos in sich haben, um einen tanzenden Stern gebären zu können."

BIBLIOGRAPHY: GEORG BRANDES

I use German and English translations:

Aesthetische Studien, Charlottenburg, 1900, original ed. 1868. The translation by Alfred Forster is incomplete.

Søren Kierkegaard, Leipzig, 1879, original ed. 1877.

Moderne Geister, Frankfurt am Main, 1882.

Menschen und Werke, Frankfurt am Main, 1894.

Henrik Ibsen. Björnstjerne Björnson. Critical Studies, New York, 1899.

Die Hauptströmungen der Literatur des neunzehnten Jahrhunderts, 6 vols. Charlottenburg, 1900. The first 4 vols. trans. Adolf Strodtmann, Vol. 5 by W. Rudow, and Vol. 6 by A. v. d. Linden. Quoted as follows:

> Vol. 1: *Die Emigrantenliteratur.*
> 2: *Die romantische Schule in Deutschland.*
> 3: *Die Reaktion in Frankreich.*
> 4: *Der Naturalismus in England.*
> 5: *Die romantische Schule in Frankreich.*
> 6: *Das junge Deutschland.*

William Shakespeare, English trans. W. Archer and Diana White, London, 1902.

Gestalten und Gedanken, Munich, 1905.

Goethe, trans. Erich Holm and Emilie Stein, Berlin, 1922.

Voltaire, trans. Otto Krieger and Pierce Butler, 2 vols. New York, 1930.

Comment:

Dr. Puls, Flensburg, "Wie Georg Brandes deutsche Literaturgeschichte schreibt," *Archiv für das Studium der neueren Sprachen,* Year XLII, *80* (1888), 1–24.

Oskar Seidlin, "Georg Brandes," *Journal of the History of Ideas, 3* (1942), 415–42, reprinted in his *Essays in German and Comparative Literature* (Chapel Hill, 1961), pp. 1–29.

Henning Fenger, *Georg Brandes' Laereår,* Copenhagen, 1955; English summary, pp. 471–74.

The introduction by Kurt Bergel to *Georg Brandes und Arthur Schnitzler: Ein Briefwechsel* (Bern, 1956), pp. 11–51.

Bengt Algot Sörensen, "Über die Schönheitsauffassung von Georg Brandes," *Jahrbuch für Aesthetik und allgemeine Kunstwissenschaft,* ed. H. Lützeler, *3* (1958), 225–44.

In the notes that follow I have thought it useful to cite the original

Danish passages, even though I read the works in German and English translation. The originals were supplied by Mrs. Iba Brown.

NOTES: GEORG BRANDES

1. *New York Times* (18 June 1914), from Bergel, p. 204.
2. *The Letters of Sir Walter A. Raleigh*, ed. Lady Raleigh (London, 1926), 2, 281. A letter to Mrs. A. H. Clough, 2 October 1905.
3. Nietzsche, *Gesammelte Briefe* (Berlin, 1905), *3*, 274. Letter dated 2 December 1887. Brandes protested against "Cultur-Missionär" in a letter of 17 December 1887, and Nietzsche defends it in a letter of 8 January 1888: *ibid.* pp. 277, 279.
4. *L'Ecole romantique en France*, trans. from the German by A. Topin, Paris, 1902.
5. *Die Emigrantenliteratur*, pp. 1, 4.
6. *Das junge Deutschland*, p. 406: "hint bibelske Glædesaar" (Brandes, *Samlede Skrifter*, Copenhagen, 1899–1910, *6*, 678).
7. See *Emigrantenliteratur*, pp. 6–16; *Die romantische Schule in Deutschland*, pp. 6–18 and *passim*.
8. *Die romantische Schule in Deutschland*, p. 2.
9. *Emigrantenliteratur*, p. 6: "den sætter Problemer under Debat" (*Samlede Skrifter, 4,* 5).
10. *Die romantische Schule in Frankreich*, p. 331: "Tendens"; "Tidsalderens Aand"; "al sand Poesis Livsblod" (*Samlede Skrifter, 6,* 55).
11. *Das junge Deutschland*, p. 359. *Kierkegaard*, p. 176.
12. *Der Naturalismus in England*, p. 137: "fra vor Tids Højde"; "Personlighedens Frigørelse fra de tilfældige Overleveringer" (*Samlede Skrifter, 5,* 379). Page 140: "være uberørt af Videnskabens Gang" (*Samlede Skrifter, 5,* 381).
13. *Emigrantenliteratur*, p. 32: "at opleve det nittende Aarhundredes Videnskabelighed"; "en ny Tro" (*Samlede Skrifter, 4,* 26). Page 102: "paa højere Udviklingsstadier af den franske Literatur" (*Samlede Skrifter, 4,* 71).
14. *Die romantische Schule in Frankreich*, p. 313: "det er Kritiken, som flytter Bjerge, alle Autoritetstroens, Fordommenes, den idéløse Magts og den døde Overleverings Bjerge" (*Samlede Skrifter, 6,* 295).
15. *Die romantische Schule in Deutschland*, p. 3.
16. See *Correspondance*, ed. Paul Krüger (Copenhagen, 1952), *1*, esp. 20–21; and *Erinnerungen: Kindheit und Jugend* (Munich, 1907), pp. 177–78, 345 ff.
17. *Reaktion in Frankreich*, p. 146: "Der fandtes i Frankrig under Kejserdømmet ingen Poesi" (*Samlede Skrifter, 5,* 122).

18. *Naturalismus in England,* pp. 162–99. *Das junge Deutschland,* pp. 384–406. *Reaktion in Frankreich,* pp. 129–45, 181–207. *Das junge Deutschland,* pp. 298–303.

19. *Emigrantenliteratur,* pp. 103, 125. Pages 47–48: "en hel Tidsalders Lidenskaber, Længsler og Kvaler har fundet deres Udtryk" (*Samlede Skrifter, 4,* 34). Pages 56–57: "Bebudelsens Poesi [er] afløst af Skuffelsens"; "Han er tungsindig og Menneskehader. Han danner Overgangen fra Goethes Werther til Byron's Giaur og Korsar" (*Samlede Skrifter, 4,* 41).

20. *Ibid.,* pp. 9–11: "I al deres Skønhed er de for uvirkelige og fordædlede til mere end ufuldkomment at afspejle den tid, i hvilken de blev til" (*Samlede Skrifter, 4,* 9).

21. For most damaging evidence see the article by Puls (pseudonym) quoted in bibliography. Puls does not see (or won't say) that some of the grotesque effects are due to retranslating from Danish.

22. *Die romantische Schule in Deutschland,* p. 191: "Stræben, Vilje, Beslutning"; "Naturside og Natside" (*Samlede Skrifter, 4,* 351).

23. *Die Reaktion in Frankreich,* pp. 197, 239–47.

24. *Der Naturalismus in England,* pp. 7, 49, 43.

25. *Ibid.,* pp. 85, 87. Page 92: "Sødme; hver Linje har en Honning-draabes Smag og Vægt" (*Samlede Skrifter, 5,* 343).

26. *Ibid.,* p. 199: "en af de ypperste og mest musikalske, som nogensinde har levet" (*Samlede Skrifter, 5,* 430).

27. *Ibid.,* pp. 226–27: "større og varigere Betydning for Menneske-aandens Frigørelse" (*Samlede Skrifter, 5,* 452).

28. *Ibid.,* pp. 294, 337, 371, 394.

29. *Die romantische Schule in Frankreich,* p. 373: "den største literære Skole vort Aarhundrede har set" (*Samlede Skrifter, 6,* 339).

30. *Ibid.,* pp. 23–24: "saa er alle de franske Romantikere Klassikere. Mérimée er en Klassiker, Gautier en Klassiker, George Sand en Klassiker, ja selv Victor Hugo er klassisk" (*Samlede Skrifter, 6,* 24).

31. *Ibid.,* p.105: "en kvindelig Genius, saa betydelig, saa fuldstændig, at aldrig før i Verdenshistorien nogen Kvinde havde vist sig i Besiddelse af saa rig en Skaberkraft" (*Samlede Skrifter, 6,* 106).

32. *Ibid.,*p. 173.

33. *Das junge Deutschland,* p. 164.

34. *Ibid.,* pp. 147, 138. Page 173: "det vittigste Menneske, der har levet" (*Samlede Skrifter, 6,* 486).

35. *Die romantische Schule in Frankreich,* p. 285. Page 307: "forstod bag Papiret at opdage Mennesket" (*Samlede Skrifter, 6,* 289). Page 309: this section seems identical with an article first published in 1869 and reprinted in *Kritiker og Portraiter,* 1870. See Fenger, pp. 432, 435.

36. Quoted by Sörensen, pp. 233-34.

37. For judgments cf. A. Bärthold, *Die Bedeutung der ästhetischen Schriften Søren Kierkegaards in Bezug auf G. Brandes's Søren Kierkegaard, ein literarisches Charakterbild* (Halle, 1879), and Aage Henriksen, *Methods and Results of Kierkegaard Studies in Scandinavia* (Copenhagen, 1951), pp. 22-30.

38. Kierkegaard, pp. 95, 188: "kan eller vil ikke forstaae at den nyere Literaturs Historie er identisk med dens Frigørelse fra Traditionens moralske og religiøse Forestillinger" (Brandes, *Søren Kierkegaard*, Copenhagen, 1877, p. 212).

39. *Henrik Ibsen. Björnstjerne Björnson* (New York, 1899), p. 4: "noget Krigerisk, Oprørsk, Voldsomt og Tungsindigt" (*Samlede Skrifter, 3*, 242), p. 28: "legemliggjorte Begreber" (Danish ed., p. 264). Page 25: "Mangel paa Motivering" (Danish ed., p. 261). Page 36: "hverken skønt eller sandt" (Danish ed., p. 271).

40. *Ibid.*, p. 69: "et medfødt Hang til hemmelighedsfuld Tro og et ligesaa oprindeligt Anlag til skærende, tør Forstandighed" (*Samlede Skrifter, 3*, 298). Page 80: "at alt som han er bleven mere nutidig, er han bleven en stedse større Kunstner" (Danish ed., p. 309).

41. *Ibid.*, p. 105: "Hedda er . . . en af Ibsens gamle romantiske Sagnskikkelser som Amazone i moderne Ridedragt" (*Samlede Skrifter, 3*, 331). Bengt is in *The Feast of Solhaus,* Gunnar in *Love's Comedy*.

42. *Ibid.*, p. 112: "at det jo dog aldeles ingen Maalestok er for en Bygmesters Storhed, om han bliver svimmel paa Vejen til et Kirketaarns Spir" (*Samlede Skrifter, 3*, 337).

43. *Ibid.*, p. 114 : "Naturalisme og Symbolisme trivedes godt i Forening" (*Samlede Skrifter, 3*, 339).

44. The Flaubert essay in *Moderne Geister* (Frankfurt, 1882), pp. 281-336. On Zola and Maupassant see *Menschen und Werke* (Frankfurt, 1894), pp. 225-60, 261-92.

45. *Französische Persönlichkeiten* (Munich, 1900), pp. 459, 465. Page 460: "fransk Poesi i det 19de Aarhundredes Slutning [er] blevet den dunkleste Poesi i Europa" (*Samlede Skrifter, 7*, 266).

46. *Menschen und Werke,* pp. 345-60, on Tolstoy.

47. On Dostoevsky see *Menschen und Werke,* pp. 309-44. Brandes' letter to Nietzsche, 16 November 1888, in *Gesammelte Briefe, 3*, 319-20: "Er ist ein grosser Poet, aber ein abscheulicher Kerl, ganz christlich in seinem Gefühlsleben und zugleich ganz *sadique*. Alle seine Moral ist was Sie Sklavenmoral getauft haben."

48. *Menschen und Werke,* pp. 300-01.

49. Cf. *Friedrich Nietzsche* (New York, n. d.), trans. A. G. Chater. I quote from *Menschen und Werke,* pp. 137-224. Page 137 (2 December

1887): "Das gescheuteste Wort, das ich bisher über mich gelesen habe."

50. *Ibid.*, pp. 191, 200–01.

51. "August Strindberg," in *Menschen und Werke*, pp. 482–502. The Correspondence of Nietzsche and Strindberg in *Gesammelte Briefe, 3*.

52. *William Shakespeare*, p. 689: "Forfatteren har ment, at naar vi besidder omtrent fyrretyve vægtige Skrifter af en Mand, saa er det udelukkende vor egen Fejl, ifald vi intetsomhelst véd om ham. Digteren har nedlagt sin hele Personlighed i disse Skrifter. Det gælder da kun om, at ve forstaar at læse, saa finder vi ogsaa ham selv i dem." (*Samlede Skrifter, 9,* 268).

53. *Ibid.*, pp. 45, 225. Page 34:"Det vilde ganske vist være urimeligt at tillægge løsrevne Repliker af forskelligartede Skuespil Værd som selvbiografiske Vidnesbyrd" (*Samlede Skrifter, 8,* 41). Page 349: "det gror indenfra, udspringer af en overmægtig Følelse i Frembringerens Sind" (Danish ed., *8,* 407). Page 363: "Alt havde han oplevet som Hamlet" (Danish ed., *8,* 424).

54. *Ibid.*, pp. 433, 141, 533.

55. *Ibid.*, p. 302: "Her alene hører vi ham bekende" (*Samlede Skrifter, 8,* 355). Page 463: "Gentleman, stor Grundejer og Tiende-Forpagter; men i ham levede Kunstner-Zigøjneren, der passede for Tatersken, endnu" (Danish ed., *8,* 538).

56. *Ibid.*, p. 555. Page 525: "en grund-angelsachsisk Nerve . . . den Nerve, der er Livsnerven i Swift, Livsnerven i Hogarth, Livsnerven i enkelte af Byrons ypperste Ting" (*Samlede Skrifter, 9,* 63).

57. *Ibid.*, p. 626: "det elskeligste, værdifuldeste, kvindelige Væsen, som Shakespeare har frembragt" (*Samlede Skrifter, 9,* 190). Page 617: "Hvad har Shakespeare ment med dette Drama?": "Hvad drev ham til at skrive" (Danish ed., *9,* 178). Pages 620–21: "Formaalsmoralen . . . Alle de værdifulde Personer begaar saaledes Bedragerier, Voldsom-heder, Løgne, ja lever et helt liv i gennemført Usandhed uden at blive ringere derved. Lasterne bestænker dem uden at plette dem . . . Rent personlige Indtryk" (Danish ed., *9,* 183–84).

58. *Ibid.*, p. 123: "Man sporer Begynderen i den Maade, hvorpaa Shakespeare her lader Begivenheder og Personer tale for sig selv uden Forsøg paa at rykke dem ind under et Hovedsynspunkt. Han skjuler sig altfor afgjort bag sit Værk" (*Samlede Skrifter, 8,* 142).

59. *Ibid.*, p. 425: "et af Shakespeares mindre interessante, ikke kunst-nerisk, men rent menneskeligt set. Det er et right, højst moralsk Melo-drama; men kun paa enkelte Punkter føler jeg Shakespeares Hjerte bankende deri" (*Samlede Skrifter, 8,* 494).

60. *Voltaire:* on Pascal, *1,* 204.

61. *Goethe*, pp. 558, 438, 396, 194; preface, pp. VI-VII.

62. *Ibid.*, p. 511: "Literaturens Historie [var] noget om Bøger. Disse Linjers Forfatter har den Svaghed og Styrke, at han interesserer sig mere for Mennesker end for Bøger og gerne ser lige tvers gennem Bogen ind i Mennesket." (Brandes, *Wolfgang Goethe,* Copenhagen, 1915, 2, 231).

63. *Das junge Deutschland,* p. 413.

BIBLIOGRAPHY:
THE ENGLISH AESTHETIC MOVEMENT

General literature on the aesthetic movement:

Albert J. Farmer, *Le Mouvement esthétique et 'décadent' en Angleterre* (1873–1900), Paris, 1931; little on criticism.

Louise Rosenblatt, *L'Idée de l'art pour l'art dans la littérature anglaise pendant la période victorienne,* Paris, 1931.

Madeleine L. Cazamian, *Le Roman et les idées en Angleterre,* Vol. 2, *L'Anti-intellectualisme et l'esthétisme (1880–1900),* Paris, 1935.

Ruth Zabriskie Temple, *The Critic's Alchemy: A Study of the Introduction of French Symbolism into England,* New York, 1953; good chapter on Swinburne.

On Swinburne: I quote *The Complete Works of Algernon Charles Swinburne,* ed. Sir E. Gosse and T. J. Wise, Bonchurch Edition (20 vols. London, 1925–27), as *B.*

The Swinburne Letters, ed. Cecil Y. Lang, Vols. 1–2, 1854–75, New Haven, 1959.

On Swinburne, general books:

Paul de Reul, *L'Œuvre de Swinburne,* Brussels, 1922.

G. Lafourcade, *La Jeunesse de Swinburne,* 2 vols. Paris, 1928.

C. K. Hyder, *Swinburne's Literary Career and Fame,* Durham, N. C., 1933.

On criticism:

A. Löhrer, *Swinburne as Kritiker der Literatur,* Zürich diss., Weida i. Thür, 1925.

Ruth C. Child, "Swinburne's Mature Standards of Criticism," *PMLA, 52* (1937), 870–79.

C. K. Hyder, "Swinburne: *Changes of Aspect* and *Short Notes,*" *PMLA, 58* (1943), 223–44; prints unpublished MSS.

T. E. Connolly, "Swinburne's Theory of the End of Art," *ELH, 19* (1952), 277–90.

Oscar Maurer, "Swinburne vs. Furnivall" in *The University of Texas Studies in English, 31* (1952), 86–96.

On Pater: I quote from the Library edition (10 vols. London, Macmillan, 1924), by abbreviated titles of the volumes:

Re. The Renaissance: Studies in Art and Poetry, 1st ed. 1873.
Mar. Marius the Epicurean: His Sensations and Ideas, 1st ed. 2 vols. 1885.
App. Appreciations, with an Essay an Style, 1st ed. 1889.
Plato Plato and Platonism, 1st ed. 1893.
Greek Greek Studies: A Series of Essays, 1st ed. 1895.
Misc. Miscellaneous Studies, ed. C. L. Shadwell, 1st ed. 1895.
Gaston Gaston de Latour, An Unfinished Romance, ed. C. L. Shadwell, 1896 (first serially in 1888).
Guardian Essays from 'The Guardian,' 1st ed. 1901 (published 1896–1900).

Uncollected articles are quoted from *Sketches and Reviews,* ed. Albert Mordell (New York, 1919), as *Ske. & Re. Uncollected Essays,* ed. T. B. Mosher, Portland, Me. (1903), contains three essays not elsewhere reprinted. There is no collection of letters.

The fullest biography, Thomas Wright, *The Life of Walter Pater* (2 vols. London, 1907), contains hardly any letters and little information except of the most external kind. Two other general books, A. C. Benson, *Walter Pater* (London, 1906), and Philip Edward Thomas, *Walter Pater: A Critical Study* (London, 1913), are slight. Arthur Symons, *A Study of Walter Pater* (London, 1932), is only a series of random remarks. L. Cattan, *Essai sur Walter Pater* (Paris, 1936), is purely descriptive. Greatly superior are three recent studies: R. V. Johnson, *Walter Pater: A Study of his Critical Outlook and Achievement,* Melbourne, 1961; a brief essay. Wolfgang Iser, *Walter Pater. Die Anatomie des Ästhetischen,* Tübingen, 1960. Germain d'Angest, *Walter Pater: L'Homme et l'Œuvre,* 2 vols. Paris, 1961; diffuse, enthusiastic, little new on criticism.

For our purposes Ruth C. Child, *The Aesthetic of Walter Pater* (New York, 1940), and Helen Hawthorne Young, *The Writings of Walter Pater: A Reflection of British Philosophical Opinion from 1860 to 1890* (Bryn Mawr College diss., 1933), are most useful. Albert J. Farmer, *Walter Pater as a Critic of English Literature: A Study of "Appreciations"* (Grenoble, 1931), is little more than a summary. Some useful material is in Arthur Beyer, *Walter Paters Beziehungen zur französischen Literatur und Kultur,* Studien zur Englischen Philologie, 73

(Halle, 1931), and in (the greatly inferior) thesis by Hans Proesler, *Walter Pater und sein Verhältnis zur deutschen Literatur.* Freiburg im Breisgau, 1917.

Among the many essays the following are of special interest to the student of criticism:

Edward Dowden, "Walter Pater," in *Essays, Modern and Elizabethan* (London, 1910), pp. 1–25.

T. S. Eliot, "Arnold and Pater" (1930), in *Selected Essays. 1917–1932* (London, 1932), pp. 379–91. Identical with "The Place of Pater" in *The Eighteen-Eighties,* ed. W. de la Mare, (Cambridge, 1930) and with "Arnold and Pater," *Bookman,* 72 (1930), 1–7. Eliot, strangely enough, considers Pater a kind of debased Arnold.

O. Elton, *A Survey of English Literature 1830–1880* (London, 1920), *I,* 279–92.

Bernhard Fehr, "Pater und Hegel," *Englische Studien, 50* (1916–17), 300–08.

————, "Walter Paters Beschreibung der Mona Lisa und Théophile Gautiers romantischer Orientalismus," *Archiv für das Studium der neueren Sprachen, 135* (1916), 80–102.

Hans Hecht, "Walter Pater: Eine Würdigung," *Deutsche Vierteljahrschrift für Literaturwissenschaft und Geistesgeschichte, 5* (1927), 550–82. A fine general essay.

Paul Elmer More, "Walter Pater," in *The Drift of Romanticism: Shelburne Essays 8th Series* (Boston, 1913), pp. 81–115. Pater is no critic.

Madeleine Cazamian, *Le Roman et les idées en Angleterre,* Vol. 2: *L'Anti-intellectualisme et l'esthétisme (1880–1900)* (Paris, 1935), pp. 119–49; good chapter on Pater.

Logan Pearsall Smith, "On Re-reading Pater," *Reperusals and Recollections* (New York, 1937), pp. 66–75.

Geoffrey Tillotson, "Arnold and Pater: Critics, Historical, Aesthetic and Unlabelled," and "Pater, Mr. Rose and the 'Conclusion' of the Renaissance," both in *Criticism and the Nineteenth Century* (London, 1951), pp. 92–123, 124–46.

NOTES:
THE ENGLISH AESTHETIC MOVEMENT

1. See this *History, 3,* 147.

2. W. Holman Hunt, *Preraphaelitism and the Preraphaelite Brotherhood,* 2 vols. London, 1890–5. W. M. Rossetti, *Dante Gabriel Rossetti: His Family Letters, with a Memoir,* 2 vols. London, 1895.

3. "The Purpose and Tendency of Early Italian Art," *The Germ*, Portland, Maine, 1898; reprint, pp. 65, 69.

4. *Ibid.*, pp. 33, 29.

5. Sir T. H. Hall Caine, *Recollections of Dante Gabriel Rossetti* (London, 1882), p. 184. Letter in *The Ashley Library* (London, 1922–36), Vol. 4 (1923), 141.

6. See John A. Cassidy, "Robert Buchanan and the Fleshly Controversy," *PMLA*, *67* (1952), 65–93, for a full account. The quotation is on p. 8.

SWINBURNE

1. *B*, *16*, 137–38.

2. *B*, *15*, 212.

3. *B*, *16*, 139.

4. Not in *B*. "Mr. George Meredith's 'Modern Love,'" *Spectator*, *35* (1862), 632–33. On Hugo, *B*, *13*, 151, 156.

5. *B*, *13*, 417, 423.

6. "Mr. Swinburne's New Poems," *Saturday Review*, 22 (1866), 145–47, quoted by Hyder, *Swinburne's Literary Career*, p. 37.

7. *B*, *16*, 369, 354.

8. *B*, *13*, 242–43.

9. MS published by C. K. Hyder, p. 233.

10. *B*, *16*, 134.

11. *B*, *16*, 395.

12. *B*, *15*, 6.

13. *B*, *13*, 244.

14. *B*, *16*, 416.

15. *B*, *14*, 161, 214–15.

16. See the scurrilous parody, "Report of the Proceedings on the First Anniversary Session of the Newest Shakespeare Society," in *B*, *11*, 198–221, and the whole polemic with Furnivall described by O. Maurer. *B*, *14*, 6; *16*, 372.

17. *B*, *13*, 4, 8, 11, 13, 14, 8.

18. On Euripides, *B*, *11*, 297; on Musset, *B*, *14*, 303 ff.; on Carlyle, e.g. *B*, *11*, 139–40. On Heine, *B*, *14*, 306–07. On Emerson, the open letter in *Letters*, 2, 274; see also *B*, *11*, 115: "A foul-mouthed Yankee pseudosopher." On J. A. Symonds, *B*, *15*, 250: "The Platonic amorist of blue-breeched gondoliers who is now in Aretino's bosom." On George Eliot, *B*, *14*, 12: "The pitiful and unseemly spectacle of an Amazon thrown sprawling over the crupper of her spavined and spur-galled Pegasus." On G. H. Lewes, *B*, *14*, 77: "The chattering duncery and impudent malignity of so consummate and pseudosophical a quack as George Henry

Lewes." In MS published by C. K. Hyder, p. 243: "The morganatic wife of H. S. H. G. Eliot." Many others.

19. *B, 15,* 120–139. "Don Juan—his magnificent masterpiece . . . the style . . . beyond all praise or blame," etc.

20. *B, 14,* 168, 169, 162, 166, 214, 188–89.

21. *B, 14,* 243, 203, 218, 235, 206, 209, 238.

22. *B, 14,* 194.

23. *B, 15,* 152, 145, 144, 143, 142, 148.

24. *B, 14,* 98.

25. *B, 14,* 102.

26. *B, 14,* 120–43, 149–54, esp. 151.

27. *B, 16,* 178 f. "There is in all these straying songs the freshness of clear wind and purity of blowing rain."

28. *B, 16,* 231, 236.

29. *B, 16,* 246.

30. *B, 16,* 342.

31. *B, 16,* 56–57.

32. *B, 15,* 348–97: "Notes on the Text of Shelley."

33. *B, 16,* 405, 408. *B, 14,* 303.

34. *B, 12,* 155, 151, 145.

35. "Modern Hellenism," in *Undergraduate Papers,* December 1857; reprinted in Lafourcade, 2, 220–23.

36. *B, 15,* 118.

37. In an early letter (1863) published in *Letters,* ed. G. W. E. Russell (London, 1896), *1,* 227–28.

38. *B, 14,* 85. Hyder, p. 236. *B, 14,* 201. Hyder, pp. 243, 234.

39. *B, 15,* 11, 19, 28, 38, 7, 46, 47–48.

40. *B, 16,* 342–45, 413–41, 418.

41. *B, 15,* 316.

42. *B, 11,* 11.

43. *B, 11,* 139, 144.

44. *B, 11,* 120.

45. *B, 11,* 239, 125–26.

46. *B, 11,* 297, 294.

47. *B, 12,* 86. See J. E. Spingarn, "The Sources of Ben Jonson's *Discoveries," Modern Philology, 2* (1905), 451–60.

48. *B, 12,* 67–68, 10.

49. *B, 14,* 57, 65, 77, 67, 69–70, 74, 58.

50. *B, 14,* 11, 5, 47–48.

51. *B, 14,* 5, 10, 354–55.

52. *B, 16,* 22. Swinburne wrote "A Note on a Question of the Hour," in *Athenaeum* (16 June 1877), denouncing *L'Assommoir.*

53. *Letters, 1,* 56–58 (1862).

54. *Ibid., 1,* 43, 32 (1859).

55. Note, e.g., that Swinburne praises Rossetti's art of translating in the same essay twice with the same striking metaphor: "The miraculous faculty of transfusion which enables the cupbearer to pour this wine of verse from the golden into the silver cup without spilling was never before given to man" (*B, 15,* 18); and "Here the divine verse seems actually to fall of itself into a new mould, the exact shape and size of the first—to be poured from one cup into another without spilling one drop of nectar" (*B, 15,* 33).

PATER

1. *A Brief Treatise on the Criticism of Poetry, Chapbook,* No. 2. March 1920.

2. *Re. p.* 125.

3. *Re. p.* 236.

4. See Bernhard Fehr, "Walter Paters Beschreibung der Mona Lisa und Théophile Gautiers romantischer Orientalismus," *Archiv für das Studium der neueren Sprachen, 135* (1917), 80–102. Mario Praz, *The Romantic Agony* (London, 1933), pp. 239–42.

5. Fehr, pp. 87–88.

6. *Ske. & Re.,* p. 3.

7. *Re.,* p. 85.

8. See this *History,* 2, 191 ff.

9. *App.,* p. 122.

10. *Greek,* p. 59.

11. *Re.,* p. VIII.

12. *Ibid.* Cf. *Dichtung und Wahrheit,* 3rd part, Book 12, in *Werke, Jubiläumsausgabe, 24,* 76.

13. *Guardian,* p. 29.

14. *Re.,* p. VII.

15. *Re.,* p. XI.

16. *Re.,* p. 76.

17. *Misc.,* p. 14.

18. *Re.,* p. 76.

19. *Re.,* p. XI.

20. *App.,* p. 43.

21. *App.,* p. 46.

22. *App.,* p. 50.

23. *App.,* p. 49.

24. *App.,* pp. 47–48.

25. *Guardian,* p. 96.

26. *App.*, p. 55.

27. *Plato*, p. 73.

28. *App.*, p. 65.

29. *App.*, p. 55.

30. *Guardian*, p. 93.

31. *App.*, p. 53.

32. I cannot see why Geoffrey Tillotson should call the Wordsworth of the "Appreciation" "a scented Wordsworth." See "Arnold and Pater," in *Criticism and the Nineteenth Century* (London, 1951), p. 119.

33. *App.*, p. 186.

34. *App.*, p. 171.

35. *App.*, pp. 183, 184.

36. *App.*, p .137. See D. K. Ziegler, *In Distinguished and Divided Worlds* (Cambridge, Mass., 1943), and Austin Warren, "The Style of Sir Thomas Browne," *Kenyon Review, 13* (1951), 674–87.

37. *Westminster Review* (1866).

38. Reprinted in *Ske. & Re.*

39. In Ward's *English Poets* (1880).

40. *App.*, p. 111.

41. *Ske. & Re.*, p. 19.

42. *App.*, p. 212.

43. *App.*, p. 213.

44. *App.*, p. 206.

45. The first edition is called *Studies in the History of the Renaissance* (1873). The 2d edition is *The Renaissance: Studies in Art and Poetry* (1877).

46. *Re.*, p. 24.

47. *Re.*, p. 86.

48. *Re.*, p. 86.

49. *Re.*, p. XII.

50. *Re.*, p. 158.

51. In *Nouveaux Lundis, 13,* 1867.

52. *Re.*, p. 170.

53. *Gaston*, p. 60.

54. *Mar., 1,* 96–97.

55. *Mar., 1,* 60.

56. *Gaston*, p. 54.

57. *Re.*, pp. XIV–XV.

58. See *Biographische Aufsätze* (1866). Cf. Wright, *Life of Walter Pater, 1,* 232. Pater did not yet know Justi's great work.

59. See Bernhard Fehr, "Walter Pater und Hegel," in *Englische Studien, 50* (1916–17), 300–08.

60. *Re.*, p. 226.

61. *Re.*, pp. 226–27.

62. *App.*, pp. 243, 249. *Goetz* dates from 1773, twenty-five years before the German romantic movement began.

63. *Re.*, p. 236.

64. *App.*, p. 249.

65. *Re.*, p. 223. *Ske. & Re.*, p. 7, *App.*, pp. 253–54.

66. *Re*, p. 74.

67. *App.*, pp. 253–54.

68. *Misc.*, p. 27.

69. *App.*, p. 242.

70. *Die Bernsteinhexe* (1838–43), and *Sidonie von Bork* (1847).

71. *App.*, p. 243.

72. *App.*, p. 246.

73. "Exposition universelle de 1855," in *Curiosités esthétiques*, ed. Jacques Crépet (Paris, Conard, 1923), p. 224.

74. *App.*, p. 257.

75. *App.*, p. 258.

76. First serially in *Belgravia* (1876).

77. Esp. *Mar.*, *1*, 144 ff.

78. *Mar.*, *1*, 145.

79. *Mar.*, *1*, 147.

80. *Mar.*, *1*, 151.

81. *Mar.*, *1*, 150.

82. *Mar.*, *1*, 146.

83. *Re.*, p. 235.

84. Pater quotes Heraclitus in the epigraph to the Conclusion, *Re.*, p. 233, and often elsewhere, e.g. *Plato*, p. 19.

85. *Re.*, p. 235.

86. *Re.*, p. 239.

87. *App.*, p. 68.

88. *App.*, p. 208.

89. *Gaston*, p. 52.

90. *Re.*, p. 137.

91. *App.*, p. 203.

92. *App.*, pp. 202–03.

93. "Le Byron de nos jours," from *Men and Women*.

94. *Re.*, p. 213.

95. *App.*, p. 171.

96. *App.*, p. 81.

97. *App.*, p. 126.

98. *App.*, p. 210.

99. *Guardian*, p. 102.
100. *Re.*, pp. 71–72.
101. *Re.*, p. 63.
102. *Re.*, p. 187.
103. *App.*, pp. 168–69.
104. *Ske. & Re.*, p. 80.
105. *Misc.*, p. 37.
106. *App.*, pp. 37–38.
107. *Re.*, p. 135.
108. *Re.*, p. 135.
109. *App.*, p. 37.
110. *Re.*, p. 130.
111. *Re.*, p. 134.
112. *Re.*, p. 3.
113. *Re.*, p. 52.
114. *Greek*, p. 32.
115. *App.*, p. 88.
116. *Greek*, p. 29.
117. *Guardian*, p. 94.
118. *App.*, p. 218.
119. *App.*, p. 62.
120. *App.*, p. 18.
121. *App.*, p. 219.
122. *Mar.*, *1*, 126.
123. *Ibid.*
124. *App.*, p. 81.
125. *App.*, p. 80.
126. *App.*, pp. 260–61.
127. *App.*, p. 41.
128. *Ibid.*
129. *App.*, p. 11.
130. *App.*, pp. 9–10.
131. *App.*, pp. 11–12.
132. *App.*, p. 17.
133. *App.*, p. 19.
134. *App.*, p. 20.
135. *App.*, pp. 24–25.
136. *App.*, p. 26.
137. *App.*, p. 37.
138. *App.*, p. 31.
139. *App.*, p. 34.
140. *Misc.*, p. 67; cf. *Guardian*, pp. 15, 36–37.

141. *App.*, p. 36.
142. *App.*, p. 38.
143. *Misc.*, p. 80.
144. *Guardian*, p. 33.
145. *Ibid.*, pp. 33–34.
146. *Ske. & Re.*, p. 110.
147. *Ske. & Re.*, p. 114.
148. *App.*, p. 72.
149. *Re.*, p. viii.
150. *Plato*, pp. 20–21.
151. *Ibid.*, p. 19.
152. *Misc.*, p. 252.
153. *Re.*, p. 199.
154. *App.*, p. 256.
155. *Plato*, pp. 9–10.
156. *App.*, p. 16.
157. *Re.*, p. 172.
158. *Ske. & Re.*, p. 15.
159. *Re.*, p. 199.
160. *Re.*, p. 198.
161. *Re.*, p. x.
162. *Guardian*, 15.
163. *Re.*, p. 49; cf. p. 35.
164. *Plato*, p. 72.
165. *App.*, p. 241.
166. *App.*, p. 261.
167. *European Literature and the Latin Middle Ages* tr. Willard R. Trask (New York, 1953), pp. 396–97. *Europäische Literatur und lateinisches Mittelalter* (Bern, 1948), p. 400: Sie sind ein Markstein in der Geschichte der literarischen Kritik und bedeuten einen Durchbruch zu einer neuen Freiheit. Die Tyrannei des Normalklassizismus ist überwunden. Die Befolgung der Regeln und die Nachahmung der Musterautoren gewährt kein Anrecht mehr auf eine gute Zensur. Nur die schöpferischen Geister zählen. Der Begriff der Tradition wird darum nicht aufgegeben, er wird umgebildet. Eine Gemeinschaft der grossen Autoren über die Jahrhunderte hinweg muss festgehalten werden, wenn überhaupt ein geistiges Reich bestehen soll. Aber es kann nur die Gemeinschaft der schöpferischen Geister sein. Das ist eine Auslese neuer Art; ein Kanon, wenn man will, aber gebunden nur durch die Idee der Schönheit, von der wir wissen, dass ihre Gestalten sich wandeln und erneuen. Darum ist das Haus der Schönheit nie fertig und abgeschlossen. Es wird weiter gebaut, es bleibt geöffnet.

BIBLIOGRAPHY:
THE OTHER ENGLISH CRITICS

On Symonds: There is no adequate monograph.
Biographies:
    Horatio F. Brown, *J. A. Symonds: A Biography.* 2d ed. London, 1903, 1st ed. 1894.
    ———,ed., *Letters and Papers of J. A. Symonds,* London, 1923.
    Van Wyck Brooks, *J. A. Symonds: A Biographical Study,* New York, 1914.
    Phyllis Grosskurth, *John Addington Symonds,* London, 1964.
For critical comment see:
    J. C. Collins' review of *Shakspere's Predecessors in the English Drama,* in *Quarterly Review, 161* (1885), 330 ff.; reprinted in *Essays and Studies* (London, 1895), 90–106.
    G. N. Giordano Orsini, "La *Introduction to the Study of Dante* di John Addington Symonds," *Giornale storico della litteratura italiana, 92* (1928), 200–02.
    ———"La Storia del Rinascimento di J. A. Symonds," *La Cultura* 6 (1927), 408–13.
    ———"John Addington Symonds e Francesco de Sanctis," *La Cultura 1* (1928), 358–66.
    ———"Symonds and De Sanctis: A Study in the Historiography of the Renaissance," *Studies in the Renaissance, 11* (1964), 151–187.
    An article in *TLS* (5 October 1940), pp. 506–07, 510.
On Wilde: I quote from the Methuen edition, 14 vols. London, 1906 ff., by title of volume, except that *De Profundis* is quoted from "the first complete and accurate version," ed. Vyvyan Holland, New York, 1950. *Intentions,* New York, 1894.
Comment is endless, but practically all is biographical and psychological. Edouard Roditi, *Oscar Wilde* (Norfolk, Conn., 1947), is the most satisfactory critical study of the work.
On sources, see:
    E. J. Bock, *Walter Paters Einfluss auf Oscar Wilde,* Bonn, 1913.
    Ernst Bendz, *The Influence of Pater and Matthew Arnold on the Prose Writings of Oscar Wilde,* Gothenburg, 1914.
    Kelver Hartley, *Oscar Wilde: L'Influence française dans son œuvre,* Paris, 1935.
Specifically on criticism, see Fritz K. Baumann, *Oscar Wilde als Kritiker der Literatur,* Zurich, 1933.
On Saintsbury: Comment on Saintsbury is scanty.

George Saintsbury: The Memorial Volume contains a "Biographical Memoir" by A. Blyth Webster, London, 1945. *A Saintsbury Miscellany* (New York, 1947) is only an American reprint of the same.

Irving Babbitt, "Are the English Critical?" in *Spanish Character and Other Essays* (Boston, 1940), pp. 21–47.

Dorothy Richardson, "Saintsbury and Art for Art's Sake in England," *PMLA, 59* (1944), 243–60; severe.

Edmund Wilson, *Classics and Commercials* (New York, 1950), pp. 306–10, 366–71.

On Shaw: I quote the Constable edition of the *Collected Works*, London, 1931. Vol 19: *The Quintessence of Ibsenism; The Perfect Wagnerite;* Vols. 23, 24, 25: *Our Theatres in the Nineties,* as *The., 1, 2, 3;* Vol. 29; *Pen Portraits and Reviews.*

There are two anthologies: *Shaw's Dramatic Criticism,* ed. John F. Matthews, New York, 1959; and *Shaw on Shakespeare,* ed. Edwin Wilson, New York, 1961.

For comment on criticism:

> E. J. West, "Shaw's Criticism of Ibsen," in *University of Colorado Studies, Series in Language and Literature, 4* (Boulder, 1953), 101–27.
>
> Sylvan Barnet, "Bernard Shaw on Tragedy," *PMLA, 71* (1956), 888–99.
>
> Albert H. Silverman, "Bernard Shaw's Shakespeare Criticism," *PMLA, 72* (1957), 722–36.

NOTES: THE OTHER ENGLISH CRITICS

J. A. SYMONDS

1. Brooks, p. 233.
2. *Essays Speculative and Suggestive* (London, 1890), *1,* 130.
3. Brown, *J. A. Symonds: A Biography,* p. 401, and *Letters,* p. 231.
4. *Shakspere's Predecessors in the English Drama* (London, 1884), pp. 262–63.
5. Introduction to *Webster Tourneur,* Mermaid ed., pp. XIII–XIV.
6. *Shakspere's Predecessors,* p. 434.
7. Brown, *J. A. Symonds: A Biography,* pp. 258–59.
8. Brown, *Letters,* pp. 73–75.
9. Brown, *J. A. Symonds,* pp. 192–93.
10. Entitled "The English Drama during the Reigns of Elizabeth and James" in *Cornhill Magazine* (1865) and *Pall Mall Gazette* (1867).
11. *Essays, 1,* 46–47.
12. *Ibid, 1,* 48, 49, 58, 60.

13. *Ibid., 1,* 52.

14. *Ibid., 1,* 54.

15. *Ibid., 1,* 78.

16. *Ibid., 1,* 67.

17. *Ibid., 1,* 56.

18. *Ibid., 1,* 80–81.

19. *Ibid.,* 2, 248, 249.

20. *Ibid., 1,* 65.

21. *Ibid.,* 2, 3.

22. *Renaissance in Italy: The Catholic Reaction* (London, 1886), 2, 398.

23. *Ibid.,* 2, 399, 396.

24. *Essays, 1,* 97, 95.

25. *Ibid., 1,* 98–99.

26. *Ibid., 1,* 102, 112.

27. *Ibid., 1,* 121–22.

28. *The Catholic Reaction,* 2, 400.

29. *Shelley* (New York, 1878), pp. 184–85.

30. Brown, *J. A. Symonds,* pp. 323–24.

31. *Walt Whitman: A Study* (London, 1893), pp. 34–35.

32. Cf. *A Problem in Greek Ethics: Being an Inquiry into the Problem of Sexual Inversion* (1883); *A Problem in Modern Ethics* (1891); and *Sexual Inversion* (1897), with Havelock Ellis.

33. *Walt Whitman,* p. 74. For comment on Whitman's letter cf. Willard Thorp in *Eight American Authors: A Review of Research and Criticism* (New York, 1956), p. 286.

34. See Orsini's article listed in the Bibliography, above. Note that in the 2d ed. (1890) the quotations from Carlyle are acknowledged. See *An Introduction to the Study of Dante* (4th ed. London, 1899), p. 156.

35. Fully documented by Orsini; see Bibliography, above.

36. See above.

37. *Shakspere's Predecessors,* pp. 94, 585.

38. *Ibid.,* p. 2.

39. *Ibid.,* pp. 17, 12.

40. *Ibid.,* pp. 29–30.

41. *Ibid.,* pp. 55, 208–09, 630.

42. *Ibid.,* p. 122.

43. *Ibid.,* pp. 260–61, 505 ff., 511.

44. *Ibid.,* pp. 574, 592, 319.

45. *Ibid.,* pp. 425, 510, 608.

46. *Ibid.,* p. 648.

WILDE

1. *De Profundis,* pp. 77, 115, 117.
2. See the bibliography, above, for source studies.
3. *Reviews* (London, 1908), pp. 172–75, 538–45.
4. *Miscellanies* (London, 1908), pp. 243–77, esp. 263–64, 274.
5. A study could be made to show that Wilde incorporated sentences, phrases and often whole paragraphs from the reviews in his most mature dialogues.
6. *The Picture of Dorian Gray* (Paris, 1908) p. 63.
7. *Intentions,* p. 210.
8. "The Soul of Man under Socialism," quoted from *Essays,* ed. H. Pearson (London, 1950), p. 262.
9. *De Profundis,* pp. 103, 106, 109, 111.
10. *Intentions,* pp. 32, 34, 39, 40, 41, 42.
11. *Essays,* ed. H. Pearson, p. 249.
12. *Intentions,* pp. 34, 156.
13. *The Picture of Dorian Gray,* p. 352.
14. *Essays,* ed. Pearson, p. 253.
15. *De Profundis,* pp. 102, 89.
16. *Intentions,* pp. 24, 53, 8.
17. *Ibid.,* p. 11. *Reviews,* p. 261.
18. *Intentions,* pp. 17, 16 ff. 101–04.
19. *Ibid.,* pp. 197, 188. *Miscellanies,* p. 176.
20. *Intentions,* p. 64. "The Portrait of Mr. W. H.," in *Essays,* ed. Pearson, p. 189.
21. *Intentions,* p. 202.
22. *De Profundis,* p. 121. *Miscellanies,* p. 32.
23. *Intentions,* p. 258.
24. *Miscellanies,* pp. 260–61. *Intentions,* pp. 43–45.
25. Letters to the editor of the *Scots Observer,* 9 July 1890, in *Miscellanies,* p. 149. *The Picture of Dorian Gray,* preface.
26. *Intentions,* pp. 197–98.
27. *Miscellanies,* p. 255.
28. *Ibid.,* p. 260. "The Soul of Man under Socialism," in *Essays,* ed. Pearson, pp. 260, 263. *Intentions,* pp. 44, 53.
29. *Intentions,* pp. 137–39, 142, 144, 147, 152.
30. *Ibid.,* pp. 139, 147, 186, 154.
31. *Reviews,* pp. 539–40; cf. *Intentions,* pp. 169–70.
32. *Intentions,* pp. 171, 206–07.

SAINTSBURY

1. *The English Critic*, London, 1952.

2. A. Blyth Webster, *G. Saintsbury, The Memorial Volume*, p. 62.

3. Stephen Potter, *The Muse in Chains* (London, 1937), p. 126.

4. Eleven lives from the thirty-five contributed to the 11th edition of the *Encyclopaedia Britannica* and the general article on French literature were reprinted as *French Literature and Its Masters*, ed. Huntington Cairns, New York, 1946.

5. Cf., e.g., Edmond Scherer, "Une Histoire anglaise de la littérature française," in *Etudes sur la littérature contemporaine, 10* (1895), 137–57. John Churton Collins, "Our Literary Guides," in *Ephemera Critica*, London, 1901.

6. *History of Criticism* (3d ed. Edinburgh, 1908), *3*, 114, 214. *History of the French Novel* (London, 1917), *2*, 297.

7. *Miscellaneous Essays* (New York, 1892), pp. 416–17. *Corrected Impressions* (New York, 1895), p. 36.

8. *History of English Prosody* (London, 1906), *3*, 332 n.

9. *Short History of English Literature* (London, 1920), p. 732.

10. *Miscellaneous Essays*, p. 84.

11. *The Later Nineteenth Century* (Edinburgh, 1923), p. 459.

12. *History of the French Novel, 2,* 26.

13. *Ibid., 2,* 355.

14. *History of Criticism, 3,* 143. *Later Nineteenth Century*, p. 12. *Minor Poets of the Caroline Period* (Oxford, 1905), *1*, 10.

15. *History of Criticism, 1,* 57; *3,* 142.

16. *Later Nineteenth Century*, p. 12. *History of English Prosody, 3,* 115. On Poe, *ibid., 3,* 484, and *Prefaces and Essays* (London, 1933), p. 323 (an article in *Dial*, December 1927).

17. *Prefaces*, p. 298.

18. *Miscellaneous Essays*, p. 322. *Essays in English Literature, 1780–1860* (London, 1890), p. 295. *A History of Nineteenth Century Literature* (New York, 1906), p. 459.

19. *Collected Essays and Papers, 1875–1920* (London, 1923), *3,* 152, 169.

20. *Ibid., 3,* 163, 170, 171.

21. *Corrected Impressions*, p. 25.

22. *Ibid.*, pp. 73–74.

23. *Prefaces and Essays*, p. 319.

24. *Miscellaneous Essays*, p. 305.

25. *Later Nineteenth Century*, pp. 463, 380. *Prefaces*, p. 296.

26. *Later Nineteenth Century,* p. 433. *A History of Elizabethan Literature* (London, 1891), p. 391.

27. *The Later Nineteenth Century,* pp. 463–64.

28. *History of the French Novel,* 2, 329. *History of Criticism, 3,* 276.

29. *Essays in English Literature, 1780–1860* p. xv.

30. *Miscellaneous Essays* p. 330.

31. *History of Criticism, 1,* 485.

32. *History of the French Novel,* 2, 287. *Miscellaneous Essays,* p. 426.

33. *History of Criticism, 1,* 472. Similarly, *History of Nineteenth Century Literature,* p. 468.

34. *Essays in English Literature, 1780–1860,* p. xviii. *History of Criticism, 3,* 609.

35. *History of Criticism, 1,* 360, 137.

36. *Minor Poets of the Caroline Period, 1,* xv.

37. *History of Criticism, 3,* 221; *1,* 158; *2,* 388.

38. *Ibid., 1,* 136–37.

39. *Ibid., 3,* 169.

40. Croce, *Estetica* (Bari, 1946), reprint, pp. 537–38, and Spingarn, *Modern Philology, 1,* (1903–04), 477 ff.

41. *History of Criticism, 3,* 143–44.

42. *Conversazioni critiche, Serie seconda* (Bari, 1942), pp. 286–87.

43. "Digiuno di filosofia," in *Estetica,* loc. cit. *History of Criticism, 3,* 141, 152 n. *A Second Scrap Book* (London, 1923), pp. 40, 57.

44. *History of English Prosody, 1,* 5; *3,* 145 n.

45. *Ibid., 3,* 465, 470, 477.

46. *Ibid., 3,* 282–83, 475.

47. *Ibid., 3,* 352.

48. *History of English Prose Rhythm* (London, 1912), pp. 21, 450.

49. *Miscellaneous Essays,* p. 417.

50. *History of the French Novel,* 2, 333.

51. *Miscellaneous Essays,* pp. 397–98.

52. *History of the French Novel, 1,* 8 n.

53. *Miscellaneous Essays,* p. 397.

54. *History of the French Novel, 1,* 375.

55. *Ibid., 1,* 90.

56. *Ibid.,* 2, 146; 2, 489; 2, 400. *A Consideration of Thackeray* (Oxford, 1931), p. 184.

57. *History of the French Novel, 1,* xiv; 408 ff.; 364 ff.; 452 ff.

58. *History of Criticism,* 2, 48 n.; *3,* 283 n.

59. *Essays on French Novelists* (2d ed. New York, 1891), p. 194.

60. *Miscellaneous Essays,* pp. 217, 246, 248.

61. *Prefaces and Essays,* pp. 277, 283.

62. *Short History of English Literature,* p. 367. Note that the image is apparently suggested by Edward Dowden's *Shakspere: His Mind and Art* (London, 1875), p. 75: "a world of the soul, a world opening into two endless vistas, the vista of meditation and the vista of passion."

63. *History of the French Novel,* 2, 460 ff.; 466 ff.

64. *The Later Nineteenth Century,* pp. 307–26, 334, 339–40, 344, cf. *Miscellaneous Essays,* p. 411

65. *History of the French Novel,* 2, 62 n. *Consideration of Thackeray,* p. 210.

SHAW

1. *Quintessence,* p. 212.

2. Cf. John Forster, *George Henry Lewes, Dramatic Essays,* ed. W. Archer and Robert W. Lowe, London, 1896.

3. *The.,* 2, 169.

4. *Quintessence,* pp. 81–83, 106–07.

5. *Ibid.,* p. 143, 148.

6. Eric Bentley, in *The Quintessence of Ibsenism* (New York, 1957), back cover.

7. *The., 1,* VIII–IX.

8. *The., 3,* 289.

9. *Fifty Caricatures,* London, 1913.

10. *The., 3,* 334–35.

11. *The.,* 2, 192; *3,* 333–34; 2, 191.

12. *The.,* 2, 205.

13. *The., 3,* 154.

14. *The., 3,* 314.

15. *The.,* 2, 299.

16. Preface to *St. Joan,* pp. LXXIII–IV.

17. Letter to *Daily News* (17 April 1905), in H. L. Mencken, *Bernard Shaw* (Boston, 1905), pp. 102 ff.

18. *The., 3,* 1, 4.

19. *The., 3,* 212 f.

20. Preface to *The Dark Lady of the Sonnets,* (London, 1914), p. 138.

21. 2 August 1905, quoted in E. J. Simmons, *Tolstoy* (Boston, 1946), p. 629 (apparently retranslated from the Russian); see the note on p. 628.

22. Preface to *Three Plays for Puritans.*

23. *The., 3,* 405 (1898).

24. *Pen Portraits,* pp. 189, 193.

25. *Ibid.,* pp. 238, 257.

26. *Ibid.,* p. 19.

27. *Ibid.,* pp. 233–34.

BIBLIOGRAPHY: THE FRENCH SYMBOLISTS

There are many accounts of the movement which pay intermittent attention to the doctrines:

A. Barre, *Le Symbolisme: Essai historique,* Paris, 1911.

E. Raynaud, *La Mêlée symboliste,* 3 vols. Paris, 1920–23.

G. Michaud, *Message poétique du symbolisme,* 3 vols. Paris, 1947. An independent volume, *La Doctrine symboliste (Documents)* (Paris, 1947), contains a useful anthology of pronouncements.

K. Cornell, *The Symbolist Movement,* New Haven, 1952.

On the aesthetic:

Bruce Archer Morrissette, *Les Aspects fondamentaux de l'esthétique symboliste,* Clermont-Ferrand, 1933; schematic, Crocean.

A. G. Lehmann, *The Symbolist Aesthetic in France, 1885–1895,* Oxford, 1950; excellent, argumentative.

On Poe in France there are several books, only partly devoted to the influence of Poe's criticism: by C. P. Cambiaire, L. Lemonnier, L. Seylaz, etc.

E. Noulet, "L'Influence d'Edgar Poe sur la poésie française," in *Etudes littéraires,* Mexico City, 1944.

Marcel Françon, "Poe et Baudelaire," *PMLA, 60* (1945), 841–59.

T. S. Eliot, *From Poe to Valéry,* New York, 1948.

Two essays in P. Mansell Jones, *The Background of Modern French Poetry* (Cambridge, 1951), make excellent points.

Joseph Chiari, *Symbolisme from Poe to Mallarmé: The Growth of a Myth,* foreword by T. S. Eliot, London, 1956; mostly concerned with showing the difference between Poe and Mallarmé; often weirdly mystical.

Patrick F. Quinn, *The French Face of Edgar Poe,* Carbondale, Ill., 1957; curious rather than convincing.

On Synesthesia:

For general phenomenon and its history, see many articles by Albert Wellek, esp. "Das Doppelempfinden in der Geistesgeschichte," *Zeitschrift für Aesthetik, 23* (1929), 14–42; "Renaissance und Barocksynästhesie," *Deutsche Vierteljahrschrift, 9* (1931), 534–84; and "Das Doppelempfinden im 18. Jahrhundert," *ibid., 14* (1936), 75–102.

Glenn O'Malley, "Literary Synaesthesia," *Journal of Aesthetics*, *15* (1957), 391–411, makes good distinctions.

On Baudelaire: I quote the Conard edition, *Œuvres complètes*, ed. J. Crépet, 19 vols. Paris, 1922–53, especially:

L'Art romantique (1925), as *AR*.
Les Fleurs du mal, (1922), as *FM*.
Curiosités esthétiques (1923), as *CE*.
Histoires extraordinaires par Edgar Poe (1932), as *HE*.
Nouvelles Histoires extraordinaires par Edgar Poe (1933), as *NH*.
Juvenilia, Œuvres posthumes, reliquiae (2 vols. 1939, 1952), as *OP*.
Correspondance générale (6 vols. 1947–53), as *CG*.
Les Paradis artificiels (1928), as *PA*.

I sometimes use the English translations in *The Mirror of Art: Critical Studies by Charles Baudelaire*, ed. Jonathan Mayne, New York, 1956; mostly a translation of *CE*, with illustrations of the pictures discussed.

New translation: *Baudelaire as a Literary Critic*. Translator and ed. Lois B. Hyslop and Francis E. Hyslop, Jr., College Park, Pennsylvania, 1964.

There is an excellent guide through the huge literature: Henri Peyre, *Connaissance de Baudelaire*, Paris, 1951.

Of general books, the following contain important discussions of the aesthetics and criticism:

Jean Pommier, *La Mystique de Baudelaire*, Paris, 1932; On correspondences, analogy, symbolism; much on aesthetics.

Georges Blin, *Baudelaire*, Paris, 1939; good on symbolism and synesthesia, esp. pp. 107 ff.

Jean Pommier, *Dans les Chemins de Baudelaire*, Paris, 1945; source studies, often far-fetched, but contains much on relations to Gautier, Banville, Flaubert, Hoffmann, etc.

Marcel A. Ruff, *L'Esprit du mal et l'esthétique baudelairienne*, Paris, 1955; good on romantic background, satanism, etc.

Lloyd James Austin, *L'Univers poétique de Baudelaire: Symbolisme et Symbolique*, Paris, 1956; persuasively argues the thesis of a development from occult symbolics to a poetic symbolism.

Books concerned with aesthetics and criticism:

André Ferran, *L'Esthétique de Baudelaire* (Paris, 1933), 734 pp.; an encyclopedic, diffuse work also on the criticism.

Giovanni Macchia, *Baudelaire, Critico,* Florence, 1939; a perceptive account of both the art and literary criticism.

Giorgio Polverini, *L'Estetica di Charles Baudelaire,* Bari, 1943; slight, Crocean.

Margaret Gilman, *Baudelaire the Critic,* New York, 1943; a chronological study of the art and literary criticism; excellent.

Otokar Levý, *Baudelaire: jeho estetika a technika,* Brno, 1947; an intelligent digest in Czech, with a brief French resumé.

On Mallarmé: I quote *Œuvres complètes,* Bibliothèque de la Pléiade, ed. Henri Mondor and G. Jean-Aubry (Paris, 1945), 1659 pp., as *O.*

Letters are quoted from *Propos sur la poésie,* ed. H. Mondor (Monaco, 1946), as *Pro.*

Other letters from H. Mondor, *Vie de Mallarmé* (2 vols. Paris, 1941), as *Vie.*

I quote when possible the very free translations from *Selected Prose Poems, Essays and Letters,* by Bradford Cook (Baltimore, 1956), changing freely in order to get nearer the original.

The best account of Mallarmé's aesthetic thought is Guy Defel, *L'Esthétique de Stéphane Mallarmé,* Paris, 1951. Hasye Cooperman (Mrs. N. B. Minkoff), *The Aesthetic of Stéphane Mallarmé* (New York, 1933), emphazises the supposed influence of Wagner.

Besides comment in the books of Lehmann, Chiari, Michaud, etc., listed above, these general books on Mallarmé contain incidental comments on the aesthetics:

E. Noulet, *L'Œuvre poétique de Stéphane Mallarmé,* Paris, 1940.

Jacques Scherer, *L'Expression littéraire dans l'œuvre de Mallarmé,* Paris, 1947; best analysis of diction and syntax.

Paul Valéry, *Écrits divers sur Stéphane Mallarmé,* Paris, 1950.

Kurt Wais, *Mallarmé: Dichtung, Weisheit, Haltung,* Munich, 1952; 2d ed., expanded and completely rewritten, of book published in 1938.

Wallace Fowlie, *Mallarmé,* Chicago, 1953.

Jacques Scherer, *Le "Livre" de Mallarmé,* Paris, 1957; reprints Mallarmé's jottings, with sympathetic introduction.

Articles:

Gardner Davies, "Stéphane Mallarmé. Fifty Years of Research," *French Studies, 1* (1947), 1–26.

Eléonore M. Zimmermann, "Mallarmé et Poe: Précisions et aperçus," *Comparative Literature, 6* (1954), 304–15.

Warren Ramsey, "A View of Mallarmé's Poetics," *Romanic Review*, 46 (1955), 178–91.

NOTES: THE FRENCH SYMBOLISTS

1. Michaud, *La Doctrine symboliste (Documents)*, p. 25: "Le véritable précurseur du mouvement actuel . . . la poésie symbolique cherche à vêtir l'Idée d'une forme sensible."

2. In the English-speaking world Arthur Symons, *The Symbolist Movement in Literature* (London, 1899), was clearly decisive. But the adoption of the term in other countries is less clearly traceable.

3. See L. Cazamian, *Symbolisme et poésie: L'Exemple anglais*, Paris, 1947; and C. Feidelson, *Symbolism and American Literature*, Chicago, 1953.

4. See this *History*, above, e.g. 2, 226 n. Sainte-Beuve, *Joseph Delorme: Pensées* XX: "[L'artiste] a reçu en naissant la clef des symboles et l'intelligence des figures." Pierre Leroux, in *La Revue Encyclopédique* (November 1831), quoted by Chiari, p. 156: "Le principe de l'art est le symbole." More on antecedents in Blin and Austin.

BAUDELAIRE

1. See the books of Pommier; G. T. Clapton, *Baudelaire and De Quincey*, Paris, 1931; Clapton, "Baudelaire and Catherine Crowe," *Modern Language Review*, 25 (1930), 286–305. On Heine see Kurt Weinberg, *Henri Heine, Romantique defroqué: Héraut du symbolisme français*, New Haven, 1954. On Delacroix's ideas see Hubert Gillot, *E. Delacroix: L'Homme—ses idées—son œuvre*, Paris, 1928.

2. *AR*, p. 404: "ce double caractère de calcule et de rêverie qui constitue l'être parfait."

3. *AR*, p. 184, introduction to Pierre Dupont, *Chants et Chansons*, 1851: "La puérile utopie de l'école de l'art pour l'art, en excluant la morale, et souvent même la passion, était nécessairement stérile."

4. In "Notes nouvelles sur Poe," *NH*, p. xix, quoted in Gautier essay, *AR*, p. 157: "*l'hérésie de l'enseignement*" . . . "La poésie . . . n'a pas d'autre but qu'Elle-même." *AR*, p. 121: "plus . . . l'art se détachera de l'enseignement et plus il montera vers la beauté pure et désintéressée."

5. *OP, 1*, 238: "un genre faux."

6. *AR*, p. 320.

7. *AR*, p. 275: "le travail journalier servira l'inspiration."

8. *CE*, p. 26: "que l'inspiration suffit et remplace le reste."

9. *AR*, p. 419: "De son absolue confiance dans le génie et l'inspiration, elle tire le droit de ne se soumettre à aucune gymnastique. Elle ignore

que le génie . . . doit, comme le saltimbaque apprenti, risquer de se romper mille fois les os en secret avant de danser devant le public; que l'inspiration, en un mot, n'est que la récompense de l'exercice quotidien."

10. *AR*, pp. 342–43: "ces théories, fautrices de paresse, qui . . . permettent au poëte de se considérer comme un oiseau bavard, léger, irresponsable, insaisissable."

11. *AR*, p. 159, from *NH*, pp. xx–xxi.

12. *OP*, 2, 63. *Fusées* X: "C'est quelque chose d'ardent et de triste, quelque chose d'un peu vague, laissant carrière à la conjecture."

13. *AR*, p. 284: "L'art est-il utile? Oui. Pourquoi? Parce qu'il est l'art . . . Je défie qu'on me trouve un seul ouvrage d'imagination qui réunisse toutes les conditions du beau et qui soit un ouvrage pernicieux."

14. *AR*, p. 311: "Le poëte est un moraliste sans le vouloir, par abondance et plénitude de nature."

15. *AR*, p. 401: "La logique de l'œuvre suffit à toutes les postulations de la morale."

16. *PA*, p. 157: "Le Beau est plus noble que le Vrai."

17. *NH*, p. xxii: "une légère impertinence . . . affectation à cacher la spontanéité, à simuler le sang-froid et la délibération . . . les amateurs de hasard, les fatalistes de l'inspiration."

18. *OP*, 2, 66: "Dans certains états de l'âme presque surnaturels, la profondeur de la vie se révèle tout entière dans le spectacle, si ordinaire qu'il soit, qu'on a sous les yeux. Il en devient le symbole."

19. *OP*, 2, 65: "Il y a des moments de l'existence où le temps et l'étendue sont plus profonds, et le sentiment de l'existence immensément augmenté . . . Cet état merveilleux." *PA*, ch. 1. *CE*, p. 251: "véritables fêtes du cerveau . . . ces beaux jours de l'esprit." The last passage refers to Poe's "Tale of the Ragged Mountains" (called "Souvenirs de M. Auguste Besloe" in Baudelaire's translation; cf. *HE*, p. 289).

20. *AR*, p. 60: "le génie n'est que *l'enfance retrouvée* à volonté." *PA*, p. 162: "le génie n'est que l'enfance nettement formulée."

21. Cf. the Projected Preface to *Fleurs du mal*: "Ce livre . . . n'a pas été fait dans un autre but que de me divertir et d'exercer mon goût passioné de l'obstacle." *FM*, p. 373.

22. *AR*, p. 305: "nous arrivons à cette vérité que tout est hiéroglyphique, et nous savons que les symboles ne sont obscurs que d'une manière relative, c'est-à-dire selon la pureté, la bonne volonté ou la clairvoyance native des âmes. Or qu'est-ce qu'un poëte . . . si ce n'est un traducteur, un déchiffreur? Chez les excellents poëtes, il n'y a pas de métaphore, de comparaison ou d'épithète qui ne soit d'une adaptation mathématiquement exacte dans la circonstance actuelle, parce que ces

comparaisons, ces métaphores et ces épithètes sont puisées dans l'inépuisable fonds de l'universelle analogie."

23. *AR*, p. 307. On hieroglyphics, see Liselotte Dieckmann, "The Metaphor of Hieroglyphics in German Romanticism" *Comparative Literature*, 7 (1955), 306–12; and E. R. Curtius, *Europäische Literatur und lateinisches Mittelalter* (Bern, 1948), esp. pp. 321 ff., 350, on ciphers, book of nature, etc.

24. *NH*, p. xx: "cet immortel instinct du Beau qui nous fait considérer la terre et ses spectacles comme un aperçu, comme une correspondance du Ciel." Cf. this *History*, *3*, 156.

25. Letter to Alphonse Toussenel (21 January 1856), in *CG*, *1*, 368: "L'imagination est la plus scientifique des facultés, parce que seule elle comprend l'analogie universelle, ou ce qu'une religion mystique appelle la correspondance."

26. *AR*, pp. 164–5: "une immense intelligence innée de la *correspondance* et du symbolisme universels, ce répertoire de toute métaphore . . . définir l'attitude mystérieuse que les objets de la création tiennent devant le regard de l'homme."

27. *CE*, p. 222: "l'immense clavier des *correspondances!*"

28. *CE*, p. 283: "Tout l'univers visible n'est qu'un magasin d'images et de signes auxquels l'imagination donnera une place et une valeur relative; c'est une espèce de pâture que l'imagination doit digérer et transformer."

29. Cf. Heine, *Werke*, ed. Ortmann, *11*, 295 (Heine's Salon of 1831): "Je crois que l'artiste ne peut trouver dans la nature tous ses types, mais que les plus remarquables lui sont révélés dans son âme, comme la symbolique innée des idées innées." Note that the same passage had been quoted by Sainte-Beuve, in *Portraits littéraires*, *2*, 256–57 (1833).

30. *CE*, p. 108: "l'artiste, qui domine le modèle, comme le créateur la création."

31. *CE*, pp. 273, 268.

32. *CE*, p. 333: "ce culte niais de la nature."

33. *AR*, p. 96: "la nature ne peut conseiller que le crime."

34. *CE*, p. 168: "la première affaire d'un artiste est de substituer l'homme à la nature et de protester contre elle."

35. *AR*, p. 399: "injure dégoûtante jetée à la face de tous les analystes, mot vague et élastique qui signifie pour le vulgaire, non pas une méthode nouvelle de création, mais une description minutieuse des accessoires."

36. *CE*, p. 284: " 'Je veux représenter les choses telles qu'elles sont, ou bien qu'elles seraient, en supposant que je n'existe pas.' L'univers sans homme. Et celui-là, l'imaginatif, dit: 'Je veux illuminer les choses avec mon esprit et en projeter le reflet sur les autres esprits.' "

37. *CE,* p. 310: "une lumière magique et surnaturelle sur l'obscurité naturelle des choses." *CE,* p. 325: "plus la matière est, en apparence, positive et solide, et plus la besogne de l'imagination est subtile et laborieuse."

38. *NH,* p. xv: "L'imagination est une faculté quasi divine qui perçoit tout d'abord, en dehors des méthodes philosophiques, les rapports intimes et secrets des choses, les correspondances et les analogies."

39. Quoted in English, *CE,* p. 279, from *The Night Side of Nature* (London, 1848), *1,* 320–21.

40. *CE,* p. 274: "C'est l'imagination qui a enseigné à l'homme le sens moral de la couleur, du contour, du son et du parfum. Elle a créé, au commencement du monde, l'analogie et la métaphore. Elle décompose toute la création."

41. *CE,* p. 275: "L'imagination est la reine du vrai, et le *possible* est une des provinces du vrai."

42. *CE,* p. 282: "Un bon tableau, fidèle et égale au rêve qui l'a enfanté, doit être produit comme un monde."

43. *CE,* p. 111: "le plus noble et le plus étrange [dessin], peut négliger la nature; il en représente une autre, analogue à l'esprit et au tempérament de l'auteur."

44. *CE,* p. 275: "Elle est positivement apparentée avec l'infini."

45. *CE,* p. 298: "son ouvrage garde fidèlement la marque et l'humeur de sa conception. C'est l'infini dans le fini. C'est le rêve! et je n'entends pas par ce mot les capharnaüms de la nuit, mais la vision produite par une intense méditation." For Schelling see this *History,* 2, 75, or cf. the same phrase in Bettina von Arnim, *Goethes Briefwechsel mit einem Kinde* (1835), *1,* 181. There was a French translation in 1843, reviewed by Sainte-Beuve in *Causeries du Lundi,* 2, 330–52 (29 July 1850).

46. *AR,* pp. 303–04: "La musique des vers de Victor Hugo s'adapte aux profondes harmonies de la nature; sculpteur, il découpe dans ses strophes la forme inoubliable des choses; peintre, il les illumine de leur couleur propre. Et, comme si elles venaient directement de la nature, les trois impressions pénètrent simultanément le cerveau du lecteur. De cette triple impression résulte la *morale des choses. . . .* La nature inanimée, ou dite inanimée; non seulement, la figure d'un être extérieur à l'homme, végétal ou minéral, mais aussi sa physionomie, son regard, sa tristesse, sa douceur, sa joie éclatante, sa haine répulsive, son enchantement ou son horreur; enfin, en d'autres termes, tout ce qu'il y a d'humain dans n'importe quoi, et aussi tout ce qu'il y a de divin, de sacré ou de diabolique.'

47. *AR,* p. 119: "C'est créer une magie suggestive contenant à la fois l'objet et le sujet, le monde extérieur à l'artiste et l'artiste lui-même."

48. *CE,* p. 97: "La bonne manière de savoir si un tableau est mélo-

dieux est de le regarder d'assez loin pour n'en comprendre ni le sujet ni les lignes. S'il est mélodieux, il a déjà un sens."

49. *AR*, p. 15: "absolument indépendante du sujet du tableau."

50. *CE*, p. 345: "le sujet fait pour l'artiste une partie du génie."

51. *CE*, p. 356.

52. *AR*, p. 112. See letter to Thoré (June 1864), in *CG*, *4*, 275–76.

53. *AR*, p. 110: "la beauté passagère, fugace, de la vie présente."

54. *AR*, p. 69: "presque toute notre originalité vient de l'estampille que le *temps* imprime à nos sensations."

55. *CE*, p. 77: "l'héroïsme *de la vie moderne.*"

56. Letter to Armand Fraisse (18 February 1860). *CG*, *3*, 39–40: "Parce que la forme est contraignante, l'idée jaillit plus intense. Tout va bien au Sonnet, la bouffonnerie, la galanterie, la passion, la rêverie, la méditation philosophique. Il y a là la beauté du métal et du minéral bien travaillés. Avez-vous observé qu'un morceau de ciel, aperçu par un soupirail, ou entre deux cheminées, deux rochers, ou une arcade, etc. . . . donnait une idée plus profonde de l'infini qu'un grand panorama vu du haut d'une montagne?"

57. *CE*, 283: "les rhétoriques et les prosodies ne sont pas des tyrannies inventées arbitrairement, mais une collection de règles réclamées par l'organisation même de l'être spirituel. Et jamais les prosodies et les rhétoriques n'ont empêché l'originalité de se produire distinctement."

58. *CE*, 328: "une poésie étrangère, empruntée généralement au passé . . . la qualité naturellement poétique du sujet qu'il en faut extraire pour la rendre plus visible."

59. *AR*, 172: "l'horrible, artistement exprimé, devienne beauté . . . la *douleur* rhythmée et cadencée remplisse l'esprit d'une *joie* calme."

60. "Le Spleen de Paris," p. xxvii, "Une Mort héroïque"; in Pléiade ed., *1*, 452.

61. Fusées XI, *OP*, *2*, 65.

62. *CE*, p. 394: Baudelaire singles out *Die Königsbraut, Meister Floh, Der Goldene Topf*, and, above all, *Prinzessin Brambilla*.

63. *CE*, pp. 385 ff.; cf. *AR*, p. 409.

64. *PA*, p. 233: "la béatitude poétique . . . un état où ils (les poëtes) sont à la fois cause et effet, sujet et objet, magnétiseur et somnambule."

65. *AR*, p. 165: "Il y a dans le mot, dans le *verbe,* quelque chose de *sacré* qui nous défend d'en faire un jeu de hasard. Manier savamment une langue, c'est pratiquer une espèce de sorcellerie évocatoire."

66. *AR*, pp. 164, 305, both quoted above. For other uses of the term see *AR*, pp. 146, 152; *CE*, pp. 7, 89, 198. For "allegory" and "emblem," see *FM*, pp. 87, 96, 142, 205; *CE*, p. 321. Excellent comment in Austin, pp. 162 ff.

67. *AR,* p. 354: "La mythologie est un dictionnaire d'hiéroglyphes vivants, hiéroglyphes connus de tout le monde."

68. *AR,* p. 217. Baudelaire quotes Wagner's "Lettre sur la Musique" prefixed to *Quatre poëmes d'opéras,* Paris, 1861.

69. *AR,* pp. 229–30: "le signe d'une origine unique, la preuve d'une parenté irréfragable, mais à la condition que l'on ne cherche cette origine que dans le principe absolu et l'origine commune de tous les êtres . . . le mythe est un arbre qui croît partout, en tout climat, sous tout soleil, spontanément."

70. See the bibliography, above, esp. the many articles by Albert Wellek.

71. *CE,* pp. 97–98. From "Höchst zerstreute Gedanken," sec. 5 of "Kreisleriana," in *Phantasiestücke in Callots Manier,* in *Werke,* ed. G. Ellinger, *1,* 56.

72. *AR,* p. 177.

73. *CE,* p. 168: "l'empiétement d'un art sur un autre."

74. *AR,* pp. 129: "tout art doit se suffire à lui-même et en même temps rester dans les limites providentielles."

75. *AR,* p. 5: "les arts aspirent, sinon à se suppléer l'un l'autre, du moins à se prêter réciproquement des forces nouvelles."

76. *Œuvres complètes,* ed. Rolland de Renéville and Jules Mouquet (Paris, 1954), Pléiade, pp. 270–71. Letter to Paul Démeny (15 May 1871): "Le Poëte se fait *voyant* par un long, immense et raisonné *dérèglement* de *tous les sens.* Toutes les formes d'amour, de souffrance, de folie; il cherche lui-même, il épuise en lui tous les poisons, pour n'en garder que les quintessences. Ineffable torture où il a besoin de toute foi, de toute force surhumaine, où il devient entre tous le grand malade, le grand criminel, le grand maudit—et le suprême Savant!—Car il arrive à *l'inconnu!*" In a similar letter to Georges Izambard (13 May 1871), he says the same in different words (ibid., p. 268): "Il s'agit d'arriver à l'inconnu par le dérèglement de *tous les sens.*"

77. *Ibid.,* p. 233: "Alchimie du verbe . . . J'inventai la couleur des voyelles!—*A* noir, *E* blanc, *I* rouge, *O* bleu, *U* vert.—Je réglai la forme et le mouvement de chaque consonne, et, avec des rhythmes instinctifs, je me flattai d'inventer un verbe poétique accessible, un jour ou l'autre, à tous les sens. Je réservais la traduction. Ce fut d'abord une étude. J'écrivais des silences, des nuits, je notais l'inexprimable." *Ibid.,* p. 234: "Je m'habituai à l'hallucination simple: je voyais très franchement une mosquée à la place d'une usine, une école de tambours faite par des anges, des calèches sur les routes du ciel, un salon au fond d'un lac; les monstres, les mystères; un titre de vaudeville dressait des épouvantes devant moi. Puis j'expliquai mes sophismes magiques avec l'hallucina-

tion des mots! Je finis par trouver sacré le désordre de mon esprit." On Rimbaud, see W. H. Frohock, "Rimbaud's Poetics," *Romanic Review, 46* (1955), 192–202, for excellent analysis.

78. *CE*, p. 229: "L'artiste ne relève que de lui-même."

79. "E. A. Poe." in *HE*, pp. xxv–xxvii. One should note that Baudelaire's first article on Poe is, in large part, a translation of an article by John M. Daniel in *Southern Literary Messenger.* See W. T. Bandy, "New Light on Baudelaire and Poe," *Yale French Studies, 10* (1953), 65–69.

80. *HE, p.* xxviii: "Sa poésie profonde et plaintive, ouvragée néanmoins, transparente et correcte comme un bijou de cristal,—par son admirable style, pur et bizarre,—serré comme les mailles d'une armure."

81. *AR,* p. 276. *CE,* pp. 97–98, 151–52, 386–88, 393–95. *PA,* pp. 201–02. On Hoffmann see the chapter in Pommier, *Dans les Chemins de Baudelaire,* pp. 297–321. On Heine, *AR,* p. 291: "sa littérature pourrie de sentimentalisme matérialiste." *CE,* p. 222: "ce charmant esprit, qui serait un génie s'il se tournait plus souvent vers le divin." *OP, 1,* 223 f., plan of an elaborate defense against Jules Janin.

82. *AR,* p. 153: "Victor Hugo, Sainte-Beuve, Alfred de Vigny, avaient rajeuni, plus encore, avaient ressuscité la poésie française, morte depuis Corneille." *AR,* 183–84: "Elle [l'école romantique] nous rappela à la vérité de l'image, elle détruisit les poncifs académiques." *AR,* p. 124: "[l'art romantique] a fait prévaloir la gloire de l'art pur."

83. *AR,* p. 359. *CE,* p. 311: "Le romantisme est une grâce, céleste ou infernale, à qui nous devons des stigmates éternels." *CE,* p. 90: "le romantisme est l'expression la plus récente, la plus actuelle du beau." This, of course, resumes Stendhal's view.

84. *CE,* p. 91: "intimité, spiritualité, couleur, aspiration vers l'infini."

85. *OP, 1,* 305: "le grand gentilhomme des décadences, qui veut retourner à la vie sauvage."

86. Letter (15 March 1865), *CG, 5,* 64: "Les *Fleurs du mal* de la veille." Baudelaire endorses a saying of Sainte-Beuve.

87. *AR,* pp. 336–40.

88. *CE,* pp. 105–06: "M. Victor Hugo laisse voir dans tous ses tableaux, lyriques et dramatiques, un système d'alignement et de contrastes uniformes. L'excentricité elle-même prend chez lui des formes symétriques . . . C'est un compositeur de décadence ou de transition, qui se sert de ses outils avec une dextérité véritablement admirable et curieuse. M. Hugo était naturellement académicien avant que de naître."

89. *CE,* pp. 106–07: "Trop matériel, trop attentif aux superficies de la nature, M. Victor Hugo est devenu un peintre en poésie."

90. *CE,* p. 247: "un grand poëte sculptural qui a l'œil fermé à la spiritualité."

91. *AR*, p. 307: "ces turbulences, ces accumulations, ces écroulements de vers, ces masses d'images orageuses." *AR*, p. 147: "il [le public] ignore les parties mystérieuses, ombreuses, les plus charmantes de Victor Hugo." *CE*, p. 345: "le roi des paysagistes." *AR*, pp. 315–16: "Victor Hugo a créé le seul poème épique qui pût être créé par un homme de son temps pour des lecteurs de son temps."

92. *AR*, p. 300: "toujours maître de lui-même, et appuyé sur une sagesse abrégée, faite de quelques axiomes irréfutables."

93. *AR*, pp. 385, 391–92. Page 390: "Un livre de charité."

94. *CG 4*, 100 (10 August 1862): "Immonde et inepte." *OP*, 2, 73: "Hugo-Sacerdoce a toujours le front penché;—trop penché pour rien voir, excepté son nombril."

95. *OP 1*, 221–22: "Dieu, par un esprit de mystification impénétrable, a amalgamé la sottise avec le génie."

96. *CG 5*, 92 (8 May 1865): "Tous les trois, mère et fils, aussi bêtes, aussi sots que le père!" *CG*, 5, 39–40 (12 February 1865): "On peut être à la fois un bel esprit et un rustre,—comme on peut en même temps posséder un génie spécial et être un sot."

97. "Au poëte impeccable, au parfait magicien ès lettres françaises, à mon très-cher et très-vénéré Maître et ami Théophile Gautier."

98. *AR*, p. 177: "la consolation par les arts, par tous les objets pittoresques qui réjouissent les yeux et amusent l'esprit."

99. *CG 2*, 345 (21 September 1859): "Je puis avouer *confidentiellement* que je connais les lacunes de son étonnant esprit."

100. "L'école païenne" (1852) in *AR*, pp. 289–97.

101. *AR*, p. 359: "il n'exprime que ce qui est beau, joyeux, noble, grand, rhythmique."

102. *CE*, p. 171: "Les singes du sentiment sont, en général, de mauvais artistes."

103. *AR*, p. 331: "Le cri du sentiment est toujours absurde." Page 160: "*La poésie du cœur.*"

104. *CG*, 5, 280(18 February 1866): "A propos du sentiment, du cœur, et autres saloperies féminines, souvenez-vous du mot profond de Leconte de Lisle: *Tous les élégiaques sont des canailles!*" Baudelaire wanted to quote this saying (nowhere in print) in the preface to *Fleurs du mal* (Conard ed. p. 372).

105. *CG*, 3, 38 (18 February 1850): "Ce maître des gandins." *OP*, 1, 227: "Mauvais poëte . . . Croque-mort langoureux." *AR*, p. 153: "féminin et sans doctrine."

106. *OP*, 2, 97: "une *grosse bête*," "lourde," "bavarde," "cette stupide créature."

107. *AR*, pp. 325–30.

108. *OP, 1,* 332: "Puissance de l'analyse racinienne."

109. *AR,* p. 168: "visionnaire passionné." Note, however, that Philarète Chasles and Sainte-Beuve made the same observation, largely in a disparaging sense: *Causeries du lundi, 2,* 450; Chasles: "Ce n'est pas un analyste, c'est mieux ou pis, c'est un voyant," quoted in E. R. Curtius, *Balzac* (2d ed. Bern, 1951), from *Journal des Débats,* 24 August 1850.

110. *AR,* p. 400: "une gageure . . . un pari . . . . l'orgue de Barbarie le plus éreinté."

111. *AR,* pp. 407–08: "Il m'eût été facile de retrouver sous le tissu minutieux de *Madame Bovary* les hautes facultés d'*ironie* et de *lyrisme* qui illuminent à outrance la *Tentation de Saint Antoine.* . . . cette faculté souffrante, souterraine et révoltée . . . évidemment la plus intéressante pour les poëtes et les philosophes."

112. *AR,* pp. 219–20: "tous les grands poëtes deviennent naturellement, fatalement, critiques. Je plains les poëtes que guide le seul instinct; je les crois incomplets . . . il est impossible qu'un poëte ne contienne pas un critique . . . je considère le poëte comme le meilleur de tous les critiques . . . Diderot, Goethe, Shakspeare, autant de producteurs, autant d'admirables critiques."

113. *CE,* p. 88: "la critique touche à chaque instant à la métaphysique."

114. *CE,* pp. 223–24: "un système est une espèce de damnation . . . Il y a dans les productions multiples de l'art quelque chose de toujours nouveau qui échappera éternellement à la règle et aux analyses de l'école."

115. *AR,* p. 198: "Il vous faut donc, pour bien représenter l'œuvre, *entrer dans la peau* de l'être créé, vous pénétrer profondément des sentiments qu'il exprime, et les si bien sentir, qu'il vous semble que ce soit votre œuvre propre."

116. *CE,* 87: "la meilleure critique est celle qui est amusante et poétique; non pas celle-ci, froide et algébrique, qui, sous prétexte de tout expliquer, n'a ni haine ni amour, et se dépouille volontairement de toute espèce de tempérament . . . pour être juste, c'est-à-dire pour avoir sa raison d'être, la critique doit être partiale, passionnée, politique, c'est-à-dire faite à un point de vue exclusif, mais au point de vue qui ouvre le plus d'horizons."

MALLARMÉ

1. *Vie,* p. 104: "Mon grand maître."

2. *O,* p. 531: "l'âme poétique la plus noble, qui jamais vécut."

3. *O,* p. 225: "le prince spirituel de cet âge."

4. *O*, p. 228: "Ainsi presque pas un des vingt morceaux qui ne soit en son mode un chef d'œuvre unique."

5. *O*, p. 230: "la théorie poétique très neuve . . . sans fondement anecdoctique . . . A savoir que tout hasard doit être banni de l'œuvre moderne et n'y peut être que feint; et que l'éternel coup d'aile n'exclut pas un regard lucide scrutant l'espace dévoré par son vol."

6. Chiari, p. 85: "Le poète idéal n'est point ce vaste épileptique que l'on nous dépeint échevelé, les yeux hagards, émettant indifféremment et d'un seul jet sous l'inspiration de je ne sais quelle Muse bavarde, des vers faciles et incohérents, mais un penseur sérieux qui conçoit fortement et que entoure ses conceptions d'images hardies et lentement ciselées."

7. See above, p. 634, n. 65.

8. *O*, p. 857: "le double état de la parole, brut ou immédiat ici, là essentiel." Also *O*, p. 368.

9. *O*, 368: "à chacun suffirait peut-être pour échanger la pensée humaine, de prendre ou de mettre dans la main d'autrui en silence une pièce de monnai."

10. *O*, 364: "la diversité, sur terre, des idiomes empêche personne de proférer les mots qui, sinon se trouveraient, par une frappe unique, elle-même matériellement la vérité. Cette prohibition sévit expresse, dans la nature . . . que ne vaille de raison pour se considérer Dieu."

11. *O*, p. 921: "sinistre digramme."

12. *O*, p. 364.

13. *O*, p. 368, 400. Page 364: "rémunère le défaut des langues."

14. *Pro*, p. 147: "un élément nouveau, à même et soi, nu et dévorant ses propres mots."

15. *Pro*, p. 75: "les mots . . . se reflètent les uns sur les autres jusqu'à paraître ne plus avoir leur couleur propre, mais n'être que les transitions d'une gamme."

16. In Edmund Gosse, *Questions at Issue* (London, 1893), p. 332.

17. *O*, p. 389: "à quelle hauteur qu'exultent des cordes et des cuivres, un vers, du fait de l'approche immédiate de l'âme, y atteint."

18. *O*, p. 368: "l'ensemble des rapports existant dans tout, la Musique." For music in the Greek sense, see the letter to Edmund Gosse (10 January 1893), in *Questions at Issue*, p. 333.

19. *O*, p. 381: "La Poésie, proche l'idée, est Musique, par excellence— ne consent pas d'infériorité."

20. *O*, p. 335: "Chez Wagner . . . je ne perçois, dans l'acception stricte, le théâtre (sans conteste on retrouvera plus, au point de vue dramatique, dans la Grèce ou Shakespeare), mais la vision légendaire

qui suffit sous le voile des sonorités et s'y mêle; ni sa partition du reste, comparée à du Beethoven ou du Bach, n'est, seulement, la musique. Quelque chose de spécial et complexe résulte: aux convergences des autres arts située, issue d'eux et les gouvernant, La Fiction ou Poésie."

21. See Charles Chassé, *Les Clés de Mallarmé,* Paris, 1954.

22. For the best analysis see Jacques Scherer, above, Bibliography.

23. *O,* p. 643: "La Musique et les lettres." A lecture given at Oxford and Cambridge in 1894. Published in 1895.

24. *O,* p. 366: "L'œuvre pure implique la disparition élocutoire de poëte, qui cède l'initiative aux mots."

25. *Pro,* p. 78: "je suis maintenant impersonnel, et non plus Stéphane que tu as connu,—mais une aptitude qu'a l'univers Spirituel à se voir et à se développer, à travers ce qui fut moi." 14 May 1867.

26. *Pro,* p. 136: "l'ouvrier disparaît (ce qui est absolument la trouvaille contemporaine)." 22 January 1888.

27. Letter to Eugène Lefébure (February 1865), in Henri Mondor, *Eugène Lefébure* (Paris, 1951), pp. 341–42: "Ce que je reproche à Taine, c'est de prétendre qu'un artiste n'est que l'homme porté à sa suprême puissance, tandis que je crois qu'on peut parfaitement avoir un tempérament humain très distinct du tempérament littéraire . . . Devant le papier, l'artiste *se fait.* Il ne croit pas par exemple qu'un écrivain puisse entièrement changer sa manière, ce qui est faux, je l'ai observé sur moi."

28. *O,* pp. 259–60: "L'homme peut être démocrate, l'artiste se dédouble et doit rester aristocrate. . . . leur nom peut-être, leurs vers, cela est faux . . . Que les masses lisent la morale, mais de grâce ne leur donnez pas notre poésie à gâter. O poëtes, vous avez toujours été orgueilleux; soyez plus, devenez dédaigneux."

29. *O,* pp. 544–45: "l'esprit français . . . répugne, en cela d'accord avec l'Art dans son intégrité, qui est inventeur, à la Légende . . . est-ce qu'un fait spirituel, l'épanouissement de symboles ou leur préparation, nécessite endroit, pour s'y développer, autre que le fictif foyer de vision dardé par le regard d'une foule!"

30. *O,* p. 394: "frappée à l'authenticité des mots et lumière, triomphale de Patrie, ou d'Honneur, de Paix." The Postscript in *National Observer* (7 May 1892), printed in E. Noulet, p. 119.

31. *O,* p. 869: "la poésie est faite pour le faste et les pompes suprêmes d'une société constituée où aurait sa place la gloire dont les gens semblent avoir perdu la notion."

32. *O,* pp. 869–70: "cette société qui ne lui permet pas de vivre, c'est le cas d'un homme qui s'isole pour sculpter son propre tombeau . . . il est en grève devant la société."

33. *O*, p. 663: "un livre qui soit un livre, architectural et prémédité."

34. *O*, p. 663: "le Livre, persuadé qu'au fond il n'y en a qu'un."

35. *O*, p. 372: "Impersonnifié, le volume, autant qu'on s'en sépare comme auteur, ne réclame approche de lecteur . . . il a lieu tout seul: fait, étant."

36. Jacques Scherer, *Le "Livre" de Mallarmé*, Paris, 1957.

37. "Le volume, malgré l'impression fixe, devient par ce jeu, mobile—de mort il devient vie." Feuillet 191.

38. *Ibid.*, p. 119.

39. *Ibid.*, p. 96.

40. *O*, p. 663: "L'explication orphique de la Terre, qui est le seul devoir du poëte."

41. *O*, p. 378: "tout, au monde, existe pour aboutir à un livre . . . l'hymne, harmonie et joie, comme pur ensemble groupé dans quelque circonstance fulgurante, des relations entre tout."

42. Scherer, *L'Expression*, pp. 155 ff., collects evidence for Mallarmé's contacts with Plato, Freemasonry, and occultism. In 1890 Mallarmé thanked Victor-Emile Michelet for his book *L'Esotérisme dans l'art* and signed: "Votre très persuadé." *Vie*, p. 222, quotes letter by Villiers de l'Isle-Adam to Mallarmé: "Quant à Hegel, je suis vraiment bien heureux que vous ayez accordé quelque attention à ce miraculeux génie." *Pro*, p. 59, denies knowledge of Buddhism.

43. *O*, p. 544: "l'esprit français, strictement imaginatif et abstrait, donc poétique."

44. *O*, p. 368: "Je dis: une fleur! . . . musicalement se lève, idée même et suave, l'absente de tous bouquets." Also, *O*, p. 857.

45. *O*, p. 400: "Evoquer, dans une ombre exprès, l'objet tu, par des mots allusifs, jamais directs."

46. *O*, p. 365: "Instituer une relation entre les images exacte, et que s'en détache un tiers aspect fusible et clair présenté à la divination."

47. *O*, pp.. 365–66: "Abolie, la prétention, esthétiquement une erreur, quoiqu'elle régît les chefs-d'œuvre, d'inclure au papier subtil du volume autre chose que par exemple l'horreur de la forêt, ou le tonnerre muet épars au feuillage; non les bois intrinsèque et dense des arbres."

48. *Pro*, p. 118: "La Poésie est l'expression, par le langage humain ramené à son rhythme essentiel, du sens mystérieux des aspects de l'existence: elle doue ainsi d'authenticité notre séjour et constitue la seule tâche spirituelle."

49. *O*, p. 646: "Oui, que la Littérature existe et, si l'on veut, seule, à l'exception de tout."

50. *Pro*, p. 59: "nous ne sommes que de vaines formes de la matière,— mais bien sublimes pour avoir inventé Dieu et notre âme . . . s'élan-

çant forcenément dans le rêve qu'elle sait n'être pas, chantant l'Ame et toutes les divines impressions pareilles qui se sont amassées en nous depuis les premiers âges, et proclamant, devant le Rien qui est la vérité, ces glorieux mensonges!"

51. *O*, p. 55:

> Idéal que nous font les jardins de cet astre,
> Survivre pour l'honneur du tranquille désastre
> Une agitation solennelle par l'air
> De paroles, pourpre ivre et grand calice clair,
> Que, pluie et diamant, le regard diaphane
> Resté là sur ces fleurs dont nulle ne se fane,
> Isole parmi l'heure et le rayon du jour!

In text, the translation of Roger Fry, from *Mallarmé, Poems* (New York, 1951), p. 55.

CHRONOLOGICAL TABLE
OF WORKS

FRANCE

1851–62	Sainte-Beuve:	*Causeries du lundi* (15 vols.)
1852	Baudelaire:	First article on Poe in *Revue de Paris*
1853	Taine:	*La Fontaine et ses fables*
1857	Baudelaire:	Review of Flaubert's *Madame Bovary*
	Champfleury:	*Le Réalisme*
	Taine:	*Les Philosophes classiques du XIXe siècle*
1858	Taine:	*Essais de critique et d'histoire*
1860	Sainte-Beuve:	*Chateaubriand et son groupe littéraire*
1861	Baudelaire:	"Victor Hugo," "Théophile Gautier"
1863–70	Sainte-Beuve:	*Nouveaux lundis*, 13 vols.
1863–95	Edmond Scherer:	*Etudes critiques sur la littérature contemporaine*, 10 vols.
1864	Taine:	*Histoire de la littérature anglaise*, 4 vols.
1865	Taine:	*Philosophie de l'art*
1866	Zola:	*Mes haines*
1867	Taine:	*De l'Idéal dans l'art*
1868	Baudelaire:	*L'Art romantique*
1871	Rimbaud:	Letter to Paul Démeny (published 1912)
1873	Rimbaud:	*Une Saison en enfer*
1880	Barbey d'Aurevilly:	*Goethe et Diderot*
	Zola:	*Le Roman expérimental*
1882	Montégut:	*Types littéraires*
1883	Bourget:	*Essais de psychologie contemporaine*, first series
	Brunetière:	*Le Roman naturaliste*
1885	Barbey d'Aurevilly:	*Les Critiques ou les juges jugés*
	Mallarmé:	"Richard Wagner"

1886	de Vogüé:	*Le Roman russe*
1887	Flaubert:	*Correspondance*, 4 vols.
1887–99	Lemaître:	*Contemporains*, 7 vols.
1887	Maupassant:	*Pierre et Jean*
1888	Anatole France:	*La Vie littéraire*, first series
	Hennequin:	*La critique scientifique*
1889	Brunetière:	*Questions de critique*
1890	Brunetière:	*L'Evolution des genres dans l'histoire*
1891	Faguet:	*Politiques et moralistes du XIXe siecle*, Vol. 1
1892	Brunetière:	*Les Epoques du theâtre français*
1893	Angellier:	*Robert Burns*, 2 vols.
1894	Jusserand:	*Histoire littéraire du peuple anglais*, Vol. 1
	Lanson:	*Histoire de la littérature française*
	Mallarmé:	"La Musique et les lettres"
	Taine:	*Derniers Essais de critique et d'histoire*
1896	Emile Legouis:	*La Jeunesse de Wordsworth*
	Texte:	*J.-J. Rousseau et les origines du cosmopolitisme littéraire*
1897	Mallarmé:	*Divagations*

ITALY

1850	De Sanctis:	"Delle Opere drammatiche di Federico Schiller"
1857	De Sanctis:	"Dell'argumento della *Divina Commedia*"
1858	De Sanctis:	"Schopenhauer e Leopardi"
1865	Imbriani:	"Un Capolavoro sbagliato"
1868–71	Carducci:	"Dello Svolgimento della letteratura nazionale"
1869	De Sanctis:	*Saggio critico sul Petrarca*
	Imbriani:	*Le Leggi dell'organismo poetico*
1870–71	De Sanctis:	*Storia della letteratura italiana*, 2 vols.
1872	Comparetti:	*Virgilio nel medio evo*
	Imbriani:	*Fame usurpate*
1874	De Sanctis:	*Saggi critici*
1876	Rajna:	*Le Fonti dell'Orlando furioso*
1877	D'Ancona:	*Le Origini del teatro in Italia*
1878–84	Bartoli:	*Storia della letteratura italiana*, 7 vols.
1880	Verga:	*Vita dei campi*
1884	Rajna:	*Le Origini dell'epopea francese*

1892	Carducci:	*Storia del Giorno*
1894	Croce:	*La Critica letteraria*
1896	Chiarini:	*Studi Shakespeariani*
1898	Capuana:	*Gli 'Ismi' contemporanei*
	Graf:	*Foscolo, Manzoni, Leopardi*

ENGLAND

1850		*The Germ,* ed. W. M. Rossetti
1852	Browning:	Introductory Essay to *Letters of Percy Bysshe Shelley*
	Dallas:	*Poetics*
1853	Arnold:	Preface to *Poems*
	Bagehot:	"Shakespeare the Man"
1855	Lewes:	*Life of Goethe*
1858	Arnold:	Preface to *Merope*
	Lewes:	"Realism in Art: Recent German Fiction"
1859–94	Masson:	*Life of John Milton,* 7 vols.
1861	Arnold:	*On Translating Homer*
1864	Bagehot:	"Wordsworth, Tennyson and Browning"
1865	Arnold:	*Essays in Criticism*
	Lewes:	"Principles of Success in Literature"
1866	Dallas:	*The Gay Science,* 2 vols.
1867	Arnold:	*On the Study of Celtic Literature*
	Pater:	"Winckelmann"
1868	Swinburne:	*William Blake*
1871	John Morley:	*Critical Miscellanies,* 2 vols.
1872	John Morley:	*Voltaire*
1873	Pater:	*Studies in the Renaissance*
1874	Stephen:	*Hours in a Library:* First Series
	Minto:	*Characteristics of the English Poets*
1875	Dowden:	*Shakespere: His Mind and Art*
	Swinburne:	*Essays and Studies*
	Ward:	*History of English Dramatic Literature*
1875–86	Symonds:	*The Renaissance in Italy,* 7 vols.
1876	Stephen:	*A History of English Thought in the Eighteenth Century,* 2 vols.
1877	Meredith:	"On the Idea of Comedy and the Uses of Comic Spirit"

1879	Arnold:	*Mixed Essays*
	Bagehot:	*Literary Studies*, 2 vols.
1880	Swinburne:	*A Study of Shakespeare*
1881	Saintsbury:	*John Dryden*
1882	Saintsbury:	*A Short History of French Literature*
1884	Symonds:	*Shakspere's Predecessors in the Drama*
1885	Arnold:	*Discourses in America*
1886	Posnett:	*Comparative Literature*
	Swinburne:	*Miscellanies*
1887	Saintsbury:	*A History of Elizabethan Literature*
1888	Arnold:	*Essays in Criticism:* Second Series
1889	Pater:	*Appreciations*
1890	Symonds:	*Essays Speculative and Suggestive,* 2 vols.
	Wilde:	*Intentions*
1891	Shaw:	*The Quintessence of Ibsenism*
1893	Symonds:	*Walt Whitman*
1895–1910	Courthope:	*A History of English Poetry,* 6 vols.
1897	Gosse:	*A Short History of Modern English Literature*
1898	Saintsbury:	*A Short History of English Literature*
	Shaw:	*The Perfect Wagnerite*
1899	Arthur Symons:	*The Symbolist Movement in Literature*
1901–04	Saintsbury:	*A History of Criticism and Literary Taste in Europe,* 3 vols.

THE UNITED STATES

1844	Lowell:	*Conversations on Some of the Old Poets*
1850	Melville:	"Hawthorne and his Mosses"
1856	Whitman:	Letter to Emerson prefixed to the second edition of *Leaves of Grass*
1870	Lowell:	*Among My Books*
1871	Whitman:	*Democratic Vistas*
	Lowell:	*My Study Windows*
1876	Lowell:	*Among My Books: Second Series*
1878	Henry James:	*French Poets and Novelists*
1879	James:	*Hawthorne*
1882	Howells:	"Henry James, Jr."

1887	Howells:	*Modern Italian Poets*
1888	James:	*Partial Portraits*
1891	Howells:	*Criticism and Fiction*
1893	James:	*Essays in London and Elsewhere*
1895	Howells:	*My Literary Passions*
1901	Howells:	*Heroines of Fiction*, 2 vols.
1907–17	Henry James:	*The Novels and Tales* (with the Prefaces)
1914	James:	*Notes on Novelists*

GERMANY

1850	Hettner:	*Die romantische Schule*
1852	Hettner:	*Das moderne Drama*
1853	Fontane:	"Unsere lyrische und epische Poesie seit 1848"
1856–70	Hettner:	*Literaturgeschichte des achtzehnten Jahrhunderts*, 6 vols.
1856	Haym:	*Wilhelm von Humboldt*
1857	Haym:	*Hegel und seine Zeit*
1863	Freytag:	*Technik des Dramas*
	Spielhagen:	"Über Objektivität im Roman"
1865	Dilthey:	"Novalis"
1870	Dilthey:	*Leben Schleiermachers*
	Haym:	*Die romantische Schule*
1872	Nietzsche:	*Die Geburt der Tragödie aus dem Geiste der Musik*
1873–74	Nietzsche:	*Unzeitgemässe Betrachtungen*, 2 vols.
1874	Otto Ludwig:	*Shakespeare-Studien*
1874–85	Hillebrand:	*Zeiten, Völker und Menschen*, 7 vols.
1877	Dilthey:	"Goethe und die dichterische Phantasie"
1878–80	Nietzsche:	*Menschliches Allzumenschliches*, 2 vols.
1880–85	Haym:	*Herder*, 2 vols.
1880	Hillebrand:	*German Thought from the Seven Years' War to Goethe's Death*
1881	Nietzsche:	*Morgenröte*
1882	Heinrich and Julius Hart:	*Kritische Waffengänge*
	Nietzsche:	*Die fröhliche Wissenschaft*
1883	Dilthey:	*Einleitung in die Geisteswissenschaften*

	Wilhelm Scherer:	*Geschichte der deutschen Literatur*
	Spielhagen:	*Beiträge zur Theorie und Technik des Romans*
1884–92	Erich Schmidt:	*Lessing*, 2 vols.
1886	Nietzsche:	*Jenseits von Gut und Böse*
1887	Otto Brahm:	*Ibsen*
1888	Nietzsche:	*Der Fall Wagner*
	Wilhelm Scherer:	*Poetik*
1889	Fontane:	Review of Hauptmann's *Vor Sonnenaufgang*
	Nietzsche:	*Götzendämmerung*
1891	Arno Holz:	*Die Kunst: ihr Wesen und ihre Gesetze*
1892	Nordau:	*Entartung*
1893	Mehring:	*Die Lessing-legende*
1899	Holz:	*Die Revolution der Lyrik*
1900	R. M. Meyer:	*Die deutsche Literatur des neunzehnten Jahrhunderts*
1905	Dilthey:	*Das Erlebnis und die Dichtung*

RUSSIA

1852	Grigoriev:	"Russian literature in 1851"
1854	Chernyshevsky:	"Aristotle's *On Poetry*"
1855	Chernyshevsky:	*The Aesthetic Relations of Art to Reality*
		"Studies in the Age of Gogol"
1856	Chernyshevsky:	Review of Tolstoy's *Childhood, Boyhood* and *Sebastopol Stories*
	Grigoriev:	"On Truth and Sincerity in Art"
1858	Dobrolyubov:	"On the Share of the People in the Development of Russian Literature"
1859	Dobrolyubov:	"What is Oblomovism?"
		"The Realm of Darkness"
	Grigoriev:	"I. S. Turgenev and his Work"
1860	Dobrolyubov:	"When Will the Day Come?"
		"A Ray of Light in the Realm of Darkness"
1861	Dobrolyubov:	"Forgotten People"
	Dostoevsky:	"Mr. — bov and the Question of Art"
	Grigoriev:	"The Development of the Idea of Nationality in Our Literature"
1862	Pisarev:	"Bazarov"

1864	Pisarev:	"The Realists"
	Grigoriev:	"The Paradoxes of Organic Criticism"
1865	Pisarev:	"The Destruction of Aesthetics"
1867	Pisarev:	"Heinrich Heine"
		Review of Dostoevsky's *Crime and Punishment*
1868	Strakhov:	*The Poverty of our Literature*
1876	Grigoriev:	*Works*, Vol. 1 (no more published)
1880	Dostoevsky:	Speech on Pushkin
1882	Strakhov:	*The Struggle with the West in Our Literature*, Vol. 1
1883	Mikhailovsky:	"A Cruel Talent"
1890	Rozanov:	"Dostoevsky's Legend of the Grand Inquisitor"
1894	Tolstoy:	Preface to Maupassant's *Stories*
	Veselovsky:	"Introduction to Historical Poetics"
1897–1906	Veselovsky:	*The Poetics of Plots*
1898	Tolstoy:	*What is Art?*
1898–99	Pypin:	*A History of Russian Literature*, 4 vols.
1904	Veselovsky:	*V. S. Zhukovsky, the Poetry of Feeling*
1906	Tolstoy:	"Shakespeare and the Drama"

INDEX OF NAMES

Adam, Paul, 74
Adamson, Robert, 185
Addison, Joseph, 54, 161
Aeschylus, 31, 56, 159, 171, 198, 240, 340, 342, 343, 356, 380, 402
Aleardi, Aleardo, Count, 130
Alexander I, Tsar of Russia, 360
Alfieri, Vittorio, 103, 114, 118, 129, 207, 321
Amiel, Henri Frédéric, 89, 91, 176, 396
Anacreon, 195
Ancona, Alessandro d', 125
Andersen, Hans Christian, 363
Andler, Charles, 337
Andreyev, Leonid, 290
Angellier, Auguste Jean, 77
Annan, Noel G., 185
Antonovich, Maxim, 260
Apollinaire, Guillaume, 456
Apuleius, 387
Aretino, Pietro, 407
Ariosto, Ludovico, 4, 105, 112, 115, 117, 118, 119, 122, 126, 129, 133, 402, 405
Aristarchus, 404
Aristophanes, 40, 54, 295, 362
Aristotle, 23, 36, 100, 107, 152, 164, 173, 221, 241, 309, 343, 404
Arnim, Achim von, 175, 259
Arnold, Matthew, 78, 84, 146, 154, *155–80*, 184, 185–86, 196, 203, 215, 235, 237, 311, 374, 378, 383, 408, 414, 417, 467; influence of, 155; concept of culture and religion, 156; theory of criticism, 156; ideal of "disinterestedness," 156; view of judicial criticism, 158; historical critic, 158; his scheme of history, 159; on adequate literatures and main currents, 160; concept of race, 161; on Celtic race, 162; on stream of history, 163; on Victorian literature, 163; poetry as criticism of life, 164; on literature and philosophy, 164; on high seriousness, 164; on natural magic, 165; on literature and morals, 166; his disparagement of poetry of reason, 166;

on art and life, 167; his emphasis on "subject," 168; on tragedy and comedy, 168; on metrics and *On Translating Homer*, 169; on the "grand style," 169; on totality and unity, 170; his "touchstones," 171–73; *Essays in Criticism* (1865), 173; views of German literature, 174; second series of *Essays*, 176; on Tolstoy, 177; essays on the English romantic poets, 177; his rankings, 179
Arnold, Thomas, 159
Aucassin and Nicolette, 386
Auerbach, Berthold, 2, 207
Aulnoy, Félicie d', 40
Aurelius, Marcus, 37, 174, 387
Austen, Jane, 210, 211, 224, 274

Babbitt, Irving, 155
Bach, Johann Sebastian, 331, 341, 432, 456
Bacon, Francis, Lord Verulam, 46, 118, 388
Bagehot, Walter, 180–85
Bain, Alexander, 142
Bakunin, Mikhail, 428
Baldensperger, Fernand, 79
Bale, John, 70
Balzac, Guez de, 50
Balzac, Honoré de, 2, *3–6*, 15, 17–18, 32, 41–43, 46, 49, 51–53, 56, 60, 63, 69, 73, 74, 82, 83, 94, 187, 216, 217, 220, 223, 224, 230, 234, 235, 274, 313, 321, 327, 334, 360, 361, 381, 412, 425, 426, 435, 450
Banville, Théodore de, 449–50
Barbey d'Aurevilly, Jules, 61, *80–82*, 85, 87, 89
Baretti, Giuseppe, 130
Bartoli, Adolfo, 127, 406
Baudelaire, Charles, 23, 26, 61, 73, 76, 82, 83, 87, 89, 90, 94, 169, 192, 216, 219, 224, 284, 351, 371, 372, 380, 381, 388, 408, 417, 426–27, 433, *434–52*, 453, 454, 458; the sources of his aesthetics, 435; relation to Poe, 435; on art for

651